Edited by
Morgan Bolling
with KC Hysmith
Sacha Madadian
and the editors of
Cook's Country

Designed by
Lindsey Timko Chandler

Foreword by
Toni Tipton-Martin

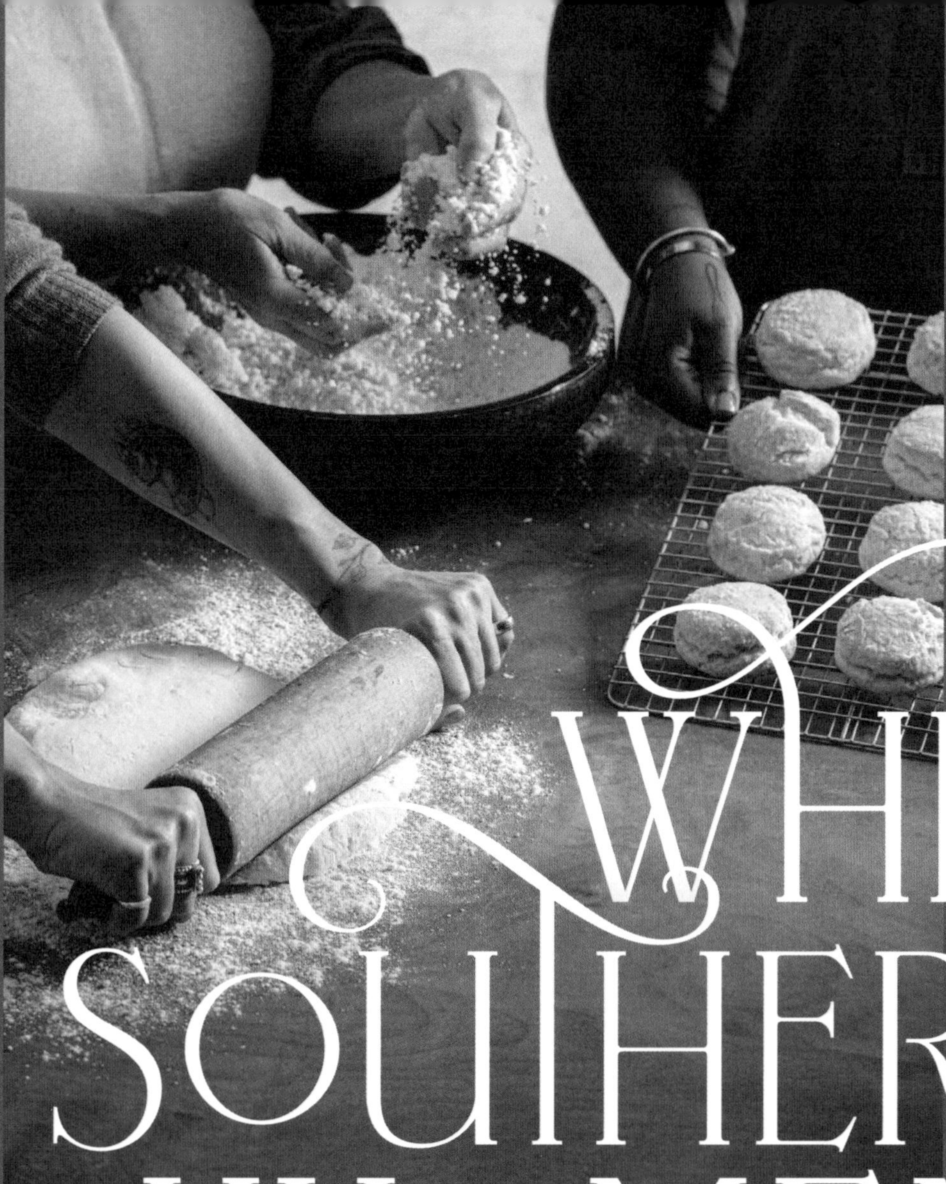

WHEN SOUTHERN WOMEN COOK

History, Lore, and 300 Recipes with Contributions from 70 Women Writers

AMERICA'S TEST KITCHEN

Library of Congress Cataloging-in-Publication Data has been applied for.

ISBN 978-1-954210-49-3

AMERICA'S TEST KITCHEN
21 Drydock Avenue, Boston, MA 02210

Printed in Canada
10 9 8 7 6 5 4 3 2 1

Distributed by Penguin Random House Publisher Services
Tel: 800-733-3000

Pictured on front cover: Baking Powder Biscuits (page 25)

Pictured on back cover (left to right): Porter Plum Pudding Layer Cake (page 448), Tomato Pie (page 146), Quick Pickled Jalapeños (page 353)

FRONT COVER

Food Styling: Catrine Kelty

Photography: Steve Klise

Featured Photographer: Steve Klise

Image Processing: Tricia Neumyer

Photo Editors: Anne Howard and Meredith Mulcahy

- facebook.com/AmericasTestKitchen
- instagram.com/TestKitchen
- youtube.com/AmericasTestKitchen
- tiktok.com/@TestKitchen
- x.com/TestKitchen
- pinterest.com/TestKitchen

AmericasTestKitchen.com
CooksIllustrated.com
CooksCountry.com
OnlineCookingSchool.com

Editorial Director, Books: Adam Kowit

Executive Food Editor: Dan Zuccarello

Project Editors: Morgan Bolling and Sacha Madadian

Consulting Historian: KC Hysmith

Senior Editors: Joe Gitter and Sara Mayer

Test Cooks: Olivia Counter, Carmen Dongo, Laila Ibrahim, José Maldonado, and David Yu

Kitchen Intern: Skye Stanger

Executive Managing Editor: Debra Hudak

Assistant Editor: Julia Arwine

Additional Editorial Support: Ann-Marie Imbornoni, Cheryl Redmond, and Rachel Schowalter

Design Director: Lindsey Timko Chandler

Photography Director: Julie Bozzo Cote

Senior Photography Producer: Meredith Mulcahy

Senior Staff Photographers: Steve Klise and Daniel J. van Ackere

Staff Photographers: Kritsada Panichgul and Kevin White

Additional Photography: Elizabeth Fuller, Joseph Keller, and Carl Tremblay

Food Stylists: Joy Howard, Sheila Jarnes, Catrine Kelty, Chantal Lambeth, Ashley Moore, Christie Morrison, Elle Simone Scott, Kendra Smith, Sally Staub, and Christine Tobin

Senior Print Production Specialist: Lauren Robbins

Production and Imaging Coordinator: Amanda Yong

Production and Imaging Specialist: Tricia Neumyer

Production and Imaging Assistant: Chloe Petraske

Copyeditor: Elizabeth Wray Emery

Proofreader: Karen Wise

Indexer: Elizabeth Parson

Editor in Chief, Cook's Country: Toni Tipton-Martin

Editorial Director, Cook's Country: Tucker Shaw

Executive Editor, Culinary Travel, Cook's Country: Bryan Roof

Executive Editor, Cook's Country: Scott Kathan

Executive Editor, Creative Content, Cook's Country: Morgan Bolling

Deputy Food Editor, Cook's Country: Nicole Konstantinakos

Deputy Editor, Cook's Country: Megan Ginsburg

Senior Editors, Cook's Country: Matthew Fairman and Jessica Rudolph

Senior Photo Test Cook, Cook's Country: Lawman Johnson

Test Cooks, Cook's Country: Mark Huxsoll, Amanda Luchtel, and Kelly Song

Executive Managing Editor, Creative Operations: Todd Meier

Art Director, Cook's Country: Maggie Edgar

Chief Executive Officer: Dan Suratt

Chief Creative Officer: Jack Bishop

Chief Content Officer: Dan Souza

Executive Editorial Directors: Julia Collin Davison and Bridget Lancaster

Senior Director, Book Sales: Emily Logan

CONTENTS

WELCOME TO AMERICA'S TEST KITCHEN

This book has been tested, written, and edited by the folks at America's Test Kitchen, where curious cooks become confident cooks. Located in Boston's Seaport District in the historic Innovation and Design Building, it features 15,000 square feet of kitchen space including multiple photography and video studios. It is the home of *Cook's Illustrated* magazine and *Cook's Country* magazine and is the workday destination for more than 60 test cooks, editors, and cookware specialists. Our mission is to empower and inspire confidence, community, and creativity in the kitchen.

All of our books are a collaborative effort, but this one, shepherded by *Cook's Country* Editor in Chief Toni Tipton-Martin and conceived by Executive Editor of Creative Content Morgan Bolling, came to life thanks to the invested care of a small all-woman editorial and design team. The manuscript arose through the tandem efforts of Morgan—who organized recipes, wrote stories, and tied in the many contributors—and Senior Editor Sacha Madadian, who shaped the content and oversaw the book's every element. Design Director Lindsey Timko Chandler's artistic vision

and layout bring Southern stories and dishes to brilliant life. Production and Imaging Specialist Tricia Neumyer made an enormous volume of images, modern and historical, of faces and of food, look their best. Debra Hudak, Julia Arwine, and Katie Kimmerer provided invaluable editorial support.

We also thank food historian KC Hysmith for her thoughtful contributions to the team and support of our mission. And, although the ATK editorial team was small, the number of Southern women voices was grand; you can find bios for the contributing essay authors on page 509. Every word (of many) was copyedited by Elizabeth Wray Emery and proofread by Karen Wise, with support from Ann-Marie Imbornoni, Cheryl Redmond, and Rachel Schowalter. Senior Print Production Specialist Lauren Robbins guided us in selecting the paper and case, and delivered the book to the printer, so we could share it with you all.

Of course, our plates would be empty without the editors and test cooks of *Cook's Country*, whose tireless efforts in the kitchen over 20 years have flavored the more than 300 Southern

recipes in this book. Additional recipes were researched, tested, and perfected by the ATK book team test cooks and editors. Steve Klise captured them with his stunning photography (find our recipe inspired by his mother's crab cakes on page 300). Special thanks is always due to Jack Bishop and Adam Kowit for their guidance overseeing the entire editorial process. Thank you also to Senior Director of Book Sales Emily Logan for her enthusiastic sales (and moral) support for this project.

To see what goes on behind the scenes at America's Test Kitchen, check out our social media channels for kitchen snapshots, exclusive content, video tips, and much more. You can watch us work (in our actual test kitchen) by tuning in to *America's Test Kitchen* or *Cook's Country* on public television or on our websites. Listen to *Proof* (AmericasTestKitchen.com/podcasts) to hear engaging, complex stories about people and food. Want to hone your cooking skills or finally learn how to bake—with an America's Test Kitchen test cook? Enroll in one of our online cooking classes.

MORGAN BOLLING, Executive Editor of Creative Content for *Cook's Country*, spearheaded *When Southern Women Cook* with a mission to highlight the unique ways food has sustained all kinds of Southern women through history and continues to feed them today. A Southern woman herself, born and raised in North Carolina, she is also a cast member of the *Cook's Country* TV show. In her 10 years at ATK, she has developed more than 100 recipes, with a specialty in barbecue and grilling. Previously, she cooked at restaurants in New York and her home state. When not developing a new recipe, there's a good chance Morgan is working with the Cambridge Women's Center, running a 5K, or planning her next pig roast.

TONI TIPTON-MARTIN, Editor in Chief of *Cook's Country* magazine, guided this project and team with her vast knowledge of Southern women's food history and her journalistic approach to sharing the stories behind America's favorite dishes. She is an award-winning food and nutrition journalist who uses cultural heritage and cooking for social change.

Toni is the author of several important books that celebrate African American cookbook history: *Juke Joints, Jazz Clubs, and Juice: Cocktails from Two Centuries of African American Cookbooks*; *Jubilee: Recipes from Two Centuries of African American Cooking*, and *The Jemima Code: Two Centuries of African American Cookbooks*. For her work, she has received the Julia Child Foundation Award, which is given to an individual (or team) who has made a profound and significant difference in the way America cooks, eats, and drinks. She is also a three-time James Beard Book Award winner, and she has earned the International Association of Culinary Professionals (IACP) Trailblazer Award, its Book of the Year Award, and Member of the Year Award. She is also the proud keeper of an incredible collection of rare cookbooks.

KC HYSMITH, PHD, served as consulting historian on the book, opening it to countless women's food stories. A Texas-bred, North Carolina–based writer, food historian, recipe developer, and photographer, KC is interested in the intersection between food, gender, and the digital landscape. She was associate editor for *Edible North Carolina: A Journey Across a State of Flavor* and co-author of Ricky Moore's *Saltbox Seafood Joint Cookbook*.

---
join our community of recipe testers

Our recipe testers provide valuable feedback on recipes under development by ensuring that they are foolproof in home kitchens. Help the America's Test Kitchen book team investigate the how and why behind successful recipes from your home kitchen.

IN THE SUMMER OF 1999,

I received an invitation to a weekend meeting in Birmingham, Alabama, from the Southern sage and award-winning journalist John Egerton, who cleverly Southernized his signature with these words: "on behalf of the add hock organizers."

Egerton's fiddling with the term ad hoc intrigued me. I looked up the definition: "A group organized for a specific purpose; a temporary opportunity to accomplish something great."

I was awed by the way that he substituted the spelling of "hoc" with the word for a fatty pig bone that spends most of its time in the mud. As a Southern California native, I reasoned that my participation would be like seasoning a kettle of simmering greens with a piece of smoky pork. I accepted the invitation to get into a little hot water by stirring the pot of Southern food history.

This call to action was anything but spontaneous. Years earlier, both author Edna Lewis and food editor Jeanne Voltz had led efforts to "establish an organization that would bring together people from all over the region and beyond who grow, process, prepare, write about, study, or organize around the distinctive foods of the South." The women failed.

Egerton, the author of the acclaimed book *Southern Food: At Home, On the Road, in History*, knew that I also shared this belief in the power of food to unify people, because he helped cultivate it. Since our chance meeting in Atlanta five years earlier, he and I bonded over our desire to untangle the knotty history and mixed messages ingrained in American race, gender, class, and food conversations.

A month after his letter arrived, I joined nearly 50 other invitees at *Southern Living* magazine's offices; by the end of the weekend we had founded the Southern Foodways Alliance, an organization dedicated to preserving, celebrating, and promoting the diverse food culture of the American South.

We gathered annually in Oxford, Mississippi, after that, listening to scholars and folks with lived experience as they challenged established notions about the region. Attendees came as strangers from all over the country and between bites of barbecued quail, corn pudding, and slaw, we grieved together about prejudice and bias. And yet, come Sunday morning, everyone departed with a sense of hope. We believed that eventually these honest conversations would bring about a kind of equity that politicians, educators, historians, and others had failed to achieve.

I reveled in the strength and power of the women I met each fall. While shopping in one of Oxford's secondhand stores, author and anthropologist Vertamae Smart-Grosvenor taught me to trust my cultural impulses, while Marcie Cohen Ferris helped me value my journalistic instincts as we crunched on North Carolina peanuts. From novelist and cookbook author Dori Sanders I learned the important art of storytelling while pondering the sweet, nuanced flavor of freshly picked South Carolina peaches. Mildred Council (aka Mama Dip) taught me to value examples of culinary excellence hidden in a pot of green beans. Ronni Lundy and I became friends while debating whether sugar belongs in cornbread. And Nathalie Dupree's "pork chop theory" of mentorship became the foundation of my passionate pursuit of culinary sisterhood.

Once I became president of the organization, one woman after another confided her frustrations about the ways Southern women were still being portrayed, in history generally, but also by SFA, specifically. The whispers turned into open criticism in 2020 when former founders, board members, alliance staff members, and others called for SFA to change its structure and programming.

When Southern Women Cook is a child of these experiences.

Written, edited, and designed by a diverse group of female changemakers, this curated collection of recipes and stories became a reality shortly after I became editor in chief of *Cook's Country*, the same month that SFA was responding to demands for progress. With past as present, we invited more than 70 bold, bright women contributors to explore the womanish side of Southern food through their particular lens. The book is by no means a complete story, but it could be the starting point for a movement.

For as long as I can remember, I have fantasized about restoring a Victorian house in the South as a place where women would come together, cook for one another, and exchange cultural stories. With this book, and my own nonprofit organization, I am reimagining that goal.

We will still want to learn more about Pardis Stitt and Subrina Collier, women who masterfully operate iconic restaurants alongside their chef husbands. More must be said about the women thriving in the beverage world—women like Ann Marshall, co-founder of High Wire Distilling; Susan Auler, a pioneer in Texas winemaking; master sommelier and award-winning hospitality group leader June Rodil; and Tahiirah Habibi, founder of the Hue Society, a group that provides uplifting cultural wine experiences. We want to dig deeper into the history- and science-based baking lessons taught by Stella Parks, Kentucky pastry chef and award-winning author of *Bravetart: Iconic American Desserts*. And we are eagerly looking forward to the day when articles describing the mouthwatering cooking of successful American men, such as James Villas and Craig Claiborne, also consider the mothers, aunties, and grandmothers who inspired them to greatness.

In the meantime, this collection, written by scholars, journalists, chefs, restaurateurs, farmers, and poets, brings you authentic truths shared by women who are resisting marginalization with determination and supporting each other with tales of female perseverance. They do so while making amazing food.

To describe this book more simply, I adapted a quote from the French feminist writer Hélène Cixous:

"We [are learning] to speak the language women speak when there is no one there to correct us."

by Toni-Tipton Martin

THROUGHOUT HISTORY,

food and cooking have sustained women as they have carved out a place for themselves in society and their communities. This is particularly poignant when you listen to women's stories in the American South; in this book, we highlight those stories, exploring how food has enabled women to overcome adversity, provide for themselves and their families, advance society, exercise their creativity, and claim their identities. It certainly has done those things for me.

I moved to Boston from North Carolina in 2014 to work on the *Cook's Country* team at America's Test Kitchen. When I first started, the brand published regional American cuisine, with a focus on what we considered (from our Northeast, coastal, mostly white perspective) country cooking. The recipes were interesting to learn about, developed with care, and delicious, but over the years, our approach evolved. We shifted from defining "American food" to exploring "how Americans eat"—a subtle but important change that broadened our storytelling and allowed us to embrace a broader narrative of what it means to be American.

In 2014, I also started volunteering at the Cambridge Women's Center, a community support space for women of all backgrounds and identities in Cambridge, Massachusetts. I come from a line of women who gave me a crash course in feminism through their lived, sometimes difficult, experiences. My mom, who wanted to be an artist, became a doctor after learning from her mother a hard lesson about the importance of creating economic independence. Their resilience inspired me, at a time when I was defining my own feminism to do something to empower women in need. I started answering a helpline (some called looking for advice; many were lonely and just looking for someone to listen) and eventually co-facilitated a support group for women and nonbinary trauma survivors, which I still do today. I learned that, like me, so many turned to art, writing, and, notably, food to navigate life's trials.

My work at *Cook's Country* and at the Women's Center fueled me, but the idea of melding my culinary career with my passion for supporting women seemed improbable. That was until Toni Tipton-Martin became *Cook's Country* editor in chief, and we began to explore this intersection of food and empowerment. It turns out, both Toni and I had been thinking a lot about how to give women space in a world that tells us to be smaller.

When Southern Women Cook is the outcome of many meaningful conversations. With Toni's journalistic approach to telling stories in *Cook's Country* magazine, we were positioned to make the book of our dreams. To start, we already had a deep archive of well-tested recipes. As I learned more than 10 years ago, we start recipe development with research, from reading cookbooks to interviewing experts. From there we cook five versions to cover different ways people make a dish. Then it all gets kind of scientific: We facilitate side-by-side taste tests until we are satisfied that a recipe is foolproof. And while this creates a recipe that is reliable, flavorful, and accessible to as many cooks as possible, it can also obscure a recipe's origins. With this book, we would bring the people and traditions that inspired us to recreate these recipes in the first place to the front.

We studied the archives to pull out the recipes that were both distinctly Southern but also windows into women's culinary experiences. And we brought on food historian KC Hysmith to help us put the recipes into context: The South is a place, as the U.S. Census Bureau defines it, but it's also, as KC taught us, well, a feeling. And so, the South in this book is vast. It includes Florida and Texas (even though each is so diverse, it could carry its own book). Within these Southern borders, we tour many corners—from the multinational Latinx communities in Miami baking festive pan de jamón and pouring out coquito to the Gullah Geechee women of the South Carolina Lowcountry celebrating their ancestral ingredients in brilliant rice dishes and deeply flavored gumbo stews.

We go back in time to capture those who built the foundations of Southern food—unnamed women firing the flames of stew stoves at Monticello; enslaved women like Marie Jean, who carried on Black and Indigenous tradition through the outdoor barbecue; chefs like Zephyr Wright, who cooked for presidents while changing history; entrepreneurial women selling handmade fried chicken to hungry railroad travelers, piping-hot fried calas or sweet pralines in New Orleans, or bowls of chili in San Antonio. And we highlight women innovating the cuisine today. These are women like Teresa Finney and Chanel Watson with cottage businesses baking Mexican conchas of every shape, flavor, and color. Like Alba Huerta, who captures the global flavors of Houston in each updated julep variation on the menu of her chic cocktail bar of the same name. Like Jordan Rainbolt, who amplifies the South's Indigenous roots through outdoor dinners and dishes like her Grit Cakes with Beans and Summer Squash, a creative take on the Three Sisters.

To tell a fuller story, we opened the writing to more than 70 Southern women—food writers, authors, journalists, historians, chefs, aficionados, and culture keepers—to cover topics close to them and their stitch in the tapestry of Southern food history. Find my fellow North Carolinian, chef Vivian Howard, writing on the painful challenges of cooking in a male-dominated world, and poet Crystal Wilkinson honoring her ancestors through her hands, through baking blackberry jam cake. Read Virginia Willis's piece on the complexities of weight management for women raised in traditional Southern society— on a traditional Southern food diet. Or learn from Carlynn Crosby about the Prohibition-era women who ruled the sea with their lucrative rum enterprises. Their stories season the recipes they appear alongside for a cookbook that, while not exhaustive, shares the tastemakers as much as it does the tastes.

Although I spent the majority of my life in the South, this book gave me a new view of what Southern food means. While it does have its fair share of recipes for fried chicken (we've included eight) and biscuits (also eight), it has so much more than that. The stories in this book show that food can be a lens through which to learn about our shared history, to pay homage to those who came before us, and to help build a better, tastier future. Cooks like Fannie Lou Hamer and Georgia Gilmore pushed the Civil Rights Movement forward through pork and slices of pound cake. Queen Maggie Bailey sent kids to school through bootlegging. Today, another queen, Dolly Parton, raises money for children's literacy through her cookbooks, and chefs like Maneet Chauhan and Asha Gomez broaden the definition of Southern food through what it means to be "Brown in the South." From them, I learned that melding a food career with women's empowerment was never improbable; food is and always has been a tool for women's empowerment. So whether it's baking messages for social justice into pies like Arley Bell or just getting the grits on the table to fuel another long day, Southern recipes represent a part of our place in a world where we increasingly take up more space.

In the trauma support group, we end each session asking women to share one way they're planning to take care of themselves in the upcoming week. Without fail, someone mentions food, whether it's to cook something healthy, enjoy ice cream, or just force themselves to eat anything at all. I hope this book gives you a little sustenance in this complex world. Yes, it can be hard, but it can also be damn delicious.

by Morgan Bolling

No.1 THE BREAD BASKET

Left to right: A worker at Flo's Kitchen shaping the famous biscuits (see page 31), Alabama Orange Rolls (page 42), Dollywood Cinnamon Bread (page 40), White Sandwich Bread (page 34), Pan de Campo (page 18).

STAFFS OF LIFE

BREADS OF CORN AND WHEAT

When you think about bread, "portability" is probably not the first word that pops into your head. We think of bread as fragile: It crumbles or it smushes, and it gets stale and moldy. But to our ancestors, baked grain was a lot easier to deal with than its predecessors, porridge and gruel. You can't exactly put gruel in your pocket and go hunting for the day. So when humans discovered that they could mix raw grain and liquid, put it near (not in) their fire, and create something edible that they could take with them, they must have thought it was pretty great. People around the world discovered this process separately, and over the millennia bread has provided sustenance for almost everyone.

With enough determination, you can make bread out of pretty much any type of seed or grain, even acorns. The materials work best if they're a bit dry and ground into powder. Whoever we are, almost all of us descend from dozens of generations of women who spent most of their days on their knees, grinding seeds or grain for their families' bread. It was a slow, laborious process, but it was essential for humanity to thrive.

In the American South, Native American women made bread from all kinds of materials—amaranth and sunflower seeds, for example—before corn made its way north from Mexico. Corn arrived sporadically in the present-day South, but it was widespread by 800 CE. Corn is amazing: It will grow almost anywhere, it's easy to plant and to harvest, and it's nutritious. Almost everywhere in the Americas, natives grew and stored corn, and they used a lot of it to make bread. They ground each day's supply fresh, as corn turns rancid quickly. Women often worked in unison, their wooden pestles keeping time in mortars made from tree stumps. They usually cooked their cakes on earthen hearths, fired hard over time.

The simplest cornbread is just ground corn and water. It's perfectly edible, if not particularly tasty. Native cooks, like good cooks everywhere, learned to improvise. Some animal fat—maybe from a bear—added tenderness. Dried fruit lent sweetness. And so on.

When Europeans arrived in the Americas after 1492, they ate corn by necessity. Spaniards learned to make tortillas, small, flat breads, from corn rather than wheat. Columbus took some back to Spain, and while Europeans never developed much taste for it, Portuguese slave traders took it with them to Africa. Corn became one of the staple foods on the Middle Passage that brought enslaved Africans to the Western Hemisphere.

Europeans craved wheat flour, the soft white powder that cooks up tender and, with some help, tall. Wheat, unlike corn, is finicky. It thrives in cool, dry climates—not exactly the situation in the South. It's difficult to harvest and process. But people loved it and were willing to sacrifice for it. The Spanish and the French on the Gulf Coast tried, without success, to grow wheat in the warm humidity. The English in the Mid-Atlantic fared much better, and soon flour mills began popping up across Virginia. Cooks—home cooks, indentured servants, and enslaved Native Americans and Africans—leavened their bread with homemade yeast or starter, sometimes left over from brewing beer.

Wheat flour became fairly common for white Southerners, particularly those with money. For enslaved people, corn remained the staple, and they received wheat flour mainly as gifts, mostly at Christmas. Enslaved women ground their families' supplies of cornmeal every day after they finished their work in the fields.

After the Civil War, industrialization changed bread baking in the South. As Linda Civitello points out on page 19, baking powder made quick breads such as biscuits possible. Standardized yeast came from companies like Fleischmann's in Cincinnati. Flour and sugar became cheaper—still a luxury for the many poor people in the region, but not so dear as before. People measured their affluence by how often they were able to have biscuits: just on Sundays, just for breakfast, or twice a day, every day.

While some Southerners made loaf bread, small breads with individual portions, such as biscuits or rolls, were more common. At their best, they came to the table hot and fresh from the oven. By the 1920s, commercial bakeries made much of the loaf bread in towns and cities, and by World War II, homemade loaf bread had almost disappeared.

As the South has become home to a population of immigrants, breads have become more diverse. Breads from Latin America, China, Vietnam, and Nigeria can all be found in Southern cities. In the 21st century, Southerners happily still eat cornbread as an accompaniment to certain dishes. But mostly they enjoy goods from wheat flour, whether it be bacon and cheese biscuits (see page 23) or conchas (see page 44). The old ways have become new, and the new ways have become standard.

by Rebecca Sharpless, PhD

professor of history at Texas Christian University and author of Grain and Fire: A History of Baking in the American South

Hoecakes

Makes 12 hoecakes ~ Total Time: 40 minutes

Hoecakes, as they're popularly called in the South, are kin to hot water cornbread, fried cornbread, and johnnycakes—all versions of earthy, naturally sweet, ever-so-slightly gritty cornmeal pancakes. There is a legend that enslaved people would cook these cakes on the hoes in the field under the hot sun; that's one explanation for how hoecakes got their name. However, food historian Rod Cofield asserts in his essay "How the Hoe Cake (Most Likely) Got Its Name" that evidence for this is limited; it's more likely that the name came from a piece of cooking equipment akin to a griddle called a "hoe."

While enslaved people certainly did make hoecakes, hoecakes are referenced in recipe collections in Virginia as early as the 17th century, which points to Native American roots. Now these cornmeal cakes are commonly found as a side dish alongside breakfast or dinner in the South. It's also traditional to serve the golden bread for New Year's, often with collard greens, to symbolize wealth for the coming year.

Some recipes for hoecakes or cornmeal cakes call for all cornmeal (no flour) and don't include leavener, so they have a denser texture. For this multipurpose recipe we were after cakes with crisp exteriors surrounding light, fluffy interiors that are delicious on their own with butter or alongside (or dipped or crumbled into) collard greens (see page 140) or straight buttermilk. To achieve this textural contrast we cut the cornmeal with a little flour and add baking powder. Pan-frying the cakes in bacon fat gives them lightly crisp edges and infuses them with plenty of smoky pork flavor (but you can substitute vegetable oil for the bacon fat, if desired). The batter will thicken slightly after sitting in step 1.

1½	cups (7½ ounces) cornmeal
½	cup (2½ ounces) all-purpose flour
2¼	teaspoons baking powder
1	teaspoon table salt
1½	cups whole milk
3	tablespoons bacon fat, divided

1 Set wire rack in rimmed baking sheet. Whisk cornmeal, flour, baking powder, and salt together in large bowl. Whisk in milk until no lumps remain. Let sit for 5 minutes.

2 Heat 1 tablespoon bacon fat in 12-inch nonstick skillet over medium-high heat until shimmering. Using ¼-cup dry measuring cup, portion 4 scant scoops of batter, evenly spaced, in skillet.

3 Cook until edges of cakes are set and first side is deep golden brown, about 1½ minutes. Flip and continue to cook until second side is golden brown, about 1 minute longer. Transfer hoecakes to prepared rack. Repeat with remaining bacon fat and batter in 2 batches. Serve.

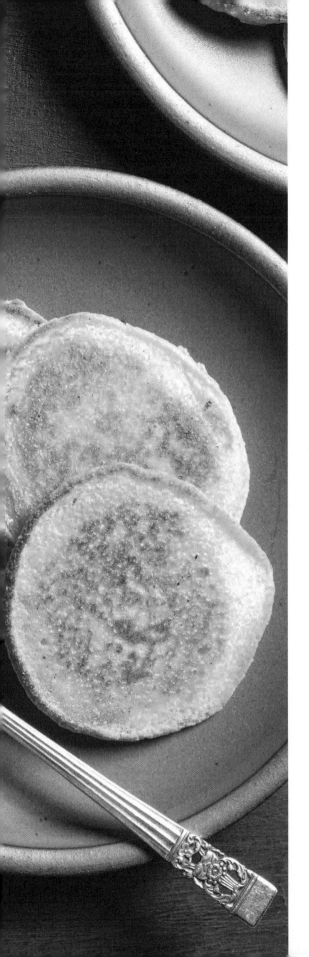

Q&A: MALINDA MAYNOR LOWERY ON INDIGENOUS FOODWAYS

From the cornbread in our skillets to the unique agricultural methods that set the South apart from the rest of the United States, Southern food as we know it exists thanks, in large part, to Indigenous foodways. To learn more about the important place corn holds in both Indigenous and Southern food traditions, we spoke with Dr. Malinda Maynor Lowery, historian, filmmaker, and member of the Lumbee tribe of North Carolina, the largest Native American tribe east of the Mississippi River.

What are Indigenous foodways and Lumbee foodways?

I would describe [them] as a very seasonally driven, vegetable-centered journey. I use that word because I can't help but think about it as a journey—of a place and a people—over time. Our food is a product of particular cultural encounters that evolve: deprivation, starvation, but also celebration. There are important ingredients, like the sweet potatoes my late husband, Willy Lowery, loved—his father built the sweet potato hill, and that's what they had to eat. There [are] also elaborate celebratory dishes that come along with coming together: chicken and pastry, chicken bog, and whole hog barbecue.

What role did corn play in these food traditions?

Corn has a similar journey. At times, it was just what was available. For example, in the wintertime in the 1950s, some Indigenous families only ate cornmeal mixed with water; not heated up, not grits, not slow cooked. [It was] similar to what soldiers ate during the Civil War, but this was in the 20th century. And we were glad to have it. Lumbee cornbread is fried, flat, and fritter-like [and uses] relatively few ingredients. Throughout the South, corn was also used by Indigenous peoples to make whiskey. Lumbee women would trade with enslaved women, cloth for corn, likely to turn into whiskey to sell and trade for the benefit of themselves, their families, and the community. There are numerous records of Lumbee women being arrested for illegal whiskey production, which gestures towards their overall independence and their agency to produce and provide in a male-dominated white world.

Could you explain food sovereignty and its importance?

Indigenous food sovereignty boils down to representation and how our contributions are given credit in American foodways. Sovereignty is asserted when a native person steps forward and self-determines how we share our culture and how we're represented. I have heard food-related memories from Lumbee born under segregation that were a combination of deprivation and joy; food sovereignty makes the latter possible despite the former. The pre-colonial foods, the origins of frybread, the fried cornbread, these *are* our foodways and these *are not* our foodways. There was and is food insecurity even in the 21st century, but people also [had] a degree of agency over what they ate, because they were growing it. That is food sovereignty.

Quick Cornbread

Serves 12   ~   Total Time: 45 minutes, plus 30 minutes cooling

Although invented in Michigan, Jiffy Corn Muffin Mix is a ubiquitous ingredient in Southern cooking. It owes its origin to a woman named Mabel White Holmes. According to the Jiffy website, Holmes's twin boys brought a friend over to their house to play, and when Holmes offered them lunch, the friend insisted on eating what his father had sent, including some unappealing biscuits. "She knew that light, flaky biscuits weren't easy to make, but these were exceptionally sad looking." So Holmes went on to create Jiffy biscuit mix, which debuted in 1930 and was marketed as "so easy even a man could do it." She was president of Jiffy until 1940 and remained invested her whole life.

Thankfully times and marketing slogans have changed. But even still, Jiffy occupies an important place in Southern food culture; the cornbread mix is used for everything from baking bread and muffins to thickening chili or making corn pudding. If you'd like to try making your own cornbread mix, this recipe is an easy way to make a big batch of dry mix to which you can add liquid ingredients anytime you want a batch of cornbread. The mix makes a nice gift.

1   cup milk

8   tablespoons unsalted butter, melted and cooled

2   large eggs

2   cups (17 ounces) Cornbread Mix (recipe follows)

1   Adjust oven rack to middle position and heat oven to 375 degrees. Spray 8-inch square baking pan with vegetable oil spray.

2   Whisk milk, melted butter, and eggs in large bowl until combined. Add cornbread mix and stir with rubber spatula until just combined and no dry mix is visible. Transfer batter to prepared pan and spread into even layer.

3   Bake until golden brown and toothpick inserted in center comes out clean, 25 to 30 minutes. Let cornbread cool in pan on wire rack for 20 minutes.

4   Remove cornbread from pan and let cool on wire rack for 10 minutes. Cut into squares and serve.

Cornbread Mix

Makes 8 cups   ~   Total Time: 10 minutes

Whisk the cornbread mix inside the container well each time before using to ensure that the ingredients are evenly distributed. This mix makes enough for four batches of cornbread. Do not use coarse cornmeal in this recipe.

6   cups (30 ounces) all-purpose flour

4   cups (20 ounces) cornmeal

2⅔   cups (18⅔ ounces) sugar

1   tablespoon table salt

2   tablespoons plus 2 teaspoons baking powder

Whisk flour, cornmeal, sugar, and salt in extra-large bowl until well combined. Sift baking powder through fine-mesh strainer over bowl. Whisk until very well combined, about 1 minute. Transfer cornbread mix to large airtight container. (Cornbread mix can be stored at room temperature for up to 2 months.)

UNDERSTANDING CORNMEAL

If you were making cornbread in the South in the 1800s, you could expect the meal to be whole-grain with big corn flavor. But as the area industrialized, finer grinds, including what we consider "standard" cornmeal today (i.e., steel-cut) became much more common in everyday baking. Still, there are producers making whole-grain and stone-ground corn-meals that have great flavor. For our baking recipes, we use regular cornmeal (steel-cut) or fine stone-ground cornmeal (regular or whole-grain). You can use either; the choice comes down to the grind size. You should avoid coarse stone-ground cornmeal—or coarse cornmeal of any label. As for color, we have tested recipes with white and yellow cornmeals and haven't noticed a significant flavor difference.

Steel-cut: Processed between steel rollers. This breaks the kernels, resulting in a sharper-textured meal. Major brands, such as Martha White, are processed in this way.

Stone-ground: Ground between stones, resulting in a softer-textured meal. We love the flavor of meals processed in this way, but stone-ground cornmeals of the coarse variety can make baked goods gritty.

Whole-grain: Ground whole, resulting in a meal made up of the bran, germ, and endosperm. Since the germ and bran contain the oil, this meal is more flavorful and more perishable than degerminated meal. It should be refrigerated or even frozen. Stone-ground cornmeal can often be whole-grain; look for the labeling on the package.

Degerminated: Stripped of its germ and bran before milling, so it is drier and less flavorful than whole-grain. Steel-cut and stone-ground cornmeals can come degerminated.

Organic: Milled from corn grown in a certified organic field.

Sweet Potato Cornbread

Serves 10 to 12   ~   Total Time: 1 hour, plus 1 hour cooling

The idea of adding ingredients such as chestnuts and potatoes to cornbread is likely as old as cornbread's history. It's thought that Native tribes did so for flavor, sure, but also to stretch the cornmeal. Chef Stephanie Tyson adds sweet potatoes to her cornbread to showcase the spuds at Sweet Potatoes (Well Shut My Mouth!!) in Winston-Salem, North Carolina. Tyson and her partner Vivián Joiner first opened their restaurant in 2003. Tyson had spent years working as an actress before moving toward the food she watched her grandmother Ora Porter cook. "Everything I saw my grandmother do, I do," Tyson says in a 2017 article in *Our State* magazine. Tyson now has two cookbooks under her belt and has twice been named a semifinalist for the James Beard Award for Best Chef Southeast. She later opened a second restaurant called Miss Ora's Kitchen in honor of her grandmother.

To speed up the cooking time in our version of sweet potato cornbread, we microwave the sweet potatoes to get them nice and soft. Cutting the cornmeal with a little bit of flour keeps the bread light, and brown sugar underscores the caramel notes of the sweet potatoes. Tyson adds a small amount of cinnamon and nutmeg to her cornbread, so feel free to do that if you'd like. At Sweet Potatoes, Tyson serves her cornbread with spicy-sweet ginger honey butter, so we follow suit. You can make this cornbread in a 10-inch cast-iron skillet or ovensafe nonstick skillet. Note that the cornbread needs to cool for 1 hour before being removed from the pan.

1½	pounds sweet potatoes, unpeeled
½	cup milk
8	tablespoons unsalted butter, melted, plus 1 tablespoon unsalted butter
4	large eggs
1½	cups (7½ ounces) cornmeal
½	cup (2½ ounces) all-purpose flour
¼	cup packed (1¾ ounces) brown sugar
1	tablespoon baking powder
½	teaspoon baking soda
1¾	teaspoons table salt

Chef Stephanie Tyson (right) with her partner, Vivián Joiner (left), co-owners of Sweet Potatoes (Well Shut My Mouth!!).

Angie Webb

1 Adjust oven rack to middle position and heat oven to 425 degrees. Prick potatoes all over with fork. Microwave on large plate until potatoes are very soft and surfaces are slightly wet, 10 to 15 minutes, flipping every 5 minutes. Immediately slice potatoes in half carefully to release steam.

2 When potatoes are cool enough to handle, scoop flesh into bowl and mash until smooth (you should have about 1¾ cups); discard skins. Whisk in milk, melted butter, and eggs. Whisk cornmeal, flour, sugar, baking powder, baking soda, and salt together in separate large bowl. Stir potato mixture into cornmeal mixture until combined.

3 Melt remaining 1 tablespoon butter in 10-inch cast-iron skillet over medium-high heat until bubbling, about 3 minutes. Swirl butter to coat bottom and sides. Pour batter into hot skillet and smooth top with rubber spatula. Bake until cornbread is golden brown and toothpick inserted in center comes out clean, 25 to 30 minutes. Let cornbread cool in skillet on wire rack for 1 hour. Loosen edges of cornbread from skillet with spatula and slide out onto cutting board. Cut into wedges and serve.

Ginger Honey Butter

Makes about ⅔ cup
Total Time: 20 minutes

This honey butter also tastes great on roasted root vegetables, boiled corn, pork chops, pancakes, muffins, biscuits, and dinner rolls.

4	tablespoons unsalted butter, softened
2	tablespoons honey
1	teaspoon grated fresh ginger
¼	teaspoon table salt

Using fork, mash all ingredients in bowl until combined. (Butter can be refrigerated for up to 3 days.)

SUGAR IN CORNBREAD

How does the South make cornbread? This question takes me back to a common-ground experiment I devised that invited friends to whip up their favorite recipe—in a plastic bag. The idea flowed from a conversation I had a long time ago with my friend and award-winning Appalachian food writer Ronni Lundy (see page 416) about whether sugar belonged in the mix. Ronni emphatically believed it did not. I argued that cornbread took on all kinds of new personality traits in the hands of enterprising cooks. My ancestors, for instance, developed a taste for sweet cornbread that we still call cornbread. Ronni called it cake.

I shared my experiment during a workshop for TerraVita Food & Drink Festival's Sustainable Classroom. The festival was founded by Colleen Minton in 2010, with a mission of "spreading the gospel of sustainable food and drink." For 10 years, the annual event featured chef demos and dinners, tasting events, and educational experiences. In addition to the cornbread activity, a diverse panel of women talked about Latinx, Native American, and New Southern cornbread traditions, about recipes as family heirlooms and as markers of identity.

Sharing your recipe for delicious cornbread with people you love comes with a bonus: It preserves your kitchen legacy. The instructions delivered by volunteers at the event went as such: "For this workshop, you are invited to re-create your favorite recipe for cornbread to share with the group. The first step is to choose a plastic bag as your 'cooking vessel' and then select a colored sticker to identify whether your bag/vessel is a cast-iron skillet, a metal or glass baking pan, or a muffin tin. Write the recipe title and baking temperature on your bag. Next, assemble your recipe. There is a wide assortment of wet and dry ingredients, leavenings, and add-ins from which you may choose, including optional ingredients such as chiles, corn, cheese, blueberries, chili powder, cinnamon, and various herbs, printed on small cards. When you're done, take your recipe with you and find a seat … Be creative and have fun!"

To complete the exercise, the audience members discussed their unique recipes and tasted delicious cornbread, still warm from the oven, made according to cultural recipes from the panelists. It was a wonderful lesson in diversity—one that honored the new creations devised when cooks tinker according to their own tastes and what's in the pantry while respecting original formulas. And these days, when discussions of recipe origins focus on authenticity, appropriation, and erasure, this activity provides a compassionate place to start the conversation.

by Toni Tipton-Martin

Fresh Corn Muffins

Makes 12 muffins   ~   Total Time: 55 minutes, plus 20 minutes cooling

One of the best things about summer in the South is the bushels of corn at the farmers' market. Of course, fresh corn is delightful straight off a boiled cob with butter or in a number of garden-fresh vegetable dishes, but if you're lucky enough to have a surplus, making sweet corn muffins packed with fresh corn is a great way to showcase the vegetable. Using equal parts flour and corn-meal gives these muffins a tender crumb that's more cakey and less crumbly than traditional versions of large-scale cornbread, which often have a higher ratio of cornmeal to flour. Microwaving cornmeal with milk until the mixture thickens to a paste-like consistency blooms the meal's flavor and softens the grain for an ultracorny muffin with a plush, not gritty, texture. When it comes to sugar, we lean toward the sweeter side here to enhance the fresh corn. Two cups of fresh corn kernels, which you should be able to get from three ears of corn, add nice pops of sweetness in each bite without weighing down the muffins. Be sure to avoid using coarse-ground cornmeals in this recipe, as they can make the muffins gritty. If you don't own a microwave, the cornmeal paste can be made in a medium saucepan over medium heat. Just be sure to whisk it constantly so that the ingredients don't scorch on the bottom of the saucepan. Try spreading warm muffins with Cardamom Brown Sugar Butter.

1½	cups (7½ ounces) all-purpose flour
1½	cups (7½ ounces) cornmeal, divided
1	cup (7 ounces) sugar
1½	teaspoons table salt
1½	teaspoons baking powder
1	teaspoon baking soda
1	cup milk
½	cup sour cream
8	tablespoons unsalted butter, melted
2	large eggs
2	cups corn (2 to 3 ears corn)

1   Adjust oven rack to middle position and heat oven to 400 degrees. Generously spray 12-cup muffin tin, including top, with vegetable oil spray. Whisk flour, 1 cup cornmeal, sugar, salt, baking powder, and baking soda together in large bowl; set aside.

2   Whisk milk and remaining ½ cup cornmeal together in medium bowl. Microwave until mixture begins to thicken to paste-like consistency, 1 to 3 minutes, whisking frequently. Whisk sour cream and melted butter into cornmeal paste. Whisk in eggs. Stir cornmeal mixture and corn kernels into flour mixture until just combined.

3   Using greased ⅓-cup dry measuring cup or #12 portion scoop, divide batter equally among prepared muffin cups; evenly distribute any remaining batter among cups (cups will be full).

4   Bake until muffins are golden brown and toothpick inserted in center comes out with few crumbs attached, 20 to 24 minutes. Let muffins cool in muffin tin on wire rack for 5 minutes. Remove muffins from muffin tin and let cool on rack for 15 minutes. Serve warm.

Cardamom Brown Sugar Butter

Makes about ⅔ cup   ~   Total Time: 20 minutes

We love this butter slathered on our Fresh Corn Muffins, but it's also good spread on toast, salmon, or chicken. We got the idea to pair cornbread with cardamom from cookbook author and restaurateur Asha Gomez. Her recipe for cardamom cornbread is in her 2016 cookbook *My Two Souths: Blending the Flavors of India into a Southern Kitchen.* In the book's introduction, Gomez says, "I call my style of cuisine 'two Souths cooking.' Its flavors and dishes are characterized and rooted in my deep affection for the resourcefulness and soulfulness of cooking both in my mother country India, in the far southern state of Kerala, and my chosen home in America's Southern culinary-savvy city of Atlanta, Georgia." Pairing cardamom with cornbread is a lovely example of how Gomez blends the food of Kerala with that of the American South.

8	tablespoons unsalted butter, softened
¼	cup packed (1¾ ounces) light brown sugar
¾	teaspoon ground cardamom
½	teaspoon table salt

Using fork, mash all ingredients in bowl until fully combined. (Butter can be refrigerated for up to 3 days.)

Corn Spoonbread

Serves 6   ~   Total Time: 1½ hours, plus 35 minutes resting and cooling

Spoonbread is a fluffy soufflé-like dish with a golden crust and a silky interior. It is rich and custardy from a high ratio of eggs and milk to cornmeal. The recipe was first published in Mary Randolph's 1824 cookbook, *The Virginia House-Wife*, which happens to be the first known regional cookbook in the Southern United States (see "Who Created the First Southern Spoon Bread?"). We admit, our version is a bit more complicated than that one: This airy spoonbread is made by cooking cornmeal in milk, cooling the mixture, stirring in egg yolks, and then folding in beaten egg whites and baking.

Soaking the cornmeal in milk for a few minutes before simmering eliminates any grittiness, and beating the egg whites with cream of tartar makes for a more stable foam and higher rise. Sautéing the fresh kernels in butter, steeping the cooked corn in milk, and then pureeing the mixture before combining it with the cornmeal intensifies the corn flavor. The silky mixture that comes out of the blender tastes like cream of corn soup—it's good enough to eat on its own! This "corn milk" creates a light, creamy texture and amazing corn taste that builds on the spoonbread of its ancestors. The resulting spoonbread has the flavors of cornbread, made from peak-season sweet corn married with something as airy and delicate as a soufflé. You can substitute frozen corn, thawed and patted dry, for fresh.

1	cup (5 ounces) cornmeal	1	teaspoon table salt
2¾	cups whole milk, divided	⅛	teaspoon cayenne pepper
4	tablespoons unsalted butter	3	large eggs, separated
2	cups corn (2 to 3 ears corn)	¼	teaspoon cream of tartar
1	teaspoon sugar		

1   Adjust oven rack to middle position and heat oven to 400 degrees. Grease 1½-quart soufflé dish or 8-inch square baking dish. Whisk cornmeal and ¾ cup milk together in bowl; set aside.

2   Melt butter in Dutch oven over medium-high heat. Add corn and cook until beginning to brown, about 3 minutes. Stir in sugar, salt, cayenne, and remaining 2 cups milk and bring to boil. Cover pot and let sit off heat for 15 minutes.

3   Transfer warm corn mixture to blender and process until smooth, about 2 minutes. Return to pot and bring to boil over medium-high heat. Reduce heat to low; add cornmeal mixture; and cook, whisking constantly, until thickened, 2 to 3 minutes. Transfer to large bowl and let cool completely, about 20 minutes. Once mixture is cool, whisk in egg yolks until combined.

4   Using stand mixer fitted with whisk attachment, whip egg whites and cream of tartar on medium-low speed until foamy, about 1 minute. Increase speed to medium-high and whip until stiff peaks form, 3 to 4 minutes. Whisk one-third of whites into corn mixture, then, using rubber spatula, gently fold in remaining whites until combined. Transfer batter to prepared dish and place in oven. Reduce oven temperature to 350 degrees and bake until spoonbread is golden brown and has risen above rim of dish, about 45 minutes. Serve immediately.

Individual Spoonbreads

In step 4, divide batter among 6 greased 7-ounce ramekins. Arrange ramekins on rimmed baking sheet and bake as directed, reducing cooking time to 30 to 35 minutes.

WHO CREATED THE FIRST SOUTHERN SPOONBREAD?

Culinary historian and food writer Debra Freeman (see page 290) says spoonbread always had ties to Virginia. The first codified version can be found in Mary Randolph's 1824 cookbook *The Virginia House-Wife* under the name "Batter Bread." (The recipe in its entirety: "Take six spoonsful of flour and three of corn meal, with a little salt; sift them and make a thin batter with flour, eggs, and a sufficient quantity of rich milk; bake it in little tin moulds in a quick oven.") Randolph's cookbook is considered one of the most influential books on American cookery and domestic life of the 19th century. Randolph, who was related to Thomas Jefferson by marriage, had much of her kitchen labor performed by enslaved people working at Monticello, and many of her recipes appear to have taken influence from Jefferson's staff.

This particular recipe sounds much like a French soufflé. And it isn't the only dish of the time with a French connection. In the book *Thomas Jefferson's Crème Brûlée: How a Founding Father and His Slave James Hemings Introduced French Cuisine to America*, author Thomas J. Craughwell reminds us that "There were no French chefs in eighteenth century Virginia," and "the mainstays of American colonial cooking were primarily meats (boiled, roasted, baked, or stewed), breads, heavily sweetened desserts, and generally overcooked vegetables." Thomas Jefferson aimed to change that.

When Thomas Jefferson was appointed U.S. minister to France, enslaved chef James Hemings accompanied Jefferson to Paris, and from 1784 to 1787, Hemings became trained in classic French gastronomy. Upon their return to Monticello, they brought back standards of French cooking, and they created new American dishes by blending French techniques with native American ingredients (eight of the formulas were written in Hemings's own hand, while others were recorded by Jefferson and Randolph but not directly attributed to any cooks). By the time Jefferson was elected president, he had earned a reputation as a culinary innovator, creating new kitchen equipment and serving lavish dinners that featured exquisite dishes and fine wines.

Jefferson did something else rare for the time: He added female cooks to the kitchen staff. "Edith Fossett was fifteen years old when she began her apprenticeship, and her sister Fanny Hern was eighteen. They would become the French chefs during Jefferson's final years," Craughwell explains. Fossett passed her skills on to her son Peter, who eventually opened a catering business in Cincinnati. And yet, we know little else about the sisters, their recipes, or their contributions to the Jefferson/Randolph culinary legacy. But we can be thankful that from France to Monticello to early cookbooks to our modern table, spoonbread survived the delicious journey.

A portrait of Mary Randolph and her book The Virginia House-Wife, *which includes the first known published spoonbread recipe (titled Batter Bread).*

Library of Congress

Pan de Campo

Serves 8 to 10   ~   Total Time: 1 hour, plus 30 minutes cooling

In 2005 the Texas state legislature declared pan de campo (known as cowboy bread) the official state bread of Texas. But it wasn't a quick decision for the sprawling state. Pan de campo has Tejano origins and was largely made in the southwest regions of the state. Throughout most of the state, it was more common to make sour-dough bread or biscuits. Ultimately, the house resolution passed with the statement, "The colorful history of the Lone Star State is inextricably associated with the romance of cowboy culture, and among the many lega-cies of this proud heritage is the delicious flat bread known as pan de campo, or cowboy bread."

In its original form, pan de campo embodied, as the resolution called it, "elegant simplicity," and was made with only flour, salt, leavener, and lard or shortening in cast-iron Dutch ovens by early settlers and vaqueros while traveling through the state. Most recipes produce breads that look like thick, flat rounds and eat like biscuits. But over the years a second type of cowboy bread has emerged that we've recreated here. It is much more akin to a coffee cake, with plenty of sugar, cinna-mon, and butter. While certainly not something that would have been made on a chuck wagon, this cake-like version of cowboy bread makes a great treat for lunch boxes or an after-school snack.

Cake

2½	cups (12½ ounces) all-purpose flour
2½	cups packed (17½ ounces) brown sugar
2	teaspoons ground cinnamon
½	teaspoon ground nutmeg
½	teaspoon baking soda
½	teaspoon table salt
6	tablespoons unsalted butter, cut into ½-inch pieces and chilled
1	cup buttermilk
2	large eggs, lightly beaten

Topping

¼	cup packed (1¾ ounces) brown sugar
2	tablespoons unsalted butter, cut into ½-inch pieces and chilled

1 **For the cake** Adjust oven rack to middle position and heat oven to 375 degrees. Grease and flour 13 by 9-inch baking dish. Process flour, sugar, cinnamon, nutmeg, baking soda, and salt in food processor until combined, about 3 seconds. Add butter and pulse until mixture resembles wet sand, about 8 pulses. Transfer to large bowl.

2 **For the topping** Return ½ cup cake mixture to now-empty processor. Add sugar and butter and pulse until mixture resembles wet sand, about 4 pulses.

3 Whisk buttermilk and eggs into remaining cake mixture until smooth. Pour into prepared dish and sprinkle with topping. Bake until toothpick inserted in center comes out clean, 25 to 30 minutes. Let cake cool in dish on wire rack for at least 30 minutes. Slice and serve.

BAKING POWDER AND ADVERTISING

Baking powder is the common ingredient in all the recipes submitted at the International Biscuit Festival in Knoxville, Tennessee. It's also the rising agent in self-rising soft wheat flour, such as products from White Lily and Martha White, prized by Southern bakers. But baking powder wasn't always so common in the South. In the antebellum (and later Jim Crow) South, enslaved women beat biscuit dough with an axe handle for 2 hours to leaven it.

Meanwhile, in the North, housewives used homemade yeast to make baked goods grow, but they were desperate to find a shortcut. And they did. The first recipes with the chemical leavener pearl ash appeared in Connecticut in 1796, in the first cook-book published in the United States, *American Cookery* by Amelia Simmons. The pearl ash made things taste a bit bitter, but it created a sensation, and in 1856, a Harvard chemistry professor patented an improvement, the first baking powder, Rumford.

Hundreds of baking powder companies sprang up in the years that followed. So did cutthroat wars for the millions of dollars at stake. Companies pumped the market with advertisements to win out the competition. Fake news was the weapon of choice for Royal, which printed thousands of articles that "proved" its competition was "poison," and bribed the Missouri legislature to pass a law saying the same.

The false advertising war ran out of steam in the 1920s. But the catchphrase "double acting" used by another brand, Calumet, stuck because it's true. Baking powder first gets to work when it combines with wet ingredients in a batter or dough, but it's that second action that keeps us mesmerized in front of the oven window, watching baked goods continue to rise after their initial puff in the oven. That puff was particularly welcome in cornmeal items that have no gluten so cannot rise via yeast. Baking powder provided the fluff that defined quick breads as we know them today.

by Linda Civitello, PhD

historian and author of Baking Powder Wars: The Cutthroat Food Fight that Revolutionized Cooking

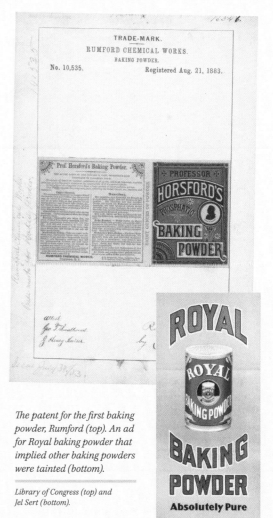

The patent for the first baking powder, Rumford (top). An ad for Royal baking powder that implied other baking powders were tainted (bottom).

Library of Congress (top) and Jel Sert (bottom).

ALL ABOUT BISCUITS

Biscuits are probably the most beloved quick bread in the South. They commonly grace breakfast tables but can be served at any meal of the day. In their book *Southern Biscuits,* Cynthia Graubart (see page 217) and Nathalie Dupree (see page 295) explain that the first biscuits were made using just flour and water; they were essentially a form of hardtack crackers meant to hold up during traveling. Lard made its way into the mix and gave way to beaten biscuits—dough pounded with a mallet, skillet, or other heavy instrument and folded to create layers that allowed the dough to slightly rise. Once baking powder became available, biscuits began to transform into something more akin to what most Southerners know today.

The ingredient list for biscuits is often simple: flour, salt, baking powder and/or soda, buttermilk, and fat. With such a short ingredient list, a lot comes down to technique. Dupree says, "I learned that biscuit making takes knowledge and technique because no one is born knowing how to make them, and few still have the joy of watching another—a mother or grandmother once upon a time—making biscuits day after day."

A baker is worth their salt only if the biscuits are light and fluffy, something that typically comes from keeping ingredients cold and avoiding handing the dough too much, which can develop gluten, leading to tough, not tender, biscuits. The study of biscuit making is worth it. "Learning to cook Southern biscuits enables freedom from commercial fast food and frozen biscuits, inferior biscuits to homemade. And it satisfies the soul," Dupree says.

Types of Biscuits

There are biscuit styles regional to every corner of the South: angel, rolled and stamped, sweetened, and layered, not to mention the many unique biscuit varieties tied to individual bakers. We focus on five important biscuits in this book: drop biscuits (objectively easy, objectively satisfying), baking powder biscuits (flaky, inspired by Edna Lewis), pat-in-the-pan buttermilk biscuits (biscuits baked in a cake pan, inspired by Virginia Willis), angel biscuits (as light and fluffy as you'll find), and cathead biscuits (our version is North Carolina Cheese Biscuits on page 30). Below we break down the ingredients and techniques that achieve these biscuit models.

Drop Biscuits

Light and fluffy interior; golden, crusty, craggy exterior

Difficulty level: ★

Shaping method: Dropped from a measuring cup

Technique. Adding melted butter to buttermilk makes the butter clump; in the oven, these clumps create steam pockets within the dough for extra fluffiness.

Baking Powder Biscuits

Hearty texture; flaky layers

Difficulty level: ★★

Shaping method: Rolled, stamped (can be dropped too)

Technique: Lard is cut into dry ingredients before liquid is added.

Pat-in-the-Pan Buttermilk Biscuits

Fluffy biscuit; high rise

Difficulty level: ★

Shaping Method: Pat in a cake pan and scored

Technique. Baking the biscuits together in a cake pan causes them to push on each other as they bake for a higher rise.

Angel Biscuits

Fluffy, cloudlike texture; shaped as angel wings

Difficulty level: ★★★

Shaping method: Rolled, stamped, shaped into wings

Technique: Using Southern biscuit flour makes them ultralight.

Cathead Biscuits

Supersize, extra-craggy, room for fillings

Difficulty level: ★

Shaping method: Dropped from a measuring cup

Technique: Fat (originally lard) is cut into dry ingredients before liquid is added. Then, the biscuits are formed quite large.

Buttermilk or Bust

For many of our recipes that call for buttermilk, we offer a substitution: clabbered (or acidulated) milk. Curious if that would work for biscuits, we tested clabbered whole, low-fat, skim, and soy milks in our biscuits—and none of them worked. Either the dough was too wet to pat into the pan and cut, or the flavor of the biscuits wasn't up to snuff. Buy buttermilk—these biscuits are worth it (if you have any left over, you can freeze it).

It's Supposed to Clump

In our recipe for Drop Biscuits (page 22), we call for stirring melted butter into buttermilk. This creates little butter clumps. They look funny, but these small butter balls melt and release steam in the oven to create light, fluffy biscuits.

Do You Really Need Biscuit Cutters?

Crafty home cooks punch out biscuits with old aluminum cans, overturned glasses, and even Mason jar rings. But using a makeshift cutter with blunt edges can compress the sides of the dough, leading to misshapen biscuits. We prefer to use biscuit cutters, round cutting tools with sharp edges that make even cuts and thus produce tall, symmetrical biscuits. Our favorite is the Ateco 5357 11-Piece Plain Round Cutter Set.

Flouring Your Biscuit Cutter

When stamping out biscuits, dip the cutter in flour as needed to prevent the dough from sticking.

Stamp but Don't Twist

We use a biscuit cutter to portion our Angel Biscuits (page 28). Twisting the cutter when stamping out biscuits pinches the dough, resulting in an uneven rise. Using a well-floured biscuit cutter and pressing down with equal pressure on both sides of the cutter (without twisting) ensures that the biscuits will rise evenly and emerge from the oven tall and fluffy.

Easy Ways to Flavor Biscuits

Dress up any biscuit recipe by adding flavorful stir-ins along with the rest of your dry ingredients. Here are some guidelines for how much to use:

¼ to ½ cup total of shredded, grated, or crumbled cheese; crumbled bacon; sliced scallions; chopped, toasted nuts; and/or dried fruit

1 tablespoon minced fresh herbs or ¾ teaspoon dried herbs

½ to ¾ teaspoon ground spices

Drop Biscuits

Makes 12 biscuits ~ Total Time: 45 minutes

One of the best starting recipes for new biscuit bakers is drop biscuits—and they're just as soul satisfying as any. Unlike rolled and stamped biscuits that typically call for carefully cutting cold fat into flour before liquid is added, drop biscuits are simply stirred together, dropped onto the baking sheet, and baked. For a drop biscuit with buttery flakes, stir together warm melted butter and cold buttermilk before incorporating the dry ingredients. This causes the butter to clump up; it looks like a mistake, but it produces pockets of steam in the oven for light, fluffy—and easy—stir-and-drop biscuits. The flavor variations here are inspired by flavors at Erika Council's Bomb Biscuits restaurant in Atlanta (see "Generations of Bomb Biscuits").

2	cups (10 ounces) all-purpose flour
2	teaspoons baking powder
½	teaspoon baking soda
1	teaspoon sugar
¾	teaspoon table salt
1	cup buttermilk, chilled
8	tablespoons unsalted butter, melted, plus 2 tablespoons unsalted butter

1   Adjust oven rack to middle position and heat oven to 475 degrees. Line rimmed baking sheet with parchment paper. Whisk flour, baking powder, baking soda, sugar, and salt together in large bowl. Stir buttermilk and melted butter together in 2-cup liquid measuring cup until butter forms clumps.

2   Add buttermilk mixture to flour mixture and stir with rubber spatula until just incorporated. Using greased ¼-cup dry measuring cup, drop level scoops of batter 1½ inches apart on prepared sheet. Bake until tops are golden brown, 12 to 14 minutes, rotating sheet halfway through baking.

3   Melt remaining 2 tablespoons butter and brush on biscuit tops. Transfer biscuits to wire rack and let cool for 5 minutes before serving.

Erika Council rolling out biscuit dough.

Peter Frank Edwards / Redux 2019

Bacon, Cheese, and Black Pepper Biscuits

Add 4 slices cooked, crumbled bacon, ¾ cup shredded sharp cheddar cheese, 2 tablespoons minced fresh chives, and 1 teaspoon pepper to flour mixture and stir to combine in step 1 before adding buttermilk mixture.

Chocolate Chip Biscuits

Increase sugar to ½ cup. Add ½ cup semisweet chocolate chips to flour mixture and stir to combine in step 1 before adding buttermilk mixture.

GENERATIONS OF BOMB BISCUITS

Restaurant owner and writer Erika Council comes from a line of women chefs. Her grandmother on her father's side was Mildred Cotton Council, the Mama behind Mama Dip's Kitchen, a beloved meat-and-three restaurant in Chapel Hill, North Carolina. Her maternal grandmother, Geraldine Dortch, cooked Sunday suppers in the 1960s and donated the proceeds to the civil rights movement.

Erika went to school for computer science but started hosting Sunday suppers of her own in Atlanta to build community and give her city a small-town feel. At one of these suppers she met Bryan Furman of B's Cracklin' BBQ, who convinced her to start doing a breakfast pop-up because her biscuits were so good. This gave way to biscuit boxes (to-go boxes of biscuits she sold to fulfill orders) and eventually a brick-and-mortar location for Bomb Biscuits, Erika's restaurant in Atlanta. Employees at the restaurant wear shirts that display the shop's slogan (and the name of Erika's cookbook), "Still We Rise," a nod to both of her grandmothers, who helped build community and acknowledge the Black presence in Southern cooking—and, of course, to biscuits themselves. (It's also hard to ignore the allusion to Maya Angelou's poem "Still I Rise.")

Most of the biscuits Erika serves are standard rolled and stamped baking powder biscuits. She offers vegan and gluten-free options so all customers can enjoy tasty biscuits. We wanted to include a drop biscuit in this book since it's such an easy starting point for biscuit bakers. But we were inspired by Erika to dress them up in two of our flavor variations. The black pepper–bacon version is inspired by her top seller, while the chocolate chip is a rotating flavor on her ever-changing menu.

by Morgan Bolling

Baking Powder Biscuits

Makes 12 biscuits ~ Total Time: 45 minutes

These baking powder biscuits are an ode to one of the most famous recipes by Edna Lewis (page 215), an icon of Southern cooking. Baking powder helps biscuits rise and become flaky; to many, baking powder–risen biscuits are the standard of Southern biscuits. But baking powder is an extra-special ingredient in Lewis's biscuits, as she was known to make her own baking powder using baking soda and cream of tartar—she thought store-bought baking powder imparted a tinny taste to baked goods. She also used lard, which was traditional at the time and gives the biscuits savoriness. And, like many Southern chefs, Lewis used Southern flour such as White Lily (see page 32) for an extra-tender biscuit.

For this version we took some liberties, such as leaving larger chunks of lard while mixing, which results in flakier biscuits. And we skip the prefab baking powder in favor of Lewis's formula. We use White Lily or Martha White flour for light, fluffy biscuits. Both White Lily and Martha White make bleached all-purpose flour, which is a lower-protein flour that develops less gluten when you work with it. If you can't find these flours, you can substitute an equal weight of cake flour. Lard is traditional, but you can substitute an equal amount of vegetable shortening. It is important to sift the flour, as it tends to clump in storage.

3	cups (13½ ounces) White Lily or Martha White flour
1	tablespoon cream of tartar
2	teaspoons baking soda
¾	teaspoon table salt
10	tablespoons lard, cut into ½-inch pieces and chilled
1	cup plus 2 tablespoons buttermilk

1   Adjust oven rack to middle position and heat oven to 450 degrees. Line rimmed baking sheet with parchment paper. Sift flour into large bowl. Whisk in cream of tartar, baking soda, and salt. Scatter lard evenly over flour mixture and use fingertips to pinch lard into flour until all pieces are flattened. Using stiff wooden spoon, stir in buttermilk until very shaggy dough forms (some bits of dry flour will remain; do not overmix).

2   Turn dough onto floured counter and, using your lightly floured hands, gently knead until dough comes together, about 30 seconds. Gently press dough into rough 6-inch round.

3   Using floured rolling pin, roll dough into 9-inch round (about ¼ inch thick). Using 2½-inch round cutter dipped in flour, stamp out 8 to 9 biscuits, making sure not to twist cutter while pressing down and dipping cutter in flour after each cut. Transfer biscuits to prepared sheet. Gather remaining dough scraps and reroll into ¾-inch-thick round. Stamp out another 3 to 4 biscuits and transfer to sheet.

4   Bake until biscuits are golden brown, about 10 minutes. Transfer sheet to wire rack and let cool for 5 minutes. Serve warm or at room temperature.

Pat-in-the-Pan Buttermilk Biscuits

Makes 9 biscuits   ~   Total Time: 1½ hours

When chef Virginia Willis (see page 249) did a demonstration at Cook's Country in August 2018, the Southern cookbook queen left us with characteristically beautiful words: "Biscuits are like people; they are better when they rise together." More than poetry, though, this sentiment referred to her preferred technique of baking biscuits touching each other on a baking sheet so they physically push each other up in the oven for a higher rise. Her demo inspired our own recipe for pat-in-the-pan biscuits. Following Willis's lead, we use low-protein cake flour for tenderness, and baking powder and baking soda for lightness and lift. We pinch bits of cold butter into these dry ingredients; the butter pieces melt in the dough during baking, producing steam that creates a fluffy interior crumb. We follow a tried-and-true Southern method for patting biscuit dough in a pan and scoring it so these biscuits can also rise together. We developed this recipe using Softasilk cake flour and a metal baking pan. This recipe can easily be doubled to yield 15 biscuits: Use a 13 by 9-inch baking pan and extend the baking time by about 15 minutes.

In the kitchen with Virginia Willis.

Angie Mosier

12	tablespoons unsalted butter, divided
4	cups (16 ounces) cake flour
2	teaspoons baking powder
½	teaspoon baking soda
2	teaspoons table salt
2	cups buttermilk, chilled

1   Cut 10 tablespoons butter into ½-inch pieces and freeze until chilled, about 15 minutes. Let 1 tablespoon butter sit at room temperature to soften. Adjust oven rack to middle position and heat oven to 450 degrees. Grease 8-inch square baking pan with remaining 1 tablespoon butter.

2   Whisk flour, baking powder, baking soda, and salt together in bowl. Add chilled butter to flour mixture and smash butter between your fingertips into pea-size pieces. Gently stir in buttermilk until no dry pockets of flour remain. Using rubber spatula, transfer dough to prepared pan.

3   Lightly sprinkle extra flour evenly over dough to prevent sticking. Using your floured hands, pat dough into even layer and into corners of pan. Using bench scraper sprayed with vegetable oil spray, cut dough into 9 equal squares (2 cuts by 2 cuts), but do not separate. Bake until golden brown on top, about 30 minutes.

4   Let biscuits cool in pan for 5 minutes. Using thin metal spatula, slide biscuits onto wire rack. Brush tops with softened butter. Let cool for 10 minutes. Pull biscuits apart at cuts and serve warm.

Angel Biscuits

Makes 16 biscuits ~ Total Time: 1¼ hours, plus 30 minutes rising

Though modest in height, angel biscuits are unbelievably light and fluffy and have the hearty yeast flavor of a dinner roll. The source of their cloudlike texture? They're made with yeast, baking powder, and baking soda—three powerful ingredients that combine to create a triple-forced lift. The biscuits are sometimes called "bride's biscuits" due to the use of three rising agents; the idea is that even a novice cook (or a new bride) can make light and fluffy biscuits on the first attempt. The dough is cut into rounds and folded in half before baking, causing the ethereally light biscuits to puff into "angel's wings" in the oven.

Angel biscuits may have been born as a use for leftover scraps of sour bread dough. In her 1846 book *Miss Beecher's Domestic Receipt-Book*, Catharine Beecher instructed cooks to "sweeten" (or neutralize) soured yeast-dough scraps with saleratus (a crude, obsolete chemical leavener similar to today's baking soda), knead in shortening, and cut the "new" dough into biscuits.

There are also theories that angel biscuits were created by White Lily or Martha White as a recipe to market their biscuit flour. Both White Lily and Martha White make bleached all-purpose flour, which is a lower-protein flour that develops less gluten when you work with it, often leading to extra-tender baked goods. If you can't find these flours, you can substitute an equal weight of cake flour.

1	cup warm buttermilk (110 degrees)
2¼	teaspoons instant or rapid-rise yeast
2¾	cups (12½ ounces) White Lily or Martha White flour
2	teaspoons baking powder
½	teaspoon baking soda
1½	teaspoons sugar
1	teaspoon table salt
8	tablespoons vegetable shortening, cut into ½-inch pieces and chilled
2	tablespoons unsalted butter, melted

1 Adjust oven racks to upper-middle and lower-middle positions and heat oven to 200 degrees. Maintain temperature for 10 minutes, then turn off oven. Line 2 rimmed baking sheets with parchment paper.

2 Stir buttermilk and yeast until yeast is dissolved. Using stand mixer fitted with paddle, mix flour, baking powder, baking soda, sugar, and salt on low speed until combined. Add shortening and mix until just incorporated, about 1 minute. Slowly mix in buttermilk mixture until dough comes together, about 30 seconds. Fit mixer with dough hook and mix on low speed until dough is shiny and smooth, about 2 minutes.

3 Knead dough briefly on lightly floured counter to form smooth ball. Roll dough into 10-inch circle, about ½ inch thick. Using 2½-inch round cutter dipped in flour, stamp out biscuits, making sure not to twist cutter while pressing down and dipping cutter in flour after each cut. Transfer biscuits to prepared sheets. Gather dough scraps and pat into ½-inch-thick round. Stamp out biscuits and transfer to sheets. Using ruler, make indentation through center of each round. Lightly brush half of each dough round with water. Fold each round in half and press lightly to adhere. Cover dough with kitchen towels and place in warm oven. Let rise until doubled in size, about 30 minutes.

4 Remove baking sheets from oven and heat oven to 350 degrees. Once oven is fully heated, remove kitchen towels and bake until biscuits are golden brown, 12 to 14 minutes, switching and rotating sheets halfway through baking. Remove from oven and brush tops with melted butter. Serve.

SHAPED BY AN ANGEL

Here's how we create Angel Biscuits' signature puffed wing shape.

1   Using ruler, make indentation through center of each round.

2   Lightly brush half of each dough round with water.

3   Fold each round of dough in half; press lightly to adhere.

North Carolina Cheese Biscuits

Makes 6 biscuits ~ Total Time: 1 hour

Cathead biscuits were born out of Appalachian frugality in a place and era (early 20th century) when butter—and free time—was an extravagance. Cooks rubbed lard into flour and leaveners, stirred in sour milk to make a wet dough, pinched off large blobs, nestled them in a cast-iron skillet, and baked them. Modern recipes typically replace the lard with shortening or now-ubiquitous butter. The resulting giant buttermilk biscuits, said to be "as big as a cat's head," are fluffy rather than flaky, with a pleasingly craggy exterior. Cooks in eastern North Carolina, like Linda Brewer of Flo's Kitchen in Wilson, North Carolina (see "#1 Biscuit Maker"), have taken to stuffing these huge biscuits with molten, gooey yellow hoop cheese, a local favorite. We love this delightfully cheesy variation.

To achieve a fluffy biscuit texture that is sturdy enough to hold a lot of cheese, we pulse chilled lard (though butter also works well) and flour in the food processor until the mixture resembles crumbly cornmeal. Next we add a generous amount of buttermilk for a wet dough; the liquid produces steam during baking for a high rise and a fluffy crumb. Hoop cheese, which is available online or in select stores in the South, is definitely worth ordering, but you can use sharp yellow cheddar. To get the cheese into the center of each biscuit, we squeeze shredded cheese into a ball, place the ball in the center of a slightly flattened circle of dough, and gently pull the circle's edges up and around the cheese to seal it inside. Since the dough is sticky, keep your hands well floured and don't be afraid to sprinkle extra flour on the biscuits to keep them from sticking. Use a light-colored cake pan.

8	ounces hoop cheese, shredded (2 cups)
2½	cups (12½ ounces) all-purpose flour, plus extra for shaping
1	tablespoon sugar
1	tablespoon baking powder
½	teaspoon baking soda
1	teaspoon table salt
4	tablespoons lard or unsalted butter, cut into ¼-inch pieces and chilled, plus 2 tablespoons melted
1½	cups buttermilk

1   Adjust oven rack to middle position and heat oven to 500 degrees. Grease light-colored 9-inch round cake pan. Working with ⅓ cup cheese, use your hands to squeeze cheese tightly into firm ball. Repeat with remaining cheese to form 5 more balls; set cheese balls aside.

2   Pulse flour, sugar, baking powder, baking soda, and salt in food processor until combined, about 6 pulses. Add chilled lard and pulse until mixture resembles pebbly, coarse cornmeal, 8 to 10 pulses. Transfer mixture to large bowl. Stir in buttermilk until just combined. (Dough will be very wet and slightly lumpy.)

3   Spread 1 cup flour in rimmed baking sheet. Using greased ½-cup dry measuring cup, transfer 6 portions of dough to prepared sheet. Dust top of each portion with flour from sheet. Using your well-floured hands, gently flatten 1 portion of dough into 3½-inch circle and coat with flour. Pick up dough and place 1 cheese ball in center. Gently pull edges of dough over cheese to enclose and pinch together to seal. Shake off excess flour and transfer, pinched side up, to prepared pan. Repeat with remaining dough and cheese, placing 5 biscuits around edge of pan and one in center. (Biscuits will be soft and will spread slightly as they sit.)

4   Brush biscuit tops with melted lard. Bake for 5 minutes, then reduce oven temperature to 450 degrees. Continue to bake until biscuits are deep golden brown, 15 to 20 minutes longer. Let biscuits cool in pan for 2 minutes, then invert onto plate. Break biscuits apart and turn right side up. Let cool for 5 minutes; serve warm.

#1 BISCUIT MAKER

Flo's Kitchen in Wilson, North Carolina, got its name from Florence Williams, a woman who knew a thing or two about cheese biscuits. She passed the recipe and restaurant down to her daughter, Linda Brewer, who now runs Flo's with a warmth that emanates like the melty cheese from her cathead biscuits. Flo's is known for their massive biscuits stuffed with warm local hoop cheese—a cheese that has some of the tanginess of cheddar but with the superb melting properties of American. If the cheese doesn't do enough for you, you can get the biscuit sandwiching slivers of country ham, bacon, fatback, fried chicken, or pork tenderloin or with a side of molasses. Whichever you pick, the biscuit will ring in under three dollars.

A staff of mostly women start making the biscuits at 3 a.m. and they're on nonstop biscuit duty: Shape, fill, bake, and repeat. It's good they start in those wee morning hours. Flo's opens its to-go window at 4 a.m. most days of the week so that anyone who is working an early shift can still power their day with biscuits.

An unmissable fixture of the restaurant is a stack of 5-gallon buckets of lard. Brewer uses it in her biscuits to give them a savory flavor and a texture firm enough to hold the copious amounts of cheese. Decorating the wall is a photo of the restaurant's matriarch, Florence Williams, who passed away at age 80. Under it reads the caption, "#1 Biscuit Maker."

The to-go window at Flo's Kitchen, open for early-morning business.

A TALE OF TWO FLOURS

For many of us from the South, biscuits evoke nostalgia. We remember the hands that made them and the brands that connect us to home and to cooking.

That connection was years in the making. It may surprise you to know that the two brands known as "Southern flour" are different in makeup. White Lily is 100 percent soft wheat, best for making light, tender biscuits. Martha White is a blend of soft and hard wheat. Technical differences aside, bakers are loyal to their brand of flour.

To explore how these flours expanded from basic commodities to respected brands is to understand the marketing of social status to women at the beginning of the 20th century. When industrial milling came South, mills produced varied grades. White Lily and Martha White were the premium products from two Tennessee mills, so were more expensive. Advertising proclaimed these to be the best flours and, even during the Depression, women were willing to pay for them. White Lily got the nickname "Sunday Best Flour," as women who could not afford it every day saved it for special meals, usually on Sunday after church.

The brands courted opinion leaders to tout the flours' quality. White Lily had the support of Mrs. Dull, *Atlanta Journal* home economics editor and cookbook author (see page 266). In the 1940s, Martha White became the sponsor of country music shows at the Grand Ole Opry and won the hearts of many, especially in the rural South, with the tagline "Goodness Gracious, It's Good!"

By the 1950s, convenience foods became more popular as women were going to work or pursuing lives outside the kitchen. Around the same time, the two companies added leavening ingredients to flour. Martha White trademarked the name "Hot Rize" for this self-rising flour, and it elicited a sense of magic; the company spread the word through a bluegrass jingle by Lester Flatt and Earl Scruggs.

Through the decades women bought less flour, but they watched more television cooking shows. In the 1970s and '80s, they tuned in to watch *New Southern Cooking with Nathalie Dupree*, underwritten by White Lily. Dupree's show gave White Lily gourmet status with home cooks and chefs.

In 2008, when bakers heard the century-old White Lily flour mill was closing in Knoxville, they emptied grocery store shelves. They were concerned the flour would not be the same even though the quality had slowly fallen for years anyway. Yet, bakers still love their Southern flour. White Lily Flour remains 100 percent soft wheat and is beloved by James Beard Award–winning authors, chefs, bloggers, and home cooks. Martha White does not have as much acclaim as a biscuit flour, but more people buy it, perhaps in part because it is easier to find outside the South despite both brands now being owned by the same company (the J.M. Smucker Company).

The truth is, however, most Southerners will tell you the best biscuit they ever had is the one they grew up eating. Turns out that it is less in the flour and more in the hands that made them all along.

by Belinda Ellis

food editor, baker, and author of Biscuits: A Savor the South Cookbook *from the University of North Carolina Press*

A White Lily flour advertisement (top), a vintage Martha White flour logo (center), and a photo of Nathalie Dupree, who made White Lily flour a household name (bottom).

Courtesy Hometown Food Company (top and center)

IT'S ALL GRAVY

In her article "The Seven Essential Southern Dishes" for *The Bitter Southerner,* cookbook author Sheri Castle (see page 150) writes, "Gravy is the apex of our sauce making. Anybody ought to be able to make an exquisite sauce with cream and butter. A cook can make exquisite gravy out of nothing." Southern cooks smother meat or biscuits with their standout gravies. Here are two very different versions for biscuit gravy, plus three additional variations.

Sawmill Gravy

Serves 6
Total Time: 25 minutes

Many food historians point to biscuits and gravy being combined for the first time in the late 1800s in southern Appalachia. Lumber was one of the main industries at the time. The theory goes that the sawmill workers would eat biscuits smothered in a calorie-dense sausage-based gravy to power them through the workday, hence the name sawmill gravy. This was before the time of commercial leaveners, so the biscuits of that era were less tender—the gravy was doing double duty in terms of flavor and texture. Nowadays this quick sausage gravy is popular at home and on brunch menus. A pile of buttery biscuits smothered with a cloak of sausage gravy is known to be the elixir for the Southerner who had a little too much bourbon the night before.

- ¼ cup all-purpose flour
- 1 teaspoon ground fennel seed
- 1 teaspoon ground sage
- 1½ teaspoons pepper
- 1½ pounds bulk pork sausage
- 3 cups whole milk

Combine flour, fennel, sage, and pepper in small bowl. Cook sausage in 12-inch nonstick skillet over medium heat, breaking up meat with wooden spoon, until no longer pink, about 8 minutes. Sprinkle flour mixture over sausage and cook, stirring constantly, until flour has been absorbed, about 1 minute. Slowly stir in milk and simmer until sauce has thickened, about 5 minutes. Season with salt and pepper to taste. Serve.

Chocolate Gravy

Serves 6 to 8
Total Time: 30 minutes

Particularly beloved in Arkansas, chocolate—yes, chocolate—gravy should be thick, rich, and sweet enough to complement a tangy biscuit. This recipe works best with natural unsweetened cocoa powder; Dutch-processed cocoa powder will result in a slightly thinner gravy. This recipe can easily be doubled; increase simmering time to 25 minutes.

- ½ cup sugar
- ½ cup natural unsweetened cocoa powder
- 1 tablespoon all-purpose flour
- ¼ teaspoon table salt
- 1½ cups water
- 1 cup whole milk
- 6 tablespoons unsalted butter, cut into ½-inch pieces and chilled
- ½ teaspoon vanilla extract

Whisk sugar, cocoa, flour, and salt together in large saucepan, then whisk in water and milk until combined. Bring to simmer over medium heat and cook, whisking frequently, until thickened and small bubbles slowly break at surface, about 15 minutes. Off heat, whisk in butter and vanilla. Serve. (Gravy can be refrigerated for up to 1 week; bring to brief simmer over medium-low heat, adjusting consistency with extra milk as needed and whisking vigorously if gravy appears broken.)

Browned Butter Chocolate Gravy

Heat butter in large saucepan over medium heat until melted, about 2 minutes. Continue cooking, stirring constantly, until butter is dark golden brown and has nutty aroma, 1 to 3 minutes; transfer butter to small heat-proof bowl. Proceed with recipe as directed in now-empty saucepan.

Orange-Rose Chocolate Gravy

Substitute ½ teaspoon rose water for vanilla. Add four 3-inch strips orange zest with milk and water. Discard zest before whisking in butter and rose water.

Spiced Chocolate Gravy

Whisk ½ teaspoon ancho chile powder, ¼ teaspoon ground cinnamon, and ⅛ teaspoon cayenne pepper into sugar mixture before adding water and milk.

White Sandwich Bread

Makes 1 loaf   ~   Total Time: 1½ hours, plus 5¾ to 6¾ hours rising and cooling

In the South, moist, fluffy slices of sandwich bread are used for far more than their namesake. Sure, you'll find the ubiquitous white bread sandwiching juicy-ripe summer tomatoes and a slathering of Duke's mayonnaise, but you'll also see it served alongside Eastern North Carolina Fish Stew (page 207) for mopping. And it's not Texas barbecue without some slices of white bread served on your plate alongside the juicy slabs of brisket. Since our sandwich bread needs to serve so many purposes, we made sure it was tender, easily sliceable, and equally good fresh or toasted. Higher-protein bread flour gives this loaf the structure it needs to rise high and just enough chew. Good white bread has a subtle richness, which we achieve with a couple tablespoons of butter. A touch of honey provides the requisite sweetness while helping the outer crust to brown. This loaf is sure to be a staple in your bread box, whether you're in the South or not.

2½   cups (13¾ ounces) bread flour

2   teaspoons instant or rapid-rise yeast

1½   teaspoons table salt

¾   cup whole milk, room temperature

⅓   cup water, room temperature

2   tablespoons unsalted butter, melted

2   tablespoons honey

1   Whisk flour, yeast, and salt together in bowl of stand mixer. Whisk milk, water, melted butter, and honey in 4-cup liquid measuring cup until honey has dissolved. Using dough hook on low speed, slowly add milk mixture to flour mixture and mix until cohesive dough starts to form and no dry flour remains, about 2 minutes, scraping down bowl as needed. Increase speed to medium-low and knead until dough is smooth and elastic and clears sides of bowl, about 8 minutes.

2   Transfer dough to lightly floured counter and knead by hand to form smooth, round ball, about 30 seconds. Place dough seam side down in lightly greased large bowl, cover tightly with plastic wrap, and let rise until doubled in volume, 1½ to 2 hours.

3   Grease 8½ by 4½-inch loaf pan. Press down on dough to deflate. Turn dough out onto lightly floured counter (side of dough that was against bowl should now be facing up). Press and stretch dough into 8 by 6-inch rectangle, with long side parallel to counter edge. Roll dough away from you into firm cylinder, keeping roll taut by tucking it under itself as you go. Pinch seam closed and place loaf seam side down in prepared pan, tucking ends as needed to match size of pan and pressing dough gently into corners. Cover loosely with greased plastic and let rise until loaf reaches 1 inch above lip of pan and dough springs back minimally when poked gently with your finger, 1 to 1½ hours.

4   Adjust oven rack to lower-middle position and heat oven to 350 degrees. Mist loaf with water and bake until deep golden brown and loaf registers at least 205 degrees, 35 to 40 minutes, rotating pan halfway through baking. Let loaf cool in pan for 15 minutes. Remove loaf from pan and let cool completely on wire rack, about 3 hours, before serving.

SHAPING SANDWICH BREAD

This supple dough is easy to shape into an even loaf.

1   Press and stretch dough into 8 by 6-inch rectangle, with long side parallel to counter edge.

2   Roll dough into firm cylinder.

3   Pinch seam closed.

4   Place dough in pan, tucking as needed.

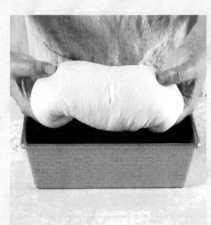

SHARING SALT-RISING BREAD

For the early settlers, who didn't have access to commercial yeast, white bread wasn't tall and fluffy like modern classic sandwich bread. The dense, yeastless, slow-rising, naturally leavened bread they made is known as salt-rising bread. The earliest known recipe is from 1778 West Virginia. The bread spread to surrounding states and eventually north to Pennsylvania and New York. As Southerners moved westward, it was even made in the Midwest and as far away as California. Despite the name, there's little to no salt in this bread. Historians don't know how it got that name; one theory is that the starter was often nestled into salt barrels to keep it warm.

Salt-rising bread was long sold in grocery stores and baked at home. But with the rise of commercial baking and modern busy schedules, it has almost disappeared entirely. Amy Dawson, farm manager and baker at Lost Creek Farm in West Virginia, is on a mission to continue this endangered baking tradition. Dawson learned to make the bread with Jenny Bardwell and Susan Ray Brown of Rising Creek Bakery in Mount Morris, Pennsylvania, which specializes in salt-rising bread. Dawson is passionate about West Virginia regional cuisine, and she bakes salt-rising bread for farm dinners. Through her commitment to baking it, she advocates for the importance of preserving culinary history.

The flavor of and process for making salt-rising bread are different from those of typical sandwich bread. Unlike sourdough starter, the salt-rising starter that makes the bread grow is made anew each time, then fermented overnight. Salt-rising bread has a flat top and dense crumb, so it's good for toast. It's cheesy, funky, and slightly sweet.

by Julia Skinner, PhD

food historian and author of Our Fermented Lives: A History of How Fermented Foods Have Shaped Cultures and Communities

Easy Crescent Rolls

Makes 16 rolls ~ Total Time: 1¼ hours, plus 2½ to 3½ hours rising

Most recipes for buttery, flaky crescent rolls call for repeated rolling and folding to layer softened butter into the dough. But as a nod to Lucille Bishop Smith, an entrepreneur who created a hot roll mix that allowed people to bake bread more easily at home (see "Business on a Roll"), we turned to an easy-to-make at-home version called butter horn rolls. These rolls are softer than traditional crescents, but they're just as rich and buttery and get some flakiness from stirring melted butter into the liquid ingredients before combining with the dry ingredients in a stand mixer. And these rolls get an extra hit of buttery flavor from a brush with softened butter, as well as a sprinkling of salt while shaping. Sure, they're not quite as easy as using hot roll mix (it's unfortunately no longer available for purchase), but they do come together relatively quickly for a crescent roll. A pizza cutter makes quick work of cutting the dough into wedges; alternatively, you can use a chef's knife or bench scraper.

2½	cups (12½ ounces) all-purpose flour
1	teaspoon instant or rapid-rise yeast
1	teaspoon table salt
½	cup half-and-half, room temperature
7	tablespoons unsalted butter, melted and cooled slightly
1	large egg plus 1 large yolk, room temperature
¼	cup (1¾ ounces) sugar
1	large egg, beaten with 1 tablespoon water and pinch table salt

1   Line rimmed baking sheet with parchment paper and spray with vegetable oil spray.

2   Whisk flour, yeast, and salt together in bowl of stand mixer. Whisk half-and-half, melted butter, egg and yolk, and sugar in 4-cup liquid measuring cup until sugar has dissolved.

3   Using dough hook on low speed, slowly add half-and-half mixture to flour mixture and mix until cohesive dough starts to form and no dry flour remains, about 2 minutes, scraping down bowl as needed. Increase speed to medium-low and knead until dough is smooth and elastic and clears sides of bowl (it will stick to bottom), about 8 minutes.

4   Transfer dough to lightly floured counter and divide in half. Knead each dough half by hand to form smooth, round ball, about 30 seconds each. Place dough balls seam side down on prepared sheet, spaced about 6 inches apart. Cover loosely with greased plastic wrap and let rise until doubled in volume, 1½ to 2 hours.

5   Line second sheet with parchment. Working with 1 dough ball at a time (keep remaining dough ball covered), press down on dough to deflate and transfer to clean counter. Press and roll dough into 12-inch circle. Using pizza cutter or chef's knife, cut circle into 8 even wedges. Starting at wide end, gently roll up each dough wedge, ending with pointed tip on bottom. Push ends toward each other to form crescent shape. Arrange crescent rolls evenly on prepared sheets (line baking sheet for rising with fresh parchment before adding crescent rolls) and reshape as needed. Cover loosely with greased plastic. Let rolls rise until nearly doubled in size and dough springs back minimally when poked gently with your finger, 1 to 1½ hours.

6   Adjust oven racks to upper-middle and lower-middle positions and heat oven to 350 degrees. Gently brush rolls with egg mixture and bake until golden brown, about 20 minutes, switching and rotating sheets halfway through baking. Let rolls cool on sheet on wire rack for 15 minutes. Serve warm or at room temperature.

BUSINESS ON A ROLL

Lucille Bishop Smith could have claimed many titles: seamstress, chef, teacher, food editor, corporation president, and, as many have called her, Texas's first African American business-woman. She was born in Texas in 1892 and graduated from Samuel Huston College (which is now Huston-Tillotson University). After college she went to work as a seamstress and cook before she took her first role lifting up her community as the teacher-coordinator for a vocational education program that was geared to train Black students in domestic service jobs.

In 1941, Smith published a box set of recipes called "Lucille's Treasure Chest of Fine Foods" to help educate people who wanted to improve their culinary skills. In the mid-1940s she created and marketed Lucille's All Purpose Hot Roll Mix, a convenience baking mix that could be used to bake pizza dough, bread, or rolls, to raise money for her church. It sold out, raising $800 (a huge amount at the time) for the church. Grocery stores began placing orders for it since this was the first all-purpose hot roll mix on the market. An article in the *Cleburne Times-Review* in 2004 stated, "The product paved the way for the convenience cooking we know today."

One of Smith's signature recipes was for chili biscuits: a biscuit stuffed with chili and topped with American cheese. They were so good, they were served at both the White House and on American Airlines flights.

Bishop-Smith served as the first food editor for *Sepia* magazine, a photo-journalistic magazine similar to *Life* that focused on Black Americans. At age 82, she assumed the role of president of her co-owned corporation, Lucille B. Smith's Fine Foods, Inc.

During a time of Jim Crow laws (which existed in Texas until 1965), Smith forged a path out of poverty for women and people of color who didn't have many opportunities. Food was her avenue for raising people up.

by Morgan Bolling

BRINGING A TASTE OF HOME TO MIAMI

Pan de jamón is a sweet and savory rolled bread popularized by Venezuelan bakeries during the early 1900s as a Christmas treat. Originally crafted from leftover bread dough, cooked ham trimmings, pepper-stuffed olives, and raisins, this traditional baked good persists to this day and travels with Venezuelans wherever they go.

In the early 1980s, my cousin Magaly Sargalski pioneered home-baking pan de jamón in Miami, Florida. Her recipe turned into a legend that gained recognition beyond Miami Dade County, especially at a time when Venezuelan cuisine was scarce. During that period, Venezuela's prosperity, driven by oil, attracted Venezuelans to the U.S. for shopping and leisure. However, the availability and demand for Venezuelan food hadn't reached its current levels, influenced by a significant migration around the turn of the millennium due to economic and political turmoil in Venezuela.

Magaly's journey into pan de jamón started informally when her mother shared one of her loaves at an office holiday potluck. This sparked a word-of-mouth phenomenon, resulting in a surge of orders for Magaly out of her home kitchen from Thanksgiving through New Year's Eve. Her reputation expanded through coverage in local magazines and newspapers, drawing attention from Venezuelan TV personalities, locals, and occasional holiday tourists who sought her culinary masterpiece year after year.

Magaly's rendition features a brioche-like bread filled with cooked ham, rendered bacon, briny olives, and plump raisins—an impressive loaf adorned with delicate braids, bows, and floral motifs, appropriate as the centerpiece of a Venezuelan holiday feast. Her vibrant kitchen during that time was a bustling operation producing more than twenty artisanal breads daily. During the holidays she shipped hundreds of breads across Florida and to Atlanta, New York, and throughout Texas.

As the years unfold, Magaly continues to honor her Venezuelan roots, limiting the baking of pan de jamón to friends, family, and a handful of devoted patrons who share the joy of this tradition. Each holiday season becomes a celebration of home, heritage, and community.

by Mercedes Golip

Caracas-born cook, recipe developer, and content creator

Pan de Jamón

Makes 1 loaf   ~   Total Time: 1½ hours, plus 1 hour 40 minutes rising and resting

Medium to thick slices of deli ham are ideal for this recipe, providing a satisfying filling. To enhance the festive appeal, Magaly trims the dough edges before assembling and places them on top of the loaf in decorative patterns—crafting ribbons, braids, and shapes by hand or using cookie cutters.

4	slices bacon
½	cup warm milk (110 degrees)
1½	teaspoons instant or rapid-rise yeast
2	tablespoons unsalted butter, melted
1½	tablespoons sugar
1	teaspoon table salt
2	large eggs
2½	cups (13¾ ounces) sifted bread flour
10	ounces deli ham
½	cup raisins
½	cup pimento-stuffed olives, patted dry
1	large egg beaten with 2 tablespoons water

1   Cook bacon in 12-inch skillet over medium-high heat until beginning to crisp, about 5 minutes. Using slotted spoon, transfer bacon to paper towel–lined plate. Reserve 2 tablespoons fat and set aside; chop bacon into 2- to 3-inch pieces; set aside.

2   Whisk milk and yeast together in bowl of stand mixer and let sit until foamy, about 10 minutes. Whisk in melted butter, 1 tablespoon reserved bacon fat, sugar, and salt. Using dough hook on medium-low speed, mix in eggs until fully incorporated. Add flour, 1 cup at a time, until cohesive dough forms and no dry flour remains, 2 to 4 minutes, scraping down bowl as needed. Increase speed to medium-high and knead until dough begins to pull away from sides of bowl, about 10 minutes, scraping down bowl as needed. Transfer dough to lightly greased large bowl. Cover tightly with plastic wrap and let rise until doubled in volume, about 1 hour.

3   Press down on dough to deflate and let rest for 10 minutes. Transfer dough to lightly floured counter and press and roll into 16 by 14-inch rectangle, about ⅛ inch thick, with short side parallel to counter edge. Save trimmings for decorating, if desired. Brush top of dough with remaining 1 tablespoon bacon fat. Arrange ham in even layer over dough, leaving ¼ inch border. Place bacon pieces evenly over ham, then sprinkle evenly with raisins and olives. Brush edge of dough with water. Roll dough away from you into firm cylinder and pinch seam and ends closed, using additional water as needed. Press loaf gently to flatten slightly (loaf should measure about 14 inches long by 4 inches wide by 2 inches high).

4   Transfer loaf to lightly greased rimmed baking sheet seam side down. Cover loosely with plastic and let rest for 40 minutes.

5   While dough rests, adjust oven rack to middle position and heat oven to 350 degrees. Just before baking, brush loaf with egg-water mixture. Bake until golden brown and loaf registers at least 200 degrees, 35 to 45 minutes, rotating pan halfway through baking. Let cool for at least 10 minutes. Slice and serve warm or at room temperature. (Pan de jamón can be refrigerated, wrapped tightly in plastic, for up to 2 days. Serve at room temperature.)

Dollywood Cinnamon Bread

Makes 1 loaf ~ Total Time: 2 hours, plus 2 hours rising

At Dollywood, a real attraction is the bread. Park patrons line up for hours at the gristmill to get freshly baked loaves of their famous yeasted bread coated in lavish amounts of butter and cinnamon sugar. They grind the flour for the bread on location. It's so good, the mill serves about 350 loaves of bread every hour! The bread is offered glazed or dusted with powdered sugar, served with apple butter, or enjoyed all by itself.

Dolly Parton herself offers a recipe for this bread in her 2006 cookbook, *Dolly's Dixie Fixin's*. (Money from sales of the cookbook went to Dolly Parton's Imagination Library, a program that gifts books to children every month.) In her recipe, she suggests using pizza dough to make it easier. And you certainly could swap in pizza dough for the bread dough in our version (simply skip steps 1 and 2), but we suggest making your own, which gives you control over the flavor and texture of the dough.

Dough

1	tablespoon unsalted butter, softened, plus 2 tablespoons melted
1⅔	cups (8⅓ ounces) all-purpose flour
1¼	teaspoons instant or rapid-rise yeast
½	cup plus 3 tablespoons warm water (110 degrees)
2	tablespoons granulated sugar
1	teaspoon table salt

Sugar Coating

½	cup packed (3½ ounces) light brown sugar
¼	cup (1¾ ounces) granulated sugar
4	teaspoons ground cinnamon
¼	teaspoon table salt
8	tablespoons unsalted butter, melted, divided

Glaze (Optional)

½	cup (2 ounces) confectioners' sugar
1	tablespoon milk

1   **For the dough** Grease 8½ by 4½-inch loaf pan with softened butter. Whisk flour and yeast together in bowl of stand mixer. Add water. Fit mixer with dough hook and mix on low speed until dough comes together and no dry flour remains, about 2 minutes, scraping down bowl and dough hook frequently. Turn off mixer, cover bowl with plastic wrap, and let dough rest for 15 minutes.

2   Add sugar, salt, and melted butter to dough and knead on medium-low speed until incorporated, about 30 seconds. Increase speed to medium and knead until dough is elastic and pulls away cleanly from sides of bowl, 6 to 8 minutes longer. Transfer dough to greased large bowl. Cover tightly with plastic and let rise until doubled in volume, about 1 hour.

3   **For the sugar coating** Meanwhile, mix brown sugar, granulated sugar, cinnamon, and salt together in shallow dish, breaking up any clumps of brown sugar. Set aside 6 tablespoons cinnamon sugar mixture. Place 4 tablespoons melted butter in second shallow dish.

4   Press dough into rough 8 by 4-inch rectangle on lightly floured counter, with long side parallel to counter edge. Using bench scraper or sharp knife, cut dough crosswise into 5 equal rectangles (about 1½ by 4 inches each). Working with 1 rectangle at a time, coat rectangles in melted butter, then coat in cinnamon sugar mixture in shallow dish. Lay crosswise in prepared pan, arranging in single layer. Cover pan loosely with greased plastic and let rise until puffy, about 1 hour (cinnamon sugar may crack during this time).

5   Adjust oven rack to middle position and heat oven to 350 degrees. Bake until top is deep brown and center of bread registers 205 to 210 degrees, about 30 minutes, rotating pan halfway through baking.

6   Meanwhile, whisk reserved 6 tablespoons cinnamon sugar mixture and remaining 4 tablespoons melted butter together. Remove loaf from oven and immediately brush with butter mixture (use all of it). Let loaf cool in pan for 15 minutes.

7   **For the glaze** If desired, whisk sugar and milk together until smooth.

8   Carefully transfer bread to platter. Let cool for 15 minutes longer. Drizzle with glaze, if using. Serve warm.

Alabama Orange Rolls

Makes 8 rolls   ~   Total Time: 1¾ hours, plus 3 to 4 hours rising and cooling

You can find pillowy, yeasted rolls filled with orange and sugar served in the bread basket alongside savory foods in many spots in Birmingham, Alabama. It's likely this trend was sparked by Mrs. Ewing Steele. Steele was hired as the baker of Vestavia Roman Rooms, an elegant Birmingham restaurant that opened in the late 1940s in a former mayor's Roman temple–inspired home. She brought her recipe from her past roles working as kitchen manager at an Episcopal church in Texas and at the Officers' Club at Fort McClellan in Alabama. Steele went on to write two cookbooks, *Secrets of Cooking* in 1970 and a follow-up, *More Secrets of Cooking* in 1980.

While they look a lot like sticky buns or cinnamon rolls, orange rolls weren't served for breakfast or dessert but rather alongside soups, salads, steaks, and the other hearty mains offered at the Vestavia Roman Rooms. The rolls became a staple at multiple clubs and restaurants around Birmingham. In our version, inspired by the ones served at All Steak Restaurant in Cullman, Alabama, we pack orange into the dough (fresh juice), filling (zest), and glaze (fresh juice). Be sure to zest the oranges before juicing them. We bake these rolls in a dark-colored cake pan to encourage better browning. If you have only a light-colored pan, increase the baking time to 45 to 50 minutes.

Dough

3   cups (15 ounces) all-purpose flour

¼   cup (1¾ ounces) sugar

2¼   teaspoons instant or rapid-rise yeast

1   teaspoon table salt

½   cup warm orange juice (110 degrees)

6   tablespoons unsalted butter, cut into 6 pieces and softened

1   large egg plus 1 large yolk

¼   cup heavy cream

Filling

½   cup (3½ ounces) sugar

2   teaspoons grated orange zest

2   tablespoons unsalted butter, softened

Glaze

¼   cup heavy cream

¼   cup (1¾ ounces) sugar

2   tablespoons orange juice

2   tablespoons unsalted butter

⅛   teaspoon table salt

1 **For the dough** Whisk flour, sugar, yeast, and salt together in bowl of stand mixer. Add orange juice, butter, egg and yolk, and cream. Knead with dough hook on medium speed until dough comes together, about 2 minutes. Increase speed to medium–high and continue to knead until dough is smooth and elastic, about 8 minutes longer (dough will be soft).

2 Transfer dough to lightly floured counter and knead until smooth ball forms, about 30 seconds. Place dough in greased large bowl, cover tightly with plastic wrap, and let rise until doubled in volume, 1½ to 2 hours.

3 **For the filling** Combine sugar and orange zest in small bowl. Transfer dough to lightly floured counter. Roll dough into 16 by 8-inch rectangle with long side parallel to counter edge. Spread butter over surface of dough using small offset spatula, then sprinkle evenly with sugar mixture. Roll dough away from you into tight, even log and pinch seam to seal.

4 Grease dark-colored 9-inch cake pan, line with parchment paper, and grease parchment. Roll log seam side down. Using serrated knife, cut log into eight 2-inch-thick rolls. Place 1 roll in center of prepared pan and remaining rolls around perimeter of pan, seam side facing center. Cover with plastic and let rise until doubled in size, 1 to 1½ hours.

5 Adjust oven rack to middle position and heat oven to 325 degrees. Bake rolls until golden brown on top and interior of center roll registers 195 degrees, 40 to 45 minutes. Let rolls cool in pan on wire rack for 30 minutes.

6 **For the glaze** Once rolls have cooled for 30 minutes, combine all ingredients in small saucepan and bring to boil over medium heat. Cook, stirring frequently, until large, slow bubbles appear and mixture is syrupy, about 4 minutes.

7 Using spatula, loosen rolls from sides of pan and slide onto platter; discard parchment. Brush glaze over tops of rolls and serve warm.

Conchas

Makes 12 conchas ~ Total Time: 2¼ hours, plus 2 to 2½ hours rising

Conchas are a lightly sweet enriched bread topped with a cookie-like crust that's scored to look like a shell (concha means "seashell" in Spanish). An ideal concha is buttery, light, and tender—perfect for a dunk in hot chocolate or coffee—yet sturdy enough to support the crispy crust. Conchas derive from brioche, brought to Mexico through the migration of European bakers in the 1800s. From there they have made their way across the border into the Southwest, and many chefs in the Southern United States are putting their own spin on conchas (see "Connecting with Conchas" on page 47).

In our version we add the flavorful, sweet topping (vanilla and chocolate are the most common versions), made from equal parts confectioners' sugar, flour, and vegetable shortening, by pressing it into a thin round to cover each bun. The high melting point of the shortening helps the iconic seashell scoring hold during baking. A butter knife makes quick work of the design, without the need for a traditional concha cutter. When the coating sets, it gives the soft bun crunch and then melts in your mouth. Conchas are best eaten the day they are made.

Dough

- 3⅔ cups (20⅛ ounces) bread flour
- 1 tablespoon instant or rapid-rise yeast
- 1¼ cups water, room temperature
- 2 large eggs, room temperature
- ¼ cup (1¾ ounces) granulated sugar
- 2 teaspoons table salt
- 13 tablespoons unsalted butter, cut into 13 pieces and softened

Sugar Crust

- 1 cup (4 ounces) confectioners' sugar
- ¾ cup (4⅛ ounces) bread flour, plus extra for rolling
- 10 tablespoons vegetable shortening
- 2 teaspoons vanilla extract
- ⅛ teaspoon table salt

1 **For the dough** Whisk flour and yeast together in bowl of stand mixer. Whisk water and eggs in 4-cup liquid measuring cup until combined. Using dough hook on low speed, add water mixture to flour mixture and mix until cohesive dough starts to form and no dry flour remains, about 2 minutes, scraping down bowl as needed. Let rest for 15 minutes.

2 Add sugar and salt to dough and knead on medium-low speed until incorporated, about 30 seconds. Increase speed to medium and, with mixer running, add butter 1 piece at a time, allowing each piece to incorporate before adding next, 4 to 6 minutes total, scraping down bowl and dough hook as needed. Continue to knead until dough is elastic and pulls away cleanly from sides of bowl, about 10 minutes longer.

3 Transfer dough to greased large bowl, cover with greased plastic wrap, and let dough rise until doubled in volume, about 1 hour.

4 **For the sugar crust** While dough rises, in clean, dry mixer bowl, combine sugar, flour, shortening, vanilla, and salt. Fit mixer with paddle and mix on low speed, scraping down bowl as needed, until mixture is homogeneous and has texture of Play-Doh, about 2 minutes. Transfer mixture to counter and divide into 12 equal pieces. Roll into balls, place on large plate, and cover with plastic; refrigerate for 30 minutes. Draw or trace 4-inch circle in center of 1 side of zipper-lock bag. Cut open seams along both sides of bag, leaving bottom seam intact so bag opens completely; set aside.

5 Line 2 rimmed baking sheets with parchment paper. Transfer concha dough to clean counter and divide into 12 equal pieces. Cover loosely with greased plastic. Working with 1 piece of dough at a time (keep remaining pieces covered), form into rough ball by bringing edges of dough together and pinching edges to seal so that top is smooth. Place ball seam side down on clean counter and, using your cupped hand, drag in small circles until dough feels taut and round. Repeat with remaining dough pieces, scraping counter clean with bench scraper as needed. Evenly space 6 dough balls on each prepared sheet. Poke any air bubbles in dough balls with tip of paring knife.

6 Cover rolls loosely with greased plastic and let rise until doubled in size, 1 to 1½ hours.

7   While rolls rise, place reserved cut bag marked side down on counter. Place ⅓ cup flour in small bowl; gently toss 1 ball of sugar crust in flour to generously coat, then open bag and place ball in center of circle. Fold other side of bag over ball and, using glass pie plate or baking dish, gently press crust to 4-inch diameter, using circle drawn on bag as guide. Carefully peel bag away from crust to remove, then place crust on top of 1 ball of concha dough, pressing gently to mold crust to dough. Repeat with remaining balls of crust and concha dough, wiping bag clean as needed. (Don't wait until after dough rises to top dough balls with crust.)

8   Using butter knife and pressing gently, score crust of each roll with series of concentric curved lines emanating from single point to create seashell pattern, being careful not to cut through topping completely.

9   Adjust oven racks to upper-middle and lower-middle positions and heat oven to 350 degrees. Bake until buns are golden brown and register at least 205 degrees, 20 to 25 minutes, switching and rotating sheets halfway through baking. Transfer sheets to wire racks and let cool for 15 minutes. Serve.

Chocolate Conchas

Reduce bread flour in sugar crust to ⅔ cup (3⅔ ounces) and add 3 tablespoons unsweetened cocoa powder.

continued   >

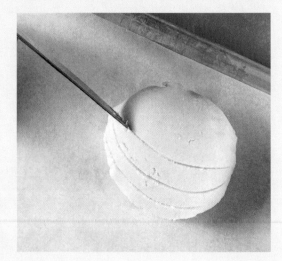

TOPPING THE CONCHAS

The sugar crust is a malleable dough that you can decorate with a knife for the trademark design.

1   Working with 1 ball of sugar crust dough at a time, toss in flour to generously coat.

2   Press dough ball to 4-inch diameter using circle on zipper-lock bag as guide.

3   Place crust on top of 1 concha, pressing crust gently to mold to dough.

4   Using butter knife and pressing gently, score crust of each roll with series of concentric curved lines emanating from single point.

CONNECTING WITH CONCHAS

When Vice President Kamala Harris visited Raleigh, North Carolina, in January 2023, she stopped into Panadería Artesenal for Mexican pan dulce (translated as "sweet bread"). On a tray piled high with treats, a fluffy concha beamed front and center.

Conchas are a round, slightly sweet bread with a cookie-like topping, sometimes brightly colored, designed to resemble a shell. Traditionally dipped into coffee, they have become a ubiquitous modern symbol of Mexican American kitsch, fashioned into dangly earrings, fluffy slippers and even a playful Spanglish meme: "Don't be self-conchas."

"I think the concha seems impressive to people, especially people who don't bake," says Teresa Finney of At Heart Panadería, the Atlanta microbakery. Finney draws from her maternal Mexican lineage and seasonal Southern ingredients. For the conchas, she experiments with both. Flavor combinations include pumpkin brown butter tangerine and hibiscus strawberry.

Teresa Finney (top) and the creative conchas she offers through her business At Heart Panadería (bottom).

Teresa Finney

She uses the umbrella term "enriched dough" to categorize the concha, though admits that isn't exact. "I love to see pan dulce being a part of the conversation. When a lot of people think about breads and pastries, the first thing that comes to mind is croissant and brioche. French foods," Finney says.

Waves of European migration to Mexico—from Spanish colonization to the late 19th century—influenced locals' adoption of nonindigenous ingredients and, eventually, baking techniques. European immigrants' panaderías helped make wheat a staple ingredient. Introduced to enriched breads like brioche, Mexican bakers made pan dulce their own, with treats like conchas.

Chanel Watson remembers visiting Mexico City with her mother, and walking to California panaderías with her Mexican abuelo for a concha as a kid. She could not get the taste of the "mesmerizing pastry" out of her head. She now makes 10 dozen a week at her Dallas home bakery, Cakelamb, perfecting the recipe over five years. The first detour she ever took: a filling of mascarpone and lemon chantilly cream. It's still her favorite. Watson's advice for making conchas at home: "They are not a perfect pastry. Focus on the process, not the end result. It's process art."

by Victoria Bouloubasis

freelance journalist, food writer, and filmmaker

Beignets

Makes 24 beignets ～ Total Time: 1 hour, plus 1 hour rising

Louisiana's official state doughnut, the beignet, is known for its airy, crisp texture and tangy yeast flavor. In 1927 the *Times-Picayune*, a New Orleans newspaper, hyped the tasty fritters: "There aren't any holes in them, [and] they are not round like in the conventional doughnut … They aren't anything that an ordinary doughnut is. The reason is that they are better."

If you can't travel to Louisiana to tear into a beignet alongside a chicory coffee, try making them at home. They take a little time but are quite easy to make. You need to use plenty of yeast and prompt it with warm water and sugar to start developing flavor right off the bat. A super-hydrated dough means lots of steam, which creates an open, honeycombed structure as soon as the beignets hit the hot oil. Since wet dough is tricky to roll out, it's helpful to let it firm up in the refrigerator and then flour the counter and baking sheet generously. After a few minutes of frying and a dusting of powdered sugar, these beignets are ready to enjoy Big Easy–style. Use a Dutch oven that holds 6 quarts or more.

1	cup warm water (110 degrees)
3	tablespoons granulated sugar, divided
1	tablespoon instant or rapid-rise yeast
3	cups (15 ounces) all-purpose flour
¾	teaspoon table salt
2	large eggs
2	tablespoons plus 2 quarts vegetable oil, divided
	Confectioners' sugar

1   Combine water, 1 tablespoon granulated sugar, and yeast in large bowl and let sit until foamy, about 5 minutes. Combine flour, salt, and remaining 2 tablespoons granulated sugar in second bowl. Whisk eggs and 2 tablespoons oil into yeast mixture. Add flour mixture and stir vigorously with spatula until dough comes together. Cover bowl with plastic wrap and refrigerate until doubled in volume, about 1 hour.

2   Set wire rack in rimmed baking sheet. Line second sheet with parchment paper and dust heavily with flour. Place half of dough on well-floured counter and pat into rectangle with your floured hands, flipping dough to coat with flour. Roll into ¼-inch-thick rectangle (roughly 12 by 9 inches). Using pizza wheel, cut dough into twelve 3-inch squares and transfer to floured sheet. Repeat with remaining dough.

3   Add remaining oil to large Dutch oven until it measures about 1½ inches deep and heat over medium-high heat to 350 degrees. Place 6 dough squares in oil and fry until golden brown, about 3 minutes, flipping halfway through frying. Adjust burner, if necessary, to maintain oil temperature between 325 and 350 degrees. Using slotted spoon or spider skimmer, transfer beignets to prepared rack. Return oil to 350 degrees and repeat with remaining dough squares. Dust beignets with confectioners' sugar. Serve immediately.

No. 2
SOUL-SATISFYING BREAKFASTS

Left to right: Kolaches (page 80), Country Ham with Red-Eye Gravy (page 66), former Village Bakery owner Mimi Montgomery Irwin (see page 82), fried chicken and waffles (see page 62), Migas (page 77).

Mimi Montgomery Irwin: John Davidson

- 54 -

Buttermilk Pancakes

Blueberry Pancakes

Chocolate Chip–Coconut Pancakes

Strawberry Vanilla Pancakes

- 56 -

Pain Perdu with Chantilly Crème

Pain Perdu with Brown Sugar and Bourbon
Chantilly Crème

Pain Perdu with Lemon Chantilly Crème

- 58 -

Quick Yeasted Waffles

Buttery Blueberry Maple Syrup

- 60 -

Fried Boneless Chicken Thighs

Spicy Lime Honey

- 64 -

Light Rolls

- 66 -

Country Ham with Red-Eye Gravy

- 68 -

Black Pepper Candied Bacon

Chipotle Candied Bacon

Five-Spice and Sesame Candied Bacon

Jerk-Inspired Candied Bacon

Rosemary Candied Bacon

- 69 -

Homemade Breakfast Sausage

- 70 -

Texas Breakfast Tacos

Texas Breakfast Tacos with Chorizo

Texas Breakfast Tacos with Potato

Salsa Roja

Homemade Taco-Size Flour Tortillas

- 74 -

Eggs Hussarde

- 77 -

Migas

- 78 -

Hash Browns

- 80 -

Kolaches

Fruit-Filled Kolaches

- 83 -

Klobásníky

THE BREAKFAST TABLE

Sunrise in the rural South is an event everyone should experience at least once. There are no mosquitoes out that early, the gnats are still sleeping, and the birds are often all you hear. If you're lucky to be near the coast, you'll notice the way the Spanish moss filters the new sunlight like an old porch screen. The stillness outside welcomes the meal that the South does best.

When I was a child growing up in a small South Georgia town, there was never a special spot in the pantry for cereal boxes and granola bars. We had no such thing. Breakfast consisted of hot grits, crispy bacon, and scrambled eggs, even on the busiest of school days. My father cooked a hot meal for my sister and me every single day, and we never went to school without being stuffed to the brim. On big test days, my mom, a second-grade teacher, would add orange juice to our repertoire to make our test scores higher. When my report card was less than impressive, I could never use a lack of morning fuel as an excuse.

The first meal of the day is different in the South, in all of the very best ways. It's the first chance to sit at the table, center yourself around the one piece of furniture that holds the whole house together, and start the day with a sense of home. Breakfast is what Southern women do to take care of those they raise and to sustain themselves.

This love affair with the first meal of the day is not mine alone. I inherited the table that my grand-mother grew up around. This piece of furniture holds the women of our family together across four generations. My grandmother ate breakfast as a child on the very same stripy tiger oak that my daughter does today, over 100 years later. It's at this table that breakfast was served during defining moments in my family long before I was born.

My grandmother's brother took a train from Atlanta after coming home from World War I, arriving in Madison, Georgia, in the middle of the night. He walked ten miles to their home with just a glow from the moon to light the way. He stunned his parents and 10 brothers and sisters by strolling up the long farm driveway as the sun rose. They had no idea he was alive, much less back from war. The dogs announced his arrival and quickly awakened the entire household. I've heard countless stories of the unexpected and bountiful breakfast that my great-grandmother prepared. It was, quite possibly, the greatest meal my grandmother and her siblings ever enjoyed. It was filled with the salted pork that was being saved for the most special of occasions, eggs from the coop, and biscuits made with the creamiest of buttermilk. It was an early morning meal where dinner plates were sprinkled with the happiest of tears as they fell in overwhelming joy and gratefulness. My table was the center of this morning rapture and held them all together as a complete family once again.

I said "I do" to my husband of 23 years at 10:30 in the morning on a mild December Saturday on a Georgia island. The decision to marry before noon was an easy one to make. We liked that eggs, mounds of bacon, scuppernong jelly, and silver dollar pancakes would outshine our wedding cake at the reception. Unlike in other parts of the country, it's not unusual for breakfast to be the highlight of just about any occasion.

Hunt breakfasts, affectionately called the Dine after the Dash, in Virginia are over-the-top ways to fill up hungry riders after their mornings of chasing fox. Breakfasts are held after the hunt, even if that falls well into the afternoon. Huge, lavish spreads filled with linens, sterling silver, breakfast casseroles, tiered cakes, stiff drinks, corn muffins, deviled eggs, and ham biscuits greet hunters with the utmost of lavish Southern hospitality.

When kickoff in Oxford, Mississippi, is before noon, breakfast takes over the most famous college tailgating locale, the Grove. Football fans do an early morning meal with sausage balls and fried chicken biscuits along with bourbon and Cokes between shouts of "Hotty Toddy" from an endless sea of red and blue.

The South's most famous golf tournament wouldn't leave patrons hungry until their pimento cheese and egg salad sandwiches are ready for lunch. A tradition of green waxed paper–wrapped breakfast sandwiches sustains devotees of the gentleman's game and those that admire azaleas nearly hypnotized to bloom on time.

No matter where in the South, or for what momentous occasion, gathering over breakfast lives on. It's a comforting and filling start that saturates the soul with a connection to the past and a craving for the day to come.

by Rebecca Lang

ninth-generation Southerner, cooking instructor, and author of eight cookbooks, including her most recent, Y'all Come Over: Charming Your Guests with New Recipes, Heirloom Treasures, and True Southern Hospitality

Buttermilk Pancakes

Makes sixteen 4-inch pancakes ~ Total Time: 50 minutes

Whether the result is called pancakes, flapjacks, griddlecakes, hotcakes, or batty cakes, it's a common scene to find batter bubbling in a greased skillet on any given morning in a Southern kitchen. The quintessential wheat flour griddlecake in the South is made with buttermilk and, according to Edna Lewis, it's the buttermilk that makes Southern baking so good. In her book *In Pursuit of Flavor*, she states, "The South has long been famous for its great hot breads and pancakes. I think the rich buttermilk or naturally soured milk, home-rendered lard, and single-acting baking powder Southern cooks always baked with have given our bread this deserved reputation." And indeed, the buttermilk in these pancakes provides a tangy flavor as well as a fluffy texture. We add a small amount of sour cream to the mix to enhance that flavor and texture further. The baking soda in these pancakes reacts with the buttermilk and sour cream to provide the perfect lift. In the early 1900s, it was common to find dark corn syrup or sorghum syrup passed around the table for topping stacks of the hot cakes. These fluffy pancakes will soak up whatever syrup you choose to drizzle them with. If you want, the pancakes can be cooked on an electric griddle. Set the griddle temperature to 350 degrees and cook as directed. If you use an all-purpose flour with a high protein content, such as King Arthur, you will need to add an extra tablespoon or two of buttermilk.

2	cups (10 ounces) all-purpose flour
2	tablespoons sugar
1	teaspoon baking powder
½	teaspoon baking soda
½	teaspoon table salt
2	cups buttermilk
¼	cup sour cream
2	large eggs
3	tablespoons unsalted butter, melted and cooled slightly
1–2	teaspoons vegetable oil

1 Adjust oven rack to middle position and heat oven to 200 degrees. Spray wire rack set inside rimmed baking sheet with vegetable oil spray; place in oven.

2 Whisk flour, sugar, baking powder, baking soda, and salt together in medium bowl. In second medium bowl, whisk buttermilk, sour cream, eggs, and melted butter together. Make well in center of dry ingredients and pour in wet ingredients; gently stir until just combined (batter should remain lumpy with few streaks of flour; do not overmix). Let batter sit for 10 minutes before cooking.

3 Heat 1 teaspoon oil in 12-inch nonstick skillet over medium heat until shimmering. Using paper towels, carefully wipe out oil, leaving thin film on bottom and sides of pan.

4 Using ¼-cup dry measuring cup, portion batter into pan in 4 places. Cook until edges are set, first side is golden brown, and bubbles on surface are just beginning to break, 2 to 3 minutes. Using thin, wide spatula, flip pancakes and continue to cook until second side is golden brown, 1 to 2 minutes longer. Serve pancakes immediately, or transfer to wire rack in preheated oven. Repeat with remaining batter, using remaining oil as necessary.

Blueberry Pancakes

You can use frozen berries: Thaw and rinse the berries and spread them out on paper towels to dry.

Sprinkle 1 tablespoon fresh blueberries over each pancake before flipping.

Chocolate Chip–Coconut Pancakes

Sprinkle 1 tablespoon semisweet chocolate chips and 1½ tablespoons sweetened shredded coconut over each pancake before flipping.

Strawberry Vanilla Pancakes

Combine 10 ounces (2 cups) finely chopped, hulled strawberries; ½ teaspoon vanilla extract; and 1 tablespoon sugar in small bowl. Sprinkle 1 tablespoon strawberry mixture over each pancake before flipping.

THE WOMAN BEHIND AUNT JEMIMA

With one of the most successful supermarket trademarks in history, Aunt Jemima brand pancake mix fed generations of American families. But who was Aunt Jemima?

The character was fictional, based on a racist mammy archetype meant to appeal to a persistent nostalgia, particularly among white consumers, for the stereotypical image of a Black woman at the stove, working for and nourishing white families. With tethers to antebellum mythology, early vaudeville revues, and other cultural touchstones of the late 19th century, the iconic image was just what the R.T. Davis Milling company wanted in 1893 to sell their new boxed pancake "ready mix." But who would play the part?

Nancy Green (1834–1923) was a Black woman from Montgomery County, Kentucky. During her early life, Green was enslaved by the wealthy Walker family, for whom she worked as a cook and housekeeper. In the years following Emancipation, she continued to work for the Walkers, eventually relocating with them to Chicago. There, the Walkers introduced Green to the marketers at Davis Milling, who tapped her to promote their pancake mix by performing cooking demonstrations—in clichéd mammy costume—at the 1893 World's Fair.

For many years, Green made appearances across the country to support the ready mix (renamed "Aunt Jemima's Pancake Flour"), while continuing to work as a housekeeper. Her portrayal of Aunt Jemima launched the brand into mainstream popularity. While Green had to act in a way that romanticized the "Old South" and the power roles that came with it, it allowed her to travel and make a decent living for decades, something that was not afforded to many Black women at the time. She was a businesswoman who used cooking skills to support herself and her career. She went on to help establish the Olivet Baptist Church and participate in fraternal organizations and charities. Nancy Green exemplifies the perseverance and tenacity that many formerly enslaved women encompassed, and her story, while unique, is representative of many. She died in 1923, at the age of 89.

Over the decades that followed, many women—including Agnes Moody, Lillian Richard, Artie Belle McGinty, and others—portrayed the fictional Aunt Jemima, before the trademark was finally retired in 2021.

by Kelley Fanto Deetz, PhD

public historian dedicated to elevating the stories of enslaved Africans and African Americans, and author of Bound to the Fire: How Virginia's Enslaved Cooks Helped Invent American Cuisine

Pain Perdu with Chantilly Crème

Serves 4 to 6 ~ Total Time: 1½ hours

Cajun and Creole cooking have been deeply influenced by French cuisine. So it's unsurprising that Louisiana cuisine has many dishes with French names, such as étouffée, maque choux, and beignets. New Orleans–style pain perdu, a dish of griddled custard-dipped bread, means "lost bread" and falls into this category. Likely inspiration for the name comes from using (rather than tossing) stale bread to make it.

Pain perdu is very similar to what Americans outside of New Orleans call French toast. In fact, many authors and recipe developers use the names interchangeably. Some vaguely distinguish the two by saying French toast is made with presliced bread, while pain perdu is made with stale loaves of bread (often French bread) that have been sliced. Others say pain perdu must have heavy cream in the custard, while French toast has milk. But there are countless recipes for both that break these respective rules; as with many dishes, the lines of what is typical or authentic have blurred to confusion. Here we opt for brioche, which makes for a rich pain perdu; however, challah can be substituted. If using challah, increase the soaking time in step 2 to 1½ minutes per side. Drying out the brioche in the oven before soaking it in a mixture of egg yolks, half-and-half, sugar, and flavorings yields a dish that is moist and custardy but doesn't fall apart. The pain perdu can be cooked all at once on an electric griddle, but may take an extra 2 to 3 minutes per side. Set the griddle temperature to 350 degrees and use the entire amount of butter for cooking. You can serve pain perdu with maple syrup or honey in addition to the chantilly crème.

Pain Perdu

14 ounces brioche, ends discarded, cut into eight 1-inch-thick slices

3 cups warm half-and-half (80 degrees)

6 large egg yolks

6 tablespoons packed light brown sugar

4 tablespoons unsalted butter, melted, plus 2 tablespoons unsalted butter, divided

2 tablespoons vanilla extract

1 teaspoon ground cinnamon

½ teaspoon table salt

Chantilly Crème

1 cup heavy cream, chilled

3 tablespoons sugar

½ teaspoon vanilla extract

Pinch table salt

1 **For the pain perdu** Adjust oven rack to middle position and heat oven to 300 degrees. Place bread on wire rack set in rimmed baking sheet. Bake bread until almost dry throughout (center should remain slightly moist), about 20 minutes, flipping slices halfway through baking. Remove bread from rack and let cool for 5 minutes. Reduce oven temperature to 200 degrees and return sheet with wire rack to oven.

2 Whisk warm half-and-half, egg yolks, sugar, melted butter, vanilla, cinnamon, and salt in large bowl until well combined. Transfer custard to 13 by 9-inch baking dish. Working with 2 slices at a time, soak bread in custard until saturated but not falling apart, 15 seconds per side. Using firm slotted spatula, transfer bread to second sheet or large platter, allowing excess custard to drip back into dish. Repeat with remaining 6 slices.

3 Melt 1 tablespoon butter in 12-inch nonstick skillet over medium-low heat. Using slotted spatula, transfer 4 slices soaked bread to skillet and cook until golden brown, 3 to 5 minutes per side (if bread is browning too quickly, reduce temperature slightly). Transfer pain perdu to prepared rack in oven to keep warm. Wipe skillet clean with paper towels. Repeat with remaining 1 tablespoon butter and remaining 4 slices soaked bread.

4 **For the chantilly crème** Using stand mixer fitted with whisk attachment, whip cream, sugar, vanilla, and salt on medium-low speed until foamy, about 1 minute. Increase speed to high and whip until soft peaks form, 1 to 3 minutes. (Chantilly crème can be refrigerated in fine-mesh strainer set over small bowl and covered with plastic wrap for up to 8 hours.) Serve pain perdu with chantilly crème.

Pain Perdu with Brown Sugar and Bourbon Chantilly Crème

Substitute light brown sugar for granulated sugar. Add 1 tablespoon bourbon to mixer with cream. Stir up to 1 additional tablespoon bourbon into chantilly crème to taste.

Pain Perdu with Lemon Chantilly Crème

Add 1 teaspoon grated lemon zest plus 1 teaspoon juice to mixer with cream.

Quick Yeasted Waffles

Serves 4 to 6　~　Total Time: 40 minutes

Waffle House's signature light-as-air, cooked-to-order waffles are made from their proprietary "sweet cream" batter. Their packaged waffle mix gives some insight into the formula: It instructs home cooks to incorporate eggs and half-and-half, a much richer combination of liquid ingredients than the standard water or milk most packaged mixes call for.

While Waffle House (see page 79) is open 24/7, you may not be lucky enough to live

close to one—or you may simply want to make waffles without leaving the house. So here we offer an all-purpose waffle recipe that's good to have in your repertoire—and almost as quick as a mix.

Our recipe doesn't call for half-and-half; we found we were able to achieve a rich waffle using a combination of whole milk, melted butter, and eggs. In another deviation from the Waffle House recipe, this waffle develops deep flavor from the addition of

yeast. We found that using a combination of yeast and baking powder and letting the batter rise for just 10 minutes results in superairy waffles. One envelope of instant yeast is 2¼ teaspoons. Even if your waffle maker has an indicator light or audio alert to let you know when the waffles are supposed to be done, we suggest following the visual cues in the recipe to determine doneness.

1¾ cups whole milk

3 tablespoons sugar

2¼ teaspoons instant or rapid-rise yeast

2 cups (10 ounces) all-purpose flour

1 teaspoon table salt

1 teaspoon baking powder

8 tablespoons unsalted butter, melted

2 large eggs

2 teaspoons vanilla extract

1 Adjust oven rack to middle position and heat oven to 200 degrees. Set wire rack in rimmed baking sheet and place sheet in oven.

2 Microwave milk in bowl until it reaches 110 degrees, 1 to 2 minutes, stirring halfway through microwaving. Whisk sugar and yeast into milk until yeast dissolves; let sit until bubbly, about 5 minutes.

3 Whisk flour, salt, and baking powder together in large bowl. Add melted butter, eggs, vanilla, and milk mixture to flour mixture and whisk until mostly smooth. Let batter sit for 10 minutes. Meanwhile, heat waffle iron according to manufacturer's instructions.

4 Whisk batter gently to deflate. Lightly coat cooking surface of waffle iron with vegetable oil spray. Cook waffles according to manufacturer's instructions until crisp, firm, and golden, 3 to 6 minutes (use about ¾ cup batter for 7-inch round Belgian waffle iron; adjust batter amount slightly as needed to spread batter to within ¼ inch of edge of iron), whisking batter between batches. Serve waffles immediately or transfer to prepared rack in oven until ready to serve.

Buttery Blueberry Maple Syrup

Serves 4 to 6 (Makes 1⅓ cups) ~ Total Time: 20 minutes

Waffle House used to offer "blueberry" waffles (that is, waffles with a blueberry-like mix-in that delivered a punch of flavor). When the waffles were removed from the menu, patrons petitioned to bring them back, lamenting that those blueberries were unlike anything else: "That sweet little dehydrated blueberry nugget is far better than its fresh counterpart. There is nowhere else in the world to find that sweet artificial blueberry, trust us we have tried. Waffle House brought back the original blueberry waffle for a limited time in 2018. What a blissful but short-lived dream it was . . . Waffle House, we miss the blueberry Waffles and we implore you to bring back America's greatest blueberry waffle," the petition read. We can't source those elusive "blueberries"—but we can offer a buttery fresh blueberry maple syrup. You can substitute thawed frozen blueberries for fresh, if desired.

7½ ounces (1½ cups) blueberries, divided

¾ cup maple syrup

¼ teaspoon ground cinnamon

¼ teaspoon table salt

2 tablespoons unsalted butter

1 teaspoon grated lemon zest plus 1 teaspoon juice

1 Combine 1 cup blueberries, maple syrup, cinnamon, and salt in small saucepan. Bring to boil over medium-high heat. Mash blueberries with potato masher and cook, stirring frequently, until blueberries have broken down and mixture is reduced and slightly thickened, about 5 minutes.

2 Off heat, stir in butter, lemon zest and juice, and remaining ½ cup blueberries until butter is melted and blueberries are softened, about 1 minute. Serve.

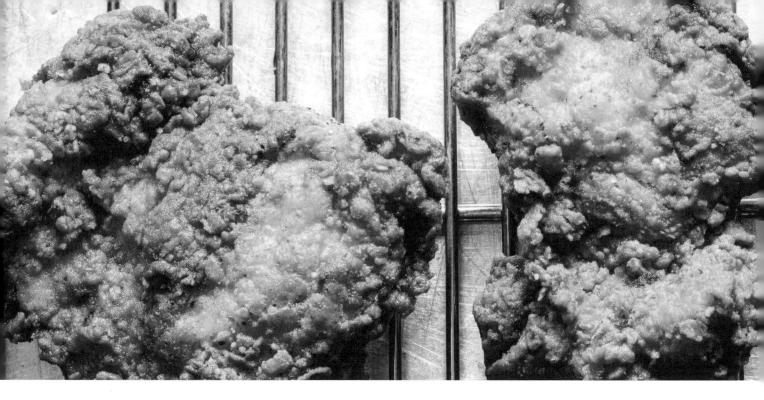

Fried Boneless Chicken Thighs

Serves 4 to 6   ~   Total Time: 1¼ hours, plus 1½ hours refrigerating

Fried chicken is the star of many Southern breakfasts: chicken and waffles, chicken biscuits, light rolls (see page 64) stuffed with fried chicken. You'll find fried chicken in the Fried and True chapter (see pages 222–233), but we wanted to offer an all-purpose savory chicken recipe tailor-made for breakfast. We use boneless, skinless chicken thighs which stay moist through cooking and are easy to cut through, so you get the perfect bite. To achieve a crispy fried coating that stands up to a pour of syrup, we call for nearly as much cornstarch as all-purpose flour in the breading. Working a small amount of liquid into the seasoned flour mix creates little hunks of breading that are rendered crunchy by the hot oil. A bit of baking powder ensures that these craggy bits are light and crispy. Use a Dutch oven that holds 6 quarts or more. We offer a recipe for Spicy Lime Honey (page 63) to cut through the richness of the chicken.

Marinade and Chicken

1	cup buttermilk
5	garlic cloves, smashed and peeled
1	tablespoon table salt
¼	teaspoon red pepper flakes
2	pounds boneless, skinless chicken thighs, trimmed
2	quarts peanut or vegetable oil for frying

Coating

1½	cups all-purpose flour
1¼	cups cornstarch
2	teaspoons celery salt
2	teaspoons ground ginger
2	teaspoons Italian seasoning
2	teaspoons granulated garlic
1	teaspoon ground coriander

2	teaspoons baking powder
2	teaspoons table salt
2	teaspoons pepper
½	teaspoon cayenne pepper
3	tablespoons buttermilk

continued   >

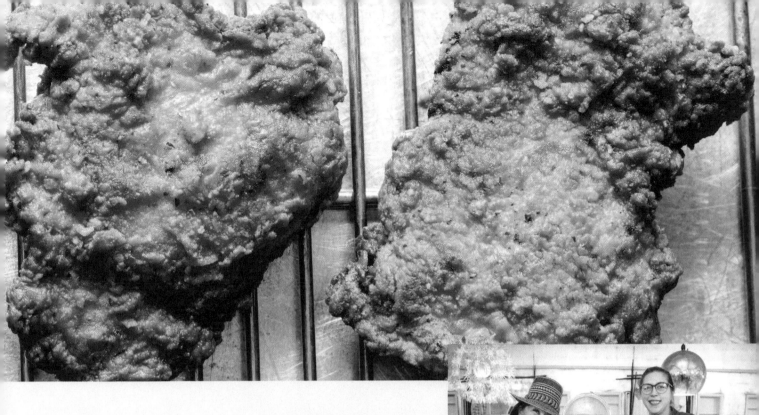

HOW TO CHICKEN YOUR WAFFLES

Chicken plus waffles plus sweet syrup will always please, but many Southern chefs are playing with this adaptable equation on their brunch menus.

Karen Carrier and Shay Widmer are the chefs of Beauty Shop in Memphis, Tennessee, a restaurant constructed in the building that was formerly Priscilla Presley's hair salon and fittingly styled like a '50s beauty shop—hair-drying chairs and all. They serve their fried chicken over a pecan waffle and switch in a sweet chile lime sauce for the syrup to perk up additions of sausage milk gravy and a sunny-side up egg.

In Nashville, Tennessee, chef and TV personality Maneet Chauhan (see page 243) features a sweet-and-spiced pakora fried chicken over a dosa waffle with mango slaw and masala syrup on her brunch menu at Chauhan Ale & Masala House.

And in New Orleans, Renee "Chef Reero" Guzman makes the meal extra-fun with a choose-your-own-adventure chicken and waffle option at Ma Momma's House of Cornbread, Chicken & Waffles. You can pick wings and/or tenders over banana nut, rum, strawberry, or even Fruity Pebbles or Cocoa Puff waffles. Drizzling decisions come down to a bourbon-spiked syrup or Ma Momma's house syrup.

For at-home chicken and waffles, start with a batch of Quick Yeasted Waffles (page 58). We suggest making the waffles first and holding them in a 200-degree oven to stay warm while you fry the chicken. Then, choose your own adventure, as they do at Ma Momma's House: Top them with Buttery Blueberry Maple Syrup (page 59), Ginger Honey Butter (page 13), Spicy Lime Honey (page 63), or whatever toppings you can conjure up on a Sunday morning.

Chefs Karen Carrier and Shay Widmer of Beauty Shop restaurant in Memphis (top), chef and TV personality Maneet Chauhan of Chauhan Ale and Masala House in Nashville (left), Renee "Chef Reero" Guzman of Ma Momma's House in New Orleans (right).

Mark Weber / The Daily Memphian (top), Brett Carlsen / The New York Times / Redux (left), and Ryan Hodgson-Rigsbee (right)

1 **For the marinade and chicken** Combine buttermilk, garlic, salt, and pepper flakes in large bowl. Add chicken to marinade and toss to coat. Cover and refrigerate for at least 1 hour or up to 24 hours.

2 **For the coating** Whisk flour, cornstarch, celery salt, ginger, Italian seasoning, granulated garlic, coriander, baking powder, salt, pepper, and cayenne together in second large bowl. Add buttermilk and, using your fingers, rub flour mixture and buttermilk together until craggy bits form throughout.

3 Working with 1 piece of chicken at a time, remove from marinade, allowing excess to drip off, then drop into flour mixture, turning to thoroughly coat and pressing to adhere. Transfer to rimmed baking sheet. Refrigerate, uncovered, for at least 30 minutes or up to 2 hours.

4 Set wire rack in second rimmed baking sheet and line half of rack with triple layer of paper towels. Add oil to large Dutch oven and heat over medium-high heat to 350 degrees. Add half of chicken to oil and fry until golden brown and registering at least 175 degrees, about 7 minutes. Adjust burner, if necessary, to maintain oil temperature between 325 and 350 degrees.

5 Transfer chicken to paper towel–lined side of rack and let drain on each side for 30 seconds, then move to unlined side of rack. Return oil to 350 degrees and repeat with remaining chicken. Transfer chicken to platter. Serve.

Spicy Lime Honey

Makes ¼ cup

Total Time: 15 minutes

¼ cup honey

2 tablespoons hot sauce

½ teaspoon grated lime zest

Stir all ingredients together in 2-cup liquid measuring cup. Microwave until sauce comes to boil, about 1 minute. Continue to microwave in 20-second intervals until sauce is reduced to ¼ cup, about 1 minute. Let cool for at least 10 minutes before serving.

SOUTHERN ROOTS, HARLEM FAME

The Wells Supper Club in Harlem, New York, which opened in 1938, is commonly credited with first concocting the dish fried chicken and waffles, serving the dinner-breakfast combo to jazz musicians in the wee hours after they'd finished their gigs. However, even though the restaurant—which has served the likes of Nat King Cole and Sammy Davis Jr.—propelled chicken and waffles into the mainstream, Wells didn't invent the pairing. Nor is chicken and waffles an exclusively Southern combination; a Pennsylvania Dutch version featuring stewed chicken dates back to the 1600s.

But the version of fried chicken and waffles that we know today is most definitely a Southern dish. According to culinary historian Adrian Miller in his book *Soul Food: The Surprising Story of an American Cuisine, One Plate at a Time*, fried chicken and waffles originated in the South on antebellum plantations: "By the early 1800s, a 'Virginia Breakfast,' a combination of fried or baked meats with any sort of hot quick bread, was the gold standard of plantation hospitality. At these meals fried chicken was a regular star, just as likely to be paired with a biscuit, cornbread, pancakes, or rolls as it was with a waffle."

Waffles themselves have a storied past. Introduced to America by English settlers and European immigrants, they gained high-society status thanks in large part to Thomas Jefferson's "waffle frolics," parties where guests would make their own waffles. At the time, waffle irons were two rigid plates attached to long handles. They were heavy, weighing in at 10 to 12 pounds, and needed to be held carefully by the cook over an open flame—not an easy task. So most of these waffle frolics moved to more heavily emphasize the frolicking (that is, eating) than the waffle making, which may have been relegated to enslaved cooks.

Over the next half century, both chicken and waffles became ways for enslaved people to participate in the economy of the antebellum South. At that time chicken was far less popular and affordable in the United States than it is today. However, it was common in the South, due at least in part to chicken's status among enslaved Black people as the only livestock permissible to cultivate. Tending chickens and selling eggs became a way to make external money. Alongside these egg vendors, "waffle women" occupied spots at markets. According to the *Atlantic Educational Journal*, these women made and sold homemade waffles, still a hard labor in the 1860s with those hefty waffle makers.

Miller says that after Emancipation, the rigorously trained and highly skilled Black cooks who would have prepared many of those "Virginia breakfasts" went on to become professional cooks for elite clientele in hotels and restaurants not only in the South, but also in the North. This presented a pathway to commercial success for Black people and propelled fried chicken and waffles into the mainstream, where they still are today.

Light Rolls

Makes 15 rolls ~ Total Time: 1½ hours, plus 2 hours 50 minutes to 3 hours 50 minutes rising and cooling

Along the coast of North Carolina, light rolls are as iconic as biscuits are in the rest of the South. According to Liz Biro for Coastal Review, these rolls, also known as lightnin' (or loitin') rolls or sometimes just hot rolls, likely trace their roots to England, as they bear similarities to the Cornish splits of Cornwall.

Typically these yeasted rolls are made without eggs and include a good amount of lard, which gives them a supple texture and savory flavor. While they're delicious straight out of the oven (especially with a schmear of butter), some people split them open and stuff them with country ham, fried chicken, or a fried pork chop for a more substantial breakfast. While the basic recipe is simple, you can find cooks in the area who fold in cheese or even make a cracklin' version, embedding fried pork skin into the dough.

This take yields tender, salty-sweet rolls that are delicious on a breakfast table or as a snack. We suggest melting the lard on the stovetop. The dough will be sticky in step 3, but the hydration will make for supersoft rolls after baking. Brushing the baked rolls with melted butter gives them a shiny coating and rich flavor.

5	cups (25 ounces) all-purpose flour
2¼	teaspoons instant or rapid-rise yeast
2	teaspoons table salt
1⅔	cups whole milk, room temperature
8	tablespoons lard, melted
2	tablespoons sugar
2	tablespoons unsalted butter, melted

1 Whisk flour, yeast, and salt together in bowl of stand mixer. Whisk milk, melted lard, and sugar in 4-cup liquid measuring cup until sugar has dissolved.

2 Using dough hook on low speed, slowly add milk mixture to flour mixture and mix until cohesive dough starts to form and no dry flour remains, about 2 minutes, scraping down bowl as needed. Increase speed to medium-low and knead until dough is smooth and elastic and clears sides of bowl, about 5 minutes.

3 Transfer dough to lightly floured counter and knead by hand to form smooth, round ball, about 30 seconds. Place dough seam side down in lightly greased large bowl or container, cover with plastic wrap, and let rise until doubled in volume, 1½ to 2 hours.

4 Make foil sling for 13 by 9-inch baking pan by folding 2 long sheets of aluminum foil; first sheet should be 13 inches wide and second sheet should be 9 inches wide. Lay sheets of foil in pan perpendicular to each

THE COASTAL CARB OF CHOICE

In North Carolina there are biscuits, cornbread, and rolls to choose from, and while you can't go wrong with any of them, it's light rolls that are the star of the show Down East—the rural waterfront communities east of Beaufort, beginning at the North River Bridge. Light rolls were prominent along the Carolina coast in the 1900s but are still made on the regular in home kitchens and sold at spots such as Davis Shore Provisions General Store in Davis, North Carolina.

These rolls go by many names, including lightning rolls, light bread, and hot rolls. They're basically yeast rolls made without eggs and they replace biscuits in these parts of the state. I didn't grow up Down East but I did frequently eat light rolls during the holidays at my Aunt Sandra and Uncle Stink's house. Truth be told, making "day after holiday sandwiches," where we'd add slivers of leftover holiday ham between the rolls, was a favorite pastime. At our local gas station chain, Nic's Pic Kwik, rolls were best accompanied by greasy, succulent pieces of perfectly fried chicken. They're also popular vehicles for the meat at barbecue joints in Eastern North Carolina, as the golden-brown crusted rolls perfectly balance the tanginess of the 'cue.

"Christmas and Easter are a given but Thanksgiving is their day to shine," says Katt Price, a Beaufort, North Carolina, native who shares Southern family recipes on her blog, *Southern Farm and Kitchen*—including Carteret County Light Rolls. The key ingredients are flour, yeast, butter, salt, and sugar, but there are minor tweaks from family to family. Older recipes call for lard (which turned to Crisco later on), but no matter what, butter brushed atop the rolls when they're fresh out of the oven is a must. "Milk and sugar is just how Granny Beulah made hers," says Price, describing the key ingredients of these rolls. "I haven't put too much thought as to why, I just see it as how we do it," she adds. "Butter on a hot light roll is my go-to right out the oven."

"Light rolls are a tradition here that will never fade," says Price. "It's a Down East woman's claim to fame, perfecting their version of the same great recipe from generation to generation."

by Jenn Rice

North Carolina culinary arts and travel journalist

SHAPING LIGHT ROLLS

1   Form piece of dough into rough ball by stretching dough around your thumb and pinching edges together so that top is smooth.

2   Place ball seam side down on clean counter and, using your cupped hand, drag in small circles until dough feels taut and round.

other, with extra foil hanging over edges of pan. Push foil into corners and up sides of pan, smoothing foil flush to pan, then spray foil with vegetable oil spray.

5   Press down on dough to deflate. Transfer dough to clean counter and divide into thirds. Cut each third into 5 equal pieces (about 3 ounces each) and cover loosely with plastic. Working with 1 piece of dough at a time (keep remaining pieces covered), form piece into rough ball by stretching dough around your thumb and pinching

edges together so that top is smooth. Place ball seam side down on clean counter and, using your cupped hand, drag in small circles until dough feels taut and round. Repeat with remaining dough pieces.

6   Arrange dough balls seam side down into 5 rows of 3 balls in prepared pan and cover loosely with plastic. Let rolls rise until nearly doubled in size and dough springs back minimally when poked gently with your finger, 1 to 1½ hours. (Unrisen rolls can be refrigerated for at least 8 hours or up

to 16 hours; let rolls sit at room temperature for 1 hour before baking.)

7   Adjust oven rack to lower-middle position and heat oven to 350 degrees. Bake until golden brown and rolls register at least 195 degrees, 25 to 30 minutes, rotating pan halfway through baking. Brush rolls with melted butter and let cool in pan on wire rack for 3 minutes. Using foil overhang, transfer rolls to wire rack and let cool for 20 minutes. Serve warm or at room temperature.

Country Ham with Red-Eye Gravy

Serves 4 ~ Total Time: 30 minutes

Ham and red-eye gravy is meant to be a simple dish, as it was born of the Southern tendency towards waste-not cooking. It's typically made by quickly pan-frying a slice of country ham before deglazing the pan with leftover coffee. The coffee thickens ever so slightly into a rich, slightly bitter sauce. Recipe developer and PBS chef Sheri Castle told us, "Red eye gravy might be the best known gravy in the South but the least eaten." We landed on a recipe that we think you'll eat an awful lot, and we hope it conjures the image Elizabeth Shestak shares in *Our State* magazine: "Redeye gravy is more than a dish; it's an ode, a love song to a personal olfactory memory—the smell of ham frying, of coffee long-brewed. It's an edible sonnet to the Southerners who came before." If country ham slices are not sold in your market, they can be sourced through online retailers. Do not confuse them with biscuit cuts, which are sliced too thin for this recipe. We prefer the flavor of lard here; an equal amount of vegetable shortening can be substituted, though the flavor will be muted. Tabasco is best here, but any Louisiana-style hot sauce will work. Serve with biscuits (see pages 20–31) or grits (see page 179).

4   (4-ounce) country ham slices, ¼ inch thick

2   tablespoons lard, divided

1   tablespoon packed brown sugar

⅓   cup brewed coffee

½   teaspoon hot sauce

1   Pat ham dry with paper towels. Heat 12-inch cast-iron skillet over medium heat for 3 minutes. Add 1 tablespoon lard and heat until just smoking. Add 2 ham slices and cook until lightly browned, about 3 minutes per side. Transfer to plate and tent with aluminum foil. Let skillet cool slightly, about 2 minutes, before repeating with remaining 1 tablespoon lard and 2 ham slices; transfer to plate.

2   Whisk sugar into fat left in skillet and cook over medium-low heat until just beginning to darken, about 30 seconds. Whisk in coffee and cook until reduced to ¼ cup, about 2 minutes. Off heat, whisk in hot sauce. Transfer gravy to small bowl. Serve ham slices, passing gravy separately.

THE HAM LADY

Nancy Newsom Mahaffey, owner of Col. Bill Newsom's Aged Kentucky Country Hams, has rightfully earned her nickname, the Ham Lady. Mahaffey learned to make country hams from working with the men in her family, who had been curing hams in Virginia since the 1600s. The family eventually made their way to Kentucky but kept the practice the same.

Mahaffey's grandfather opened a country store in Kentucky on New Year's Day 1917. Initially the store didn't sell hams; most families at the time cured them at home. But as that practice fell out of fashion, selling hams at the store became the main source of revenue. "Eventually, the groceries weren't selling but the hams were. It was the end of the mom-and-pop grocery era, and at the same time, the new generation had lost the rabbit's foot on curing hams," Mahaffey said in an interview for *Garden & Gun*. And the praise rolled in. Even James Beard wrote about their country hams in American Airlines' in-flight magazine, *American Way*, and then in his columns and books.

Mahaffey's father inherited the store from his father and eventually she inherited it. She didn't intend to, but her dad retired after a fire destroyed their grocery store, and her brother lived out of state. Mahaffey advanced their mail-order business that continues strong today.

The Ham Lady, Nancy Newsom Mahaffey, showing off her curing hams at Col. Bill Newsom's.

Nancy Newsom Mahaffey

Today, Mahaffey still uses her family's method, one she refers to as "old-fashioned weather-curing" (meaning she times curing the hams with the seasons without using air conditioning or heat), which she explains makes for a more complex ham. In addition to the country ham, Mahaffey sells other gourmet goods such as prosciutto and smoked sausages.

There's a lot of history behind Col. Bill Newsom's Aged Kentucky Country Hams. The future? Mahaffey expressed in the *Garden & Gun* interview that while she could potentially pass the business to her son, she wants her children to follow their own path. "If someone else took over, it would have to be someone who loves the process, the heritage, the history—all those things that go into it. Somebody that's down to earth and doesn't want the millions, but more the old-fashioned flavor."

To honor Mahaffey and other women in the pork industry, we offer recipes for three Southern pork-based breakfasts in these pages: country ham with red-eye gravy, candied bacon, and breakfast sausage.

by Morgan Bolling

Black Pepper Candied Bacon

Serves 4 to 6 ~ Total Time: 45 minutes

For our sugar-and-spiced bacon, we sprinkle strips with brown sugar and black pepper. Baking the slices in the oven allows for more even cooking and the ability to make a bigger batch. The sugar contributes a lovely caramel-toffee background flavor along with its sweetness, and a bit of black pepper provides the punch of spice. We prefer center-cut bacon for this recipe, which is more uniform in thickness than traditional bacon. If your bacon has a range of thicknesses, place thinner slices on one tray and thicker pieces on the other for more even cooking. Do not substitute dark brown sugar here.

¼   cup packed light brown sugar
1   teaspoon pepper
12   ounces center-cut bacon, halved crosswise

1   Adjust oven racks to upper-middle and lower-middle positions and heat oven to 350 degrees. Combine sugar and pepper in bowl. Arrange bacon on 2 aluminum foil–lined rimmed baking sheets and sprinkle with sugar mixture. Using fingers, spread sugar mixture evenly over one side of slices.

2   Bake bacon until dark brown and sugar is bubbling, 20 to 25 minutes, switching and rotating sheets halfway through baking. Set wire rack over triple-layer of paper towels. Remove sheets from oven as bacon finishes cooking and transfer bacon to prepared rack. Let cool for 5 minutes before serving.

Chipotle Candied Bacon

Add ½ teaspoon chipotle chile powder, ½ teaspoon ground cumin, and ¼ teaspoon garlic powder to sugar mixture.

Five-Spice and Sesame Candied Bacon

Add 1 teaspoon five-spice powder to sugar mixture. After spreading sugar over bacon, sprinkle slices with 1 tablespoon sesame seeds.

Jerk-Inspired Candied Bacon

Add 1 tablespoon minced fresh thyme, 1½ teaspoons ground allspice, ¾ teaspoon granulated garlic, ½ teaspoon dry mustard, and ⅛ teaspoon cayenne pepper to sugar mixture.

Rosemary Candied Bacon

Add 1 tablespoon minced fresh rosemary to sugar mixture.

Homemade Breakfast Sausage

Serves 6 to 8 ~ Total Time: 30 minutes

Making breakfast sausage, also often called "country sausage," became a way for farmers in the 1800s to use up less desirable pig parts while making a hearty, protein-rich breakfast. In her book, *Breakfast: A History*, Heather Arndt Anderson surmises that adding sage to uncured pork sausage is what set apart breakfast sausage from other types. It's unclear why it was added, but it could have been because the smell of sage would help mask the smell of unrefrigerated meat, or because sage may have been thought to prevent illness. Nowadays, sage is added because of its lasting signature breakfast sausage flavor; a plate of biscuits and gravy wouldn't feel right without a hint of sage. Making your own breakfast sausage is quick and allows you to control exactly what spices go into it. Avoid lean or extra-lean ground pork; it makes the sausage dry, crumbly, and less flavorful. Try this breakfast sausage as the filling for a biscuit breakfast sandwich.

2	pounds ground pork
2	tablespoons minced fresh sage or 2 teaspoons dried
1	tablespoon maple syrup
1½	teaspoons minced fresh thyme or ½ teaspoon dried
1½	teaspoons pepper
1	teaspoon table salt
1	garlic clove, minced
⅛	teaspoon cayenne pepper
2	tablespoons vegetable oil, divided

1 Gently mix pork, sage, maple syrup, thyme, pepper, salt, garlic, and cayenne together in bowl with hands until well combined. Divide meat mixture into 12 lightly packed balls, then gently flatten into 3-inch patties, about ½ inch thick. (Patties can be refrigerated for up to 24 hours.)

2 Heat 12-inch cast-iron skillet over medium heat for 5 minutes. Add 1 tablespoon oil and heat until just smoking. Brown half of patties, 3 to 5 minutes per side. Transfer patties to paper towel–lined plate and tent loosely with aluminum foil.

3 Wipe skillet clean with paper towels. Repeat with remaining 1 tablespoon oil and patties. Serve.

BREAKFAST WITH A SIDE OF LIVERMUSH

Sausage isn't the only ground meat specialty of the Southern breakfast table. The name "livermush" could use a rebrand, but try a slice of this pan-fried pork loaf, cooked until crispy with a tender, rich inside, and you'll find it's deeply comforting food.

Livermush is a mixture, or mush (a type of cornmeal pudding), of pork liver, pork meat, spices, and enough cornmeal to bind it. This North Carolina dish likely traces its roots back to pon hoss, a German dish of pork scraps, starch, and spices. It's most present in the foothills region on the western side of the state. In her essay for Extra Crispy, "Why Livermush Matters to North Carolina," Sheri Castle explains the pork mixture was often made at home until the Great Depression, when company and country stores began selling this affordable product. Despite its humble status, livermush isn't a far cousin from elegant French pâté and terrine, both of which add liver to a bound meat product, Castle notes. But livermush wouldn't make sense on a charcuterie platter as much as it does next to fried eggs on a breakfast plate.

While livermush hasn't made it far outside western North Carolina, it has a deep following there, with annual festivals featuring such events as livermush eating contests and pageants. Not fully sold on the meat mixture? That's OK. Castle says, "Food that's weird to people who've never heard of it isn't weird to those who grew up eating it. Livermush matters to people who matter to me. I am from western North Carolina, and I know my place."

by Morgan Bolling

Texas Breakfast Tacos

Serves 4 to 6 ~ Total Time: 30 minutes

We did Texas-style breakfast tacos the right way, from the homemade tortillas to the salsa roja topping. Be sure to follow the visual cues when making the eggs, as your pan's thickness will affect the cooking time. If you're using an electric stovetop for the eggs, heat a second burner on low and move the skillet to it when it's time to adjust the heat. This recipe makes enough filling for twelve 6-inch tacos.

12	large eggs
½	teaspoon table salt
¼	teaspoon pepper
6	slices thick-cut bacon, cut into ½-inch pieces
1	small onion, chopped fine
1	jalapeño chile, stemmed, seeded, and minced
1	recipe Homemade Taco-Size Flour Tortillas (page 73)
1	recipe Salsa Roja (page 72)
	Shredded Monterey Jack cheese
	Thinly sliced scallions
	Lime wedges

1 Whisk eggs, salt, and pepper in bowl until thoroughly combined and mixture is pure yellow, about 1 minute. Set aside.

2 Cook bacon in 12-inch nonstick skillet over medium heat until crispy, 8 to 10 minutes. Pour off all but 2 tablespoons fat from skillet (leaving bacon in skillet). Add onion and jalapeño and cook until vegetables are softened and lightly browned, 4 to 6 minutes.

3 Add egg mixture and, using heat-resistant rubber spatula, constantly and firmly scrape along bottom and sides of skillet until eggs begin to clump and spatula leaves trail on bottom of skillet, 1½ to 2½ minutes.

4 Reduce heat to low. Gently but constantly fold egg mixture until clumped and slightly wet, 30 to 60 seconds. Season with salt and pepper to taste. Fill tortillas with egg mixture and serve immediately, passing salsa, Monterey Jack, scallions, and lime wedges separately.

ONLY AS GOOD AS THE TORTILLA

The best breakfast tacos demand freshly made tortillas. But there aren't many people learning how to make tortillas by hand anymore. No one in my family could make them. I was fortunate that a neighbor woman taught me. Before my neighbor's tortilla coaching, the ones I made were simply terrible.

Making tortillas isn't a skill you can learn from reading or even watching. You have to get your hands into the masa (dough). Both corn and flour tortillas are popular, but they are made very differently.

Corn tortillas are the quintessential bread of the Americas. Around the hearth, stove, or table, the people of the Americas have been sharing corn tortilla–making techniques for millennia. The original kitchen tools needed for making corn tortillas were stone mortars, clay griddles, fire, water, and hands, mostly women's hands. These days, we use heavy cast-iron tortilla presses to flatten the masa evenly and quickly (don't bother with the aluminum or plastic tortilla presses). A double sheet of plastic helps release the uncooked tortilla from the cast iron press.

Flour tortillas, however, were developed after colonization, when wheat flour was brought to the Americas. A rolling pin, a clean surface, and extra flour are needed for making flour tortillas. The masa is stretchy and cannot be pressed like corn tortillas. My trick is to make the flour tortilla masa a day in advance and store it in the fridge, so the wheat gluten has time to relax for easier rolling and, therefore, thinner tortillas.

My two pieces of advice for novice tortilla makers are: First, a tortilla has three sides. Lay a tortilla on the hot griddle, flip once, then the final time. That's it. Second, keep practicing. Accept bad tortillas—you'll mess up hundreds. The trial and error task (and messy hands) of tortilla making is essential to becoming a breakfast taco master.

After filling a basket with hot, freshly made tortillas, I always come away with new thoughts, goals, and just a little more confidence.

by Melissa Guerra

food historian, authority on the foodways of the Americas, and eighth-generation Texan living on a cattle ranch

Texas Breakfast Tacos with Chorizo

Mexican-style chorizo and Spanish-style chorizo are not interchangeable. Be sure to use Mexican-style chorizo for this recipe. Mexican chorizo is usually sold raw.

Substitute 8 ounces Mexican-style chorizo sausage, casings removed, for bacon. Cook chorizo in skillet over medium heat, breaking up meat with wooden spoon, until well browned, 6 to 8 minutes, before adding onion and jalapeño.

Texas Breakfast Tacos with Potato

Omit bacon. Melt 2 tablespoons unsalted butter in skillet over medium heat. Add 1 (8-ounce) russet potato, peeled and cut into ½-inch cubes, and ¼ teaspoon salt and cook until tender, 6 to 8 minutes, before adding onion and jalapeño.

Salsa Roja

Serves 6 (Makes about 1½ cups)
Total Time: 25 minutes

This salsa is a welcome addition to our Texas Breakfast Tacos, but it can also be served with tortilla chips or as a flavorful accompaniment to pork, chicken, or fish. To make this salsa even spicier, you can reserve and add the chile seeds to the blender before processing all the ingredients.

1	pound plum tomatoes, cored and chopped
2	garlic cloves, chopped
1	jalapeño chile, stemmed, seeded, and chopped
2	tablespoons chopped fresh cilantro
1	tablespoon lime juice
1	teaspoon table salt
¼	teaspoon red pepper flakes

1 Combine tomatoes and garlic in bowl and microwave, uncovered, until steaming and liquid begins to pool in bottom of bowl, about 4 minutes. Transfer tomato mixture to fine-mesh strainer set over bowl and let drain for 5 minutes.

2 Combine jalapeño, cilantro, lime juice, salt, pepper flakes, and drained tomato mixture in blender. Process until smooth, about 45 seconds. Season with salt to taste. Serve warm. (Salsa can be refrigerated for up to 3 days. Cover and microwave briefly to rewarm before serving.)

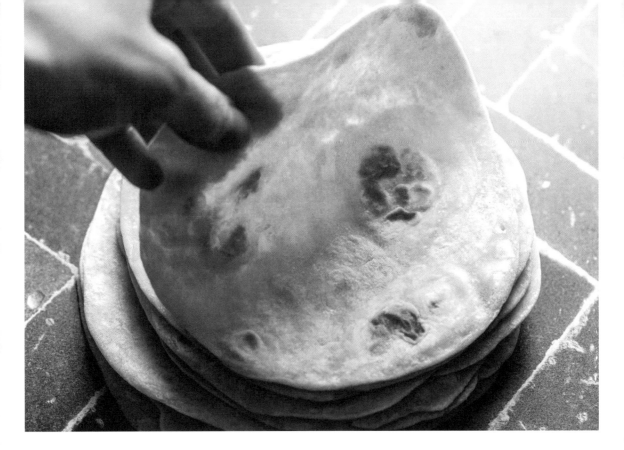

Homemade Taco-Size Flour Tortillas

Makes twelve 6-inch tortillas

Total Time: 50 minutes, plus 30 minutes chilling

Lard can be substituted for the shortening.

2	cups (10 ounces) all-purpose flour
1¼	teaspoons table salt
5	tablespoons vegetable shortening, cut into ½-inch chunks
⅔	cup warm tap water
1	teaspoon vegetable oil

1   Combine flour and salt in large bowl. Using your fingers, rub shortening into flour mixture until mixture resembles coarse meal. Stir in water until combined.

2   Turn dough onto counter and knead briefly to form smooth, cohesive ball. Divide dough into 12 equal portions, about 2 tablespoons each; roll each into smooth 1-inch ball between your hands. Transfer to plate, cover with plastic wrap, and refrigerate until dough is firm, at least 30 minutes or up to 2 days.

3   Cut twelve 6-inch squares of parchment paper. Roll 1 dough ball into 6-inch circle on lightly floured counter. Transfer to parchment square and set aside. Repeat with remaining dough balls, stacking rolled tortillas on top of each other with parchment squares between.

4   Heat oil in 12-inch nonstick skillet over medium heat until shimmering. Wipe out skillet with paper towels, leaving thin film of oil on bottom. Place 1 tortilla in skillet and cook until surface begins to bubble and bottom is spotty brown, about 1 minute. (If tortilla is not browned after 1 minute, turn heat up slightly. If it browns too quickly, reduce heat.) Flip and cook until spotty brown on second side, 30 to 45 seconds. Transfer to plate and cover with clean dish towel. Repeat with remaining tortillas.

To Make Ahead   Cooled tortillas can be layered between sheets of parchment paper, covered with plastic wrap, and refrigerated for up to 3 days. To serve, discard plastic, cover tortillas with clean dish towel, and microwave at 50 percent power until heated through, about 20 seconds.

Eggs Hussarde

Serves 4 ~ Total Time: 2½ hours

This recipe is inspired by the original from Brennan's (see "Q&A: Ti Adelaide Martin on Her Mother, the Matriarch of New Orleans Restaurants" on page 76). It's an ultrarich dish similar to eggs Benedict but made supersavory with a very deep, meaty, umami-forward sauce called marchand de vin. The particularly lemony hollandaise helps balance the toppings. The marchand de vin will yield more than you need; save extra sauce for a future batch or as an accompaniment to steaks, chops, and roasts.

Marchand de Vin

2	tablespoons vegetable oil
1	pound 85 percent lean ground beef
1	onion, chopped
1	carrot, peeled and chopped
2	tablespoons tomato paste
4	cups beef broth
8	sprigs fresh thyme, plus 1 teaspoon minced fresh thyme
4	garlic cloves, smashed and peeled
3	bay leaves
2	teaspoons black peppercorns
2	tablespoons unflavored gelatin
2	tablespoons unsalted butter
4	ounces cremini mushrooms, trimmed and chopped fine
1	shallot, minced
¼	ounce dried porcini mushrooms, rinsed and minced
⅓	cup dry red wine
1	teaspoon red wine vinegar
¼	teaspoon table salt

Hollandaise

3	large egg yolks
2	tablespoons lemon juice
½	teaspoon table salt
¼	teaspoon cayenne pepper
16	tablespoons unsalted butter, melted and still hot (180 degrees)

Eggs Hussarde

2	tomatoes, cored and halved crosswise
4	English muffins, split
8	slices Canadian bacon
2	tablespoons distilled white vinegar
2	teaspoons table salt
8	large eggs
2	tablespoons minced fresh chives
	Coarse sea salt

1 **For the marchand de vin** Heat oil in large saucepan over medium-high heat until shimmering. Add ground beef and cook, breaking up meat with wooden spoon, until well browned, 8 to 10 minutes. Stir in onion and carrot and cook until softened and lightly browned, 5 to 7 minutes. Stir in tomato paste and cook until paste starts to darken slightly, about 30 seconds. Stir in broth, thyme sprigs, garlic, bay leaves, and peppercorns, scraping up any browned bits. Bring to simmer and cook until reduced to 3 cups, about 25 minutes.

2 Strain broth through fine-mesh strainer into bowl, pressing on solids to extract as much liquid as possible; discard solids. Let liquid settle for 5 minutes, then skim fat from surface using wide, shallow spoon. Sprinkle gelatin over broth in bowl and let sit until softened, about 5 minutes.

3 Melt butter in now-empty saucepan over medium heat. Add cremini mushrooms, shallot, and porcini mushrooms and cook until softened, about 5 minutes. Stir in minced thyme and cook until fragrant, about 30 seconds. Stir in reserved broth mixture and wine, bring to simmer, and cook until reduced to 1 cup, 10 to 15 minutes. Off heat, stir in vinegar and salt and season with pepper to taste. Cover to keep warm. (Sauce can be refrigerated for up to 3 days or frozen for up to 1 month; bring to gentle simmer over medium-low heat before serving.)

4 **For the hollandaise** Process egg yolks, lemon juice, salt, and cayenne in blender until frothy, about 10 seconds, scraping bottom and sides of blender jar as needed. With blender running, slowly add hot butter and process until hollandaise is emulsified, about 2 minutes. Adjust consistency with hot water as needed until sauce slowly drips from spoon.

5 **For the eggs hussarde** Adjust oven rack 6 inches from broiler element and heat broiler. Arrange tomato halves cut side up on 1 side of rimmed baking sheet and broil until tomatoes begin to soften, about 10 minutes. Arrange English muffins split side up on empty side of sheet and broil until tomatoes are spotty brown and muffins are golden brown, 2 to 4 minutes. Place 1 slice bacon on each muffin half and broil until heated through, about 1 minute. Remove sheet from oven and tent with aluminum foil to keep warm.

6 Add water to 12-inch skillet until two-thirds full. Add vinegar and salt and bring to boil over high heat. Crack 2 eggs into each of 4 cups. Carefully pour all eggs into skillet. Cover skillet, remove from heat, and let sit until egg whites are set but yolks are still slightly runny, 4 minutes. (For firmer eggs, cook 2 to 3 minutes longer.) Using slotted spoon, transfer eggs to paper towel–lined plate.

7 Arrange 2 muffin halves on each serving plate and spoon 1 tablespoon marchand de vin evenly over top of each muffin half. Arrange 1 egg on top of each muffin half, then spoon hollandaise evenly over top. Sprinkle with chives and sea salt and serve with tomatoes.

Q&A: TI ADELAIDE MARTIN ON HER MOTHER, THE MATRIARCH OF NEW ORLEANS RESTAURANTS

Ella Brennan first entered the culinary world in 1943 as a teenager working for her brother, Owen Brennan, at a restaurant in New Orleans's French Quarter. When Owen opened another spot, the Vieux Carré, Ella was dissatisfied with the food quality. So Owen challenged her to fix it. And that she did. By 18, she was managing the restaurant, overseeing everything from inventory to staff training to hiring and firing. She traveled to New York and Europe for inspiration and focused her vision for haute New Orleans cuisine, making the restaurant's stuffy French menu more regionally vibrant and spotlighting elements of Creole cooking. The Vieux Carré thrived. When Owen passed away suddenly in 1955, Ella carried out plans they had to move the restaurant to a larger space. She renamed it Brennan's.

Brennan's became an iconic New Orleans restaurant. It is the birthplace of bananas Foster (see page 425) and eggs hussarde.

In the 1970s, a family dispute with Owen's widow forced Ella out of Brennan's, so she went on to open Commander's Palace with her other siblings. Commander's Palace became a giant among New Orleans's pedigreed restaurants. Commander's has earned seven James Beard Awards, and it has served as a training ground for some of the city's finest chefs.

Ella Brennan passed away in 2018 at the age of 92. Her daughters, Ti Adelaide Martin and Lally Brennan, and her son, Alex Brennan-Martin, are now proprietors of her restaurants.

Staff and patrons gave Ella the nickname "Hurricane Ella." We asked Martin about her mom's nickname.

Your mom was named Hurricane Ella, presumably due to her demand for excellence. What did she think of the term?
The Hurricane Ella nickname came from Mom's relentlessness. She just pushed, all the time. She was giving her all, and she wanted you to do the same. And that was not just for the business's sake; she believed it was best for you.

It sounds like a legacy that still lives on in the restaurant.
Yes, we have a sign that says, "You Will Not Suffer the Curse of Low Expectations." She pushed everyone but maybe had a soft spot for women.

Can you think of other lessons that women can learn from her personal philosophy?
Be prepared to take care of yourself financially. Young women working for her, like Nancy Oswald, who is the largest Ruth's Chris franchisee owner-operator, were pushed to learn everything about the business. [Editor's note: Ruth's Chris Steak House was founded by another titan of New Orleans's restaurants, Ruth Fertel, in 1965. She built a business that spans the globe from a small steakhouse with an "original recipe for success: perfect steak, warm hospitality, and good times that never stop rolling."]

Migas

Serves 4 ~ Total Time: 30 minutes

Another classic Tex-Mex breakfast, migas combines scrambled eggs with chiles, onion, and fried tortilla pieces. It has a delightful mix of textures with fluffy eggs enveloping those crisp-chewy tortillas.

Tex-Mex migas is different from the Spanish and Portuguese dishes with the same name. Migas means "crumbs" in Spanish, and in most parts of Spain, migas would bring to mind a dish of stale bread that has been rehydrated with water and olive oil, often with garlic and sometimes with sausage or another pork product. And in central Mexico, migas can refer to a rich soup made with torn bolillos (a type of bread) and flavored with garlic, peppers, and plenty of pork. How all these dishes came to have the same title is unclear, but they do share this principle of repurposing a bread product into something delicious and satisfying.

For this version, we fry the tortillas in oil before adding the eggs, which infuses the scramble with toasted-corn flavor. A mix of onion, red bell pepper, and briny pickled jalapeños gives the dish a Tex-Mex backbone. Cooking over two heat levels produces soft, fluffy egg curds. First turning the heat to medium-high creates steam to puff up the curds and then turning the heat down to low ensures they don't overcook. Shredded Monterey Jack cheese, folded in at the end, makes for creamy, cohesive eggs. It's important to follow the visual cues when making the eggs, as your pan's thickness will affect the cooking time. If you're using an electric stove, heat a second burner on low and move the skillet to it when it's time to adjust the heat. For a spicier dish, use the larger amount of jarred jalapeños.

8	large eggs
½	teaspoon table salt, divided
¼	teaspoon pepper
3	tablespoons vegetable oil
6	(6-inch) corn tortillas, cut into 1 by ½-inch strips
1	onion, chopped fine
1	small red bell pepper, stemmed, seeded, and chopped fine
1–2	tablespoons minced jarred jalapeños
1½	ounces Monterey Jack cheese, shredded (⅓ cup), plus extra for serving
1	tablespoon chopped fresh cilantro
	Salsa

1 Whisk eggs, ¼ teaspoon salt, and pepper in bowl until thoroughly combined, about 1 minute; set aside.

2 Heat oil in 12-inch nonstick skillet over medium-high heat until shimmering. Add tortillas and remaining ¼ teaspoon salt and cook, stirring occasionally, until golden brown, 4 to 6 minutes. Add onion, bell pepper, and jalapeños and cook, stirring occasionally, until vegetables are softened, 5 to 7 minutes.

3 Add egg mixture and, using heat-resistant rubber spatula, constantly and firmly scrape along bottom and sides of skillet until eggs begin to clump and spatula leaves trail on bottom of skillet, 30 to 60 seconds.

4 Reduce heat to low and gently but constantly fold egg mixture until clumped and still slightly wet, 30 to 60 seconds. Off heat, gently fold in Monterey Jack and cilantro. Serve immediately, passing salsa and extra Monterey Jack separately.

Hash Browns

Serves 4 to 6   ~   Total Time: 1½ hours

The way people define the geographic boundaries of the South varies, but one claim is that you can tell you're in a Southern state by the number of Waffle Houses per capita. And while Waffle House gets its name from the pile of waffles you can order, Southerners know the smothered and covered hash browns are one of the best bites on the menu.

The breakfast and late-night rushes at Waffle House have trained the people who work there to be some of the fastest cooks in America. To make their famed hash browns, these practiced short-order cooks keep a mound of crispy shredded spuds cooking on their flat-top griddles. They're flipping and turning (while smothering and covering the hash browns with toppings) all hours of the day.

That said, most home cooks don't have a griddle that big and turn to either frozen hash browns or cooking shredded potatoes in a skillet. But there are moments in life when you want more hash browns than a skillet can accommodate. We worked on a recipe that makes crispy hash browns in the oven, so you can serve a group of up to six.

Using medium-starch Yukon Gold potatoes creates a textural balance of crispy yet moist (not gummy). Shredding the potatoes and soaking them gets rid of excess starch. Squeezing them dry then removes moisture that would inhibit browning and crisping. Flipping sections of the hash browns with a metal spatula before returning the sheet to the oven creates a delightful mix of crispy and creamy, an outcome similar to that achieved on a hot griddle. We prefer to use the shredding disk of a food processor to shred the potatoes, but you can also use the large holes of a box grater. Like the beloved Waffle House hash browns, these are great smothered, covered, and/ or chunked (topped with sautéed onions, sliced American cheese, or chopped ham, respectively).

3   pounds Yukon Gold potatoes, unpeeled

6   tablespoons extra-virgin olive oil

1   teaspoon table salt

¼   teaspoon pepper

1   Adjust oven rack to middle position and heat oven to 450 degrees. Fit food processor with shredding disk. Halve or quarter potatoes as needed to fit through processor hopper, then shred potatoes. Transfer potatoes to large bowl and cover with cold water. Let sit for 5 minutes.

2   One handful at a time, lift potatoes out of water and transfer to colander; discard water. Rinse and dry bowl.

3   Place one-quarter of shredded potatoes in center of clean dish towel. Gather ends of towel and twist tightly to wring out excess moisture from potatoes. Transfer dried potatoes to now-empty bowl. Repeat 3 more times with remaining potatoes.

4   Add oil, salt, and pepper to potatoes and toss to combine. Lightly spray 16 by 11-inch rimmed baking sheet with vegetable oil spray. Distribute potatoes in even layer on sheet, but do not pack down. Bake until top of potatoes is spotty brown, 32 to 35 minutes.

5   Remove sheet from oven. Flip hash browns with metal spatula. Return sheet to oven and continue to bake until deep golden brown on top, 6 to 8 minutes longer. Season with salt and pepper to taste. Serve.

TUCKING INTO FOOD AND THOUGHTS AT WAFFLE HOUSE

The illuminated black letters, each encased in yellow boxes, of the Waffle House sign are a beacon in the night sky; they promise comfort in the form of breakfast, burgers, and diner classics.

If you listen to Southern rappers, you might think the always-open—24/7 365 days a year—chain's an epic rodeo for post-club shenanigans. In reality, that's hardly the case. Even, especially, in those lost hours, Waffle House has served as a safe space with good food for women for over half a century. A warm public space where you can sit with a bottomless cup of coffee—and nobody asks questions—is a strong refuge when life is too much.

Every Waffle House surely holds more stories than ways to order hash browns (reportedly 1,572, 864 ways)! Just as much as the Waffle House classic can "smother" and "cover" an impending hangover at the end of a girls' night out, it refills the tanks of the woman working late, whether on a big report, saving lives, cleaning buildings, or long-haul trucking.

You might see a mother feeding her children waffles or cheeseburgers at odd hours; maybe, depending on her domestic situation, it was the only place they could go. Like Edward Hopper's *Nighthawks*, they're suspended in amber, killing time, listening to the Flava Fry sizzling whatever's on the grill and the songs pouring from the jukebox. Those children think it's an adventure; the mother wonders if it's safe to go home.

Everything isn't that dire, of course. Sometimes tucking into a booth with your thoughts or a book is a quick escape. Knowing someone else is not only doing the cooking (maybe the fluffiest Toddle House Omelet or a balanced All-Star Special) but that they're also cleaning it up when you're done offers serenity.

I remember sitting at the counter in a pink Chanel suit between the church service and public memorial for Tammy Wynette pushing a half-eaten whole-wheat Texas Patty Melt around the plate. My tears dropped onto the Formica for the lady whose songwriting showed me so much about joy when life sucks. While I'm feeling untethered, a fresh iced tea with two lemons and a smile arrives to ground me.

The servers, whether tattooed or with hair piled to heaven, know without asking. They've seen it all, and understand, recognizing who needs to be left to their thoughts, given a "Hon, how ya doin'?," or engaged in a little snappy back-and-forth. The uniform might be genuine polyester, but that black apron serves more like a black belt in the human condition, developed shift after shift, night after night.

Sure, at times Waffle House can feel like the punched-down after-party's after-party: people talking too loud, jukebox banging hip-hop, hard rock, Skynyrd, and tush-pushin' country. But there's also an understanding: You're safe here. Inhale, exhale, figure it out, reset your sails and your compass. In those moments, the jukebox pours out a "Tennessee Whiskey," "Anything But Mine," or "Thinking Out Loud," or something by Patsy Cline. Or maybe it's Chaka or Whitney's "I'm Every Woman," Whitney or Dolly's "I Will Always Love You," or, always relevant, Aretha's "Respect."

by Holly Gleason

Nashville-based writer and artist development consultant

Kolaches

Makes 16 kolaches ~ Total Time: 1½ hours, plus 2 hours 50 minutes rising and cooling

Sibling to a Danish and a brioche, a kolache is a palm-size round of sweetened bread with a dollop of sweet cheese or fruit filling in the center and a streusel topping. Czech immigrants brought kolaches to Texas in the late 19th century. Today, these pastries are so popular in parts of the Lone Star State that multiple towns claim the title "kolache capital" and there are annual kolache festivals and kolache chain restaurants, such as Kolache Factory, throughout the state.

This recipe is inspired by the kolaches served by Denise Mazal, a Czech expat and the classically trained chef behind Little Gretel restaurant in Boerne, Texas. We visited her a little over a decade ago and were impressed by her kolaches, which were subtly sweet, buttery, and tender, a texture she achieves with a dough enriched by milk, melted butter, eggs, and extra egg yolks. We watched her let the dough rise before punching it down and shaping each kolache. As she baked, Mazal described a Czech wedding tradition in which the bride-to-be bakes 1,000 kolaches for the wedding to prove to her betrothed that she will keep him well fed (to be a woman . . .).

Mazal closed Little Gretel to retire, but you can mail-order Mazal's kolaches at lovekolaches.com. She makes a version with sweetened farmer's cheese and peach, poppy seed and almond, and plum jam and streusel. Here we offer versions you can make yourself with a sweetened cream cheese or fruit filling. Do not use nonfat ricotta cheese in this recipe. In step 1, if the dough hasn't cleared the sides of the bowl after 12 minutes, add up to 2 tablespoons more flour, 1 tablespoon at a time. In step 6, to prevent sticking, reflour the bottom of the measuring cup (or drinking glass) after making each indentation.

Dough

- 1 cup whole milk
- 10 tablespoons unsalted butter, melted
- 1 large egg plus 2 large yolks
- 3½ cups (17½ ounces) all-purpose flour
- ⅓ cup (2⅓ ounces) sugar
- 2¼ teaspoons instant or rapid-rise yeast
- 1½ teaspoons table salt

Cheese Filling

- 6 ounces cream cheese, softened
- 3 tablespoons sugar
- 1 tablespoon all-purpose flour
- ½ teaspoon grated lemon zest
- 6 ounces (¾ cup) whole-milk or part-skim ricotta cheese

Streusel

- 2 tablespoons plus 2 teaspoons all-purpose flour
- 2 tablespoons plus 2 teaspoons sugar
- 1 tablespoon unsalted butter, cut into 8 pieces and chilled
- 1 large egg, beaten with 1 tablespoon milk

1 **For the dough** Grease large bowl. Whisk milk, melted butter, and egg and yolks together in 2-cup liquid measuring cup (butter will form clumps). Whisk flour, sugar, yeast, and salt together in bowl of stand mixer. Fit stand mixer with dough hook, add milk mixture to flour mixture, and knead on low speed until no dry flour remains, about 2 minutes. Increase speed to medium and knead until dough clears sides of bowl but still sticks to bottom, 8 to 12 minutes.

2 Transfer dough to prepared bowl and cover with plastic wrap. Adjust oven racks to upper-middle and lower-middle positions. Place bowl of dough on lower rack and place loaf pan on bottom of oven. Pour 3 cups boiling water into loaf pan, close oven door, and let dough rise until doubled in size, about 1 hour.

3 **For the cheese filling** Using clean, dry mixer bowl and paddle, beat cream cheese, sugar, flour, and lemon zest on low speed until smooth, about 1 minute. Add ricotta and beat until just combined, about 30 seconds. Transfer to bowl, cover with plastic, and refrigerate until ready to use.

4 **For the streusel** Combine flour, sugar, and butter in bowl and rub between your fingers until mixture resembles wet sand. Cover with plastic and refrigerate until ready to use.

5 Line 2 rimmed baking sheets with parchment paper. Punch down dough and transfer to lightly floured counter. Divide into quarters and cut each quarter into 4 equal pieces. Form each piece into rough ball by pulling dough edges underneath so top is smooth. On unfloured counter, cup each ball in your palm and roll into smooth, tight ball. Arrange 8 dough balls on each prepared sheet and cover loosely with plastic. Place sheets on oven racks. Replace water in loaf pan with 3 cups boiling water, close oven door, and let dough balls rise until doubled in size, about 1½ hours.

6 Remove sheets and loaf pan from oven. Heat oven to 350 degrees. Grease and flour bottom of ⅓-cup dry measuring cup (or 2¼-inch-diameter drinking glass). Make deep indentation in center of each dough ball by slowly pressing until cup touches sheet. (Perimeters of balls may deflate slightly.)

7 Gently brush kolaches all over with egg-milk mixture. Divide filling evenly among kolaches (about 1½ tablespoons per kolache) and smooth with back of spoon. Sprinkle streusel over kolaches, avoiding filling. Bake until golden brown, about 25 minutes, switching and rotating sheets halfway through baking. Let kolaches cool on sheets for 20 minutes. Serve warm.

Fruit-Filled Kolaches

Combine 10 ounces frozen pineapple, blueberries, or cherries; 5 tablespoons sugar; and 4 teaspoons cornstarch in bowl. Microwave, covered, until bubbling and thickened, about 6 minutes, stirring halfway through microwaving. Mash with potato masher. Let cool completely and substitute for cheese filling.

KLOBÁSNÍKY NOT KOLACHES

Driving east from my home in Austin to my birthplace of Houston along US Route 77 and Interstate 10, there are almost as many billboards advertising kolaches and klobásníky as there are Texas bluebonnets blooming in the spring. However, in the stretches between those billboards and in the surrounding counties are small towns where Texas Czechs, including my family, are home baking a tastier, more traditional version of the pastries.

Whether meat market barbecue, hoppy beer, smoked sausages, or kolaches, foods of Texas's Czech community have been of particular interest in food media. But it is the misunderstood pastry known as a klobásník in Czech (usually misnamed a sausage kolache by commercial bakeries) that may be the current darling.

Certainly thousands of klobásníky (the plural of klobásník) are sold daily across Texas and increasingly across the United States at mom-and-pop shops and national (but Texas-based) chains such as the Kolache Factory and Shipley Do-Nuts. Hungry commuters buy them to eat in the car and they're a familiar sight at office meetings, Saturday morning sports practices, and Sunday morning church gatherings. In Austin, there are at least two dozen bakeries serving them. Some are "artisanal" bakeries and some are chain establishments, but their offerings, with fillings such as barbecued brisket or sausage-egg-cheese, cannot be called traditional.

The now-closed Village Bakery, which opened in 1952 in the overwhelmingly Czech town of West, Texas, claimed to have invented the klobásník and even trademarked the name, but there are mentions in Czech-language newspapers of the pastry being made by home cooks that predate the bakery by decades. My great-aunts will tell you they remember taking klobásníky out to the fields to eat on breaks from picking cotton on their family farms well before the bakery opened.

A traditional klobásník, like those portable lunches made by my great-grandmother 80 years ago, wraps soft, yeasty, milk-and-butter-enriched double-risen dough around smoky, garlicky homemade or Texas Czech meat market–made sausage and is liberally brushed with butter during the baking process.

The dough absorbs the rich flavor of the butter from the outside and the smoky aroma and fatty juiciness of the sausage from the inside in a way that distinguishes the finished product from mass-produced doughnut shop "sausage kolaches." Smoked and fresh sausages are a hallmark of Czech cuisine. Immigrants to Texas brought recipes for a variety of sausages, and their descendants still make them, using every part of a pig in different combinations.

Some versions include barley or rice; some use head meat or offal such as heart and liver. But the sausage ("klobase" in Czech) inextricably associated with klobásníky is the most basic: generally a 1-pound, horseshoe-shaped link of coarsely ground pork meat (or pork and beef) flavored simply with salt, garlic, pepper, and sometimes paprika.

A meticulous cook "peels" the casing off the sausage before slicing it into pieces for klobásníky. And Texas cooks do not skimp on butter, buttering the pan, buttering the rising dough balls, and also buttering the finished pastries when they come out of the oven.

Most often, Texas Czechs would eat klobásníky at a family or community gathering, either baking the pastries themselves or picking up several dozen at a local bakery for an extended family Christmas party, funeral reception, or heritage group meeting.

For such events, klobásníky might be one offering in a lunch spread, served alongside foods such as chicken soup with homemade, fine-cut noodles; pimento cheese and chicken salad sandwiches; pickles; and sliced summer sausage.

Typical recipes in community cookbooks make a batch of no less than six dozen klobásníky, ensuring plenty for historically large Texas Czech families. As successive generations in the community have fewer children, smaller families might make one pan of klobásníky on the weekend, wrap each klobásník individually in freezer paper or plastic wrap, and store them in a zipper-lock bag in the freezer for their kids to grab and microwave for breakfast.

This recipe makes one dozen but can easily be multiplied for parties or holidays.

by Dawn Orsak

fourth-generation Texas Czech and author of the forthcoming cookbook Kolach Culture: Cooking in Texas Czech Kitchens

Klobásníky

Makes 12 rolls　～　Total Time: 1½ hours, plus 1½ to 2¼ hours rising

These are Dawn Orsak's real-deal klobásníky (Texas Czech–style sausage rolls), not to be confused with a savory kolache. One envelope of instant yeast is 2¼ teaspoons. You can find Prasek's brand Smoked Pork and Beef Sausage at H-E-B grocery stores in Texas or online at Praseks.com. If you can't find Prasek's sausage, you can substitute a 14- or 16-ounce ring link of kielbasa. Removing the casing in step 3 will work best with chilled sausage (though you needn't remove the casing if you're using kielbasa).

½	cup whole milk
4	tablespoons salted butter, softened and cut into 4 pieces, plus 2 tablespoons melted, divided
1	large egg plus 1 large yolk
2	tablespoons sugar
2¼	teaspoons instant or rapid-rise yeast
½	teaspoon table salt
2¼	cups (11¼ ounces) all-purpose flour
1	(1-pound) ring link Prasek's Smoked Pork and Beef Sausage, chilled

1　Using stand mixer fitted with whisk attachment, mix milk, softened butter, egg and yolk, sugar, yeast, and salt on medium speed until thoroughly combined, about 1 minute (some small lumps of butter will remain). Fit stand mixer with dough hook. Add flour and mix on low speed until no dry flour remains, about 2 minutes, scraping down bowl as needed. Increase speed to medium and knead until dough is smooth and elastic and clears sides of bowl but sticks to bottom, about 3 minutes.

2　Transfer dough to lightly greased counter and knead by hand to form smooth, round ball, about 30 seconds. Place dough seam side down in lightly greased large bowl, cover tightly with plastic wrap, and let rise until doubled in size, 1 to 1½ hours.

3　Meanwhile, cut sausage into 2 equal lengths. Cut each length into 3 equal pieces, each about 3 inches long. Slice each piece in half lengthwise to form 12 equal pieces. Using paring knife, peel casing from sausage pieces; discard casing and set sausage aside.

4　Adjust oven rack to middle position and heat oven to 375 degrees. Grease 13 by 9-inch baking pan with 2 teaspoons melted butter. Transfer dough to lightly greased counter, divide into 12 equal pieces (about 1⅔ ounces each), and cover loosely with plastic. Working with 1 piece of dough at a time (keep remaining pieces covered), form dough into rough ball. Place ball seam side down on counter, then loosely cup dough with your palm and roll in circles against counter to form smooth, tight ball. Cover with plastic.

5　Working with 1 dough ball at a time, place ball seam side up on counter. Using your fingertips, press ball into 4 by 5-inch rectangle. Place 1 piece of sausage cut side up in center of dough, with long side of sausage parallel to long side of rectangle. Bring edges of dough up and around sausage and pinch seams to seal, completely encasing sausage. Arrange shaped klobásníky seam side down in 3 rows of four in prepared pan. Brush klobásníky with 2 teaspoons melted butter, cover with plastic, and let rise again until puffy, 30 to 45 minutes.

6　Bake until tops of klobásníky are light golden brown, 15 to 20 minutes, rotating pan halfway through baking. Brush with remaining 2 teaspoons melted butter and let cool for 10 minutes. Serve warm.

To Make Ahead　Klobásníky can be stored in airtight container at room temperature for up to 2 days or frozen. To freeze, wrap individual klobásníky in plastic wrap and freeze in zipper-lock bag for up to 3 months; thaw before serving or reheating. To reheat, wrap individual klobásníky in paper towels and microwave for about 30 seconds.

No.3 EAT WITH YOUR HANDS

Left to right: Natchitoches Meat Pies (page 118), Pimento Cheese (page 95), Truffled Egg Salad (page 106), Southern Cheese Straws (page 88), West Virginia Pepperoni Rolls (page 116).

CHEESE STRAWS

A SYMBOL OF SOUTHERN HOSPITALITY

Of all the savory morsels you might pop into your mouth at a festive gathering in the South, nothing says "Southern hospitality" as eloquently as a cheese straw. But not just any cheese straw.

Julia Reed, the late chronicler of Southern food and politics, railed against those "ubiquitous and taste-less parmesan-coated puff pastry twists found in every gourmet shop in Manhattan" in her 2008 collection of reflections on the delightful quirks of Southern entertaining, *Ham Biscuits, Hostess Gowns, and Other Southern Specialties.*

Cheese straws, to Reed's way of thinking, meant the kind perfected by her mother and practically every other matriarch she knew from her Mississippi Delta upbringing: "ridged rectangular wafers made of the heavenly combination of cheddar, butter, flour, and cayenne pepper that melts in your mouth and is best made with an old-fashioned cookie press. They're crunchy in texture, sharp in flavor; there's almost nothing I'd rather eat."

That lusty flavor profile fits well alongside other stalwarts of the Southern sideboard: salted and sugared pecans, deviled eggs, ham-stuffed biscuits, pimento cheese finger sandwiches, and pickled shrimp on toothpicks.

The reasons for cheese straws' enduring popularity are clear. They wash down easily with the stiffest cocktail or the sweetest tea. They're neat to eat and easy to transport. They're passed on silver trays at weddings, packed in tins for gift-giving, and offered as a snack any time of day or night to make guests feel welcomed and special, when a bowl of chips or Cheez-Its just won't do.

How the cheese straw became so deeply intertwined with Southern culture is less clear. One common theory is that they were born out of thrift, as a way of stretching cheese with leftover biscuit dough in the hot, humid South. Centuries-old recipes for crispy European snacks such as British biscuits and Italian biscotti could have had an influence.

"I think that cheese straws became so wildly popular in the South because they would keep (most Southern homes didn't have air conditioners until the late 1960s), because they're good, and possibly most importantly, because they are so good with drinks," writes the culinary historian John Martin Taylor (aka Hoppin' John) in a 2008 article in *Gastronomica*. "And drink we do! How could we not in this godawful heat?"

In Taylor's research, the first published recipe for Cayenne Cheese Straws he came across was in the 1887 edition of *The White House Cookbook*. *The New Dixie Cook-Book*, published in Atlanta in 1893, offered several versions, including one that suggested two serving styles: "piled on a plate, crossing them in pairs and tying with ribbons of different colors; or, bake in 8-inch lengths and serve log-cabin style"; the instructions were accompanied by a sketch to illustrate the styles. At the turn of the century, numerous cheese straw recipes appeared in New Orleans cookbooks in chapters laden with heavy hors d'oeuvres and cocktails. Nowadays, most every Southern recipe collection, it seems, has at least one cheese straw recipe or a close cousin. Recipes tend to be similar, although nuances and deviations abound: Some call for a shot of Worcestershire or Tabasco. Others swap out part of the cheddar with Parmesan, or all of it with blue cheese. Sometimes, instead of fussy sticks pushed out of the star tip of a cookie press or pastry bag, the dough is made into "cheddar cheese coins" that are shaped like a slice-and-bake cookie. Edna Lewis simply rolled cheesy dough out as for pie dough, then cut it in thin strips. And "hot cheese olives," a bridge club standby from the 1950s, are made by encasing pimento-stuffed olives in that familiar pastry. And, no surprise, the contributor is most often a woman.

In *The Southern Foodways Alliance Community Cookbook*, Georgia food writer Damon Lee Fowler deemed cheese straws "a standard for any hostess worth her iced tea."

Not all cheese straw artisans are so forthcoming in their instructions. "Delta cooks are incredibly protective of their recipes; nowhere is this more apparent than with cheese straws," inveterate Mississippi hostess and storyteller Gayden Metcalfe wrote in her hilarious 2005 collection of recipes and essays, *Being Dead Is No Excuse: The Official Southern Ladies Guide to Hosting the Perfect Funeral*. While ingredient lists are similar from one recipe to the next, proper technique is essential. Metcalfe noted how one matron offered to give private lessons at her house rather than part with her late mother-in-law's recipe.

Mastering cheese straws requires a level of finesse that has allowed generations of Southern women to show off their creativity and ingenuity and, in some cases, build businesses. Mary Margaret Yerger of Yazoo City, Mississippi, was among the trailblazers. As a widow with young children, she supported her family by catering weddings and running the local school lunch programs. At cafeteria meetings, she often brought cheese straws. As she approached retirement, one of those regular recipients, a woman who'd started a small business selling her home-made hush puppy mix, urged her to consider turning those treats into a cottage industry. And with the help of sons Hunter and Robbie, Yerger did just that. The brothers installed a mechanical extruder in her home kitchen and outfitted it with dies to mimic the shapes of the ones she'd previously squeezed out by hand. In 1991, the Mississippi Cheese Straw Factory rolled out their first 40-pound batch.

Today, the factory's 35,000-square-foot facility churns out upwards of 3,000 pounds a day to ship all over the country and beyond. They've expanded their line to include a variety of sweet "cookie straws," as well as savory variations on the traditional formula, flavored with sriracha and Asiago cheese. With more women with busy lives seeking shortcuts to entertaining, competition has soared as well. Nowadays, tins and bags of cheese straws are sold in gift stores and some supermarkets all over the South, and by mail order across the internet. And with most, there's an origin story that begins with a family recipe and a mom with a knack for hospitality.

by Susan Puckett

James Beard Award–nominated food journalist and editor who has authored or collaborated on more than a dozen books, including her culinary travelogue, Eat Drink Delta: A Hungry Traveler's Journey Through the Soul of the South

Southern Cheese Straws

Makes about 48 cheese straws   ~   Total Time: 1 hour, plus 20 minutes cooling

"Next to the ham hock, I'd argue that cheese straws qualify as the culinary mascot of the South," author Ashley English says in her book *Southern from Scratch: Pantry Essentials and Down-Home Recipes Inspired by Southern Appalachia*. Likely made as a way to preserve cheese, these delicate, crumbly, buttery crackers have long garnered a loyal following in the South. For the ultimate savory cheesy profile, we use a generous helping of extra-sharp cheddar cheese along with a little cayenne, which adds pleasant heat—just enough to make our straws irresistible alongside a glass of sweet tea, or a cocktail if you choose. Using a food processor to buzz the grated cheese, chilled butter, flour, and baking powder together results in crackers with a short, extra-tender texture. Many Southern recipes call for a cookie press to fashion the straws into the signature long, ridged shape. Since some don't own a cookie press, we call for rolling the dough into a square and adding ridges with a fork before cutting it into strips and baking. Flour the counter and the top of the dough as needed to prevent sticking.

8	ounces extra-sharp cheddar cheese, shredded (2 cups)	¾	teaspoon table salt
1½	cups (7½ ounces) all-purpose flour	¾	teaspoon paprika
8	tablespoons unsalted butter, cut into 8 pieces and chilled	½	teaspoon baking powder
		¼	teaspoon cayenne pepper
		3	tablespoons ice water

1   Adjust oven rack to middle position and heat oven to 350 degrees. Line rimmed baking sheet with parchment paper. Process cheddar, flour, butter, salt, paprika, baking powder, and cayenne in food processor until mixture resembles wet sand, about 20 seconds. Add ice water and process until dough ball starts to form, about 25 seconds.

2   Transfer dough to lightly floured counter. Knead briefly until dough fully comes together, 2 to 3 turns. Using your hands, pat dough into rough 4 inch square. Roll dough into 10 inch square, about ¼ inch thick, flouring counter as needed to prevent sticking.

3   Position dough so 1 side is parallel to counter edge. Using rounded side of fork, drag tines across entire surface of dough to make decorative lines.

4   Using pizza cutter or chef's knife, trim away and discard outer ½ inch of dough to make neat square. Cut dough into 3 equal pieces perpendicular to decorative lines. Working with 1 section of dough at a time, cut into ½-inch-wide strips in direction of lines.

5   Evenly space cheese straws on prepared sheet, about ½ inch apart. Bake until edges of straws are light golden brown, 30 to 35 minutes, rotating sheet halfway through baking. Let straws cool completely on sheet. Serve. (Straws can be stored at room temperature for up to 1 week.)

SHAPING THE STRAWS

There's no need for a cookie press for these easy-to-shape straws.

1 Roll dough into 10-inch square, then drag tines of fork across dough to make decorative lines.

2 Cut square into thirds, then cut each rectangle into ½-inch-wide strips with pizza cutter.

Parmesan–Black Pepper Cheese Straws

Reduce extra-sharp cheddar to 1½ cups. Add 1 cup grated Parmesan to food processor with flour in step 1. Substitute 1 teaspoon black pepper for cayenne pepper.

Appetizer Biscuits

Makes about 28 biscuits ~ Total Time: 1 hour

Diminutive biscuits split and stuffed with country ham or slathered with Red Pepper Jelly (page 370) or Beer Cheese (page 92) are an essential component of a Southern appetizer spread. One type of biscuit in particular occupies a place of historical pride for Southerners: beaten biscuits.

These biscuits were first made before baking powder and baking soda were commercially available, so the cook was required to beat the dough as a way of leavening it. By hitting it with a mallet, a rolling pin, or the back of an axe, cooks trapped air pockets in the tough dough. It was often a task relegated to enslaved women since it was so labor intensive. The process also developed gluten, a protein that trapped the air pockets as the biscuits rose in the oven. The result was a cross between a biscuit and a cracker, crunchy and firm on the exterior with a flaky, semisoft interior.

Some bakers continue to make beaten biscuits the traditional way—a labor of love given the work involved. And while the process doesn't make for the type of biscuits we often think of today, beaten biscuits have hard-earned layers, a nicely firm texture, a slight rise, and a mild flavor, making them well suited for filling with country ham or smothering with gravy or jam. Some chefs now make beaten biscuits with the help of a stand mixer, food processor, or other piece of equipment in place of hand beating. Similarly, this recipe takes some modern turns, calling for a little baking powder and the use of a food processor to help us achieve a pastry with some layers and a cracker-like crunch.

2½	cups (12½ ounces) all-purpose flour
1	tablespoon sugar
2	teaspoons baking powder
1	teaspoon table salt
8	tablespoons unsalted butter, cut into ½-inch pieces and chilled
1	cup whole milk, chilled

1 Adjust oven rack to middle position and heat oven to 350 degrees. Line rimmed baking sheet with parchment paper. Pulse flour, sugar, baking powder, and salt in food processor until combined, about 3 pulses. Add butter and pulse until reduced to pea-size pieces, 10 to 12 pulses.

2 Transfer mixture to large bowl. Add milk and stir with rubber spatula until shaggy dough forms. Transfer dough to heavily floured counter and knead until dough comes together fully and feels smooth, with few small butter flecks still visible, 8 to 10 turns.

3 Roll dough into 11-inch circle about ½ inch thick. Using floured 2-inch round cutter, stamp out 22 to 23 biscuits. Reroll scraps once to similar thickness and stamp out 5 to 6 more biscuits. Space biscuits evenly on prepared sheet (7 rows of 4). Prick each biscuit 3 times with tines of fork.

4 Bake until tops are light golden brown, 27 to 30 minutes, rotating sheet halfway through baking. Let biscuits cool on sheet for 5 minutes, then transfer to wire rack. Serve warm or at room temperature.

Beer Cheese

Serves 10 (Makes about 2½ cups)
Total Time: 25 minutes

This creamy cheese spread is so deeply embedded in Kentucky cuisine that there is a Beer Cheese Trail—featuring multiple stops to sample this regional favorite—in Winchester, Kentucky, and even an annual beer cheese festival. Garin Pirnia, author of *The Beer Cheese Book* puts it well: "Beer cheese is to Kentuckians like bagels are to New Yorkers."

Many point to beer cheese first being served at the Driftwood Inn in Winchester, Kentucky, in the late 1930s as a complimentary offering to encourage beer sales. It became a trend. Alongside a recipe for beer cheese in her cookbook from 1940, *Out of Kentucky Kitchens*, author Marion W. Flexner says, "In the days when free lunches were served in Kentucky saloons with every five cent glass of beer, we were told of a wonderful beer cheese that decked every bar."

For this version we boil beer to cook off some of its sharpness (although this step is considered a point of contention to some). We then process sharp cheddar cheese with garlic, hot sauce, Worcestershire sauce, and mustard (all of which were in Flexner's recipe) until smooth before slowly drizzling in the beer. Serve beer cheese cold on Appetizer Biscuits (page 90), with crackers, or as a dip for crudités.

½	cup mild lager, such as Budweiser
1	pound sharp or extra-sharp cheddar cheese, shredded (4 cups)
¼	cup finely chopped onion, rinsed and patted dry
2	tablespoons ketchup
1	tablespoon Dijon mustard
1	tablespoon Worcestershire sauce
1½	teaspoons hot sauce
1	garlic clove, minced

1   Bring beer to boil in small saucepan over high heat. Reduce heat to medium-low and simmer for 1 minute. Transfer to small bowl and let cool completely.

2   Process cheddar, onion, ketchup, mustard, Worcestershire, hot sauce, and garlic in food processor until smooth, about 1½ minutes. With processor running, slowly drizzle in beer and continue to process until very smooth, about 1 minute longer. Serve immediately, or transfer to bowl, cover with plastic wrap, and refrigerate until firm, about 2 hours.

Roast Country Ham

Serves 12 to 15   ~   Total Time: 5¾ hours, plus 30 minutes resting

To make an archetypical country ham, we scrub off the mold, trim off the skin, and score the surface. We place the ham fat side up in a roasting pan, add water, and cover the pan with aluminum foil to ensure a moist ham. After baking we apply a brown sugar glaze, return the ham to the oven to set the glaze, and let it rest on a carving board before slicing and serving it with Appetizer Biscuits (page 91). Use a ham aged six months or less for this recipe. Mold on country ham is not a sign of spoilage; it is a natural effect of the curing and aging process.

1 (13- to 15-pound) 3- to 6-month-old bone-in country ham
½ cup packed light brown sugar
1 tablespoon dry mustard
2 teaspoons pepper

1 Adjust oven rack to middle position and heat oven to 325 degrees. Using clean, stiff-bristled brush, scrub ham under cold running water to remove any surface mold. Transfer ham to cutting board and trim off dry meat, skin, and all but ¼ inch of fat. Using sharp knife, cut slits ½ inch apart in crosshatch pattern in fat cap of ham, being careful not to cut into meat.

2 Transfer ham to large roasting pan fat side up, add 4 cups water, and cover pan tightly with aluminum foil. Roast until thickest part of meat registers 140 degrees, 4 to 5 hours. Remove ham from oven, discard foil, and increase oven temperature to 450 degrees.

3 Combine sugar, mustard, and pepper in bowl and rub over top of ham. Return ham to oven and cook, uncovered, until glazed and lacquered, 12 to 17 minutes. Transfer ham to carving board and let rest for 30 minutes before carving and serving.

COUNTRY HAM PRIMER

Country ham is an intrinsic part of the culture in the Southeastern and Midwestern United States, and it's made by large-scale producers and individuals alike. These regions fall within the Ham Belt, a latitudinal strip that circles the globe through Western Europe, Southeastern China, and the Southeastern United States, where the weather is conducive to ham preservation. The production facilities for the most famous cured hams fall within it.

How It's Made The process has three stages: curing, salt equalization, and aging. Trimmed hams are rubbed with salt, sugar, and spices and dry-cured to draw out the moisture. This happens around November; the temperature for curing should be below 40 degrees. Hams are usually aged for at least three months. Shorter-aged hams taste less salty, while longer-aged hams are saltier and funkier. Commercial producers use temperature-monitored warehouses known as "ham houses."

When springtime temperatures rise to 50 to 60 degrees, the ham goes through a month-long salt equalization period during which the warmer temperatures allow the salt and sugar to migrate throughout. Then some, but not all, hams are cold-smoked.

How It's Prepared and Served Some people eat country ham raw and sliced paper-thin. However, the USDA doesn't sign off unilaterally on this. Producers can either undergo microbial testing or label ham as not a ready-to-eat product; most choose the latter. Thicker slices can be pan-fried, used to make a red-eye gravy (see page 66), and served for breakfast.

If you buy a whole uncooked country ham, you will likely need to first scrub mold and residue from the exterior. This mold is harmless; many producers assert that mold growth correlates with complex flavor.

How to Buy and Store It If you live outside the Southeastern and Midwestern United States, where country ham is found in stores year-round, you can order it. Storage varies based on what form of country ham you purchase. In a cool, dry environment, you can hang an uncooked country ham in its original packaging to continue aging, or you can store it in the fridge or freezer for up to one year.

PIMENTO CHEESE: PÂTÉ OF THE SOUTH

While pimento cheese is now as ubiquitous in the South as the term "y'all," it was born above the Mason-Dixon line. Largely the brainchild of industrial food manufacturers and resourceful home cooks alike, it has a history that branches across the country.

In the 1870s two key ingredients—cream cheese and canned pimentos—started to gain traction in the prepackaged food industry. Dairy farmers in New York started producing French-style Neufchâtel cheese, which was eventually manufactured into cream cheese. Around the same time, sweet peppers from Spain known as "pimientos" (the "i" was later dropped in the United States) started gaining popularity in the Americas. Viewed as a high-end, imported good, they soon found their way into American agriculture and recipes. And soon enough, the two ingredients married. In 1908, Good Housekeeping (based in Massachusetts at the time) ran a recipe combining cream cheese and minced pimentos, flavored with mustard and chives. It wasn't quite the pimento cheese we know and love today, but well on its way.

With published recipes such as this (as well as ones for pimento-infused dressing and even a salad of peanut butter and pimentos), the pimento became the vogue vegetable in the early 1900s. Georgia and California vied for top pimento production, with Georgia using marketing campaigns like festivals and pageants that celebrated the vegetable as a way to get a leg up.

Another reason for Georgia's growing pimento prowess over California's was less glamorous, however. In her article "Pimento-cracy" published in the Oxford American, Dr. Cynthia R. Greenlee writes, "The South's oppressively low pay shifted that dynamic; pickers plucked peppers for pittances and tossed them in sacks like cotton, and Georgia's canning workers earned 20 cents an hour to the California plant laborer's 38 ... Many of those workers were Black women and men."

Eventually, between the inexpensive labor and agricultural and processing innovations, both cream cheese and pimentos became inexpensive and widely available. Due to their popularity, it wasn't long before commercial manufacturers (mostly in Wisconsin and New York) were running the peppers through mechanical choppers to churn out pimento cheese for the masses. Sandwiches featuring the spread became a staple at soda fountains across the country. And with the onset of World War I and the need to feed soldiers cheaply and quickly, pimento cheese became a mainstay.

By the late 1940s, packaged pimento cheese began to wane in popularity. But Southern cooks had taken a particular liking to the spread and started making it from scratch, turning the manufactured product into a home kitchen staple. Why it stayed in the South specifically is hard to say. Food writer Hanna Raskin credits the Southern popularity of pimento cheese with marketing efforts from Duke's mayonnaise. Kathleen Purvis (see page 493) of the Charlotte Observer theorizes it may have been because pimento cheese didn't spoil quickly (when made with Southern hoop cheese; see page 30) so it could be packed for lunch in the heat. Or it may have been thanks to the Masters golf tournament, held in Augusta, Georgia, at which iconic pimento cheese sandwiches are served; legend has it a husband and wife, Hodges and Ola Herndon, brought homemade sandwiches to the tournament in the late 1940s and sold them to the crowd for a quarter each.

Over the last 20 years or so, pimento cheese has picked up a following outside the South once again, and, like many Southern staples, it has been played with in different contexts. Sure, it is still eaten as an appetizer or sandwich spread, but you can find it stirred into grits or macaroni and cheese (see page 334), as a burger topping, as a flavoring for kettle chips, or even rolled into sushi at certain high-end Southern restaurants. However pimento cheese landed in the South, it's now at the heart of Southern food culture.

by Kelly Song

Cook's Country *test cook and journalist*

Pimento Cheese

Serves 10 (Makes about 3 cups)
Total time: 25 minutes

Don't substitute preshredded cheese here; it includes added starches (meant to prevent the shreds from sticking together) that will result in a dry spread.

⅔ cup mayonnaise
2 tablespoons cream cheese, softened
1 teaspoon lemon juice
1 teaspoon Worcestershire sauce
¼ teaspoon cayenne pepper
1 pound sharp yellow cheddar cheese
⅓ cup pimentos, patted dry and minced

1 Whisk mayonnaise, cream cheese, lemon juice, Worcestershire, and cayenne together in large bowl.

2 Shred half of cheddar on large holes of box grater. Shred remaining cheddar on small holes of box grater. Stir pimentos and cheddar into mayonnaise mixture until thoroughly combined. Serve. (Pimento cheese can be refrigerated for up to 1 week.)

Smoked Pimento Cheese

Substitute smoked cheddar cheese, shredded on small holes of box grater, for the finely shredded sharp cheddar cheese.

Hot Cheddar Crab Dip

Serves 6 ~ Total Time: 45 minutes

This dip is inspired by crab au gratin, a French-influenced Louisiana Cajun dish. For an irresistibly creamy hot dip, we begin by making a base that's essentially a traditional French Mornay sauce (a cheese-laden cream sauce) boldly flavored with distinctly Cajun ingredients. Take care when sourcing the two star ingredients; high-quality cheddar and the best crabmeat available will add incomparable depth to the already flavorful base of this dip. Aged cheddars are not only salty and sharp but also pleasantly sour and buttery. We prefer freshly cooked and picked unpasteurized crab here, but we also like the test kitchen's winning refrigerated pasteurized crabmeat, Phillips Premium Crab Jumbo. It's fresh-tasting and sweet, with a pleasant, mild brininess. Lump, backfin (special), and claw meat all work well here. Shred the cheese on a box grater. This recipe can easily be doubled to serve a crowd. The finished dip goes great with a little extra Worcestershire and some Tabasco sauce on top. Serve with toasted baguette slices or crackers.

2	tablespoons unsalted butter	¼	teaspoon pepper
½	cup finely chopped onion	1½	tablespoons all-purpose flour
¼	cup finely chopped celery	⅔	cup whole milk
¼	cup finely chopped red bell pepper	2	teaspoons Worcestershire sauce
2	garlic cloves, minced	6	ounces sharp or extra-sharp cheddar cheese, shredded (1½ cups), divided
2	teaspoons fresh thyme leaves, divided	8	ounces crabmeat, picked over for shells
1	teaspoon table salt	1	teaspoon paprika
½	teaspoon cayenne pepper		

1 Adjust oven rack 8 inches from broiler element and heat broiler. Melt butter in medium saucepan over medium heat. Add onion, celery, and bell pepper and cook until softened, 5 to 7 minutes. Stir in garlic, 1 teaspoon thyme, salt, cayenne, and pepper and cook until fragrant, about 30 seconds. Sprinkle flour over vegetables and cook, stirring constantly, for 1 minute.

2 Slowly whisk in milk and Worcestershire and bring to simmer. Cook until sauce thickens, about 2 minutes. Whisk in half of cheddar until melted. Off heat, gently stir in crabmeat. Transfer crab dip to shallow broiler-safe 1-quart baking dish.

3 Sprinkle remaining cheddar over crab dip, followed by paprika. Broil until cheese is well browned, 3 to 5 minutes. Remove dish from oven and sprinkle dip with remaining 1 teaspoon thyme. Let dip cool for 5 minutes. Serve.

Women picking crabmeat at Milbourne Oyster Company in Crisfield, Maryland, 1940.

Collections of the Maryland State Archives

CRAB SHELLS BY THE SEASHORE

Deviled crab means a couple different things depending on where you are in the South. In Florida, deviled crab croquettes can be found within the Cuban, Italian, and Spanish communities in Ybor City. These bites are akin to Maryland crab cakes, but they come in an oblong shape and have more breading to hold them together so they can be eaten out of hand.

In the other Gulf states and the South Carolina Lowcountry, deviled crab takes a different form. Crabmeat is mixed with butter or cream sauce and seasonings and stuffed back into a cleaned-out crab shell. It's then topped with bread crumbs or crackers and baked or broiled. This concept likely originated from free and enslaved Black women in port cities in Colonial America who would make loads of these, carefully picking the crab meat from freshly caught crabs and repurposing the shells as a serving vessel. They would then fill wicker baskets with them and go down to the docks to sell them to fishermen and loggers for lunch.

If you can procure clean crab shells, you can fill them with our Hot Cheddar Crab Dip, top them with buttery bread crumbs, and broil them on an aluminum foil–lined baking sheet. These will be creamier and cheesier than what the women sold in the port cities but will still be a delicious nod to them.

by Morgan Bolling

Chile con Queso

Serves 8 to 10 (Makes 4 cups) ~ Total Time: 30 minutes

This creamy cheese dip is often at the center of parties in Texas. The most widespread recipe combines Ro-Tel diced tomatoes and chiles with Velveeta, which is then microwaved. We use a mixture of Monterey Jack and Colby cheeses for bold cheese flavor, but to replicate the consistency of a queso made with Velveeta, we also incorporate evaporated milk; its built-in stabilizers ensure a smooth-melting base. This very cheesy magma has some extra smokiness from chipotle chiles in adobo. You can substitute ¾ cup canned diced tomatoes (drained) and 1 tablespoon chopped canned green chiles for the Ro-Tel tomatoes. Serve with tortilla chips. The dip can be refrigerated for up to 24 hours. To rewarm cooled dip, microwave in 20-second bursts, stirring at each interval, until melted.

8 ounces Monterey Jack cheese, shredded (2 cups), room temperature	1 tablespoon minced canned chipotle chile in adobo sauce
4 ounces Colby cheese, shredded (1 cup), room temperature	2 garlic cloves, minced
2 tablespoons vegetable oil, divided	1 (10-ounce) can Ro-Tel Original Diced Tomatoes & Green Chilies, drained
1 onion, chopped fine	1 (12-ounce) can evaporated milk
	2 tablespoons water

Place Monterey Jack, Colby, and 1 tablespoon oil in blender; set aside. Heat remaining 1 tablespoon oil in medium saucepan over medium-high heat until shimmering. Add onion and cook until golden brown, about 5 minutes. Stir in chipotle and garlic and cook until fragrant, about 30 seconds. Stir in tomatoes and cook until hot, about 2 minutes. Transfer to serving bowl.

2 Add evaporated milk and water to now-empty saucepan and bring to boil. Pour hot milk mixture over cheese in blender, cover, and process until smooth, about 30 seconds. Pour cheese into serving bowl with tomato mixture and stir to combine. Season with salt and pepper to taste. Let sit for 10 minutes to thicken slightly. Serve.

To Serve Out of a Slow Cooker Transfer dip to 1½- to 5-quart slow cooker and set cooker to warm or low setting for up to 2 hours. Dip will thicken slightly over time; adjust consistency with hot water as needed, whisking in 2 tablespoons at a time.

QUESO AND LADY BIRD JOHNSON

While its exact birthplace is unknown, chile con queso, the Texan party favorite, originated in Mexico and made its way across the border in the late 1800s. At this time, the dish was a tangle of roasted long green chile strips melted with white cheese. It was served as a side dish and not an appetizer.

As chile con queso evolved in the United States, it was next presented as a sauce to go over toast, like Welsh rarebit. Texans took it a step further and offered the creamy sauce with fried corn tortillas. These recipes for chile con queso, however, were made with cheddar or American cheese, and not Velveeta, the easy-melting brick processed cheese.

In 1939, Mrs. Myron Hinkle of Lubbock, Texas, shared her version in the cookbook *What'll I Cook*, published by the First Christian Church of Lubbock. Hers called for a block of Velveeta to be melted with the canned tomatoes and green chile peppers sold under the brand name Ro-Tel. This was the first published occurrence of what is now a party classic, and Texans have loved it ever since.

Indeed, when native Texans President Lyndon Johnson and Claudia "Lady Bird"

Lady Bird Johnson in central Texas.

Austin American-Statesman

Johnson were in Washington, queso became a frequent addition to White House menus. Its presence, however, was not well received by all. For instance, the White House head chef, a Frenchman named René Verdon, was said to have referred to the cheese dip as "chile concrete."

It's not known if it was the processed cheese that caused Verdon's aversion, though when Mrs. Johnson submitted her queso recipe to the *Washington Post*, hers called for aged cheddar cheese, not processed cheese. When prepared as written, this recipe was thick and sludgy since it didn't have any starches or liquids, both of which Velveeta provides, to create a smooth sauce.

What's curious is that other queso recipes attributed to Mrs. Johnson are made with processed cheese. Was the aged cheese in this one recipe an attempt to mollify Verdon and create something more sophisticated? That is a mystery, but when it comes to queso, processed cheese is an easy path to a pot of liquid gold.

by Lisa Fain

food writer, cookbook author, and voice behind the James Beard Award–winning food blog Homesick Texan

Vidalia Onion Dip

Serves 6 to 8 ~ Total Time: 1 hour

In 1986, the Vidalia Onion Act was passed by the Georgia legislature. The act specifies that only those sweet onions grown within a 20-county area can earn the trademarked name Vidalia. These sweet onions have inspired a yearly festival with a recipe contest, fried blooming Vidalia onions galore, onion-decorated wares, and a Miss Vidalia Onion competition.

In her *Bitter Southerner* article "Blood Sweat & Tears," Shane Mitchell (see page 156) explains how Vidalias were originally bred from Texas Early Grano 951C, a Texas sweet onion, and YB986, an agrarian name for a flat White Bermuda onion. But in Georgia, the soil is low in sulfur, which helped this already mild onion eat sweeter and less sharp.

Some people enjoy Vidalias raw like apples. President Jimmy Carter was known to slice them up and eat them on crackers smeared with peanut butter. While we don't necessarily endorse swapping your apple a day for a Vidalia a day, we do recommend this creamy, cheesy Georgia dip. It's usually made by combining cheese, mayonnaise, and finely chopped Vidalias and baking the mixture until warm and bubbly. Here we use a whole lot of Vidalias to let them shine through. We prefer the sharp flavor of cheddar cheese to milder Swiss, but cheddar tends to separate during baking, turning the dip greasy. Adding just ½ cup of American cheese, which is more stable when melted, to the cheddar keeps the dip together as it bakes. A few scallion greens both in the dip and sprinkled on top add color and accentuate the onion flavor. Delicate Vidalias are now available nationwide, so displaced Southerners (and those who prefer a more mild onion) can use them for their cooking. However, sweet onions such as Texas 1015, Maui, or Walla Walla will work here. Do not use regular yellow onions. Serve with crackers or tortilla chips.

2	Vidalia onions, finely chopped (2 cups)
6	ounces sharp cheddar cheese, shredded (1½ cups)
¾	cup mayonnaise
2	ounces American cheese, chopped (½ cup)
¼	cup thinly sliced scallion greens, divided

1 Adjust oven rack to middle position and heat oven to 375 degrees. Combine onions, cheddar, mayonnaise, American cheese, and 2 tablespoons scallions in bowl. Transfer to 1-quart casserole dish.

2 Bake until browned and bubbly, about 25 minutes. Let cool for 10 minutes. Top with remaining 2 tablespoons scallions. Serve.

Fire Crackers

Serves 6 to 8   ~   Total Time: 30 minutes, plus 1 hour resting

Fire crackers are also known as Alabama fire crackers or comeback crackers—an apt name because they keep you coming back for more. That's because when you give saltines a generous coating of fat and bold flavorings, magic happens. These irresistible crackers are great on an appetizer tray, served as a snack at a party or a church potluck, or as an accompaniment to soups and chilis.

Letting the saltines sit with oil, ranch dressing mix, and some extra flavorings (to boost the ranch profile) for at least 1 hour (but preferably 24 hours) seasons the crackers and changes their texture. Then, baking the saltines turns them golden brown and gives them a flaky texture and toasty flavor.

We developed this recipe using Hidden Valley Original Ranch Salad Dressing & Seasoning Mix. Two sleeves of saltines weigh about 8 ounces and contain about 72 crackers. Three teaspoons of red pepper flakes add modest heat to these crackers; feel free to increase or decrease the amount, if desired. This recipe can easily be doubled.

¾	cup vegetable oil
1	(1-ounce) package ranch dressing mix
2-4	teaspoons red pepper flakes
1	teaspoon dried dill
1	teaspoon garlic powder
8	ounces saltines

1   Add oil, ranch dressing mix, pepper flakes, dill, and garlic powder to 1-gallon zipper-lock bag. Seal bag and knead mixture with hands until well combined. Add saltines and reseal bag. Shake and turn gently until crackers are thoroughly coated. Let sit, turning bag occasionally, for at least 1 hour or up to 24 hours.

2   Adjust oven racks to upper-middle and lower-middle positions and heat oven to 250 degrees. Spread saltines into single layer over 2 rimmed baking sheets. Bake until light golden brown and slightly puffed, 20 to 25 minutes. Let crackers cool on sheets for at least 10 minutes before serving. (Fire crackers can be stored at room temperature for up to 1 week.)

Barbecue Fire Crackers

Omit dill. Substitute 1 tablespoon chipotle chile powder for red pepper flakes. Add 2 tablespoons packed brown sugar to zipper-lock bag with oil.

Lemon-Pepper Fire Crackers

Add 2 teaspoons grated lemon zest and 1 teaspoon pepper to zipper-lock bag with oil.

BENNE WAFERS

A SIGNATURE BENNE SEED TREAT

In the 19th century, three sweets developed and sold by Black women along the streets of Charleston invoked the beauty of the nutty, earthy, sweet benne seed: benne cake, benne stick, and benne brittle. One, however, rose above: The benne wafer, known then as benne cake, became the Lowcountry's signature sweet.

The benne seed is a cousin to the modern sesame seed, but it contains about 15 percent less oil. It arrived in the United States with enslaved Africans through the transatlantic slave trade, and it was grown and pressed for oil that was commonly used for cooking. The seeds themselves were an integral ingredient in soups and confections—in particular, they were the heart of what we know today as benne wafers.

According to author and historian Dr. David Shields, African American women sweetened the earliest forms of these confections with molasses which, prior to the Civil War, was a less expensive alternative to sugar. Sometimes they flavored them with lemon. Benne cake was especially popular from the 1850s to 1890s and became a source of income for newly freed Black Gullah Geechee women—particularly those who were older, and some of whom were single, as evidenced by photographs from the era.

By the 1890s, however, benne seeds were no longer grown as an oil crop, and the benne wafer disappeared from the carts of these vendors. That is, until the early 1900s, when African American bakers Elizabeth Mitchell and Maum Chloe began selling their confections in theaters across Charleston. In 1938, the first documented example of what was now called "benne wafers," for their thin profile and crispy texture, emerged at the Old Slave Mart Museum in Charleston, a business opened in 1938 by a white woman named Miriam Wilson. The African American history of the benne wafer was undeniable, however. Further, historians credit Black cooks during the 20th century with adding ingredients such as flour, cream, butter, and sugar, which had become more accessible to them, and cite Black children's love for a flatter, crispier sweet.

Throughout the Lowcountry, benne wafers are sold in packages at novelty tourist shops and local markets, featured on restaurant menus throughout Charleston, and immortalized in cookbooks that convey the region's varied foodways. In *Gullah Geechee Home Cooking: Recipes from the Matriarch of Edisto Island*, Emily Meggett (see page 162) detailed her own recipe for benne cookies, a common name for the wafer, which she prepared for more than 100 descendants during her 90 years of life. Mrs. Meggett advocates for a wafer that's "thin and crisp," speaking to the light, sweet essence of the region's favorite treat.

by Kayla Stewart

James Beard Award–winning food writer and journalist, and cookbook author, including co-author with Emily Meggett of Gullah Geechee Home Cooking

Savory Benne Wafers

Makes about 50 wafers ～ Total Time: 1 hour, plus 1 hour 20 minutes chilling and cooling

If there is a single food item that has molded the culinary heritage of Lowcountry, Charleston, South Carolina, it would be the benne seed, which has a 300-year history in the United States (see "Benne Wafers: A Signature Benne Seed Treat"). Although less common than sweet benne wafers, there are savory versions (sometimes referred to as benne seed cocktailers). These salty wafers showcase the earthiness and roasted flavor of benne seeds, but they're mild enough to pair with cheese, dips, or spreads. While true benne wafers use benne seeds, of course, most home cooks don't have easy access to heirloom benne seeds. We tested our recipe with both benne seeds and easier-to-find sesame seeds and found that toasting the sesame seeds is essential to create enough flavor to match their benne seed counterparts.

If you don't have a 2¼-inch round cutter or shot glass, you can use a pizza cutter or a large knife to cut the dough into 2-inch squares. If you're not able to find benne seeds locally, you can order them online from Anson Mills or opt for sesame seeds. If using sesame seeds, toast them in a skillet (without any oil) set over medium heat, shaking the pan occasionally to prevent scorching, until they become a deep golden brown, 3 to 5 minutes.

1	cup (5 ounces) all-purpose flour
1	teaspoon baking powder
¼	teaspoon baking soda
½	teaspoon kosher salt
⅛	teaspoon cayenne pepper
8	tablespoons unsalted butter, cut into ½-inch pieces and chilled
¼	cup milk, chilled
½	cup plus 1 tablespoon benne seeds or toasted sesame seeds, divided
2	teaspoons flake sea salt

1 Process flour, baking powder, baking soda, kosher salt, and cayenne in food processor until combined, about 5 seconds. Scatter butter over top and pulse until butter pieces are no larger than peas, about 10 pulses. Add milk and ½ cup benne seeds and pulse until dough forms large clumps and no dry flour remains, 10 to 12 pulses.

2 Transfer dough to lightly floured counter and knead briefly until it comes together. Divide dough in half and form each half into 5-inch disk, wrap disks tightly in plastic wrap, and refrigerate for at least 1 hour or up to 24 hours.

3 Adjust oven rack to middle position and heat oven to 375 degrees. Line 2 rimmed baking sheets with parchment paper.

4 On lightly floured counter, roll each dough disk into 13-inch round of even 1⁄16-inch thickness. Sprinkle 1½ teaspoons benne seeds evenly over each dough round. Using rolling pin, gently press benne seeds into dough. Using 2¼-inch round cutter or shot glass, cut 17 to 20 smaller rounds from each large dough round. Gather remaining dough from both large rounds and roll into 1 round of even 1⁄16-inch thickness. Cut 10 to 16 smaller rounds to yield about 50 total (do not reroll scraps a second time).

Arrange cut rounds in single layer on prepared sheets. Prick each round twice with fork and sprinkle evenly with flake salt.

5 Bake rounds, 1 sheet at a time, until golden brown, 8 to 10 minutes, rotating sheet halfway through baking. Let wafers cool completely on sheet, about 20 minutes. Serve. (Wafers can be stored at room temperature for up to 5 days.)

Old Bay Benne Wafers

Add 1½ teaspoons Old Bay Seasoning to flour mixture in step 1. Omit flake sea salt. Sprinkle wafers with ½ teaspoon Old Bay Seasoning in step 4.

Basic Deviled Eggs

Makes 12 eggs ~ Total Time: 40 minutes

"Eggs are big business in the South," Jeanne Voltz says in her book *The Flavor of the South: Delicacies and Staples of Southern Cuisine.* Southern states make up four of the top ten states in U.S. egg production. Before the commercial era, she explains, both farm women and city folks would raise flocks of laying hens to produce eggs for their families. Perhaps this is why eggs are found in so many Southern bites; they were an affordable way to stretch a meal and could be transformed in so many ways.

One of the most iconic Southern egg dishes is the deviled egg. The Southern Foodways Alliance website has captured memories and recipes from a mix of Southerners who participated in their 2004 Deviled Egg Recipe Competition. Several of the highlights recall the ways that some mothers nurtured their families with deviled eggs. The project also shares some deviled egg folk wisdom known to grandmothers.

Robert Croft recalls that his mother would mail order a hundred "straight run" biddies from a hatchery or the Sears Roebuck catalog every spring, and by mid-summer the family had more eggs than they knew what to do with. She'd often make deviled eggs for the kids as an after-school snack. Ernest L. Lewis says his mother would package deviled eggs in a cardboard box to bring to church potlucks or picnics, and he knew "that to 'squash the top' of this container was to court her wrath." And Lucinda Hougland tells about how her grandmother would always lay the cartons of eggs sideways the night before boiling her eggs to center the yolks.

A handful of contributors mention calling them "stuffed" or "dressed" eggs. Luci Lyler Anderson says her mom would never let anyone call them "deviled" since they were destined to be served at Sunday dinner or church suppers.

Few foods inspire the same common nostalgia as the deviled egg. Or are as adaptable. Some recipes are as simple as mashing the yolks of hard-cooked eggs with mayonnaise and salt before stuffing them back into the hollowed-out whites. But some call for mixing in herbs, lemon, hot sauce, or mustard. And many chefs make even more elaborate twists. Here we have a basic but balanced classic recipe plus a couple of flavor variations. Make them your own however you like.

6	Hard-Cooked Eggs (recipe follows)	1½	teaspoons lemon juice
3	tablespoons mayonnaise	1	teaspoon Dijon mustard
1	tablespoon minced fresh parsley, plus 12 small whole parsley leaves for garnishing		Pinch cayenne pepper

1   Slice each egg in half lengthwise with paring knife. Transfer yolks to bowl; arrange whites on serving platter. Mash yolks with fork until no large lumps remain. Add mayonnaise and use rubber spatula to smear mixture against side of bowl until thick, smooth paste forms, 1 to 2 minutes. Add minced parsley, lemon juice, mustard, and cayenne and mix until fully incorporated. Season with salt to taste.

2   Transfer yolk mixture to small, heavy-duty plastic bag. Press mixture into 1 corner and twist top of bag. Using scissors, snip ½ inch off filled corner. Squeezing bag, distribute yolk mixture evenly among egg white halves. Garnish each egg half with parsley leaf and serve.

Bacon and Chive Deviled Eggs

Cook 2 finely chopped slices bacon in 10-inch skillet over medium heat until crispy, 5 to 7 minutes. Using slotted spoon, transfer bacon to paper towel–lined plate. Reserve 1 tablespoon fat. Make filling, reducing mayonnaise to 2 tablespoons. Add reserved fat and ⅛ teaspoon salt. Substitute fresh chives for parsley and 2 teaspoons distilled white vinegar for lemon juice. Stir in three-quarters of bacon and sprinkle remaining bacon on filled eggs.

Chipotle Deviled Eggs with Radishes and Cilantro

Omit cayenne. Substitute cilantro for parsley, lime juice for lemon juice, and 2 teaspoons minced canned chipotle chile in adobo for mustard. Add 2 finely chopped radishes to filling.

Deviled Eggs with Curry Powder

Add 1 teaspoon curry powder with cayenne in step 1.

Hard-Cooked Eggs

Makes 2 to 8 eggs
Total Time: 30 minutes

Start timing after adding the last egg to the boiling water. This recipe works equally well with as few as two eggs and as many as eight eggs. The timing changes when more than eight eggs are cooked at once.

2–8   large eggs

1   Bring 12 cups water to boil in large saucepan over high heat. Fill large bowl halfway with ice and water.

2   Using spider skimmer or slotted spoon, gently lower eggs into boiling water and cook for 7 minutes for soft-cooked eggs or 13 minutes for hard-cooked eggs. Transfer eggs to ice bath and let cool for 5 minutes.

3   To peel, gently tap 1 egg on counter to crack shell all over. Begin peeling off shell at wider end of egg, making sure to break membrane between shell and egg white. Under gently running water, carefully peel membrane and shell off egg. Repeat with remaining eggs. Serve.

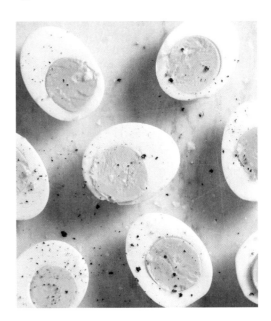

Truffled Egg Salad

Serve 4 to 6 ~ Total Time: 45 minutes

Egg salad is commonly served for a light lunch in the South. But this version takes inspiration from the truffled egg salad served during afternoon tea at Fearrington House Restaurant, a part of the idyllic Fearrington Village in Pittsboro, North Carolina. Keebe Fitch, who opened McIntyre's Books, an independent bookstore in the Village, says that the English custom of serving fresh-brewed tea and a menu of petite sandwiches, pastries, and jam has been part of the Fearrington experience for as long as she can remember. Her parents R.B. and Jenny Fitch initially established Fearrington as a "coming together place." The tea is just one way the family continues to express Southern hospitality.

"I love seeing customers come in on weekends, some wearing fascinators. You just know they are going to tea," says Fitch. Fearrington's dainty bite of truffled egg salad is served on challah with cornichons and arranged on a tiered china platter. It is a far cry from the heartier menus served in early American tea rooms.

To make a truffled egg salad, we stir in truffle oil, tangy Dijon mustard, and a splash of Tabasco sauce. A manual pastry blender makes quick work of chopping the eggs and blending the salad. If you don't have one, simply chop the eggs with a knife before stirring them together with the remaining ingredients. We recommend using our recipe for Hard-Cooked Eggs and cooking eight eggs all at once. If you'd like, follow the presentation at Fearrington and serve the egg salad on toasted challah with extra cornichons.

8	Hard-Cooked Eggs (page 105)	½	teaspoon table salt
⅓	cup mayonnaise	½	teaspoon pepper
1	tablespoon Dijon mustard	¼	cup chopped cornichons
1	tablespoon truffle oil	2	tablespoons minced fresh chives
½	teaspoon Tabasco sauce		

Using pastry blender, chop eggs, mayonnaise, mustard, truffle oil, Tabasco sauce, salt, and pepper in bowl until combined and egg whites are cut into rough ¼-inch pieces. Stir in cornichons and chives. Serve.

Deviled Egg Salad

Increase mustard to 2 tablespoons and Tabasco sauce to 2 teaspoons. Omit truffle oil. Substitute ¼ cup minced celery for chives.

A 1940 postcard from a destination tea room on the Tennessee side of the Great Smoky Mountains.

SETTING THE SCENE FOR SOUTHERN TEA ROOMS

The tea may have been iced, but the lunches and dinners in Southern tea rooms were warm, homey, and usually prepared by women. Tea rooms attracted diners for these qualities, but they were important for another reason as well. In the early 1900s, restaurants were male strongholds; if they welcomed women, often it was only alongside a man. Tea rooms served as gathering spaces that were open to women, not only as visitors but also as business owners.

With sweet names such as the Shady Lawn, the Green Shutter, or the Country Parson's, tea rooms offered charm not found in the average eat-and-run lunch room. Their interiors often featured ruffled curtains likely sewed by the proprietor, colorfully painted furniture, and an atmosphere of restful leisure. Some tea rooms in the South fashioned themselves after high-society clubs in the North, particularly those in trendy Manhattan. The Gypsy Inn in Florida, for example, styled itself as "The Greenwich Village of St. Petersburg" and welcomed all kinds of colorful people.

Most tea rooms were operated by white women, but some were Black-owned. And Black women played an important role in Southern tea room kitchens, expertly turning out favorites such as fried chicken, beaten biscuits, and waffles.

While women customers were typical, men also appreciated the tea rooms' welcoming comfort and good food. A 1948 contributor to *Gourmet's Guide to Good Eating* noted that the Little Tea Shop in Memphis, Tennessee, attracted businessmen with its special dish of corn sticks and sliced chicken covered with gravy.

Tea rooms served as spaces not only for meals but for socializing and celebratory events, such as wedding showers, college reunions, and bridge club parties. They became a place women could host, gossip, and eat. And the option to open a tea room and run it how they saw fit allowed many single (and non-single) women a chance to obtain financial independence and express individualism.

by Jan Whitaker

writer and consumer historian, with a focus on department stores and restaurants, and author of the book Tea at the Blue Lantern Inn: A Social History of the Tea Room Craze in America

Boiled Peanuts

Serves 16 (Makes about 4 quarts)
Total Time: 6½ hours, plus 2 hours cooling

If you haven't tried boiled peanuts, you're in for a treat. Whereas roasting peanuts until crunchy brings out their nuttiness, boiling softens them until very tender, drawing out their sweetness and resulting in a plump, juicy, salty-sweet snack. If you want to pronounce them properly, most Southerners leave off the "ed," calling their bag "boil' peanuts." They're sold at roadside stands and gas stations around the South, and they're a great snack for a road trip.

While boiled peanuts are often thought of as inherently Southern, in her article "The Global Love of Boiled Peanuts" for the *Bitter Southerner,* food historian Dr. Julia Skinner (see page 35) calls their history "as rich and complex as the spices they're often cooked in." Skinner explains that peanuts are indigenous to South America but were brought to Europe and eventually to regions of Africa through colonization. When Africans were enslaved in the United States, they brought the cooking technique of boiling peanuts with them. Today, in addition to the American South (where billions of pounds of peanuts are still grown annually, mostly in Georgia), you can find versions of boiled peanuts in Senegal, Nigeria, China, India, and Hawaii. "So while the peanut itself is indigenous to the Americas," Skinner writes, "the cooking process is African, and this process has spread around the world, the result of intercontinental trade, colonization, slavery, and immigration."

Most recently, Southern fine dining chefs have taken to mixing them into inventive dishes such as boiled peanut hummus, or pickled boiled peanuts as a topper for red snapper. This version is an intro to the rustic, snackable original. To be accessible to everyone, it doesn't rely on the traditional green (freshly dug) peanuts. However, you can use green peanuts, which are available late summer and early fall, if you wish; reduce the cooking time to about 2 hours. To eat boiled peanuts, pop off the shell and suck out the peanut and any of the seasoned liquid left within it.

2   pounds raw, shell-on peanuts

2   gallons water

1   cup table salt

Combine peanuts, water, and salt in 12-quart stockpot. Bring to boil over high heat. Reduce heat to low, cover, and simmer until peanuts are tender, about 6 hours, stirring occasionally. Remove from heat and let peanuts cool completely in water, about 2 hours. Drain and serve.

Candied Pecans

Serves 20 (Makes about 5 cups)   ~   Total Time: 1 hour minutes, plus cooling

Americans love to debate the proper way to pronounce "pecan." Perhaps it's because pecans are the only major nut native to our soil. It's our nut, after all, so we should get to decide what it's called. But is it "puh-KAHN," "pee-KAHN," "PEE-can" or some other variation?

Native pecans were eaten and traded by Native Americans for millennia, most heavily around the Mississippi Valley in what is now the American South, and in Texas and Northern Mexico. The modern word comes from the Algonquin languages, and they had some half a dozen different spellings, from pakaani to pagan to pa'kan, that referred either to nuts in general or to hard-shelled nuts such as the pecan.

Differences in how we refer to this particular nut, then, have been baked into our language from the start, so it's fitting that there's still no consensus on how to say "pecan." But whether or not we can agree on a pronunciation, at least now we've agreed on a spelling, and surely most of us can agree on another thing: Pecans are delicious—buttery and eminently snackable, especially in sweets such as pralines (see page 404) and candied pecans.

For our recipe for candied pecans, we use egg whites mixed with a little water and salt for the coating, which gives the nuts a perfect, even crunch. (We've found that oil, melted butter, and other common coatings make for greasy hands and spotty coverage.) Slow-roasting the nuts at a low temperature ensures they cook completely without scorching the exterior. To double this recipe, simply adjust the oven racks to the upper-middle and lower-middle positions and bake the pecans on two baking sheets, switching and rotating the sheets halfway through baking.

1	large egg white	½	cup sugar
1	tablespoon water	2	teaspoons ground cinnamon
1	teaspoon table salt	1	teaspoon ground ginger
1	pound unsalted pecans	1	teaspoon ground coriander

1   Adjust oven rack to upper-middle position and heat oven to 300 degrees. Line rimmed baking sheet with parchment paper and coat with vegetable oil spray. Whisk egg white, water, and salt together in large bowl. Add pecans and toss to coat. Drain thoroughly in colander, 4 to 5 minutes.

2   Mix sugar, cinnamon, ginger, and coriander in large bowl. Add drained pecans and toss to coat. Spread pecans evenly on prepared sheet and bake until dry and crisp, 40 to 45 minutes, rotating sheet halfway through baking. Let pecans cool completely. Break pecans apart and serve. (Pecans can be stored at room temperature for up to 3 weeks.)

PEANUTS

Nut, Not So Much

Although "nut" is in the name, peanuts are actually legumes, edible seeds that grow in pods (their shells). Unlike tree nuts, such as pecans, almonds, and walnuts, peanuts grow below the surface of the soil.

Peanuts originated in South America, traveled to Africa with Portuguese explorers, and then came to North America on British ships carrying enslaved Africans. Today the United States is one of the top three producers worldwide—thanks mostly to our collective love of Peanut Butter (page 371). But the protein-packed peanut shines in its pure form in recipes for Boiled Peanuts (page 108) as well.

Peanuts are available year-round, in both raw and dry-roasted forms. Store peanuts in an airtight container in a cool, dry cupboard or in the freezer for up to six months.

A Peanut by Any Other Name

Depending on where you live in the country, you might consider a goober to be a goof, or maybe you recall the concession stand candy, but for many in the South, a goober is an unadulterated peanut. Goober is derived from the word "nguba" in Kongo and Kimbundu languages, a lasting reminder of the journey peanuts made with enslaved people from Africa (where they are beloved). Like the popularity of peanuts, their word infiltrated the South. Southerners have also called peanuts "pindar," derived from mpinda in Kongo, but the name has fallen out of fashion, leaving goober as a favorite. Other names used for the not-nut include earthnut and groundnut, unsurprising since the legume doesn't grow on trees.

Raw Peanuts & Green Peanuts

Peanuts are categorized based on their post-dig processing.

Green Peanuts This refers to peanuts that are freshly dug; they have a high moisture content and should be refrigerated to extend their short shelf life (usually 7 to 10 days). They are only available May through November.

Raw Peanuts This refers to green peanuts that have been air dried to remove much of their moisture. It extends their shelf life greatly, so you can find these in stores year-round.

Varieties of Peanuts Grown in the Southern United States

If you haven't thought much about peanut varieties before, you'll find each has a different ideal application.

Runner

The most common type of peanut grown in the United States (accounting for more than 85 percent of U.S. peanuts), runners are the go-to peanut for peanut butter. They're grown primarily in Alabama, Florida, Georgia, Oklahoma, and Texas.

Virginia

Virginia peanuts have large kernels and are most commonly sold as snacking peanuts, both in and out of their shells. As their name implies, they're grown in Virginia, as well as in the Carolinas and Texas.

Spanish

These peanuts have a reddish-brown skin and a higher oil content than the other peanut varieties. They're used primarily for candies and snacks. They're most commonly grown in Oklahoma and Texas.

Valencia

Accounting for less than 1 percent of peanut production in the United States, Valencias have three to four small kernels per shell. They have a slightly sweet flavor, which makes for great boiled peanuts. They're the prime choice for natural peanut butter. Most Valencias are grown in New Mexico.

A Snack and a Sipper

One of the easiest Southern treats to prepare is salted peanuts in Coca-Cola. Kaitlyn Yarborough puts it deliciously in an article for *Southern Living*: "Peanuts in Coca-Cola is a union predestined by the stars—the sweetness of the Coca-Cola perfectly complementing the saltiness of the peanuts. A fizzy sip followed by a satisfying crunch." And she's right; if you were to put out a tray of glass Coke bottles and tiny bags of salted peanuts at a Southern party, guests would be very happy.

According to the National Peanut Federation, the practice may have come about in the 1920s when workers, who didn't want to handle their snack with dirty hands, would open a packet of peanuts and pour them into their Coke so they could snack and drink at the same time.

It's just about as simple as it sounds, but there are some ground rules: Glass bottles of Coke are preferred over plastic. Use salted peanuts: no unsalted or lightly salted nuts here. Sip on the Coke carefully: The true pros are able to tilt the bottle so only one or two salty peanuts come along with each sip of Coke.

Pickled Shrimp

Serves 6 to 8   ~   Total Time: 1¼ hours, plus 3 hours pickling

Before there was refrigeration, pickling was a common practice for preserving a load of shrimp. One of the earliest recipes for the dish appears in a "receipt" book assembled by a well-to-do planter's wife. Her book was published in 1984 to give modern audiences a glimpse into daily life in an early American household. The 1770 book is titled *A Colonial Plantation Cookbook: The Receipt Book of Harriott Pinckney Horry*.

While pickling shrimp is thought to have come from England, the practice may also have been imported from the West Indies, where the practice of marinating fish is a familiar concept known as escabeche or ceviche: Take a flavorful dressing with a good amount of vinegar and toss in cooked shrimp to marinate. The shrimp take on the nuanced flavor of the dressing while staying crisp and sweet. Today, pickled shrimp are often served as an hors d'oeuvre or first course. The shrimp in this recipe need to be refrigerated for at least 3 hours before serving.

2 pounds extra-large shrimp
   (21 to 25 per pound), peeled and deveined

1 teaspoon table salt, plus salt for cooking shrimp

8 cups ice

1 cup cider vinegar

¼ cup sugar

2 garlic cloves, smashed and peeled

3 bay leaves

1 teaspoon whole allspice berries

1 teaspoon coriander seeds

½ teaspoon red pepper flakes

1 cup extra-virgin olive oil

¼ cup capers, minced

2 tablespoons Dijon mustard

2 tablespoons minced fresh dill

1 tablespoon hot sauce

1 tablespoon Worcestershire sauce

1 cup thinly sliced red onion

1 lemon, cut into 6 wedges

1 Combine 4 cups cold water, shrimp, and 2 teaspoons salt in Dutch oven. Set pot over medium-high heat and cook, stirring occasionally, until water registers 170 degrees and shrimp are just beginning to turn pink, 5 to 7 minutes.

2 Remove pot from heat, cover, and let sit until shrimp are completely pink and firm, about 5 minutes. Drain shrimp in colander. Rinse shrimp under cold water, then pat dry with paper towels.

3 Combine vinegar, sugar, garlic, bay leaves, allspice, coriander seeds, and pepper flakes in large bowl and microwave until hot, about 2 minutes. Stir to dissolve sugar. Let cool completely. Whisk in oil, capers, mustard, dill, hot sauce, Worcestershire, and salt until combined.

4 Stir onion, lemon wedges, and shrimp into vinegar mixture until thoroughly combined. Push to submerge shrimp in marinade, then place small plate on top to keep shrimp submerged. Cover and refrigerate, stirring occasionally, for at least 3 hours or up to 2 days. To serve, remove shrimp from marinade using slotted spoon.

Diane Wilson in her Texas home.

TEXAS WOMEN SHRIMPERS

As Southerners cook and eat our beloved Gulf shrimp, we should give thanks to the hardworking shrimpers hauling the nets and delivering their delicious harvests to our tables. Traditionally, shrimping has been a male domain, but there are women who've transcended the barriers.

Diane Wilson is an exceptional woman in more ways than one. A fourth-generation shrimper in Seadrift, Texas, she assisted her father as a schoolgirl and, by her twenties, was captain of her own shrimp boat. She thinks of the bay waters as a nurturing grandmother and loves the solitary saltwater work. In 1989, learning of the toxic contamination levels in her beloved bays and the threats to sea life and to fisherfolks' health and livelihood, Wilson sprang into action and never looked back. Leading the local fight for clean water for decades (while raising five children), she was plaintiff in a Clean Water Act suit against Formosa Plastics. The case was settled in 2019 for $50 million to fund marine environmental cleanup. In 2023, Wilson was awarded the international Goldman Prize for grassroots environmental activism.

After a 27-year career in property management, Nicole (Nikki) Johnson-Kunz joined forces with her octogenarian father-in-law, Captain Jerome "Pops" Kunz, the oldest working shrimper on the Texas coast. Worried about him working alone on his boat in Galveston Bay, she resolved to ride along, just in case. Along the way, she learned the ropes and became a valued professional deckhand, performing all the physical tasks required for shrimping. She's known as the Shrimp Diva—she wears full makeup while she works, and her boat gear is distinctively pink. She and Pops shrimp every day of the season and are the subject of an online documentary series.

by MM Pack

food writer, historian, and private chef

Shrimp Rémoulade

Serves 4 to 6   ~   Total Time: 45 minutes, plus 1 hour chilling

Rémoulade comes from the word "remolas," which is a northern French dialect word meaning horseradish. It's thought that this piquant sauce came to New Orleans from France, though Louisiana has put its own spin on it. It's a creamy, tangy condiment that serves as a seafood accompaniment, a dip for fried delights, or a robust sandwich spread. Another common way of eating the sauce is to toss it with plump, juicy shrimp to make shrimp rémoulade, a satisfying Creole appetizer.

Letting poached shrimp sit in the pungent stir-together rémoulade allows the mild seafood flavor to blend with the bright sauce. We serve the shrimp rémoulade in lettuce leaves, as is common. If using shrimp treated with sodium or preservatives, reduce the salt in step 1 to ½ teaspoon. Buy refrigerated prepared horseradish, not the shelf-stable kind, which contains preservatives and additives.

Shrimp

1½   pounds jumbo shrimp (16 to 20 per pound), peeled, deveined, and tails removed

Table salt for cooking shrimp

Rémoulade

⅔   cup mayonnaise

¼   cup finely chopped celery

¼   cup finely chopped green bell pepper

3   tablespoons minced cornichons

2   scallions, sliced thin

1   tablespoon lemon juice, plus lemon wedges for serving

1½   teaspoons prepared horseradish, drained

1   teaspoon spicy brown mustard

1   teaspoon ketchup

1   garlic clove, minced

½   teaspoon paprika

½   teaspoon Worcestershire sauce

¼   teaspoon table salt

¼   teaspoon pepper

⅛   teaspoon cayenne pepper

½   head Bibb lettuce (4 ounces), leaves separated

Hot sauce

1 **For the shrimp** Combine 3 cups cold water, shrimp, and 1½ teaspoons salt in Dutch oven. Set pot over medium-high heat and cook, stirring occasionally, until water registers 170 degrees and shrimp are just beginning to turn pink, 5 to 7 minutes.

2 Remove pot from heat, cover, and let sit until shrimp are completely pink and firm, about 5 minutes. Drain shrimp in colander. Rinse shrimp under cold water, then pat dry with paper towels. Transfer shrimp to large bowl and refrigerate until ready to use.

3 **For the rémoulade** Combine all ingredients in bowl.

4 Fold rémoulade into shrimp until combined. Season with salt and pepper to taste. Cover and refrigerate to let flavors blend, about 1 hour. Serve over lettuce with lemon wedges and hot sauce.

West Virginia Pepperoni Rolls

Makes 16 rolls ~ Total Time: 2 hours, plus 2 hours rising

A classic West Virginia pepperoni roll is a fluffy yeasted dough stuffed with batons of pepperoni sticks or fistfuls of sliced pepperoni and baked until golden. Courtney Balestier, a writer and expert on Appalachia, will tell you that even with a short ingredient list, pepperoni rolls serve a role in the region that's greater than the sum of their parts. In her article "The Poetry of Pepperoni Rolls" in *Appalachian Review*, Balestier says, "The pepperoni roll, really, is a poem: self-contained, complete, economical in every sense of the word." This simple baked good is a veritable handheld meal. The first known record of pepperoni rolls is from the 1920s, when an Italian baker named Giuseppe Argiro made them to sell to coal miners in Fairmont, West Virginia. A symbol of Appalachia's hardworking people, they continue to be served at restaurants and in home kitchens nearly a century later. "We do not tend to glorify the poor, and we do not tend to glorify the working class. These are concepts very much tied, through reality and rhetoric, to Appalachia, but in general, we Americans do not tend to lavish respect on those who make something out of nothing or on the satisfying meal they've managed to stretch from limited ingredients," Balestier asserts.

To make pepperoni rolls at home, we slice pepperoni sticks into wedges and microwave them, reserving the flavorful rendered oil. Next we make a simple dough of all-purpose flour, yeast, milk, and a little sugar, flavored with the reserved oil. Tossing the pepperoni wedges with flour helps them adhere better to the dough when they're rolled inside (avoiding gaping holes in the rolls' centers). Brushing the surface with an egg wash and sprinkling it with sesame seeds gives the rolls their signature look.

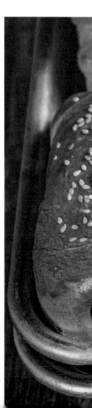

4   (7- to 8-ounce) sticks pepperoni, 8 inches long

1½   cups water

1   cup whole milk

2   tablespoons plus 2 teaspoons sugar

6⅔   cups (33⅔ ounces) plus 1 table-spoon all-purpose flour, divided, plus extra as needed

1   tablespoon instant or rapid-rise yeast

2   teaspoons table salt

1   large egg beaten with 1 tablespoon water

4   teaspoons sesame seeds

1   Line rimmed baking sheet with parchment paper. Cut pepperoni sticks in half crosswise, then cut each half in half lengthwise. Slice each quarter lengthwise into four 4-inch wedges. (You should have 64 wedges.) Place pepperoni in large bowl and microwave until fat is rendered, about 3 minutes. Using tongs, transfer pepperoni to paper towel–lined plate; reserve 3 tablespoons pepperoni oil. Do not wash bowl.

2   Combine water, milk, and sugar in 4-cup liquid measuring cup. Microwave until temperature registers 110 degrees, 1 to 2 minutes. Stir in reserved pepperoni oil.

3   Using stand mixer fitted with dough hook, mix 6⅔ cups flour, yeast, and salt on low speed until combined, about 30 seconds. With mixer running, slowly add water mixture until incorporated. Increase speed to medium and mix until dough is shiny and smooth and pulls away from sides of bowl, about 8 minutes. (If dough appears wet, add additional flour 1 tablespoon at a time.) Turn dough onto lightly floured counter and knead briefly to form cohesive ball. Transfer dough to reserved bowl and turn to coat with residual pepperoni oil in bowl. Cover with plastic wrap and let rise in warm place until doubled in volume, 50 to 60 minutes.

4   Transfer dough to lightly floured counter and divide into 16 equal (3½-ounce) pieces. Working with 1 piece at a time (keep remaining pieces covered with plastic), form dough into balls, cover with plastic, and let rest for 5 minutes.

5   Toss pepperoni wedges with remaining 1 tablespoon flour to coat. Working with 1 dough ball at a time, use hands to press ball into 6 by 4-inch rectangle. Starting along short side of rectangle, lay 4 pieces of pepperoni side by side, ½ inch apart, and roll into tight cylinder, pinching seam to seal. Leave ends of rolls open. Arrange rolls seam side down on prepared sheet, end to end, ½ inch apart and 4 per row. Cover with plastic and let rise until doubled in size, 50 to 60 minutes. Adjust oven rack to middle position and heat oven to 375 degrees.

6   Brush rolls with egg mixture and sprinkle with sesame seeds. Bake until golden brown, 24 to 28 minutes. Transfer sheet to wire rack and let cool for at least 15 minutes. Serve. (Baked and cooled rolls can be wrapped in plastic, placed in zipper-lock bag, and frozen for up to 1 month. To reheat, adjust oven rack to middle position and heat oven to 350 degrees. Remove plastic and wrap each roll in foil. Bake directly on oven rack until heated through, 35 to 45 minutes.)

Natchitoches Meat Pies

Makes 16 pies ～ Total Time: 2¼ hours, plus 1 hour chilling

It doesn't take much time living in Louisiana to understand that Natchitoches meat pies are pronounced NACK-a-tush meat pies. The name comes from the city of Natchitoches, Louisiana, which got its name from the Natchitoches Native American tribe. Not unlike empanadas from Latin America, beef patties from Jamaica, or Cornish pasties from England, these hand pies have a flaky crust with a savory filling of ground meat and spices. Natchitoches meat pies are typically stuffed with a combination of beef and pork flavored with the holy trinity: onions, green bell peppers, and celery. And they're deep-fried for an extra-crispy crust.

Culinary historians argue about the origins of these fried turnovers. Since they resemble empanadas, many historians trace their origins to 18th-century Spanish outposts not far from Natchitoches; other scholars point to their similarity to French-Canadian tourtières and connect them to the French Canadians who settled the region. James Lasyone, of Lasyone's Meat Pie Restaurant, offered a theory close to the first one in a 1996 issue of *Gourmet*: "I believe it was cooks on boats from far away who made the meat pies. People in town liked them, learned how to make them, and never forgot them." In the 1940s, when Lasyone was young, the pies were sold from street carts, but when that tradition faded, it was hard to get one of these local delicacies unless you knew a woman who was making them out of her house. James was a butcher and sold meat to these women for their pies; he eventually tried his hand at making them himself and started selling them out of the window of his shop.

James passed away in 2015, but his daughters Angela Lasyone and Tina Lasyone Smith took over Lasyone's, and they co-own the business today. They're not new to the restaurant; after their dad opened it, their mom JoAnn kept the books while Tina and Angela learned the ropes of rolling out the dough, stuffing, frying, and selling the meat pies. Now, more than half a century after their father started selling meat pies, Tina and Angela are keeping up the tradition and selling them alongside some newer additions such as a crawfish pie variation.

For this recipe, you can make the dough and the filling up to 24 hours ahead and refrigerate them separately. You can also shape and fill the pies, refrigerating them for up to 24 hours before frying, so meat pies are an approachable lunch for all. Use a Dutch oven that holds 6 quarts or more.

Filling

5	teaspoons vegetable oil, divided
12	ounces 85 percent lean ground beef
12	ounces ground pork
1½	teaspoons table salt, divided
1	teaspoon pepper, divided
1	small onion, chopped fine
1	small green bell pepper, stemmed, seeded, and minced
1	celery rib, chopped fine
6	scallions, white parts minced, green parts sliced thin
3	garlic cloves, minced
¼	teaspoon cayenne pepper
2	tablespoons all-purpose flour
1	cup chicken broth

Dough

4	cups (20 ounces) all-purpose flour
2	teaspoons table salt
1	teaspoon baking powder
8	tablespoons vegetable shortening, cut into ½-inch pieces
1	cup chicken broth
2	large eggs, lightly beaten
1	quart vegetable oil for frying

1 **For the filling** Heat 2 teaspoons oil in 12-inch skillet over medium-high heat until just smoking. Add beef, pork, 1 teaspoon salt, and ½ teaspoon pepper and cook, breaking up pieces with spoon, until no longer pink, 8 to 10 minutes. Transfer meat to bowl.

2 Add remaining 1 tablespoon oil to now-empty skillet and heat over medium-high heat until shimmering. Add onion, bell pepper, celery, scallion whites, remaining ½ teaspoon salt, and remaining ½ teaspoon pepper and cook until vegetables are just starting to brown, 3 to 5 minutes. Stir in garlic and cayenne and cook until fragrant, about 30 seconds.

3 Return meat and any accumulated juices to skillet with vegetables. Sprinkle flour over meat and cook, stirring constantly, until evenly coated, about 1 minute. Add broth, bring to boil, and cook until slightly thickened, about 3 minutes. Transfer filling to bowl and stir in scallion greens. Refrigerate until completely cool, about 1 hour. (Filling can be refrigerated for up to 24 hours.)

4 **For the dough** Process flour, salt, and baking powder in food processor until combined, about 3 seconds. Add shortening and pulse until mixture resembles coarse cornmeal, 6 to 8 pulses. Add broth and eggs and pulse until dough just comes together, about 5 pulses. Transfer dough to lightly floured counter and knead until dough forms smooth ball, about 20 seconds. Divide dough into 16 equal pieces. (Dough can be covered and refrigerated for up to 24 hours.)

5 Line rimmed baking sheet with parchment paper. Working with 1 piece of dough at a time, roll into 6-inch circle on lightly floured counter. Place ¼ cup filling in center of dough round. Brush edges of dough with water and fold dough over filling. Press to seal, trim any ragged edges, and crimp edges with tines of fork. Transfer to prepared sheet. (Filled pies can be covered and refrigerated for up to 24 hours.)

6 Adjust oven rack to middle position and heat oven to 200 degrees. Set wire rack in second rimmed baking sheet. Add oil to large Dutch oven until it measures about ¾ inch deep and heat over medium-high heat to 350 degrees. Place 4 pies in oil and fry until golden brown, 3 to 5 minutes per side, using slotted spatula or spider skimmer to flip. Adjust burner, if necessary, to maintain oil temperature between 325 and 350 degrees. Transfer pies to prepared wire rack and place in oven to keep warm. Return oil to 350 degrees and repeat with remaining pies. Serve.

No.4
FROM THE GARDEN

Left to right: Cowboy Caviar (page 148), Tomato Pie (page 146), Green Beans with Ham and Potatoes (page 142), Watermelon Salad (page 128).

FROM FIELDS TO FEASTS

HONORING BLACK WOMEN IN SOUTHERN FARMING

Deep in the heart of America's culinary landscape lies the unique tapestry of Southern cuisine—a mosaic woven with tradition, innovation, and the indelible mark of women who toiled the land and raised the future generations who built this country. If there are no farmers, there is no food. The legacy of Black Southern women farmers, who refused to be relegated to the kitchen, is a story of resilience, adaptation, and the relentless pursuit of flavor. When it comes to modern representation of farming heritage as well as community activation and social ingenuity in the farming space, the stories of Black women often go untold. These women support entire food systems and do double, even triple, duty as keepers of the flame, upholding the communities in which they live and preserving farming systems that reach beyond the legacy of enslavement and sharecropping, for all around them.

Among these notable figures is Samantha "Foxx" Winship of Mother's Finest Urban Farm in Winston-Salem, North Carolina. She is a passionate advocate for sustainable agriculture and community empowerment. Through her urban approach to farming, Winship not only grows fresh produce but also cultivates connections within her community, bridging the gap between farm and table. After turning to beekeeping and agriculture to help her children learn about nature's beauty and complexity, she extended that knowledge to school-age children's programming and summer camps on her property. The honey, tonics, elderberry syrup, and community-supported agriculture (CSA) boxes she produces from her urban family farm feed the community and foster a sense of belonging and shared purpose.

Gabrielle E.W. Carter, a culture preservationist and founder of Tall Grass Food Box in Durham, North Carolina, shows unwavering commitment to community-driven food systems. By sourcing produce from Black farmers across the state, Carter supports local agriculture and preserves the region's rich agricultural heritage. Her Revival Taste Collective community dinners and seed-saving (see page 129) efforts exemplify Southern hospitality and solidarity. Along with her great-grandfather, Carter also records her family's stories to preserve and underscore the importance of Black land ownership.

Dori Sanders, a founding member of the Southern Foodways Alliance and second-generation South Carolinian peach farmer, embodies the deep-rooted connection between land and food in Southern culture. As a best-selling author of a cookbook and several novels, the nonagenarian is a champion of and a role model for contemporary Black women farmers. Since 1915, Sanders Peach Farm in York County, South Carolina, has sustained the family and serves as a symbol of generational continuity. Sanders persists despite numerous challenges, including the increasing unpredictability of weather and the economic pressures of maintaining a small-scale farm in a globalized food market.

Long before Shirley Sherrod held her former position as Georgia State Director of Rural Development for the U.S. Department of Agriculture, she empowered Black communities to reclaim their land and heritage through her advocacy for community land trusts in her home state. Her tireless efforts to promote food justice and equity have impacted Southern food culture and inspired future generations to continue the fight for a more just and sustainable food system.

Through her work, Shorlette Ammons, program director of Farm Aid, has championed small-scale farmers' rights and promoted sustainable agriculture practices across the South. The North Carolina native comes from a lineage of farmers, cooks, and storytellers. In her essay in *Edible North Carolina: A Journey across a State of Flavor*, she writes, "The older I get, the closer I feel to the ways and experiences of home that led me to my work in the food systems of North Carolina. Despite this state's difficult histories that I confront daily, I recognize the significance that land, food, and farming have for my future and the people I love."

These five women are among the many who have shaped entire food systems, consequently influencing Southern food culture along the way. May we continue to honor them and inspire future generations through culinary storytelling.

by Nikki Miller-Ka

chef and food and travel writer based in North Carolina

Buttermilk Coleslaw

Serves 4 to 6   ~   Total Time: 20 minutes, plus 1½ hours salting and chilling

Historians trace the linguistic origins of coleslaw to the Dutch "kool" (meaning cabbage) and "sla" (meaning salad), as the Dutch likely brought a version of the dish with them to the United States in the 17th century. Generations later, the dish became coleslaw (notably, a recipe without cabbage is just a "slaw") and adopted ingredient variations as it was prepared and eaten by other cultural groups who likely already had a shredded vegetable salad in their own culinary heritage. Thanks to the combination of sugar, salt, and acids, coleslaw is already on its way to being a type of pickle, which means it keeps for a relatively long time. In the South, especially in South Carolina, some home cooks make a dish called "permanent slaw," a seemingly everlasting dish that keeps in the fridge for weeks or months and is sometimes even topped off with additional cabbage and dressing (similar to the way pickles are made in certain cultures). Classic buttermilk coleslaw doesn't keep that long, but it still earns a permanent spot as picnic side dish and church lunch offering. It also adds delightful crunch as a topping for fish tacos, a trick we learned from Food Network chef Kardea Brown's cookbook, *The Way Home: A Celebration of Sea Islands Food and Family with over 100 Recipes*.

That said, homemade coleslaw is prone to becoming watery and wilted. For a crisp coleslaw with a buttermilk dressing that clings to the cabbage instead of collects in the bottom of the bowl, you need to salt and drain the cabbage first. This process removes excess water and softens the cabbage to a pickle-crisp texture. For a hefty and tangy dressing, this recipe combines buttermilk, mayonnaise, and sour cream. To save time, shred the cabbage in a food processor fitted with a slicing disk. If you don't have a food processor, slice the cabbage wedges crosswise ⅛ inch thick. Shred the carrots on the large holes of a box grater.

½   head red or green cabbage, quartered, cored, and shredded (6 cups)

¼   teaspoon table salt, plus salt for salting cabbage

1   carrot, peeled and shredded

½   cup buttermilk

2   tablespoons mayonnaise

2   tablespoons sour cream

2   tablespoons minced fresh parsley

1   small shallot, minced

½   teaspoon cider vinegar

½   teaspoon sugar

¼   teaspoon Dijon mustard

⅛   teaspoon pepper

1   Toss cabbage and 1 teaspoon salt in colander set over large bowl and let sit until wilted, at least 1 hour or up to 4 hours. Rinse cabbage under cold running water. Press, but do not squeeze, to drain, and blot dry with paper towels.

2   Combine cabbage and carrot in large bowl. In separate bowl, whisk buttermilk, mayonnaise, sour cream, parsley, shallot, vinegar, sugar, mustard, pepper, and salt together. Pour dressing over vegetables and toss to combine. Refrigerate until chilled, about 30 minutes. Serve. (Coleslaw can be refrigerated for up to 2 days.)

Buttermilk Coleslaw with Scallions and Cilantro

Omit mustard. Substitute 1 tablespoon minced fresh cilantro for parsley and 1 teaspoon lime juice for vinegar. Add 2 thinly sliced scallions to dressing in step 2.

Lemony Buttermilk Coleslaw

Substitute 1 teaspoon lemon juice for vinegar. Add 1 tablespoon minced fresh chives and 1 teaspoon minced fresh thyme to dressing in step 2.

Red Slaw

Serves 4 to 6 ~ Total Time: 15 minutes,
plus 30 minutes chilling

Much like the regional variations of barbecue, coleslaws also differ from place to place. In Lexington, North Carolina, both the barbecue sauce and coleslaw are flavored with tomatoes. Over in Kentucky, some home cooks use ketchup instead of mayonnaise. As Dana Bowen writes in her article "East vs. West: North Carolina Pulled Pork" for *Saveur*, the "ketch-up-spiked slaw" pairs perfectly with "such robustly flavored meat," and has the added bene-fit of withstanding hot Southern temperatures better than mayonnaise-based recipes. Finely chopped rather than shredded cabbage is both traditional and practical, as it makes the slaw eas-ier to pile on a barbecue sandwich. Adding just a tablespoon of oil makes the cabbage more tender. Cider vinegar provides tanginess, while hot sauce and black pepper add a spicy kick. Cutting the cabbage by hand results in evenly sized pieces, but you can also prep it in a food processor; cut the cabbage into 1-inch pieces and pulse it in two batches until it's finely chopped.

½	cup ketchup
¼	cup cider vinegar
¼	cup sugar
1	tablespoon vegetable oil
1	teaspoon hot sauce
1	teaspoon table salt
¾	teaspoon pepper
1	small head green cabbage (1¼ pounds), halved, cored, and chopped fine (6 cups)

Whisk ketchup, vinegar, sugar, oil, hot sauce, salt, and pepper together in large bowl. Stir in cabbage until well combined. Cover and refrigerate until chilled, at least 30 minutes or up to 2 days. Season with salt and pepper to taste. Serve.

Pickled Cucumber and Onion Salad

Serves 4 to 6 ~ Total Time: 15 minutes,
plus 1 hour chilling

This dish is so simple it barely counts as a recipe, and it's one you might have learned by watching and listening as your mom or grandmother tasked you with peeling the cucumbers as she whisked the dressing. It seems that all Southern women know how to make this dish—and know to make it when cucumbers are perfectly in season. The refreshing side of cucumbers and onion falls somewhere on the spectrum between a salad and a pickle. This version is inspired by Vivian Howard's recipe for Everyday Cucumbers in her book *Deep Run Roots: Stories and Recipes from My Corner of the South*. Cider vinegar tempered with water and sugar provides a bright, not-too-sharp dressing. Peeled regular cucumbers—as opposed to English or pickling cucumbers—provide the best crunch. Allowing the cucumbers and thinly sliced onion to sit in the dressing for at least an hour provides time for the flavors to meld and the vegetables to soften slightly.

½   cup cider vinegar

¼   cup water

2   tablespoons sugar

1½   teaspoons table salt

½   teaspoon pepper

1   pound cucumbers, peeled, halved lengthwise, and sliced ⅛ inch thick (about 3 cups)

1   cup thinly sliced onion

Whisk vinegar, water, sugar, salt, and pepper together in medium bowl. Add cucumbers and onion and toss to combine. Cover and refrigerate for at least 1 hour. Use slotted spoon to serve. (Salad can be refrigerated for up to 3 days.)

Tomato Salad with Onion

Serves 4 to 6 ~ Total Time: 15 minutes, plus 1 hour resting

Ripe summer tomatoes need nothing more than a little olive oil, vinegar, salt, and pepper to help them taste their best. We like to add sliced onion to the mix to accent the sweetness and tartness of the tomatoes. Sweet Vidalia onion provides just enough pungency without overpowering the other flavors. Fruity cider vinegar calls out the tomatoes' sweetness. Letting the dressed salad sit for an hour allows the flavors to meld and draws liquid out of the tomatoes that mixes with the dressing to become an elixir so tasty that, when the tomatoes themselves are gone, you'll want to pick up the bowl and drink the dregs.

¼   cup extra-virgin olive oil

3   tablespoons cider vinegar

1   teaspoon table salt

1   garlic clove, minced

¼   teaspoon pepper

2   pounds vine-ripened tomatoes, cored

1   small Vidalia onion, quartered through root end and sliced thin crosswise

1   Whisk oil, vinegar, salt, garlic, and pepper together in large bowl. Halve tomatoes through core, cut into 1-inch wedges, then cut wedges in half crosswise.

2   Add tomatoes and onion to vinaigrette and fold gently with rubber spatula to combine. Let salad sit for 1 hour at room temperature, stirring once after 30 minutes. Serve. (Salad can be refrigerated for up to 2 days.)

Watermelon Salad

Serves 4 to 6 ~ Total Time: 30 minutes, plus 1 hour draining and chilling

Much like tomatoes were given the sweet-pie treatment long ago (see page 146), other common Southern fruits are often treated like vegetables, serving as the base for savory seasonal salads. This summery dish pairs sweet watermelon with salty feta and briny olives. To enhance the flavor and texture of the fresh melon, we macerate it in sugar for 30 minutes, driving off excess moisture to prevent a watery salad. A simple dressing of white wine vinegar and olive oil lets the bold flavors of the salad shine, and soaking sliced shallot in the vinegar before tossing it in the bowl tames its bite. Finally, plenty of fresh torn basil and a pinch of red pepper flakes round out this summery side.

6	cups seedless watermelon, cut into 1-inch pieces
1½	teaspoons sugar, divided
1	shallot, sliced into thin rings
3	tablespoons white wine vinegar
½	teaspoon table salt, divided
¼	teaspoon red pepper flakes
1	English cucumber, peeled, quartered lengthwise, seeded, and cut into ½-inch pieces
½	teaspoon pepper
3	tablespoons extra-virgin olive oil
½	cup pitted kalamata olives, chopped coarse
½	cup fresh basil leaves, torn
3	ounces feta cheese, crumbled (¾ cup)

1 Toss watermelon with 1 teaspoon sugar in large bowl, transfer to colander set in sink, and let drain for 30 minutes. Wipe out bowl. Combine shallot, vinegar, ¼ teaspoon salt, pepper flakes, and remaining ½ teaspoon sugar in separate bowl and let sit while watermelon drains.

2 Pat cucumber and drained watermelon dry with paper towels and transfer to now-empty bowl. Using fork, remove shallot from vinegar mixture and add to bowl with watermelon. Add pepper and remaining ¼ teaspoon salt to vinegar mixture and slowly whisk in oil until incorporated. Add dressing and olives to bowl with watermelon and toss to combine. Refrigerate for at least 30 minutes or up to 4 hours.

3 Add basil to salad and toss to combine. Season with salt and pepper to taste. Transfer to serving platter and sprinkle with feta. Serve.

The women of Sow True Seed cooperative in Asheville, North Carolina.

Mackenzie Crosson / Sow True Seed

SOUTHERN SEED SAVING AND SEED COMPANIES

Saving seeds from garden produce for use year after year is not just a Southern tradition, it's an important part of Southern gardening heritage. This historical method is used by cultural groups all over the world: Indigenous peoples of the South in addition to colonists, enslaved peoples, and other immigrant communities brought and cultivated fruits, vegetables, grains, herbs, and edible flowers that were important to their respective cultural food traditions.

Starting in the 18th century, Southerners could also order seeds from seed and nursery trade catalogs. These mail-order catalogs were started rather informally by fellow seed savers who wanted to trade seeds with other farmers and gardeners, but they quickly grew into large enterprises and became an integral part of the region's agricultural economy. Over time these catalogs evolved to include illustrations, gardening designs, and planting advice. As the nation expanded, so too did access to new and exciting seed and plant varieties; meanwhile, the original practice of seed saving and the preservation of traditional heirlooms waned. Generations later, this shift in focus spurred numerous seed savers and gardeners to create new, Southern-focused seed catalogs.

Founded in 2009 by gardener and food activist Carol Koury, Sow True Seed, based in Asheville, North Carolina, is an employee-owned cooperative committed to open-pollinated seeds and regenerative agriculture. While customers can buy new seeds from the cooperative each season, Sow True Seed encourages gardeners to practice seed saving and teaches workshops to prevent seed extinction.

Southern Exposure Seed Exchange is another cooperative based out of Mineral, Virginia, that sources seeds from small farms and specializes in varieties suited to the Southeast. The cooperative was founded in the early 1980s by Patty Wallens and her husband Jeff McCormack. McCormack's training as a biologist and his position at the University of Virginia helped connect them to other local seed savers, and Wallens came up with the co-op's slogan: "Saving the Past for the Future." The first Southern Exposure Seed Catalog came out in 1983 and featured only a handful of varieties. It quickly grew to include other heirloom varieties that the founders learned about from neighbors, friends, and customers. Some of their specially curated heritage seed collection includes Bowling Red Okra, Hen Peck Collards, and the Whippoorwill Southern Pea, a cowpea that was originally brought to the Americas from Africa during the transatlantic slave trade and was grown by Thomas Jefferson at his estate Monticello.

Since 1999, Florida-born Ira Wallace has been one of the worker/owners of the Exchange and has served as a garden educator for fellow Southerners from Georgia to Virginia. Wallace is also well known as the matriarch of the Heirloom Collard Project, an organization that documents, celebrates, and cultivates heirloom collard varieties in the South. While seed saving remains a labor-intensive process, the resources for modern-day gardeners are growing faster than ever with the shared goal to preserve Southern seed heritage.

by KC Hysmith

Peach and Burrata Salad

Serves 4 to 6   ~   Total Time: 20 minutes

This salad highlights one of the most succulent rewards of summertime in the South: peaches. Here we use our Preserved Peaches in Syrup (page 366), but you can substitute fresh peaches; simply swap in two large, ripe, cored peaches and slice them into ¾-inch wedges.

Whichever you use, you'll quickly toss the peach slices in a little vinegar before assembling the rest of the salad. For ease, we cut the creamy burrata cheese into pieces right on the serving platter before arranging the peaches around the dish and sprinkling everything with salt and pepper. Bite-size slices of salty prosciutto, sweet fresh basil, and some olive oil top off this salad for a summertime treat—and if you use the preserved peaches, it can be enjoyed year-round!

1	pint Preserved Peaches in Syrup (page 366), drained and cut into ¾-inch wedges
2	teaspoons white wine vinegar
1	(8-ounce) ball burrata cheese
½	teaspoon flake sea salt
½	teaspoon cracked pepper
2	ounces thinly sliced prosciutto, torn into bite-size pieces
7	fresh basil leaves, torn
2	tablespoons extra-virgin olive oil

1   Gently toss peaches with vinegar in bowl; set aside. Place burrata in center of large platter and cut into 8 to 10 pieces. Distribute burrata evenly on platter. Distribute peaches among burrata pieces. Sprinkle burrata and peaches with salt and pepper.

2   Distribute prosciutto and basil among peaches and burrata. Drizzle with oil and serve.

Killed Salad

Serves 4 ~ Total Time: 20 minutes

Killed salad (also called "kilt" salad, wilted salad, or smothered lettuce) is a traditional springtime Appalachian side dish (see "Appalachian Salad"). This salad is made by pouring hot bacon fat over torn fresh lettuce and chopped onions or ramps to warm and barely wilt the greens. It was typically made with the first leafy lettuces that popped up in the garden or with foraged wild substitutes such as dandelion greens if the garden was a little behind. Six slices of bacon and 3 tablespoons of bacon fat enhance rather than overpower the lettuce. With its sturdy texture, green leaf lettuce holds up well under the hot dressing. Other firm greens such as escarole, romaine, and red leaf lettuce can be substituted for the green leaf lettuce, if desired. If ramps (see page 133) are in season at your local market, you can substitute them for the scallions in this salad. Cider vinegar cuts the richness of the bacon fat, and sugar tempers the acidity of the vinegar.

1	head green leaf lettuce (12 ounces), torn into bite-size pieces
4	scallions, sliced thin
6	slices bacon, cut into ½-inch pieces
½	cup cider vinegar
3	tablespoons sugar
1	teaspoon table salt
½	teaspoon pepper

1   Combine lettuce and scallions in large bowl. Cook bacon in 10-inch nonstick skillet over medium heat until crispy, 6 to 8 minutes. Using slotted spoon, transfer bacon to paper towel–lined plate. Pour off all but 3 tablespoons fat from skillet (if you don't have 3 tablespoons, supplement with vegetable oil).

2   Return skillet to medium heat. Whisk in vinegar, sugar, salt, and pepper and bring to boil.

3   Once boiling, immediately pour hot dressing over lettuce-scallion mixture and toss to combine. Season with salt and pepper to taste. Serve, sprinkling with bacon.

APPALACHIAN SALAD

Fancy a dish of chickentoe, anyone?

For centuries people have foraged the forests of Appalachia for foods, from mushrooms to tree fruits. It's a tradition that's carried on today—and not just out of desperation (or, in the case of foods such as ramps, trendiness). The fact is, this mountain range is dense with wild foods. Many of them are impossible to grow in gardens, which makes them more prized.

Darrin Nordahl, author of *Eating Appalachia: Rediscovering Regional American Flavors*, describes chickentoe as "a dainty vegetable … a member of the purslane family, the leaves are fleshier and juicier than more familiar salad greens, and they have a pleasantly crisp texture. The flavor is quite mild, however, tasting like young green lettuce."

The most common way to serve chickentoe (also called spring beauty) is to "kill" it—that is, to douse it in hot bacon fat, wilting the leaves and adding deep country flavor. But chickentoe season is fleeting—mid-March to early April—and it's next to impossible to cultivate the stuff the rest of the year. Bacon, however, knows no season, and the technique works well with other lettuces, too, as in our Killed Salad.

by KC Hysmith

Grilled Ramps

Serves 4 ~ Total Time: 30 minutes

Ramps—also known as wild leeks, wild garlic, or ramson—are a member of the onion family native to North America. They taste slightly more pungent than the more familiar alliums, with hints of garlic and chives. These tender, aromatic leeks sprout up in woodlands as far-flung as Canada, Missouri, Minnesota, and, of course, the South. You can find them, briefly, in the shady woodlands of the Appalachian Mountains, from West Virginia to North Carolina, during the spring (the season starts in late March or early April and is over by early May). In addition to having a fleeting season, ramps are under threat from inexperienced harvesters and overpicking.

But never fear, ramps can stay on the menu so long as you follow a few guidelines. First, if you're lucky enough to have a ramp patch, follow the advice of Michelle Baumflek, a North Carolina–based research biologist, in a USDA Forest Service article by Deena C. Bouknight: "At least leave some of the bottom of the bulb part, where the roots are, in the ground and then the ramps have a better chance of growing back."

Second, for the rest (and most) of us, you should buy ramps only from your local farmers' market when they're in season. Encouraging moderate and respectful harvesting will ensure that everyone can enjoy ramps for many more seasons to come.

Once procured, ramps are delicious raw or cooked. They can be used in applications that call for onions, leeks, or scallions. We like them sautéed in butter and tossed with pasta, as well as pickled in a simple vinegar mixture. They're also delicious grilled as we've shown here.

A simple toss in oil, salt, and pepper is all the ramps need, but grilled lemon makes a beautiful presentation and provides a welcome tart finish. The ramp greens will char quickly, so watch them carefully. Serve with grilled steak, chicken, or fish, or chop them up and add to salads.

5   ounces ramps, trimmed
1   tablespoon extra-virgin olive oil
1   lemon, quartered

1a **For a charcoal grill** Open bottom vent completely. Light large chimney starter filled with charcoal briquettes (6 quarts). When top coals are partially covered with ash, pour evenly over half of grill. Set cooking grate in place, cover, and open lid vent completely. Heat grill until hot, about 5 minutes.

1b **For a gas grill** Turn all burners to high, cover, and heat grill until hot, about 15 minutes. Leave primary burner on high and turn off other burner(s).

2   Clean and oil cooking grate. Toss ramps with oil. Arrange ramps on grill, perpendicular to grate bars, with whites over hotter side of grill and greens over cooler side. Place lemon quarters over hotter side of grill. Grill until ramp whites are softened and lightly charred and lemons are well charred, turning ramps as needed, about 5 minutes.

3   Flip ramps so greens are over hotter side of grill and cook, turning as needed, until greens are blistered and charred, about 15 seconds. Transfer ramps and lemon quarters to platter. Season ramps with salt and pepper to taste. Serve, squeezing with lemon juice.

CHEROKEE NATION AND RAMPS

It's March, and as I move off a well-worn path in the Great Smoky Mountains, I notice the smell. Pungent, fresh, green. People new to harvesting assume that ramps grow quickly, like the leafy lettuces in grocery stores. But Cherokee people know that a ramp patch takes its time—nearly 10 years!—to make its home patch. It also needs to be with family; harvesting more than 10 percent of this patch can cause irreparable damage.

Cherokee people have been working with ramps for millennia, carefully monitoring patches, harvesting small amounts, and cutting only the leaves so that the bulb remains intact for future harvests. In return, this first spring green brings nutrition, life, and a powerful flavor that revitalizes the store of winter foods. Cherokees from all three nations (Cherokee Nation and United Keetoowah Band in Oklahoma; Eastern Band of Cherokee Indians in North Carolina) cook ramps with eggs as a quintessential spring meal. They also pickle, freeze, and dry ramps to use all year.

Today, ramps are threatened by inexperienced and uncaring harvesters while Cherokee people are threatened at gunpoint by the National Parks Service for their yearly cultivations of ramps, which was recently made illegal following a flawed study that excluded Cherokee harvesting methods. But even as the climate becomes more chaotic and our foods become more rare, Cherokee people continue to orient our current actions to the future, tracking the changing climate, teaching about heritage plant life cycles, and, as we have always done, growing.

by Courtney Lewis, PhD

enrolled citizen of the Cherokee Nation and associate professor at Duke University, reshaping the academic landscape by bolstering Native American studies

Squash Casserole

Serves 6 to 8 ~ Total Time: 1¼ hours

One of the most beloved side dishes in classic meat and three restaurants and on home menus alike is squash casserole. Made from a combination of mild summer squash, melted cheese, mayonnaise or sour cream, and a crunchy Ritz Cracker topping, the dish is traditionally baked in a casserole, although some modern cooks have updated the dish to make it a bit more refined. Bridgette A. Lacy is one such cook. In *Sunday Dinner: A Savor the South Cookbook*, the journalist and Southern storyteller relied on memories of shopping at the local farmers' market with her mother for a new, inspired version that calls for stuffing the squash with the traditional ingredients rather than baking it casserole-style.

We stick close to the original here, offering a few other important tips to ensure your squash is supremely flavorful. To prevent the yellow squash—by nature a watery vegetable—from throwing off too much liquid, we cook it (along with some onions) in a skillet. This preemptively drives off moisture and softens the vegetables. Rather than switching to a separate baking dish, we stir cheese, mayonnaise, and scallions directly into the skillet with the softened squash. The final touches: sprinkling crushed Ritz Crackers on top and moving the skillet to the oven to melt the cheese and brown the topping. Using a mix of intense sharp cheddar and creamy, silky American cheese creates a rich, smooth sauce. Two types of peppers, black and cayenne, add just enough heat to contrast with the sweet squash.

2	tablespoons extra-virgin olive oil
3	cups thinly sliced onion (3 onions)
1	teaspoon table salt, divided
2	pounds yellow summer squash, halved lengthwise and sliced ¼ inch thick
2	garlic cloves, minced
6	ounces sharp cheddar cheese, shredded (1½ cups)
2	ounces American cheese, chopped (½ cup)
½	cup mayonnaise
4	scallions, sliced thin
½	teaspoon pepper
	Pinch cayenne pepper
30	Ritz Crackers, crushed coarse

1 Adjust oven rack to middle position and heat oven to 375 degrees. Heat oil in 12-inch ovensafe skillet over medium-high heat until shimmering. Add onions and ¼ teaspoon salt and cook until onions are lightly browned, about 6 minutes.

2 Add squash, garlic, and remaining ¾ teaspoon salt and cook until any liquid exuded by squash has evaporated and squash is tender, about 10 minutes. Reduce heat to low and stir in cheddar, American cheese, mayonnaise, scallions, pepper, and cayenne until fully combined, about 2 minutes.

3 Off heat, use rubber spatula to scrape down sides of skillet. Scatter crackers over top. Transfer skillet to oven and bake until bubbling around edges and hot throughout, about 18 minutes. Let cool for 10 minutes. Serve.

Creamed Corn

Serves 4 to 6 ～ Total Time: 40 minutes

After rice, one of the most important agricultural crops in Southern history is corn, and it's at the heart of Southern cookbooks. Skillet-fried corn is a classic: It's made with fresh corn kernels and their milk sautéed in bacon drippings and thickened with a flour-and-water mixture. In creamed corn, heavy cream provides the milky gravy instead. Either version is delicious, but the seasonal favorite takes on a unique character when reimagined as fried creamed corn, a dish created by chef and author Jennifer Hill Booker; she relies on bacon fat, butter, flour, *and* cream. Booker learned French cooking at Le Cordon Bleu College of Culinary Arts in Paris, and she demonstrates her passion for fusing the best of two culinary words in her cookbooks, *Field Peas to Foie Gras: Southern Recipes with a French Accent* and *Dinner Déjà Vu: Southern Tonight, French Tomorrow.* With so many variations of creamed corn, we found that simple is the best introduction to this staple. Cooking the fresh corn kernels with water (and no salt) tenderizes the corn and brings out its sweet flavor. Pureeing some of the corn gives the dish body. And adding a small amount of cream provides a creamy texture without added thickeners.

9 ears corn, kernels cut from cobs (6¾ cups)	¼ cup heavy cream
1¼ cups water	1⅛ teaspoons salt
	¼ teaspoon pepper

1   Combine corn and water in large saucepan and bring to boil over high heat (bubbles will be noticeable around sides of saucepan). Reduce heat to low, cover, and cook until corn is crisp-tender, about 20 minutes, stirring occasionally.

2   Remove from heat and transfer 1½ cups corn mixture to blender. Add cream, salt, and pepper and process until smooth, about 1 minute. Stir pureed corn mixture into corn mixture in saucepan. Season with salt and pepper to taste. Serve. (If your creamed corn looks thin, return it to low heat and cook gently until thickened slightly, about 3 minutes.)

VICTORY GARDENS

In times of war, Southerners helped sow the seeds of victory in their home gardens. Starting in World War I, rations coupled with labor shortages that made it hard to harvest produce and transport it to local markets resulted in an amazing nationwide civil project: the victory garden. When the United States entered World War II in the 1940s, most Southerners still lived on farms or in rural areas and knew how to cultivate a home garden, but residents living in urban regions needed a little more support. The 1942 print campaign "Gardens for U.S. at War" first introduced the concept of victory gardens, complete with tips for growing and patriotic calls to action. War Service Gardens, as they were more officially known, also helped provide nourishment to Southerners in other stressful moments, such as the H1N1 flu pandemic of 1918. Campaign materials encouraged communities to work together to grow fruits and vegetables for themselves. Modern-day gardening archives, including the Cherokee Garden Library at the Atlanta History Center and Martha Blakeney Hodges Special Collections at the University of North Carolina Greensboro, hold artifacts and garden club records detailing which specific varieties of seeds thrived best in Southern growing zones.

   Due in part to the South's culinary affinity for corn and corn-based dishes, the crop was a staple of many Southern victory gardens. Growing local corn not only provided everyday Americans an opportunity to be part of the national war effort, but also ensured that Southerners could partake in classic dishes, including creamed corn, even when normal agricultural production was disrupted.

by KC Hysmith

A print for World War II victory gardens.

Library of Congress

Esquites

Serves 6 to 8 ~ Total Time: 1 hour

According to Indigenous Nahuatl legend, esquites were created by Tlazocihuapilli, the only female deity who ruled the Mesoamerican peoples known as Xochimilcas. Today, both men and women prepare and sell this classic street food, but the delicious origin story makes esquites even richer. Charred corn is layered with rich, tangy crema; salty cotija cheese; chili powder; and lime juice to make a salad in which every bite consists of the ideal ratio of flavors and textures. Here we achieve charring on the kernels by cooking them in a small amount of oil in a covered skillet. The kernels in contact with the skillet's surface brown and char, and the lid traps steam and prevents the kernels from popping out of the hot skillet. We cook the corn in two batches to allow more kernels to make contact with the skillet and brown. If desired, substitute plain Greek yogurt for the sour cream. We like serrano chiles here, but you can substitute a jalapeño chile that has been halved lengthwise and sliced into ⅛-inch-thick half-moons. Adjust the amount of chiles to suit your taste. If cotija cheese is unavailable, substitute feta cheese.

3	tablespoons lime juice, plus extra for seasoning (2 limes)
3	tablespoons sour cream
1–2	serrano chiles, stemmed and cut into ⅛-inch-thick rings
1	tablespoon mayonnaise
¾	teaspoon table salt, divided
2	tablespoons plus 1 teaspoon vegetable oil, divided
8	ears corn, kernels cut from cobs (6 cups), divided
2	garlic cloves, minced
½	teaspoon chili powder
4	ounces cotija cheese, crumbled (1 cup)
¾	cup coarsely chopped fresh cilantro
3	scallions, sliced thin

1   Combine lime juice, sour cream, serrano(s), mayonnaise, and ¼ teaspoon salt in large bowl. Set aside.

2   Heat 1 tablespoon oil in 12-inch nonstick skillet over high heat until shimmering. Add half of corn and spread into even layer. Sprinkle with ¼ teaspoon salt. Cover and cook, without stirring, until corn touching skillet is charred, about 3 minutes. Remove skillet from heat and let stand, covered, for 15 seconds, until any popping subsides. Transfer corn to bowl with sour cream mixture. Repeat with 1 tablespoon oil, remaining corn, and remaining ¼ teaspoon salt.

3   Return skillet to medium heat and add remaining 1 teaspoon oil, garlic, and chili powder. Cook, stirring constantly, until fragrant, about 30 seconds. Transfer garlic mixture to bowl with corn mixture and toss to combine. Let cool for at least 15 minutes.

4   Add cotija, cilantro, and scallions and toss to combine. Season salad with up to 1 tablespoon extra lime juice and salt to taste. Serve.

MY NEW SOUTHERN-LATINO GARDEN

When I moved to the South from Guatemala, nothing made more sense to me than to plant my own vegetable garden. It became a place of reverence, where my hands could literally grab on to the soil of my new home. The desire wasn't to produce enough food to feed my family—although that became a later goal. What I yearned for was a place where I could lift my spirit and feel safe, an outdoor chapel where I could freely shape dreams until they became a reality.

Working between vines of field peas, corn, and heirloom tomatoes gave me purpose; harvesting potatoes and green beans fed my soul as much as it did my belly. Ultimately, the food of our Indigenous ancestors, grown in the South, with my own hands, tied me to this land and its people, and opened up my seat at the Southern table.

Growing deep roots is invariably the most important aspect of settling into a new place. For first-generation immigrants, it means starting from seed, often in unwelcoming terrain. Armed with the tools of tenacity and patience, we learn to care for our nascent roots and grow. Ultimately, after a few seasons, subsequent generations collect the fruits of such labor and become entrenched, no longer strangers, but part of the landscape.

What immersion looks like for many immigrants: It often entails learning the language, the culture, and the culinary traditions of our new home to make multigenerational immigration successful. Those who don't plant deep roots in a new homeland will never feel grounded. As it is with edible plants, if roots are shallow, the plant will ultimately succumb to the weakest gust of air, a tiny pest, or a bad rainfall. But when it is allowed to grow in rich earth and cast a wide net underground, the plant flourishes and overcomes obstacles.

My new Southern–Latino garden, brimming with tomatillos, okra, chiles, and collard greens, continues to keep me grounded and reminds me that I am home.

by Sandra A. Gutierrez

journalist, award-winning food writer, historian, professional cooking instructor, and author of four cookbooks

Grit Cakes with Beans and Summer Squash

Serves 4 ~ Total Time: 1¾ hours, plus 9 hours brining and chilling

This is Jordan Rainbolt's take on cooking the Three Sisters, a concept in Indigenous traditions that refers to the symbiotic agricultural relationship of squash, corn, and beans. Many Indigenous chefs combine them in a Three Sisters stew, but Rainbolt's approach here is an elegant plated dinner: With the corn, she makes grit cakes; with the beans, she blends up a sumac-spiced creamy puree; and with the squash, she pickles zucchini while cooking yellow summer squash until it's lightly browned. It's complex in flavor, and delicious. Raimbolt developed this recipe with reddish Wade's Mill Bloody Butcher Grits. You can use whatever coarse-ground grits are local to you.

Beans

- 3 tablespoons kosher salt for brining
- 1 cup dried black tepary beans or any dried black bean variety, picked over and rinsed
- 1 teaspoon kosher salt
- 1 garlic clove, minced
- 1 teaspoon ground sumac, plus extra for serving

Grit Cakes

- 3 cups water
- 1 cup coarse-ground grits
- 2 teaspoons kosher salt
- 2 tablespoons extra-virgin olive oil

Pickled Zucchini

- 1 (8-ounce) zucchini, halved lengthwise, then sliced crosswise into ½-inch-thick rounds
- 2 teaspoons black peppercorns
- ½ cup maple vinegar or cider vinegar
- ½ cup water
- 2 tablespoons kosher salt
- 2 tablespoons sugar
- 2 garlic cloves, smashed and peeled
- 1 sprig fresh dill, plus extra coarsely chopped dill for serving

Yellow Squash

- 1 (8-ounce) yellow summer squash, seeded and chopped
- 1 tablespoon extra-virgin olive oil, plus extra for drizzling
- 1 teaspoon kosher salt
- 1 teaspoon pepper
- 1 teaspoon sugar

1 **For the beans** Dissolve 3 tablespoons salt in 2 quarts cold water in large container. Add beans and soak at room temperature for at least 8 hours or up to 24 hours. Drain and rinse well.

2 **For the grit cakes** Heat 3 cups water in large saucepan over high heat. Slowly whisk grits and salt into saucepan until no lumps remain, about 1 minute. Reduce heat to low and cook, covered, and stirring frequently, until thick and creamy, about 45 minutes (add extra water, ¼ cup at a time, as needed if grits get too dry and start to stick to bottom of saucepan).

3 Line 8-inch square baking pan with parchment paper and grease parchment. Transfer hot grits to prepared pan, spread into even layer, and let cool completely. Cover grits and refrigerate until completely chilled, at least 1 hour or up to 2 days.

4   Meanwhile, combine drained beans, 3 cups water, 1 teaspoon kosher salt, garlic, and sumac in large saucepan and bring to boil over high heat. Reduce heat to medium and simmer, covered, until beans are tender, about 1 hour.

5   **For the pickled zucchini** Meanwhile, place zucchini in medium heatproof bowl; set aside. Heat peppercorns in 8-inch skillet over medium heat until fragrant, about 3 minutes. Add vinegar, ½ cup water, salt, sugar, and garlic and bring to simmer over medium-high heat. Reduce heat to low and cook, whisking often, until sugar is dissolved, about 1 minute. Immediately pour mixture over zucchini. Add dill and let sit at room temperature for at least 45 minutes. (Pickles can be refrigerated for up to 1 week.)

6   Drain beans in colander, reserving cooking liquid. (Drained beans can be refrigerated for up to 3 days. Alternatively, beans can be cooled, transferred to zipper-lock bags, and frozen for up to 1 month.) Transfer beans to blender and process until smooth, about 1 minute, adding up to ¼ cup reserved liquid (add additional warm water if needed to measure ¼ cup) as needed to enable beans to blend.

7   **For the yellow squash** Adjust oven rack to middle position, heat oven to 400 degrees, and place 12-inch cast-iron skillet on oven rack. Toss squash with oil, salt, pepper, and sugar in large bowl.

8   Once oven is heated, using oven mitts, remove skillet from oven. Add squash to skillet and bake until squash is lightly browned, about 10 minutes.

9   Using 3½-inch round cutter, cut 4 circles from chilled grits, reserving scraps for another use. Heat oil in 12-inch skillet over medium-high heat until shimmering. Add grit cakes and cook until golden brown, about 3 minutes per side. Transfer grit cakes to 4 serving plates. Spread bean paste evenly over cakes. Divide pickled zucchini and roasted squash evenly among cakes. Top with chopped dill. Sprinkle with extra sumac and drizzle with extra oil. Serve.

Q&A: JORDAN RAINBOLT ON AMPLIFYING THE SOUTH'S NATIVE ROOTS

Jordan Rainbolt grew up in Kansas City and has taken her cooking skills to Korea for culinary school and, in 2019, to Charlotte, North Carolina, to work in restaurants. In 2021, as the COVID-19 pandemic started to ease a bit, Rainbolt was inspired to do something "that had more meaning to her." She founded Native Root in Winston-Salem, North Carolina, which hosts pop-ups and communal outdoor dinners that highlight Indigenous traditions. We chatted to learn more about her work.

Can you tell me about Native Root?
Native Root is a concept I started in 2021. The ethos is to bring people together, and go back to what community actually means. My mother is of Cherokee and Choctaw descent, so I wanted to pay homage by using Indigenous ingredients of the region but also pulling in a global-meets-local approach. Native Root is now a pop-up restaurant and ghost kitchen. I also create food for private events. We do a lot of different things throughout the entire state, but we're based in Winston-Salem.

Your tagline is "Indigenous roots of the South." Can you tell me about what that means?
Southern cuisine is thought of as a very specific style of food compared to that of the rest of the world. So I wanted to dig deeper into what the food of this region and of the rest of the South actually means. A lot of Southern cuisine is based on Indigenous ingredients and technique—even something as primal as cooking over live fire. This is something I like to pull into many of my menus. When Southern cooking meant Indigenous cooking, it wasn't about specific recipes. It was more about using the abundance of the land. That's kinda been lost, and [I'm] trying to pull in different ways to revive that.

Can you talk to me about your take on the Three Sisters?
I love creating menus based around the Three Sisters. It connects to the tradition of companion planting and how people did that before they had larger food access. I especially love making this in North Carolina because the seasons are so long; corn, beans, and squash grow almost all year round here. I love that this dish has different textures and flavors but they come together really nicely.

   If you have the ability, it's great to source the ingredients from purveyors you believe in or that are local. I used a coarse Bloody Butcher grit. Bloody Butcher corn is an heirloom plant that was almost lost, but some chefs revived it. I buy it locally. Tepary beans are considered an ancient bean. They have a creamy texture inside, but they have a really nice chew. I opted for pickling zucchini because it's a traditional preservation technique. And then the roasted summer squash is a nice contrast.

Stewed Collards

Serves 6 to 8   ~   Total Time: 2½ hours

This emblematic Southern recipe is made by braising collard greens with a salty smoked pork product. Over a long cooking time, the pork and greens intermingle and turn the cooking water into a supersavory broth known as potlikker (see page 142) that some consider the best part of the dish. Adding two smoked ham hocks provides deeply smoky pork flavor. Plus, after a long braising time, it is easy to pull savory little chunks of meat off the hocks to add back to the greens. Cooking the greens in the controlled heat of the oven, rather than on the stove, makes for silky, evenly cooked collard greens. We love serving these with a few dashes of our Pepper Vinegar (page 344) in addition to or instead of the hot sauce.

Whatever you do, don't throw out the potlikker.

2	pounds collard greens	3	garlic cloves, smashed and peeled
2	tablespoons unsalted butter		
1	onion, chopped	2¼	teaspoons table salt
6	cups water	2	teaspoons sugar
2	(12-ounce) smoked ham hocks	⅛	teaspoon red pepper flakes
			Hot sauce

1 Adjust oven rack to lower-middle position and heat oven to 300 degrees. Trim collard stems to base of leaves; discard trimmings. Cut leaves into roughly 2-inch pieces. Place collards in large bowl and cover with water. Swish with your hand to remove grit. Repeat with fresh water as needed until grit no longer appears in bottom of bowl. Remove collards from water and set aside (you needn't dry them).

2 Melt butter in large Dutch oven over medium heat. Add onion and cook until lightly browned, 6 to 8 minutes. Add water, ham hocks, garlic, salt, sugar, and pepper flakes and bring to boil over high heat. Add collards (pot may be full) and stir until collards wilt slightly, about 1 minute. Cover, transfer to oven, and cook until collards are very tender, about 1½ hours.

3 Transfer ham hocks to cutting board and let cool for 10 minutes. Remove meat from ham hocks, chop, and return to pot; discard skin and bones. Season collards with salt to taste. Serve with hot sauce.

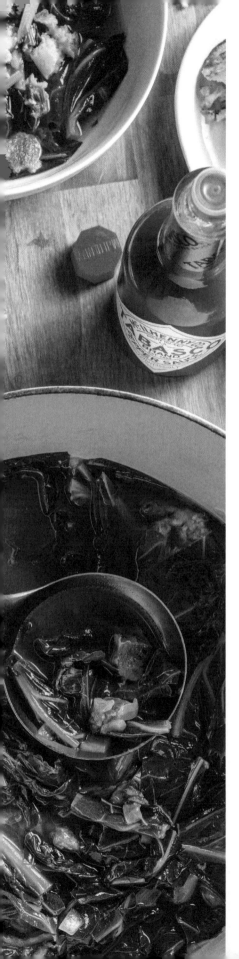

WHAT'S THE DIFFERENCE BETWEEN SOUTHERN AND SOUL?

A bar in Decatur, Georgia, changed how I cook collard greens.

I'm an Army brat. Globe-trotting with my dad definitely shaped my palate and cooking, but my foundational skills came from my grandmothers, aunt, and great-aunt. They taught me to season greens with pork, pepper vinegar, and crushed red pepper—an unwritten family formula that's certainly common in North Carolina, yet there's something unique about the taste we Chavises achieve that's been ours for five generations or more.

But one day I went to Victory Sandwich Bar for a bite and ordered a side of collards. Twang balanced the greens' earthy selves. The heat French-kissed me. A soft sweetness left an afterglow. I had to ask.

"Hard cider and apple cider vinegar," the waitress told me when she came back from the kitchen with an answer.

A British drink is now a key ingredient in my Southern Black family's greens.

Exchanges like this make it challenging to distinguish Southern and soul food. Who taught what to whom is a tangled, incomplete history. Biscuits can trace roots back to British scones. Using small amounts of meat to season vegetables—such as ham hocks in collards—is an African technique. For millennia, Native Americans have ground corn into cornmeal to make bread. Southern and soul claim them all.

Both cuisines share a fridge full of nutritious ingredients: shrimp, catfish, black-eyed peas, sweet potatoes, tomatoes, peaches, pecans, watermelon, okra. Yet Southern food and soul food each bear an unfair stereotype of being bad for you.

People started using the term "soul food" in the '60s, part of an emerging Black American identity. Seasoning is heavier, and there are more bones, more offal. As people left the South during the Great Migration, including Gullah Geechee Girl herself Vertamae Smart-Grosvenor, soul food evolved into a distinct cuisine that's since become regionalized: Take Chicago's fried fish and spaghetti, with Italian American influence. Black moms who moved to California combined soul with Mexican American cuisine, and now Los Angeles has a Black tacos scene. Entrepreneurs like Alisa Reynolds and Barbara "Sky" Burrell fill tortillas with ground turkey and cheese (weeknight comfort food), oxtails, and jerk shrimp. Across the South, chefs invite diners to make fresh connections with soul food's multicultural taproot. At one of Deborah VanTrece's Atlanta restaurants, Twisted Soul, the menu features dishes such as stewed pork neck bones with johnnycakes, and catfish ballotine with hoppin' John and green tomato choka (a Trinidadian-inspired side).

Southern food's evolved too. Much of it happens through the people who move to the region. Jiyeon Lee (see page 317), chef and co-owner of Heirloom Market BBQ in Atlanta, introduces Korean flavors in her kimchi slaw, gochujang-rubbed smoked pork, and Korean barbecue sauce. Chef and cookbook author Asha Gomez (see page 15), born in south India, became Atlanta famous for her Kerala fried chicken.

These cuisines ground you. In 2020, as we faced isolation from the COVID-19 pandemic and increased racial strife, people cooked and ate more of them. There's an existing constant diners know: Southern and soul food both provide comfort.

by Shaun Chavis

food and health journalist and cookbook editor

Green Beans with Ham and Potatoes

Serves 6 to 8   ~   Total Time: 1½ hours

Collard greens aren't the only green vegetable that, when stewed, come with a shot from the pot. Green beans are surprisingly versatile, and boiling them with potatoes and pork for nearly an hour turns them uniquely silky-soft and infuses them with deliciously salty, meaty, full flavor. And as a bonus, you get to drink rich potlikker when they're done. Two smoky ham hocks and a hefty dose of salt amplify the flavor of the liquid. Adding the potatoes partway through cooking and leaving the lid on the pot the whole time yields evenly cooked potatoes and silky-smooth green beans.

1	tablespoon vegetable oil
1	onion, halved and sliced thin
4	cups water
1½	pounds green beans, trimmed and cut into 1½-inch lengths
2	(12-ounce) smoked ham hocks
3	garlic cloves, crushed and peeled
2¼	teaspoons table salt
1	pound red potatoes, unpeeled, cut into 1-inch pieces
1	teaspoon cider vinegar (optional)

1   Heat oil in Dutch oven over medium-high heat until shimmering. Add onion and cook until translucent, about 4 minutes.

2   Add water, green beans, ham hocks, garlic, and salt and bring to boil. Reduce heat to low, cover, and simmer for 20 minutes. Stir in potatoes, cover, and continue to simmer until potatoes are tender, about 30 minutes longer, stirring halfway through simmering.

3   Off heat, remove ham hocks and let cool for 5 minutes, then remove meat from bones. Chop meat and return it to pot; discard skin and bones. Gently stir in vinegar, if using, to avoid breaking up potatoes. Season with salt and pepper to taste. Serve.

DRINK THE POTLIKKER

Considered liquid gold in many corners of the South, potlikker (also styled "pot liquor") is the brothy liquid left behind after boiling greens (most often collards) or beans; it's often seasoned with salt and pepper in addition to some type of smoked meat such as fatback, a ham hock, or bacon. In addition to containing high amounts of essential vitamins and minerals captured from the leafy greens during the cooking process, potlikker is also known for its delicious salty and savory taste and slick mouthfeel. Most serve potlikker with some type of cornbread for dipping or dunking, while devotees sip (or shoot) a shot of the hot broth plain. While collards originally come from Europe, cooking them low and slow, as well as the consumption of the resulting potlikker, points to what Dr. Jessica B. Harris calls the "African American experience" and a nutritional necessity for enslaved peoples, who were often recipients of the leftover broth.

While mid-20th century Southern (male) politicians might have brought potlikker into the national spotlight with their debates over the proper spelling, origins, and method of consuming the broth, it was almost assuredly Southern women gently stirring those pots of greens and making sure the potlikker was never wasted. Mary Mac's Tea Room in Atlanta, opened by Mary MacKenzie in 1945, still serves complimentary cups of potlikker with "cracklin' cornbread." When describing how non-Southerners react to this Southern staple for an article in the North Carolina magazine *Our State*, Sheri Castle makes it clear: "You can lead a body to potlikker, but you can't make them dunk." Perhaps they haven't met *Cook's Country* editor in chief Toni Tipton-Martin, who is well known for her catchphrase: "Drink the potlikker."

Tamatar and Bhindi Dal Tadka

Serves 4 to 6 ~ Total Time: 1 hour

This recipe for dal finished with tadka was developed by chef Preeti Waas. Tadka refers to a cooking technique that blooms whole spices in ghee or oil to infuse or top a dish. Tadka is made with different spices in different regions of India: In northern India, where Waas's parents are from, it's more typical to use cumin seeds, but in southern India, where Waas spent most of her childhood, mustard seeds and fenugreek seeds are the primary tadka spices. In certain areas of western India, there's a spice mix of five seeds called panch phoran. This blend has cumin seeds, fennel seeds, fenugreek seeds, nigella seeds, and mustard seeds. Waas makes her tadka with this spice mix as a way to bridge northern and southern Indian cooking. If you can't find panch phoran, substitute equal parts of fennel seeds, cumin seeds, brown mustard seeds, nigella seeds, and fenugreek seeds. Serve over basmati rice.

Okra Dal

4½	cups water
2	cups chana dal, picked over and rinsed
1	pound okra, trimmed and sliced into 1-inch pieces
1	tomato, cored and chopped
½	onion, chopped fine
1	tablespoon ground coriander
2½	teaspoons table salt
½	teaspoon Kashmiri chili powder

Tadka

2	tablespoons ghee
2	tablespoons panch phoran
1	garlic clove, minced
½	tomato, cored and chopped
½	teaspoon table salt
1	teaspoon lemon juice

1   **For the okra dal** Combine all ingredients in large Dutch oven. Bring to boil over medium-high heat, then reduce heat to low, cover, and cook, stirring occasionally, until the dal is tender (it should still hold its shape but break apart between two fingers), 40 to 50 minutes.

2   **For the tadka** Meanwhile, melt ghee over medium heat in small saucepan. Add panch phoran and cook until fragrant, about 1 minute. Add garlic and cook for 30 seconds longer. Add tomato and salt and continue to cook until tomato just begins to break down, about 2 minutes longer. Remove from heat, add lemon juice, and stir to combine.

3   Stir tadka into cooked dal. Season with salt to taste. Serve.

Q&A: PREETI WAAS ON COOKING UNCOMPROMISINGLY INDIAN

Born and raised in southern India, Preeti Waas is an award-winning chef and owner of the restaurant Cheeni in Durham, North Carolina. Waaṣ started baking when she was young using a pressure cooker and a British cake-baking cookbook. This developed into a culinary career that has spanned private chef, café owner, caterer, baker, and cooking class instructor.

You owned a café in the late 2000s, you worked in restaurants, you even spent some time selling homemade chocolate chip cookies. Now you own and operate your restaurant, Cheeni. How has your cooking evolved?

I am not somebody who likes to fade into the background. That is completely contrary to my personality. But I kind of let go of my Indianness. For a bit, I was lost, I was floundering here, and I didn't have a network. Everything was about my kids and my family, so I was just trying to be the mom that they needed. But then as my children were grown and leaving the house, I finally felt comfortable enough to lean into my Indianness. It turns out if anybody asked me for advice at 51 years old, I would say always go back to your roots because that's where you're most comfortable and authentic. So [with Cheeni] I started making home-cooked Indian food. And for that I was a James Beard semifinalist.

Can you speak to how you've thought about your menu?

So many global food restaurants in the South are still trying to straddle that line between [honoring] their culture but also trying to appease the American palate. To me that is a waste. I'm either all in or all out. So for me, if I'm going to open an Indian restaurant, I'm going to serve the kind of food that I actually grew up eating, not what people expect. So there will be no tikka masala on my menu because that's not even Indian (it was invented in Scotland). Now, there's nothing wrong with the Indian curry house model; it's been around for a long time and it's popular for a reason. But to say that a country as large as India, with over a billion people with 23 different states and as many languages and hundreds more dialects, can be encapsulated within one menu with tikka masala and saag paneer is a travesty. I'm Indian. Why would I represent my country that way? So the cuisine that I choose to offer is true to me. It's my Indian and it's my authentic version of Indian.

Do you identify as Southern?

I have lived in the South since 2006. I will take the Southern association because it seems to be associated with everything to do with food and foodways and family and nourishment and agriculture and all of those things.

Can you talk about the okra and dal recipe?

I love dal; dal is comfort food. My children love dal. It is something that they associate most with being little and when they were sick. The first time my daughter came home from college, all she wanted was dal and rice. Now in India, typically it's part of a spread; there [are] like five different things on the plate. Like in a Punjabi meal we would have roti and dal and maybe some other sides, including okra. Okra is called bhindi, which means lady fingers. With this recipe, I cook the okra down with the dal, which adds such a silkiness to the sauce. This dish is one that's always on my restaurant's menu.

Tomato Pie

Serves 8 ~ Total Time: 2 hours, plus 2 hours salting, chilling, and cooling

Modern Southerners likely would not recognize the early 19th-century recipes for tomato pie, which were once a much sweeter affair. These recipes substituted both green and ripe red tomatoes for other more traditional pie fruits such as peaches and gooseberries and instructed bakers to add spoonfuls or teacupfuls of sugar to the filling. A recipe published in an 1855 issue of the *Fayetteville Observer* newspaper suggested that "pies made in this way can be scarcely distinguished from peach, and are delicious." The popular *Dixie Cook-Book*, published in 1883, included a recipe for Southern Tomato Pie sweetened with sugar, nutmeg, and cinnamon. Over time, as society shifted to view the tomato more as a vegetable (rather than the fruit it actually is), recipes adapted to feature the ingredient with more savory flavors.

The more contemporary Southern version still holds the pie shape but instead is enriched with mayonnaise, cheese, and herbs (it's a far cry from the Philadelphia tomato pie that's more akin to pizza without cheese). It's likely a creation of midcentury cookbook and magazine food editors looking for new ways to use easy and accessible ingredients.

Today it's a summertime favorite. And still, chefs continue to put their own spin on the classic. Ashley Christensen (see page 153) peels her tomatoes before assembling the pie and suggests adding a tablespoon of horseradish to the filling in her cookbook for her iconic Raleigh, North Carolina, restaurant, *Poole's: Recipes and Stories from a Modern Diner*. Durham chef Sara Foster plays on the concept in her recipe for Heirloom Tomato Tarts with Goat Cheese and Fresh Rosemary in her book *Sara Foster's Casual Cooking: More Fresh Simple Recipes from Foster's Market*. She opts for a puff pastry crust that she tops with goat cheese and slices of colorful heirloom tomatoes. Nashville-born, DC-based chef and TV personality Carla Hall makes more of a cobbler by topping summer tomatoes with torn homemade garlic bread chunks and baking until golden brown.

Here we offer a basic formula for the party-worthy pie, but feel free to adapt it as you like. For the best results, use a variety of ripe, in-season tomatoes with a fragrant aroma and flesh that yields slightly when gently pressed. Avoid sharp cheddar, which tends to clump when baked.

2½	pounds tomatoes, cored and sliced ¼ inch thick
½	teaspoon table salt
1	recipe Single-Crust Pie Dough (page 456)
8	ounces mild cheddar cheese, shredded (2 cups), divided
4	scallions, sliced thin
½	cup mayonnaise
2	tablespoons plus 2 teaspoons cornstarch
1	tablespoon minced fresh chives

1 Arrange tomatoes on paper towel–lined baking sheet and sprinkle with salt. Let sit for 1 hour, flipping tomatoes halfway through salting and replacing paper towels. Press tomatoes with additional paper towels until dry.

2 Roll dough into 12-inch circle on floured counter. Loosely roll dough around rolling pin and gently unroll it onto 9-inch pie plate, letting excess dough hang over edge. Ease dough into plate by gently lifting edge of dough with your hand while pressing into plate bottom with your other hand.

3 Trim overhang to ½ inch beyond lip of plate. Tuck overhang under itself; folded edge should be flush with edge of plate. Crimp dough evenly around edge of plate. Wrap dough-lined plate loosely in plastic and refrigerate until firm, about 30 minutes. Adjust oven rack to lower-middle position and heat oven to 350 degrees.

4 Line chilled pie shell with double layer of aluminum foil, covering edges to prevent burning, and fill with pie weights. Bake on foil-lined rimmed baking sheet until edges are set and just beginning to turn golden, 25 to 30 minutes, rotating sheet halfway through baking. Remove foil and weights, sprinkle ¼ cup cheddar over bottom of crust, and continue to bake crust until golden brown and crisp, 10 to 15 minutes longer. Transfer sheet to wire rack. (Crust must still be warm when filling is added.)

5 Combine scallions, mayonnaise, cornstarch, and remaining 1¾ cups cheddar in bowl. Separate tomato slices into 3 groups, keeping best-looking slices together for final layer. Shingle one group of tomatoes in even layer on bottom of pie crust. Spread half of mayonnaise mixture evenly over top. Repeat layering with second group of tomatoes and remaining mayonnaise mixture. Shingle final group of tomatoes on top. Bake until filling is bubbling around edges and crust is golden brown, 1 to 1¼ hours. Let pie cool until filling is set, about 30 minutes. Sprinkle with chives, and serve.

Cowboy Caviar

Serves 6 to 8 ~ Total Time: 15 minutes, plus 1 hour resting

Contrary to what its name suggests, cowboy caviar, sometimes known as Texas caviar, is composed of "pickled" black-eyed peas, not fish roe. This salad shares origins with other pea dishes, such as hoppin' John, that were originally crafted from a combination of African culinary tradition and Southern ingredients. However, the "rebranding" of this dish is credited to Helen Corbitt, Neiman Marcus culinary director in the 1940s, who first put the dish on the downtown Dallas store's café menu. While Corbitt was born in New York, her recipe resonated with Texans, and like its fancier namesake, the dish was right at home in a party spread—its bright colors and creamy-crisp texture make it an excellent accompaniment to a variety of dishes, and even better, it can be prepared well in advance. It's a colorful blend: Canned black-eyed peas are punctuated by scallions, chopped red and green bell peppers for sweetness and color, celery for vegetal crunch, and two minced jalapeños for heat. A pile of chopped parsley and cilantro freshens up the canned beans. Red wine vinegar provides the punchy acidity in Texas caviar's signature dressing and essentially pickles the black-eyed peas. Note that the salad needs to sit for at least 1 hour for the flavors to meld, but the longer it sits, the better it will taste. If you prefer a spicier salad, reserve and stir in some of the jalapeño seeds.

⅓	cup red wine vinegar	1	red bell pepper, stemmed, seeded, and chopped
3	tablespoons vegetable oil	1	green bell pepper, stemmed, seeded, and chopped
1	tablespoon sugar		
2	garlic cloves, minced	2	jalapeño chiles, stemmed, seeded, and minced
1	teaspoon table salt		
½	teaspoon pepper	1	celery rib, chopped fine
2	(15-ounce) cans black-eyed peas, rinsed	¼	cup chopped fresh cilantro
6	scallions, sliced thin	¼	cup chopped fresh parsley

1   Whisk vinegar, oil, sugar, garlic, salt, and pepper together in large bowl.

2   Add black-eyed peas, scallions, bell peppers, jalapeños, celery, cilantro, and parsley and toss to combine. Season with salt and pepper to taste. Let sit for at least 1 hour before serving.

IN THE GARDEN, WE GROW SISTERHOOD

Sittin' in my grandma Ruby's livin' room as she reminisces about her childhood in Oklahoma, specifically in Rentiesville, Fame, and Eufaula. I am enveloped in the scents of home—fresh cornbread from the oven, collard greens simmerin', and the earthy aroma of black-eyed peas. At 97, Grandma Ruby, a former nurse and a matriarch, shares stories of living on the farm. I hold her hands, firm yet soft and gentle, as she shares family tales of generations of healers, ranchers, and cowboys. Our family's roots run deep in this red soil, and our culture thrives in the warmth of her kitchen and on the family farm.

As a fifth-generation Black Oklahoman, I grew up surrounded by bounty yet seldom saw my culture reflected in the mainstream narrative, and I felt trapped in the margins of society. To reclaim my purpose, I created NativSol Kitchen, wellness programs fueled by African foods and nutrition. NativSol provides my community with resources to shop and cook for health. My roots and food culture as well as those of other Southern Black folks from our ancestral homeland on the shores of Nigeria in West Africa hold the keys to protecting and healing our community, from erasure from mainstream wellness traditions and from the ills of the Western colonized diet and lifestyle.

To extend that mission, I founded WANDA (Women Advancing Nutrition, Dietetics, and Agriculture), a movement to empower and unite Black women and girls specifically to transform our food and agricultural system. We host farm-to-table Sisterhood Suppers, which gather Black women to make nourishing meals with African heritage foods and to share our stories. The garden is central to these meals; it's a symbol of hope and regeneration. You see, in the garden, growin' food isn't just about fillin' our bellies but also feedin' our souls. Those black-eyed peas? They're the coins we use to pay for a taste. And the greens? Well, they're like the dollar bills, bringin' prosperity to our plates. We spice up our lives with onions, tomatoes, and bell peppers. The garden-powered dinners remind us "we are all that we got."

As part of the Sisterhood, we dream of a new world where Black women and girls play lead roles in farm and health sectors. This nods to our intertwined ancestral callings as growers and healers and lets us follow the path of women farmers and food justice activists and educators while we look toward the future through recipes created by cooks such as Michelle Braxton, blogger and author of *Supper with Love: Vibrant, Delicious, and Comforting Plant-Forward and Pescatarian Recipes for Every Day.*

When we create the menu, like Grandma Ruby and other matriarchs, we ensure we are not on it. We honor our ancestors' wisdom, and nourish our bodies, minds, and souls with self-love. We reclaim our foodways because diabetes and heart disease are not our heritage. Our food is our medicine, and we *will* leave a legacy of generational health—the highest form of wealth.

by Tambra Raye Stevenson

scholar, food justice advocate, and founder of WANDA and NativSol Kitchen

Three-Bean Salad

Serves 4 to 6 ~ Total Time: 30 minutes

Three-bean salad is such a Southern summertime classic, you can find it premade in the grocery store. Store-bought versions may be convenient, but they can also be mushy and sugary. Here's our fresh take. First, we blanch fresh Romano beans and yellow wax beans until they're crisp-tender. Canned kidney beans round out our trio, so we avoid the need to soak and simmer dried beans for hours. Letting the garlic and onion sit in the vinaigrette tames the garlic and quick-pickles the onion. A touch of honey in the dressing adds the appropriate sweetness to recall the classic formula, and a generous amount of parsley folded in just before serving contributes a lively finish. Set up the ice bath before cooking the wax and Romano beans.

¼ cup cider vinegar

3 tablespoons extra-virgin olive oil

1 tablespoon honey

1 garlic clove, minced

½ teaspoon table salt, plus salt for cooking beans

⅛ teaspoon pepper

½ small red onion, sliced thin

8 ounces yellow wax beans, trimmed and halved on bias

8 ounces Romano beans, trimmed and halved on bias

1 (15-ounce) can red kidney beans, rinsed

¼ cup minced fresh parsley

1 Whisk vinegar, oil, honey, garlic, salt, and pepper together in large bowl. Stir in onion and set aside.

2 Bring 4 quarts water to boil in large pot over high heat. Fill large bowl halfway with ice and water. Add wax beans, Romano beans, and 1 tablespoon salt to boiling water and cook until crisp-tender, 3 to 5 minutes. Drain beans, then transfer immediately to ice bath. Let beans cool completely, about 5 minutes, then drain again and pat dry with paper towels.

3 Add wax and Romano beans, kidney beans, and parsley to vinaigrette and toss to coat. Season with salt and pepper to taste, and serve.

APPALACHIAN BEANS TALK

When those of us raised on foundational Appalachian cuisine talk of beans so beloved that one wonders whether they're magic beans, we aren't aiming to grow a storybook beanstalk: We're sharing our eternal longing for a heavenly meal. Any discussion of the art and ingenuity of Appalachian cookery must include beans, which, along with corn and squash, form the Three Sisters crops (see page 138).

Our beans are special. They're heirloom beans—pole, bush, and runner varieties with lyrical names such as Half-Runners, Pink Tips, Cornfield, and Greasy Cut-Shorts—that flourish in the mountainous terrain, generous rain, and short growing season that distinguish our geography and gardening. We leave them to grow until the hulls are bulging with mature beans cinched in by ropy strings that must be pulled away. The plump, meaty beans inside remind us that they are a vital source of nourishing protein, not merely a green vegetable side dish.

Unlike flimsy filet beans (such as the slender French haricot verts) that need only a wisp of steam or quick blanch to turn them crisp-tender, the proper way to coax the deep flavor and nutrients from our robust beans is to simmer them until meltingly tender. We serve our beans bathed in beautifully seasoned potlikker as fully wrought as rich soup, the color of strong tea, and laced with umami. Uninformed cooks, who perhaps have never even seen heirloom beans, much less feasted on them, mistakenly describe our soft beans as overcooked, but they are in fact, perfectly prepared. Undercooked mature beans are chalky and inedible, just as overcooked filet beans are watery mush. Understanding the different techniques is analogous to knowing when to braise beef short ribs instead of searing a steak.

No green bean from a store-bought tin can or microwaveable pouch can touch the flavors and textures of our storied local beans. Like the beloved foodways of other regions and cooks, nothing can replace or replicate the taste of right here.

by Sheri Castle

food writer, cooking instructor, and host of PBS's The Key Ingredient

Southern-Style Baby Lima Beans

Serves 4 to 6 ~ Total Time: 1¼ hours

The beauty of this recipe is in its simplicity: Frozen baby lima beans are cooked low and slow, seasoned with a few strips of bacon and wedges of onion in the pot. The resulting beans and their smoky, thick, peppery broth are complex and deeply comforting. Stirring occasionally as the beans cook emulsifies the bacon fat into the broth, giving it a silky texture. This dish is great as a side or as a main course served over white rice (see our Everyday White Rice on page 160). Do not thaw the baby lima beans before cooking.

4	slices bacon, cut into ½-inch pieces
4	cups chicken broth
1½	pounds frozen baby lima beans
1¼	cups water
1	onion, halved
1	teaspoon pepper
¾	teaspoon table salt

1 Cook bacon in large saucepan over medium heat until lightly browned and fat has rendered, 7 to 10 minutes. Add broth, lima beans, water, onion, pepper, and salt. Bring to boil over high heat.

2 Reduce heat to medium-low and simmer, uncovered and stirring occasionally, until beans just begin to break down and liquid is thickened, about 1 hour (liquid will continue to thicken as it sits). Discard onion. Season with salt and pepper to taste. Serve.

PERUVIAN IMPORTS

Lima beans, which originated in Guatemala, have been cultivated in Lima, Peru, for centuries—hence the name—and are a staple food there. By the 1500s, what we now call Peru had found trading partners throughout South, Central, and North America and also in Europe. As the beans were introduced to North America, they were adapted into regional recipes. Many versions of Native American succotash use this large, nutritious bean. Lima beans remain especially popular in the dishes of the American South.

Some cooks use the terms "lima beans" and "butter beans" interchangeably, as the two beans come from the same plant. But other cooks know butter beans as the more mature larger white beans that are typically sold dried or canned, and baby lima beans as the smaller, greener beans that are typically sold frozen or canned.

Sweet Potato Casserole

Serves 6 to 8   ~   Total Time: 1¾ hours

The story of the sweet potato starts in South and Central America. Over many generations, Indigenous groups learned to cultivate the root vegetable and slowly expanded its growing region all the way to the South. Later, enslaved people found solace in the tuber because it resembled and could be cooked similarly to the local yams from back home. This connection with the West African crop is likely the reason why many Americans continue to confuse and conflate American-grown sweet potatoes with yams, especially around holidays such as Thanksgiving, when the ingredient is part of many customary dishes. Due to their association with the transatlantic slave trade, sweet potatoes were often deemed lesser and carried disparaging racial connotations. Nonetheless, many of the first cookbooks authored by Black Americans featured recipes for sweet potatoes, including Malinda Russell's 1866 *A Domestic Cook Book*, which featured the root in a recipe for Baked Pudding made with eggs, sugar, and nutmeg. Sweet potato recipes, including the beloved sweet potato pie, remain staples of Southern and especially Black Southern foodways. Cookbook author Dori Sanders, author of *Dori Sanders' Country Cooking: Recipes and Stories from the Family Farm Stand*, includes a recipe for a sweet potato pie that she brightens with orange juice.

Today, the root remains a crucial agricultural crop in several Southern economies, including North Carolina, which ranks first in the production of the orange-fleshed tuber and grows nearly half of the country's sweet potatoes. To honor this long history, this classic sweet potato casserole aims for elegance and simplicity. Butter and cream add richness to the sweet potato puree, while cinnamon, orange zest (just like Sanders suggests), and a pinch of cayenne round out the flavors. Once the sweet potatoes are spread in a soufflé dish, a sprinkle of a simple sugar–orange zest topping and a quick turn under the broiler creates a crisp, caramelized crust.

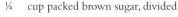

¼ cup packed brown sugar, divided

1 teaspoon grated orange zest, divided, plus 2 tablespoons juice

3 pounds sweet potatoes, peeled and cut into 1½-inch pieces

4 tablespoons unsalted butter, cut into 6 pieces

¼ cup heavy cream

1 teaspoon table salt

½ teaspoon ground cinnamon

¼ teaspoon pepper

⅛ teaspoon cayenne pepper

1 Adjust oven rack to middle position and heat oven to 400 degrees. Mix 3 tablespoons sugar and ½ teaspoon orange zest in small bowl until thoroughly combined; set aside.

2 Lay two 24 by 12-inch sheets of heavy-duty aluminum foil perpendicular to each other inside rimmed baking sheet. Place sweet potatoes in center of foil and sprinkle with remaining 1 tablespoon sugar. Fold opposite sides of foil toward each other and crimp edges to seal tightly. Put sheet in oven and bake until sweet potatoes are tender, about 1 hour longer. Remove sheet from oven and heat broiler.

3 Carefully open 1 end of foil pouch, taking care to avoid escaping steam, and pour potatoes and accumulated liquid into food processor. Add butter, cream, salt, cinnamon, pepper, cayenne, orange juice, and remaining ½ teaspoon orange zest and process until completely smooth, 30 to 60 seconds, scraping down sides of bowl as needed.

4 Transfer potato puree to 2-quart soufflé dish and sprinkle evenly with reserved sugar-zest mixture. Broil until topping is lightly browned and bubbling, 2 to 4 minutes. Serve.

WHEN SERVICE IS JOY

I have a theory that the majority of professional chefs cook for one of two reasons: They either grew up eating really well, or they grew up scraping the char off of their toast and sneaking seasoning into their food. I can say with tremendous gratitude that I grew up in the former scenario.

Though both of my parents were truly excellent cooks jointly revered by friends and neighbors for their food-focused talents, my mother was the true natural. While my father rigidly followed the text of cookbooks and culinary mags, my mother cooked with a freedom that I would later find in my own kitchen DNA. Though she loved cookbooks and any article she could read about food, they served as inspiration more than guidance. The one book she referenced most of all was one she referred to as the "red book," which sat on a shelf too high for me to reach as a kid. It always held a bit of mystique to me. I never saw her use it, but I always felt its presence.

The freedom with which my mom cooked was a thing of beauty, but it was also a symbol of her service to our family. My father was a long-haul truck driver, so Mom's ingrained sense of service to our family was called upon more often than not. She was incredibly busy, working full-time as a real estate agent, and filling all of the roles of a mother to two young children as best she could. I remember how she would make breakfast for us: with hot rollers in her hair, taking business calls on the landline with its 20-foot cord, ironing a blouse for the day, and whipping my hair into pigtails as she buttered the whole-wheat toast for the foil-wrapped egg sandwiches she would arm us with for school. Before the same sun had set and after Mom had spent a full day at the office, my brother and I would sit at the bar that looked into the kitchen, scribbling at our home-work and watching my mom cook with the enthusiasm that most bring to prepare a holiday meal—but with the ease of acknowledging it was just a Wednesday, and this was just oven-roasted lamb with the mint-vinegar sauce "from the red book."

When I think about why I am a cook, I think about my mother. I think about what a treasure it is that she finds joy and release where she also finds service. This is the gift she has given me, both through nature and through nurture. In celebration of my 40th birthday, my mother also gave me the gift of the red book, which her great-grandmother gifted her when she married my father. As I studied this 600-page tome, I realized that it didn't contain anything close to a road map of my mother's talents. Its pages were packed with hundreds of simply written recipes, and sections for menu planning, shopping on a budget, timetables for roasting and braising, and even a section dedicated to high-altitude cookery.

The book, first issued in 1942, is titled *The Modern Family Cook Book*. In coming to know this book as my own, I realize that its name is unimportant and its value lies not in what is printed on its pages, but rather in the impressions of the hands that have held it, the rubs and rips and spills from its travels from kitchen to kitchen, and the invaluable scribbles on the most-visited pages. It is a time capsule of stories told through the lives of each of its keepers. It is joy and release, and it is service.

by Ashley Christensen

North Carolina chef, proprietor of AC Restaurants, and cookbook author

No.5

R I C E
O R
G R I T S

Left to right: Boudin Balls (page 158), Shrimp and Grits (page 180), Mashama Bailey at her Savannah restaurant The Grey (see page 164), Fried Whole Branzino with Grits (page 182), Gullah Lowcountry Red Rice (page 174).

RICE IS LIFE

Where my family comes from, we serve rice with a special spoon. If you're born lucky, it gets passed down to you, or gifted as a wedding present. This long-handled sterling spoon showed up on the sideboard in my great-aunt's formal dining room for two o'clock dinner, especially on Sundays when company was coming. Originally intended for basting meats or serving stuffing in Georgian-era England, that use changed on arrival in colonial-era Charleston, where the export of a short-grain rice called Carolina Gold made some people incredibly wealthy, and forced others to toil from dawn to dusk in the flooded fields of the Lowcountry tidal basin. A rice that's dainty, easily broken. Difficult to harvest and winnow, all while dodging death by poisonous snakes, lurking alligators, and malarial mosquitoes.

A handwritten manuscript of recipes by Eliza Lucas Pinckney, compiled in 1756, contains the first method for boiling fluffy white rice grown as a plantation crop in the Carolinas—harder than you'd think in a kitchen where everything was cooked on a wood-fired hearth. She instructed to "avoid stirring the rice once 'tis in the sauce-pann for one turn with a spoon will spoil all" (good advice that sticks with us, even today). Her daughter, Harriott Pinckney Horry, added more dishes in her own recipe collection from 1770—rice bread, rice pudding, and a rice flour "journey cake," the 18th-century equivalent of flatbread. By the time Sarah Rutledge

published *The Carolina Housewife* in 1847, she references "rice birds" as a particular delicacy. This was a colloquial term for the migrating bobolinks that landed in fields and gobbled up grain. None of these lady authors properly acknowledged who truly did the cooking in their households. While many enslaved cooks are remembered only by their first names (Daphne, Mary-Ann, Ebba) in these early records, they played an enduring role in defining the recipes that belong to what historian Karen Hess referred to as the Carolina rice kitchen.

In 1866, caterer and baker Malinda Russell became the first free Black woman to publish a cookbook; her recipes include a comforting rice milk dessert beloved by earlier generations of Southerners that coincidentally bears a neighborly resemblance to Mexican horchata, Puerto Rican arroz con leche, and Jamaican rice porridge. More recently, Judith A. Carney's *Black Rice: The African Origins of Rice Cultivation in the Americas* centers the enslaved experience in the Atlantic world. A large portion of traditional ingredients and dishes—perloo or pilau, hoppin' John, shrimp and crab rice, bog and hash—have been traced back to West Africa's Guinea Coast, also known as the Rice Coast, where slave traders kidnapped agrarians skilled in growing the crop. Beyond the Carolinas, Creole cooks in New Orleans gave us calas, gumbo, jambalaya, and red beans and rice.

It needs saying that rice was closely associated with racism and classism in the city my ancestors helped found. In my own lifetime, I can recall certain Charleston relatives who refused to eat dishes associated with Black culture, even though they employed a housekeeper or nanny or cook also born on the peninsula. And yet, thankfully, this hypocritical behavior wasn't sufficient to erase one of our most significant regional cuisines. My favorite dish from childhood is a forcemeat called liver pudding. Don't be fooled by the name, this is a savory side similar to Pennsylvania Dutch scrapple or Cajun boudin sausage. A lesson in diaspora cooking, liver pudding contains red pepper seeds for heat, and rice as a binder for the hog innards that were minced together with fatty bits and then shaped in a terrine or roulade. Yes, this springs from a classic French charcuterie technique, as some of the first rice planters were descended from Huguenot refugees, but it mostly lives on in the kitchens of the Gullah Geechee, coastal descendants of those original enslaved cooks. I like to think of liver pudding as the Lowcountry's pâté de campagne; it appeared most frequently on my parents' table with breakfast grits, but I love it fried to a crisp whenever one of the few butchers who still makes it shares a batch with me.

Rice is no longer a strict culinary dichotomy in the South, as the region has begun to welcome more diversity in its dishes, extending to Pakistani cholay biryani, Filipino arroz caldo, Korean bibimbap, and Senegambian jollof, the original version of what Gullah Geechee people call red rice. At any given time, I now have a dozen or so rice varieties stored in my kitchen cupboard, long and short grains brought back from journeys to other rice cultures. Riz blanc from the Camargue in southern France, riso vialone nano from Verona, aromatico grano largo fino purchased in Uruguay, aged heirloom basmati from India. More domestic varieties grown in Arkansas, Louisiana, and Texas. And sometimes even a gift from growers, both Black and white, involved in the complicated rice revival going on in the Lowcountry. I serve Carolina Gold like a risotto.

My rice spoon? Already passed it on to a younger sister.

by Shane Mitchell
author, including of the forthcoming book
The Crop Cycle: A History with Southern Roots
(Bitter Southerner Publishing), and five-time
James Beard Award–winning journalist

Boudin Balls

Makes about 30 balls ~ Total Time: 4¼ hours, plus 4 hours chilling

To say that Cajun boudin is a pork sausage doesn't do it justice—this mix of spiced pork, rice, and liver is a hallmark of Cajun cuisine. When made into sausage links, the boudin is fully cooked before it gets stuffed into the casings, and the preferred method of consumption is to bite off the top of the casing and squeeze the soft, heavily seasoned mixture directly into your mouth. But if company is coming, you can spread it on crackers or ball it up, roll it in breading, and fry it into delectable morsels known as boudin balls.

The history of boudin is just as rich as its flavor. Boudin's roots can be traced back to the Acadians (or "les Cadiens"), a group of French expatriates who came to Nova Scotia, which was known as Acadia at the time, in 1604. Eventually expelled to different parts of the United States in 1755, many ended up scattered throughout Louisiana, where they became known as Cajuns and made use of the land's bounty by hunting and fishing—and cooking. Among the foods they brought to the region was boudin blanc, a white sausage made from pork (or veal or chicken), bread, cream, mirepoix (onions, celery, and carrots), and spices. Because rice was abundant in Louisiana, over time it replaced the bread as the starchy filler.

Today boudin is sold in all manner of markets, grocery stores, and gas stations throughout Louisiana. Boudin-maker Beverly Giardelli—whose aunt and uncle Eunice and Clement Hebert opened C. Hebert's Slaughter House & Meat Market in 1959 in Abbeville, Louisiana—uses 50-pound sacks of rice and cooks it "the old fashioned way" on the stove. Despite the sausage's starch-filled interior, there is nothing subtle about the best boudin. Simmering chunks of heavily marbled pork shoulder in water with the holy trinity, salt, garlic, smoked paprika, white and black pepper, and cayenne creates a deep base of flavor. Using some of that liquid (now pork stock) to cook the rice infuses the grains with flavor. To make the boudin balls, we simply chill the filling, portion it into spheres, and then bread (we use panko) and fry them. This crowd-pleasing version is an absolute treat. Pork butt roast is often labeled Boston butt in the supermarket. Do not trim the pork butt; the rendered fat is utilized in the recipe. This recipe was developed with Diamond Crystal kosher salt; if using Morton, which is denser, decrease the amount to 2½ tablespoons. You can find chicken livers in the refrigerated meat section of your supermarket or at your local butcher shop. Use a Dutch oven that holds 6 quarts or more. Serve with Rémoulade (recipe follows).

2	pounds boneless pork butt roast, cut into 2-inch pieces	2	teaspoons pepper
4	cups water, plus extra as needed	1½	teaspoons cayenne pepper
1	onion, chopped coarse	12	ounces chicken livers, patted dry and trimmed
1	green bell pepper, stemmed, seeded, and chopped coarse	1⅓	cups long-grain white rice
1	celery rib, chopped coarse	9	scallions, sliced thin (1¼ cups)
3½	tablespoons kosher salt	1	cup all-purpose flour
6	garlic cloves, smashed and peeled	4	large eggs
1	tablespoon smoked paprika	2½	cups panko bread crumbs
1	tablespoon white pepper	2	quarts peanut or vegetable oil for frying

1   Combine pork, water, onion, bell pepper, celery, salt, garlic, paprika, white pepper, pepper, and cayenne in large Dutch oven. Bring to boil over medium-high heat. Reduce heat to low, cover, and simmer until pork is tender, about 2 hours. Stir in chicken livers and cook until cooked through, about 10 minutes.

2   Set fine-mesh strainer over large bowl. Using slotted spoon or spider skimmer, transfer pork, vegetables, and chicken livers to rimmed baking sheet. Strain pork cooking liquid through prepared strainer and transfer any remaining solids to sheet with pork. Spread pork mixture into even layer and let cool completely, about 30 minutes.

3   Meanwhile, let cooking liquid settle for 5 minutes. Using wide, shallow spoon, skim off and reserve 3 tablespoons fat from surface; discard remaining fat. Measure out and reserve 3 cups cooking liquid; discard excess liquid. (Add extra water as needed to yield 3 cups.)

4   Place rice in fine-mesh strainer and rinse under running water, agitating rice with your hand every so often, until water running through rice is almost clear, about 1½ minutes. Bring 2 cups reserved cooking liquid and rice to boil in large saucepan over medium-high heat. Reduce heat to low, cover, and simmer until rice is tender and liquid has been absorbed, about 20 minutes. Off heat, let sit, covered, for 10 minutes.

5   Working in 3 batches, pulse cooled pork mixture in food processor until coarsely ground and slightly tacky, about 6 pulses; transfer to large bowl. Fold in remaining 1 cup reserved cooking liquid, rice, scallions, and reserved fat until thoroughly combined. Cover and refrigerate boudin filling until completely chilled, at least 4 hours or up to 2 days.

6   Place flour in shallow dish. Beat eggs in second shallow dish. Spread panko in third shallow dish. Line rimmed baking sheet with parchment paper. Measure ¼-cup portions of boudin mixture and, using your

lightly moistened hands, roll into balls. Transfer boudin balls to prepared sheet (you should have about 30 balls). Working with 1 ball at a time, dredge in flour, dip in eggs, and coat with panko, pressing gently to adhere; return balls to prepared sheet. (Balls can be refrigerated for up to 24 hours or frozen on sheet until solid, then transferred to zipper-lock bags and stored in freezer for up to 1 month; thaw frozen balls overnight in refrigerator before frying.)

7   Line second rimmed baking sheet with triple layer of paper towels. Add oil to clean Dutch oven until it measures about 1½ inches deep and heat over medium-high heat to 350 degrees. Using slotted spoon or spider skimmer, gently lower 10 balls into hot oil and cook until golden brown, about 6 minutes, rotating balls halfway through frying. Adjust burner, if necessary, to maintain oil temperature between 325 and 350 degrees. Transfer balls to prepared sheet and let drain. Return oil to 350 degrees and repeat with remaining balls in 2 more batches. Serve.

Rémoulade

Makes 1½ cups   ~   Total Time: 5 minutes

A typical Louisiana-style rémoulade is a tangy, creamy, mayo-based sauce often containing some or all of the following: chopped celery, scallions, parsley, pickles, and capers, as well as horseradish, ketchup, mustard, and a bit of cayenne or hot sauce. For a zingy dipping sauce, we like a simplified one—one that requires no chopping. The cool, bright heat of the horseradish, Dijon mustard, and hot sauce balances the richness of the sausage in our Boudin Balls, and the smooth sauce lightly coats the crispy spheres without competing with the texture and complexity of the boudin. It's equally delicious as a sauce for any crispy fried snack. Buy refrigerated prepared horseradish, not the shelf-stable kind, which contains preservatives and additives. We like to make this rémoulade with Crystal Hot Sauce; you can substitute other Louisiana-style hot sauces, but start with less and add to taste.

1⅓   cups mayonnaise

3   tablespoons prepared horseradish

2   tablespoons Worcestershire sauce

2   tablespoons Crystal Hot Sauce

1   tablespoon Dijon mustard

½   teaspoon pepper

Whisk all ingredients together in bowl. (Rémoulade can be refrigerated for up to 1 week.)

Everyday White Rice

Makes 6 cups ~ Total Time: 40 minutes

Rice has been an agricultural staple across the South since the 18th century. Beginning with African-grown rice in the 1700s, waves of immigrant groups brought new strains of rice to the South's fertile coastal growing zones, including resilient shinriki rice brought by the Japanese to Texas and sticky rice varieties brought by the Hmong people to North Carolina.

No matter the variety, rice may seem simple, but a perfectly cooked pot of it—even common long-grain white rice—can be awfully elusive. Long-grain rice is an essential side for many Southern recipes, serving as a landing pad to soak up Smoky Chicken, Sausage, and Shrimp Gumbo (page 196) and a neutral accompaniment to dampen the tang of South Carolina Barbecue Hash (page 190). This reliable recipe for steamed long-grain white rice is light and perfectly tender throughout, yet clumps together slightly. Rinsing off the excess starch before cooking is key to the desired finished texture. Three cups of water for 2 cups of raw rice is just enough liquid to cook the rice through without leaving it wet. Two finishing tricks guarantee success: letting the rice sit, still covered, off the heat for 10 minutes so any extra moisture is absorbed, and gently fluffing the rice with a fork to break up any big masses.

2 cups long-grain white rice

3 cups water

½ teaspoon table salt (optional)

1 Place rice in fine-mesh strainer and rinse under running water, agitating rice with your hand every so often, until water running through rice is almost clear, about 1½ minutes.

2 Combine rice; water; and salt, if using, in large saucepan and bring to simmer over high heat. Stir rice with rubber spatula, dislodging any rice that sticks to bottom of saucepan.

3 Cover, reduce heat to low, and cook for 20 minutes. (Steam should steadily emit from sides of saucepan. If water bubbles out from under lid, reduce heat slightly.)

4 Off heat, let rice sit, covered, for 10 minutes. Gently fluff rice with fork. Serve.

To double this recipe Increase rice to 4 cups and water to 6 cups. In step 2, use Dutch oven instead of large saucepan. After rice comes to simmer, cover pot, transfer to middle rack of 350-degree oven, and bake for 20 minutes. Remove from oven and continue with step 4.

Chicken Bog

Serves 6 to 8 ~ Total Time: 1¾ hours

Some say chicken bog earned its regional moniker due to the "wet" consistency of the rice, while others believe it's a reference to the dish's geographical origins in the salt marsh regions that run along the South Carolina coast. And a few argue that the chicken just gets "bogged down" in the rice. In the early 20th century, South Carolina girls' groups, PTAs, and the wives of members of men's associations such as the Masons hosted "chicken bogs," the name given to large outdoor gatherings where chicken bog and other Lowcountry dishes were served.

Chicken bog—a one-pot porridge-like mélange of chicken, smoky sausage, and white rice—is a delicious dish packed with savory taste in every last bite. To get in on that flavor, this recipe relies on pilaf-like rice cooked in a deeply flavorful broth with generous chunks of chicken and sausage. Chicken thighs provide both juicy meat and maximum flavor. Browning the thighs and then setting them aside allows the skin's rendered fat to infuse chicken flavor into the onion and kielbasa. Adding a little garlic to the chicken broth creates an aromatic brew. A bowl of this bog is perfectly seasoned and "bogged down"—in the best way—with flavor.

6	(5- to 7-ounce) bone-in chicken thighs, trimmed
1½	teaspoons table salt, divided
1¼	teaspoons pepper, divided
1	tablespoon vegetable oil
8	ounces smoked kielbasa sausage, cut into ½-inch-thick rounds
1	onion, chopped fine
3	garlic cloves, minced
4	cups chicken broth
2	cups long-grain white rice

1   Pat chicken dry with paper towels and sprinkle with ½ teaspoon salt and ¼ teaspoon pepper. Heat oil in Dutch oven over medium heat until just smoking. Cook chicken skin side down until browned, 5 to 8 minutes. Transfer chicken to plate; discard skin.

2   Pour off all but 1 tablespoon fat from pot and return to medium heat. Add sausage and onion and cook until onion is translucent and sausage begins to brown, 3 to 5 minutes. Add garlic and cook until fragrant, about 30 seconds. Add broth, chicken, remaining 1 teaspoon salt, and remaining 1 teaspoon pepper and bring to boil. Reduce heat to low, cover, and simmer until chicken is tender, about 30 minutes.

3   Remove chicken from pot and set aside. Stir rice into pot, cover, and continue to cook over low heat until rice is tender, about 20 minutes.

4   Shred chicken with 2 forks into bite-size pieces; discard bones. Gently fold shredded chicken into rice mixture. Remove from heat and let sit, covered, for 10 minutes. Serve.

THE MATRIARCH OF EDISTO ISLAND

When we arrived at Emily Meggett's tidy yellow home on Edisto Island, South Carolina, Ms. Emily, as everyone called her, waited at the side door, eager to start cooking. Guests were not welcome at her home, only friends and family, but Ms. Emily was quick to say that everyone who walked through her front gate instantly became friends and family. After a warm greeting, Ms. Emily and Toni Tipton-Martin approached the kitchen counter to begin making hoppin' John based on a recipe from Ms. Emily's 2022 cookbook, the *New York Times* bestseller *Gullah Geechee Home Cooking*. The house was filled with the aromas of smoky bacon slowly simmering with cabbage on the stovetop and chicken thighs braising in the oven. Ms. Emily began dispensing kitchen wisdom as quickly as she'd hand a stranger a warm biscuit. "A little sugar in the cabbage takes away the bitterness—about 1 tablespoon per head of cabbage." And "Spooning the cooking liquid over chicken helps the skin brown." Ms. Emily handed Toni a knife and placed a fresh ham hock on the cutting board. "Split the ham hock in half," she said, turning the hock upright. "Cut close to the bone." Toni complied and easily split the hock in two.

Ms. Emily called Edisto Island her home for her entire life. She often drove around the island handing out meals to friends and those who couldn't provide for themselves due to illness or financial hardship. At Christmas she dropped off lima beans to islanders she called her "little people." When she brought her car to the mechanic, the trunk was filled with hot meals, and in return she was charged nothing for the repairs. She insists that there is something special about Edisto Island. "Across the [McKinley] bridge is a little bit of heaven. Everybody here loves everybody." Standing at the kitchen sink, Ms. Emily rinsed her Sea Island red peas in three changes of water. "Floating peas are dead peas," she said. "Keep rinsing until the peas don't float." She added the peas to a large pot and covered them with plenty of water. She rinsed Toni's split ham hock in two changes of water to "remove the blood" before also adding it to the pot. The peas simmered for just over an hour until they were tender. In the meantime, Ms. Emily turned her attention to a hunk of skin-on salt pork. She preferred the salt pork to bacon in her hoppin' John. As a child, she said, when her family didn't have salt on hand, they used to scrape the salt off a hunk of salt pork to season their grits. Hoppin' John kitchen wisdom from the matriarch of Edisto Island.

All four burners and the oven were in use, and Ms. Emily moved with purpose and sure of her steps. She barked out loving, quick commands: "Rinse this." "Hand me that pot." "Chop this onion." Ms. Emily passed away in 2023 at age 90. Her friends and family would tell you, she didn't play around in the kitchen.

Emily Meggett on the porch of her home on Edisto Island, South Carolina.

Hoppin' John

Serves 4 to 6   ~   Total Time: 2½ hours

While its mysterious name has a lot of proposed origins, hoppin' John is without question an icon of the Southern table. The earliest published recipe appeared in *The Carolina Housewife*, a recipe book written by Sarah Rutledge in 1847. A wealthy, white Charlestonian, Rutledge called for red peas, a staple crop of the Sea Island Gullah Geechee people, and relied on the one-pot cooking method used in African cooking tradition. While the author might have been an aficionado of the locally grown cow pea, she more likely obtained this recipe from an enslaved or formerly enslaved person. The pork-enriched rice-and-pea dish (and variations using the similarly sized black-eyed pea) spread across the South and eventually became a cherished meal consumed on New Year's Day to ensure prosperity and good luck. This recipe is inspired by a cook-through with Ms. Emily Meggett (see "The Matriarch of Edisto Island"). Split the ham hock in half so that it cooks through at about the same rate as the peas. Adding the optional smoky pieces of ham hock to the hoppin' John lends an extra savory note, but feel free to leave it out if you prefer your rice and peas with less meat. Note that not all salt pork is sold with its rind on. Do not rinse the rice before cooking. You can use long grain white rice or regional Carolina Gold rice in this recipe. We use Rollen's Raw Grains Carolina Gold rice, which you can purchase online at rollensrawgrains.com.

Peas

1	cup Sea Island red peas
1	smoked ham hock, split in half vertically along bone
1	tablespoon table salt

Hoppin' John

6	ounces salt pork, rind removed, rinsed, patted dry, and cut into ¾-inch pieces
¼	cup vegetable oil or lard
1	cup chopped onion
3	scallions, sliced ½ inch thick
1½	cups long-grain or Carolina Gold rice
1	teaspoon table salt
¾	teaspoon pepper
¾	teaspoon granulated garlic
½	teaspoon onion powder

1   **For the peas** Place peas in medium bowl and cover with water. Slosh peas around with your hand to knock off loose dirt. Let peas settle, then pour off excess water along with any floating peas; repeat rinsing and pouring off excess water until no peas float.

2   Combine rinsed peas, 4 quarts water, ham hock, and salt in Dutch oven. Bring to boil over high heat. Reduce to medium-low, cover, and simmer until peas are tender, 50 minutes to 1 hour.

3   Reserve 2¼ cups pea cooking liquid and transfer ham hock pieces to plate to cool. Drain peas in colander in sink. (Cooked peas can be refrigerated for up to 24 hours or frozen for up to 1 month. Thaw before proceeding with recipe.) When cool enough to handle, chop ham hock meat into ½-inch pieces and reserve ¾ cup for hoppin' John, if desired (reserve remaining ham for another use or discard).

4   **For the hoppin' John** Combine salt pork and oil in large saucepan. Cover and cook over medium heat until pork is evenly browned, 10 to 12 minutes, stirring occasionally and being mindful of splatter. (Pork will initially stick to bottom of pot but will eventually release as it browns.)

5   Add onion and scallions to salt pork and cook until softened, about 3 minutes. Stir in rice until grains are evenly coated with oil and cook, stirring often, until edges of rice are translucent, about 2 minutes. Stir in salt; pepper; granulated garlic; onion powder; cooked peas; reserved pea cooking liquid; and chopped ham hock, if using, and bring to simmer. Once simmering, cover pot with sheet of aluminum foil, then cover with lid. Reduce heat to low and cook for 20 minutes without removing lid.

6   Off heat, let hoppin' John sit, covered, for 10 minutes. Fluff rice with carving fork. Transfer to shallow serving dish. Serve.

Shrimp Middlins

Serves 6 to 8   ~   Total Time: 1½ hours

Mashama Bailey, James Beard Award–winning chef and co-founder of renowned Savannah, Georgia, restaurant The Grey, has built a reputation on thoughtful preparations of Southern ingredients. Her seasonal menu features regional bites such as pickled oysters, smoked collard greens, succotash, crab Louie, and hoppin' John, but her approach to each is distinctly her own, reflective of both her upbringing in New York and Georgia and her international training.

Bailey's fatigue with the misogyny she faced in professional kitchens was a catalyst for the success she has today. In her book *Black, White, and The Grey: The Story of an Unexpected Friendship and a Beloved Restaurant*, written with her restaurant partner John "Johno" Morisano, she says, "If you want to cook at a certain level, you need to enter the boy's club … As a woman in these kitchens, I learned quickly that I had to establish my boundaries, protect my personal space, and set what I believed to be acceptable standards of personal behavior from my male colleagues." Eventually that standard meant seeking mentorship at East Village restaurant Prune under chef Gabrielle Hamilton. Hamilton helped Bailey find her culinary voice and also put her in touch with Johno; together they opened The Grey in a restored Jim Crow–era Greyhound bus terminal in Savannah.

When Bailey visited the property the first time, Johno showed her around, pointing out the segregated entrances, waiting rooms, and restrooms. Though she expected to feel sadness in the face of the structure's history, she instead felt pride—she could use this restaurant to change the narrative. "It was going to be important to me to support other Black people going forward, recognize the contributions of Black people in the past, and acknowledge all of the sacrifices that Black people have made," Bailey writes.

One of the dishes that fulfills her vision, and one often appears on The Grey's ever-changing menu, is middlins. Middlins are broken grains of rice, also called rice grits, and they have a long history in the South. Carolina Gold rice, an heirloom grain originally cultivated by enslaved laborers in the Lowcountry (see page 156), is especially brittle and prone to breakage during the milling process. Deemed unsellable, these broken grains were given to enslaved cooks. Traditionally middlins are cooked like rice or grits, but they have a chewier texture and a starchy creaminess. They're typically served alongside a main dish, such as fried fish or seafood stew.

Bailey cooks hers like a risotto. She starts with a base of sautéed celery, onion, and shallot bolstered with tomato paste and saffron for sweet depth. Then she toasts Carolina Gold middlins in olive oil with the vegetables, deglazes with white wine, and ladles in her homemade shrimp stock, stirring and continually adding stock until the rice is al dente. She adds chopped shrimp and red snapper to cook in the rice, and finishes the dish with butter and a shower of fresh herbs. This version follows Bailey's lead closely, simplifying a step or two: It uses a near-hands-off risotto method and just shrimp for the seafood.

4	tablespoons unsalted butter, divided
1	pound extra-large shrimp (21 to 25 per pound), peeled and deveined, shells reserved, shrimp cut into ½-inch pieces
2	tablespoons tomato paste, divided
8	cups water
1	tablespoon table salt, divided
¼	cup extra-virgin olive oil
1	onion, chopped fine
1	celery rib, chopped fine
2	shallots, minced
2	cups Carolina Gold rice middlins or rice grits
⅛	teaspoon cayenne pepper
¾	cup dry white wine
¼	cup chopped fresh parsley
2	tablespoons minced fresh chives
2	teaspoons lemon juice, plus extra for seasoning
1	teaspoon chopped fresh tarragon

1   Melt 1 tablespoon butter in large saucepan over medium heat. Add reserved shrimp shells and cook, stirring occasionally, until shells are spotty brown, about 7 minutes. Stir in 1 tablespoon tomato paste and cook for 30 seconds. Add water and bring to boil. Reduce heat to low, cover, and simmer for 5 minutes.

2   Strain shrimp stock through fine-mesh strainer set over bowl, pressing on solids to extract as much liquid as possible; discard solids. You should have about 8 cups stock. Return stock to saucepan, cover, and keep warm over low heat.

3   Toss shrimp with 1 teaspoon salt and set aside. Heat oil in large Dutch oven over medium heat until shimmering. Add onion, celery, shallots, and 1 teaspoon salt and cook, stirring occasionally, until translucent, about 10 minutes. Add middlins and cook, stirring frequently, until edges of grains are translucent, about 2 minutes. Add remaining 1 tablespoon tomato paste and cayenne and cook until tomato paste is evenly distributed, about 1 minute.

4   Add wine and cook, stirring frequently, until wine is nearly absorbed, about 2 minutes. Stir in 7 cups warm stock and remaining 1 teaspoon salt and bring to simmer. Reduce heat to low, cover, and simmer, stirring occasionally, until nearly all liquid has been absorbed and rice is just al dente, about 20 minutes.

5   Add shrimp and cook, stirring constantly, until mixture is creamy and shrimp are cooked through, about 3 minutes. Stir in parsley, chives, lemon juice, tarragon, and remaining 3 table-spoons butter. Season with salt and lemon juice to taste. Stir in additional stock to loosen texture as needed. (Texture should be somewhat loose; it will thicken slightly as it sits.) Serve.

Cajun Rice Dressing

Serves 8 to 10   ~   Total Time: 1½ hours

Flip through any Louisiana church or community cookbook and you'll see at least a half dozen recipes for Cajun rice dressing, each woman's recipe differing slightly with a little of this or a bit of that. Born and raised in Terrebonne Parish in South Louisiana, chef and author Melissa A. Martin says in her book, *Mosquito Supper Club: Cajun Recipes from a Disappearing Bayou*, that this "offal-heavy" dressing can be eaten alone, with sides, and is "always on the table for Thanksgiving and Christmas." The recipe details change from kitchen to kitchen, but the basics—rice, ground meat, and chicken livers—stay the same. This dressing doesn't taste strongly of liver; the underutilized ingredient simply adds a signature savoriness. You can find chicken livers in the refrigerated meat section of your supermarket or at your local butcher shop. If you prefer, you can use a food processor to chop the chicken livers; it will take about six pulses to finely chop them. For a spicier dish, use the larger amount of cayenne pepper.

6	tablespoons unsalted butter, divided
3	slices bacon, chopped
2	green bell peppers, stemmed, seeded, and chopped fine
2	onions, chopped fine
1	celery rib, chopped fine
12	scallions, cut into ½-inch pieces, divided
4	garlic cloves, minced
1	tablespoon chopped fresh thyme
2	teaspoons table salt, divided
1¾	teaspoons pepper, divided
1	pound ground pork
8	ounces chicken livers, trimmed and chopped fine
1	tablespoon paprika
1½	teaspoons granulated garlic
½	teaspoon celery salt
¼–½	teaspoon cayenne pepper
3	cups chicken broth
1	recipe Everyday White Rice (page 160)
	Hot sauce

1   Melt 4 tablespoons butter in Dutch oven over medium-high heat. Add bacon and cook until almost crispy, about 3 minutes.

2   Add bell peppers, onions, celery, half of scallions, garlic, thyme, ¾ teaspoon salt, and 1 teaspoon pepper and cook until vegetables have softened, about 7 minutes, stirring occasionally.

3   Add pork, chicken livers, paprika, granulated garlic, celery salt, cayenne, ¾ teaspoon salt, ½ teaspoon pepper, and remaining 2 tablespoons butter and cook, breaking up meat with spoon, until mixture begins to fry in its own fat and fond develops on bottom of pot, 12 to 15 minutes, stirring occasionally.

4   Stir in broth, scraping up any browned bits. Stir in remaining scallions and bring to boil. Reduce heat to medium-low and simmer until slightly reduced, about 15 minutes.

5   Off heat, add rice, remaining ½ teaspoon salt, and remaining ¼ teaspoon pepper and stir until thoroughly combined. Season with salt and pepper to taste. Serve with hot sauce.

Red Beans and Rice

Serves 8 to 10 ~ Total Time: 3¼ hours

Countless cultures across the world have some version of beans and rice—including Ghanaian waakye, Japanese azuki beans and rice, and Indian rajma chawal—in their culinary playbook. The simple but flavorful combination of grain and legume provides important nutrients, accessible calories, and endless variations. In many Southern Creole kitchens, red beans and rice was (and is) a Monday night dish. The hambone saved from Sunday dinner was simmered on the back burner, its marrow flavoring the red beans and thickening the broth. Today, however, most home cooks don't have leftover hambones. For porky, salty flavor, we cook four strips of bacon and add onion, bell pepper, and celery to the rendered fat, followed by garlic and spices. To ensure that the beans turn out tender and taste meaty, we simmer them in both water and chicken broth before adding smoky, spicy andouille sausage. Half an hour is just enough time for the sausage to impart great flavor to the beans without becoming too tough. Serve this Louisiana classic any night of the week. In order for the bean starch to thicken the cooking liquid, maintain a vigorous simmer in step 1.

Beans

4	slices bacon, chopped
1	small onion, chopped fine
1	green bell pepper, stemmed, seeded, and chopped fine
1	celery rib, minced
4	garlic cloves, minced
7	cups chicken broth
7	cups water
1	pound (2½ cups) dried red kidney beans, picked over and rinsed
4	bay leaves
1	teaspoon minced fresh oregano
1	teaspoon minced fresh thyme
1	teaspoon pepper
½	teaspoon table salt
½	teaspoon cayenne pepper
8	ounces andouille sausage, halved lengthwise and sliced ¼ inch thick

Rice

3	cups long-grain white rice
2	tablespoons vegetable oil
4½	cups water
1½	teaspoons table salt

Hot sauce

1 **For the beans** Cook bacon in Dutch oven over medium heat until crispy, about 7 minutes. Add onion, bell pepper, and celery and cook, stirring frequently, until softened, about 8 minutes. Stir in garlic and cook until fragrant, about 30 seconds. Add broth, water, beans, bay leaves, oregano, thyme, pepper, salt, and cayenne and bring to boil over high heat. Reduce heat to medium and simmer vigorously, stirring occasionally, until beans are soft and liquid thickens, 2 to 2½ hours.

2 Stir in sausage and cook until liquid is thick and creamy, about 30 minutes.

3 **For the rice** Meanwhile, place rice in fine-mesh strainer and rinse under running water, agitating rice with your hand every so often, until water running through rice is almost clear, about 1½ minutes.

4 Heat oil in large saucepan over medium heat. Add rice; cook, stirring constantly, for 1 to 3 minutes, until rice is lightly toasted. Add water and salt; bring to boil, swirling pan to blend ingredients.

5 Reduce heat to low, place dish towel folded in half over pan, and cover pan. Cook until liquid is absorbed, about 15 minutes.

6 Turn off heat and let rice stand on burner, covered, to finish cooking, about 15 minutes longer. Fluff rice with fork. Season beans with salt and pepper to taste. Serve over rice, passing hot sauce separately.

RICE AND BEANS: EL MATRIMONIO

Comfort comes in many forms: warm sunshine on your face, a tender hug, the smells wafting out of your family's kitchen, the full belly that follows. Rice and beans are ubiquitous across Latin America and the Caribbean, with seemingly limitless variations. In Cuban congrí and Jamaican rice and peas, beans and rice are cooked together with aromatics in the same pot. But more often, beans are stewed separately and served atop white rice.

In Puerto Rico, rice and beans are sometimes referred to as a matrimonio (marriage), marking the profound harmony of these two ingredients. This combination nourished me often when I grew up in Atlanta, filling not only my stomach but also my soul, reminding me of my ancestral roots. I grew up in a humble household, and like many similar families, we used mostly processed ingredients. Canned beans, jarred sofrito (a core ingredient in Puerto Rican cuisine), and packets of sazón spice blend formed the base of the beans I started preparing for my family when I was in middle school. I began by heating olive oil in a saucepan and adding the aforementioned convenience ingredients along with tomato sauce, pimento-stuffed olives, and chopped potatoes. My mother's family preferred red kidney beans, whereas my father liked pink beans, the sauce thickened with canned pumpkin.

Today, rice and beans remains the most comforting combination I can imagine. The shortcut ingredients are definitely convenient and have good flavor. But slow-cooking dried beans that are seasoned with homemade sofrito and sazón, studded with fresh calabaza, and served over rice is much closer to what my ancestors made and brings me more satisfaction.

In many ways, Puerto Rican arroz con habichuelas (rice and beans) is an extension of indigenous Taíno and African foodways, with ingredients introduced by colonization that were creatively adapted. Beans and legumes thrive on the land and were an essential component of the Taíno diet. The iconic legumes for arroz con habichuelas are dark red kidney beans, which are known locally as colorá (or habichuelas coloradas). They are larger than other common varieties and have a creamy texture and rich flavor.

Most Puerto Ricans I know are "arroceros"—rice lovers—who will mound their plate with white rice regardless of what they layer it with. Stewed beans can stand on their own. But nothing beats beans and rice. Rice was brought to the island during Spanish colonization and ultimately cultivated by enslaved African workers who brought knowledge of rice cultivation from their native countries. Among the most traditional preparations is arroz con tocino, where white rice is cooked with rendered salt pork and a bit of fresh garlic, adding richness and dimension that enhances the flavor of what it's served with.

I've been preparing the recipes for rice and beans that follow for years, but I've never previously written them down, because they'd become so intuitive. Between the lines of the ingredients and preparation, though, is an archive of history and adaptation and, above all, what tastes good to you.

by Von Diaz

writer; documentary producer exploring the intersections of food, culture, and identity; and author of Coconuts and Collards: Recipes and Stories from Puerto Rico to the Deep South

Habichuelas Guisadas con Calabaza

Serves 4 to 6 ~ Total Time: 1¾ hours, plus 6 hours soaking

This version of Puerto Rican stewed red beans by Von Diaz includes calabaza squash instead of more common potatoes for its flavor and the rich color it adds. While red beans are inherently delicious, sofrito is the foundation of classic habichuelas guisadas. Sofrito, which is European in origin, is traditionally pounded or ground into a paste in Puerto Rico, reflecting indigenous and African influence. It typically contains onions, garlic, bell pepper, and culantro (which is called chadon beni in the Caribbean and sawtooth coriander elsewhere). The sofrito is sautéed in olive oil or lard; for this recipe, using olive oil and jamón de cocinar for extra porky oomph works well.

Tomato sauce, chicken broth, and water slowly cook the dried beans. Pimento-stuffed green olives fill out the beans with balanced pops of sweetness and brininess. A splash of red wine vinegar and some cilantro provide vibrancy and citrusy freshness.

We prefer to use homemade sofrito and sazón here, but you can use store-bought sofrito and/or sazón. If using store-bought products, taste the stew in step 4 before seasoning with salt and vinegar to taste. If you can't find jamón de cocinar, you can substitute an equal volume of chopped ham steak. Calabaza is typically sold precut in Latin and Asian grocery stores. Kabocha, butternut squash, or sugar pumpkin are good substitutes for calabaza (no need to peel the kabocha; butternut and pumpkin should be peeled). Serve with Arroz con Tocino (page 171) or Everyday White Rice (page 160) and with lime wedges, if desired.

8	ounces (1¼ cups) dried red kidney beans, picked over and rinsed	1	bay leaf
2	tablespoons extra-virgin olive oil	1	tablespoon kosher salt
½	cup finely chopped jamón de cocinar (about 4 ounces)	1	pound seeded calabaza squash, cut into 1-inch pieces (2½ cups)
½	cup Sofrito (recipe follows)	½	cup pimento-stuffed green olives
1	tablespoon Sazón (recipe follows)	2	teaspoons red wine vinegar, plus extra for seasoning
1	tablespoon tomato paste	¼	teaspoon pepper
1	(8-ounce) can tomato sauce	½	cup fresh cilantro leaves
2	cups chicken broth		

continued >>

1 Cover beans with at least 2 inches water in large bowl and soak at room temperature for at least 6 hours or up to 24 hours. Drain well.

2 Heat oil in Dutch oven over medium heat until shimmering. Add jamón and cook until lightly browned, 3 to 5 minutes. Stir in sofrito and cook, stirring often, until liquid is evaporated, 3 to 5 minutes.

3 Stir in sazón and tomato paste and cook until mixture begins to darken in color, about 30 seconds. Stir in tomato sauce, scraping up any browned bits. Add broth, 2 cups water, bay leaf, salt, and drained beans. Bring to boil over high heat. Cover, reduce heat to medium-low, and simmer until beans are completely tender but not falling apart, 40 to 50 minutes.

4 Stir in calabaza and olives. Add extra water (up to 1 cup) if liquid has reduced below level of beans. Bring to simmer over medium-high heat. Cover, reduce heat to low, and cook until calabaza is fork-tender but not falling apart, 10 to 15 minutes. Stir in vinegar and pepper. Season with salt and vinegar to taste and sprinkle with cilantro. Serve.

Sofrito

Makes 2¼ cups ~ Total Time: 10 minutes

This recipe is adapted from *Coconuts and Collards* by Von Diaz. For an easy-to-make sofrito we employ the food processor to quickly break down the classic mix of aromatics and herbs. If you can't find ajíes dulces or ajíes amarillos, you can substitute half of a red, orange, or yellow bell pepper. Culantro, also called chadon beni and sawtooth coriander, has long leaves with jagged edges and a stronger, earthier flavor than cilantro. You can find it in the produce section of most Latin markets, as well as in Asian markets. If you can't find culantro, substitute cilantro.

1 red bell pepper, stemmed, seeded, and quartered
3 ajíes dulces or ajíes amarillos, stemmed, seeded, and chopped coarse
6 large garlic cloves, peeled
1 large onion, chopped coarse
6 fresh culantro leaves and tender stems, chopped coarse
6 sprigs fresh cilantro, chopped coarse

Process bell pepper, ajíes dulces, and garlic in large (14-cup) food processor until mixture is smooth, about 1 minute, scraping down sides of bowl as needed. Add onion and process until smooth, about 30 seconds. Add culantro and cilantro and process until herbs are finely minced, about 30 seconds. (Sofrito can be refrigerated for up to 1 week or frozen for up to 3 months.)

Sazón

Makes about ½ cup
Total Time: 5 minutes

This recipe is adapted from *Coconuts and Collards* by Von Diaz. You can find ground annatto in the spice aisle of well-stocked supermarkets, in Latin markets, or online. If you can't find annatto, you can substitute paprika.

2	tablespoons table salt
2	tablespoons ground annatto
1	tablespoon garlic powder
1	tablespoon onion powder
1	tablespoon ground cumin
1	tablespoon ground turmeric
½	teaspoon pepper

Combine all ingredients in bowl. (Sazón can be stored at room temperature for up to 3 months.)

Arroz con Tocino

Serves 4 to 6 ~ Total Time: 1 hour

This garlicky rice that is studded with bits of salty pork is not only intensely satisfying on its own but also makes the perfect accompaniment to Habichuelas Guisadas con Calabaza (page 169). Remove the rind of the salt pork to eliminate the chewy bits and then rinse the pork to tame the saltiness and funk. Cooking the pork over moderate heat keeps it from browning too quickly, allowing ample time for the plentiful fat to fully render. Toasting the rice briefly in the hot liquid fat helps it cook up fluffier. Finally, resting the rice after steaming ensures that each grain is fully cooked and tender throughout. Salt pork can vary in taste and aroma, so rinse it well and pat it dry with a clean towel before dicing, and adjust the salt to taste. If you can't find salt pork, you can substitute diced thick-cut bacon. Note that not all salt pork is sold with its rind on. Any short-grain white rice will work here; this recipe was developed with sushi rice. Do not rinse the rice before cooking as it will retain moisture and become mushy.

5½	ounces salt pork, rind removed, rinsed, patted dry, and chopped into ½-inch pieces
1	teaspoon extra-virgin olive oil
1	large garlic clove, minced
2	cups short-grain white rice
3	cups water

1   Cook salt pork and oil in large saucepan over medium heat, stirring often, until pork is browned and fat has rendered, 7 to 10 minutes. Add garlic and cook until fragrant, about 30 seconds. Add rice and cook, stirring frequently, until edges of grains are translucent, about 2 minutes.

2   Stir in water and bring to boil over high heat. Reduce heat to medium-low and simmer, uncovered, until liquid falls below surface of rice and rice is dotted with small bubbling holes, 7 to 10 minutes.

3   Reduce heat to low, cover, and cook for 17 minutes. Off heat, let rice rest, covered, for at least 10 minutes. Check to ensure rice is fully cooked; if rice is slightly underdone, let sit, covered, until fully tender, 5 to 10 minutes longer. Fluff rice with fork and season with kosher salt to taste. Serve.

Chicken and Shrimp Jambalaya

Serves 6   ~   Total Time: 2 hours

A one-pot meal featuring components and culinary traditions from the multicultural melting pot of Louisiana's history, jambalaya is a delightful mix of African, Spanish, and French cuisines. The dish's similarities to the West African red-hued jollof rice can't be missed, though the combination of sweetness, spice, and smoke makes jambalaya unique to Louisiana and the South. This recipe uses chicken thighs, which not only ensures moist meat but also avoids the need to cut up a whole chicken as is traditionally done. Classic andouille sausage contributes spice and smoke. Simmering the rice in a combination of chicken broth and clam juice adds the requisite brininess of the Creole classic, and some tomato paste boosts the tomato flavor without overwhelming the other components (traditional Cajun versions of this dish omit the tomatoes). Adding the raw shrimp to the pot just 5 minutes before the rice is finished keeps them perfectly tender. To prevent the dish from becoming greasy, remove excess fat from the chicken thighs and trim the skin. Be sure to stir the rice gently when cooking in step 5; aggressive stirring will make the rice gluey.

1¼	pounds bone-in chicken thighs, trimmed
¼	teaspoon table salt
⅛	teaspoon pepper
1	tablespoon extra-virgin olive oil
8	ounces andouille sausage, halved lengthwise and sliced ¼ inch thick
1	onion, chopped fine
1	celery rib, chopped fine
1	red bell pepper, stemmed, seeded, and chopped fine
5	garlic cloves, minced
1	teaspoon minced fresh thyme or ¼ teaspoon dried
¼	teaspoon cayenne pepper
2	teaspoons tomato paste
1½	cups chicken broth
1	(8-ounce) bottle clam juice
1	(14.5-ounce) can diced tomatoes, drained
2	cups long-grain white rice
1	pound large shrimp (26 to 30 per pound), peeled, deveined, and tails removed
3	tablespoons minced fresh parsley

1   Adjust oven rack to middle position and heat oven to 350 degrees. Pat chicken dry with paper towels and sprinkle with salt and pepper.

2   Heat oil in Dutch oven over medium-high heat until just smoking. Brown chicken on both sides, 6 to 8 minutes; transfer to large bowl. Add sausage to fat left in pot and cook until lightly browned, about 5 minutes; transfer to bowl with chicken.

3   Pour off all but 2 tablespoons of fat left in pot. Add onion, celery, and bell pepper and cook until softened, 5 to 7 minutes. Stir in garlic, thyme, and cayenne and cook until fragrant, about 30 seconds. Stir in tomato paste and cook for 1 minute. Stir in broth and clam juice, scraping up any browned bits.

4   Stir in tomatoes, chicken, and sausage with any accumulated juices and bring to simmer. Reduce heat to medium-low, cover, and cook for 20 minutes.

5   Thoroughly stir in rice. Cover, transfer pot to oven, and cook until all of rice is tender and liquid has been absorbed, 20 to 30 minutes, gently stirring rice from bottom of pot to top every 10 minutes.

6   Transfer chicken to carving board. Stir shrimp into rice, cover, and continue to cook in oven until shrimp are opaque throughout, 5 to 7 minutes. Let chicken cool slightly, then pull into large chunks using 2 spoons; discard skin and bones.

7   Gently stir shredded chicken and parsley into rice and season with salt and pepper to taste. Cover and let sit until chicken is heated through, about 5 minutes. Serve.

LEARNING FROM LEAH CHASE

I remember the first time I met Leah Chase. We were both attending an American Dietetic Association meeting in New Orleans. It was the late 1990s, and I had heard about the confident young bride who challenged her in-laws to turn their sandwich shop—a po' boy powerhouse—into a fine dining establishment. Dooky Chase's restaurant defied segregation, becoming a place where jazz greats, such as Duke Ellington, Sarah Vaughan, and Ray Charles, enjoyed legendary meals featuring gumbo z'herbes, shrimp Clemenceau, and Creole jambalaya studded with ham, sausage, and shrimp. During the early 1960s, it was a mecca for mixed-race political gatherings, Freedom Riders, and civil rights leaders, including Dr. Martin Luther King Jr.

But now, the chef and revolutionary, who has been described as a "champion for women," left her usual post in the kitchen, and was chatting with me in the dining room, between visits to customers' tables. We talked about her love of special occasions and fine dining, her passion for community, and the reason why she exhibited Black art in her restaurants—because museums had refused to install the works, she said.

Our relationship grew over the years. We shepherded the Southern Foodways Alliance together, she as its first president. I was her vice president. Devotion to community building, social justice, and culinary excellence were our shared passions. Discussions of faith, ambition, perseverance, and strength framed our relationship. One afternoon, when I volunteered to drive her to mass at the Catholic church on the University of Mississippi campus, she encouraged me to persevere through the trials I was experiencing as I tried to get food industry publishers to invest in my work. These words, which she took from the title of a book for women business owners, have defined my career ever since: "Think like a man. Act like a lady. Work like a dog."

by Toni Tipton-Martin

Gullah Lowcountry Red Rice

Serves 4 to 6   ~   Total Time: 1¾ hours

Gullah Lowcountry red rice, a tomato and pork pilaf (or "purloo" in the Lowcountry) that is similar to West African jollof rice, should be fluffy, with a flavor that's at once rich and bright. Chef Kardea Brown, Charleston-born and of Gullah Geechee descent, says the rice has intense tomato flavor but avoids tasting too acidic thanks to the addition of a dash of sugar. This version starts with a rich base created by rendering the fat from salt pork and browning smoked sausage in that fat. Rinsing the red rice thoroughly removes excess starch that could otherwise turn the finished dish gummy; baking the rice cooks it gently and evenly to ensure it is uniformly fluffy. Pureed fresh tomatoes lend brightness, while tomato paste offers depth and savory complexity. This recipe uses Carolina Gold rice, traditionally cultivated by the Gullah Geechee in the Lowcountry and coveted for its fluffiness and intensely nutty aroma and flavor. We used Rollen's Raw Grains Carolina Gold rice, which you can purchase online at rollensrawgrains.com. Carolina Gold is standard in this dish, but another long-grain white rice can also be used. Look for a fatty piece when purchasing the salt pork so it renders enough fat for sautéing. Note that not all salt pork is sold with its rind on.

1½	cups Carolina Gold rice
2	tomatoes (12 ounces), cored and quartered
4	ounces salt pork, rind removed, rinsed, patted dry, and cut into ½-inch pieces
8	ounces smoked sausage, cut in half lengthwise and sliced ¼ inch thick
1	cup chopped onion
1	cup chopped green bell pepper
¼	cup tomato paste
1¼	cups chicken broth
1	teaspoon sugar (optional)
1	teaspoon pepper
1	teaspoon granulated garlic
½	teaspoon table salt
½	teaspoon onion powder
¼	teaspoon cayenne pepper

1   Adjust oven rack to middle position and heat oven to 350 degrees. Place rice in fine-mesh strainer and rinse under cold running water for 1½ minutes. Shake strainer vigorously to remove all excess water; set aside.

2   Process tomatoes in food processor until smooth, about 30 seconds, scraping down sides of bowl as needed. Transfer tomatoes to liquid measuring cup; you should have 1½ cups (if necessary, spoon off excess or top off with water so that volume equals 1½ cups).

3   Cook salt pork in Dutch oven over medium heat, stirring often, until pork is browned and fat has rendered, 10 to 12 minutes. Increase heat to medium-high, add sausage, and cook until browned, about 3 minutes. Add onion and bell pepper and cook until nearly softened, about 3 minutes. Stir in rice until grains are evenly coated with fat and cook, stirring often, until edges of rice are translucent and vegetables are softened, about 4 minutes. Stir in tomato paste and cook until darkened, about 1 minute.

4   Stir in broth; pureed tomatoes; sugar, if using; pepper; granulated garlic; salt; onion powder; and cayenne and bring to boil, scraping up any browned bits. Cover pot with sheet of aluminum foil, then cover with lid. Transfer to oven; bake for 35 minutes.

5   Remove rice from oven and let stand, covered, for 10 minutes. Fluff rice gently with fork, and let stand, uncovered, for an additional 5 minutes. Serve.

Calas

Serves 8　～　Total Time: 1½ hours, plus 6 hours chilling

In the late 19th century, Creole street vendors sold fresh, hot calas (pronounced ka-LA), announcing their wares with cries of: "Belle calas! Tout chauds!" (which translates to "Beautiful calas! Still hot!"). These small fried cakes were made with readily available ingredients, including boiled and cooled rice, sugar, eggs, and spices. They are similar to Beignets (page 48), which are served with cafe au lait at the French Market, but Calas existed in the shadows where they might have stayed without Poppy Tooker. The author, food historian, and radio host led a crusade in 2013 to "save the calas." She told stories about their history and taught students to make them in cooking classes. Rice growing traditions of West Africa came to the South through the transatlantic slave trade, including making calas. Both emancipated and enslaved women sold calas in French-ruled Louisiana; for the enslaved, selling calas was a vital way to earn money to buy their freedom. The tradition continued after the abolition of slavery, and calas served as an important aspect of Black women's entrepreneurial successes in New Orleans. The fritters are a must-try when in New Orleans. After mixing the batter and letting it rest, be sure to give the bowl a stir, scraping all the way to the bottom to even out the mixture. Some of the calas might flip on their own as they fry. Use a Dutch oven that holds 6 quarts or more.

1	cup long-grain or medium-grain white rice
1⅔	plus cups plus ½ cup water, divided
3	large eggs, lightly beaten
6	tablespoons (2⅔ ounces) sugar
2¼	teaspoons instant or rapid-rise yeast
1	teaspoon table salt
1	teaspoon vanilla extract
¼	teaspoon ground nutmeg
1¼	cups (6¼ ounces) all-purpose flour
2	quarts peanut or vegetable oil for frying
	Confectioners' sugar

1　Place rice in fine-mesh strainer and rinse under running water, agitating rice with your hand every so often, until water running through rice is almost clear, about 1½ minutes. Bring rice and 1⅔ cups water to boil in medium saucepan over high heat, stirring occasionally with rubber spatula to dislodge any rice that sticks to bottom of saucepan. Cover, reduce heat to low, and simmer for 30 minutes.

2　Transfer rice to large bowl and mash with potato masher until most grains have been crushed, about 1 minute. Let cool for 5 minutes. Whisk in remaining ½ cup water, eggs, sugar, yeast, salt, vanilla, and nutmeg until well combined and no lumps of rice larger than ¼ inch remain. Gently fold in flour until just combined. Cover with plastic wrap and refrigerate for at least 6 hours or up to 24 hours.

3　Adjust oven rack to middle position and heat oven to 200 degrees. Set wire rack in rimmed baking sheet and line half of rack with triple layer of paper towels. Add oil to large Dutch oven until it measures about 1½ inches deep and heat over medium-high heat to 375 degrees.

4　Stir batter well. Transfer heaping tablespoon of batter to oil, using second spoon to ease batter out of spoon; repeat portioning until there are 10 calas in oil. Fry until calas are deep golden brown, about 4 minutes, flipping once halfway through frying. Adjust burner, if necessary, to maintain oil temperature between 350 and 375 degrees.

5　Using spider skimmer or slotted spoon, transfer calas to prepared wire rack; roll briefly so paper towels absorb grease. Transfer sheet to oven to keep warm. Return oil to 375 degrees and repeat with remaining batter in 2 batches. Dust calas with confectioners' sugar and serve immediately.

GIVING THE WOMEN WHO MAKE GRITS THEIR DUE

When I set out to write a book about grits, my research—which took me down back roads, into gristmills and home kitchens, through history, and eventually to the plate—led me to many stories about women. The ones who cook and serve grits, the ones who carried the dish through generations, and the ones who mill the corn.

Milling corn is labor-intensive and muscle-wearing. When worked through a stone-on-stone mill, grits maintain a nuanced flavor—earthy, sweet, and of the place the corn is grown. Operating the mill can be a fine dance, putting machinery and user in sync. There are very few women who operate gristmills, maybe a handful here in the South. In Mississippi, there are two, both of whom have their businesses because of Georgeanne Ross.

Ross came to milling almost by accident. Her husband, Freddie, was a tinkerer who collected machines. He showed her how to work a mill and then restored an old Meadows Mill for her. She milled cornmeal at home and gave it away—until it landed in the hands of a Memphis chef, who offered to buy more. Other chefs followed suit and her business grew, reaching more than 60 accounts. She eventually had to take a break and sell her first business when her mother had a stroke. (It still exists and is operated by another woman.) But chefs such as John Currence of Oxford's City Grocery kept calling, and eventually she fired up the mill again, naming the new business The Original Grit Girl.

When I met Ross in 2017, she was training an apprentice, Brittany Barnes, who runs The Original Grit Girl today. Ross told me then, "I want to keep it with the girls, you know?" Hauling 50-pound sacks of corn, running and repairing the mill, packaging—it's tough on the body. Just like standing over the stove, stirring pot after pot of grits.

Women's hands may not dominate the industry of milling, but as I learned in my travels, they are certainly the ones who keep the grits coming.

by Erin Byers Murray

award-winning food writer, author, and cookbook editor, and editor in chief of The Local Palate *magazine, which celebrates the food culture of the South*

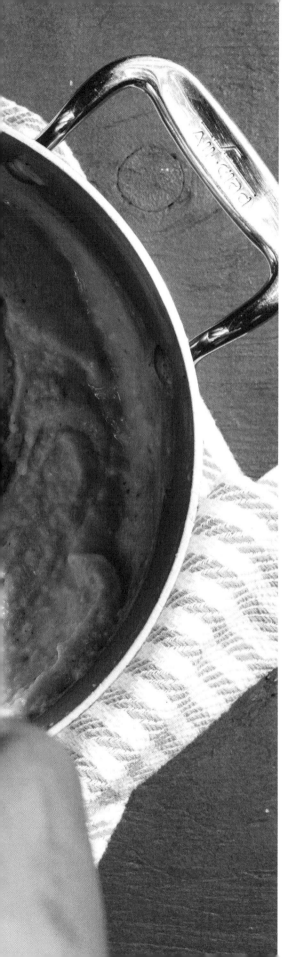

Extra-Cheesy Grits

Serves 4 to 6   ~   Total Time: 45 minutes

Before creamy, hearty grits became a Southern staple, they were known as grist, a dish of nixtamalized corn that Native Americans introduced to European colonists. The stone-ground grain resembled hominy; the Native Americans used it as currency, and they shared its preparation methods with the foreign settlers. Grits became so well loved in the United States that there's an entire region named after them: The "Grits Belt" spans from Texas to Virginia, where grits abound in diners and on weeknight dinner tables alike. In recent history, grits have taken on yet another identity. They've transformed from a simple mixture of water and ground corn to a creamy, savory— and often cheesy—culinary staple. These extra-cheesy grits benefit from flavor-boosting ingredients inspired by macaroni and cheese. Worcestershire sauce, Dijon mustard, and hot sauce add complexity and savoriness, while cooking the grits in a mixture of milk and water provides both creaminess and thorough hydration. Using extra-sharp cheddar and a hint of Parmesan allows the cheesy flavors to shine through. These ultrasavory grits are as flavorful as they are versatile; pair them with bacon and runny eggs for breakfast, spoon them next to a pile of greens (see page 140), or simply enjoy them by the bowlful with extra hot sauce. This recipe uses widely-available supermarket medium-ground grits. If you use more coarsely ground grits, such as the regional brands sold throughout the South, you will need to increase the simmering time in step 1 to about 50 minutes.

2¼   cups whole milk

2   cups water, plus extra for thinning

½   teaspoon table salt

½   teaspoon pepper

1   cup grits

6   ounces extra-sharp cheddar cheese, shredded (1½ cups)

2   ounces Parmesan cheese, grated (1 cup)

2   tablespoons unsalted butter

2   teaspoons Dijon mustard

2   teaspoons hot sauce, plus extra for seasoning

2   teaspoons Worcestershire sauce

1   Bring milk, water, salt, and pepper to boil in medium saucepan over medium-high heat. Slowly whisk in grits. Reduce heat to low, cover, and simmer, whisking often, until grits are thick and creamy, about 25 minutes. (Add extra water, 2 tablespoons at a time, if grits become too stiff while cooking.)

2   Whisk cheddar, Parmesan, butter, mustard, hot sauce, and Worcestershire into grits until cheese is melted, about 1 minute. Off heat, season with salt, pepper, and hot sauce to taste. Serve.

Shrimp and Grits

Serves 4 ~ Total Time: 1 hour 20 minutes

According to Nathalie Dupree, author of an entire cookbook devoted to the dish, "grits are embedded in the region's biracial culture and celebrated in poetry, song, and story." Nonetheless, despite the lauded dish's importance, shrimp and grits weren't a mainstay on Southern restaurant menus until the 1980s, when a slew of male chefs began to tout a revolutionary New Southern cuisine first introduced by Dupree in her 1986 cookbook, *New Southern Cooking*. In reality, the humble dish of sautéed shrimp and creamy grits wasn't a trend; it had always been about the ingenuity of the working class in home kitchens, particularly women, and a reliance on regional ingredients.

Originally called shrimp and hominy, the earliest published recipe for the dish appears in the 1930 book *Two Hundred Years of Charleston Cooking*. People living in Charleston, South Carolina, around this time would have likely eaten their grits with tiny, flavorful "creek shrimp" caught in the nearby creeks and rivers. Shrimpers and everyday citizens alike enjoyed the flavorful combination; as Dupree says, "many hands" (Black, brown, and white) prepared the dish over time. And other cultural groups, including Jewish housewives who served grits with fried salt herring, adapted the recipe to suit their culinary needs.

Shrimp and grits is a hallowed Southern dish, and this homage makes only a few changes to the tried-and-true formula. The grits are not typically toasted in butter first, but doing so coaxes out rich corn flavor. Cooking the grits for a little longer than usual ensures an ultracreamy texture. Making a quick shrimp stock using the shrimp shells gives the sauce deep shrimp flavor. Sautéing the shrimp in the fat

left over from cooking the bacon creates a bold base of flavor and releases some of the shrimp's moisture, so when you stir the shrimp back in at the end to finish cooking through, they won't dilute the sauce.

Grits

3	tablespoons unsalted butter, divided
1	cup grits
2¼	cups whole milk
2	cups water
¾	teaspoon table salt

Shrimp

3	tablespoons unsalted butter, divided
1½	pounds extra-large shrimp (21 to 25 per pound), peeled and deveined, shells reserved
1	tablespoon tomato paste
2¼	cups water
3	slices bacon, cut into ½-inch pieces
1	garlic clove, minced
½	teaspoon table salt
½	teaspoon pepper
2	tablespoons all-purpose flour
1	tablespoon lemon juice
½	teaspoon Tabasco sauce, plus extra for serving
4	scallions, sliced thin

1 **For the grits** Melt 1 tablespoon butter in medium saucepan over medium heat. Add grits and cook, stirring often, until fragrant, about 3 minutes. Add milk, water, and salt. Increase heat to medium-high and bring to boil. Reduce heat to low; cover; and simmer, whisking often, until thick and creamy, about 25 minutes. Off heat, stir in remaining 2 tablespoons butter and season with salt and pepper to taste. Cover to keep warm.

2 **For the shrimp** Meanwhile, melt 1 tablespoon butter in 12-inch nonstick skillet over medium heat. Add reserved shrimp shells and cook, stirring occasionally, until shells are spotty brown, about 7 minutes. Stir in tomato paste and cook for 30 seconds. Add water and bring to boil. Reduce heat to low, cover, and simmer for 5 minutes.

3 Strain shrimp stock through fine-mesh strainer set over bowl, pressing on solids to extract as much liquid as possible; discard solids. You should have about 1½ cups stock (add more water if necessary to equal 1½ cups). Wipe skillet clean with paper towels.

4 Cook bacon in now-empty skillet over medium-low heat until crispy, 7 to 9 minutes. Increase heat to medium-high and stir in shrimp, garlic, salt, and pepper. Cook until edges of shrimp are just beginning to turn pink but shrimp are still translucent in center and not cooked through, about 2 minutes. Transfer shrimp mixture to bowl.

5 Melt 1 tablespoon butter in now-empty skillet over medium-high heat. Whisk in flour and cook for 1 minute. Slowly whisk in shrimp stock until incorporated. Bring to boil, reduce heat to medium-low, and simmer until slightly thickened, about 5 minutes.

6 Stir in shrimp mixture, cover, and cook until shrimp are cooked through, about 3 minutes. Off heat, stir in lemon juice, Tabasco, and remaining 1 tablespoon butter. Season with salt and pepper to taste. Serve shrimp over grits, sprinkled with scallions, passing extra Tabasco separately.

Fried Whole Branzino with Grits

Serves 2 to 4 ~ Total Time: 1¼ hours

This recipe is from Kentuckian Antoinette Johnson, cookbook author and winner of *America's Test Kitchen: The Next Generation*. A clever spin on a Southern classic, it's an example of Johnson's stylish but approachable cooking that honors her roots. To speed preparation, she uses quick-cooking grits. You can also ask your fishmonger to prepare the fish. This recipe calls for sharp white cheddar, but other types of cheddar can be used. Serve with Texas Pete's Hot Sauce. Use a Dutch oven that holds 6 quarts or more.

Branzino

- 2   teaspoons kosher salt
- 2   teaspoons garlic powder
- 1   teaspoon pepper
- ½   teaspoon paprika
- 1   cup all-purpose flour
- 2   (1- to 1½-pound) whole branzino, about 15 inches long, scaled, gutted, gills removed, fins snipped off with scissors
- 2   tablespoons yellow mustard
- 1   quart vegetable oil for frying

Grits

- 2   cups water
- 2   cups heavy cream
- ½   teaspoon kosher salt
- 1   cup quick-cooking grits
- 4   ounces white sharp cheddar cheese, shredded (1 cup)
- 1   ounce Parmesan cheese, grated (½ cup)
- 4   tablespoons unsalted butter, cut into 4 pieces
- 1   teaspoon garlic powder
- 1   teaspoon onion powder
- ¼   teaspoon pepper

   Hot sauce
   Lemon wedges

1 **For the branzino** Adjust oven rack to middle position and heat oven to 200 degrees. Set wire rack in rimmed baking sheet. Combine salt, garlic powder, pepper, and paprika in small bowl. Place flour in shallow dish, add 2 teaspoons spice mixture, and whisk to combine. Rinse each branzino under cold running water and pat dry inside and out with paper towels. Using sharp knife, cut each fish in half crosswise. Make three ½-inch-deep slashes about 1 inch apart along skin sides of each fish. Sprinkle remaining spice mixture evenly over both exterior and interior cavity of each piece. Brush both sides of each piece evenly with ½ tablespoon mustard. Working with 1 piece at a time, coat both sides lightly with flour mixture, shaking off excess, and place on prepared wire rack.

2 Set second wire rack in second rimmed baking sheet. Heat oil in Dutch oven over medium-high heat until it registers 350 degrees. Using tongs, add 1 piece fish to oil, holding for 5 to 10 seconds below surface of oil to set coating before gently releasing into oil. Adjust burner, if necessary, to maintain oil temperature between 350 and 375 degrees. Fry branzino until golden brown, crisp, and registers 140 degrees, 3 to 5 minutes per side. Using 2 spatulas, carefully remove piece from oil and place on prepared wire rack. Season with salt to taste. Transfer fish to oven, return oil to 350 degrees, and repeat with remaining fish.

3 **For the grits** Bring water, cream, and salt to boil in medium saucepan over high heat. Whisk in grits. Cover, reduce heat to low, and cook, whisking occasionally, until grits are tender and have consistency of thick pancake batter, 5 to 7 minutes. Off heat, add cheddar, Parmesan, butter, garlic powder, onion powder, and pepper and stir until cheddar and butter have melted. Season with salt to taste. (Adjust consistency with 1 to 2 tablespoons water as needed). Divide grits evenly among individual plates, spreading into even layer. Place fish on top. Serve, passing hot sauce and lemon wedges separately.

SOUTHERN ROOTS ON SCREEN

Antoinette Johnson is the season 1 winner of *America's Test Kitchen: The Next Generation*, a cooking show featuring home cooks competing to appear on *America's Test Kitchen* and write their own cookbook. Johnson's Southern roots in Kentucky, her family, and motherhood informed her cooking on the show, while also grounding her winding journey of culinary expression.

Nightly family dinners, prepared by her mother, sparked Johnson's interest and adventures in cooking, and she grew determined to learn the tools of the trade. She documented her journey on Instagram, and she explains in her cookbook *Mostly Homemade: 100 Recipes to Help You Save Time and Money While Eating Better* that she had her share of "cooking eras." There was the homestyle Southern era, the plant-based era, and the everything-from-scratch homesteading era, all of which she learned new skills and recipes from. Despite moving through eras, Johnson's culinary voice always comes back to her Southern roots, and she leans toward sharing quick recipes with ingredients of the region.

These recipes took on new meaning when Johnson became a mother. "It's amazing how a pint-size food critic can inspire a whole new perspective on what it means to cook with love and purpose." The responsibility of feeding another mouth at home brought new intentionality to her cooking, she says. This included nutritional considerations and using flavors to please various palates. With all her experience, she was prepared to take her hobby to TV and compete on *The Next Generation*, where she impressed the judges with dishes in her distinctive voice, colored by her history and her life with her daughter, Royce.

At this point Johnson has catered overseas and cooked for huge events, but she might be most proud of having earned the title of family cook at all of her family's Southern gatherings.

No.6
IN THE
STEW
POT

Left to right: Viet-Cajun Shrimp Boil (page 208), Carne Guisada (page 204), Eastern North Carolina Fish Stew (page 207), a chili stand in Haymarket Plaza, San Antonio, 1933 (see page 202), Delta Hot Tamales (page 218).

SOUTHERN COMFORT

Bubbling, steaming, and brimming with goodness, stews conjure comfort. They can be as simple as a seafood boil (see page 208) or as layered as a Brunswick stew (see page 188), but regardless of the contents they are warming and deeply flavorful. These are dishes you typically make at home, as stewing is a cooking method that magically transforms food scraps, tough cuts of meat, and bones from useless to edible, and allows you to stretch ingredients that you might not have quite enough of—such as two strips of bacon, which can be just enough to make a pot of stewed beans special. The feeling is home too. You want to sit with it, hold the bowl in your hands close to your face, spoon it or slurp it, or simply breathe it in.

For me, stews are dishes that uniquely bridge my ancestral and my physical homes. My mother isn't from the South, but that's where she raised me, and so the stews I grew up with were from her native Puerto Rico, such as sancocho, a combination of different meats and starchy vegetables like cassava and plantains. My favorite was asopao, a traditional rice stew of shrimp or chicken seasoned with garlic, oregano and cumin, tomatoes, olives, and capers—simple and satisfying. And so when I encountered Southern jambalaya (see page 172), which is basically a less soupy asopao, I added it to the growing list of dishes that connect the South to the Caribbean.

They are contiguous regions but are considered separate worlds; that said, the relationship between the Caribbean and the South is undeniable. Much more like sister colonies, one fed the other; ingredients and ideas that simmered in the Caribbean were transmitted, informing Southern food and culture. The Caribbean was the terminus through which ingredients from Europe and other global colonies—particularly in Africa and Asia—were cultivated before arriving on the American continent.

Take gumbo (see page 196), which is undoubtedly among Louisiana's most prized dishes: Its history is inextricably tied to the transatlantic slave trade and the African people and ingredients forcibly brought to the United States. While folks today will start with a roux to thicken the stew, okra was the original thickener. In fact, the word "gumbo" is derived from West African terms for okra, and the vegetable itself can be traced back there (see page 351).

The blend of cultures and ingredients in the South made it a region primed for the cultivation of different stews, but just as important is the method itself. Stewing is likely the most popular cooking method on earth as it has an easily replicable formula that can be produced even in the most challenging conditions. The South is, perhaps, an ideal environment for stewing, as a region with a paradoxical propensity for both agricultural abundance and poverty, with the hot temperatures lending themselves to outdoor kitchens and low-and-slow cooking. The ingredients that distinguish stew from soup with their thickening properties—roux or okra or starchy mix-ins such as rice, potatoes, or root vegetables—are trademark of or cultivated in the South. And really, the stew is only as good as the sop; biscuits and cornbread are great on their own, but they're pure magic when paired with thick, rich, flavorful stew.

But perhaps stew's most enduring tie to the South is the communal aspect of the dish, particularly for enslaved people, whom we now affirm as being the primary architects of the Southern culinary lexicon. The dishes they developed stemmed from African traditions, adapted to make the most of limited ingredients in a way that would nourish the most people. To this day, a stew is not a quick meal prepared for one, and unlikely to be prepared on a weekday without substantial prep or a slow cooker.

Like the recipes across this book, we so often associate stews with the women in our lives—in my case, my mother—and with comfort. To comfort is to care, and to perhaps replace a feeling of pain with that of pleasure, of contentment. There are moments in life, well known by BIPOC women, where the weight of the world is more than you can bear, and there's no clear solution. Those are the moments when we need comfort most, and a stew feels like a warm hug from the inside out.

by Von Diaz

writer; documentary producer exploring the intersections of food, culture, and identity; and author of Coconuts and Collards: Recipes and Stories from Puerto Rico to the Deep South

Brunswick Stew

Serves 4 to 6   ~   Total Time: 1½ hours

Brunswick stew is a fixture at many Southern barbecues; it's common to find a pot of the rich, tomato-based stew full of assorted meats and vegetables simmering near smoking pits. Because there is no definitive Brunswick stew, many cooks use it as a kitchen sink dump-all. Writer Roy Blount Jr. famously said, "Brunswick stew is what happens when small mammals carrying ears of corn fall into barbecue pits."

He was joking, of course, but at the root is truth: Brunswick stews vary from town to town and kitchen to kitchen, and they were first made with whatever meats were available, including game. As for town of origin—that will be a forever debate among Brunswick enthusiasts. A historical marker in Brunswick, Virginia points to Jimmy Matthews as the inventor in the early 1800s. Debra Freeman points out in a 2020 article for *Southern Grit* that James "Jimmy" Matthews may have been an enslaved Black man. Meanwhile, many people hold that Brunswick, Georgia, is the birthplace of Brunswick stew. It is also very likely Native Americans were making a similar stew with wild game well before the Southern states were colonized.

We don't take a stand on what defines Brunswick stew, but we think it's a must-know Southern dish, and we aimed to make a simple yet complexly flavored version. We start by browning ketchup to give the sauce depth. We like chicken thighs for their deep flavor and reliably tender meat and kielbasa sausage for its smokiness. Staggering the addition of potatoes, tomatoes, lima beans, and corn to the pot ensures that all the vegetables finish cooking at the same time.

1	tablespoon vegetable oil
1	onion, chopped fine
¾	cup ketchup
4	cups water, divided
2	pounds boneless, skinless chicken thighs, trimmed
1	pound russet potatoes, peeled and cut into ½-inch chunks
8	ounces kielbasa sausage, sliced ¼ inch thick
6–8	tablespoons cider vinegar
2	tablespoons Worcestershire sauce, divided
1	tablespoon yellow mustard
1	teaspoon garlic powder
1	teaspoon table salt
1	teaspoon pepper
¼	teaspoon red pepper flakes
1	cup canned crushed tomatoes
½	cup frozen lima beans
½	cup frozen corn

1   Heat oil in Dutch oven over medium-high heat until shimmering. Add onion and cook until softened, 3 to 5 minutes. Add ketchup and ¼ cup water and cook, stirring frequently, until fond begins to form on bottom of pot and mixture has thickened, about 6 minutes.

2   Add chicken, potatoes, kielbasa, 6 tablespoons vinegar, 1½ tablespoons Worcestershire, mustard, garlic powder, salt, pepper, pepper flakes, and remaining 3¾ cups water and bring to boil. Reduce heat to low, cover, and simmer until potatoes are tender, 30 to 35 minutes, stirring frequently.

3   Transfer chicken to plate and let cool for 5 minutes, then shred into bite-size pieces with 2 forks. While chicken cools, stir tomatoes, lima beans, and corn into stew and continue to simmer, uncovered, for 15 minutes. Stir in shredded chicken and remaining 1½ teaspoons Worcestershire and cook until warmed through, about 2 minutes. Season with salt, pepper, and remaining vinegar (up to 2 tablespoons) to taste. Serve.

STEW STOVES

Most of today's cooks do their cooking in an indoor kitchen, standing at a four-burner cooktop in a stove made of metal and fueled by electricity, induction, or natural gas. This mighty kitchen centerpiece houses a large oven under the stovetop.

Southern women in the colonial era were cooking over wood fires, outdoors and then indoors, while Native American women made bread in freestanding ovens made of clay. Next came indoor kitchens centered on brick or stone fireplaces, often with wood or charcoal ovens built into an adjacent wall. Using various cooking vessels made of glazed clay or cast iron and large spits for roasting meats, cooks in colonial-era kitchens produced an extraordinary range of dishes. The work of wrangling flames was intense, especially for women wearing long, voluminous skirts. Same for the challenges of bending to reach pots suspended over the fire or crouching down to tend to an array of dishes tucked among glowing coals.

For wealthy households such as the Governor's Palace in Williamsburg, Virginia, Hampton House near Baltimore, and Thomas Jefferson's Monticello, one technological solution to these challenges was the stew stove, known in French as a potager. The stew stove was a rectangular masonry box constructed of brick or stone mortared right into the kitchen wall and floor. Built waist-high and with two to eight stew-holes, the stew stove allowed cooks to stand up as they worked, using copper and other delicate cookware to fry, sauté, and season dishes with a finer hand and at the same time. Stew stoves enabled the cook to manage the level of heat much more easily, using grates and trivets of various shapes and heights to elevate a fish poacher or place a copper sauté pan closer to the heat.

Thomas Jefferson included stew stoves in his designs for the initial kitchens in Monticello's South Pavilion, completed in 1770. When Jefferson headed to Paris as the United States minister to France in 1784, he took along young James Hemings, an enslaved member of his household, in order for Hemings to learn the cuisine of France. Hemings returned with a professional batterie de cuisine, featuring copperware for the kitchens at Monticello, and Jefferson began a major renovation of his grand home, which was completed in 1809. The new kitchen included a fine potager with eight stew-holes and a large set kettle that maintained a hot water supply.

According to the Monticello website, archaeologists excavating the South Pavilion have discovered the original kitchen fireplace, along with evidence of a crane to suspend iron cooking pots, a bake oven, at least two generations of kitchen counters (or dressers), and two generations of stew stoves. Dr. Leni Sorensen, who studies, teaches, and cooks early American foods, presents history-themed dinners that feature Mary Randolph's recipes, explore Jefferson's culinary legacy, and demonstrate period cooking in the Monticello kitchen, which includes a stew stove.

by Nancie McDermott

North Carolina food writer, cooking teacher, and author of Southern Soups and Stews: From Burgoo and Gumbo to Etoufée and Fricasse *and 13 other titles*

South Carolina Barbecue Hash

Serves 8 to 10   ~   Total Time: 3 hours

This South Carolina specialty is a far cry from the crispy potato hash you may be acquainted with. The comforting concoction features shreds of pork stewed in a tangy barbecue sauce; it's often served over rice and is somewhere on the spectrum between a stew and a gravy. Traditionally it was made with liver and other organ meats. In her article "Hash, South Carolina's Greatest Contribution to Barbecue Canon, Fading Across Lowcountry" for the *Post and Courier,* Hanna Raskin (see page 281) calls it a "gravy of secondary pig parts."

This classic dish has roots tracing to before the Civil War. It developed out of the customary practices surrounding hog slaughters; the stew, often made by enslaved people, was a way to use every part of the pig, including the head, liver, and other internal organs.

Since it was typically made in large cast-iron pots and could feed crowds, hash was often served at political rallies. And it became a working person's food with hash houses popping up to sell lunch to local mill workers. But as Brunswick Stew (page 188) became more popular, and liver and other organ meats waned in popularity, it became a more localized dish. However, there are still chefs in South Carolina who keep hash on their menus. Some use leftover barbecue beef or pork, grind it, and season it with barbecue sauce (either ketchup- or mustard-based, depending on where in the state you live). Others make something closer to early versions and use liver.

In most parts of South Carolina, hash is considered a side dish to accompany barbecue, not a meal unto itself, but in some restaurants you can order it as a standalone dish. For our version, we braise pork butt in chicken broth, adding chicken livers to give the dish a complex, savory boost. Yellow mustard, Worcestershire sauce, and hot sauce cut through the richness of the pork. Served over white rice, this saucy dish is hard to beat. Instead of chopping the chicken livers by hand, you can use a food processor; it will take about six pulses to get them finely chopped.

3 pounds boneless pork butt roast, trimmed and cut into 1½-inch chunks

4 cups chicken broth

8 ounces chicken livers, trimmed and chopped fine

1 large onion, chopped coarse

6 scallions, cut into 1-inch pieces

3 garlic cloves, peeled

1 tablespoon pepper

2 teaspoons table salt

½ teaspoon cayenne pepper, plus extra for seasoning

1¼ cups yellow mustard

⅓ cup cider vinegar

3 tablespoons packed brown sugar

1 teaspoon hot sauce

1 teaspoon Worcestershire sauce

Everyday White Rice (page 160)

1   Adjust oven rack to lower-middle position and heat oven to 300 degrees. Combine pork, broth, livers, onion, scallions, garlic, pepper, salt, and cayenne in Dutch oven. Bring to boil over high heat. Transfer to oven and cook, uncovered, until fork inserted into pork meets little resistance, 2 to 2½ hours.

2   Transfer pot to stovetop. Using potato masher, mash pork until finely shredded. Stir in mustard, vinegar, sugar, hot sauce, and Worcestershire. Bring to boil over medium-high heat. Reduce heat to medium-low and simmer until slightly thickened, about 10 minutes. Season with salt, pepper, and extra cayenne to taste. Serve over rice.

CELEBRATING THE QUEEN OF CHITLINS

Of the offal eaten in the South, liver might be the most common (see "Breakfast with a Side of Livermush" on page 69), but chitlins tell a story of Southern culinary resourcefulness and innovation. If you're not sure what chitlins (or "chitterlings," as they're more commonly called north of the Mason-Dixon line) are, we're talking about pig intestines.

While dining on pig intestines might deter some, aficionados appreciate their distinctive aroma during cooking—a scent often tempered with heaps of onion. And the cooked dish is equally pungent. Chitlins have a chewy texture with a savory flavor that allows them to take on a lot of the flavorings they're cooked with. They're traditionally boiled or fried, or sometimes stuffed, and jazzed up with apple cider vinegar and hot sauce.

Cooking and eating chitlins comes from the Southern principle of leaving no part of the hog behind. While they were originally eaten mostly by those who needed to stretch a meal, including enslaved and low-income people, they're beloved by many today. In fact, the cultural significance of chitlins is celebrated annually at the Chitlin' Strut in Salley, South Carolina, a festival that's more than half a century old. There's a parade, a hog calling contest, a beauty pageant, a dancing contest for attendees to strut their stuff, and, of course, lots of cooked chitlins.

No one person promotes chitlins more than the self-proclaimed Queen of Chitlins, Shauna Anderson. Chitlin connoisseur and author of *Offal Great: A Memoir from the Queen of Chitlins,* Anderson says in an interview with the *Washington Post* that "she was representing 400 years of slavery and oppression" in her craft. Anderson was born in Washington, DC, to musician parents who were treated as second-class citizens, even at their gigs. Her forebearers were enslaved and then went on to own land in Virginia. Anderson was primarily raised by her grandmother, Virginia Battle, who taught her how to clean and cook chitlins and, thus, taught her empowerment.

Once she grew up, Anderson spent over a decade working for the IRS before opting to sell cleaned chitlins as a way to bring in supplemental income. Cleaning is one of the most intimidating parts of cooking chitlins, so this removed a huge barrier to entry for many people wanting to continue the chitlin cooking tradition. Seeing the demand, she turned her passion for chitlins into her profession. She opened the Chitlin' Market, which sold cleaned, ready-to-cook chitlins. And she went on to start a website with a mail-order component.

In 2003, Anderson donated the records of opening her historic market to the Smithsonian as documents to help showcase African American food and culture. Anderson says, "It [cleaned chitlins] brings the elite, rich and famous together, with the poor and hungry. It has one common bond. Food that was once trashed and buried was dug up, cleaned and cooked for nourishment to the African American slaves. It was survival food."

Unfortunately, the physical market was shut down by the county in 2007 and the location was rezoned to be residential instead of retail. And yet, Anderson continues to champion the renaissance of chitlins from a maligned staple to a celebrated delicacy. Her efforts solidify chitlins as a symbol of cultural pride, honoring the legacy of a dish steeped in resilience.

by Morgan Bolling

Shauna Anderson illustrated in her branding.

Anacostia Community Museum, Smithsonian Institution

Kentucky Burgoo

Serves 4 to 6 ~ Total Time: 3 hours

A Kentucky favorite, burgoo is a hunter's stew, the kind that originally made use of whatever meat—squirrel to rabbit—was caught and vegetables were harvested. It boasts a slowly building heat and a compelling tangy quality. Its flavor isn't a far cry from that of Brunswick Stew (page 188). Nowadays the protein of choice is often mutton (older lamb than what is typically available at the store), which gives the stew a more gamey flavor.

Some attribute burgoo's creation to Gus Jaubert, a Frenchman who fed the stew to soldiers during the Civil War, while others link it to the cooking of formerly enslaved people or trace it to Native American hunting stews. The name "burgoo" is thought to have come from someone mishearing "bird stew" or "barbecue."

For our version, we traveled to Moonlite Bar-B-Q Inn, a restaurant in Owensboro, Kentucky, known in part for their burgoo. The restaurant was originally owned by husband and wife Catherine and Hugh "Pappy" Bosley, who bought it in 1963. On the Moonlite website, their grandson explains that Pappy drove a cab while also holding a job at Fleischman's Distillery. Catherine worked at a different distillery, Glenmore Distillery, as a foreman. Pappy got laid off from Fleischman, so they bought Moonlite for $50,000, in part because it was near Catherine's mother's house. At the time, Moonlite had 30 seats counting the stools nestled under the counter. But under their ownership, it expanded to a 350-seat restaurant, a processing plant, a catering company, and a wholesale and mail-order business for their barbecue and related products. While running the restaurant with her family, Catherine kept the foreman job at Glenmore. She wanted to make sure the family had steady income, just in case. Catherine and Pappy both passed away in 2003, but today their children, grandchildren, and great-grandchildren run the business; four generations have carried on their business prowess.

For burgoo matching the familiar, cozy flavor and meatiness you can get at Moonlite, we made a few adaptations for a home kitchen. We use chicken thighs and lamb shoulder chops—a deviation from the mutton used at Moonlight, but easier to find around the country. Plus, lamb chops are a good stewing cut that becomes nearly as tender as mutton when simmered a long time. Worcestershire sauce adds unusual tang and savory depth, while a healthy dose of black pepper gives it just enough spice. This version includes traditional vegetables: tomatoes, potatoes, corn, and lima beans. We opted for frozen corn and beans to reduce the amount of prep work. A splash of lemon juice at the end brightens the meaty stew. If you can't find lamb shoulder chops, you can substitute 1½ pounds of boneless leg of lamb or boneless beef chuck-eye roast, cut into 1½ inch pieces.

2   pounds bone-in chicken thighs, trimmed

3   pounds lamb shoulder chops (blade or round bone), ½ inch thick, trimmed

1¼   teaspoons pepper, divided

1   teaspoon table salt

1   tablespoon vegetable oil, plus extra as needed

2   onions, chopped

2   tablespoons all-purpose flour

2   garlic cloves, minced

6   cups chicken broth

1   (14.5-ounce) can diced tomatoes

¼   cup Worcestershire sauce

1½   pounds Yukon Gold potatoes, peeled and cut into ½-inch pieces

1½   cups frozen corn

1½   cups frozen baby lima beans

¼   cup lemon juice (2 lemons)

1   Adjust oven rack to lower-middle position and heat oven to 300 degrees. Pat chicken and lamb dry with paper towels and sprinkle with ½ teaspoon pepper and salt. Heat oil in Dutch oven over medium-high heat until just smoking. Cook chicken until browned on both sides, 8 to 10 minutes; transfer to large plate. Pour off all but 1 tablespoon fat from pot and reserve (you should have 2 tablespoons; if necessary, supplement with extra oil). Heat fat left in pot until just smoking. Brown half of chops on both sides, 8 to 10 minutes; transfer to plate. Repeat with 1 tablespoon reserved fat and remaining chops; transfer to plate.

2   Heat remaining 1 tablespoon reserved fat in now-empty pot, add onions, and cook until softened, about 5 minutes. Stir in flour and garlic and cook for 1 minute. Slowly whisk in broth, scraping up any browned bits and smoothing out any lumps. Stir in tomatoes and their juice and Worcestershire and bring to simmer. Nestle chicken and lamb into pot along with any accumulated juices. Cover, transfer pot to oven, and cook until chicken and lamb are very tender and chicken registers at least 195 degrees, about 1½ hours.

3   Transfer chicken and lamb to cutting board, let cool slightly, then shred into bite-size pieces using 2 forks; discard skin and bones.

4   Add potatoes to stew and simmer over medium heat until tender, about 15 minutes. Stir in corn, lima beans, chicken, and lamb and simmer until heated through, about 5 minutes. Stir in lemon juice and remaining ¾ teaspoon pepper and season with salt to taste. Serve.

KENTUCKY DERBY STEW

At the Kentucky Derby, amid the glamor of fancy hats and horse races, a less heralded but equally vital tradition thrives: the serving of burgoo. In an article for Tasting Table, "Burgoo and the Kentucky Derby History," Priya Krishna indicates that this hearty stew, rich in history and flavor, first became intertwined with horse racing in the early 1800s at livestock sales. Beyond animal trading sites, these sales evolved into social and political hubs. Cooks saw an opportunity, and they began making large batches of burgoo to sell to the crowds.

As horse-racing events gained prominence, they naturally inherited the culinary customs of the livestock sales, with burgoo becoming a staple. This tradition was firmly established when the Kentucky Derby started in 1875. Since then, burgoo has been an integral part of the Derby experience. Keeneland Race Course, which hosts Derby qualifiers, has served its unique burgoo recipe since the 1930s, and it turns out upwards of 100 gallons of burgoo each day during race week.

ALL ABOUT BROTH

While some are made simply with water, most stews call for broth. We use mostly chicken broth in these Southern stews. Making chicken broth from scratch is a simple process of gently cooking bones and aromatics in water, and great homemade broth is like liquid gold. It is a building block of flavor that can improve everything you cook—not only stews, but sauces, bean dishes, and more. While you can certainly use store-bought chicken broth for all of the recipes in this book, we've provided a classic, soul-warming recipe to make for stew or to have on hand to deepen all your dishes.

Chicken Broth

Makes 8 cups
Total Time: 5½ hours

This classic broth calls for gently simmering a mix of chicken backs and wings in water for several hours and requires almost no hands-on work. The long, slow simmer helps the bones and meat release both flavor and gelatin, resulting in a full-bodied broth. If you have a large pot (at least 12 quarts), you can double this recipe to make 1 gallon.

4	pounds chicken backs and wings
3½	quarts water
1	onion, chopped
2	bay leaves
2	teaspoons table salt

1   Heat chicken and water in large stockpot or Dutch oven over medium-high heat until boiling, skimming off any scum that rises to surface. Reduce heat to low and simmer gently for 3 hours.

2   Add onion, bay leaves, and salt and continue to simmer for 2 hours.

3   Strain broth through fine-mesh strainer into large pot or container, pressing on solids to extract as much liquid as possible. Discard solids. Let broth settle for about 5 minutes, then skim off fat. (Broth can be refrigerated for up to 4 days or frozen for up to 2 months.)

Freezing Broth

To save extra broth, we either store it in an airtight container in the refrigerator for up to four days or freeze it for up to two months using one of these methods.

Muffin Tin
Divide broth among muffin cups and freeze. Once frozen, transfer broth portions to zipper-lock bag.

Ice Cube Tray
Pour broth into ice cube trays and freeze. After cubes have frozen, transfer them to zipper-lock bag.

Zipper-Lock Bag
Line 4-cup measuring cup with zipper-lock bag; pour in cooled broth. Seal, pressing out air, and lay bag flat to freeze.

Storing and Reheating Stews

As much as you might want to clean up, do not transfer hot foods straight to the refrigerator. This can increase the fridge's internal temperature to unsafe levels, which is dangerous for all the other food stored there. Letting the stew cool on the counter for an hour helps its temperature drop to about 75 degrees, at which point you can transfer it safely to the fridge.

To reheat stews, we prefer to simmer them gently on the stovetop, but a spin in the microwave works, too. Cover the dish to prevent a mess. Note that while most stews freeze just fine, those that contain dairy or pasta do not—the dairy curdles as it freezes, and the pasta turns bloated and mushy. Instead, make and freeze the dish without including the dairy or pasta. After thawing and heating the stew, stir in uncooked pasta and simmer until just tender, or stir in dairy and heat gently until hot (do not boil).

ALL ABOUT ROUX

The French technique of making a roux—cooking fat and flour together—thickens a lot of Southern gravies and stews, giving them body. Here we break down the basics.

Different Types of Roux

In French cooking, roux is often cooked only briefly, to a white, blond, or light brown shade. Butter is often the fat of choice. But in Southern cooking (particularly Cajun and Creole), roux is cooked for a much longer time, to a much darker brown, in order to add a toasty, nutty flavor to dishes. In this case, oil (or bacon fat) is typically employed.

The darker the roux, the more pronounced its flavor, but the darker it gets, the more compromised its thickening power becomes—so it's important to cook roux to the specified color. If you shortchange the cooking time for the dark roux in a gumbo recipe, you'll end up with a gluey, gloppy dish without that deep flavor that characterizes gumbo.

The Right Whisk for Roux

Making a roux shouldn't be scary, but it is serious business—you're whisking hot ingredients in a hot pot, so choosing the right whisk is important. If you have a flat whisk in your kitchen for sauces, you can use it here. But most of us want one whisk for all tasks. Whisks measuring less than 11 inches bring your hand too close to the heat when making a roux or pan sauce in a tall pot. Look for a whisk measuring between 11 inches and 11.5 inches.

Whisks come in a variety of shapes, from narrow French whisks to wide balloon whisks. Something in between, what we call "skinny balloons," with medium-size heads, offer an ideal combination of coverage and maneuverability. They scrape sauce from the perimeters of a pan while covering a good amount of territory in each swoop. (To boot, you can use these all-purpose whisks for all tasks, including baking.)

Finally, count the wire loops. The more wire loops a whisk has, the more even and consistent the coverage it provides. Look for whisks with at least 10 flexible loops.

Balloon Whisk

Skinny Balloon Whisk

Roux Hue

Cook the roux, whisking constantly, until it is the color of milk chocolate.

Getting started

Halfway there

Finished

Smoky Chicken, Sausage, and Shrimp Gumbo

Serves 10 to 14 ~ Total Time: 4¾ hours

Gumbo—the landmark dish that *Mosquito Supper Club: Cajun Recipes from a Disappearing Bayou* author Melissa M. Martin says is "like a religion" in Louisiana—comes from the word for okra ("gombo") in West African languages. It's a full-bodied soup that's thickened in one of three ways: from the naturally gelling mucilage in okra; from filé, a seasoning from ground sassafras tree leaves introduced to gumbo by Chocktaw Native Americans; or from a dark roux (see page 195). It's a "melting pot dish," as Stanley Dry writes in the article "A Short History of Gumbo," published by the Southern Foodways Alliance; it's one that crosses class and regional barriers.

The first documented references to gumbo in the United States appeared at the start of the 19th century. Okra (or ochra) gumbo and okra soup were often interchangeable terms in early African American cookbooks. They were flavored with ham and a rich broth made from simmering beef or poultry bones. Abby Fisher (see page 355) included a recipe for ochra gumbo in her 1881 book, *What Mrs. Fisher Knows About Old Southern Cooking*. Her version's savory and alluring flavor derives from a broth made by boiling a beef shank, and okra is her preferred thickener. Creole chef, cooking teacher, and restaurateur Lena Richard (see "Lena Richard's Gumbo House" on page 199) included a recipe for okra gumbo thickened with both a roux and filé in her 1939 cookbook, though it's uncommon to work all three thickeners into a single pot. Years later, author and TV chef Leah Chase (see page 173), the "Queen of Creole Cuisine," added ham, veal, and sometimes sausage to hers.

For our version, an intensely savory pork-and-chicken stock lays the foundation. We like to use a roux, and we cook the flour dark and fast in preheated oil. The milk chocolate–colored roux gives this gumbo its signature deep, roasted flavor and alluring color. Sourcing Cajun pork products from Louisiana completes the robust, smoky profile.

While this is our recipe, we truly believe the common refrain that "gumbo is personal." Chances are, if you're a Louisianian—whether you're surrounded by brackish bayous on tendrils of land fading into the great gulf or you can trace your Creole ancestry back to the names on crypts in 200-year-old New Orleans cemeteries—you have a family gumbo. You make a version of the one you love so much because that's the one your loved ones made and because their loved ones did too. So, some advice if it's your first time making gumbo: Take your time and enjoy the process. And, after you've made it once, improvise with bits of diced ham or crabmeat until the dish is your own.

You will need a 7-quart or larger Dutch oven or a large, heavy-bottomed stockpot for this recipe. You can substitute 3 pounds of mixed bone-in, skin-on chicken pieces for the whole chicken. Making the roux quickly, as called for here, requires constant attention and whisking, so monitor it closely, and be sure to have your prepped vegetables at the ready. We strongly recommend using good-quality Louisiana andouille and smoked sausage, such as those from Jacob's World Famous Andouille. Bourgeois Meat Market is another good online resource for smoked sausages. In a pinch, you can substitute kielbasa for either or both. The saltiness of the final dish will vary depending on the pork products you use, so liberal seasoning with additional salt before serving may be necessary. We like to serve this gumbo with Crystal Hot Sauce.

continued   >

1	(3-pound) whole chicken, giblets discarded
1¼	cups plus 2 tablespoons vegetable oil, divided
12	cups chicken broth
2	(12-ounce) smoked ham hocks
3	onions (1 halved, 2 chopped), divided
1½	pounds large shrimp (26 to 30 per pound), peeled, deveined, tails removed, and shells reserved
16	garlic cloves (6 smashed, 10 minced), divided
4	bay leaves, divided
1½	cups all-purpose flour
2	green bell peppers, stemmed, seeded, and chopped
3	celery ribs, chopped
1	tablespoon sugar
1	tablespoon Tony Chachere's Original Creole Seasoning
2½	teaspoons pepper
1	teaspoon smoked paprika
1	teaspoon white pepper
1	pound Jacob's World Famous andouille sausage, quartered lengthwise and sliced ½ inch thick
12	sprigs fresh thyme
1	pound Jacob's World Famous smoked sausage, sliced ¼ inch thick
12	ounces fresh or frozen okra, caps trimmed, cut into ½-inch pieces
	Everyday White Rice (page 160)
8	scallions, sliced thin

1   Pat chicken dry inside and out with paper towels. Heat 2 tablespoons oil in 7-quart or larger Dutch oven over medium-high heat until just smoking. Add chicken and cook, turning as needed, until well browned on all sides, 10 to 12 minutes. Add broth, ham hocks, halved onion, reserved shrimp shells, smashed garlic, and 2 bay leaves and bring to simmer over high heat. Reduce heat to low, cover, and simmer until chicken registers at least 160 degrees in breasts and thighs, 40 to 45 minutes.

2   Off heat, transfer chicken to cutting board and let cool slightly. Pull meat from bones, shred into bite-size pieces with 2 forks, and transfer to bowl; refrigerate meat while finishing stock. Add skin and bones to stock and bring to simmer over medium-high heat. Reduce heat to medium-low, cover, and simmer until ham hocks are tender, 1 to 1½ hours.

3   Off heat, transfer ham hocks to cutting board and let cool slightly. Strain stock through fine-mesh strainer set over large bowl (you should have about 12 cups stock; add water as needed to make up the difference). Shred ham hocks into bite-size pieces and transfer to bowl with chicken meat (keep refrigerated); discard skin and bones. Skim excess fat from surface of stock using large spoon or ladle; set aside. (Cooled stock and shredded meats can be refrigerated separately for up to 3 days or frozen for up to 1 month; thaw before using.)

4   Heat remaining 1¼ cups oil in now-empty, dry Dutch oven over medium-high heat until just smoking. Add flour and cook, whisking constantly, until roux is color of milk chocolate, 8 to 14 minutes. (Roux will begin to smoke during final few minutes of cooking.) Reduce heat to medium and add bell peppers, celery, sugar, Creole seasoning, and chopped onions. Cook, stirring and scraping bottom of pot often, until vegetables are softened, about 10 minutes.

5   Stir in pepper, paprika, white pepper, and minced garlic and cook until fragrant, about 2 minutes. Add reserved stock, andouille sausage, thyme sprigs, and remaining 2 bay leaves, scraping up any browned bits. Bring to simmer over medium-high heat. Cover, reduce heat to low, and simmer for 1 hour.

6   Meanwhile, cook smoked sausage in 12-inch nonstick skillet over medium-high heat until browned, 7 to 10 minutes. Using slotted spoon, transfer sausage to plate; set aside.

7   Add okra, shredded chicken and ham, and browned sausage to gumbo and cook, covered, until okra is tender, 20 to 25 minutes. Add shrimp and cook, uncovered, until opaque, about 5 minutes. Off heat, skim excess fat from surface of gumbo. Discard bay leaves and thyme sprigs. Season with salt and pepper to taste. Serve over rice, sprinkled with scallions.

LENA RICHARD'S GUMBO HOUSE: A NEIGHBORHOOD REFUGE AND NATIONALLY CELEBRATED RESTAURANT

In February 1949, Lena Richard's Gumbo House opened to anticipation and applause from the New Orleans community. The restaurant, with just 12 tables, sat on the border of a historically Black middle-class neighborhood in New Orleans and a white one. It was one of the only Black-owned and -operated white-tablecloth restaurants in Jim Crow New Orleans. Some contemporary examples existed, but not many, and those included Dooky Chase's Restaurant and Hayes' Restaurant. The Gumbo House's chef and proprietor, Lena Richard, was a celebrated figure, having published *New Orleans Cook Book* in 1940, which had earned her national attention.

On opening night of the Gumbo House, Richard gave away 110 gallons of her famous gumbo filé, the house specialty. For some, one mouthful of her savory, soupy stew of shrimp, oysters, and crabs was enough to win them over as loyal customers. Soon, she was selling 54 gallons of gumbo a week in addition to the other Creole and Southern dishes on the menu. There was no lack of enthusiasm for her fare. When interviewing with the *New Orleans Item,* Richard told the story of one insatiable Dillard University professor who ate four bowls of gumbo in one sitting. She clarified, "That's about one quart"—a large helping, and proof of his ardor for Richard's cooking.

The Gumbo House was a rare and special place where Black community members could enjoy a restaurant meal—an experience regularly denied to them because of racial segregation laws. Although unjustly barred from the hallowed dining rooms of Antoine's and New Orleans's other renowned white-owned restaurants, Black patrons could gather in the cozy dining room at the Gumbo House knowing that their business was welcome and appreciated, the space imbued with a sense of kinship and community. And just like at Antoine's, they could enjoy oysters Rockefeller—in this case, Lena Richard's famous scalloped oysters that were a menu favorite among diners at the Travis House in Williamsburg, Virginia, where she worked as head chef from 1943 to 1944.

February 2024 marked the 75th anniversary of the opening of Lena Richard's Gumbo House. Through her visionary work there, as well as her inspiring career as a cookbook author, culinary educator, and community advocate, Richard should be remembered as a nationally celebrated culinary authority in the Jim Crow era. She paved the way for the next generation of Black women chefs to pursue their dreams.

by Ashley Rose Young, PhD

historian of the American Food History Project at the Smithsonian's National Museum of American History, specializing in race, ethnicity, and gender in American food culture

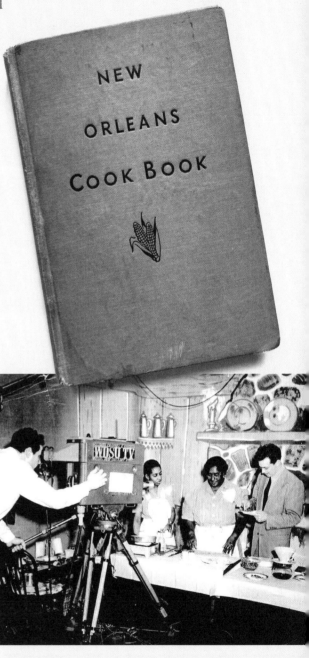

Lena Richard's celebrated cookbook (top). Richards, with her daughter, filming her cooking show that aired on local station WDSU-TV (bottom).

Wikimedia Commons (top) and Newcomb Archive, Vorhoff Library Special Collections, Tulane University (bottom)

Lowcountry Shrimp and Okra Stew

Serves 8 to 10   ~   Total Time: 4 hours 50 minutes

For me, okra and shrimp stew represents home. Its ingredients reflect a wise use of the land and sea, and its cooking methods and simple techniques reveal a cultural wisdom that simmers up both deep flavors and emotions. When I make the thick stew, which is well known in the Carolina Lowcountry, I'm instantly reminded of my childhood home and memories of happily slurping up second helpings. I'm also surprised that so few people outside the region know about the long-simmered, complexly flavored mix of vegetables and seafood. Making okra and shrimp stew takes a bit of time, but the investment is worth it. This is a dish that is meant to be shared among family, friends, and community.

Okra and shrimp stew is a gumbo-style dish, but unlike the more familiar Louisiana-style gumbos (see page 196), our gumbos in the Lowcountry do not rely on a deep-brown roux or filé powder for flavor and texture. Instead, just the bright-green okra, with its sticky, slimy character, serves as a natural thickener. These stews often start with a flavorful, slow-simmered broth or stock made from a large smoked ham bone. Ham stock is a familiar element in African American cookery. In some Lowcountry kitchens, it is common to see a pot of stock simmering all day on the back burner of the stove, ready for use as a flavorful base for hoppin' John, slow-cooked lima beans, and collard greens as well as in soups, stews, and gumbos.

And while some cooks reserve their soups, stews, and gumbos for when the weather is cooler, I grew up eating this meal all year round, served with simple white rice.

If you can find medium shrimp (41 to 50 per pound), use those and leave them whole. Look for meaty ham hocks. If you buy the test kitchen's preferred brand of andouille sausage, Jacob's World Famous Andouille, which tends to be thicker than other products, halve it lengthwise before slicing it crosswise.

by Amethyst Ganaway

chef and food writer specializing in the culture and foodways of the American South and the African diaspora

4	quarts water
1–1¼	pounds smoked ham hocks
1	onion, quartered
1	bay leaf
1	tablespoon vegetable oil
12	ounces andouille sausage, sliced ¼ inch thick
1	pound fresh or frozen okra, caps trimmed, cut into ½-inch pieces
1	(14.5-ounce) can diced tomatoes
1½	cups frozen baby lima beans
4	garlic cloves, minced
2	teaspoons table salt
1	teaspoon pepper
1	teaspoon granulated garlic
1	teaspoon onion powder
½	teaspoon paprika
1	pound large shrimp (26 to 30 per pound), peeled, deveined, and tails removed, cut into thirds
	Everyday White Rice (page 160)

1   Combine water, ham hocks, onion, and bay leaf in large Dutch oven and bring to boil over high heat. Reduce heat to medium-low; cover, with lid slightly ajar; and simmer until ham hocks are fork-tender, 2½ to 3 hours.

2   Off heat, transfer ham hocks to cutting board. Let ham hocks rest until cool enough to handle; discard onion and bay leaf from broth. Transfer broth to large bowl; measure out 8 cups broth (add enough water to equal 8 cups if necessary; reserve any excess for another use). Remove ham from bones, discard bones, and cut ham into bite-size pieces. (Broth and chopped ham can be refrigerated separately for up to 2 days. If fat solidifies on top of broth after chilling, you can discard fat before proceeding, if preferred.)

3   Heat oil in now-empty pot over medium-high heat until shimmering. Add sausage and cook until lightly browned on both sides, about 5 minutes. Add okra, tomatoes and their juice, beans, minced garlic, salt, pepper, granulated garlic, onion powder, paprika, reserved broth, and ham to pot. Bring to boil over high heat.

4   Reduce heat to medium and cook at strong simmer until reduced by about half and thickened to stew-like consistency, 55 minutes to 1 hour 5 minutes, stirring occasionally. Reduce heat to low, stir in shrimp, and cook until shrimp are just cooked through, about 3 minutes. Off heat, season with salt and pepper to taste. Serve over rice.

THE GULLAH INFLUENCE ON LOWCOUNTRY CUISINE

While the marshy, coastal area of South Carolina known as the Lowcountry charms tourists, it offers much more than a beach vacation. Its rich history and cuisine are also worth exploring. The Lowcountry is home to the Gullah, or Gullah Geechee, people. Descendants of West Africans who were sought after for their rice-farming skills and enslaved on coastal plantations on the mainland and throughout the Sea Islands, the Gullah applied African cooking techniques to ingredients that were accessible to them, namely fresh seafood; wild game; and African foods imported during the slave trade, including rice, okra, peanuts, and benne seeds. Many Gullah dishes, such as Frogmore stew, hoppin' John, and shrimp and grits, are now known outside the Lowcountry and eaten throughout the South and beyond.

Chefs, writers, and historians who grew up on Gullah cuisine educate diners and bring recognition to this style of cooking through various endeavors. On TV you may see Gullah cook Kardea Brown. She started a pop-up, New Gullah Supper Club, inspired by her grandmother's and mother's cooking, and now hosts a Food Network show called *Delicious Miss Brown*. Sallie Ann Robinson is a chef, a culinary historian, a sixth-generation Gullah from Daufuskie Island, South Carolina, and the self-proclaimed Gullah Diva. After writing two cookbooks about Gullah cooking, she now runs tours of the island that help fund her nonprofit, Daufuskie Island Gullah Heritage Society, which helps refurbish Gullah homes. Finally, the late Emily Meggett (see page 162) published a cookbook in 2022, *Gullah Geechee Home Cooking* that was a *New York Times* bestseller. Today the Lowcountry remains defined by Gullah cuisine and traditions (they're even celebrated annually at the Original Gullah Festival in Beaufort, South Carolina), which is a testament to the tight-knit Gullah community, and their commitment to carrying on their culture.

THE CHILI QUEENS

In San Antonio from the late 19th to the early 20th centuries, the chili queens stood as iconic local figures, delighting soldiers, residents, drivers, and tourists in this frontier town by serving their spicy dishes in open-air stands, notably the Military Plaza. These Mexican women, who made a living and gained autonomy through serving, were hailed as "ever-attentive, always-jolly, bright, bewitching creatures" by the *Daily Express* in 1894.

The chili-slinging trade was a tremendous effort involving hauling cookware, prepping in the wee hours of the morning, cooking all day, packing up, and doing it all over again. And the vendors didn't serve just chili; the menus at these stands included a range of Mexican dishes, all of which leaned on the flavors of dried and fresh chiles, cumin, and/or coriander. In addition to operating in open-air stalls, some established fondas, or cafes, within their homes.

In *Texas Home Cooking: 400 Terrific and Comforting Recipes Full of Big, Bright Flavors and Loads of Down-Home Goodness*, Cheryl and Bill Jamison write, "The chili queens hawked their goods from stands lining the plaza that was the nighttime hangout of every drifter, drinker, and rowdy in the wide-open San Antonio of the time. These were the customers, and the ladies competed for their favor by flirtation as well as fare. They might pin a rose over your heart, as one did to Stephen Crane, or hint at multiple ways to spice up your life. Whatever the means, the chili queens kept you coming back for more." Then, as San Antonio transformed into commercial hub, chili stands gained national recognition.

However, by the end of the 19th century, city authorities started pushing the chili stands out of the main plazas due to sanitary concerns and urban development. Escalating regulations and dwindling profits led to the closure of most stands by 1943. But their legacy is a testament to the entrepreneurial spirit of the women of San Antonio. In their honor, we offer our Chili con Carne, a Texas chili using meat and no beans.

by Morgan Bolling

Chili con Carne

Serves 6   ~   Total Time: 3½ hours

Chili con carne is a Texas chili that people have strong feelings about: It can't have beans. It should get its flavor and color from dried chiles ground at home. And some people claim it's absolutely not Texas chili if there's tomato, while others say you can add a little for body.

The Aztecs made batches of chili in northern Mexico before the 1500s. Before Texas was part of the United States, the cowboys working on the cattle ranches owned by the Spanish would make chili with lean Longhorn meat, dried chiles, and water. The simmering time and chile flavors made the tough meat more palatable.

We think our version would get the Texas seal of approval. We select dried chiles that are moist and pliant, like dried fruit. Adding bacon lends sweetness and smokiness. Thickening with masa harina (common in Texas chili) or cornstarch helps, too, making for a smoother, softer, and more appealing sauce. And, while we know some Texans won't agree with this call, we include crushed tomatoes for extra body and acidity.

You should count on one-half to a full pound of trimmings from your chuck roast, so start with a four-pound roast to end up with three to three and a half pounds of beef cubes. If you like your chili spicier, use the larger amount of jalapeños. You can also boost the heat with a pinch of cayenne, a dash of hot sauce, or some crumbled pequín chiles near the end of cooking. The chili tastes best if made in advance and reheated. Serve it with warm pinto or kidney beans (since there are definitely no beans in the stew!), cornbread, chips, corn tortillas, tamales, Everyday White Rice (page 160), biscuits, or just plain crackers. Top with any of the following garnishes: chopped fresh cilantro leaves, finely chopped white onion, diced avocado, shredded cheddar or Jack cheese, and/or sour cream.

3   dried ancho chiles, toasted, stemmed, seeded, and ground, or 3 tablespoons ancho chile powder

3   dried New Mexican chiles, toasted, stemmed, seeded, and ground, or 3 tablespoons New Mexican chile powder

2   tablespoons cumin seeds, toasted and ground

2   teaspoons dried oregano, preferably Mexican

7½   cups plus ⅔ cup water, divided

1   (4-pound) boneless beef chuck-eye roast, trimmed and cut into 1-inch cubes

2   teaspoons table salt

8   slices bacon, cut into ¼-inch pieces

1   onion, chopped fine

5   garlic cloves, minced

4–5   small jalapeño chiles, stemmed, seeded, and minced

1   cup canned crushed tomatoes or plain tomato sauce

2   tablespoons lime juice

5   tablespoons masa harina or 3 tablespoons cornstarch

1   Combine ancho chile powder, New Mexican chile powder, cumin, and oregano in small bowl and stir in ½ cup water to form thick paste; set aside. Toss beef cubes with salt; set aside.

2   Cook bacon in large Dutch oven over medium-low heat until fat renders and bacon crisps, about 10 minutes. Remove bacon with slotted spoon to paper towel–lined plate; pour off all but 2 teaspoons fat from pot into small bowl; set aside. Increase heat to medium-high and brown beef on all sides in 4 batches, about 5 minutes per batch, adding up to 2 teaspoons reserved fat to pot as needed. Transfer beef to large bowl. Reduce heat to medium and add 3 tablespoons reserved bacon fat to now-empty pan. Add onion and cook until softened, 5 to 6 minutes. Add garlic and jalapeño and cook until fragrant, about 1 minute. Add chile paste and cook until fragrant, 2 to 3 minutes. Add bacon and browned beef, tomatoes, lime juice, and 7 cups water; bring to simmer. Continue to cook at steady simmer until meat is tender and sauce is dark, rich, and starting to thicken, about 2 hours.

3   Mix masa harina with remaining ⅔ cup water (or cornstarch with 3 tablespoons water) in small bowl to form smooth paste. Stir paste into pot and simmer until thickened, 5 to 10 minutes. Season generously with salt and pepper to taste. Serve immediately or cool slightly, cover, and refrigerate overnight or for up to 5 days. Reheat before serving.

Carne Guisada

Serves 8 to 10 ~ Total Time: 3¼ hours

Carne guisada means "stewed meat." It's a bold and satisfying stew eaten in many Latin American countries. Recipes can vary wildly, but they nearly always include a few core ingredients: beef, broth, chiles, cumin, oregano, tomatoes, bell pepper, and potatoes.

Ours is inspired by the carne guisada we ate at Irma's Original in Houston, Texas. Chef Irma Gonzalez Galvan started a sandwich shop in Houston after her husband was murdered and she needed to support her children. She turned the shop into a Mexican restaurant and decorated the space with her own personal furniture to make it feel homey.

Using a modest amount of liquid and adding some flour gives the dish body, making it equally delicious as a taco filling or served with beans and rice. Note that you are browning only half the beef in step 1. If your Dutch oven holds less than 6 quarts, you may need to brown the beef in batches to avoid overcrowding the pot. This recipe yields enough filling for about 24 tacos.

3	pounds boneless beef chuck-eye roast, trimmed and cut into 1-inch pieces
1½	teaspoons table salt, divided
½	teaspoon pepper
2	tablespoons vegetable oil
2	onions, chopped
2	tablespoons tomato paste
4	garlic cloves, minced
1	tablespoon chili powder
1	tablespoon dried oregano
2	teaspoons ground coriander
1½	teaspoons ground cumin
1	tablespoon all-purpose flour
1	(14.5-ounce) can diced tomatoes, drained
1	cup chicken broth
1	pound Yukon Gold potatoes, peeled and cut into ½-inch pieces
2	green bell peppers, stemmed, seeded, and cut into ¼-inch strips
24	(6-inch) flour tortillas, warmed
	Fresh cilantro leaves
	Lime wedges

1 Adjust oven rack to lower-middle position and heat oven to 325 degrees. Pat beef dry with paper towels and sprinkle with ½ teaspoon salt and pepper. Heat oil in Dutch oven over medium-high heat until just smoking. Add half of beef and cook until browned on all sides, 7 to 10 minutes; transfer to plate.

2 Reduce heat to medium-low, add onions and remaining 1 teaspoon salt to pot, and cook until softened, about 5 minutes. Stir in tomato paste, garlic, chili powder, oregano, coriander, and cumin and cook until fragrant, about 30 seconds. Stir in flour and cook for 1 minute. Stir in tomatoes and broth and bring to simmer, scraping up any browned bits. Stir in all of beef and any accumulated juices. Cover, transfer pot to oven, and cook for 1½ hours.

3 Remove pot from oven and stir in potatoes and bell peppers. Cover, return pot to oven, and continue to cook until beef and potatoes are tender, about 45 minutes longer.

4 Season with salt and pepper to taste. Spoon small amount of stew into center of each tortilla, top with cilantro, and serve with lime wedges.

COOKING IN A WEIRD WORLD

I've worked in restaurants for more than 25 years. First I was a server. Then—because I thought it might suit my interests as a writer—I became a cook. I was in New York. It was the early 2000s. So yes, I was one of a few women in kitchens full of men. But my gender didn't feel like my handicap, the country twang of my accent did. It's not to say that I didn't experience the kind of sexism that people get fired for today. My sous chef at wd~50 told me they only kept me around because I was attractive, and my supervisor at Spice Market named me Delta because he said I looked like a flight attendant in my commis hat. But on both occasions, and pretty much every other time I was made to feel small while working in restaurant kitchens, I was just grateful I didn't get called a redneck.

No matter who we are, we have something to prove. I grew up the youngest of four girls and left home at fourteen to attend an all-female boarding school, so my formative years led me to believe that women ruled the world. I can't mark the moment I knew things to be different, but I can tell you I was thrilled that my father wasn't able to help me move into my dorm at Salem Academy my freshman year. My mom, a soft-spoken Nancy Reagan look-alike, could pass as polished. My dad, who always looked like he had just rolled out of a tobacco field (because he had), could not. Above all else I didn't want my classmates to know I was a country bumpkin before I had the chance to prove them wrong.

That chip on my shoulder softened as I found my footing in not one but two boarding schools, and all but disappeared when I was an undergraduate at NC State. But when I was a fledgling cook in the Big Apple, my insecurities around where I came from reared their head once again. All I wanted was to be taken seriously, but my managers as well as my peers gawked at the way I pronounced certain, impossible to avoid words like "line" (because we cooked on one) or "cooler" (because that's where we stored food). One night I responded to a call for a ticket with "steel working" rather than "still working." The ridicule that followed forced me into a new accent as well as a new kitchen. There I fooled a few people into believing I was from New Zealand, but for the most part things were the same. My work ethic, speed, and finesse on the line were not worth mentioning, but the way I wore my uniform and the way I talked were the punchlines for a lot of jokes.

After a few years of moving laterally between garde manger, sauté, and grill but never moving into leadership in the kitchens where I cooked, I tucked my tail between my legs and moved home. Back in Eastern North Carolina I opened a restaurant that I believed would be a stopgap for me, an opportunity to gain experience and build a nest egg for my next chapter. I never in a million years guessed the restaurant would become a phenomenon and that my accent would be my calling card.

From the beginning we were busy. Guests came from all the little rural communities around Kinston for the spectacle: At the time, people didn't open much of anything in our poor corner of the state, so when a fancy-pants, too-big-for-her-britches chef moved home from New York City to show country folks how to eat, attendance was practically mandatory. No matter how much they complained about the price of dinner, people paid it over and over again to watch me toil, stir, and—on hard nights—shed a few tears in my open kitchen.

Six years in, a childhood friend and I created a PBS series called *A Chef's Life*.

The show told the story of my restaurant through the farmers and traditions that were the foundation for the food we served. It was a big, award-winning hit in the PBS world and as a result my community swelled with pride under its spotlight and I got the opportunity to write books, make more TV, and open more restaurants. These are things you would expect the star of a National TV show to enjoy. For a while I did enjoy them. I was so wrapped up in promoting books, filming specials, and opening new restaurants that I had no idea that as soon as I stepped away from the stove at Chef & the Farmer's, rumors started to fly. Now, more than five years later, the story that stuck, the untruth that people in my town continue to share with anyone who will listen, is that I abandoned my elderly parents, moved to Charleston, and lost custody of my children. I never moved. I am an active and present mom and I am going out to dinner with my parents for their 63rd wedding anniversary tonight.

Part of me thinks that if I were a man on a book tour, a man opening new restaurants, or a man who decided he didn't want to be on TV anymore, my rural community would see me as strategic and successful. How else do you explain how in a matter of media minutes I went from hometown hero to disgraced disappointment by doing nothing but grow my business outside my hometown? Therein lies the answer I guess. My community and I share the same handicap. We live in a place with few opportunities. If you can, you leave. I did once. Who could blame them for believing I'd do it again.

by Vivian Howard

chef and restaurateur, cookbook author, writer, and PBS TV personality from Deep Run, North Carolina

Eastern North Carolina Fish Stew

Serves 8 ~ Total Time: 1¼ hours

When cast-iron stew pots come out of the cabinet in Lenoir County, North Carolina, the safe bet is that a fish stew is on the way. Here's how the food-focused party (referred to as a "fish stew") goes down: First, the cook renders bacon or salt pork in a large pot, then layers in onions, potatoes, and chunks of white fish and adds water, tomato, and red pepper flakes. It's essential to not stir the stew as it cooks to keep the fish from breaking up. A final addition: poached eggs. The stew is ladled into bowls and served with sliced white bread to mop up the spicy broth.

The origins of this egg addition are murky. We asked Kinston, North Carolina, chef Vivian Howard, and she speculated, "A frugal farmer probably went fishing and wanted to stretch the fish he got."

While it's related to a dish called fish muddle that's more common, fish stew itself is not widely known outside of a small area in eastern North Carolina—though Howard has made it a mission to spread the word. She created a program, #FishStewRescue, in which she partnered with other chefs to sell fish stew at their restaurants to raise funds for the local community after Hurricane Matthew brought major destruction to the area in 2016. "Fish stew tells a story of our place in the world, and our resourcefulness, and our hospitality," Howard says in an article for *Garden & Gun* titled "Help Eastern North Carolina with Fish Stew."

If you'd like to make the stew at home, wherever you live, any mild, firm-fleshed white fish, such as bass, rockfish, cod, hake, haddock, or halibut will work well. Serve with soft white sandwich bread or saltines.

6	slices thick-cut bacon, cut into ½-inch-wide strips
2	onions, halved and sliced thin
1½	teaspoons table salt
½	teaspoon red pepper flakes
6	cups water
1	(6-ounce) can tomato paste
1	pound red potatoes, unpeeled, sliced ¼ inch thick
1	bay leaf
1	teaspoon Tabasco sauce, plus extra for serving
2	pounds skinless white fish fillets, 1 to 1½ inches thick, cut into 2-inch chunks
8	large eggs

1 Cook bacon in Dutch oven over medium heat until crispy, 9 to 11 minutes, stirring occasionally. Add onions, salt, and pepper flakes and cook until onions begin to soften, about 5 minutes.

2 Stir in water and tomato paste, scraping up any browned bits. Add potatoes and bay leaf. Increase heat to medium-high and bring to boil. Reduce heat to medium and cook at vigorous simmer for 10 minutes.

3 Reduce heat to medium-low and stir in Tabasco. Nestle fish into stew but do not stir. Crack eggs into stew, spacing them evenly. Cover and cook until eggs are just set, 17 to 22 minutes. Season with salt to taste. Serve, passing extra Tabasco separately.

VIET-CAJUN CULINARY CROSSROADS IN HOUSTON AND NOLA

Viet-Cajun cuisine, a fusion of Vietnamese and Cajun flavors, has become a prominent part of the South's culinary landscape. The end of the Vietnam War in 1975 marked the beginning of a significant migration of Vietnamese refugees to California, Texas, and Louisiana. Drawn to the Gulf Coast's seafood industry due to its resemblance to that of coastal Vietnam, these immigrants quickly became a substantial part of the region's fishing community. According to chef Nini Nguyen in an article for *Food & Wine*, today Vietnamese immigrants make up about one-third of Gulf Coast fishers.

During this initial migration, the Vietnamese community in New Orleans found a familiar sense of home in the city's French Quarter, with its similar coffee culture (see page 478) and humid climate. Many began opening restaurants following the local food customs, meaning they served Cajun or Creole food, not Vietnamese food. Cajun cuisine, originating from South Louisiana, is known for its hearty, rustic dishes such as jambalaya (see page 172) and boudin (see page 158), and is heavily influenced by French Acadian and Southern cooking styles. There is a deep connection to rice and crawfish. On the other hand, Creole cuisine, from New Orleans, is more cosmopolitan, with diverse European, African, and Native American influences.

Today, Houston is known as the epicenter of Viet-Cajun cooking (though New Orleans definitely still has imprints of it). This resulted from two catastrophic events: Hurricane Katrina in 2005 and the Deepwater Horizon oil spill in 2010, both of which resulted in a substantial relocation of the Vietnamese community from New Orleans to Houston. To stand out in this new, bustling city in Texas, Vietnamese cooks developed Viet-Cajun cuisine. This unique blend combines traditional Louisiana dishes with Vietnamese innovation, captivating the tastes of a diverse Texan population.

by Morgan Bolling

Viet-Cajun Shrimp Boil

Serves 10   ~   Total Time: 1¾ hours

One hallmark of Viet-Cajun cuisine in Houston and New Orleans is large seafood boils. Big batches of seafood are flavored with Cajun seasoning as well as aromatics common in Southeast Asia, such as ginger and lemongrass.

This recipe lends itself well to an outdoor cooking setup with a propane burner and large stockpot, but it works indoors too. Note that you will need a stockpot that is 24 quarts or larger for the shrimp boil. If you don't have a large enough pot, you can split the shrimp boil ingredients evenly between two smaller pots. Several large, deep pans or platters can be used instead of the disposable roasting pans.

We use shrimp as opposed to often-used crawfish as they are much easier to source. If possible, purchase extra-large, head-on shrimp that are wild caught in the United States and pick them up as close to party time as is practical. If you can't find head-on shrimp, substitute 6 pounds headless extra-large shrimp. With a seafood boil, freshness and quality are key.

Be sure to use the crab boil seasoning mix that comes as a loose, powdered seasoning blend rather than the kind with whole spices in a net bag. Any smoked sausage (such as andouille or kielbasa) will work in this recipe. Serve with crusty French bread for sopping up the garlic butter.

Shrimp Boil

- 3 pounds small red potatoes, unpeeled
- 2 pounds smoked sausage, cut into 3-inch lengths
- 6 celery ribs, cut into 1-inch pieces
- 2 onions, halved
- 1 cup Zatarain's Crawfish, Shrimp, and Crab Boil
- ½ cup paprika
- ¼ cup cayenne pepper
- ¼ cup celery salt
- ¼ cup table salt
- 3 lemons, halved
- 4 ears corn, husks and silk removed, cut into thirds
- 8 pounds extra-large head-on shrimp

Garlic Butter

- ¼ cup fish sauce
- ¼ cup lime juice (2 limes)
- ¼ cup orange juice
- 8 garlic cloves, smashed and peeled
- 2 (2-inch) pieces ginger, peeled and chopped coarse
- 1 lemongrass stalk, trimmed to bottom 6 inches and chopped coarse
- 24 tablespoons (3 sticks) unsalted butter
- 2 tablespoons Zatarain's Crawfish, Shrimp, and Crab Boil
- 2 tablespoons sugar
- 2 tablespoons lemon pepper seasoning
- 1 tablespoon celery salt
- 2 (18 by 14-inch) disposable aluminum roasting pans

1 **For the shrimp boil** Add 2½ gallons water, potatoes, sausage, celery, onions, crab boil, paprika, cayenne, celery salt, and salt to large stockpot (at least 24 quarts). Squeeze lemon juice into pot, add lemon rinds, and stir to combine ingredients. Bring to boil over high heat. Reduce heat to medium-high and cook until potatoes are fully tender, about 15 minutes. Off heat, add corn and shrimp and let steep until shrimp are cooked through, about 7 minutes.

2 **For the garlic butter** Meanwhile, combine fish sauce, lime juice, and orange juice in bowl; set aside. Process garlic, ginger, and lemongrass in food processor until very finely minced, about 20 seconds, scraping down sides of bowl as needed. Melt butter in large saucepan over medium heat. Add garlic mixture, crab boil, sugar, lemon pepper, and celery salt and cook until sizzling rapidly, about 3 minutes. Remove from heat and set aside.

3 Using spider skimmer, transfer shrimp boil to roasting pans, draining well and discarding lemons and onions. Stir fish sauce mixture into garlic-butter mixture and drizzle evenly over shrimp boil. Stir to coat shrimp boil ingredients in garlic butter. Serve.

Stuffed Turkey Wings

Serves 4 ~ Total Time: 3 hours

Laura's II is a soul food institution in Lafayette, Louisiana, that rose from the ashes, quite literally. Owned by Madonna Broussard, the restaurant is run by three generations of women with family, community, and heirloom recipes at its heart. It was founded by Broussard's grandmother Laura, who opened the original Laura's in her home in 1968. As the city's first plate lunch house, the restaurant appealed to working-class residents, providing a square meal for a good price. Sadly, Laura's home was destroyed in a fire in the 1970s. The legacy continued, however, with Madonna's mother Dorothy and Madonna herself, who later reopened the restaurant as Laura's II.

While the location has changed, the food remains true to Laura's spirit of cooking. The still-packed establishment, complete with a homey dining room and charming windows lined with venetian blinds, serves up a series of decadent entrées inspired by Laura's recipes. In the lineup are crispy pork chops, shrimp fricassee, a luscious gravy, and, most famously, Laura's stuffed turkey wings.

Much like the original version, the wings are a marvel to behold. Two pounds each, golden brown, and braised in their own juices, the dish divorces the poultry from its often-bland reputation. The main source of flavor comes from the area along the drumette, which is "stuffed" with a mixture of garlic cloves and flavor-packed spices. This wing is braised to fall-off-the-bone tenderness in a rich gravy before being served over rice.

Following tradition, the next generation of Broussards is already stepping up in the business, including Madonna's daughter, who spearheads the restaurant's marketing efforts. With their prevailing family spirit and equally steadfast customer base, it's clear why the Broussards fought so hard to establish their restaurant's roots.

For our take on the turkey wings at Laura's, we "stuff" the wings by making slits in the drumettes and flat portions of the separated wings. We then rub them inside and out with a spice mixture of paprika, cayenne, granulated garlic, onion powder, celery salt, salt, and pepper and put halved garlic cloves in the slits. Browning the wings gives them beautiful color, creates flavorful fond in the pot, and tempers the cayenne's raw heat. From there we add a bit of flour to the fat left in the pot to make a caramel-colored roux and then soften a mix of onion, bell pepper, celery (aka the holy trinity), and aromatics in the roux. After their braise in the oven, the wings are fall-off-the-bone tender and draped in an astonishingly complex and delicious gravy.

Serve these as the Broussard women do, with rice (see Everyday White Rice on page 160).

Spice Mix

1¾	teaspoons paprika
1	teaspoon granulated garlic
¾	teaspoon table salt
¾	teaspoon pepper
½	teaspoon onion powder
½	teaspoon celery salt
¼	teaspoon cayenne pepper

Turkey

4	(12- to 16-ounce) whole turkey wings, cut at joints into flats and drumettes, wingtips discarded
12	garlic cloves, peeled (8 halved lengthwise, 4 smashed)
¼	cup vegetable oil
¼	cup all-purpose flour
1	cup finely chopped green bell pepper
1	cup finely chopped onion
¼	cup finely chopped celery
1	tablespoon chopped fresh thyme
3	cups chicken broth

1   **For the spice mix** Combine all ingredients in bowl. Measure out 1½ teaspoons spice mix and set aside.

2   **For the turkey** Adjust oven rack to middle position and heat oven to 300 degrees. Make one 1-inch-long incision, about ½ inch deep, on either side of each drumette bone and one 2-inch-long incision, about ½ inch deep, between bones on underside of each flat. Sprinkle wings inside and out with remaining 4 teaspoons spice mix. Stuff 1 piece halved garlic into each slit of each drumette and 2 pieces into slit of each flat.

3   Heat oil in Dutch oven over medium-high heat until shimmering. Add wings and cook until browned on both sides, about 10 minutes. Transfer wings to plate. Reduce heat to medium and add flour to fat left in pot. Cook, stirring often, until roux is caramel-colored, about 3 minutes.

4   Add bell pepper, onion, celery, thyme, smashed garlic, and reserved spice mix and cook, stirring occasionally and scraping up any browned bits, until vegetables are just beginning to soften, about 5 minutes.

5   Stir in broth and bring to simmer. Nestle wings into broth mixture. Cover, transfer pot to oven, and cook for 1 hour. Remove pot from oven and flip wings. Cover, return pot to oven, and continue to cook until tender, about 45 minutes longer.

6   Transfer wings to clean plate. Bring gravy to boil over high heat and cook until slightly thickened, about 7 minutes. Off heat, season with salt and pepper to taste. Return wings to pot and gently turn to coat with gravy. Serve.

Beef Yakamein

Serves 6   ~   Total Time: 3¼ hours

Yakamein (also known as old sober) is a boldly seasoned, spicy noodle soup of dark broth, noodles, chopped beef, boiled egg, and scallions that's purported to cure even the nastiest of hangovers.

Thanks mostly to the tireless efforts of chef Linda Green, known around New Orleans as the Yakamein Lady, this irresistible brew is becoming increasingly easy to find. In the years since Hurricane Katrina hit in 2005, she's cooked yakamein into a popular resurgence, ladling out her soup to the likes of the late Anthony Bourdain, winning an episode of Food Network's *Chopped*, and garnering profiles in publications such as the *New York Times* and *Rolling Stone*.

Green's yakamein is a fusion of Creole, Asian, and soul food cuisines. Winston Ho, a University of New Orleans graduate student researching Chinese American history, theorizes that yakamein is of Chinese American origin. The dish, he says, "is an improvised noodle soup, which the Cantonese created in the late 1800s from whatever ingredients they could find in North America—spaghetti noodles instead of Chinese noodles for example." So Cantonese restaurants in cities across America (including San Francisco, New Orleans, New York, and Baltimore) were the first to serve yakamein. And some of these places still have Americanized noodle dishes descended from the original Cantonese noodles, such as "yock" or "yock in a box" in southeastern Virginia, among others. The name, spelled many different ways, loosely translates as "an order of noodles." Ho points out that the original Cantonese soup would've been very different from what you can find now in soul food places across New Orleans (yakamein is made with Creole spices and a soy sauce–heavy broth and finished with hot sauce).

When asked about the Chinese influence in New Orleans food in a 2009 interview by chef and food writer Gisele Perez, the famed chef of Dooky Chase's Restaurant and "Queen of Creole Cuisine" Leah Chase (see page 173) explained that Chinese and African Americans commingled their food traditions while living side by side. Yakamein became a dish influenced by the many cultures of the great city of New Orleans.

And so yakamein spread and evolved, from Chinese restaurants in the once-bustling New Orleans Chinatown to their Black patrons and then to Black-owned Creole and soul food bars and restaurants. One such establishment, Bean Brothers Bar, is where Shirley Green, Linda Green's mother and culinary inspiration, sold her yakamein. Shirley passed her closely guarded, wildly popular recipe to Linda. And Linda in turn has served it up for countless others at the jazz festival, in local museums, and at surprise events outside her home. Her efforts have immensely widened yakamein's mysterious appeal.

Linda—who has shared her recipe with only her daughter—continues to guard the family secret. But for those who can't just walk down the street to order a bowl, we quilted together this recipe to make at home.

Smaller chuck-eye roasts (such as the one called for in this recipe) are sometimes sold pre-packaged and labeled as chuck steak. If you can find only chuck roasts larger than 2 pounds, you can ask the butcher to cut a smaller roast for you or cut your own 2-pound roast and freeze the remaining meat for another use. Sriracha or Tabasco can be substituted for the Crystal Hot Sauce, if desired. We developed this recipe with Kikkoman Soy Sauce and Better Than Bouillon Roasted Beef Base. Monosodium glutamate, an umami-enhancing seasoning that gives this yakamein broth a savory boost, is sold under the brand name Ac'cent. Look for it in the spice aisle next to the seasoning salts.

1 (2-pound) boneless beef chuck-eye roast, trimmed

2 teaspoons kosher salt

2 teaspoons pepper

2 tablespoons vegetable oil

1 onion, chopped

1 green bell pepper, stemmed, seeded, and chopped

1 celery rib, chopped

4 garlic cloves, minced

1 tablespoon Tony Chachere's Original Creole Seasoning

1 tablespoon sugar

1 teaspoon onion powder

½ teaspoon Ac'cent (optional)

8 cups beef broth

¼ cup soy sauce, plus extra for serving

12 ounces spaghetti

3 Hard-Cooked Eggs (page 105), halved

6 scallions, sliced ¼ inch thick

   Crystal Hot Sauce

1 Pat beef dry with paper towels and sprinkle with salt and pepper. Heat oil in large Dutch oven over medium-high heat until shimmering. Add beef and cook until well browned on all sides, 8 to 12 minutes. Transfer beef to plate.

2 Add onion, bell pepper, and celery to fat left in pot and cook until softened, 5 to 7 minutes. Add garlic; Creole seasoning; sugar; onion powder; and Ac'cent, if using, and cook until fragrant, about 1 minute. Stir in broth and soy sauce, scraping up any browned bits. Return beef to pot and bring to boil over high heat. Cover, reduce heat to low, and simmer until beef is tender, 1½ to 2 hours.

3 Transfer beef to cutting board and let cool until easy to handle, at least 20 minutes. Use wide spoon to skim excess fat from broth. Set colander over large bowl. Strain broth through colander, pressing on solids to extract all liquid. Discard solids in colander. Return broth to pot; cover and keep warm over low heat.

4 Meanwhile, bring 3 quarts water to boil in large saucepan. Add pasta and cook until fully tender. Drain pasta and return it to saucepan. Cover and set aside.

5 Using chef's knife, chop beef into approximate ¾-inch pieces. Divide pasta evenly among 6 serving bowls. Divide beef, eggs, and scallions evenly among serving bowls on top of pasta. Ladle hot broth into serving bowls to cover pasta (about 1½ cups each). Serve, passing hot sauce and extra soy sauce separately.

Chicken and Pastry

Serves 4 to 6 ~ Total Time: 1¼ hours

We first ate chicken and pastry—a hearty Southern take on chicken soup featuring tender shreds of chicken and chewy strips of pastry in an ultrasavory stock—at Red's Little School House in Grady, Alabama, in 2016, back when it was owned by Debbie Deese. The food there is pure Southern comfort, as is the reincarnated schoolhouse, a relic that functioned as a one-room school from 1910 to 1960 only to be reborn as a restaurant in 1985. Inside are wide-plank floors, some with old-fashioned square-cut nails, which creaked beneath our feet. A dusty chalkboard, framed by portraits of former presidents, lists the day's offerings. Wooden tables and red checkered drapes subtly disguise this building's former identity. And while Deese has retired, the restaurant continues to serve comforting classics such as chicken and pastry.

To prepare a flavorful base for chicken and pastry, we brown chicken thighs before pouring in broth and water. For the soup's trademark pastry dumplings, we take a cue from Edna Lewis's recipe (see "Southern Cooking with Style") and cut the dough into attractive diamonds. Once stirred in and simmered, these diamond-shaped pastries become tender and their starch thickens the soup, giving it a rich, velvety consistency. Keep the root ends of the onion halves intact so the petals don't separate during cooking and the onion is easy to remove from the pot.

1½	cups (7½ ounces) all-purpose flour
2	teaspoons baking powder
½	teaspoon table salt
1	teaspoon pepper, divided
½	cup milk
2	tablespoons unsalted butter, melted, plus 1 tablespoon unsalted butter
2	pounds bone-in chicken thighs, trimmed
4	cups chicken broth
1	cup water
1	onion, peeled and halved through root end
1	celery rib, halved crosswise

1   Combine flour, baking powder, salt, and ½ teaspoon pepper in large bowl. Combine milk and melted butter in second bowl (butter may form clumps). Using rubber spatula, stir milk mixture into flour mixture until just incorporated. Turn dough onto lightly floured counter and knead until no flour streaks remain, about 1 minute. Return dough to large bowl, cover with plastic wrap, and set aside.

2   Pat chicken dry with paper towels and sprinkle with remaining ½ teaspoon pepper. Melt remaining 1 tablespoon butter in Dutch oven over medium-high heat. Add chicken, skin side down, and cook until golden brown, 3 to 5 minutes. Flip chicken and continue to cook until golden brown on second side, 3 to 5 minutes longer.

3   Add broth and water, scraping up any browned bits. Nestle onion and celery into pot and bring to boil. Reduce heat to low, cover, and simmer for 25 minutes.

4   Meanwhile, roll dough into 12-inch square, about ⅛ inch thick. Using pizza cutter or knife, cut dough lengthwise into 1-inch-wide strips, then cut diagonally into 1-inch-wide strips to form diamonds (pieces around edges will not be diamonds; this is OK).

5   Off heat, transfer chicken to plate and let cool slightly. Discard onion and celery. Return broth to boil over medium-high heat and add pastry. Reduce heat to low, cover, and simmer, stirring occasionally, until pastry is tender and puffed, about 15 minutes. While pastry cooks, shred chicken into bite-size pieces with 2 forks; discard skin and bones.

6   Stir chicken into stew and cook, uncovered, until warmed through and stew has thickened slightly, 2 to 4 minutes. Season with salt and pepper to taste. Serve.

SOUTHERN COOKING, WITH STYLE

Edna Lewis in 1971.

John T. Hill

Until Edna Lewis broke her ankle in the 1970s, she didn't have the time to write the cookbook her editor wanted—one infused with her personal story, giving texture, urgency, and humanity to the recipes she hoped to share.

A descendant of formerly enslaved people, Lewis grew up on a subsistence farm in rural Virginia and made a life as a farmer, a seamstress, and a celebrated New York City chef before legendary cookbook editor Judith Jones convinced her to compile her recipes and share her wisdom. After all, what else would she do with herself while her ankle was in a cast?

That book, *The Taste of Country Cooking*, published in 1976, became a cornerstone of the American cookbook shelf; Julia Child, Alice Waters, and Craig Claiborne praised its pure recipes and intimate tone.

At Café Nicholson, the New York restaurant where she cooked in the 1950s, Lewis was known for comforting meals (roast chicken was a specialty) presented with a chic flourish (cheese soufflé on the side). It was this sense of style that inspired her to cut her dumplings into diamond shapes, as we do in our Chicken and Pastry; it's a small bit of elegance in a homespun dish.

Lewis died in 2006, having accomplished the goal she articulated to the *New York Times* in 1989: "As a child in Virginia, I thought all food tasted delicious. After growing up, I didn't think food tasted the same, so it has been my lifelong effort to try and recapture those good flavors of the past." And to present them, with a flourish.

Smothered Chicken

Serves 4   ~   Total Time: 1½ hours

While it may have been called a fricassee or a stew over the centuries, smothered chicken—from the recipe published by Lettice Bryan in *The Kentucky Housewife* in 1839 (see "Smothering: A Timeless Technique") to ours here—is pretty much always made and flavored the same, with a few variations in ingredients and methods. We start with chicken parts rather than a whole bird. We brown the pieces and then shallow-braise them in a savory gravy built from chicken broth, flour, sautéed onions, celery, garlic, and dried sage. A splash of cider vinegar brightens the sauce and helps the chicken's flavor shine. This dish is best served with rice (find Everyday White Rice on page 160), but it's also good with potatoes. You may substitute ground sage for the dried sage leaves, but decrease the amount to ¼ teaspoon.

3   pounds bone-in chicken pieces (split breasts cut in half, drumsticks, and/or thighs), trimmed

1½   teaspoons table salt, divided

¾   teaspoon pepper, divided

½   cup plus 2 tablespoons all-purpose flour, divided

¼   cup vegetable oil

2   onions, chopped fine

2   celery ribs, chopped fine

3   garlic cloves, minced

1   teaspoon dried sage leaves

2   cups chicken broth

1   tablespoon cider vinegar

2   tablespoons minced fresh parsley

1   Pat chicken dry with paper towels and sprinkle with ½ teaspoon salt and ¼ teaspoon pepper. Spread ½ cup flour in shallow dish. Working with 1 piece at a time, dredge chicken in flour, shaking off excess, and transfer to plate.

2   Heat oil in Dutch oven over medium-high heat. Cook half of chicken skin side down until browned, 5 to 8 minutes. Flip chicken and brown on second side, about 5 minutes; transfer to plate. Repeat with remaining chicken; transfer to plate.

3   Pour off all but 2 tablespoons fat and return pot to medium heat. Add onions, celery, remaining 1 teaspoon salt, and remaining ½ teaspoon pepper and cook until softened, 6 to 8 minutes. Stir in garlic, sage, and remaining 2 tablespoons flour and cook until vegetables are well coated with flour and garlic is fragrant, about 1 minute. Whisk in broth, scraping up any browned bits.

4   Nestle chicken into sauce, add any accumulated juices from plate, and bring to boil. Reduce heat to low, cover, and simmer until breasts register 160 degrees and drumsticks/thighs register 175 degrees, 30 to 40 minutes.

5   Transfer chicken to serving dish. Stir vinegar into sauce and season with salt and pepper to taste. Pour sauce over chicken, sprinkle with parsley, and serve.

SMOTHERING: A TIMELESS TECHNIQUE

Fricassee, braise, stew, and smothered are culinary cousins in the hearts and bellies of Southerners. Add in that "smothered" translates to "étouffée" in French, and we have a banquet of closely related, and much beloved, slow-cooking techniques practiced by home cooks.

Although it's challenging to draw a straight line from its inception to the chicken dish we know today, smothering as a technique has been around for ages—it was just called something else. Fricassee appears in print in the 14th century and outlines the process we still identify as smothering: flouring and browning chicken or rabbit in fat, adding a liquid, vegetables, and seasonings, and cooking slowly until tender. Mrs. John Burroughs of Philadelphia recorded a recipe for "A Frickasie" of chicken in 1734, seven years before the first American cookbook was published by Hannah Glasse, *The Art of Cookery Made Plain and Easy*, which contained a recipe "To Make a Brown Fricassee" with rabbits and chickens. The term "fricassee" probably fell out of favor over time, perceived as formal and fussy, and smothered took its place in the Southern vernacular.

Fast-forward 100 years, and we have Lettice Bryan to thank for most likely being the first American to publish a recipe titled Smothered Chicken in a cookbook. *The Kentucky Housewife*, published in 1839, reigns as one of the most thorough early cookbooks printed in the United States, and the first cookbook written in the state.

Bryan, while raising a family of nine children (she went on to raise a total of 14), chronicled more than 1,300 recipes in her popular cookbook. Written for an upper-class woman overseeing "domestics or slaves," her recipes reflect a typical household of the day growing and raising the majority of its food. Prepared in a hearth-centered kitchen, Bryan's recipes were written in the style of the day, which listed ingredients and brief instructions in paragraph form. Her recipe "To Smother Chickens Brown" is as viable today as it was at its creation.

by Cynthia Graubart

James Beard Award–winning cookbook author and culinary television producer

TO SMOTHER CHICKENS BROWN.

Take two half grown chickens, split them open on the backs, and beat them flat with a roller. Season them with salt, pepper, mace, lemon, and sifted sage, and fry them a light brown in lard. Stew some trimmings of beef, veal, or poultry, in a very little water, till the gravy is extracted; then strain the liquid into a sauce-pan, add to it two ounces of butter, two spoonfuls of flour, two minced onions, a small handful of mint, chopped fine, a tea-spoonful of pepper, and a glass of sweet cream; put in your chickens, simmer them a few minutes, and serve up all together.

Lettice Bryan's smothered chicken recipe in her cookbook The Kentucky Housewife.

Library of Congress, Rare Book and Special Collections Division

Delta Hot Tamales

Serves 6 to 8   ~   Total Time: 1¾ hours, plus 30 minutes soaking

Hot tamales—rich, spicy meat wrapped in flavorful corn dough—are a favorite in the Mississippi Delta.

These are a bit different than the Mexican tamales you may first think of, which are wrapped in corn husks and steamed, but they were hugely influenced by Mexican migrant workers helping with the cotton harvest in the Delta in the early 1900s. The dish took new root with a new cooking method—stewing, rather than steaming—to yield a spicy, moist tamale and plenty of cooking liquid to serve with it. Today hot tamales are sold all over the Delta, and they've even inspired a documentary (see "The Mississippi Delta Hot Tamale Trail").

You're unlikely to find Delta-style hot tamales outside Mississippi, though, so we went to the source, following the Hot Tamale Trail from Clarksdale to Greenville and sampling tamales in restaurants, blues clubs, and even people's homes. While the tamales we tasted varied wildly in flavor and texture, the process of making them was similar. You can find versions with pork, turkey, or other meats, but many we tried started with beef—either round, brisket, or ground beef—which was browned with spices and fat (usually lard) before being chilled and then shaped into logs. Most sources began with self-rising cornmeal, combined with spices and mixed into a batter or paste before cooking. After rolling the meat inside the cornmeal or extruding it through a machine to make a corn dog–like cylinder, they rolled the tamales with moistened corn husks (or "shucks").

For our tamales, we got great flavor from ground beef. And, though untraditional, we combine the seasoned stewing liquid with a cornstarch slurry for a glazy sauce. Use a saucepan that holds 4 quarts or more, with at least 5-inch sides. Corn husks can be found in the international aisle of grocery stores or ordered online. You can substitute unsalted butter for the lard.

24	corn husks
1½	tablespoons chili powder
1	tablespoon paprika
1	tablespoon table salt
2	teaspoons ground cumin
2	teaspoons sugar
¾	teaspoon pepper
¾	teaspoon cayenne pepper
2½	cups (12½ ounces) yellow cornmeal
1	tablespoon baking powder
12	tablespoons lard, cut into 12 pieces
½	teaspoon baking soda
1	pound 85 percent lean ground beef
2	garlic cloves, minced
2	tablespoons cornstarch combined with 2 tablespoons cold water

1   Place husks in large bowl and cover with hot water; soak until pliable, about 30 minutes. Combine chili powder, paprika, salt, cumin, sugar, pepper, and cayenne in bowl.

2   While husks are soaking, pulse cornmeal and baking powder in food processor until combined, about 3 pulses. Add lard and 1½ tablespoons spice mixture and pulse to chop lard into small pieces, about 8 pulses. Add 1¼ cups water and process until dough forms, about 30 seconds. Reserve ½ cup cornmeal mixture. Divide remaining cornmeal mixture into 24 equal portions, about 1½ tablespoons each, and place on plate.

3   Dissolve baking soda in 2 tablespoons water in large bowl. Add beef, garlic, reserved ½ cup cornmeal mixture, and 1½ tablespoons spice mixture and knead with your hands until thoroughly combined. Divide meat mixture into 24 equal portions, about 1½ tablespoons each, and place on plate.

4   Remove husks from water and pat dry with dish towel. Working with 1 husk at a time, lay husk on counter, smooth side up, with long side parallel to counter edge and wide end oriented toward right. Using small offset spatula, spread 1 portion of cornmeal mixture in 3½-inch square over lower right corner of husk, flush to bottom edge but leaving ¼-inch border on right edge.

5   Place 1 portion of meat mixture in log across center of cornmeal (end to end), parallel to long side of husk. Roll husk away from you and over meat mixture so cornmeal mixture surrounds meat and forms cylinder; continue rolling to complete tamale. Fold tapered end (left side) of tamale up, leaving top open. Using scissors, trim tapered end of tamale to align with filled end (if tapered end hangs over). Set tamales aside seam side down.

6   Stack tamales on their sides in groups of 6 and tie into bundles with kitchen twine. Add remaining 2 tablespoons spice mixture to large saucepan. Stand tamales, open ends up, in pot (walls of pot should clear tops of tamales). Add about 5½ cups water to pot to come within 1 inch of tops of tamales, being careful not to pour water into tamales.

7   Bring water to boil. Cover, reduce heat to low to maintain gentle simmer, and cook until tamales are firm and beginning to pull away from husks, about 30 minutes. Using tongs and slotted spoon, carefully transfer tamales to serving platter and remove twine.

8   Return liquid to simmer over medium heat. Whisk in cornstarch slurry and cook until slightly thickened, about 1 minute. Serve sauce with tamales.

THE MISSISSIPPI DELTA HOT TAMALE TRAIL

In the 1940s, when the late Elizabeth Scott and her husband, Aaron, started selling tamales from a cart on Nelson Street in Greenville, Mississippi, they went for 20 cents a dozen. Eight decades later, Scott's Hot Tamales is a thriving walk-up and mail-order business, selling a dozen of their legendary Delta-style hot tamales for 14 dollars a pop. Prices may have changed, but Delta tamales are still very much the same—and, to the surprise of many, just barely resemble their Latin American cousins.

Elizabeth Scott's story is part of *The Mississippi Delta Hot Tamale Trail,* a multimedia documentary project published online by the Southern Foodways Alliance in 2005, and just one of many oral histories that help trace the history of what outsiders consider a culinary conundrum.

Most people agree that tamales arrived in the Delta along with Mexican migrant laborers who traveled along the Mississippi River to work the cotton harvests in the early part of the 20th century. For the past century, the keepers of this unique culinary adaptation continue to be primarily Black Deltans who have not only made the dish their own but also established it as an important part of the state's culinary and cultural fabric.

In the Delta, recipes vary slightly from place to place and person to person. Most use beef, but some prefer turkey. Hunting season calls for deer tamales. Past that, Mississippi tamales are surprisingly specific. The basic signifiers of a Delta-style tamale are that they tend to be smaller than Latin American-style tamales; they're not steamed but simmered in a spice-infused water; they have a gritty texture from the use of cornmeal instead of the traditional corn flour or masa; they often have considerably more spice; and they are usually served with juice that is the by-product of simmering. (Fans of Barbara Pope's tamales at the White Front Café in Rosedale know to bring their own containers if they want to take home more of the juice.)

In the spring of 2012, three friends, Valerie Lee, Anne Martin, and Betty Lynn Cameron, affectionately known as the Hot Tamale Mamas, got together to start a tamale festival in Greenville. Then-Mayor Chuck Jordan proclaimed the city as the Hot Tamale Capital of the World, and the first-annual Delta Hot Tamale Festival was held later that fall. Held every October, the festival is still going strong and is the best way to enjoy Mississippi Delta hot tamales and get to know the people who make them.

by Amy C. Evans

artist, writer, and former lead oral historian for the Southern Foodways Alliance whose stories and paintings appear in A Good Meal Is Hard to Find: Storied Recipes from the Deep South, *which she co-wrote with Martha Hall Foose*

No.7
FRIED
& TRUE

Left to right: Puffy Tacos (page 240), One-Batch Fried Chicken (page 224), Crispy Fried Shrimp (page 236), Crab Croquettes (page 234),

THE TASTES OF
SOUTHERN FRIED FOODS
AND THE LEGACIES WORTH KNOWING

Oh, the joy of fried foods, so bad for us, "they" say, and yet so very good—tasty, crispy, succulent, and greasy. For Southern women, past and present, the joy and delight of cooking and eating fried foods have made them a mainstay on household dinner menus—especially on Sundays after worship service. Women have showcased their cooking skills through fried foods—through the layering of flavors and the at-once light and airy and crunchy-crispy textures enveloping chicken, fish, pies, and other tasty treats. Those skills have been a vehicle for women to begin new business ventures. In fact, fried foods made and sold by women, especially Black women, have raised significant funds for houses of worship and have even funded political movements. Yet in earlier days of our society, these women cooks were often relegated to the margins as unimportant, their earnings considered merely "pin money" that contributed little to the overall family economy.

But small bits of pocket change these funds were not. In some cases, this money was the key to economic freedom. Take, for instance, the Gordonsville, Virginia waiter carriers of the late 19th century, a multigenerational group of Black women who transported fried chicken and other foods (fried pies, cakes, boiled eggs, fruit, tea, and coffee, biscuits, sandwiches, fried ham—what a feast!), often on large platters held on their heads, to sell to travelers at the local railroad depot. In an interview during the town's centennial celebration in 1970, Isabella Winston told a reporter for the *Orange County Review* that she was a third-generation waiter carrier, having learned the business from her mother, Maria Wallace. The waiter carriers sold chicken wings and backs for 5 cents while the choicer pieces of meat, the breasts and legs, sold for 10 cents. As the trains pulled into the station, the women would rush to the platform and raise up their platters, selling all their foods. The practice only waned when excessive regulations and the lure of air conditioning forced them to cease competing with local tavern owners.

Many of these women provided better lives for their families. Winston's mother, for example, built their family home from the money she made from her fried chicken enterprise. Another waiter carrier, Hattie Edwards, opened an eatery called Hattie's Inn, where she sold sodas, candies, cakes, and pies to people looking to socialize and hang out. She also served the community by feeding those in need, using her restaurant's leftovers. Several other Black women like Winston and Edwards listed themselves in the census as chicken vendors and indicated they were "head of household," residing in properties they either rented or owned.

Very few early entrepreneurial experiences of Black women—or any women for that matter—have been documented. In this way, the Gordonsville women are notable. Though it was relatively common to find women selling foodstuffs at most every small-town whistle-stop, we still only have a smattering of their stories. We should know more, for example, about Black women like the photographed unknown "negro girl in the most tawdry slip [sic] and of extreme vulgarity" who offered "at the [Richmond, Virginia] station rolls & chicken legs." Or Julia Brown, along with her daughter Lizzie, of Corinth, Mississippi, who sold fried chicken and fruit-pie lunches. These and many more women formed the bedrock for later Black Southern women like Georgia Gilmore (see page 419) of Montgomery, Alabama,

who sold fried chicken, fish, and pork chop sandwiches, pound cakes, sweet potato pies, and other goodies to raise funds to support the Montgomery bus boycott during the Civil Rights Movement.

Because the Black woman who sold fried and other foods for capital did not accumulate the type of wealth that would be documented in primary sources like county and municipal deed records, tax assessments, records, wills, inventories, or succession records, their achievements often go unremarked upon and are largely dismissed. But the life experiences of the Gordonsville waiter carriers—Bella Winston, Maria Wallace, Laura Swift, Lucy Washington, Frances Taylor, Adeline Daniel, Hattie Edwards, and Mary Vest—and many others like them form a narrative about Black Southern women's uses of fried foods that is worth knowing.

by Psyche A. Williams-Forson, PhD

scholar of African American food and foodways, and author of several books, including Building Houses Out of Chicken Legs: Black Women, Food, and Power

One-Batch Fried Chicken

Serves 4 ~ Total Time: 1 hour,
plus 2 hours brining and chilling

This is a great starter recipe for anyone wanting to try their hand at frying bone-in chicken for the first time. It teaches basic principles you can reference when pursuing other fried chicken recipes.

Brining is a way to flavor the chicken deeply and ensure it will stay moist through high-heat frying, and it's a favorite technique of many Southern cooks. This chicken is soaked in a mixture of buttermilk and salt. But that's not where the seasoning ends: As a nod to an old KFC marketing slogan that claimed the chicken was made with 11 herbs and spices, we add Italian seasoning (dried oregano, thyme, basil, rosemary, and sage), granulated garlic, ground ginger, celery salt, and both white and black pepper to the dredging flour. A little bit of baking powder in the flour mix keeps the coating crunchy, not tough.

Once the chicken is brined and the dredge mixed up, we rub several tablespoons of buttermilk into the seasoned flour to create a shaggy coating that, after a rest on the chicken in the refrigerator, adheres nicely to the skin and fries up into a satisfying, crunchy crust. This chicken cooks nice and fast in one batch. Covering the pot for the first half of the cooking time allows the oil, which drops in temperature when the chicken is added, to quickly heat up again. Letting the pieces fry undisturbed for a while before turning them allows the coating to set almost entirely around each piece. And there you go: a one-batch recipe for fried chicken that's easy enough for a beginner but tastes like it was made by an expert. Use a Dutch oven that holds 6 quarts or more. To take the temperature of the chicken pieces, take them out of the oil and place them on a plate; this is the safest way and provides the most accurate reading.

Chicken

2	cups buttermilk for brining
1	tablespoon table salt for brining
3	pounds bone-in chicken pieces (2 split breasts cut in half crosswise, 2 drumsticks, and 2 thighs), trimmed
1½	quarts peanut or vegetable oil for frying

Coating

3	cups all-purpose flour
3	tablespoons white pepper
1	tablespoon pepper
1	tablespoon celery salt
1	tablespoon granulated garlic
1	tablespoon ground ginger
1	tablespoon Italian seasoning
1	tablespoon baking powder
½	teaspoon table salt
6	tablespoons buttermilk

1   **For the chicken** Whisk buttermilk and salt in large bowl until salt is dissolved. Submerge chicken in buttermilk mixture. Cover and refrigerate for at least 1 hour or up to 24 hours.

2   **For the coating** Whisk flour, white pepper, pepper, celery salt, granulated garlic, ginger, Italian seasoning, baking powder, and salt together in large bowl. Add buttermilk and, using your fingers, rub flour mixture and buttermilk together until craggy bits form.

3   Set wire rack in rimmed baking sheet. Working with 2 pieces of chicken at a time, remove from buttermilk mixture, allowing excess to drip off, then drop into flour mixture, turning to thoroughly coat and pressing to adhere. Transfer to prepared rack, skin side up. Refrigerate, uncovered, for at least 1 hour or up to 2 hours.

4   Set second wire rack in second rimmed baking sheet and line with triple layer of paper towels. Add oil to large Dutch oven until it measures about 1 inch deep and heat over medium-high heat to 350 degrees. Add all chicken to oil, skin side down, in single layer (some slight overlap is OK) so that pieces are mostly submerged. Cover and fry for 10 minutes, rotating pot 180 degrees after 5 minutes. Adjust burner, if necessary, to maintain oil temperature around 300 degrees.

5   Uncover pot (chicken will be golden on sides and bottom but unset and gray on top) and carefully flip chicken. Continue to fry, uncovered, until chicken is golden brown and breasts register 160 degrees and drumsticks/thighs register 175 degrees, 7 to 9 minutes longer. (Remove pieces from pot as they reach correct temperature.) Transfer chicken to paper towel–lined rack and let cool for 10 minutes. Serve.

BRINE BEFORE YOU FRY

Poultry loses moisture when it's cooked, so brining—soaking meat in salinated water or other liquids such as buttermilk (for flavor)—can be a great way to keep it from drying out. Brining not only seasons the meat but also promotes a change in the structure of its muscle proteins. As the salt is drawn into the meat, the protein structure of the meat is altered, creating gaps that increase its ability to hold on to water and stay juicy and tender during high-heat frying. To brine, dissolve the salt called for in water or buttermilk in a container large enough to hold the brine and chicken. Submerge the meat completely in the brine. Cover and refrigerate, following the times in the recipe (do not brine for longer or the meat will become overly salty). Remove the meat from the brine and get to coating!

THE BEST
FRIED CHICKEN

In 2005, Willie Mae's Restaurant earned the prestigious America's Classic Award from the James Beard Foundation, in large part because of the restaurant's popular fried chicken. The recipe is carefully guarded and many cooks have tried to re-create it. Most agree the chicken is based on a wet and highly seasoned batter that produces what is often described as a "shatteringly crisp" crust.

For nearly 50 years, Willie Mae Seaton, who originally established the business in 1957 as a bar, barbershop, and beauty salon in New Orleans's historic Tremé neighborhood, eluded guests and critics alike who tried to crack the code on her secret recipe.

Unfortunately, Hurricane Katrina caused severe damage to Willie Mae's and the local icon closed. It reopened in 2007 with the help of the Southern Foodways Alliance and other organizations. After that, the Food Network and Travel Channel ordained Willie Mae's recipe "America's Best Fried Chicken," according to the Willie Mae's Restaurant website.

Seaton passed away in 2015 at age 99, but her great-granddaughter, Kerry Seaton Stewart, keeps Willie Mae's legacy alive. She has taken the reins of the operation in New Orleans and also heads up a Willie Mae's outpost in Venice, California. And, if the restaurants aren't enough of a testament to the appeal of her crisp fried chicken, Goldbelly, the online food delivery company, satisfies cravings for Willie Mae's chicken and several Southern side dishes for hungry diners nationwide.

by Toni Tipton-Martin

Lard-Fried Chicken

Serves 4 ~ Total Time: 1¼ hours, plus 30 minutes chilling

The practice of frying chicken in pork fat has been popular in Southern cooking for centuries; in fact, Mary Randolph's (see page 17) 1824 fried chicken recipe calls for cooking in bubbling-hot lard. Cooks have taken spins on this fat-flavoring concept ever since. In 2003, Edna Lewis partnered with Alabama-born chef Scott Peacock to publish *The Gift of Southern Cooking*. The book contains Lewis's recipe for Southern pan-fried chicken, which blends fried chicken styles typical in both Virginia and Alabama. The chicken is first brined and then soaked in buttermilk—the Alabama part. Then Lewis inserts her signature Virginia style by adding a bit of country ham cooked in butter to the frying lard. The result is fried chicken that's extra rich and savory.

Our lard-fried chicken has a light yet substantial crust that comes from dipping the chicken pieces in flour, then water, and then back in flour. It's important to keep the lard between 300 and 325 degrees to ensure that the coating on the chicken becomes golden brown all over and doesn't develop any off-flavors (which can happen when lard is heated to higher temperatures). Draining the fried chicken on paper towels ensures the savory chicken isn't greasy.

Lard isn't the only animal fat you can use to fry, and Tiffany Derry fries everything—including her famous chicken—in duck fat at her restaurant Roots Chicken Shak in Plano, Texas. She's served the ultraflavorful chicken at the White House twice. If you feel so inclined to follow Derry's lead, swap out the lard for an equal amount of duck fat. Use a Dutch oven that holds 6 quarts or more.

3	pounds bone-in chicken pieces (2 split breasts cut in half crosswise, 2 drumsticks, and 2 thighs), trimmed
5	teaspoons kosher salt, divided
1	tablespoon pepper
1½	cups all-purpose flour
1½	teaspoons baking powder
4	cups water
2	pounds lard for frying

1 Sprinkle chicken all over with 2 teaspoons salt and pepper. Whisk flour, baking powder, and remaining 1 tablespoon salt in large bowl until combined. Place water in medium bowl.

2 Working with 1 piece of chicken at a time, dredge chicken in flour mixture, shaking off excess; dunk in water, letting excess drip off; then dredge again in flour mixture, pressing to adhere. Transfer to large plate and refrigerate, uncovered, for at least 30 minutes or up to 2 hours.

3 Set wire rack in rimmed baking sheet and line half of rack with triple layer of paper towels. Melt lard in large Dutch oven and heat over medium-high heat to 350 degrees. Add all chicken to lard, skin side down, in single layer (some slight overlap is OK) so pieces are mostly submerged. Fry for 10 minutes, rotating pot 180 degrees after 5 minutes. Adjust burner, if necessary, to maintain oil temperature between 300 and 325 degrees.

4 Carefully flip chicken and continue to fry until golden brown and breasts register 160 degrees and drumsticks/thighs register 175 degrees, 5 to 9 minutes longer. (Remove pieces from pot as they reach correct temperature.) Transfer chicken to paper towel–lined side of prepared rack and drain for about 10 seconds per side, then move to unlined side of rack. Let cool for 10 minutes. Serve.

North Carolina Dipped Fried Chicken

Serves 4 ~ Total Time: 1½ hours, plus 1½ hours brining and chilling

When we tried dipped chicken, a North Carolina style of fried chicken, at Frankie's Chicken Shack (see "Keys to the (Fried Chicken) Kingdom"), we knew we needed to dip into this recipe. The chicken features a deeply seasoned, craggy coating that stays crunchy even after the chicken's signature dip in a spicy red sauce that has the tangy notes of a North Carolina barbecue sauce (see page 332). One sauce essential: Texas Pete Original Hot Sauce (which is actually a North Carolina specialty). For our version, we combine the hot sauce with Worcestershire sauce, oil, molasses (to balance the heat), and cider vinegar. We deep-fry in 350-degree peanut oil until the coating is crispy; we then dip the sog-proofed chicken in the sauce. Use a Dutch oven that holds 6 quarts or more. You'll need one 12-ounce bottle of Texas Pete Original Hot Sauce for this recipe.

Chicken

- ½ cup table salt for brining
- ¼ cup sugar for brining
- 3 pounds bone-in chicken pieces (split breasts cut in half crosswise, drumsticks, thighs, and/or wings), trimmed
- 1¼ cups all-purpose flour
- ¾ cup cornstarch
- 2 teaspoons pepper
- 1 teaspoon table salt
- 1 teaspoon granulated garlic
- 1 teaspoon baking powder
- 3 quarts peanut or vegetable oil for frying

Sauce

- 1¼ cups Texas Pete Original Hot Sauce
- 5 tablespoons Worcestershire sauce
- 5 tablespoons peanut or vegetable oil
- 2 tablespoons molasses
- 1 tablespoon cider vinegar

1 **For the chicken** Whisk 2 quarts cold water, ½ cup salt, and sugar in large bowl until salt and sugar are dissolved. Submerge chicken in brine, cover, and refrigerate for at least 1 hour or up to 4 hours.

2 Whisk flour, cornstarch, pepper, salt, granulated garlic, and baking powder together in large bowl. Add 2 tablespoons water to flour mixture; using your fingers, rub flour mixture and water together until water is evenly incorporated and shaggy pieces of dough form.

3 Set wire rack in rimmed baking sheet. Working with 1 piece of chicken at a time, remove from brine, letting excess drip off; dredge chicken in flour mixture, pressing to adhere. Transfer to prepared rack. Refrigerate chicken, uncovered, for at least 30 minutes or up to 2 hours.

4 Set second wire rack in second rimmed baking sheet and line half of rack with triple layer of paper towels. Add oil to large Dutch oven until it measures 2 inches deep and heat over medium-high heat to 350 degrees. Add half of chicken to pot, skin side down, and fry until breasts register 160 degrees and drumsticks/thighs/wings register 175 degrees, 13 to 16 minutes. (Remove pieces from pot as they reach correct temperature.) Adjust burner, if necessary, to maintain oil temperature between 325 and 350 degrees.

5 Transfer chicken to paper towel–lined side of prepared rack. Let chicken drain on each side for 30 seconds, then move to unlined side of rack. Return oil to 350 degrees and repeat with remaining chicken. Let chicken cool for 10 minutes.

6 **For the sauce** Meanwhile, whisk all ingredients together in bowl. Microwave, covered, until hot, about 2 minutes, stirring halfway through microwaving.

7 Dip chicken in sauce, then transfer to shallow platter. Spoon any remaining sauce over top. Serve.

KEYS TO THE (FRIED CHICKEN) KINGDOM

Linda Dillard delights in sharing the history of dipped chicken, made famous by her parents. Her late father, Benjamin Franklin Cureton Sr. started a burger and dog business in Salisbury, North Carolina, in 1942. Fried chicken was only an afterthought. But the chicken soon proved to be the most popular item on the menu, and the business came to be known as Frankie's Chicken Shack—"Frank's" to locals. To keep up with demand, Cureton needed to fry some chicken well before the customers arrived, and he looked for a way to keep the chicken warm. Cureton's wife, Nannie Mae Stevenson-Cureton, suggested rewarming the chicken in a sauce and developed the hot, vinegary concoction ("dip") that became their trademark. Stirred together in 5-gallon buckets, the dip, Dillard says, was called "the keys to the kingdom." So protective of the recipe was the family that when it was time for Dillard's brother, Benjamin Franklin Cureton Jr., to learn it himself, he grabbed a pencil and paper, but his mother was quick to tell him that the secret formula must never be written down, only memorized.

Frankie's fame spread well beyond Salisbury. Even Duke Ellington and his musicians stopped by whenever they were in town. In 1986, Cureton Sr. handed over the business to Dillard and her brother, who ran it for another 18 years. The business eventually closed for good in 2004.

Today, Dillard makes her chicken by coating pieces with seasoned flour and then dropping them into the oil with the kind of confidence that only 40 years of frying chicken can produce. She needs no timer to know when it's done. After pulling them out of the oil, she pours the hot, spicy dip over the craggy pieces of chicken, and the sharp aroma of vinegar cuts the air.

Nashville Hot Fried Chicken

Serves 4 to 6 ~ Total Time: 1½ hours, plus 30 minutes brining

Nashville's hot fried chicken has become a popular phenomenon outside of the city for those chasing heat via lip-burning sauce brushed on crunchy-coated chicken. To make the famous, sweat-inducing treat at home, we "bloom" dried spices (cook them in oil for a short period) to bring out their complexity. This includes a hefty dose of cayenne pepper, and a healthy amount of hot sauce in the brine to flavor the chicken from the start. If you want even more fire, we offer an extra-hot version that mimics the Nashville original (it's not our default since it's definitely not for the faint of heart). Chicken quarters take longer to cook than smaller pieces. To ensure that the exterior doesn't burn before the inside cooks through, keep the oil temperature between 300 and 325 degrees while the chicken is frying. Use a Dutch oven that holds 6 quarts or more.

½	cup hot sauce for brining
½	cup table salt for brining
½	cup sugar for brining
1	(3½- to 4-pound) whole chicken, giblets discarded, quartered
3	tablespoons peanut or vegetable oil
1	tablespoon cayenne pepper
1	teaspoon table salt, divided
½	teaspoon paprika
½	teaspoon sugar
¼	teaspoon garlic powder
2	cups all-purpose flour
½	teaspoon pepper
3	quarts peanut or vegetable oil for frying

1   Whisk 2 quarts cold water, hot sauce, ½ cup salt, and ½ cup sugar in large bowl until salt and sugar dissolve. Submerge chicken in brine, cover, and refrigerate for at least 30 minutes or up to 1 hour.

2   Heat 3 tablespoons oil in small saucepan over medium heat until shimmering. Add cayenne, ½ teaspoon salt, paprika, sugar, and garlic powder and cook until fragrant, about 30 seconds. Transfer to small bowl.

3   Set wire rack in rimmed baking sheet. Remove chicken from brine and dry thoroughly with paper towels. Combine flour, pepper, and remaining ½ teaspoon salt in large bowl. Dredge chicken pieces 2 at a time in flour mixture. Shake excess flour from chicken and transfer to prepared rack. (Do not discard flour.)

4   Adjust oven rack to middle position and heat oven to 200 degrees. Set second wire rack in second rimmed baking sheet. Heat 3 quarts oil in large Dutch oven over medium-high heat to 350 degrees. Return chicken pieces to flour mixture and turn to coat. Fry half of chicken, adjusting burner as necessary to maintain oil temperature between 300 and 325 degrees, until deep golden brown and breasts register 160 degrees and legs register 175 degrees, 20 to 25 minutes. (Remove pieces from pot as they reach correct temperature.) Drain chicken on second prepared rack and place in oven to keep warm.

5   Return oil to 350 degrees and repeat with remaining chicken. Stir spicy oil mixture to recombine and brush over both sides of chicken. Serve.

Extra-Hot Fried Chicken

In step 2, increase oil to ¼ cup, cayenne to 3½ tablespoons, and sugar to ¾ teaspoon, and add 1 teaspoon dry mustard.

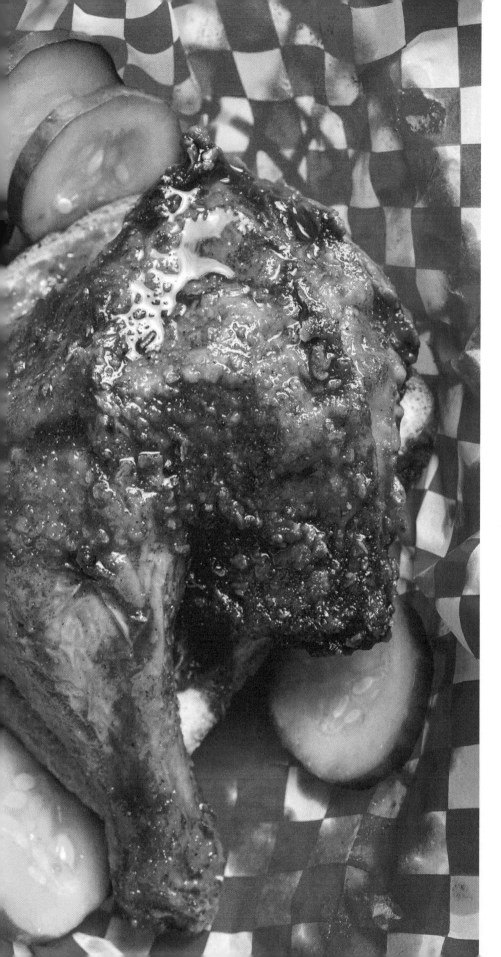

THE PRINCE OF SHACKS AND THE PRINCESS OF CHICKEN

Prince's Hot Chicken Shack got its start in 1945, when, according to legend, Thornton Prince—who was especially fond of women—angered his girlfriend by coming home late one too many times. Intending to teach him a lesson, she doused his chicken dinner with hot peppers and spices. But her payback ended up birthing a culinary icon: Prince liked the chicken, and the seed of Prince's Hot Chicken Shack was planted. Thornton soon opened a restaurant to sell this ultraspicy chicken.

After a couple passes of hands within the family, the current proprietor is, deservedly, a woman: Thornton's grandniece André Prince Jeffries took over the business in the 1980s. She was named Nashvillian of the Year in 2022 by *Nashville Scene*. In the accompanying article, Jeffries states, "I give the credit to a woman … she came up with what I call 'revenge chicken.'" Prince Jeffries runs the business with her two daughters, who currently do the bookkeeping and other management. Her niece Kim Prince operates a food truck outpost in Los Angeles, Hotville Chicken.

The story sounds like a country music song—fitting, as there are many Grand Ole Opry stars who have made Prince's famous. Country singers used to (and still do) drop in after their shows for late-night snacks of the blazingly hot chicken. Word spread, and now everybody in Nashville (and beyond), it seems, has a taste for the cayenne-infused heat and crispy texture of hot chicken.

Chicken-Fried Chicken

Serves 4　~　Total Time: 1 hour, plus 1½ hours brining and chilling

In the extended branches of the fried-chicken family tree, chicken-fried chicken ranks as a distant cousin (once or twice removed). If anything, the thinly pounded cutlet is more closely related to a German schnitzel or an Italian breaded scallopini (though typically not as thin). Much like these other flattened and fried cuts, chicken-fried chicken is only complete when topped with its telltale sauce, white cream gravy.

While the exact origins of Southern chicken-fried chicken remain obscure, we know it earned its name from chicken-fried steak, which is a thin piece of beef prepared in the manner of fried chicken: dredged in seasoned flour and fried in a shallow skillet until golden crisp. Chicken-fried steak, naturally, begets chicken-fried chicken: chicken that is fried, not like chicken, but like chicken-fried steak. It's pounded thin, and similar to the use of tougher pieces of beef for chicken-fried steak, this preparation turns a lean chicken breast into a hearty, satisfying staple at roadside eateries, cafés, and diners across the South.

After brining the chicken in buttermilk, coating it and then letting that coating hydrate in the refrigerator creates a breading that won't fall off while frying. We make the peppery milk gravy in a saucepan while the chicken cooks so they're ready at the same time.

Use a gentle hand when pounding the chicken to ensure that it doesn't tear. If you don't have a 12-inch cast-iron skillet, use a large Dutch oven instead, and increase the oil for frying by 1 cup.

Chicken

- 4　(6- to 8-ounce) boneless, skinless chicken breasts, trimmed
- 2　cups buttermilk
- 4　teaspoons table salt for brining
- 2　tablespoons pepper, divided
- 1　teaspoon cayenne pepper, divided
- 1½　cups all-purpose flour
- 1¼　cups cornstarch
- 2　teaspoons baking powder
- 2　teaspoons table salt
- 3　cups peanut or vegetable oil for frying

Gravy

- 2　tablespoons unsalted butter
- 2　tablespoons all-purpose flour
- 2　cups milk, plus extra as needed
- 1　teaspoon table salt
- 1　teaspoon pepper

1 **For the chicken** Using meat pounder, gently pound each chicken breast to even ¼-inch thickness between 2 sheets of plastic wrap. Whisk buttermilk, 4 teaspoons salt, 1 tablespoon pepper, and ½ teaspoon cayenne together in large bowl. Submerge chicken in brine, cover, and refrigerate for at least 1 hour or up to 24 hours.

2 Set wire rack in rimmed baking sheet. Whisk flour, cornstarch, baking powder, salt, remaining 1 tablespoon pepper, and remaining ½ teaspoon cayenne together in bowl. Working with 1 piece of chicken at a time, remove chicken from brine and transfer to flour mixture. Turn to coat, pressing firmly on coating to adhere. Transfer chicken to prepared wire rack. Reserve remaining flour mixture. Refrigerate chicken, uncovered,

for at least 30 minutes or up to 2 hours. (If you plan to refrigerate chicken for longer than 30 minutes, refrigerate reserved flour mixture as well.)

3 Set second wire rack in second rimmed baking sheet and line half of rack with triple layer of paper towels. Heat oil in 12-inch cast-iron skillet over medium-high heat to 375 degrees. (To take oil temperature, carefully tilt skillet so oil pools on 1 side).

4 Working with 2 pieces of chicken at a time, return chicken to flour mixture and turn to coat, pressing firmly on coating to adhere. Carefully place chicken in hot oil (pieces may overlap slightly; this is OK), and cook until well browned on first side, 3 to 5 minutes, adjusting heat as needed to maintain oil temperature between 325 and 350 degrees. Using tongs, carefully flip chicken and continue to cook until well browned on second side, 3 to 5 minutes longer. Transfer chicken to paper towel–lined side of rack and let drain on each side for 30 seconds, then move to unlined side of rack. Repeat with remaining 2 pieces of chicken. Let chicken cool slightly, about 5 minutes.

5 **For the gravy** Meanwhile, melt butter in large saucepan over medium heat. Whisk in flour until smooth. Slowly add milk, whisking constantly until smooth, about 30 seconds. Bring to simmer and cook, whisking often, until gravy has thickened, 1 to 2 minutes. Adjust consistency as needed with extra milk, 1 tablespoon at a time. Off heat, whisk in salt and pepper. Serve gravy over chicken.

Crab Croquettes

Makes 18 croquettes ~ Total Time: 1½ hours, plus 3 hours chilling

There are many relatives of crab croquettes in the South. Maryland crab cakes (see page 300) are similar, although they're typically less creamy and bready. Tampa has its own version that comes from Spanish, Cuban, and Italian immigrant communities and uses deviled crab (see page 97).

This featured take, however, is a Spanish-style croquette inspired by Suire's Grocery & Restaurant, located deep in Louisiana's bayou country. We set out to create a home version of fried crab croquettes in the same crunchy-creamy Spanish style found in the region (see "Cajun Country Cooking"). It starts with a thick béchamel (a simple cooked sauce of fat, flour, and milk) to bind everything together. The béchamel is seasoned with chopped onion, bell pepper, and garlic, and to that we add the crabmeat, along with scallions, spicy Creole seasoning, and vinegary Tabasco hot sauce for a bold boost of flavor. Refrigerating the mixture for 3 hours helps it firm up before being shaped into croquettes. For supercrisp exteriors that reveal soft, creamy interiors, we bread the crab croquettes with a standard three-step breading procedure before deep-frying them.

Fresh crabmeat makes the best croquettes, but refrigerated canned crabmeat, often found at the supermarket fish counter, is the next best thing. Use a Dutch oven that holds 6 quarts or more.

CAJUN COUNTRY COOKING

Sitting alongside a breezy stretch of Highway 35 in Kaplan, Louisiana, Suire's Grocery & Restaurant is flanked on each side by grassy flats and farmlands. It's a squat, tin-roofed building painted with happy caricatures of crawfish, crabs, turtles, and, most notably, a smiling alligator wearing a chef's toque and apron near the front door. Suire's is split down the middle: The right side serves as the grocery store, and the left side serves as the dining room, where the tablecloths are patterned with red and black crawfish and the pepper shakers are filled with cayenne. The dining room walls are plastered with faded local news clippings, restaurant write-ups, and photos of hunters posing with their trophies.

Lisa Frederick behind the counter at Suire's Grocery and Restaurant.

The menu at Suire's represents a broad swath of Cajun home cooking, with everything from alligator po' boys to crawfish étouffée to brown sugar–glazed fig cake made with local figs. Recently, Suire's has begun to draw in tourists in search of true Cajun food. As the menu states, "If you want country cooking, come to the country."

Opened on October 4, 1976, by Mary Oels and Newton Suire, Suire's is now owned and operated by their daughters, Lisa Frederick and Joan Suire. Joan recalls her parents telling her when she was 19 years old, "If we buy the store, you're running it." She's been involved with it ever since.

In the beginning, Newton, who was a rice farmer all his life, would cook at Suire's in the early morning, leave to go tend the farm, and then come back to cook again in the afternoon. "He was the real cook in the family," Joan says. She says that all the recipes are family secrets, which they don't care to share. Lisa took over the cooking when Newton was unable to carry on.

At Suire's, the shrimp gumbo is complex and redolent of sweet seafood, and the boudin sausage is peppery and bold. The turtle sauce picante—a tomato-and-roux-based turtle stew—has a nice kick to it. And the crab croquettes that inspired our recipe have a crunchy exterior that cracks between your teeth to reveal a soft, creamy crab-filled interior. And while all the dishes served at Suire's are complex, they aren't overly complicated. Lisa wouldn't share exact recipes, but she gave us some of her kitchen wisdom: "You don't have to put in the kitchen sink to make the food taste good."

Croquettes

4	tablespoons unsalted butter
½	cup finely chopped onion
½	cup finely chopped green bell pepper
3	garlic cloves, minced
1¼	teaspoons table salt
1	cup all-purpose flour, divided
1½	cups whole milk
8	ounces lump crabmeat, picked over for shells
3	scallions, sliced thin
1	teaspoon Tabasco sauce
1	teaspoon Tony Chachere's Original Creole Seasoning, plus extra for sprinkling
½	teaspoon pepper
2	large eggs
2	cups panko bread crumbs
1½	quarts vegetable oil for frying

Dipping Sauce

½	cup mayonnaise
2	teaspoons Tabasco sauce
½	teaspoon Worcestershire sauce

1 **For the croquettes** Melt butter in large saucepan over medium heat. Add onion, bell pepper, garlic, and salt and cook until vegetables are softened, about 5 minutes.

2 Stir in ½ cup flour until no dry flour remains; cook for 1 minute, stirring often. Slowly whisk in milk; continue to whisk 1 minute longer to ensure no lumps of flour remain. Cook until bubbles begin to break surface and mixture is thickened to consistency of paste, 1 to 2 minutes.

3 Off heat, stir in crab, scallions, Tabasco, Creole seasoning, and pepper until well combined. Transfer to 8-inch square baking dish and refrigerate, uncovered, until fully chilled and firm, about 3 hours (or cover with plastic wrap once cooled completely and refrigerate overnight).

4 **For the dipping sauce** Whisk mayonnaise, Tabasco, and Worcestershire together in bowl; refrigerate until ready to serve.

5 Place remaining ½ cup flour in shallow dish, beat eggs together in second shallow dish, and place panko in third shallow dish. Divide croquette mixture into 18 heaping 2-tablespoon portions (about 1½ ounces each) and place on rimmed baking sheet. Roll portions between your hands to make balls, then shape into 2-inch-long ovals.

6 Working with few croquettes at a time, dredge lightly in flour, shaking off excess; roll in beaten egg, allowing excess to drip off; and coat with panko. Return to sheet. (Croquettes can be covered with plastic wrap and refrigerated for up to 3 hours.)

7 Line large plate with triple layer of paper towels. Heat oil in large Dutch oven over medium-high heat to 375 degrees. Place 9 croquettes in oil and fry until golden brown, about 2 minutes per side. Transfer to prepared plate. Return oil to 375 degrees and repeat with remaining 9 croquettes. Sprinkle lightly with extra Creole seasoning and serve with dipping sauce.

Crispy Fried Shrimp

Serves 4 to 6 ~ Total Time: 1¼ hours

Crispy deep-fried shrimp can be found all over the South. Calabash-style fried shrimp was born in the 1930s in the fishing community of Calabash, North Carolina. When fishermen returned home with their catch, families would wait for them on shore to purchase the fish. Eventually the community started setting up "fish camps" right there alongside the water, where they would communally batter and fry seafood that had been freshly caught. You can still get this type of shrimp locally.

Down in Louisiana you can get fried shrimp with the monikers "Cajun," "Creole," or "Bayou-style." All of them typically have a good dose of seasoning in the breading. There are also tempura-fried shrimp at Japanese restaurants and crispy salt-and-pepper shrimp at Chinese restaurants. And you'll come across a more generic version of Southern-fried shrimp pretty much anywhere.

This recipe doesn't replicate a particular style, but it's definitely inspired by the crispy, well-seasoned versions you can find in the South. Extra-large shrimp (21 to 25 per pound) can withstand enough time in the hot oil for the coating to become nicely browned and crisp. The tails make for an attractive presentation and they're a nice handle for dipping as well. Coating the shrimp with salt, pepper, granulated garlic, and cayenne flavors them inside and out. A batter of seasoned flour, egg, and water and a coating of panko bread crumbs quickly form a crisp exterior in the hot oil.

For a creamy hybrid of the classic cocktail and tartar sauces served with fried shrimp, we combine ketchup and horseradish with mayo, Worcestershire, lemon juice, cayenne, and Old Bay seasoning. Use a Dutch oven that holds 6 quarts or more.

Sauce

- ½ cup ketchup
- ½ cup mayonnaise
- ¼ cup prepared horseradish
- 2 teaspoons Worcestershire sauce
- 1 teaspoon lemon juice
- ½ teaspoon Old Bay seasoning
- ½ teaspoon cayenne pepper

Shrimp

- ½ cup all-purpose flour
- ½ cup water
- 2 large eggs
- 1¼ teaspoons table salt, divided
- ½ teaspoon pepper, divided
- 2 cups panko bread crumbs
- 1 teaspoon granulated garlic
- ¼ teaspoon cayenne pepper
- 1½ pounds extra-large shrimp, (21 to 25 per pound), peeled, deveined, and tails left on
- 1½ quarts vegetable oil for frying

1 **For the sauce** Whisk all ingredients in bowl until combined; set aside.

2 **For the shrimp** Whisk flour, water, eggs, ½ teaspoon salt, and ¼ teaspoon pepper in bowl until no lumps remain. Spread panko in shallow dish.

3 Combine granulated garlic, cayenne, remaining ¾ teaspoon salt, and remaining ¼ teaspoon pepper in small bowl. Pat shrimp dry with paper towels and sprinkle with spice mixture.

4 Working with 1 shrimp at a time, hold shrimp by tail and dip into batter, letting excess drip back into bowl, then coat with panko, pressing gently to adhere. Arrange breaded shrimp on rimmed baking sheet. Refrigerate while heating oil (breaded shrimp can be refrigerated for up to 2 hours).

5 Line platter with triple layer of paper towels. Add oil to large Dutch oven until it measures about 1 inch deep and heat over medium-high heat to 350 degrees. Add one-third of shrimp, one at a time, to hot oil. Fry, stirring gently to prevent shrimp from sticking together, until shrimp are golden brown, 1 to 2 minutes after adding last shrimp.

6 Transfer shrimp to prepared platter. Return oil to 350 degrees and repeat with remaining shrimp in 2 more batches. Serve immediately with sauce.

To make ahead At end of step 4, freeze breaded shrimp on sheet until firm, then transfer to zipper-lock bag and freeze for up to 1 month. Do not thaw before cooking; increase cooking time by 1 to 2 minutes.

AS SOUTHERN AS SWANEE

Long after the Civil War, even during the 1930s and 1940s, numerous Southern restaurants relied on plantation imagery and racist stereotypes in their menus and advertising. It seemed that this tone-setting was meant as a sort of nostalgic nod to the ways of the past and the image of what the South used to be.

Pack Memorial Library in Asheville, North Carolina, has a menu from 1937 featuring "Fried Southern Shrimp (As Southern as Swanee)." The menu was part of the "Southern Mammy Dinners," a special service that ran at Creighton's restaurant during the height of public nostalgia for the "Old South" and all things *Gone with the Wind*, which was first published just a year earlier, in 1936. The menu featured "Gone with the Wind Plates" such as the "Mammy" (featuring goose liver mousse, tomatoes, lettuce, pickles, and saltines), the "Rhett Butler" (tomato stuffed with shrimp, Thousand Island dressing, and lettuce), and the "Scarlett" (a plate of chicken salad, deviled eggs, and peanut butter and jam sandwiches).

As Marcie Cohen Ferris points out in her book *The Edible South: The Power of Food and the Making of an American Region*, this sort of menu was not uncommon at the time and such themed dishes supported the false narrative of the Lost Cause, the belief that the Civil War was not, in fact, about slavery, but about Southern rights and heroism. The Old Southern Tea Room in Vicksburg, Mississippi, had a menu with a mammy character illustrated on the front as well as a photo of the owner's daughter dressed in antebellum clothing. Mammy's Cupboard, a roadside restaurant built in the 1940s in the shape of a mammy still stands on US Highway 61 south of Natchez, Mississippi.

While this advertising likely drew in regular customers as well as fans of the famous novel, it also perpetuated stereotypes and contributed to the larger practice of casual racism that was prevalent at the time. These historical menus serve as important reminders of how food and cooking can be used as tools for both progress and oppression.

by Morgan Bolling with
KC Hysmith

Fried Catfish

Serves 4 to 6 ~ Total Time: 55 minutes

Mississippi is one of the biggest producers of farmed catfish in the United States, and the Mississippi River and its tributaries are popular, productive destinations for catfish fishing. It's rare to visit a restaurant there that doesn't have fried catfish on the menu. The fish's firm texture (similar to that of grouper or sea bass) and mild flavor give it broad appeal, but for most aficionados, deep-fried catfish is the only way to go. At its best, fried catfish has a crispy, thin cornmeal crust; perfectly cooked, sweet flesh; and just enough spice to make it interesting.

We like to process half of the cornmeal to a fine powder to give the coating just the right texture. For fish that cooks evenly and has a high ratio of crunchy coating to fish, we halve the fillets to make catfish "tenders" before dunking them in hot sauce–laced buttermilk and dredging them in the cornmeal coating. Use a Dutch oven that holds 6 quarts or more. If your spice grinder is small, grind the cornmeal in batches or process it in a blender for 60 to 90 seconds. Serve with Comeback Sauce (recipe follows).

2	cups buttermilk	1	teaspoon cayenne pepper
1	teaspoon hot sauce	4	(6- to 8-ounce) catfish fillets, halved lengthwise along natural seam
2	cups cornmeal, divided		
4	teaspoons table salt	2	quarts peanut or vegetable oil for frying
2	teaspoons pepper		
2	teaspoons granulated garlic		Lemon wedges

1   Set wire rack in rimmed baking sheet and line half of rack with triple layer of paper towels. Whisk buttermilk and hot sauce together in shallow dish. Process 1 cup cornmeal in spice grinder to fine powder, 30 to 45 seconds. Whisk salt, pepper, granulated garlic, cayenne, remaining 1 cup cornmeal, and ground cornmeal together in second shallow dish.

2   Pat catfish dry with paper towels. Working with 1 piece of catfish at a time, dip catfish in buttermilk mixture, letting excess drip off; dredge in cornmeal mixture, shaking off excess; and transfer to large plate.

3   Add oil to large Dutch oven until it measures about 1½ inches deep and heat over medium-high heat to 350 degrees. Working with 4 pieces of catfish at a time, add catfish to oil. Adjust burner, if necessary, to maintain oil temperature between 325 and 350 degrees. Fry catfish until golden brown and crispy, about 5 minutes. Transfer catfish to paper towel–lined side of prepared rack and let drain for 1 minute, then move to unlined side of rack. Return oil to 350 degrees and repeat with remaining catfish. Serve with lemon wedges.

Comeback Sauce

Serves 4 to 6 (Makes about 1 cup)
Total Time: 10 minutes

Somewhere between rémoulade and Thousand Island dressing amped with hot sauce, this Southern condiment is thought to have gotten its name from the phrase, "y'all come back now"—and from the idea that it's so delicious, people to come back to eat it. Comeback sauce is often credited to Greek immigrants in Mississippi in the 1930s or 1940s. But in his article "The Sauce That Barbecue Lost," Robert F. Moss points to an announcement in the *Kansas City Star* in 1906 with an African American organization promoting a picnic in which a reverend would barbecue meats "with his come back sauce on the side."

We would happily eat this sauce on fried catfish or alongside a plate of smoked meats. It would also be delightful served as a spread on sandwiches, as a dipping sauce, or as a rich salad dressing. For this version, ketchup and chili sauce add sweetness, raw onion lends some bite, and Worcestershire and lemon juice brighten it up. Processing the sauce in a blender gives it a silky texture.

½	cup mayonnaise
⅓	cup chopped onion
2	tablespoons vegetable oil
2	tablespoons chili sauce
1	tablespoon ketchup
2½	teaspoons Worcestershire sauce
2½	teaspoons hot sauce
1	teaspoon yellow mustard
1	teaspoon lemon juice
1	garlic clove, minced
¾	teaspoon pepper
⅛	teaspoon paprika

Process all ingredients in blender until smooth, about 30 seconds. Sauce can be refrigerated for up to 5 days.

Puffy Tacos

Serves 6 to 8　～　Total Time: 1½ hours

Ask an outsider about San Antonio's charms, and you'll likely hear about the downtown Riverwalk, the vibrant nightlife, and, of course, the iconic Alamo. But ask a local and you'll get an earful about puffy tacos. Puffy tacos are traditionally made by deep-frying and shaping fresh masa de maíz (finely ground hominy) until it puffs into a light, crispy taco shell, giving you a delicious amalgamation of textures and flavors.

The ubiquitous tacos are so important here that the mascot for the San Antonio Missions minor league baseball team is, yes, Henry the Puffy Taco. Until prefab taco shells became the national Tex-Mex norm in the 1960s, most tacos in South Texas were of a similar puffy ilk. Cooks in Houston, Corpus Christi, Austin, and many other, smaller south Texas towns have been dropping fresh tortillas into frying oil and forming them into pockets for ground meat fillings for generations, sometimes calling them "crispy" or "crunchy" tacos—both equally apt descriptors.

Maria Lopez-Rambo, co-owner of Ray's Drive Inn, says the puffy taco came about as a mistake made by her great-grandmother, Maria Rodriguez Lopez. While frying tostadas, she wasn't paying attention and let the tortilla inflate; she then dropped a stick she was using to keep the tortillas from sticking together into the inflated tortilla. The dough puffed around the utensil, creating the first puffy taco. This culinary mishap is now a staple at Ray's Drive Inn. (In an article for *Texas Monthly*, "The Delicate History of the Puffy Taco," Lopez-Rambo acknowledges this story has been passed down through the generations so it may be a bit, well, inflated.)

Many San Antonio fans of the dish cite Diana Barrios Treviño's restaurant, Los Barrios, as having the best in the city. Barrios Treviño starts with fresh masa de maíz to create a moist masa dough. She uses a tortilla press to stamp portions of masa dough into 6-inch tortillas and then drops them one at a time into the deep-fryer. The tortillas puff up with air, ballooning as Barrios Treviño flips and shapes them with two spatulas into the familiar taco-shell shape—except a bit puffier. She pulls the shells from the oil to drain upside down before stuffing them with a simple ground meat filling.

For ease, we fry in a saucepan, which requires a modest amount of oil, and the pan's profile makes the tacos easy to shape. For a flavorful filling, picadillo made with ground beef, green bell pepper, onion, garlic, and cumin fits the bill. We used Maseca Instant Masa Corn Flour for our taco shells. The dough should not be sticky and should have the texture of Play-Doh. If the dough cracks or falls apart when pressing the tortillas, just reroll and press again.

Picadillo

12	ounces 85 percent lean ground beef
½	russet potato (4 ounces), peeled and cut into ¼-inch pieces
1	teaspoon pepper
¾	teaspoon table salt
1	onion, chopped fine
1	small green bell pepper, stemmed, seeded, and chopped fine
3	garlic cloves, minced
1½	teaspoons ground cumin
2	teaspoons all-purpose flour
¾	cup water

Taco Shells

2½	cups (10 ounces) masa harina
1	teaspoon table salt
1⅔	cups warm water
2	quarts vegetable oil for frying
	Shredded iceberg lettuce
	Chopped tomato
	Shredded sharp cheddar cheese
	Hot sauce

1 **For the picadillo** Combine beef, potato, pepper, and salt in 12-inch nonstick skillet. Cook over medium-high heat until meat and potato begin to brown, breaking up meat with spoon, 6 to 8 minutes. Add onion and bell pepper and cook until softened, 4 to 6 minutes. Add garlic and cumin and cook until fragrant, about 30 seconds.

2 Stir in flour and cook for 1 minute. Stir in water and bring to boil. Reduce heat to medium-low and simmer until thickened slightly, about 1 minute. Season with salt and pepper to taste. Remove from heat, cover, and keep warm.

3 **For the taco shells** Mix masa harina and salt together in medium bowl. Stir in warm water with rubber spatula. Using your hands, knead mixture in bowl until it comes together fully (dough should be soft

and tacky, not sticky), about 30 seconds. Cover dough with damp dish towel and let rest for 5 minutes.

4 Divide dough into 12 equal portions, about ¼ cup each, then roll each into smooth ball between your hands. Transfer balls to plate and keep covered with damp dish towel. Cut sides of 1-gallon zipper-lock bag, leaving bottom seam intact.

5 Set wire rack in rimmed baking sheet and line rack with triple layer of paper towels. Add oil to large saucepan until it measures 2½ inches deep and heat over medium-high heat to 375 degrees.

6 When oil comes to temperature, enclose 1 dough ball at a time in split bag. Using glass pie plate (so you can see size of tortilla), press dough flat into 6-inch circle (about ⅛ inch thick).

7 Carefully remove tortilla from plastic and drop into hot oil. Fry tortilla until it puffs up, 15 to 20 seconds. Using 2 metal spatulas, carefully flip tortilla. Immediately press down in center of tortilla with 1 spatula to form taco shape, submerging tortilla into oil while doing so. Using second spatula, spread top of tortilla open about 1½ inches. Fry until golden brown, about 1 minute. Adjust burner, if necessary, to maintain oil temperature between 350 and 375 degrees.

8 Transfer taco shell to prepared rack and place upside down to drain. Return oil to 375 degrees and repeat with remaining dough balls.

9 Divide picadillo evenly among taco shells, about ¼ cup each. Serve immediately, passing lettuce, tomato, cheddar, and hot sauce separately.

FRYING THE TACO SHELLS

You'll need two metal spatulas to shape these shells.

1 Lower 1 tortilla into hot oil. Tortilla will begin to puff up in 15 to 20 seconds.

2 Using 2 metal spatulas, flip tortilla over, being careful not to pierce or tear tortilla.

3 Shape tortilla into shell with wide mouth. Nudge shell into oil and fry until golden.

Gobi Manchurian

Serves 4 ~ Total Time: 1 hour

Gobi Manchurian, a multinational dish with roots in Chinese immigrant communities in Kolkata, India, features cauliflower battered and fried until crisp and then served with or tossed in a flavorful, spicy sauce. In recent years the dish has proven popular in Indian restaurants across the United States, including those in Southern cities, for its powerful flavors and mix of crisp and soft textures. Fans love it as a side dish or shared snack.

Our version is inspired by a visit to Chai Pani, a restaurant in Asheville, North Carolina, owned by husband-and-wife chefs Meherwan and Molly Irani. Meherwan Irani is part of Brown in the South, a collaborative dinner series showcasing Indian chefs in the South (see "More Than a Dinner Series").

These delightfully crisp cauliflower florets are fried in a light batter coating made from water, cornstarch, flour, baking powder, and salt. After frying, they're tossed in a spicy, tangy sauce made from ketchup, chili-garlic sauce, garlic, ginger, scallions, and lots of freshly squeezed lime juice. A whole 2½-pound head of cauliflower should yield 1 pound of florets. You can also buy precut florets if available. Use a Dutch oven that holds 6 quarts or more.

Sauce

- ¼ cup ketchup
- 3 tablespoons water
- 2 tablespoons soy sauce
- 1 tablespoon chili-garlic sauce
- 2 teaspoons lime juice, plus lime wedges for serving
- ¾ teaspoon pepper
- ½ teaspoon ground cumin
- 2 tablespoons vegetable oil
- 3 scallions, white and green parts separated and sliced thin
- 1 tablespoon grated fresh ginger
- 3 garlic cloves, minced

Cauliflower

- 1 cup water
- ⅔ cup cornstarch
- ⅔ cup all-purpose flour
- 1 teaspoon table salt
- 1 teaspoon baking powder
- 1 pound (1½-inch) cauliflower florets (4 cups)
- 2 quarts peanut or vegetable oil for frying

1 **For the sauce** Combine ketchup, water, soy sauce, chili-garlic sauce, lime juice, pepper, and cumin in bowl. Heat oil in small saucepan over medium-high heat until shimmering. Add scallion whites, ginger, and garlic and cook, stirring frequently, until fragrant, about 1½ minutes. Stir in ketchup mixture and bring to simmer, scraping up any bits of ginger mixture from bottom of saucepan. Transfer sauce to clean large bowl.

2 **For the cauliflower** Whisk water, cornstarch, flour, salt, and baking powder in large bowl until smooth. Add cauliflower florets to batter and toss with rubber spatula to evenly coat; set aside.

3 Line baking sheet with triple layer of paper towels. Add oil to large Dutch oven until it measures about 1½ inches deep and heat over medium-high heat to 375 degrees.

4 Using tongs, add florets to hot oil 1 piece at a time. Cook, stirring occasionally to prevent florets from sticking together, until coating is firm and very lightly golden, about 5 minutes. Adjust burner, if necessary, to maintain oil temperature between 300 and 325 degrees. Using spider skimmer, transfer florets to prepared sheet. Let sit for 5 minutes.

5 Add cauliflower and scallion greens to bowl with sauce and toss to combine. Transfer to platter and serve with lime wedges.

MORE THAN A DINNER SERIES

The Brown in the South dinner series started after the 2017 Southern Foodways Alliance Symposium. Vishwesh Bhatt and Meherwan Irani, two chefs who have restaurants in the South and from India, conceived the idea after speaking about the commonalities between India and the American South. These two invited other Southern Indian chefs to create a dinner party series playing with fusions of the two cuisines. The first dinner, which took place in Asheville, North Carolina, at Chai Pani in 2018, featured five chefs: Bhatt, Irani, Maneet Chauhan, Asha Gomez, and Cheetie Kumar.

Chauhan went on to host the next party at her restaurant in Nashville, Chauhan Ale & Masala House. It was a "family-style supper that celebrated the late-summer garden bounties of both Tennessee and India," Chandra Ram wrote in an article for *Food & Wine* magazine. Samantha Fore brought her take on Southern tomato pie, which she described as Sri Lankan cheese toast flavored with chile pepper and onion. Kerala-style fried chicken and Indian sloppy joes also accented

Asha Gomez preparing food for a Brown in the South dinner.

Thomas Payne

conversations about identity and belonging at the event.

Priya Krishna, author of *Indian-ish: Recipes and Antics from a Modern American Family*, did not attend the Brown in the South gatherings, but she is extremely proud of these chefs who are serving "boundary-breaking" dishes that reveal the similarities between Indian cuisine and the cooking of the American South: "okra, fried chicken, pickles." We asked the Dallas native, whose cookbook celebrates her mom's style of "accessible and innovative Indian-American dishes," to share her thoughts about blending her Indian and Southern heritage. Here's what she had to say: "The truth is, *Indian-ish* was a placeholder title . . . but [we] realized that it was really the perfect way to describe how I felt about my identity, and the recipes in the book. I am Indian, but I am also so much more. There is a recipe for matar paneer, but there's also a recipe for a dump cake, which originates from the South. I grew up with Tex Mex, dal, Texas bluebonnets, and Diwali celebrations. My identity—and my cookbook—encompasses all of that. Being Indian doesn't make me less Southern, just as being Southern doesn't make me less Indian." The dishes crafted by all these chefs perfectly capture that final sentiment.

by Morgan Bolling

Fried Okra

Serves 4 to 6 ~ Total Time: 45 minutes, plus 30 minutes chilling

In her book *Delilah's Everyday Soul: Southern Cooking with Style*, Delilah Winder exclaims, "All this talk about slime makes me laugh, actually. Okra only acquires this texture when it's overcooked, and, in truth, it is probably the only vegetable we don't overcook in the South!" That's why, Winder explains, okra is so good fried—because it cooks so quickly that way.

Fried okra can be found throughout the South. The vegetable is also popular in Indian cuisine, so Chef Vimala Rajendran developed a version for her Chapel Hill, North Carolina restaurant, Vimala's Curryblossom Café. Rajendran halves okra pods and deep-fries them until crisp before dusting them with chaat masala, a spice mix that is tangy, tart, and a touch warming. This crunchy, spiced, salty item is one of the most popular on Rajendran's menu. (Another reason to love her: In one of her many acts of service to her community, Rajendran keeps a donation jar on the café's counter to support anyone who wants to eat but is unable to pay.)

Our recipe for quick-fried okra is tender and well seasoned inside, with a buttermilk dredge and a crunchy cornmeal coating bolstered with cornstarch, which adds a light, crispy effect; and flour, which creates the gluten structure that ensures that the coating stays put. Garlic powder and cayenne season the dredge. While we prefer the flavor and texture of fresh okra in this recipe, you can substitute frozen cut okra, thawed and thoroughly patted dry, for fresh. We recommend frying in three batches if using frozen okra. Use a Dutch oven that holds 6 quarts or more.

⅔	cup buttermilk
1	large egg
¾	cup cornmeal
½	cup cornstarch
¼	cup all-purpose flour
1½	teaspoons table salt
1	teaspoon garlic powder
½	teaspoon cayenne pepper
¼	teaspoon pepper
1	pound okra, stemmed and cut into 1-inch pieces
3	quarts peanut or vegetable oil for frying
	Lemon wedges
	Hot sauce

1   Line rimmed baking sheet with parchment paper. Whisk buttermilk and egg together in shallow dish. Whisk cornmeal, cornstarch, flour, salt, garlic powder, cayenne, and pepper together in second shallow dish. Working in batches, dip okra in buttermilk mixture, letting excess drip back into dish. Dredge in cornmeal mixture, pressing firmly to adhere; transfer to prepared sheet. Refrigerate, uncovered, for at least 30 minutes or up to 4 hours.

2   Meanwhile, adjust oven rack to middle position and heat oven to 200 degrees. Set wire rack in second rimmed baking sheet and line with triple layer of paper towels. Add oil to large Dutch oven until it measures about 2 inches deep and heat over medium-high heat to 375 degrees. Carefully add half of okra to oil and fry, stirring as needed to prevent sticking, until okra is golden and crisp, 2 to 4 minutes. Adjust burner if necessary to maintain oil temperature between 350 and 375 degrees. Using spider skimmer or slotted spoon, transfer okra to prepared rack. Season with salt to taste and transfer to oven to keep warm.

3   Return oil to 375 degrees and repeat with remaining okra. Serve immediately with lemon wedges and hot sauce.

Q&A: VIMALA RAJENDRAN ON MAKING FOOD FOR EVERYBODY

Modern Southern cuisine is as diverse as a well-stocked spice rack. While early Southern cookbooks and restaurants often failed to capture this diversity, or intentionally only highlighted a narrow palate, today they are decidedly global thanks to the multicultural foodways shared by new generations of Southerners. One perfect example of this delicious evolution can be found at Vimala's Curryblossom Café in Chapel Hill, North Carolina, which is owned and operated by Vimala Rajendran, who immigrated from India to the South in the 1980s. Vimala and her homestyle cooking have become a culinary staple of the area as well as a comfort for many in the diverse community. Around Chapel Hill, there's a well-known saying: "When Vimala cooks, everybody eats."

What's important to you about cooking?

It started with me as a child being hungry all the time. The food would never be prepared on time and so getting involved became a necessity. It was impossible to keep me out of the kitchen. It brings me the greatest joy to bring food to the table. Sambar, a lentil and vegetable stew, was one of the first dishes I loved as a child and so I put all of those memories in the same dish that's made at the restaurant.

Who in the community do you cook for?

I am placed here in the South, I owe to the soil that I've sent roots down into, and that soil includes the people who surround me no matter where they came from or how long they've lived around me. I had been preparing my own food [and serving it] out of my kitchen door and onto my neighborhood streets, because sharing what was nostalgic to me was important. I would share stories and memories about why the food was important, too. I refer to myself as a culinary chameleon; as I was bringing my food out to others who had never experienced it, I was watching their reactions and trying to learn from them and, soon, cooking their food for them, too. So I've cooked for local schools, for community garden groups, churches, the campus Hillel, and many more. Every year for Martin Luther King Jr. Day, the restaurant has a tradition of giving away chai and hot chocolate on the sidewalk to the marchers from Peace Plaza to First Baptist Church.

So you're known not just for your cooking but also for feeding people in your community. How are these two actions intertwined?

Our food isn't just about what we serve, but who we serve. My restaurant occupies the space that was Chapel Hill's first desegregated ice cream shop. This is historic, sacred ground I stand on and I take that as a high privilege, and privilege always comes with the responsibility to make yourself available to serve others. So my way to serve others is to make food that seems familiar. Cooking and feeding people are intertwined because food sovereignty is very important; it means being able to access food that is familiar to ours even when we are displaced. There are more refugees now than ever before. So when I have refugees, say, from nine different countries, Ghana, Syria, Pakistan, Yemen, and others, I can make halal food in flavors they're familiar with—more garlic, maybe no ginger even, and onions and tomatoes—and they've said, "This tastes like home." The definition of food sovereignty is when food can taste like home.

Churros with Mexican Chocolate Sauce

Makes 18 churros ~ Total Time: 1½ hours

There's a lot to love about churros: These fluted pastries are fried until crisp on the outside and soft on the inside, at which point they're rolled in a cinnamon-sugar coating and served with a side of rich, warm chocolate sauce for dipping. The lightly crisp pastry, inviting fragrance of cinnamon, and slightly bitter edge of chocolate pair perfectly with a steaming mug of coffee.

Many recipes call for piping the cooled dough directly into hot oil, but this process can feel a little stressful. In this recipe we call for piping the still-warm dough onto a baking sheet and refrigerating the churros for a few minutes to firm them up. This makes the process of transferring them to the oil easy. A combination of cocoa powder and unsweetened chocolate keeps the sweetness of our sauce in check, while a bit of chipotle chile powder adds heat and a little cinnamon contributes warmth.

We used a closed star #8 pastry tip, ⅝ inch in diameter, to create deeply grooved ridges in the churros. You can use any large closed star tip of similar diameter, though your yield may vary slightly. To keep the eggs from scrambling, it's important to mix the dough for 1 minute in step 2 before adding them. Use a Dutch oven that holds 6 quarts or more.

Churros

- 2 cups water
- 2 tablespoons unsalted butter
- 2 tablespoons plus ½ cup sugar (3½ ounces), divided
- 1 teaspoon vanilla extract
- ½ teaspoon table salt
- 2 cups (10 ounces) all-purpose flour
- 2 large eggs
- 2 quarts vegetable oil for frying
- ¾ teaspoon ground cinnamon

Sauce

- 1¼ cups (8¾ ounces) sugar
- ⅔ cup whole milk
- ¼ teaspoon table salt
- ¼ teaspoon ground cinnamon
- ¼ teaspoon chipotle chile powder
- ⅓ cup (1 ounce) unsweetened cocoa powder, sifted
- 3 ounces unsweetened chocolate, chopped fine
- 4 tablespoons unsalted butter, cut into 8 pieces and chilled
- 1 teaspoon vanilla extract

1 **For the churros** Line rimmed baking sheet with parchment paper and spray with vegetable oil spray. Combine water, butter, 2 tablespoons sugar, vanilla, and salt in large saucepan and bring to boil over medium-high heat. Off heat, add flour all at once and stir with rubber spatula until well combined with no streaks of flour remaining.

2 Transfer dough to bowl of stand mixer. Fit mixer with paddle and mix dough on low speed until cooled slightly, about 1 minute. Add eggs, increase speed to medium, and beat until fully incorporated, about 1 minute.

3 Transfer warm dough to piping bag fitted with ⅝-inch closed star pastry tip. Pipe 18 (6-inch) lengths of dough onto prepared sheet, using scissors to snip dough at tip. Refrigerate, uncovered, for at least 15 minutes or up to 1 hour.

4 **For the sauce** Meanwhile, heat sugar, milk, salt, cinnamon, and chile powder in medium saucepan over medium-low heat, whisking gently, until sugar has dissolved and liquid starts to bubble around edges of saucepan, about 6 minutes. Reduce heat to low, add cocoa, and whisk until smooth.

5 Off heat, stir in chocolate and let sit for 3 minutes. Whisk sauce until smooth and chocolate is fully melted. Whisk in butter and vanilla until fully incorporated and sauce thickens slightly. (Sauce can be refrigerated for up to 1 month; gently warm in microwave, stirring every 10 seconds, until pourable, before using.)

6 Adjust oven rack to middle position and heat oven to 200 degrees. Set wire rack in second rimmed baking sheet and place in oven. Line large plate with triple layer of paper towels. Add oil to large Dutch oven until it measures about 1½ inches deep and heat over medium-high heat to 375 degrees.

MAKING (BIG AND) LITTLE WAVES

"Heart Driven" is painted on one wall of Cocoa Cinnamon, a coffee shop in Durham, North Carolina, co-founded by wife and husband, Areli Barrera Grodski and Leon Grodski Barrera.

They started their business on what they refer to as their "espresso bike"; the two converted a bike and pedaled between farmers' markets to sell coffee. But this operation was weather-dependent and took a lot of strength (both mental and physical). So with help from an investor, they opened their brick-and-mortar shop Cocoa Cinnamon. Today they have three physical locations, one of which includes its own coffee microroaster, Little Waves, a bustling operation that produces 1,800 pounds of coffee weekly.

In their businesses, Areli and Leon center community: They emphasize fair trade principles, equitable hiring practices, and fostering connections with women and minority coffee producers. According to the article "A Deeper Roast: Little Waves Coffee" in *Walter Magazine*, as of December 2023 they paid their staff a base of $17.60 per hour, well above the $7.25 minimum wage in the country.

These entrepreneurs also put love into their churros. The freshly fried treats can be tossed in cinnamon sugar, cardamom sugar, or any number of other rotating flavors. You can get them made into an ice cream sandwich complete with rainbow sprinkles or snack on them alongside sipping chocolate. In a piece for *HuffPost* by Garin Pirnia, Areli explained that adding churros to the menu in 2017 was a purposeful choice: "It was a delicious, simple gesture to the Latino community that this was the place for them."

Warm churros are not the only thing adding to the sense of place in their spaces. The husband and wife duo decorate their spaces with Mexican oilcloths and paper stars. While speaking on the *Discover Durham* podcast, Areli noted, "I feel like the design for all three locations has always been intentional. Mostly from a perspective of thinking of how do you say things without saying them? How do you get people to feel things without saying things?" The shops are also adorned with work by local artists.

Also artistic are their drinks. Sometimes they offer a drink called La Frida, which is made with mole syrup and topped with rose petals. It's from a family recipe and named after Frida Kahlo. They make Amuleto (vanilla bean latte) "to honor how the Olmecs [an Atzec group] used the vanilla orchid flower as protection." And their rotating wonder menu tells stories of people, places, and ingredients reflected in their drinks. They have achieved acclaim with these homages: Little Waves was recognized as *Roast Magazine*'s microroaster of the year in 2022.

by Morgan Bolling

Areli Barrera Grodski at her Durham coffee shop Cocoa Cinnamon.

7   Gently drop 6 churros into hot oil and fry until dark golden brown on all sides, about 6 minutes, turning frequently for even cooking. Adjust burner, if necessary, to maintain oil temperature between 350 and 375 degrees. Transfer churros to prepared plate for 30 seconds to drain off excess oil, then transfer to wire rack in oven. Return oil to 375 degrees and repeat with remaining dough in 2 more batches.

8   Combine cinnamon and remaining ½ cup sugar in shallow dish. Roll churros in cinnamon sugar, tapping gently to remove excess. Transfer churros to platter and serve with sauce.

Fried Peach Pies

Makes 8 hand pies ~ Total Time: 2 hours, plus 20 minutes chilling

The massive, peach-shaped water tower looming over Clanton, Alabama, heralds Peach Park, a roadside retail attraction and restaurant that serves as the spiritual center of Alabama's peach-producing region. Out front, an open-air market sells fresh produce (peaches, mostly) and peach-based pantry products; inside, a long cafeteria case houses meat-and-three fare (preludes, perhaps, to peach ice cream and peach cobbler). Portraits of the reigning Miss Peach and her younger counterparts Junior Miss Peach, Young Miss Peach, and Little Miss Peach honor their regal stone-fruit court.

Husband and wife owners Gene and Frances Gray started Peach Park as a roadside fruit stand. Frances started to make peach ice cream to expand their business. From here, it didn't take long for fried peach hand pies to become a star attraction. Rumor has it these sweet, warm pies were something the duo started cooking as a way to use up overripe peaches, too soft and ugly to sell as is but still full of peach flavor. If so, thank goodness for those ugly peaches because these handheld fried peach pies emerge from the hot oil with a warm crust that's both tender and crumbly wrapped around a delicious thick peach filling.

Our inspired version is made by cooking sliced peaches with sugar and a pinch of salt on the stovetop before gently mashing the fruit and letting it thicken. The soft dough made with melted butter holds up under the hot oil. The addition of baking powder and milk in our dough helps achieve the dainty, almost cake-like crumble for the crust. You can substitute 20 ounces frozen peaches for the fresh peaches; increase the cooking time in step 1 to 15 to 20 minutes. Use a Dutch oven that holds 6 quarts or more.

4	ripe peaches, peeled, halved, pitted, and cut into ½-inch wedges
½	cup (3½ ounces) sugar
1	teaspoon table salt, divided
2	teaspoons lemon juice
2	cups (10 ounces) all-purpose flour
2	teaspoons baking powder
6	tablespoons unsalted butter, melted and cooled
½	cup whole milk
2	quarts peanut or vegetable oil for frying

1 Combine peaches, sugar, and ¼ teaspoon salt in medium saucepan. Cover and cook over medium heat, stirring occasionally and breaking up peaches with spoon, until tender, about 5 minutes.

2 Uncover and continue to cook, stirring and mashing frequently with potato masher to coarse puree, until mixture is thickened and measures about 1⅔ cups, 7 to 13 minutes. Off heat, stir in lemon juice and let cool completely.

3 Line rimmed baking sheet with parchment paper. Pulse flour, baking powder, and remaining ¾ teaspoon salt in food processor until combined, about 3 pulses. Add melted butter and pulse

until mixture resembles wet sand, about 8 pulses, scraping down sides of bowl as needed. Add milk and process until no floury bits remain and dough looks pebbly, about 8 seconds.

4 Turn dough out onto lightly floured counter, gather into disk, and divide into 8 equal pieces. Roll each piece between your hands into ball, then press to flatten into round. Place rounds on prepared sheet, cover with plastic wrap, and refrigerate for 20 minutes.

5 Working with 1 dough round at a time, roll into 6- to 7-inch circle about ⅛ inch thick on floured counter. Place 3 tablespoons filling in center of circle. Brush edges of dough with water and fold dough over filling to create half-moon shape, lightly pressing out air at seam. Trim any ragged edges and crimp edges with fork to seal. Return pies to prepared sheet, cover with plastic, and refrigerate until ready to fry. (Pies can be covered and refrigerated for up to 24 hours.)

6 Line platter with triple layer of paper towels. Add oil to large Dutch oven until it measures about 1½ inches deep and heat over medium-high heat to 375 degrees. Gently place 4 pies in hot oil and fry until golden brown, about 3 minutes, using spider skimmer or slotted spoon to flip halfway through frying. Adjust burner, if necessary, to maintain oil temperature between 350 and 375 degrees. Transfer pies to prepared platter. Return oil to 375 degrees and repeat with remaining 4 pies. Let cool for 10 minutes before serving.

SOUTHERN WOMEN AND WEIGHT

I was in junior high school then. We were piled into the car on a family excursion and, like always, I had my head in a book when my aunt reached over and poked the pooch of my belly. She wanted to see if it was me or my ballooning khaki pants that caused the roundness. My face still burns hot at the memory.

My adolescent insecurity wasn't solely fueled by family members assessing and evaluating my body. In Macon County, Georgia, Southern girls were meant to be well-mannered, petite, and pretty. We would hear "clean your plate," and then, in the next breath, "act like a lady," which tacitly implied not cleaning your plate. It's an uncomfortable paradox of admonitions: As "Southern ladies," we are meant to cherish food, but also to minimize ourselves. And I was a sturdy kid, broad-shouldered. Not tall and thin like my younger sister, not petite and fine-boned like my mother. Where did I fit?

From *Gone with the Wind* to the latest comedy featuring Madea, there are a million stereotypes regarding weight and Southern women of all races, and nothing shines a light on the expectations placed on Southern women more clearly than the food we prepare and consume—dishes that traditionally have been fried in fat and laced with sugar and salt. If modern social media culture prides itself on the freedom of not caring what other people think (or at least an illusion of not caring), traditional Southern society is the exact opposite. Traditional Southern society cares deeply about what other people think.

Southern food and cooking has long been about hospitality and abundance. Originally, it was the work of enslaved Africans, and later emancipated labor, who made the famed plantation hospitality possible. We can also trace many Southern foods we love today to those who brought their foodways and culinary skills with them during their forced journey to America centuries ago. These foods spread beyond the über-wealthy elites to the rest of Southern society.

Out of the tragic truth of slavery grew the myth of a plump, happy Black cook. Mammy, a caricature of an African American woman, signaled home and comfort for white popular culture. Her equally mythical white counterpart was the lady of the plantation who no longer existed: a nonworking, fair-skinned, and dainty creature placed high in an ivory tower, the proverbial Southern belle. She was fragile and flirtatious, yet sexually innocent. She was beautiful, but delicate and risky to touch. She was a fictional character based on the desires and expectations projected onto women by straight, white, ruling-class Christian men—a tidy package of racism, misogyny, and ageism.

As a Southern white, gay woman and professional cook and food writer who's struggled with weight for much of my life, it's been a journey to get a handle on loving a place that doesn't always love me back. I'm finished with minimizing and making myself small. Instead I strive to value strength over stereotypes, to help make the modern South a better place for women—mind, body, and spirit—through good and good-for-you recipes. And not to be concerned about the unrealistic expectations of others.

Because frankly, my dear, I don't give a damn.

by Virginia Willis

James Beard award–winning cookbook author, Southern chef, TV personality, and speaker

No.8

SANDWICH
ICONS

Left to right: Surry Ground Steak Sandwiches (page 265), Ultimate BLT Sandwiches (page 264), Lemongrass Chicken Banh Mi (page 260), Pickle-Brined Fried Chicken Sandwiches (page 272), Ham and Swiss Football Sandwiches (page 277).

MAKE ME A SANDWICH

On a steamy August afternoon in 1999, my husband Bruce and I pulled our car off of Interstate 25 in Pueblo, Colorado, to visit with the parents of one of his college friends. We'd just dropped our freshman son at the University of Denver and were making our way back home to Texas. Though the men spend most of the conversation traveling down memory lane, I am enjoying the banter. Behind them, the mother can be seen in the kitchen reaching in and out of the refrigerator pulling open drawers, and rooting around in the cupboard. When the time comes to say our goodbyes, she hands Bruce a brown paper bag. "A little something for the road," she says. A few minutes later, we are back in the car, and I am surprised by what's inside: two pieces of cold fried chicken; buttered slices of white bread, crusts removed, cut in half diagonally, wrapped in wax paper; two slices of pound cake.

To anyone else this gesture of hospitality might have simply seemed kind. And it was. But for me, a student of history, the meal also reflected an unspoken holdover from African American life in the segregated South. I couldn't help thinking about the danger and inconvenience my ancestors experienced while traveling and being unable to find a safe place to stop and eat during the waves of the Great Migration. They packed everything they might need to feed themselves on the road, a habit we have come to know as the "shoebox lunch."

Contemplating Southern sandwiches brought this memory back. The combination of bread and a protein combined into a portable meal is a classic expression of the sandwich as we know it. According to the legend surrounding its creation in 1762, John Montagu, the 4th Earl of Sandwich, was a gambler. He didn't want to stop playing cards to eat. So he asked a servant to bring him two slices of bread with a slice of beef in between; no need to leave the table. In a similar way, the buttered bread and chicken care package Bruce and I received that day ensured that we wouldn't need to stop on the road for a bite to eat.

The more I thought about the various foods that cooks, generally, and Southern cooks, specifically, put between two slices of bread, the more surprising nuances I observed across gender, race, and class. Stay with me.

Sammys such as Vietnamese banh mi, Chinese roujiamo, Mexican tortas, and Cuban sandwiches reflect the influence global cuisines have on the South. Creole specialties—po' boys, oyster loaves, and muffalettas—and pulled (or chopped) pork sandwiches that differ by state, are banners for regional representation.

Chipped beef, the club, the Dagwood, and the Elvis may all seem hearty, meaty, and, yes, manly, while finger sandwiches made with delicate fillings and spreads, cut into triangles, and the crusts removed, reflect a time when ladies gathered at fancy luncheons or afternoon tea, and nibbled on canapés, miniature ham biscuits, and petit fours. Some modern Southern cooks also see finger sandwiches as an expression of minimalist cooking; a rejoinder to muggy, hot Southern summers when no one wants to cook at the lake, a fun addition to a wedding reception, and even as condolence food, says Carrie Morey, founder of Callie's Hot Little Biscuit in Charleston.

In her book *Callie's Biscuits and Southern Traditions: Heirloom Recipes from Our Family Kitchen*, Morey writes: "It's a message saying that you acknowledge their pain, that you are there for them, that you are thinking of them, and that if you could do anything in the world that would help ease their anguish, they just need to tell you what that is."

Sandwiches can also be entrepreneurial. At Brenda's Bar-B-Q Pit, a family-owned and -operated restaurant in Montgomery, Alabama, since 1942, fried fish sandwiches and pig ear sandwiches keep the community "feelin' good."

In Houston, Michelle Wallace, a pitboss and contestant on Bravo's *Top Chef*, established the B'tween Sandwich Co., a dining pop-up with menus that highlight her more modern experience cooking over fire: smoked porchetta with collard green salsa verde, shrimp biscuit with mango, charcuterie sando, and smoked crab and blue corn biscuit. And, at the same time that social media misogynists have created a snarky meme suggesting that women belong in the kitchen and should serve men with sandwiches, Sicily Sierra, who lives in North Carolina, founded the Sandwich Ministry, a program that teaches women and others not only how to make delicious sandwiches, but also to find agency and empowerment through culinary education.

Think of that the next time a man tells you to go "make me a sandwich."

by Toni Tipton-Martin

Cuban Sandwiches

Serves 4 ~ Total Time: 40 minutes

In Tampa, Florida, the Cuban sandwich is an enduring source of pride, sustenance, and fierce debate. Connoisseurs take strong stands on each element. Cuban sandwiches are derived from mixto sandwiches, which were popular in Cuba more than a century ago. They were a common lunch for laborers in the cigar factories and were made with a variety of meats that could survive in paper sacks at room temperature. No mayonnaise, tomato, or lettuce.

Today's Cuban sandwich features the basic elements of roasted spiced pork, ham, Swiss cheese, dill pickles, and yellow mustard on a special soft bread that's pressed and toasted until golden brown. In Tampa, the sandwiches also include Genoa salami. That sandwich, which was created by Victor Padilla and Jolie Gonzalez-Padilla, is celebrated at the annual Ford International Cuban Sandwich Festival—a massive two-day event at Centennial Park in Tampa's Ybor City neighborhood, featuring music, performances and, in 2019, a winning attempt at a world record for the longest Cuban sandwich—183 feet.

To make Tampa-style Cuban sandwiches that rival the regional favorites at the festival, go for the full experience with homemade versions of two of the key ingredients: the bread and the pork. For the filling, we build the sandwich in the traditional order: deli ham, Cuban roast pork, Genoa salami, Swiss cheese, and finally pickles. Taking a cue from some creative cooks at the festival, we include a swipe of flavorful mojo sauce (from our Cuban Roast Pork with Mojo on page 256) on the bottom slice of bread for complexity and brightness. A less traditional smear of mayonnaise keeps the sandwich moist. To achieve the classic pressed and crispy-edged crust, we use a heavy Dutch oven to weigh down the sandwiches.

Don't have the time to make your own Cuban bread? You can substitute four 7- to 8-inch soft white Italian-style sub rolls or two 15-inch loaves of soft supermarket Italian or French bread. Do not use a thick-crusted rustic or artisan-style loaf or a baguette. To make slicing the roast pork easier, be sure to chill it thoroughly beforehand. Mojo and mayonnaise aren't typical ingredients in Tampa-style Cuban sandwiches, but they make nice additions.

1 recipe Cuban Bread (page 257)

¼ cup mojo from Cuban Roast Pork with Mojo (page 256) (optional)

¼ cup mayonnaise (optional)

12 ounces thinly sliced deli ham

10 ounces thinly sliced pork from Cuban Roast Pork with Mojo (2 cups) (page 256)

3 ounces thinly sliced deli Genoa salami with peppercorns

6 ounces thinly sliced deli Swiss cheese

16 dill pickle chips

¼ cup yellow mustard

4 tablespoons unsalted butter, cut into 4 pieces, divided

1 Adjust oven rack to middle position and heat oven to 200 degrees. Set wire rack in rimmed baking sheet. Cut bread in half crosswise, then cut each piece in half horizontally.

2 Brush bread bottoms with mojo, if using, and spread with mayonnaise, if using. Layer on ham, followed by pork, salami, Swiss cheese, and pickles, overlapping and/or folding meats as needed to keep them from overhanging sides of bread. Spread mustard on bread tops. Cap sandwiches with bread tops.

3 Melt 1 tablespoon butter in 12-inch nonstick skillet over medium-low heat. Place 2 sandwiches in skillet, right side up, in alternating directions, and spread far apart. Place heavy Dutch oven on top and cook until bottoms of sandwiches are uniformly golden brown and feel firm when tapped, 5 to 7 minutes, rotating sandwiches in skillet as needed. (You will need to flip sandwiches to tap them.)

4 Transfer sandwiches to cutting board. Melt 1 tablespoon butter in now-empty skillet. Return sandwiches to skillet toasted side up. Place Dutch oven on top and continue to cook until second side is uniformly golden brown and feels firm when tapped, 3 to 5 minutes longer.

5 Transfer toasted sandwiches to prepared wire rack and place in oven to keep warm. Wipe skillet clean with paper towels. Repeat with remaining 2 tablespoons butter and remaining 2 sandwiches. Cut sandwiches in half on steep diagonal and serve.

THE CUBAN AT THE COLUMBIA

Columbia Restaurant in Ybor City has been sourcing bread for their sandwiches, which they consider the definitive Cuban sandwiches, from La Segunda Bakery for nearly 100 years. Opened in 1903 as Columbia Saloon, the restaurant originally served as a tasting room for Florida Brewing Company. Andrea Gonzmart Williams is the fifth-generation owner of this restaurant that now spans an entire city block.

Gonzmart Williams explains how the restaurant originally served mixto sandwiches—a more simple ham and cheese sandwich and predecessor to the Cuban—but as Ybor City evolved, so did the sandwiches, and the neighborhood became, according to most historians, the birthplace of the Cuban sandwich we know today. Accordingly, Columbia shifted to making the Cuban, which she calls "truly a representation of everyone that immigrated to Ybor City at the turn of the century."

She says that the ham came from the Spaniards, the roast pork and bread from the Cubans, the salami from the Italians, and the mustard and pickles from the Germans. Swiss cheese represents Ybor City "because it is a melting pot," Gonzmart Williams explains.

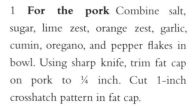

Cuban Roast Pork with Mojo

Serves 6 to 8 ~ Total Time: 4 to 5½ hours, plus 12¾ hours salting and resting

Cuban roast pork is delicious as a dinner centerpiece or as a meaty filling to Cuban Sandwiches (page 254). It should be tender, juicy, and infused with the mojo (a zesty Cuban marinade) flavors of citrus, garlic, oregano, and cumin. For juicy pork, we use an overnight dry rub for seasoning instead of a wet marinade. And to achieve meat that's both ultratender and beautifully bronzed, first we braise the pork and then roast it uncovered to caramelize its exterior.

Avoid buying a boneless pork butt wrapped in netting; it will contain smaller lobes of meat rather than one whole roast. The pork will take longer to cook in a stainless-steel pot than in an enameled cast-iron Dutch oven. If you're using a stainless-steel pot, place a sheet of aluminum foil over the pot before affixing the lid. If you plan to make sandwiches with the leftovers, it is best to slice only what you want to serve and then slice the chilled leftover pork for the sandwiches. You will need about 10 ounces, or 2 cups, of pork and ¼ cup of mojo for the sandwiches. If serving as a main dish, garnish with raw onion to cut through the richness.

Pork

⅓	cup kosher salt
⅓	cup packed light brown sugar
1	tablespoon grated lime zest (2 limes)
1	tablespoon grated orange zest
3	garlic cloves, minced
2	teaspoons ground cumin
2	teaspoons dried oregano
½	teaspoon red pepper flakes
1	(5-pound) boneless pork butt with fat cap

Mojo

⅓	cup extra-virgin olive oil
6	garlic cloves, minced
⅓	cup pineapple juice
⅓	cup orange juice
⅓	cup lime juice (3 limes)
1	tablespoon yellow mustard
1¼	teaspoons ground cumin
1	teaspoon kosher salt
¾	teaspoon pepper
¾	teaspoon dried oregano
¼	teaspoon red pepper flakes
	Thinly sliced onion rounds

1 **For the pork** Combine salt, sugar, lime zest, orange zest, garlic, cumin, oregano, and pepper flakes in bowl. Using sharp knife, trim fat cap on pork to ¼ inch. Cut 1-inch crosshatch pattern in fat cap.

2 Place pork on large double layer of plastic wrap. Sprinkle pork all over with salt mixture. Wrap pork tightly in plastic, place on plate, and refrigerate for at least 12 hours or up to 24 hours.

3 Adjust oven rack to middle position and heat oven to 325 degrees. Unwrap pork; transfer to Dutch oven, fat side up; and pour 2 cups water around pork. Cover, transfer to oven, and cook until meat registers 175 degrees in center, 2½ to 3 hours.

4 Uncover pork and continue to cook until meat registers 195 degrees in center and fork slips easily in and out of meat, 45 minutes to 1¾ hours longer. Transfer pork to carving board, tent with aluminum foil, and let rest for 45 minutes.

5 **For the mojo** While pork rests, heat oil and garlic in small saucepan over low heat, stirring often, until tiny bubbles appear and garlic is fragrant and straw-colored, 3 to 5 minutes. Let cool for at least 5 minutes. Whisk pineapple juice, orange juice, lime juice, mustard, cumin, salt, pepper, oregano, and pepper flakes into cooled garlic oil.

6 Slice pork as thin as possible (some meat may shred; this is OK) and transfer to serving platter. Serve with onion and mojo.

Cuban Bread

Makes two 15-inch loaves
Total Time: 1 hour 20 minutes, plus
13¾ hours resting and cooling

At La Segunda Bakery (see "The Cuban at the Columbia" on page 255), the pan Cubano is airy and light, with a paper-thin crust—just right for sandwiches or for buttering and eating. This recipe achieves a fluffy interior crumb with a "sponge" of flour, yeast, and water that ferments overnight before being added to the rest of the ingredients. This step helps create the carbon dioxide bubbles that give the finished bread its characteristic airy texture. Lard, a traditional addition to Cuban bread, adds a very subtle savory flavor (not sweet or yeasty like a typical sandwich loaf). In Cuban sandwiches, it beautifully complements the pork and ham.

You can substitute shortening for the lard, if desired. Cover the loaves with a rectangular disposable aluminum roasting pan for the first part of baking; the pan traps steam, which then condenses on the bread. This moisture gelatinizes the starches on the outside of the bread, creating golden loaves that are cottony on the inside and crisp on the outside. Overnight fermentation of the sponge provides extra flavor, but if you're strapped for time, you can ferment the sponge for at least 1 hour or up to 4 hours at room temperature instead. Be gentle when slashing the shaped loaves or they will bake up wide and squat.

As a table bread, these loaves are best eaten warm, but for Cuban sandwiches, two-day-old bread is still acceptable.

Sponge

¼ cup water

¼ cup (1¼ ounces) all-purpose flour

½ teaspoon instant or rapid-rise yeast

Dough

3 cups (15 ounces) all-purpose flour

2 teaspoons instant or rapid-rise yeast

1½ teaspoons table salt

1 cup warm water (110 degrees)

¼ cup lard

1 (16 by 12-inch) rectangular disposable aluminum roasting pan

1 **For the sponge** Whisk all ingredients with fork in liquid measuring cup until consistency of thin pancake batter. Cover with plastic wrap and refrigerate overnight (sponge will rise and collapse).

2 **For the dough** Whisk flour, yeast, and salt together in bowl of stand mixer. Add warm water, lard, and sponge. Fit mixer with dough hook and mix on low speed until no dry flour remains, about 2 minutes, scraping down bowl as needed. Increase speed to medium and knead for 8 minutes. (Dough will be sticky and clear sides of bowl but still stick to bottom.)

3 Turn dough onto lightly floured counter, sprinkle top with flour, and knead briefly to form smooth ball, about 30 seconds. Transfer dough to greased large bowl and turn to coat. Cover with plastic and let dough rise at room temperature until doubled in volume, about 45 minutes.

4 Line rimless baking sheet with parchment paper. Turn dough onto floured counter and cut into 2 equal pieces, about 14 ounces each.

5 Working with 1 piece of dough at a time, flatten into 10 by 6-inch rectangle with long side parallel to counter's edge. Fold top edge of rectangle down to midline, pressing to seal. Fold bottom edge of rectangle up to midline, pressing to seal. Fold dough in half so top and bottom edges meet; pinch seam and ends to seal. Flip dough seam side down and gently roll into 15-inch loaf with tapered ends.

6 Transfer loaf, seam side down, to 1 side of prepared sheet. Repeat shaping with second piece of dough and place about 3 inches from first loaf on other side of sheet. Cover loosely with plastic and let rise at room temperature until puffy, about 30 minutes. Adjust oven rack to middle position and heat oven to 450 degrees.

7 Using sharp paring knife in swift, fluid motion, make ⅛-inch-deep lengthwise slash along top of each loaf, starting and stopping about 1½ inches from ends. Cover loaves with inverted disposable pan. Bake for 20 minutes. Using tongs, remove disposable pan and continue to bake until loaves are light golden brown and centers register 210 degrees, 10 to 12 minutes longer.

8 Transfer loaves to wire rack and let cool for 30 minutes. Serve warm.

Shrimp Po' Boys

Serves 4　~　Total Time: 1½ hours

Though numerous variations of this iconic Southern sandwich exist in different parts of the region, they were all born from working-class mealtime needs: easy, affordable, and filling. Historians still debate the origins of the term "po' boy," but most agree that the name comes from a Southern pronunciation of the phrase "poor boy," or the working-class boys and men for whom the sandwiches were first made. While other fillings—including roast beef, ham, and other fried seafood—can be used, a po' boy stuffed with crispy fried shrimp is a New Orleans classic, especially when served on pillowy bread slathered with a pungent rémoulade.

For our at-home take, we start by tossing the shrimp in a flour, cornmeal, and Creole seasoning mixture. To ensure that the batter stays put when fried, we then dip the shrimp in a paste-like batter of beaten eggs bolstered with a bit of the Creole-seasoned dry mixture, dredge them again in the flour mixture, and let them rest in the refrigerator. New Orleans–style French bread is difficult to find outside of Louisiana and the surrounding states. In a pinch, you can use any locally available soft white sub rolls.

Use refrigerated prepared horseradish, not the shelf-stable kind, which contains preservatives and additives. Frank's RedHot Original Cayenne Pepper Hot Sauce is best here. Use a Dutch oven that holds 6 quarts or more. Do not refrigerate the breaded shrimp for longer than 30 minutes, or the coating will be too wet. It may seem like you're spreading a lot of rémoulade on the bread, but it will be absorbed by the other ingredients.

Rémoulade

- ⅔　cup mayonnaise
- 2　tablespoons prepared horseradish
- 1　tablespoon Worcestershire sauce
- 1　tablespoon hot sauce
- ¼　teaspoon pepper

Shrimp

- 2　cups all-purpose flour
- ¼　cup cornmeal
- 2　tablespoons Creole seasoning
- 4　large eggs
- 1　pound medium-large shrimp (31 to 40 per pound), peeled, deveined, and tails removed
- 2　quarts peanut or vegetable oil for frying
- 4　(8-inch) lengths New Orleans–style French bread, split
- 2　cups shredded iceberg lettuce
- 2　large tomatoes, cored and sliced thin
- 1　cup dill pickle chips

1　**For the rémoulade** Whisk all ingredients together in bowl. Set aside.

2　**For the shrimp** Set wire rack in rimmed baking sheet. Whisk flour, cornmeal, and Creole seasoning together in shallow dish. Whisk eggs and ½ cup flour mixture together in second shallow dish.

3　Place half of shrimp in flour mixture and toss to thoroughly coat. Shake off excess flour mixture, dip shrimp into egg mixture, then return to flour mixture, pressing gently to adhere. Transfer shrimp to prepared wire rack. Repeat with remaining shrimp. Refrigerate shrimp for at least 15 minutes or up to 30 minutes.

4　Line large plate with triple layer of paper towels. Add oil to large Dutch oven until it measures about 1½ inches deep and heat over medium-high heat to 375 degrees. Carefully add half of shrimp to oil. Cook, stirring occasionally, until golden brown, about 4 minutes. Using slotted spoon or spider skimmer, transfer shrimp to prepared plate. Return oil to 375 degrees and repeat with remaining shrimp.

5　Spread rémoulade evenly on both cut sides of each bread. Divide lettuce, tomatoes, pickles, and shrimp evenly among bread. Serve.

MELBA'S PO' BOY SHOP: GENEROUS WITH MORE THAN SHRIMP

There can't be too many places where you could put in a load of laundry, grab an overstuffed shrimp po' boy (they advertise 30 shrimp in every sandwich), and attend Pulitzer-winning novelist Colson Whitehead's book signing all in the same spot on the same day. But on the right day at Melba's in New Orleans, you could do just that.

When we walked into the restaurant, it was clear that this is no typical po' boy shop. On one side is a wall showcasing dozens of books and a sign that reads: "Get a book in Melba's Golden Bookcase, get a FREE daiquiri or turkey leg or red beans or . . ." At the bar, there are signs advertising free daiquiris with the purchase of a children's book. What's going on at Melba's?

The person behind Melba's unique literary spirit is Jane Wolfe, founder and co-owner along with her husband Scott Wolfe. The two have an incredible story (one you can read about in their book *From GED to Harvard Then Inc. 500: How Two Teens Went from GEDs to Building the Fastest Growing Business in New Orleans*). They married when Jane got pregnant in high school, got their GEDs, and eventually established a small empire of local grocery stores: Wagner's. (New Orleans folks may remember the slogan: "You can't beat . . . Wagner's meat.") When Hurricane Katrina obliterated every single Wagner's location, the devastated couple quickly changed tack, going into the roofing business. Half a dozen years later, they were back on their feet. Jane—by this time a grandmother herself—seized the opportunity to fulfill a dream to finish her education, parlaying continuing education studies at Tulane University into a master's from Harvard Divinity School.

She still brings that passion to Melba's. For Jane, Melba's literacy program (which has brought in the aforementioned Pulitzer Prize winner Colson Whitehead, a National Book Award Winner, Obama's speech writer, and the Clintons), isn't simply about getting as many books into people's hands as possible; it's an extension of her lifelong goal of using her businesses to do good in her community. There's the bottom line—the necessity of the business turning a profit—and then there's what Jane calls the "all-important second bottom line." This she sums up in two commandments: "Love thy neighbor" and "Be fruitful and share." It's what drove her to give free ice cream cones out to kids who got As on their report cards; to push for higher wages for all of their employees; and to eventually start a literacy program that has "given away more than 20,000 books and connected world-famous people and celebrity authors with Melba's everyday customers." Jane puts it best in her book: "I … saw an opportunity to do far more than open pocket books. In an area of deep poverty, I wanted to open minds."

Jane has done and continues to do just that. She shows the impact one family can have on its community, by feeding it; by employing, educating, and empowering its people; and by always leading her business with a spirit of love and generosity.

THE PO' BOY AND THE BANH MI: TWINS IN NEW ORLEANS

The po' boy is at least a century old, but for the last 45 or so years, it's been evolving alongside its long-distance twin: the Vietnamese banh mi. Indeed, the sandwiches—hailing from two places that could hardly be farther apart—bear enough resemblance to one another that when people in the Crescent City first encountered the banh mi, they came to know it as a "Vietnamese po' boy." And both have fed the city's working class, whether sold from street cart or corner store.

What the sandwiches have most in common is the bread. New Orleans–style "French bread" and Vietnamese "baguettes" are not identical, but they have so much in common—French lineage; a shape vaguely like a baguette; a soft, light, tender, uniform crumb; and a uniquely delicate, thin, crisp crust—that there are places around the Big Easy where they are used interchangeably.

We were first clued in to this overlap on a trip to Today's Cajun Seafood in New Orleans, where chef Huong Vu (Rose) Nguyen (see page 297) served us a perfect fried shrimp po' boy. It seemed like simply another textbook example of the city's best-known sandwich, but when we asked Nguyen where she sourced her French bread, she presented a large box of freshly baked rolls from Dong Phuong Bakery, the city's most heralded Vietnamese bakery.

Dong Phuong, a James Beard Award–winning bakery owned by Huong Tran and opened by her grandmother in the early 1980s, most famously uses their bread to make the banh mi they sell at their location in New Orleans East. But they also deliver thousands of loaves to restaurants around the area daily, and the bread seamlessly subs in for New Orleans's other famous sandwich loaf.

Further examination revealed other restaurants capitalizing on the similarity between the two sandwiches: from Banh Mi Boys, where they serve po' boys and banh mi alongside each other and encourage customers to mix and match ingredients, to MoPho, where they serve mash-ups of the two called a Po Mi. We'd love to try every version of each.

Lemongrass Chicken Banh Mi

Serves 4 ~ Total Time: 1½ hours, plus 1 hour marinating

As a nod to the connection between the po' boy and the banh mi (see "The Po' Boy and the Banh Mi: Twins in New Orleans"), we offer this recipe for a lemongrass chicken banh mi. Grilled chicken po' boys are a popular variety in New Orleans. We marinate boneless, skinless chicken thighs for at least an hour, but preferably 24 hours, in order to season them and infuse them with lemongrass flavor. A hot skillet gives the chicken char (you can substitute a grill pan for those appealing marks). We slice the meat, drizzle it with lime juice, and then layer it on a sandwich with mayonnaise; Maggi Seasoning, an umami-packed liquid that's a favorite of Vietnamese cooks; crunchy pickles; fresh cucumber; cilantro; and jalapeño. The result: a sandwich with big (and Big Easy) flavor and textures.

We suggest looking for banh mi rolls—a distinctive style of soft white roll with a thin, extra-crisp crust and an even, resilient crumb—at your local Vietnamese bakery or restaurant. Or you can use New Orleans–style French bread. In a pinch, you can use any locally available soft white sub rolls. Maggi Seasoning is available online or in Asian markets. We like to use Kewpie mayonnaise for these banh mi.

2	lemongrass stalks, trimmed to bottom 6 inches and sliced thin
1	shallot, quartered
¼	cup packed brown sugar
3	tablespoons fish sauce
3	tablespoons oyster sauce
4	garlic cloves, smashed and peeled
1	tablespoon toasted sesame oil
1	tablespoon sriracha
1	teaspoon five-spice powder
1¾	pounds boneless, skinless chicken thighs, trimmed and pounded ¼ inch thick
2	tablespoons vegetable oil, divided
1	tablespoon lime juice
¾	cup mayonnaise
4	(8-inch) banh mi rolls, lightly toasted and split
1	cup Banh Mi Pickles (recipe follows), drained and squeezed dry
½	English cucumber, halved lengthwise and sliced on bias ¼ inch thick
1	cup fresh cilantro leaves and stems, trimmed and cut into 2-inch lengths
1	large jalapeño chile, stemmed, halved, and sliced on bias ¼ inch thick
	Maggi Seasoning

1   Process lemongrass, shallot, sugar, fish sauce, oyster sauce, garlic, sesame oil, sriracha, and five-spice in blender until smooth, about 1 minute. Add chicken to large zipper-lock bag, pour marinade over chicken, and toss well to thoroughly coat. Refrigerate for at least 1 hour or up to 24 hours.

2   Heat 1 tablespoon vegetable oil in 12-inch nonstick skillet over medium-high heat until shimmering. Place half of chicken in skillet (allowing any excess marinade to drip back into bag) and cook until chicken is deeply browned with charring in spots and registers 170 to 175 degrees, 3 to 5 minutes per side (reducing heat as necessary if chicken begins to get too dark). Transfer chicken to cutting board and tent with

aluminum foil. Wipe skillet clean and repeat with remaining 1 tablespoon vegetable oil and remaining chicken. Let chicken rest for 5 minutes. Slice ¼ inch thick and drizzle with lime juice.

3   Spread mayonnaise evenly on both cut sides of each roll. Divide pickles, cucumber slices, cilantro, jalapeño slices, and chicken evenly among rolls. Drizzle sandwich fillings with Maggi Seasoning to taste.

4   Starting from corner of 16 by 12-inch sheet of parchment paper, immediately wrap each sandwich tightly. Let sandwiches rest in parchment for 5 minutes. To serve, cut sandwiches in half through parchment and unwrap as you eat.

Banh Mi Pickles

Makes 1 pint   ~   Total Time: 20 minutes, plus 1 hour pickling

Look for daikon radish at Asian markets. Turnip can be substituted for the daikon. For convenience, you can use bagged shredded carrots. If you have a mandoline with a julienne blade or a julienne peeler, you can use it to make quick work of the vegetable prep.

3   carrots, peeled and julienned (2 cups)

4   ounces daikon radish, peeled and julienned (1 cup)

¼   cup plus 1 teaspoon sugar, divided

5   teaspoons table salt, divided

1   cup distilled white vinegar

¼   cup water

1   Toss carrots, daikon, 1 teaspoon sugar, and 1 teaspoon salt together in bowl. Massage vegetables gently with your fingers until juices begin to pool in bottom of bowl, about 2 minutes. Let sit for 5 minutes. Drain vegetables in colander and rinse with cold water. Drain thoroughly. Transfer to 2-cup jar.

2   Whisk vinegar, water, remaining ¼ cup sugar, and remaining 4 teaspoons salt until sugar dissolves. Pour into jar until vegetables are covered with brine. (Reserve any excess brine for another use.) Refrigerate for at least 1 hour or up to 1 month.

Tomato Sandwiches

Serves 4 ~ Total Time: 40 minutes

Food journalist Kathleen Purvis said in the *Charlotte Observer*, "Of all the foods that define Southernness, the tomato sandwich may be right up there with grits as the true dividing line."

Real Southerners know the best tomato sandwich relies on little more than white bread, your favorite mayonnaise (Duke's if you're south of the Mason-Dixon), and peak-season summer tomatoes. This recipe adds a bit to the formula by marinating the tomatoes in extra-virgin olive oil, red wine vinegar, and salt and then using some of the tangy marinade to liven up the mayonnaise. Why? The simple Southern archetype isn't so successful if you can't get amazing tomatoes or the right mayonnaise. Dressing the tomatoes allows more people to eat delicious tomato sandwiches no matter their locale or climate.

Buy the best tomatoes you can find that are no more than 2 inches in diameter. The tomatoes should smell fruity and feel heavy for their size. You're more likely to break up the tomatoes if you toss them with the marinade in a bowl; combining them in a zipper-lock bag is gentler. And if you're wondering what to do with your empty Duke's mayonnaise jar, consider following one elderly customer's lead. According to the *Washington Post*, a devoted Southerner wrote to the company requesting a few old-style glass Duke's mayonnaise jars to hold her eventual cremains.

If you want to steer further away from the traditional, you can take a cue from Katie Button (see "Mayo and All i Oli") and, for a garlicky kick, try Homemade Garlic Mayo (recipe follows) on your sandwich instead of conventional mayo.

3   tablespoons extra-virgin olive oil
1   tablespoon red wine vinegar
¾   teaspoon table salt
1   pound mixed ripe tomatoes, cored and sliced ¼ inch thick
½   cup mayonnaise
8   slices hearty white sandwich bread, toasted

1   Whisk oil, vinegar, and salt together in medium bowl; transfer marinade to 1-gallon zipper-lock bag. Add tomatoes to bag, press out air, seal bag, and gently turn to coat tomatoes with marinade. Lay bag flat on counter and let sit for 10 minutes.

2   Transfer tomato slices to now-empty bowl, leaving marinade in bag. Combine 1½ tablespoons marinade with mayonnaise in small bowl. Discard remaining marinade.

3   Place toast on cutting board. Spread 1 tablespoon mayonnaise mixture on 1 side of toast. Shingle tomatoes evenly on 4 slices of toast, covering as much of toast as possible. Season tomatoes with pepper to taste. Top tomatoes with remaining 4 slices of toast, mayonnaise side down. Cut sandwiches in half. Serve.

Homemade Garlic Mayo

Makes 1½ cups
Total Time: 15 minutes

Our mayo is the easy kind, using the "egg and food processor shortcut," as Katie Button says. Do not substitute olive oil for the vegetable oil; the mayo will turn out bitter. A little Dijon and some cayenne pepper give this version kick. This recipe contains raw or undercooked egg, which comes with inherent risks.

1	large egg
4	teaspoons lemon juice
1½	teaspoons Dijon mustard
1	garlic clove, minced
¾	teaspoon table salt
¼	teaspoon sugar
	Pinch cayenne pepper
1½	cups vegetable oil
2	tablespoons extra-virgin olive oil

Process egg, lemon juice, mustard, garlic, salt, sugar, and cayenne in food processor until combined, about 5 seconds. With processor running, slowly drizzle in vegetable oil until emulsified and mixture is thick, about 2 minutes. Scrape down sides of bowl with rubber spatula and continue to process 5 seconds longer. Transfer to airtight container and whisk in olive oil. Cover and refrigerate until ready to use. (Mayo can be refrigerated for up to 1 week.)

MAYO AND ALL I OLI

I'm a mayo fan. Learning from my Southern parents, I would smear two pieces of bread with mayonnaise and fill it with raw Vidalia onions and a sprinkle of salt and pepper. The crunchy sweetness of the onion with a binder of tangy, creamy mayo—that's heaven. When I was a kid, my dad and I stood in the kitchen together with a knife in the mayo jar, smearing a dollop onto each bite of a hard-boiled egg. Whether on tomato sandwiches or BLTs, mayonnaise matters, especially to Southerners. So much so that I've witnessed people raise their voices when defending their favorite brands.

As I came into my culinary own, exploring, making, and falling in love with Spanish food, my affinity grew for mayo's Spanish counterpart. It's similar in consistency, but built on garlic and olive oil; "all i oli" is Catalan for garlic and olive oil. Traditionally, one emulsifies the olive oil and garlic slowly by hand, using a mortar and pestle. I have to confess, I have never made all i oli this way—mainly because you have to have unthinkable patience to work olive oil into garlic, one drop at a time, to yield perfectly creamy emulsification without the saving grace of an egg to bind it together, or a food processor to save your arms a workout. While most people (like me) take the egg and food processor shortcut, you can tell the difference when it's done right.

Handmade all i oli is thicker, almost stands up, and has a greenish hue with little bits of the garlic pieces remaining. Of course, you can taste the difference too! When I was living on the Costa Brava, I was introduced to all i oli alongside a giant paella of fideos (short noodles), cuttlefish, cigalas (a small lobster relative), and mussels. The dish is called fideuà. While some believe it should be so flavorful that all i oli isn't necessary, the garlic condiment offers a complex level of umami and creaminess that I simply won't give up.

What I love most about traveling and learning about new foods is that I can take the teachings back home and see how they impact my history, my story, and my Asheville, North Carolina, restaurant menus. I will never make mayonnaise without a hefty amount of garlic in it. This has forever changed the way I enjoy a Vidalia onion sandwich, for the better. My husband is from Spain and now our kids get to experience these sandwiches from my youth through the lens of our combined Spanish American family cultures.

by Katie Button

James Beard Award–nominated chef, restaurateur, business owner, and author of the cookbook Cúrate: Authentic Spanish Food from an American Kitchen

Ultimate BLT Sandwiches

Serves 4   ~   Total Time: 55 minutes

In her article "The Complete(ish) History of the BLT" for *Saveur*, Farideh Sadeghin says "BLT" became part of our food conversations with the rise of diners in the 1940s in the United States; waitstaff used the abbreviation to quickly communicate orders to the chef in these bustling environments. The sandwich's popularity surged after World War II with the growth of supermarkets, which meant seasonal items such as tomatoes became accessible year-round.

In the South, these pork-enhanced sandwiches are kissing cousins to the classic tomato sandwich. Merritt's Grill in Chapel Hill, North Carolina—home to "simply the best BLT in town"—calls their version the Love Sandwich. The previous owners, Robin and Bob Britt, started making their BLT in 1992 at this gas station–turned–lunch counter with a focus on using the best ingredients available: homemade bread, vine-ripened tomatoes, and high-quality crispy bacon. And while Robin has passed away and new owners Paula and John Toogood have taken over Merritt's, the sandwich recipe is still their most popular menu item.

Because of the BLT's simplicity, this recipe calls for high-quality ingredients and intentional construction. We enhance the mayonnaise with some basil and lemon juice to add interest. Toasted potato bread offers both crunch (on the outside) and plush, slightly sweet softness (on the inside).

Choose fresh tomatoes that are about 2 inches in diameter. Since broiler outputs vary, keep an eye on the toasting in step 3. You may need more than one package to get 16 slices of bacon. Do not substitute thick-cut bacon in this recipe.

16	slices bacon
3	vine-ripened tomatoes
2	tablespoons extra-virgin olive oil
1	tablespoon red wine vinegar
¼	teaspoon table salt
¼	teaspoon pepper
½	cup mayonnaise
¼	cup chopped fresh basil
1½	teaspoons lemon juice
	Pinch cayenne pepper
8	slices potato sandwich bread
1	head Bibb lettuce (8 ounces), leaves separated

1   Adjust oven rack 6 inches from broiler element and heat oven to 400 degrees. Arrange bacon in single layer on aluminum foil–lined rimmed baking sheet, overlapping slightly as needed to fit. Bake until bacon is deeply browned and crispy, 25 to 30 minutes, rotating sheet halfway through baking. Transfer bacon to paper towel–lined plate; discard bacon fat and foil. Heat broiler.

2   Meanwhile, core tomatoes and cut into sixteen (¼-inch-thick) slices (you may have some left over). Whisk oil, vinegar, salt, and pepper together in shallow dish. Add tomatoes and turn gently to coat with vinaigrette. Whisk mayonnaise, basil, lemon juice, and cayenne together in bowl.

3   Arrange bread on now-empty sheet. Broil until lightly browned on 1 side only, 1 to 2 minutes.

4   Transfer bread, toasted side down, to cutting board. Spread basil mayonnaise evenly on untoasted sides of bread (use all of it). Break bacon slices in half. Shingle 4 bacon halves on each of 4 bread slices, followed by 2 lettuce leaves, 4 tomato slices, 2 more lettuce leaves, and 4 more bacon halves. Top sandwiches with remaining bread slices, mayonnaise side down. Cut sandwiches in half, corner to corner. Serve.

Surry Ground Steak Sandwiches

Serves 6 ~ Total Time: 35 minutes

North Carolina's Surry County, which sits along the state's northern border with Virginia, is made up of the towns Pilot Mountain, Elkin, Mount Airy, and Dobson. It is also the proud home of the ground steak sandwich. This no-nonsense regional specialty consists of ground beef cooked with flour and water (or milk) and served on a bun. It is a "loose meat" sandwich, meaning the meat is never formed into a patty—think sloppy joe without the sauce. It's often cited as a relic of the Great Depression, when making meat go further was a necessity, and is believed to have originated at the former Canteen restaurant in Mount Airy in the early 1930s. A proper Surry County–style ground steak sandwich is seasoned with only salt and pepper and then topped with a slice of tomato, coleslaw, and a little mayonnaise, making it simple and straightforward in flavor.

If you want a little extra (besides the traditional tomato, coleslaw, and mayo) on your ground steak at Dairy Center in Mount Airy, you can order it "all the way," meaning topped with chopped onions. Other stops along the Surry Ground Steak Trail serve the sandwich on buttery Texas toast or with an added swipe of zesty mustard.

Martha Sue's is a restaurant just outside of downtown Mount Airy where the food is homey and the atmosphere is classic Americana. In the morning, the kitchen is run by Wilma Fleming, a proud octogenarian who has been cooking professionally for more than 40 years. She describes herself as a "dump cook: I just dump it and cook it. Nothing fancy. Just plain country." Fleming cooks her ground steak mixture until it's the consistency of gravy.

This version serves six people with a pound of meat and employs a cast-iron skillet to sauté (rather than boil) the rich 80 percent lean ground beef with pepper and salt. To achieve the fine texture of the slaw traditionally served on this sandwich, we shred the cabbage using the shredding disk of the food processor (or the large holes of a box grater) and add a tablespoon of sugar so that it is just sweet enough to complement the rich beef.

You will need 6 to 8 ounces of cabbage to yield 1½ cups of shredded cabbage. Serve these sandwiches with finely chopped onion and yellow mustard.

Slaw

2	tablespoons mayonnaise
1	tablespoon sugar
1	tablespoon distilled white vinegar
½	teaspoon table salt
⅛	teaspoon pepper
1½	cups shredded green cabbage

Ground Steak

1	pound 80 percent lean ground beef
1¾	teaspoons pepper
1	teaspoon table salt
¼	cup all-purpose flour
¾	cup water
¼	cup mayonnaise
6	hamburger buns, toasted and buttered
6	tomato slices

1 **For the slaw** Whisk mayonnaise, sugar, vinegar, salt, and pepper together in bowl. Add cabbage and toss to coat; refrigerate until ready to use.

2 **For the ground steak** Cook beef, pepper, and salt in 12-inch cast-iron skillet over medium heat, breaking up meat with wooden spoon, until beef is no longer pink, 7 to 10 minutes. Mash beef with potato masher until fine-textured, about 1 minute.

3 Sprinkle flour over beef and cook, stirring constantly, until flour has been absorbed, about 1 minute. Slowly stir in water and cook, scraping up any flour sticking to skillet, until mixture has thickened and becomes cohesive, 2 to 4 minutes.

4 Spread mayonnaise evenly on bun bottoms. Divide beef mixture among bun bottoms, then top with tomato slices, coleslaw, and bun tops. Serve.

HENRIETTA DULL'S PATH TO SOUTHERN COOKING CELEBRITY

Henrietta Stanley Dull was born in the small town of Stanley's Mill in rural southeast Georgia, with one foot in the 19th century and one in the 20th. The daughter of a miller, she was raised on stone-ground cornmeal, and she would become the South's earliest cooking celebrity.

Through her weekly recipes and columns in the *Atlanta Journal* newspaper, Mrs. S. R. Dull (her pen name) guided cooks through the Depression, job loss, World War II, and war rationing, and she helped them transition from old wood stoves to gas and then to electric.

Hardship was something Dull knew personally, as she was left with a young family to support when her husband died, so she turned to selling sandwiches to church members; the effort evolved into catering, cooking classes sponsored by Atlanta Gas Light, and finally writing about food in the newspaper and later in her 1928 classic cookbook, *Southern Cooking*, which was so successful regionally it was republished in 1941 for a larger national audience.

The book documented the ups and downs and disparities of the South, for among recipes for dainty pineapple fritters, ladies' luncheon tomato aspic, and fine-grained angel food cake, you will find simple corn pone, information on cooking for disabled family members at home, and instructions for wringing a chicken's neck and then frying it up for supper.

Like other authors of her time, Dull was fastidious about no shortcuts, taking the time to do things right, and accurate measurements. Although the home economics movement began much earlier in the Northeast, Dull was its pioneer down south. With calm assurance, she crafted recipes that had been rooted in "a little of this and a dab of that," and in so doing, preserved Southern cooking for generations to come. She died in 1964 at 100 years old and is buried at Westview Cemetery in Atlanta.

by Anne Byrn

food writer and bestselling cookbook author

Bacon, Lettuce, and Fried Green Tomato Sandwiches

Serves 4   ~   Total Time: 1¼ hours, plus 1 hour salting

While you may have come across fried green tomatoes in the Southern United States, it wasn't until Fannie Flagg's 1987 novel *Fried Green Tomatoes at the Whistle Stop Cafe* came out—and even more impactful, the movie adaptation in 1991—that this dish turned into a culinary sensation. Restaurants across the South added them to their menus, and the demand for green tomatoes soared. According to Flagg, "If there is such a thing as complete happiness, it is knowing that you are in the right place." We can't promise this BLT-inspired sandwich complete with fried green tomatoes will transport you to the right place—or guarantee eternal happiness—but, darn, does it taste good.

Look for green tomatoes that are about 3 inches in diameter. It's best to slice the tomatoes close to ⅛ inch thick if possible, but as long as they're less than ¼ inch thick they will work well in this sandwich. Crunchy panko bread crumbs boldly seasoned with Old Bay ensure a crisp and flavorful fried green tomato. A tangy, spicy mayo slathered on a big, soft brioche roll; a pile of bacon; shredded lettuce; and the crispy fried tomatoes make for a sandwich that is far better than the sum of its already delicious parts.

3	green tomatoes
1	tablespoon sugar
1½	teaspoons table salt, divided
½	cup mayonnaise
2	teaspoons Tabasco sauce
1½	cups all-purpose flour
1½	cups panko bread crumbs
1	tablespoon Old Bay seasoning
4	large eggs
1½	cups vegetable oil for frying
4	large brioche sandwich rolls, split and toasted
12	slices cooked bacon, halved
2	cups shredded iceberg lettuce

1   Core tomatoes and cut off rounded top and bottom. Slice tomatoes into twelve ⅛- to ¼-inch-thick slices (you may have some left over). Line rimmed baking sheet with triple layer of paper towels. Place tomatoes on prepared sheet and sprinkle both sides with sugar and 1 teaspoon salt. Cover tomatoes with triple layer of paper towels and let sit for 1 hour.

2   Meanwhile, whisk mayonnaise and Tabasco together in bowl; set aside.

3   Whisk flour, panko, Old Bay, and remaining ½ teaspoon salt together in large bowl. Beat eggs together in shallow dish. Remove top layer of paper towels from tomatoes. Transfer tomatoes to flour mixture and toss to coat. Remove remaining paper towels from sheet and wipe sheet dry. Return tomatoes to now-empty sheet. Working with 1 slice at a time, dip tomatoes in egg, allowing excess to drip off, and return to flour mixture, pressing firmly so coating adheres. Return tomatoes to sheet.

4   Line large plate with triple layer of paper towels. Add oil to 12-inch nonstick skillet and heat over medium-high heat to 350 degrees. Fry half of tomatoes until golden and crispy, about 2 minutes per side, reducing heat as needed. Using tongs, transfer fried tomatoes to prepared plate. Return oil to 350 degrees and repeat with remaining tomatoes.

5   Spread 1 tablespoon mayonnaise mixture on each roll bottom, then follow with 6 half-slices bacon and 3 fried tomatoes, overlapping slightly in center. Toss lettuce with remaining ¼ cup mayonnaise mixture in bowl and divide evenly among sandwiches. Cover with roll tops and serve.

Fried Onion Burgers

Serves 4 ~ Total Time: 30 minutes, plus 35 minutes salting and resting

The fried onion burger is a specialty in Oklahoma and parts of northern Texas. It's like a regular hamburger but with a crispy, onion-laced side. To make it, give the onion some TLC. A mandoline makes quick work of slicing the onion thin. Squeezing the salted onion slices until they're as dry as possible ensures that they adhere to the patties. Next, as is typical, we set a ball of meat on top of each mound of onion and then press the patties down into the onion to help it stick. Layering the burgers in a buttered skillet onion side down browns the onion and seals it onto the burgers. When the onion crust is caramelized and slightly crisp underneath, it's time to flip the burgers and turn up the heat to finish cooking and get a nice sear. These burgers are traditionally served with yellow mustard and slices of dill pickle.

1	large onion, halved and sliced ⅛ inch thick
1½	teaspoons table salt, divided
¾	teaspoon pepper, divided
1	pound 85 percent lean ground beef
1	tablespoon unsalted butter
1	teaspoon vegetable oil
4	slices American cheese (4 ounces)
4	hamburger buns, toasted if desired

1 Toss onion with 1 teaspoon salt in colander and let sit for 30 minutes, tossing occasionally. Transfer onion to clean dish towel, gather edges, and squeeze onion dry. Sprinkle with ½ teaspoon pepper.

2 Divide onion mixture into 4 equal mounds on rimmed baking sheet. Divide ground beef into 4 equal portions, then gently shape into balls. Place beef balls on top of onion mounds and flatten beef firmly so onion adheres and patties measure ¼ inch thick.

3 Sprinkle patties with remaining ½ teaspoon salt and remaining ¼ teaspoon pepper. Melt butter and oil in 12-inch nonstick skillet over medium heat. Using spatula, transfer patties to skillet onion side down and cook until onion is deep golden brown and beginning to crisp around edges, 8 to 10 minutes. Flip patties, increase heat to high, and continue to cook until well browned on second side, about 2 minutes longer. Transfer burgers to platter and let rest for 5 minutes. Place 1 slice American cheese on each bun bottom. Serve burgers on buns.

A TASTE OF OKLAHOMA TRADITION IN TEXAS

Tucked away in the Fort Worth Stockyards, Hooker's Grill is a beacon of culinary tradition. It was founded by mother-daughter duo Ruth and Kathryn Hooker. In an interview with *Texas Country Reporter*, Ruth jokes about using the family's name for a restaurant, saying, "I had thought forever, I thought, maybe I shouldn't call it 'Hooker's,' but we do have fun with it."

Initially, the Hookers' aim was to bring the famous Oklahoma fried onion burger to Texas, and they have done it well; the burger has been named "best burger in Fort Worth" by the local paper. According to Ruth, this burger was developed in Oklahoma during the Depression when meat was very expensive; the fried onions stretched the ingredients and made something delicious.

The menu at Hooker's Grill includes a number of other comforting sandwiches: fried bologna, Coney dogs, grilled PB&Js, patty melts, and BLTs. Plus, Ruth serves another beloved dish from Oklahoma and Native American communities, a frybread taco (Hooker's calls it the "Indian Taco").

Ruth is a member of the Choctaw Nation, and this is just one of the ways she brings her heritage into the restaurant. Ruth's family's handprints are pressed into the foundation. And the phrase "chi pisa la chike," meaning "until we meet again," adorns the wall.

by Morgan Bolling

Muffulettas

Serves 8 ~ Total Time: 1 hour, plus 3 hours resting, cooling, and pressing

This iconic NOLA sandwich, packed with richness and piquant flavor, stacks cured meats, cheese, and olive salad inside a puffy round of bread. The sandwich came to New Orleans with Sicilian immigrants (see "Sicilian Women in New Orleans") and the Southern Italian–inspired flavors shine.

It can be hard to find bread rounds big enough just anywhere, so we start with (semi) homemade bread by baking store-bought pizza dough into sandwich rounds. We top our bread with sesame seeds as they do at Central Grocery, the birthplace of NOLA's version of muffuletta. The olive salad consists of capers, giardiniera, garlic, herbs and spices, and a splash of vinegar in addition to the olives; it's briny, bright, and tangy and elevates this sandwich above other cold cut varieties. For the cold cuts we use mortadella, salami, and hot capicola for kick, as well as aged provolone cheese. Alternating layers of meats and cheese gives the stacked sandwich stability, so it's easier to eat. We press the assembled sandwiches for an hour to allow the olive salad to soak into the bread. You will need one 16-ounce jar of giardiniera to yield 2 cups drained. If you like a spicier sandwich, increase the amount of pepper flakes to ½ teaspoon. If you don't have a heavy Dutch oven, use two 5-pound bags of flour or sugar to weigh down the wrapped muffulettas.

2	(1-pound) balls pizza dough
2	cups drained jarred giardiniera
1	cup pimento-stuffed green olives
½	cup pitted kalamata olives
2	tablespoons capers, rinsed
1	tablespoon red wine vinegar
1	garlic clove, minced
½	teaspoon dried oregano
¼	teaspoon red pepper flakes
¼	teaspoon dried thyme
½	cup extra-virgin olive oil
¼	cup chopped fresh parsley
1	large egg, lightly beaten
5	teaspoons sesame seeds
4	ounces thinly sliced Genoa salami
6	ounces thinly sliced aged provolone cheese
6	ounces thinly sliced mortadella
4	ounces thinly sliced hot capicola

1   Form dough balls into 2 tight round balls on oiled baking sheet, cover loosely with greased plastic wrap, and let sit at room temperature for 1 hour.

2   Meanwhile, pulse giardiniera, green olives, kalamata olives, capers, vinegar, garlic, oregano, pepper flakes, and thyme in food processor until coarsely chopped, about 6 pulses, scraping down sides of bowl as needed. Transfer to bowl and stir in oil and parsley. Let sit at room temperature for 30 minutes. (Olive salad can be refrigerated for up to 1 week.)

3   Adjust oven rack to middle position and heat oven to 425 degrees. Keeping dough balls on sheet, flatten each into 7-inch disk. Brush tops of disks with egg and sprinkle with sesame seeds. Bake until golden brown and loaves sound hollow when tapped, 18 to 20 minutes, rotating sheet halfway through baking. Transfer loaves to wire rack and let cool completely, about 1 hour. (Loaves can be wrapped in plastic and stored at room temperature for up to 24 hours.)

4   Slice loaves in half horizontally. Spread one-fourth of olive salad on cut side of each loaf top and bottom, pressing firmly with rubber spatula to compact. Layer 2 ounces salami, 1½ ounces provolone, 3 ounces mortadella, 1½ ounces provolone, and 2 ounces capicola in order on each loaf bottom. Cap with loaf tops and individually wrap sandwiches tightly in plastic.

5   Place rimmed baking sheet on top of sandwiches and weigh down with heavy Dutch oven for 1 hour, flipping sandwiches halfway through pressing. Unwrap and slice each sandwich into quarters and serve. (Pressed, wrapped sandwiches can be refrigerated for up to 24 hours. Let come to room temperature before serving.)

SICILIAN WOMEN IN NEW ORLEANS

Sicilian influence at the Creole table can be traced as far back as the 19th century, when agricultural workers who had been unable to find work or enough food during the slow unification of Italy made their way to south Louisiana to work in the sugarcane fields. They settled in New Orleans's French Quarter (often called Little Palermo in those days), and they immediately began to influence the food by selling produce in the French Market or butchering meat in the Halle des Boucheries, or Butcher's Market. Later they established pasta businesses and developed innovative recipes. The Sicilians imported machines that extruded pasta that

was dried and sold in "macaroni factories" and in restaurants that offered the pasta dressed with traditional Sicilian tomato sauce. New Orleans women began to make their own version of pasta sauce using a roux to thicken the sauce instead of thickening it by long cooking—a sauce known today as red gravy. Anonymous women cooked in French Quarter restaurants fronted by their husbands, including po' boy shops that served meatball or Italian sausage sandwiches sauced with this red gravy.

And of course, they served the towering muffuletta. While multiple Sicilian immigrants claim to have invented this sandwich

in New Orleans, that is mostly bold marketing of the technique of building a sandwich traditionally made by women in Sicily for their husbands to eat in the fields. The Sicilian version is typically simpler— soft, seeded bread; tomato; cheese; some olive oil and anchovy—but still contains vibrant savory flavors. The New Orleans muffuletta without a doubt reflects its roots. With this sandwich, Sicilian women made a lasting impact on New Orleans cuisine.

by Liz Williams

author, podcaster, and founder of the National Food & Beverage Foundation

Pickle-Brined Fried Chicken Sandwiches

Serves 4 ~ Total Time: 1 hour, plus 6½ hours brining and chilling

Brining chicken in pickle juice may sound a bit odd, but it just makes sense. The juice is already salty and acidic—two characteristics that make for a good fried chicken brine. Chef Sara Foster, owner of the beloved Foster's Market in Durham, North Carolina, makes a mean pickle-brined fried chicken, which can be found in her cookbook *Foster's Market Favorites: 25th Anniversary Collection*. In addition to great flavor, she touts the utility of using pickle juice: "The end of a pickle jar (which I greet quite often) makes an easy excuse for this dish, and this dish makes an easy excuse to open a new jar of pickles. It's a cycle I'm not keen to break."

   For our take on this technique, we wanted to put the pickle front and center, so we call for adding the brine in three stages. First, we soak boneless chicken thighs in pickle juice fortified with fresh dill, garlic, and dry mustard. Next we dredge the thighs in a seasoned flour mixed with a little pickle brine for a flavorful coating; the brine also creates bits of flour that fry up craggy and crisp. To top off these sandwiches, we mix mayonnaise, chopped pickles, finely chopped red onion, more dill and garlic, a pinch of cayenne, and a table-spoon of pickle brine for a creamy, crunchy, pickle-y topping. This sandwich in three words? Crispy, tangy, and delicious. A 24-ounce jar of pickles is large enough to yield the 1¼ cups plus 1 tablespoon of brine needed for this recipe. Use a Dutch oven that holds 6 quarts or more.

Dill Pickle Topping

¼	cup mayonnaise
¼	cup chopped kosher dill pickles, plus 1 tablespoon brine
½	small red onion, chopped fine
2	tablespoons minced fresh dill
2	garlic cloves, minced
	Pinch cayenne pepper

Chicken Sandwiches

4	(3- to 5-ounce) boneless, skinless chicken thighs, trimmed
1¼	cups kosher dill pickle brine, divided
8	sprigs fresh dill, plus 2 tablespoons minced fresh dill
6	garlic cloves, smashed and peeled
5	teaspoons dry mustard, divided
5	teaspoons kosher salt, divided
5	teaspoons pepper, divided
1¼	cups all-purpose flour
½	cup cornstarch
2	teaspoons granulated garlic
1	teaspoon baking powder
3	cups vegetable oil for frying
¼	cup mayonnaise
4	hamburger buns
2	cups shredded iceberg lettuce

Buffalo Pickle-Brined Fried Chicken Sandwiches

Omit dill pickle topping, mayonnaise for bun bottoms, and lettuce. Toss 4 thinly sliced celery ribs, ½ cup crumbled blue cheese, and ¼ cup mayonnaise together in medium bowl. Whisk ½ cup Frank's RedHot Original Cayenne Pepper Hot Sauce and 4 tablespoons melted unsalted butter together in separate medium bowl. Toss each piece of fried chicken in hot-sauce mixture before placing chicken on bun bottoms. Top with celery topping, ¼ cup celery leaves, and bun tops before serving.

Chili Crisp Pickle-Brined Fried Chicken Sandwiches

Omit dill pickle topping, mayonnaise for bun bottoms, and lettuce. Microwave ½ cup rice vinegar, 1 tablespoon sugar, 1 tablespoon toasted sesame oil, 1 tablespoon soy sauce, and 2 teaspoons kosher salt in liquid measuring cup, stirring occasionally, until sugar is dissolved and mixture is hot, 1 to 2 minutes. Pour vinegar mixture over ½ English cucumber, halved lengthwise and sliced thin, in medium bowl. Let cucumber mixture cool completely, then refrigerate until ready to serve. Combine ½ cup mayonnaise, 2 tablespoons chili crisp, 1 tablespoon water, and ¼ teaspoon sugar in separate medium bowl. Toss each piece of fried chicken in mayonnaise mixture before placing on bun bottoms. Top with drained sesame-pickle topping and bun tops before serving.

1   **For the dill pickle topping** Combine all ingredients in bowl and refrigerate until ready to serve. (Topping can be refrigerated for up to 2 days.)

2   **For the chicken sandwiches** Combine chicken, 1 cup pickle brine, dill sprigs, smashed garlic, 1 tablespoon mustard, 1 tablespoon salt, and 1 tablespoon pepper in bowl. Cover with plastic wrap and refrigerate for at least 6 hours or up to 12 hours.

3   Set wire rack in rimmed baking sheet. Whisk flour, cornstarch, granulated garlic, baking powder, minced dill, remaining 2 teaspoons mustard, remaining 2 teaspoons salt, and remaining 2 teaspoons pepper together in second bowl. Add remaining ¼ cup pickle brine to flour mixture and rub between your fingers until tiny craggy bits form throughout.

4   Working with 1 piece of chicken at a time, remove chicken from brine and transfer to flour mixture. Using your hands, toss chicken in flour mixture, pressing on coating to adhere and breaking up clumps, until coated on all sides. Transfer chicken to prepared wire rack. Discard brine. Refrigerate for at least 30 minutes or up to 2 hours.

5   Heat oil in Dutch oven over medium-high heat to 350 degrees. Carefully add chicken and fry until chicken is golden brown and registers at least 175 degrees, 8 to 12 minutes, flipping chicken halfway through frying. (Adjust heat as needed to maintain oil temperature between 325 and 350 degrees.) Transfer chicken to paper towel–lined plate.

6   Spread mayonnaise evenly on bun bottoms. Place chicken on bun bottoms, then top with dill pickle topping, lettuce, and bun tops. Serve.

Chicken Salad with Fresh Herbs

Serves 6   ~   Total Time: 1 hour, plus 2½ hours cooling and chilling

While it wasn't invented in the region, chicken salad has a deep history in the South. You can find versions of it in early cookbooks such as Sarah Rutledge's *The Carolina Housewife* and Abby Fisher's *What Mrs. Fisher Knows About Old Southern Cooking*. Both call for making a homemade mayo (the only option then) with egg yolks and oil, and Rutledge calls out that it can be eaten with cold meats, other fowl, or even shrimp or oysters.

Women throughout the South put their own spin on signature chicken salads, and Stacy Brown's Chicken Salad Chick menu is a prominent example. The restaurant chain's motto is "Every chick has a story." Brown started by selling chicken salad door-to-door in Alabama, but the health department squashed the operation with the prohibition of the sale of food cooked in a home kitchen. Demand was outgrowing her home kitchen anyway, so she decided to open the first brick-and-mortar restaurant in 2008. Today, the chain has more than 250 locations. Brown named each chicken salad after a woman in her life. There's Fancy Nancy, which is "dressed up" with apples, grapes, and pecans. And Buffalo Barclay, which comes with a little anecdote on the menu: "Let's be honest, lending your name to a Buffalo recipe isn't the most flattering opportunity for a chick. But Barclay isn't most chicks. She's my unflappable next door neighbor who always looks on the sunny side of things." Other options include Olivia's Old South, Lauryn's Lemon Basil, and Fruity Fran.

For chicken salad as consistently delicious as Brown's, we pound chicken breasts to an even thickness; place them in a baking dish with a little olive oil, salt, and pepper; cover them; and steam them, hands-off, in the oven. A creamy classic mayo dressing, including bright lemon juice, crunchy celery, and tons of fresh herbs holds everything together. For variety, make a version with curry powder and dried apricots, or a take featuring grapes and nutty toasted walnuts. These salads can be served in a sandwich or over lettuce.

2	pounds boneless, skinless chicken breasts, trimmed
1	tablespoon extra-virgin olive oil
¾	teaspoon table salt, divided
½	teaspoon pepper, divided
⅔	cup mayonnaise
¼	cup finely chopped celery
3	tablespoons chopped fresh chives
4	teaspoons chopped fresh tarragon
1	tablespoon chopped fresh dill
1	tablespoon lemon juice

1   Adjust oven rack to middle position and heat oven to 350 degrees. Cover chicken with plastic wrap. Using meat pounder, gently pound thickest part of each breast to ¾-inch thickness.

2   Toss chicken, oil, ¼ teaspoon salt, and ¼ teaspoon pepper together in 13 by 9-inch baking dish. Arrange chicken in single layer in dish and cover tightly with aluminum foil. Bake until chicken registers 160 degrees, 28 to 32 minutes. (When checking temperature, carefully open foil so steam escapes away from you.) Transfer chicken to large plate and let cool for 15 minutes; discard any accumulated juices. Refrigerate chicken until completely cooled, about 30 minutes.

3   Cut chicken into ½-inch pieces. Combine chicken, mayonnaise, celery, chives, tarragon, dill, lemon juice, remaining ½ teaspoon salt, and remaining ¼ teaspoon pepper in bowl. Cover with plastic and refrigerate for at least 2 hours to allow flavors to meld. Serve. (Salad can be refrigerated for up to 2 days.)

Chicken Salad with Curry Powder and Dried Apricots

Omit chives, tarragon, and dill. Add ½ cup finely chopped dried apricots, 6 tablespoons toasted slivered almonds, 4 thinly sliced scallions, and 2 teaspoons curry powder to bowl in step 3.

Chicken Salad with Grapes and Walnuts

Omit tarragon and dill. Add 1 cup halved seedless red grapes; 6 tablespoons walnuts, toasted and chopped; and 3 tablespoons chopped fresh parsley to bowl in step 3. Substitute Dijon mustard for lemon juice.

Ham and Swiss Football Sandwiches

Serves 6   ~   Total Time: 1¼ hours

At first glance, football sandwiches look like simple ham sliders. But these tailgate favorites have a devout following among Southern sports fans who know that description wouldn't do them justice. Personal recipes are common in Junior League and other community cookbooks, but most follow a similar formula: Layer ham and cheese or other meats in slider rolls with mustard. Then stir together a rich onion, butter, and poppy seed sauce to brush onto the rolls before baking. As they bake, the sandwiches soften and steam and the butter soaks into the rolls to flavor them.

For a quick, tasty version of the sauce, we microwave chopped onion with butter and poppy seeds. Worcestershire and garlic powder whisked into the melted butter mixture enhance the savory-sweet flavors of the sauce. We spread mustard on the sliced rolls, arrange the bottoms in a baking dish, and layer ham and Swiss on each before placing the tops on the sandwiches and brushing each with the poppy seed sauce. We spoon the remaining sauce over all of the sandwiches and let them sit for 10 minutes to soak up the flavors. Covering and baking the sandwiches for 20 minutes melts the cheese, while a few minutes uncovered in the oven crisps the tops nicely. In almost no time at all, the sandwiches emerge melty, warm, and ready for game day. We prefer the soft white dinner rolls found in the bakery section of the supermarket, but dinner-size potato rolls will also work in this recipe.

12	square soft white dinner rolls
6	tablespoons yellow mustard, divided
12	thin slices deli Black Forest ham (8 ounces)
12	thin slices deli Swiss cheese (8 ounces)
4	tablespoons unsalted butter
2	tablespoons finely chopped onion
1	tablespoon poppy seeds
2	tablespoons Worcestershire sauce
1	teaspoon garlic powder

1   Adjust oven rack to middle position and heat oven to 350 degrees. Slice rolls in half horizontally. Spread ¼ cup mustard on cut sides of roll tops and bottoms. Arrange roll bottoms, cut side up and side by side, in 13 by 9-inch baking dish. Fold ham slices in thirds, then once in half; place 1 slice on each roll bottom. Fold Swiss like ham, then place over ham. Season with pepper to taste and cap with roll tops.

2   Combine butter, onion, and poppy seeds in bowl. Microwave until butter is melted and onion is softened, about 1 minute. Whisk Worcestershire, garlic powder, and remaining 2 tablespoons mustard into butter mixture until combined. Generously brush tops and edges of sandwiches with all of butter mixture. Spoon any remaining solids over sandwiches.

3   Cover dish with aluminum foil and let sit for 10 minutes to allow sandwiches to absorb sauce. Bake for 20 minutes. Uncover and continue to bake until cheese is melted around edges and tops are slightly firm, 7 to 9 minutes longer. Let cool for 10 minutes. Serve warm.

To make ahead   Sandwiches can be brushed with sauce, covered, and refrigerated for up to 24 hours. Let come to room temperature before cooking.

Pastrami and Swiss Football Sandwiches

Substitute 36 thin slices (8 ounces) deli peppered pastrami brisket for ham. Fold pastrami in thirds and use 3 slices per sandwich. Top pastrami with 1 pound sauerkraut, drained and squeezed dry, before adding Swiss.

No.9
SKILLET SUPPERS & CASSEROLE COMFORT

Left to right: Pad Thai (page 299), Cider-Brined Pork Chops with Apples and Onions (page 294), Pan-Seared Maryland-Style Crab Cakes (page 300), Cast Iron Baked Chicken (page 283).

SURVIVAL COOKING

SKILLETS PRODUCE DINNER AND HOPE

When the National Weather Service issued its first flash flood emergency warning for eastern Kentucky on July 26, 2022, it wasn't even raining in Whitesburg. But a river gauge on Main Street showed the North Fork Kentucky River was already about five feet higher than normal, and raring to swell upward with the coming storm.

One foot of rain fell on Whitesburg overnight, submerging the gauge and mustering a historic flood that rampaged through the streets, ripped the freezers off the walls of the local IGA, and charged into homes where people were sleeping, sloshing over handmade quilts.

More than 2,000 people were rescued by neighbors and first responders, including one septuagenarian who clung to her porch roof for hours. Across the affected area, 43 people died.

"I ran out in chest-high water," remembers Penny Vaccaro of Whitesburg, who was scooped up by a neighbor in a kayak.

Like most people who fled the flood, Vaccaro didn't bring anything with her when she left the house. The waters consumed wedding albums, family Bibles, baby blankets, and cast-iron skillets, handed down with cornbread advice and scrubbing tips from one generation to the next. But Vaccaro was determined to get her cookware back.

"It was just a mess," Vaccaro said of the scene she confronted when the flood receded. Mud coated everything in the kitchen; a blender in a knee-high cabinet was still lidded but filled with filthy water. Amid that wreckage, Vaccaro's grown son found and pried free the skillet in which Vaccaro had so many times fried chicken and simmered red gravy.

"I didn't care if anything came out of there, save that pan," said Vaccaro, who salvaged eight plastic bins of belongings before her destroyed home was torn down.

Home cooks have always had special relationships with their cast-iron skillets. "I don't know another kind of cookware that has such strong recipe associations, or that people have passed down as heirlooms," cookbook author Sheri Castle, who grew up in another corner of Appalachia, has been quoted as saying. "I don't know anyone who tells such tales about Teflon, and none of us have our grandmother's Revere Ware."

Generally, the attachment to cast iron is attributed to the past. Personal culinary histories are etched into every skillet, as anyone tasked with scouring away the skin of last night's pan-fried trout can attest. The family meal remains a fleeting art form, and a skillet is a durable connection to bygone suppers and the expertise and emotions that went into them.

Honestly, though, the same could be said about a Bundt pan or a wooden spoon. Once we've crossed into the kitchen magic circle, just about any appliance or implement has the power to evoke memories and warm feelings (although a skillet still has the upper hand when it comes to cornbread).

What the cast-iron skillet represents—to Vaccaro, and to all the home cooks who cling proudly to their skillets—isn't longing for the past, but faith in the future. The cast-iron skillet is a bulwark against uncertainty; a 7.9-pound, indestructible assurance that life will proceed beyond any present distress and despair.

In other words, the 2022 floods were horrific. For the survivors who lost their prized cast-iron skillets to them, they were worse.

Louis Pizitz, founder of the foundational department store in Birmingham, Alabama, acknowledged as much in a 1923 newspaper ad celebrating the opening of a new Pizitz location. Introductory sale items included a 79-cent preserving kettle described as "good [and] heavy," and a 99-cent six-quart boiler touted as "strong." But only the 19-cent cast-iron skillet was guaranteed to "last a lifetime."

Nowadays, with foundries turning out cast iron that's enameled and factory-imprinted with American flags, a skillet can cost a day's wages. But one of the reasons that cast-iron skillets became fixtures in Southern pantries when the region was deeply impoverished was their affordability. In 2024 dollars, a 19-cent price tag works out to $3.51—which makes the promise of forever a pretty good return.

Perhaps because cast iron is linked to eternity, whether by department store owners or home cooks imagining grandbabies someday using their skillets, these pans have a way of popping up in potentially lethal circumstances. During the U.S. Civil War, soldiers such as John G. Lindsey of the North Carolina 60th fried salt pork in them. In 1862, Lindsey abandoned his "grub" skillet at the Missionary Ridge battlefield, coincidentally about 30 miles east of the Tennessee town where genre powerhouse Lodge Cast Iron would later be founded.

In 1906, he dug it up.

"Of course, he will treasure it as the dearest souvenir of his life," the *Knoxville Sentinel* reported.

Women in dangerous situations were known to wield skillets themselves as weapons, warding off intruders and abusive husbands. In 1952, when Robert H. Clamp showed up at his wife's Atlanta prayer meeting, drunk and armed, she subdued him with a cast-iron pan.

Legendary food writer Henrietta Dull of Georgia wrote a 1930 column about frying chicken: "A heavy, deep skillet distributes the heat to all parts, and gives a uniform cooking. There is also less danger of scorching." The same applies to a number of skillet suppers, such as baked chicken and blackened fish; they can be made in other heavy pans, whether stainless steel or nonstick-coated, but you can near guarantee goodness with a cast-iron skillet. Dull further comments, "Occasionally someone bobs up and announces that we do not have good old-time cooking. And then I get so peeved and would like to broadcast to the world that we do. WE DO!"

And, with cast-iron skillets, we always will.

by Hanna Raskin

founder of the Food Section, *an award-winning newsletter covering food and drink across the American South, and James Beard–honored former food editor of the Post and Courier in Charleston, South Carolina*

Blackened Salmon

Serves 4   ~   Total Time: 50 minutes

Blackening is the process of coating quick-cooking proteins in a robust Cajun spice blend and flash-cooking them in a ripping-hot cast-iron skillet until the fat and spices smoke and char—but don't completely burn. The technique was popularized in the 1980s by chef Paul Prudhomme, who used fish.

Today many other Southern—particularly New Orleans—chefs include blackened fish on their menus because the technique imparts tons of flavor, both from the spices and from the blackening. At Commander's Palace, one of the restaurants from restaurateur Ella Brennan (see page 76), current executive chef Meg Bickford serves "bronzed red-fish"; the fish is seared in cast iron and served over roasted fennel, confit onions, blistered tomatoes, greens, satsuma, and saffron beurre blanc. Chef Martha Wiggins uses blackened catfish, along with other dishes on the menu at Café Reconcile, to train the next generation of chefs. The restaurant provides paid on-the-job culinary training to at-risk individuals ages 16 to 24. Saint Lucian chef Nina Compton, a finalist on Bravo's *Top Chef*, fills the menu at New Orleans's Compère Lapin with dishes featuring local ingredients that reflect her ancestral tastes and classical training. She demonstrates her skills blackening a variety of foods—from slow-cooked, seasoned, and blackened octopus to pig ears with smoked aioli.

Here we blacken salmon, which is somewhat firm, readily available for most at the supermarket, and an ideal canvas for a boldly flavored spice blend. For the best results, choose salmon fillets of the same size and thickness; to ensure uniform pieces of fish, you can purchase a whole center-cut salmon fillet and cut it into four equal pieces yourself. Use a well-seasoned cast-iron skillet (see page 285) to prevent the fish from sticking and to ensure that the blackening seasoning adheres. This cooking technique will create a good amount of smoke, so be sure to turn on your exhaust fan or open a window prior to cooking.

2 teaspoons paprika

2 teaspoons kosher salt

¾ teaspoon garlic powder

¾ teaspoon onion powder

½ teaspoon dried oregano

½ teaspoon dried thyme

½ teaspoon pepper

½ teaspoon white pepper

½ teaspoon cayenne pepper

4 (6- to 8-ounce) skin-on salmon fillets, 1 to 1½ inches thick

4 tablespoons unsalted butter, melted, divided

   Lemon wedges

1   Adjust oven rack to middle position and heat oven to 325 degrees. Combine paprika, salt, garlic powder, onion powder, oregano, thyme, pepper, white pepper, and cayenne in small bowl.

2   Place salmon in single layer on large plate. Brush salmon all over with 2 tablespoons melted butter and sprinkle all over with spice mixture (use all of it).

3   Heat 12-inch cast-iron skillet over high heat for 5 minutes. Carefully place salmon in skillet skin side up (skillet handle will be very hot). Cook until very dark brown on bottom, about 1 minute.

4   Using tongs, carefully flip salmon, transfer skillet to oven, and bake until center is still translucent when checked with tip of paring knife and registers 125 degrees (for medium-rare), 12 to 16 minutes. Transfer to serving platter skin side down and pour remaining 2 tablespoons melted butter over salmon. Serve with lemon wedges.

Cast Iron Baked Chicken

Serves 4 ~ Total Time: 1¼ hours

Many Southern chefs turn to their cast-iron skillets to fry chicken. But Sema Wilkes, former owner of the legendary Mrs. Wilkes Dining Room in Savannah, Georgia, explains in her cookbook that her baked chicken recipe is "proof-positive that we Southerners don't fry all of our birds." She calls her recipe "a backdoor favorite with locals."

The dish is a staple on menus in Southern and soul-style restaurants from the Atlantic to Gulf coasts. It's dished up with mashed potatoes and gravy or macaroni and cheese, green beans, and other table sides at the now-closed Bertha's Kitchen, a James Beard America's Classics Award–winner in Charleston, South Carolina, and Mikki's Soul Food Cafe in Houston, Texas.

A cast-iron skillet is key for its superior heat retention and ability to produce ultra-crisp chicken skin. For our version of baked chicken, we like to preheat the skillet in the oven since it brings this thick pan up to temperature more evenly than the stove. We spice our chicken with paprika, onion powder, and granulated garlic. Sprigs of thyme and some butter mingle with the pan juices to create a silky sauce to spoon over the chicken.

2 teaspoons paprika

2 teaspoons table salt

1 teaspoon pepper

½ teaspoon onion powder

½ teaspoon granulated garlic

3 pounds bone-in chicken pieces (2 split breasts, 2 drumsticks, 2 thighs, and 2 wings with wingtips discarded), trimmed

2 tablespoons unsalted butter

6 sprigs fresh thyme

1   Adjust oven rack to middle position, place 12-inch cast-iron skillet on rack, and heat oven to 450 degrees. Combine paprika, salt, pepper, onion powder, and granulated garlic in bowl. Pat chicken dry with paper towels and sprinkle all over with spice mixture.

2   When oven is heated, carefully remove hot skillet. Add butter, let it melt, and add thyme sprigs. Place chicken in skillet skin side down, pushing thyme sprigs aside as needed. Return skillet to oven and bake for 15 minutes.

3   Remove skillet from oven and flip chicken. Return skillet to oven and bake until breasts register 160 degrees and drumsticks/thighs register at least 175 degrees, about 15 minutes longer.

4   Let chicken rest in skillet for 10 minutes. Transfer chicken to platter and spoon pan juices over top. Serve.

Tamale Pie

Serves 4 to 6   ~   Total Time: 1¼ hours

Tamale pie, popular in Southern border states and beyond, pulls inspiration from Mexican tamales. The dish of juicy, spicy sautéed ground meat under a cornmeal crust is assisted by convenience items such as canned beans and frozen corn. And because it comes in comforting casserole form, it's much quicker than traditional tamales to put together. Author Jean Anderson points to the dish's surge in popularity during World War I and World War II in *The American Century Cookbook: The Most Popular Recipes of the 20th Century*. But there was pressure during that time for women to save meat; Anderson notes that a 1918 booklet called *Conservation Recipes* offers five versions of tamale pie—all meatless. She explains that after World War II, it became "the darling of potluck suppers," with meat added back in. The straight sides of a deep cast-iron skillet make it an excellent cooking vessel for the pie's hearty layers; its superior heat retention offers even, steady cooking, guaranteeing that the filling remains moist while the topping develops a golden brown crust.

¼	cup vegetable oil, divided
1	pound ground pork
6	scallions, white and green parts separated and sliced thin
2	tablespoons chili powder
1	tablespoon minced fresh oregano or 1 teaspoon dried
1	teaspoon table salt, divided
1	(15-ounce) can black beans, rinsed
1	(14.5-ounce) can diced tomatoes
1	cup frozen corn
½	cup chicken broth
4	ounces pepper Jack cheese, shredded (1 cup)
¾	cup (3¾ ounces) all-purpose flour
¾	cup (3¾ ounces) cornmeal
¾	teaspoon baking powder
¼	teaspoon baking soda
¾	cup buttermilk
1	large egg

1   Adjust oven rack to middle position and heat oven to 400 degrees. Heat 10-inch cast-iron skillet over medium heat for 5 minutes. Add 1 tablespoon oil and heat until just smoking. Add ground pork and cook, breaking up meat with wooden spoon, until just beginning to brown, about 5 minutes.

2   Stir in scallion whites, chili powder, oregano, and ¼ teaspoon salt and cook until fragrant, about 1 minute. Stir in beans, tomatoes and their juice, corn, and broth. Bring to simmer and cook until mixture has thickened slightly, 5 to 7 minutes. Off heat, stir in pepper Jack until well combined. Season with salt and pepper to taste.

3   Whisk flour, cornmeal, baking powder, baking soda, scallion greens, and remaining ¾ teaspoon salt together in large bowl. In separate bowl, whisk buttermilk, egg, and remaining 3 tablespoons oil until smooth. Stir buttermilk mixture into flour mixture until just combined. Pour batter over meat mixture and smooth into even layer. Transfer skillet to oven and bake until topping is golden brown and toothpick inserted into center comes out clean, 15 to 20 minutes, rotating skillet halfway through baking. Let casserole cool for 10 minutes before serving.

CARING FOR CAST IRON

When a long-simmered stew simply won't do, skillet-cooked meats and comforting baked casseroles are often what's for dinner in the South. The skillet is particularly multipurpose—you can fry, bake, or sauté in it. Different skillets serve different purposes, and we use nonstick, traditional stainless, and cast iron in these recipes. But there's something special—if a bit high maintenance—about cast iron. It retains heat well. It gets better over time, developing a natural slick patina called seasoning that releases food easily. And it is virtually indestructible.

Cleaning a Cast-Iron Skillet
This is the way to keep your skillet in its best shape.

1 Clean After Every Use Wipe interior surface of still-warm skillet with paper towels to remove any excess food and oil. Rinse under hot running water, scrubbing with non-metal brush or nonabrasive scrub pad to remove any traces of food. (Use small amount of soap if you like; rinse well.)

2 Lightly Oil After Each Cleaning Dry skillet thoroughly (do not drip-dry), then heat over medium-low heat until all traces of moisture have evaporated. Add ½ teaspoon oil to pan and use paper towels to lightly coat interior surface with oil. Continue to wipe surface with oiled paper towels until it looks dark and smooth and no oil residue remains. Let pan cool completely.

Seasoning a Cast-Iron Skillet
Sometimes your pan is in need of some extra TLC so it looks slick and is nonstick.

Stovetop Repair
Heat skillet over medium-high heat. Using paper towels dipped in 2 tablespoons oil and held with tongs, wipe surface until oil smokes and there is no remaining oil residue. Repeat oil application 3 to 5 times, making sure oil smokes and letting skillet cool slightly after each application.

Oven Repair
Heat oven to 500 degrees. Using paper towels, rub 1 tablespoon (for 12-inch skillet) or 2 teaspoons (for 10-inch skillet) oil over surface. Using clean paper towels, thoroughly wipe out excess oil (surface should look dark and smooth). Place skillet in oven for 1 hour. Using potholders, remove skillet from oven and let cool completely.

A Note on Oil: Flaxseed oil is ideal, though other vegetables oils work.

Keftedes

Serves 4 to 6 ~ Total Time: 1 hour

The Greek influence on Southern cuisine is significant. In the 1850s and 1860s, there was a major wave of Greek immigrants to the United States. Many landed in New York, while others went through Southern ports such as New Orleans and Charleston. By 1866, the first Greek Orthodox church was established in New Orleans.

According to Jennifer Kornegay in her article "Friends to Strangers" for *Bitter Southerner*, more than 400,000 Greeks immigrated to the United States between 1880 and 1920. Many were leaving behind a struggling economy, so they moved to cities that had industrial opportunities. It was common for immigrants to open fruit stands since they required little capital, but soon they entered the restaurant sector. Kornegay wrote this about Greek immigrants in the early 1900s in Alabama: "They created a South-meets-Mediterranean food philosophy that was born out of their desire to assimilate, but also to honor their heritage by imbuing what they presented their customers with pieces of their home culture—from distinct flavors to high levels of hospitality."

Most Greek restaurants at the time didn't go all out with Greek flavors; rather, they served the Southern-style food of the community, slipping in a Greek dish here and there. Assimilating more to the local culture would foster a broader customer base, they thought. And some feared they'd be putting a target on their backs; a lot of these restaurants opened during the Civil Rights Movement in Alabama, a time when immigrants often faced persecution.

Today, the Greek culinary legacy is proud and thrives in the South. New Orleans's annual Greek festival features mezedes (small plates), Greek wines, and a baklava ice cream sundae. Alabama is the original home of the fast-casual chain Zoës Kitchen, founded in Homewood in 1995 by Zoë and Marcus Cassimus. The chain, before being acquired by Cava Group, grew to have locations across the country. Even Mississippi's comeback sauce, which is also now served all over the South and which you'll find with our Fried Catfish (page 238) is rumored to have Greek-restaurant origins.

Keftedes are bright herb and warm spice–packed meatballs that are served in Greek spots across the South (and elsewhere in the country). They're standard Greek mezedes, providing welcome savory bites among the other fresh dishes. This version makes keftedes the meal, matching the keftedes with the typical creamy yogurt sauce as well as generous planks of zucchini. Different versions use ground lamb, beef, or pork, or a combination. Here, we use equal parts beef and pork for robust meaty flavor. Mashing yogurt, water, and torn bread pieces together creates a panade to bind the meatballs for easier shaping and for keeping them tender and juicy through cooking.

Sauce

- ½ cup plain Greek yogurt
- 1 tablespoon lemon juice
- 1 tablespoon chopped fresh mint
- 1 garlic clove, minced

Meatballs

- 2 slices hearty white sandwich bread, torn into 1-inch pieces
- ⅓ cup plain Greek yogurt
- 2 tablespoons water
- 3 scallions, minced
- ¼ cup minced fresh mint, dill, and/or cilantro
- 1 large egg
- 2 garlic cloves, minced
- 2 teaspoons ground cumin
- 1¼ teaspoons table salt, divided
- ¼ teaspoon pepper
- ⅛ teaspoon cinnamon
- 1 pound 93 percent lean ground beef
- 1 pound ground pork
- 2 tablespoons extra-virgin olive oil
- 1½ pounds zucchini, halved lengthwise and cut on bias into 2- to 3-inch lengths

1 **For the sauce** Combine all ingredients in bowl and season with salt and pepper to taste. (Sauce can be refrigerated for up to 4 days.)

2 **For the meatballs** Mash bread, yogurt, and water in large bowl to smooth paste. Stir in scallions, mint, egg, garlic, cumin, 1 teaspoon salt, pepper, and cinnamon. Add beef and pork and knead with hands until uniformly combined. Pinch off and roll mixture into 2-inch round meatballs (about 26 meatballs total). Transfer meatballs to large plate, cover loosely with plastic wrap, and refrigerate until firm, 15 to 30 minutes.

3 Heat oil in 12-inch nonstick skillet over medium-high heat until just smoking. Add meatballs and cook, gently shaking skillet and turning meatballs as needed, until browned on all sides and cooked through, 10 to 12 minutes. Using slotted spoon, transfer meatballs to serving platter.

4 Add zucchini, cut side down, to fat left in skillet and sprinkle with remaining ¼ teaspoon salt. Cook over medium-high heat, turning as needed, until tender and deep golden brown, 6 to 10 minutes. Serve meatballs with zucchini and yogurt sauce.

CAT CORA'S SOUTHERN GREEK UPBRINGING

Cat Cora, restaurateur celebrated as the first female Iron Chef and host of multiple cooking shows, is not often recognized for her Southern roots. But in her memoir *Cooking As Fast As I Can: A Chef's Story of Family, Food, and Forgiveness*, we learn how deep they run.

Born in Mississippi and adopted by Virginia Lee and Spiro "Pete" Cora, Cat was raised in a household where Greek cuisine mingled with Southern traditions. Her father, an American-born son of Greek immigrants, and her mother, a full-time nurse who always cooked from scratch, introduced Cat to a hybrid culinary world. "My parents loved and cooked fusion food long before anyone had ever heard of it: Greek and southern," Cat writes. When visiting her Aunt Inez and Uncle George in Jackson, Mississippi, Cat enjoyed her aunt's traditional Southern food spread while her uncle made recipes such as biscuits and feta.

Her grandfather, also Pete Cora, ran a restaurant called the Coney Island Café a name Cat says he chose because it sounded American. And her godfather, Peter J. Costas, ran a pizza place (where Cat's parents met) before opening a white tablecloth restaurant, the Continental.

Going to school at the Culinary Institute of America in Hyde Park, New York, and working in restaurants in Northern California added accent to Cat's culinary, professional, and personal identity, but her cooking maintained its foundation in the Southern and Greek experience, as seen in her first book, *Cat Cora's Kitchen: Favorite Meals for Family and Friends*, which includes recipes from Fish Roe Spread with Crostini to Southern-Style Greens and Greek Butter Cookies, all with Greek translations.

Cora's memoir also recounts stories of Cora overcoming immense hardship, navigating her identity in the South, and starting her nonprofit. Cat Cora is an Iron Chef living in California, but her grit grew in her Southern Greek household.

by Morgan Bolling

M'sakhan

Serves 4 to 6 ~ Total Time: 1¼ hours

In her book *Arabiyya: Recipes from the Life of an Arab in Diaspora*, chef and activist Reem Assil (see "From Gaza to Mississippi, with Love") says, "I often joke that while we don't have a nation-state, we most certainly have a national dish." Palestine's national dish, m'sakhan, is usually a big communal affair: Diners tear off pieces of warm, pillowy taboon bread that's slathered with olive oil–simmered onions piled on a platter and wrap them around succulent chunks of roast chicken sprinkled with tangy sumac. M'sakhan's cultural significance runs deep, to the olive tree that's at the heart of both this dish (which is made to celebrate the olive harvest and test the quality of the oil) and Palestinian identity itself. According to Palestinian American educator and chef Awad Awad, olive trees traditionally figure into m'sakhan's every component: The olive oil–enriched flatbread is baked in clay-and-stone taboon ovens that are fueled by olive wood and dried olive pulp, and the chicken and onions are cooked in generous glugs of olive oil. Awad shares a famous Palestinian saying, "A good m'sakhan should have olive oil dripping from your elbows," and this version keeps olive oil central to the dish. Our recipe uses chicken pieces instead of the traditional whole chicken and naan in place of taboon, but we hope you enjoy this marvelous dish as intended: with your hands and with your friends. Afghan or Indian naan and pocketless Greek pita are close substitutes for taboon bread, but any flatbread can be used. Use a good-quality, flavorful extra-virgin olive oil. Palestinian olive oil can be purchased online.

⅓	cup slivered almonds or pine nuts
5	tablespoons extra-virgin olive oil, divided, plus extra for drizzling
3	pounds bone-in chicken pieces (split breasts cut in half, drumsticks, and/or thighs), trimmed
1½	teaspoons table salt, divided
¾	teaspoon pepper
1½	pounds red onions, chopped
¼	cup sumac, divided
2	teaspoons baharat
3	naans
¼	cup chopped fresh parsley

FROM GAZA TO MISSISSIPPI, WITH LOVE

I found my Gazan roots in the fertile U.S. soil of Mississippi. I had helped organize a high school visit to the Deep South in the late '90s on a quest for a truth about America that I sensed but could not see in the suburbs of Boston. I was a first-generation Palestinian-Syrian, fresh off a sobering trip to Palestine, where I witnessed the destruction of my mother's birthplace while American leaders were celebrating an Israel-Palestine peace process. I felt deeply betrayed by America and yearned to reconnect to a place that I was supposed to call home.

Mississippi's dusty potholed streets lined with grain fields immediately reminded me of the rubbled roads I once stood on in Gaza. I learned that, unlike the fables told in history books, the Civil Rights Movement was a struggle eerily similar to the Palestinian intifada of the '80s. Men and women on the front lines of both resistance movements put their lives at risk to defend their right to exist.

It was on this trip that I would find my journey as an Arab in America so deeply intertwined with the struggle against racism and social injustice. The late civil rights activist Hollis Watkins Muhammad planted in me a seed of wisdom that to sustain the fight for freedom, we must tap into the collective care and love that are rooted in our cultural traditions. I later learned to know this as "sumoud," Arabic for steadfastness, which describes the Palestinian struggle to live freely and safely, in dignity.

Today, as a community organizer and chef, I am continuously inspired by the determination of diasporic communities to strengthen their bonds to place and people and to cultivate home away from home no matter where they find themselves. Okra brought from Africa during enslavement is much like smuggled wild za'atar—a plant Israel forbids Palestinians to forage on their own land—brought over by Palestinians to grow in the West Bank of New Orleans. In

Texas, we celebrate the yearly olive harvest and cook pots of olive oil–steeped m'sakhan at a time Palestinians cannot access their own olives in the West Bank and Gaza. Our matriarchs carry the recipes from one generation to the next, with their hard-working hands and animated stories. As the author of the cookbook *Arabiyya*, which translates to Arab woman, I am proud to strengthen that lineage for my child's generation. The continuity of Indigenous Palestinian knowledge from the homeland to the American South is liberatory.

As we continue these traditions, we not only assert our communities' ancestries and legacies but also stay connected to our humanity. May our roots continue to grow, together, with no boundaries, to create fertile ground for our collective liberation.

by Reem Assil

award-winning speaker, cookbook author, and chef/owner of Arab street corner bakery Reem's California, working at the intersection of food, community, and social justice

1   Line bowl with double layer of paper towels. Cook almonds and 1 tablespoon oil in 12-inch ovensafe skillet over medium heat, stirring frequently, until almonds are golden brown, 3 to 5 minutes. Using slotted spoon, transfer almonds to prepared bowl; set aside.

2   Adjust 1 oven rack to lower-middle position and second rack 6 inches from broiler element. Heat oven to 475 degrees. Pat chicken dry with paper towels and sprinkle with 1 teaspoon salt and pepper. Add 1 tablespoon oil to fat left in skillet and heat over medium-high heat until just smoking. Place chicken skin side down in skillet and cook until skin is well browned and crisp, 8 to 10 minutes. Transfer chicken to large plate.

3   Pour off fat from skillet and wipe skillet clean with paper towels. Add onions, remaining 3 tablespoons oil, and remaining ½ teaspoon salt to now-empty skillet. Cook over medium heat, stirring occasionally and scraping up any browned bits, until onions soften and start to stick to bottom of skillet, 8 to 10 minutes. Off heat, stir in 2 tablespoons sumac and baharat.

4   Arrange chicken skin side up on top of onions and pour any accumulated juices around chicken. Transfer skillet to lower rack in oven and cook until breasts register 160 degrees and drumsticks/thighs register 175 degrees, 15 to 20 minutes.

5   Remove skillet from oven (handle will be hot). Transfer chicken to clean plate, tent with aluminum foil, and let rest while preparing naans.

6   Heat broiler. Arrange naans in even layer on rimmed baking sheet (pieces may overlap slightly) and broil on upper rack until lightly toasted, about 2 minutes. Transfer naans to cutting board, spread onions evenly over top, and sprinkle with 1 tablespoon sumac. Cut each naan in quarters and arrange on serving platter. Arrange chicken pieces on top of naan and sprinkle with almonds, parsley, and remaining 1 tablespoon sumac. Drizzle with extra oil and serve.

FANNIE'S FREEDOM FARM

While food delivers joy, pleasure, and nutrition, it is also political; one of the greatest illustrations of that is the civil rights leader Fannie Lou Hamer's Freedom Farm Cooperative.

Born in rural Mississippi in 1917, Hamer was deeply politically active, and she co-founded the Freedom Democratic Party and the National Women's Caucus. However, she grew frustrated with the political process, and she moved on to focus on economic activism. She purchased 40 acres of land in Mississippi in 1967 after receiving a $10,000 donation from the nonprofit Measure for Measure, and with that she opened the Freedom Farm Cooperative (FFC).

"If you give a hungry man food, he will eat it. If you give him land, he will grow his own food," Hamer famously said when describing the ethos and goals of the cooperative, which included access to affordable housing, addressing nutritional needs, and increasing self-sustainability and creative income opportunities for Black Americans.

By 1972, Hamer purchased another 640 acres, and she created a pig bank; Hamer believed that as long as people had access to pork, they would not starve. Unfortunately by 1976, the FFC closed. Floods, droughts, and tornadoes in those four years crippled the organization. Crops were not profitable, which resulted in unpaid property taxes. Additionally, the FFC did not receive any state financial support (although white-owned farms did). Investors pulled out, as Hamer was not able to fundraise due to her declining health in those years. In 1977, she died from breast cancer. Although the Freedom Farm Cooperative did not live on, it served as a blueprint for what the Black community can do to pull together resources to feed its inhabitants.

by Debra Freeman

award-winning writer, executive producer and host of the documentary Finding Edna Lewis, *and host of the IACP award–winning podcast* Setting the Table

Fannie Lou Hamer at the Democratic National Convention in 1964.

Library of Congress

Roasted Pork Shoulder with Peach Sauce

Serves 8 to 12   ~   Total Time: 5¼ to 6¼ hours, plus 12 hours salting

Emily Meggett (see page 162) wrote in her book *Gullah Geechee Home Cooking:* "At this house there are no guests—just friends and family." There are a few guidelines for a Southern holiday: Make all guests feel like family. Prepare more than you think you'll need, just in case. Don't worry if things aren't perfect. Decide before guests arrive if you're willing to share your recipe. Dress the table as well as you dress yourself. And cook for the joy of sharing it with others. This recipe for roasted pork shoulder is worthy of a holiday table, and its payoff is far greater than the work put in.

We rub a flavorful bone-in pork butt with brown sugar and salt, then leave it to rest overnight. The sugar dries out the exterior and helps boost the browning in the oven. We treat the cast-iron skillet as a roasting pan, elevating the pork on onions and adding water to the skillet, which keep the pork's drippings from burning. A fruity peach sauce with sweet and sour elements cuts the slow-roasted pork shoulder's richness. Pork butt roast is often labeled Boston shoulder, Boston butt, or pork butt in the supermarket. Add more water to the skillet as necessary during the last hours of cooking to prevent the fond from burning. This recipe requires refrigerating the salted meat for at least 12 hours before cooking.

1   (6- to 8- pound) bone-in pork butt, trimmed

⅓   cup kosher salt

⅓   cup packed light brown sugar

2   teaspoons pepper

1   onion, sliced into ½-inch-thick rounds

2   cups water

1   pound frozen peaches, cut into ½-inch pieces

2   cups dry white wine

½   cup granulated sugar

5   tablespoons unseasoned rice vinegar, divided

2   sprigs fresh thyme

1   tablespoon whole-grain mustard

1   Using sharp knife, cut slits in surface of fat layer of roast, spaced 1 inch apart, in crosshatch pattern, being careful to cut down to but not into meat. Combine ⅓ cup salt and brown sugar in bowl, then rub mixture evenly over roast. Wrap roast tightly with plastic wrap and refrigerate for at least 12 hours or up to 24 hours.

2   Adjust oven rack to lowest position and heat oven to 325 degrees. Brush any excess salt mixture from surface of roast and sprinkle with pepper. Arrange onion rounds in single layer on bottom of 12-inch cast-iron skillet and place roast fat side up on top. Add water to skillet. Transfer skillet to oven and roast, basting twice during cooking, until pork is extremely tender and meat near (but not touching) bone registers 190 degrees, 4 to 5 hours. Remove skillet from oven (handle will be hot). Transfer roast to carving board, tent with aluminum foil, and let rest while making peach sauce.

3   Being careful of hot skillet handle, discard onion rounds and transfer remaining juices to fat separator. Let liquid settle for 5 minutes, then measure out and reserve ¼ cup jus; discard fat and remaining jus. (If necessary, add water as needed to equal ¼ cup.)

4   Bring reserved jus, peaches, wine, granulated sugar, ¼ cup vinegar, and thyme sprigs to simmer in now-empty skillet over medium-low heat. Cook, stirring occasionally, until reduced to 2 cups, about 30 minutes. Stir in any accumulated meat juices. Off heat, discard thyme sprigs. Using potato masher, mash portion of peaches to thicken sauce as desired. Stir in mustard and remaining 1 tablespoon vinegar and season with salt and pepper to taste.

5   Using sharp paring knife, cut around inverted T-shaped bone until it can be pulled free from roast (use clean dish towel to grasp bone). Using serrated knife, slice roast thin. Serve with sauce.

Shrimp Curry

Serves 4　～　Total Time: 40 minutes

Zephyr Wright (1915–1988) was a Black woman who, like Dolly Johnson and Elizabeth McDuffie before her, cooked for the president. She attended to Lyndon B. Johnson and his family from 1942 (when LBJ was serving in the House of Representatives) until the end of his presidency in 1969. She is known for her friendship with Johnson and her influence on his civil rights policies (see "The Taste of Equality").

But it was Wright's cooking, and her mastery of Southern cooking in particular, that made her somewhat of a celebrity in LBJ's dinner-party circle. Sam Rayburn, Speaker of the House at the time, called Wright, "the best Southern cook this side of heaven."

A favorite is her simple formula for shrimp curry (curries became well loved in the South thanks to the influence of English colonists, merchants, and slave traders, many of whom had colonial ties or experience in South Asia and Southeast Asia). Her instructions call for steaming a pound of shrimp before stirring them into a sauce made with curry powder, ginger, onion, butter, chicken bouillon, a little sugar for balance, milk, and lemon juice. The short ingredient list results in a creamy dish with rich curry flavor.

Inspired by Wright's personal story and this dish, we developed a recipe for shrimp curry that is scaled to serve four people and cooked in one pan for weeknight ease. For an accurate measurement of boiling water, bring a kettle of water to a boil and then measure out the desired amount. If preferred, you can substitute 1 cup of chicken broth for the boiling water and chicken bouillon cube (omit step 1). Serve over Everyday White Rice (page 160).

1	cup boiling water
1	(½-ounce) chicken bouillon cube
2	pounds extra-large shrimp (21 to 25 per pound), peeled, deveined, and tails removed
1	teaspoon table salt, divided
¼	teaspoon pepper
2	tablespoons unsalted butter
1	small onion, chopped fine
1	tablespoon all-purpose flour
1½	teaspoons curry powder
½	teaspoon sugar
½	teaspoon ground ginger
1	cup whole milk
2	teaspoons lemon juice

1　Combine boiling water and bouillon cube in liquid measuring cup and stir to dissolve bouillon; set aside.

2　Sprinkle shrimp with ½ teaspoon salt and pepper. Melt butter in 12-inch skillet over medium heat. Add onion and remaining ½ teaspoon salt and cook until onion is softened, about 5 minutes.

3　Stir in flour, curry powder, sugar, and ginger and cook for 1 minute. Add milk and reserved bouillon mixture and bring to simmer. Add shrimp and cook, stirring occasionally, until shrimp are opaque and just cooked through, 2 to 4 minutes. Off heat, stir in lemon juice and season with salt and pepper to taste. Serve.

THE TASTE OF EQUALITY

Zephyr Wright wasn't just a great cook. She is also known as a civil rights advocate who influenced some of President Lyndon B. Johnson's political decisions.

When the Johnsons traveled between Texas and Washington, D.C., Wright joined them. But as the group passed through the Jim Crow South, Wright and other Black staffers were not allowed to stay in hotels or enter restaurants, even when the Johnsons insisted. Wright eventually put her foot down and refused to go on the segregated trips. Her experiences gave LBJ an up-close view of the South's humiliating practices, and when he signed the Civil Rights Act of 1964, Wright stood by his side. After signing, Johnson handed Wright the pen and said, "You deserve this more than anyone else."

by Morgan Bolling

Zephyr Wright baking bread in the White House.

Associated Press, *1961*

Cider-Brined Pork Chops with Apples and Onions

Serves 4 ~ Total Time: 1½ hours, plus 8 hours brining

This recipe is inspired by Nathalie Dupree's pork chops—and pork chop theory (see "A Conversation between Women: Nathalie Dupree and Toni Tipton-Martin"). Dupree's recipe involves searing two gloriously large 2-inch-thick bone-in pork chops on the stove and finishing them in the oven until they're just barely pink and juicy inside. To go with the pork, Dupree sautés apples and onions in separate skillets, each with a knob of butter and some fresh sage. The result is pork chops worthy of a special occasion with this rich, complex (in taste, not procedure) apple-onion condiment. Since Dupree's thick pork chops require a special order from a butcher, we developed a recipe with the same delicious flavor and learned technique that can be pulled off with thinner boneless chops. We sear the cider-brined chops and then build the apple and onion topping in the same skillet to infuse them with some pork flavor. We add a little extra cider before finishing the pork chops in the oven to make a flavorful pan sauce. Sweet apples, such as Gala, Fuji, or Braeburn, work here; they should remain unpeeled. Sweet onions, such as Maui or Walla Walla, will work here in place of the Vidalias.

5   cups apple cider, divided
2   tablespoons table salt for brining
1   tablespoon pepper for brining
4   (6- to 8-ounce) boneless pork loin chops, 1 inch thick
¾   teaspoon sugar
2   tablespoons vegetable oil
4   tablespoons unsalted butter, cut into 4 pieces, divided
3   Vidalia onions, halved and sliced thin
1   teaspoon table salt
½   teaspoon pepper
2   large apples, cored and cut into ½-inch wedges
2   teaspoons minced fresh sage
1   tablespoon cider vinegar

1   Whisk 4 cups cider, 2 tablespoons salt, and 1 tablespoon pepper in large bowl until salt is dissolved, about 1 minute. Arrange pork chops in single layer in 13 by 9-inch baking pan. Pour brine over pork chops. Cover and refrigerate for at least 8 hours or up to 24 hours.

2   Adjust oven rack to middle position and heat oven to 400 degrees. Place chops on rimmed baking sheet lined with double layer of paper towels. Place double layer of paper towels on top of chops and press firmly to blot excess liquid. Let chops sit at room temperature for 10 minutes while towels absorb moisture; discard towels, then pat chops dry with clean paper towels. Using kitchen shears, snip layer of fat surrounding each chop in 2 places, about 2 inches apart. Sprinkle sugar evenly over 1 side of each chop.

3   Heat oil in 12-inch ovensafe nonstick skillet over medium-high heat until just smoking. Place chops in skillet in single layer, sugar side down, and cook until bottoms of chops are well browned, about 2 minutes; transfer chops to large plate, browned side up. Wipe skillet clean with paper towels.

4   Melt 2 tablespoons butter in now-empty skillet over medium heat. Stir in onions, salt, and pepper and cook, stirring often, until onions are softened and well browned, 14 to 18 minutes. Push onions to 1 side of skillet. Add apples to now-empty side of skillet and cook, flipping occasionally, until well browned, about 8 minutes, stirring onions occasionally. Stir apples into onion mixture until evenly combined. Off heat, add remaining 1 cup cider.

5   Nestle pork chops into onion mixture, browned side up. Transfer skillet to oven and roast until thickest part of each chop registers 130 to 135 degrees, about 9 minutes. Transfer chops to carving board and let rest for 5 minutes.

6   Stir sage into onion mixture and bring to boil over medium-high heat. Cook until liquid is slightly thickened, about 1 minute. Off heat, stir vinegar and remaining 2 tablespoons butter into onion mixture until butter is melted and fully incorporated; season with salt and pepper to taste. Divide onion mixture evenly among serving plates and top with pork chops. Serve.

A CONVERSATION BETWEEN WOMEN:
NATHALIE DUPREE AND TONI TIPTON-MARTIN

Nathalie Dupree is a chef, author of 14 cookbooks, television host, and beloved Southern cooking instructor. Toni Tipton-Martin invited Nathalie to the *Cook's Country* kitchen in 2023 to prepare pork chops from her 2012 book, *Mastering the Art of Southern Cooking* (you can watch the video on AmericasTestKitchen.com) and to share her pork chop theory. Here's a snapshot of their rich conversation.

Toni   Nathalie, I cannot tell you how excited I am to have you here with me, exploring these discussions about women and our place in the world, and our place in the food world—what we've managed to achieve sometimes in the face of so many obstacles. You are my friend and also you've been a mentor to me. And also, you're an icon. I thought (without getting teary), we could chat a little bit about some of the things we often talk about.

Nathalie   Yes, and there is that sense that white women and Black women historically didn't have a dialogue, but I do think—or maybe I like to think—that they did. Food is power; whoever controls the food has the power. You know the woman that burns her husband's toast or doesn't get his bacon crisp—that's a sign of control and vice versa. Who controls it? Does the man that controls crispy bacon have more power or does the woman that doesn't make it crispy have more power? There's a constant struggle in food and relationships.

Toni   In my reading of the Southern narrative, I could see that contradiction. In my study of their real dynamic, what I realized is that, with all due respect, that though white woman might have set the table, chosen the linens, and controlled the flour, until that Black woman put the food on the plate, there was no party. And *that* was the ultimate expression of the power. You can have hospitality and you can invite people in, but you don't have any power. And so I think what both of us have done in our work is try to bring that message forward.

....

Toni   So at one point, you've got a restaurant, you're a culinary instructor, you're writing. What's motivating you?

Nathalie   I suppose I don't know how to say no [laughs]. But also I was just doing all these opportunities that came to me. Julia Child came to my graduation, not because of me, and I got to meet her. I went up to her and said, "I'm graduating today. What should I do with my degree?" She said we need cooking schools in America. And that's what I did.

Toni   That connection you have with Julia reminds me so much of my connection to Edna Lewis, as you know. And that little seed that is planted woman-to-woman. You don't really know what it is doing as it's growing and you have all these experiences that are watering and nurturing it, and one day it just reveals itself.

Nathalie   That's it exactly.

Toni   So you know I invited you here to make pork chops because I wanted us to be able to talk about your pork chop theory. Can you tell me a little bit about that?

Nathalie   Yes, Shirley Corriher and I were both running for the board of an organization, and we were from the same town, and she had been my student. I didn't want to compete with her nor did she want to compete with me, so we came up with this theory that satisfied us both as the reason why we could both run and not be competitive with each other. Shirley is the chemist, so she probably came up with it. It's, "One pork chop in the pan goes dry." It does. It's hard to cook one pork chop but if you have two, the fat from one feeds the other. It's about women of course, women sharing the spotlight, finding a way to work together.

Toni   It's empowering and encouraging and uplifting one another. It's terrific. I love it.

Bourbon Chicken

Serve 4 ~ Total Time: 40 minutes

Bourbon chicken—tender morsels of dark meat slathered in a sticky, sweet-savory sauce—is a popular offering at Asian- and Cajun-themed fast-casual restaurants all over the United States, especially in mall food courts, where it is famously served as samples. But this adaptation is inspired by the exceptional bourbon chicken served at Today's Cajun Seafood run by Huong Vu (Rose) Nguyen and her husband Hao (Howie) in the Faubourg Marigny neighborhood of New Orleans (see "A Crescent City Gem"). The intense umami presence in the soy-based sauce keeps the sugar in check, making the dish irresistible. The couple keeps their recipe closely guarded, so if you're in New Orleans be sure to try it for yourself. Here's our best attempt at replicating their delicious chicken at home.

For the sauce, brown sugar adds complex sweetness and subtle notes of molasses that balance the saltiness of the soy sauce. Toasted sesame oil rounds things out with a rich, roasty depth, and minced garlic and grated ginger infuse the sauce with their fresh, pungent bite. A shot of bourbon imparts aromatic top notes of vanilla and caramel (and earns the dish its name). The pieces of boneless chicken thighs benefit from the Chinese technique of velveting in which they're tossed in a combination of cornstarch and some of the sauce mixture before sautéing. This technique not only ensures that they stay ultra-tender and juicy but also helps thicken the sauce, bestowing it with an attractive glossy sheen. A little cider vinegar stirred in at the end adds brightness. Use a good-quality soy sauce for this recipe. Serve with rice.

½ cup soy sauce

½ cup packed brown sugar

¼ cup water

2 tablespoons bourbon

1 teaspoon toasted sesame oil

½ teaspoon pepper

2 pounds boneless, skinless chicken thighs, trimmed and cut into 1-inch pieces

2 tablespoons cornstarch

2 tablespoons vegetable oil

2 garlic cloves, minced

1 teaspoon grated fresh ginger

2 teaspoons cider vinegar

1 Combine soy sauce, sugar, water, bourbon, sesame oil, and pepper in 2-cup liquid measuring cup. Microwave until hot, about 2 minutes. Whisk to dissolve sugar. Toss chicken, cornstarch, and 2 tablespoons soy sauce mixture in bowl until thoroughly combined.

2 Heat vegetable oil in 12-inch nonstick skillet over medium-high heat until shimmering. Add chicken (skillet will be full) and cook, stirring occasionally, until browned and cooked through, about 10 minutes.

3 Stir in garlic, ginger, and remaining soy sauce mixture. Bring to boil and cook until sauce is syrupy and rubber spatula dragged through it leaves wide trail before filling back in, 6 to 8 minutes. Off heat, stir in vinegar. Serve.

A CRESCENT CITY GEM

Neon signs hanging in the graffiti-tagged windows promise "Po-Boys," "Jambalaya," "HOT BOUDIN," and "Yaka Mein." One handwritten sign reads, "Now serving Pho." The menu is a beautiful mash-up of cultures: shrimp and sausage gumbo, smothered pork chops, boiled crawfish, General Tso's chicken, baked spaghetti, and bourbon chicken. Though very few restaurants in New Orleans actually serve bourbon chicken, there's a legend (based on a theory) that the teriyaki-style dish was named after Bourbon Street.

New Orleans is known for its modernized takes on blended cuisines—its culinary influences range from the home cooking of the descendants of French settlers in rural Louisiana to the foods of enslaved West Africans, Vietnamese refugees, Spanish and Chinese immigrants, and Native Americans. This restaurant somehow serves all these things and none of them at the same time. And as Huong Vu (Rose) Nguyen, who owns and operates Today's Cajun Seafood with her husband Hao (Howie), will tell you, everything on the menu is good.

Howie refers to both himself and Rose as "boat people," the name given to the nearly 800,000 refugees who fled Vietnam from the period after the war to 1995. In the United States, Howie studied psychology, worked on an offshore oil rig, and then taught ESL (English as a second language) in New Orleans public schools. Rose worked for years in her brother's restaurant, China Ruby, in St. Bernard Parish.

Following Hurricane Katrina, the couple lived in Houston for a year with their children. They returned to their neighborhood in New Orleans East and joined the rebuilding effort. In 2007, Howie, Rose, and Rose's brother opened Today's Cajun Seafood with a diverse menu, building a loyal clientele of regulars. When asked why his restaurant sells bourbon chicken, Howie answered pragmatically, "It's Bourbon Street. People like it."

Like so many other restaurant owners, Howie and Rose closed for a short time during the pandemic, but today the dining room is bustling. As with each of their past hardships, they continue to respond with grace, kindness, warmth, and an uncommon understanding of the power of hospitality, overfilling plates with comfort food and making life better for their community.

Rose and Howie (top) and their restaurant Today's Cajun Seafood (bottom).

Pableaux Johnson

GRANDMA'S PAD THAI

Pad thai's rise to fame around the world, particularly within the American South, is no accident; its inception and subsequent popularity are intertwined with longstanding intentional nation-building efforts and the resilience of Thai culture and people, both domestically and abroad.

For the past 40 years, pad thai has reigned as the top-selling dish at my family's Thai restaurant in Royal Palm Beach, Florida. This restaurant's woman-powered team, led by my grandmother, great-aunt, and their four sisters, has stir-fried nearly a million portions of pad thai since their arrival to the United States in the late 1970s. In archived news clippings from the 1990s, writers coined the dish "famous pad thai," and even then recognized it as the "most requested dish."

So, how did pad thai come to be so popular in such a small Florida town? Its story traces back to 1818, when American missionaries first set foot in what was then known as Siam, long before pad thai's creation. Although the region was never formally colonized, early American involvement compelled Prime Minister Plaek Phibunsongkhram to embrace Western ideals on behalf of the nation as defense against colonization. This transformative era, marked by economic challenges and rice field flooding in the 1930s, saw not only the renaming of the country from Siam to Thailand, but also the birth of the world's most famous national dish: pad thai. In the wake of the flooding, Phibunsongkhram introduced rice noodles, a calorie-dense and cost-efficient alternative to rice itself (it used only 50 percent of the grain), and then championed pad thai as both a food source and a symbol of nation-building. According to Phibunsongkhram, a country with a strong national dish could project a unified image internationally.

As American military influence throughout the region continued to grow during the Cold War, United States troops developed a fondness for Thai food. This newfound affinity, coupled with the post-war tourism boom in the region, led to a surge in American visitors to Thailand who returned to the States with their Thai culinary "discoveries."

As Americans began visiting Thailand, a parallel trend emerged: Thais slowly started immigrating to the United States. By the late 1970s, around 5,000 Thais, including my family, had moved to America and gradually opened Thai restaurants, starting with Bangkok Market in 1972 in Los Angeles. It wasn't until the 1980s that Thai restaurants began to emerge in the South, with my grandparents among the first to open one in South Florida in 1986. At first these restaurants primarily served immigrant Thais who were missing home, but it wasn't long before these restaurants became hot spots, and the appetite for the sweet-salty-sour-spicy goodness of pad thai made its mark throughout South Florida and beyond.

Meanwhile, Thailand saw a valuable opportunity to strengthen its economy by expanding its global presence. In 2002, the Thai government launched the Global Thai Program. Under this initiative, the state offered training programs and grants to Thai chefs interested in establishing restaurants abroad. The strategic move catapulted Thai cuisine to global phenomenon and pad thai to superstar-status.

Though not completely ideal, the success that my family's restaurant has found in the American South owes much to pad thai, and the dish's journey to near icon-status is a testament to the power of gastrodiplomacy, cultural exchanges, and the pursuit of economic opportunities that go beyond borders.

by Ali Domrongchai

Florida-born, North Carolina-raised food writer and recipe developer based in Brooklyn, New York

Pad Thai

Serves 4 to 6　~　Total Time: 1 hour

This recipe by Ali Domrongchai is an adaptation of her grandmother's. Pad thai translates to "stir-fried noodles," so there are countless ways to make it. Pad thai with chicken and shrimp is the most popular order at Ali's family's restaurant, but feel free to play around with proteins.

Tamarind is a sweet-sour fruit responsible for the zesty tang in many Thai recipes. When Thais first immigrated to America, they were unable to get tamarind, so some used ketchup to replicate it. You can substitute an equal amount of ketchup for the tamarind concentrate here. We developed this recipe with Erawan brand rice noodles, Healthy Boy brand soy sauce, Squid brand fish sauce, and JHC brand palm sugar. The amount of time required to soak the noodles will vary by brand. If you can't find Thai thin soy sauce you can substitute any soy sauce. Thai thin soy sauce tends to be lighter and thinner than other soy sauces; it also contains some sugar. You can use dark brown sugar instead of the palm sugar.

8　ounces (¼-inch-wide) rice noodles

7　tablespoons plus 2 teaspoons vegetable oil, divided

2　tablespoons Thai thin soy sauce

1　tablespoon cornstarch

8　ounces boneless, skinless chicken thighs, trimmed and sliced crosswise into ¼-inch-thick strips

5　tablespoons (2 ounces) palm sugar

3　tablespoons fish sauce

2　tablespoons tamarind concentrate

1　teaspoon paprika

4　ounces large shrimp (26 to 30 per pound), peeled, deveined, and tails removed

7　ounces firm tofu, cut into ½-inch cubes and patted dry

1　large shallot, sliced thin

4　garlic cloves, minced

3　scallions, white and green parts separated and sliced thin, plus extra for garnish

3　large eggs, lightly beaten

2　ounces (1 cup) bean sprouts

¼　cup roasted, unsalted peanuts, chopped coarse (optional)

　　Red pepper flakes (optional)

　　Lime wedges

1　Lay noodles in 13 by 9-inch baking dish and cover with warm tap water. Let noodles soak until pliable and almost tender, 15 to 30 minutes, separating noodles with tip of paring knife to prevent sticking. Drain noodles well, then toss with 2 teaspoons oil.

2　Meanwhile, whisk soy sauce and cornstarch together in medium bowl until combined. Add chicken, toss to coat, and refrigerate for at least 10 minutes or up to 1 hour.

3　Bring palm sugar and 1 tablespoon water to simmer in small saucepan over medium-low heat, stirring and breaking and mashing to dissolve sugar. (Do not let mixture caramelize). Off heat, stir in fish sauce, tamarind concentrate, paprika, and ¼ cup water; set aside.

4　Heat 1 tablespoon oil in 14-inch flat-bottom wok over medium-high heat until just smoking. Add shrimp and spread into even layer. Cook, without stirring, until shrimp turn pink around edges, about

30 seconds. Flip shrimp and cook until opaque pink on second side, about 30 seconds. Off heat, use slotted spoon to transfer shrimp to large plate.

5　Return wok to medium-high heat and add 2 tablespoons oil. Add chicken (including any excess marinade) and cook, stirring often, until golden, 4 to 5 minutes. Off heat, use slotted spoon to transfer chicken to plate with shrimp.

6　Wipe wok clean with paper towels. Return wok to medium-high heat and add 2 tablespoons oil. Add tofu and stir-fry until golden, 3 to 5 minutes. Off heat, use slotted spoon to transfer tofu to plate with chicken and shrimp.

7　Return wok to medium-high heat and add 1 tablespoon oil. Add shallot, garlic, and scallion whites and cook, stirring, until fragrant, about 30 seconds. Add noodles and stir-fry until coated in oil-shallot mixture, about 30 seconds. Add palm sugar mixture and toss to coat noodles. Cover and cook until noodles are tender, about 1 minute. Uncover noodles and continue to cook until sauce has thickened.

8　Stir noodles, then push to 1 side of wok. Add remaining 1 tablespoon oil and eggs to empty side of wok and cook, stirring frequently, until eggs are just set, about 45 seconds. Add chicken, shrimp, tofu, scallion greens, and bean sprouts and cook, stirring, until combined, about 30 seconds. Transfer to serving platter. Sprinkle with peanuts and pepper flakes, if using. Serve with lime wedges.

Pan-Seared Maryland-Style Crab Cakes

Serves 4   ~   Total Time: 45 minutes, plus 1 hour chilling

Of course, crab cakes are inevitably associated with Maryland. These specific crab cakes are inspired by Susan Klise, mother of *Cook's Country* senior staff photographer Steve Klise. She is a longtime Maryland resident who has been making crab cakes this way for decades. Rather than broiling or deep-frying, Klise prefers to pan-fry her crab cakes in a combination of extra-virgin olive oil and butter, which gives them crisp, rich browning. While some claim crab cakes should taste only of crab, these have some welcome extra verve thanks to a feisty trio of condiments (Dijon mustard, Worcestershire sauce, and hot sauce), plus a handful of thinly sliced scallion. Be gentle when folding the crab to avoid breaking up the large lumps. If you can't find jumbo lump crabmeat, regular lump crabmeat can be substituted. This recipe can easily be doubled. You will need a nonstick skillet with a tight-fitting lid for this recipe.

Crab Cakes

½   cup mayonnaise

1   large egg

2   tablespoons minced fresh parsley

1   scallion, sliced thin (optional)

2   teaspoons Dijon mustard

2   teaspoons Worcestershire sauce

2   teaspoons Old Bay seasoning

½   teaspoon Tabasco sauce or 1 teaspoon Frank's RedHot Original Cayenne Pepper Hot Sauce

⅛   teaspoon cayenne pepper

½   cup panko bread crumbs

8   ounces jumbo lump crabmeat, picked over for shells

8   ounces backfin or claw crabmeat, picked over for shells

1   tablespoon extra-virgin olive oil

1   tablespoon unsalted butter

Cocktail Sauce

½   cup ketchup

¼   cup prepared horseradish

1½   teaspoons lemon juice

½   teaspoon pepper

½   teaspoon Tabasco sauce or 1 teaspoon Frank's RedHot Original Cayenne Pepper Hot Sauce

½   teaspoon Worcestershire sauce

¼   teaspoon table salt

1   **For the crab cakes** Whisk mayonnaise; egg; parsley; scallion, if using; mustard; Worcestershire; Old Bay; Tabasco; and cayenne together in large bowl. Stir in panko until incorporated. Gently fold in jumbo lump and backfin crabmeat, taking care not to break up large pieces. Divide crab mixture into 4 equal balls, about 1 scant cup or 5¾ ounces each, and place on plate. Cover with plastic wrap and refrigerate for at least 1 hour or up to 24 hours.

2   **For the cocktail sauce** Meanwhile, whisk all ingredients together in bowl; set aside for serving. (Sauce can be refrigerated for up to 24 hours.)

3   Heat oil in 12-inch nonstick skillet over medium heat until shimmering. Add butter and cook until melted. Add crab cakes to skillet (do not flatten), cover, and cook until well browned on first side, about 5 minutes. Flip crab cakes and continue to cook, uncovered, until well browned on second side, about 5 minutes longer. Remove from heat, cover, and let sit until heated through, about 3 minutes. Serve with cocktail sauce.

Cheese Enchiladas

Serves 4   ~   Total Time: 1¼ hours

Many Texas chefs showcase their signature version of cheese enchiladas—recipes from different regions of Mexico and Texas-bred spins—on their menus. Iliana de la Vega, chef and co-owner of the Austin restaurant El Naranjo, serves enfrijoladas oaxaqueñas. For this dish, the tortillas are smothered in black bean sauce spiced up with pasilla de Oaxaca chiles. At Nixta, also in Austin, owners Edgar Rico and Sara Mardanbigi serve an enchilada potosina taco: a tortilla stuffed with potato and chorizo puree and duck fat refried beans, topped with a mix of ingredients including queso enchilado, an aged cheese (queso añejo) that has a rind rubbed with chiles.

Travel to San Antonio, and you can try a handful of different enchiladas from Roy Royes and his late wife Evelyn Reyes of Panchito's; their cheese version leans on American cheese for an ultra-creamy eating experience. In Houston, Sylvia Casares, known as the city's Enchilada Queen, serves 19 different types of enchiladas at the two locations of her Sylvia's Enchilada Kitchen. One of the most simple: the Morelia that's stuffed with cheese and topped with a spicy red chile sauce, lettuce, onion, and radishes.

Our cheese enchiladas are also simple and easily pulled together from the contents of your cupboard and fridge. We use a heavy dose of chili powder, which packs the bold red sauce with serious spice and earthiness. We cook the chili powder in the skillet along with onion, tomato paste, and garlic for more intensity. Feel free to add beans, vegetables, or shredded meat to your enchiladas if you'd like.

2	tablespoons vegetable oil
1	onion or red onion, chopped fine, divided
3	tablespoons chili powder
4	teaspoons tomato paste
4	garlic cloves, minced
3	tablespoons all-purpose flour
3	cups chicken or vegetable broth
12	(6-inch) corn or flour tortillas, warmed
1	pound Monterey Jack cheese, shredded (4 cups), divided
	Lime wedges (optional)

1   Adjust oven rack to middle position and heat oven to 450 degrees. Heat oil in 12-inch skillet over medium heat until shimmering. Add three-quarters of onion and cook until softened, 3 to 5 minutes. Stir in chili powder, tomato paste, and garlic and cook until fragrant, about 30 seconds. Stir in flour and mash into skillet with wooden spoon until well combined, about 30 seconds. Gradually add broth, whisking constantly to smooth out any lumps. Bring to simmer and cook until thickened slightly, about 4 minutes.

2   Spread 1 cup sauce in bottom of 13 by 9-inch baking dish. Spread ¼ cup cheese across center of 1 warm tortilla, tightly roll tortilla around filling, then place seam side down in prepared dish. Repeat with remaining 11 tortillas (2 columns of 6 tortillas will fit neatly across width of dish).

3   Pour remaining sauce over top of enchiladas and sprinkle with remaining 1 cup cheese. Cover dish with lightly greased aluminum foil and bake until cheese is melted, about 10 minutes. Uncover and continue to bake until sauce is bubbling around edges, about 5 minutes. Let cool for 10 minutes, then sprinkle with remaining onion. (Cooled enchiladas can be refrigerated for up to 2 days or frozen for up to 1 month.) Serve with lime wedges, if using.

Macarona Béchamel

Serves 10 to 12 ~ Total Time: 2½ hours, plus 1 hour 10 minutes cooling

This recipe is from chef Sarah Cole (see "Egyptian-Southern Food Memories"). It's an adaptation of her Taeta's (grandmother), Aunt Alice's, and mother's recipes. If preferred, you can substitute bison or lamb for the beef. You can use cider vinegar in place of the red wine vinegar, if desired. Use a broiler-safe baking pan for this recipe.

Tomato-Meat Sauce

3 tablespoons vegetable oil

3 large onions, chopped fine

1½ teaspoons table salt, divided

8 garlic cloves, minced

2 pounds 90 percent lean ground beef

1 tablespoon ground cumin

2 teaspoons ground coriander

¼ teaspoon ground allspice

1 (28-ounce) can tomato sauce

1 (15-ounce) can crushed tomatoes

2 teaspoons red wine vinegar

Béchamel

¾ cup all-purpose flour

6 tablespoons vegetable oil

1 tablespoon pepper

¾ teaspoon table salt, plus salt for cooking pasta

2¾ cups whole milk

3 large eggs

1 pound penne

1 **For the tomato-meat sauce** Heat oil in Dutch oven over medium-high heat until shimmering. Add onions and ¾ teaspoon salt and cook, stirring occasionally, until golden brown, about 10 minutes. Add garlic and cook until fragrant, about 30 seconds. Add beef and cook, breaking up meat with wooden spoon, until well browned, 7 to 10 minutes.

2 Stir in cumin, coriander, allspice, and remaining ¾ teaspoon salt and cook until fragrant, about 30 seconds. Add tomato sauce and crushed tomatoes. Bring to boil, reduce heat to medium-low, and simmer until flavors have melded, about 20 minutes, scraping bottom of pot regularly. Stir in vinegar and cook for 5 minutes longer. Season with salt and pepper to taste. Remove from heat and allow to cool while making béchamel. (Sauce can be refrigerated for up to 3 days.)

3 **For the béchamel** Whisk flour, oil, pepper, and salt together in medium saucepan. Cook over medium heat, whisking frequently, until flour turns golden, 5 to 8 minutes.

4 Slowly whisk in milk until no lumps remain (mixture will be very thick). Remove from heat and let cool completely, about 45 minutes. Once béchamel is completely cooled, whisk in eggs until fully combined.

5 Adjust oven rack 6 inches from broiler element and heat oven to 350 degrees. Bring 4 quarts water to boil in large pot. Add pasta and 1 tablespoon salt and cook, stirring frequently, until just al dente. Drain pasta completely.

6 Combine tomato-meat sauce and pasta in now-empty pot. Stir in 1 cup béchamel. Transfer pasta mixture to 13 by 9-inch baking pan. Smooth top with rubber spatula. Scoop remaining béchamel over top and spread using rubber spatula.

7 Transfer pan to oven and bake until top is puffed and starting to crack around edges, about 45 minutes. Heat broiler and broil until browned on top, about 3 minutes. Remove from oven and allow to cool, about 25 minutes. Cut into portions and serve.

EGYPTIAN-SOUTHERN FOOD MEMORIES

My mom moved from Egypt to Demopolis, Alabama, to flee religious persecution in the early 1980s. This story always sparks the question, "How?", to which she responds with a joke that she and her younger sister acted so badly during the flight out that the pilot tossed them from the plane and they landed in Demopolis. While some assume she was a mail-order bride, the real story involves a bag of potatoes.

Demopolis was a stopping point where Mom reunited with her cousin Philip, a traveling minister who organized a celebratory dinner for her arrival. My father, the produce manager at the local grocery at the time, helped her pick out a bag of potatoes—and managed to invite himself to dinner. After many dates and marriage, my mom has called Alabama home for 41 years.

This Egyptian woman found a supportive group of people who welcomed her, helped her find work, a place in their congregation, and ultimately a home within their town. My mom says Demopolis isn't that different from where she grew up. Her family didn't have much; they lived a simple but full life centered around family, friends, home, and food, which is exactly what her new life entailed.

But despite these similarities, she sought ways to remain connected to the culture she was forced to leave behind. Food became a way for her to celebrate her heritage and share it with her new family. Our dinner table held both traditional Egyptian dishes and Southern staples. Some Egyptian dishes were saved for special occasions when she was able to source ingredients from her older sister in New Jersey.

But there were certain Egyptian dishes that became Mom's go-tos, as the ingredients were familiar staples in our rural Alabama town. Macarona béchamel is one such example, an Egyptian comfort dish that is similar to a Southern casserole. This bake was always on rotation, and it was an easy one for her to share with neighbors, to cook when we had friends coming over, or to add to a potluck spread. It consists of noodles, a rich tomato-meat sauce, and a creamy béchamel, all baked to perfection.

Funny enough, my mom doesn't love being in the kitchen. But she will always go out of her way to make sure people are fed abundantly, in true Egyptian fashion. It allows her to express herself. And now that I've started my own food venture, Abadir's, sharing our family recipes and Egyptian-Southern memories, food has become our way of communicating. Her story and all the dishes I grew up loving inspired me to connect to my own heritage.

by Sarah Cole

owner and head chef of Abadir's in Greensboro, Alabama

Savory Noodle Kugel

Serves 8 to 10   ~   Total Time: 2 hours

Sweet kugels are traditionally served with Jewish holiday meals, but savory kugels—made with egg noodles, onions, and eggs—make a great side dish any night of the week.

Skye Estroff (see "Jewish and Southern Culinary Traditions") learned to add Vidalia onions to her kugel from her grandma, Anita Estroff, known in the family as Nini. If you search online, you can find a video of Nini beating Bobby Flay in a sweet potato casserole cook-off. She was also a proud winner of the local Vidalia Onion Cook-Off. We are happy to borrow Nini's wisdom by adding Vidalia onions to our kugel. We caramelize the onions in rendered chicken fat (schmaltz) to build a savory base and then add parsley, salt, pepper, and eggs. We toss the egg mixture with still-warm noodles to thicken the eggs slightly so they cling to the noodles rather than sink to the bottom of the casserole. To achieve the characteristic crunchy top, we give the baked casserole a quick pass under the broiler. Look for rendered chicken fat in the frozen food section of larger supermarkets; if you can't find it you can swap in extra-virgin olive oil (the resulting casserole will not be as savory). Use a broiler-safe baking dish for this recipe.

3	tablespoons rendered chicken fat	6	large eggs
3	Vidalia onions, chopped fine	2	tablespoons minced fresh parsley
1½	teaspoons table salt, divided, plus salt for cooking pasta	¾	teaspoon pepper
		1	pound wide egg noodles

1   Adjust 1 oven rack to middle position and second rack 6 inches from broiler element. Heat oven to 350 degrees. Grease broiler-safe 13 by 9-inch baking dish. Heat rendered chicken fat in 12-inch skillet over medium-low heat until shimmering. Add onions and ½ teaspoon salt and cook, stirring occasionally, until caramelized, 30 to 40 minutes. (Caramelized onions can be refrigerated for up to 3 days.)

2   Transfer onions to large bowl and let cool for 10 minutes. Whisk eggs, parsley, 1 teaspoon salt, and pepper into onions; set aside.

3   Bring 4 quarts water to boil in large pot. Add noodles and 1 tablespoon salt and cook, stirring often, until al dente. Reserve 3 tablespoons cooking water, then drain noodles and let cool for 5 minutes. Whisk reserved cooking water into onion mixture. Stir still-warm noodles into onion mixture until well combined.

4   Transfer noodle mixture to prepared dish. Bake on lower rack until set, about 20 minutes. Remove kugel from oven and heat broiler. Broil kugel on upper rack until top noodles are browned and crisp, 1 to 3 minutes, rotating dish as needed for even browning. Serve.

To make ahead   Kugel can be fully assembled, covered, and refrigerated up to 24 hours in advance. Increase baking time to 25 minutes.

JEWISH AND SOUTHERN CULINARY TRADITIONS

The Southern community is one in which everyone seems to know everyone. When you're Southern and Jewish, everyone *actually* knows everyone by family name, line of work, and if there's a good cook in the family. It's a tight-knit subculture that is particularly personal to me.

My great-great-grandparents fled the pogroms of Russia and came directly to rural Georgia and South Carolina. I know from their stories that assimilating in small towns where they were the only Jewish people was a challenge, but it was one they overcame. They found food to be the universal connector in this unfamiliar culture. Don't get me wrong, there are other Jewish people in the South, but it is much more uncommon to find the families of Jewish people who immigrated here and have not left in the generations since.

Fast-forward to my experience growing up in suburban Atlanta, and it was still a rarity to come from this background. My bat mitzvah served as a crash course in Jewish tradition to my public school peers. When I was involved in international Jewish youth groups, they were intrigued by my Southern drawl. Let's just say, no one was accustomed to my family's familiar phrasings like "L'Chaim and Go Dawgs!"

My coexistence would mystify people. It was my party trick. I found acceptance by sharing this new archetype of person with others. By way of language but also with food.

I grew up accustomed to an amalgamation of these two cuisines. There was squash casserole at every Shabbat dinner with matzah meal baked in to substitute for bread crumbs. Vidalia onions were braised with every brisket.

My college roommates would snack on my Grammy's homemade mandel bread; my friends would post up at my grandparents' football tailgates at UGA with a generous spread of deviled eggs, cheese straws, pimento cheese, and bagels, too.

Interpretations of Jewish food in the restaurant space have generally shared the deli-side of our cuisine, but there is a subcategory that has not yet been expressed to the masses. This mash-up of Jewish and Southern cultures is my family's comfort food. When you're fortunate enough to have the two worlds collide, your whole community becomes mishpucha (Yiddish word for "family").

by Skye Estroff

TV and podcasting producer and personality, connecting people through food

Southern Chicken Spaghetti

Serves 8 ~ Total Time: 1¾ hours, plus 15 minutes cooling

Lisa Fain, known as the Homesick Texan, defines Tex-Mex chicken spaghetti as "baked pasta with chicken and chile con queso" on her website. Typically this dish features shredded chicken, cheese, and some mix of mushrooms, peppers, and onions (and sometimes canned Ro-Tel tomatoes) intertwined in baked spaghetti.

According to Fain's research, the earliest recorded recipe dates back to 1931. It was published in the *Amarillo Daily News* and featured a simple combination of chicken, cheese, and noodles, seasoned with a liberal dose of chili powder. The recipe evolved to include canned cream of mushroom soup and Velveeta, products of the convenience-food boom of the 1920s and 1930s that underscored the era's casserole culture.

But this casserole's history isn't limited to Texas. *New York Times* food editor and restaurant critic Craig Claiborne noted his mother's influence on his version of the dish—a childhood favorite—in his 1987 book, *Craig Claiborne's Southern Cooking*. Claiborne speculated about its origins and compared the rich flavors of the dish to those of an authentic Italian ragù bolognese, due to its creamy tomato base and savory ground meat. His mother, Mary Kathleen Craig Claiborne, was "famous for it up and down the Mississippi Delta," he said.

We keep chicken spaghetti easy by starting with a rotisserie chicken. Breaking the spaghetti in half makes the dish easier to serve and eat. A creamy sauce made with butter, flour, chicken broth, and half-and-half is flavored with mushrooms and other vegetables. A combination of American and cheddar cheeses gives this pasta bake an ultracreamy consistency with plenty of cheese flavor. For a spicier dish, use the larger amount of cayenne pepper. Use Dutch oven that holds 6 quarts or more.

1	pound spaghetti
1½	teaspoons table salt, plus salt for cooking pasta
8	ounces deli American cheese, shredded (2 cups)
4	ounces sharp cheddar cheese, shredded (1 cup)
3	tablespoons unsalted butter, divided
12	ounces white mushrooms, trimmed and sliced ¼ inch thick
1	red bell pepper, stemmed, seeded, and chopped
1	onion, chopped
3	tablespoons all-purpose flour
3	cups chicken broth
2	cups half-and-half
½	teaspoon pepper
¼–½	teaspoon cayenne pepper
2	cups shredded rotisserie chicken

1   Bring 4 quarts water to boil in Dutch oven. Loosely wrap half of pasta in dish towel, then press bundle against corner of counter to break pasta in half; repeat with remaining pasta. Add pasta and 1 tablespoon salt to boiling water and cook until al dente. Drain pasta and rinse thoroughly under cold running water; set aside. Clean and dry pot.

2   Adjust oven rack to middle position and heat oven to 350 degrees. Combine American cheese and cheddar in bowl; set aside. Melt 1 tablespoon butter in now-empty pot over medium-high heat. Add mushrooms, bell pepper, and onion and cook until softened and liquid has evaporated, 8 to 10 minutes. Transfer vegetables to separate bowl and set aside.

3   Melt remaining 2 tablespoons butter in again-empty pot over medium heat. Add flour and cook, whisking constantly, for 1 minute. Slowly whisk in broth, half-and-half, pepper, cayenne, and salt, scraping up any browned bits and smoothing out any lumps. Bring to simmer and cook until sauce is thickened, 6 to 8 minutes.

4   Off heat, whisk 2 cups cheese mixture into sauce until smooth. Stir in spaghetti, vegetables, and shredded chicken until well combined.

5   Transfer mixture to 13 by 9-inch baking dish, spread into even layer, and cover tightly with greased aluminum foil. Bake until sauce is bubbling around edges, 25 to 30 minutes. Remove foil, sprinkle remaining 1 cup cheese mixture over top, and bake, uncovered, until cheese is melted, about 5 minutes. Let cool for 15 minutes before serving.

A LOVE LETTER TO COMMUNITY COOKBOOKS

For a long time, it was rare for women to see their own name in print. But in the 1860s, when home cooks started selling booklets of their recipes to raise money for Civil War soldiers, that's what happened. Women's names were recorded next to their recipes, each dish reflecting an individual and shared cultural history that gave us a glimpse into what was happening at home.

As community cookbooks gathered steam over the following century, it seems nearly every school, church, and civic organization—no matter their size—published a collection of recipes. Now, many of us turn to these books for very specific dishes. In *River Road Recipes: The Textbook of Louisiana Cuisine*, the bestselling book from the Baton Rouge Junior League, I like the Mexican casserole with hominy, and in the community cookbook from my middle school there's a hash brown casserole that is perfect for Sunday brunch.

Community cookbooks have brought women together for good causes for more than 150 years, and even in the digital era it still means something to sign your name to a recipe and share it with the world—or even with just your neighbors.

My grandma was one of those neighbors who was always sharing recipes. Her goulash appears in my favorite community cookbook, a collection of family recipes my mom printed off and assembled in a three-ring binder one Christmas 20 years ago. That's where you'll find our own spin on the Mexican casserole—we make it with layers of flour tortillas—alongside other comfort-food dishes that aren't fancy enough for a "real" cookbook but are treasured in ours: chicken and dumplings, pumpkin pie cake, tamale pie.

These are the dishes I make when I'm feeling nostalgic about home, but I also reach out for these community-powered books, these everyday recipes, when I want a reminder of all the cooks, everywhere, who feed and comfort their loved ones, then and now. Behind their names, I see wartime pantries and overloaded work schedules, their holiday favorites and the hopes that their children will one day make these recipes even after they're gone. These women contributed more to the world than these recipes, and these cookbooks hold those memories, too.

by Addie Broyles

food writer; author of the Invisible Thread, *a weekly newsletter about the things that connect us that we cannot see; and native of the Missouri Ozarks*

King Ranch Casserole

Serves 6 to 8 ~ Total Time: 2 hours

King Ranch just might be the most famous casserole in Texas, one packed with tender shreds of chicken, corn tortillas, and spicy tomatoes bound in a rich, cheesy sauce.

The casserole comes premade and sold in H-E-B supermarkets around the state, and was a familiar addition to community and Junior League cookbooks, as well as ladies' magazines. The dish became popular during the 1940s and 1950s when cooking with convenience and canned foods helped women get dinner on the table fast. But despite its name, there is no evidence that the comforting dish is linked to King Ranch, a 825,000-acre ranch in South Texas that dates back to the mid-19th century.

In a 1989 *Texas Monthly* article titled "Texas Primer: King Ranch Casserole," Anne Dingus notes that the dish resembles chilaquiles, a Mexican dish of tortillas smothered in sauce. She also observed that, "Not only is King Ranch casserole the most requested dish at the 1886 Room, Austin's premier ladies' lunch spot, but it is also popular at trendy Brazos on Greenville Avenue in Dallas, where needy singles demand it at the end of particularly punishing work weeks." The owner of Brazos termed the casserole "mom food."

For this version, we suggest—as many cooks today do—forgoing the traditional canned soups and instead stirring together a rich gravy from butter, flour, and chicken broth. To avoid soggy tortillas, we crisp corn tortillas in the oven, which prevents them from disintegrating into mush during baking. Then, we build a mildly spicy sauce with sautéed onions, jalapeños, and Ro-Tel tomatoes. Instead of discarding the liquid from the tomatoes, we reduce it to intensify the flavor. And for an added boost of corn flavor, we sprinkle crushed Fritos over the casserole and bake it until just lightly browned. If you can't find Ro-Tel tomatoes, substitute 2 cups of canned diced tomatoes and two stemmed, seeded, and finely chopped jalapeño chiles. Monterey Jack can be substituted for the Colby Jack here.

12	(6-inch) corn tortillas
	Vegetable oil spray
1	tablespoon unsalted butter
2	onions, chopped fine
2	jalapeño chiles, stemmed, seeded, and minced
2	teaspoons ground cumin
2	(10-ounce) cans Ro-Tel Original Diced Tomatoes & Green Chilies
5	tablespoons all-purpose flour
3	cups chicken broth
1	cup heavy cream
4	(6-ounce) boneless, skinless chicken breasts, trimmed, halved lengthwise, and cut crosswise ½ inch thick
1	pound Colby Jack cheese, shredded (4 cups)
2	tablespoons minced fresh cilantro
6	ounces Fritos corn chips, crushed (2¼ cups)

1   Adjust oven racks to upper-middle and lower-middle positions and heat oven to 450 degrees. Arrange tortillas on 2 rimmed baking sheets and lightly spray both sides of tortillas with oil spray. Bake until slightly crisp and browned, about 12 minutes. Let tortillas cool slightly, then break into bite-size pieces. Adjust upper rack to middle position (oven rack will be hot).

2   Heat butter in Dutch oven over medium-high heat. Add onions, jalapeños, and cumin and cook until lightly browned, about 8 minutes. Add tomatoes and their juice and cook until most of liquid has evaporated, about 10 minutes. Stir in flour and cook for 1 minute. Add broth and cream, scraping up any browned bits and smoothing out any lumps, bring to simmer, and cook until thickened, 2 to 3 minutes. Stir in chicken and cook until no longer pink, about 4 minutes. Off heat, add Colby Jack and cilantro and stir until cheese is melted. Season with salt and pepper to taste.

3   Scatter half of tortilla pieces in 13 by 9-inch baking dish (or similar size casserole dish) set in rimmed baking sheet. Spoon half of filling evenly over tortilla pieces. Scatter remaining tortilla pieces over filling, then top with remaining filling. (Unbaked casserole can be wrapped tightly in aluminum foil and refrigerated for up to 24 hours; increase covered baking time to 30 minutes.)

4   Cover dish with foil and bake on upper rack until filling is bubbling, about 15 minutes. Remove foil, sprinkle with Fritos, and bake until lightly browned, about 10 minutes. Let casserole cool for 10 minutes before serving.

Cornbread Dressing

Serves 10 to 12 ~ Total Time: 2 hours

In *The Twisted Soul Cookbook: Modern Soul Food with Global Flavors*, author, chef, and Atlanta restaurateur Deborah Van Trece includes the following: "This book is dedicated to all the women in my life who have shaped me and given me a strong foundation." And among all the creative spins she takes to breathe new life into Southern and soul food classics—think deviled egg po' boy, Boursin cheese grits, lobster beignets with vanilla bean rémoulade, and deep-fried fish bone brittle (one of Toni Tipton-Martin's favorites)—she offers a Cajun cornbread dressing that we can't resist. Cornbread dressing is dotted with fresh vegetables and andouille sausage and baked with just enough eggs and savory chicken broth to achieve a cohesive, set dish. Her dressing (generally in the South, folks say "dressing"; Northerners tend to call the dish "stuffing") is also seasoned with fresh herbs and seasoning salt. Ours relies on Creole seasoning for oomph. We brush it with melted butter before baking to give the dressing a rich, crisp, golden top. We developed this recipe using Quaker Yellow Cornmeal.

Cornbread

1½	cups (7½ ounces) all-purpose flour
1½	cups (7½ ounces) cornmeal
3	tablespoons sugar
1	tablespoon baking powder
1	teaspoon table salt
1¾	cups whole milk
3	large eggs
6	tablespoons unsalted butter, melted

Dressing

2	tablespoons unsalted butter, plus 4 tablespoons unsalted butter, melted
12	ounces andouille sausage, cut into ¼-inch pieces
2	onions, chopped
2	green bell peppers, stemmed, seeded, and chopped
2	celery ribs, chopped
4	slices bacon, cut into ¼-inch pieces
1	tablespoon Tony Chachere's Original Creole Seasoning
2	garlic cloves, minced
3	cups chicken broth
1	cup whole milk
3	large eggs, lightly beaten
¾	cup chopped fresh parsley
½	teaspoon pepper

1 **For the cornbread** Adjust oven rack to middle position and heat oven to 425 degrees. Spray 13 by 9-inch baking dish with vegetable oil spray.

2 Whisk flour, cornmeal, sugar, baking powder, and salt together in large bowl. Whisk milk, eggs, and melted butter together in second bowl. Whisk milk mixture into flour mixture until just about combined. Transfer batter to prepared dish. Bake until cornbread is golden brown and toothpick inserted in center comes out clean, about 20 minutes.

3 **For the dressing** While the cornbread bakes, melt 2 tablespoons butter in 12-inch nonstick skillet over medium-high heat. Add andouille, onions, bell peppers, celery, and bacon to skillet and cook until vegetables are softened, about 8 minutes. Add Creole seasoning and garlic and cook until fragrant, about 1 minute. Transfer sausage mixture to large bowl.

4 Turn hot cornbread onto rimmed baking sheet and break into small pieces with two forks. (Cooled, crumbled cornbread can be transferred to zipper-lock bag and stored at room temperature for up to 24 hours.)

5 Transfer crumbled cornbread to bowl with sausage mixture. Add broth, milk, eggs, parsley, and pepper and stir to combine. Transfer dressing to now-empty dish and spread into even layer (do not pack down). Using side of rubber spatula or wooden spoon, create ridges about ½ inch apart on top of dressing.

6 Brush top of dressing with remaining 4 tablespoons melted butter. Bake until browned and crisped on top and heated through, about 35 minutes. Let cool for 10 minutes and serve.

To make ahead At end of step 5, let dressing cool completely. Cover baking dish with plastic wrap and refrigerate for up to 24 hours or wrap in additional layer of aluminum foil and freeze for up to 1 month. To serve, thaw overnight in refrigerator if frozen. Proceed with step 6, extending baking time by 15 minutes and covering with foil for final 10 minutes of cooking if top begins to get too dark.

No.10

OUTDOOR COOKING (& EATING)

Left to right: Backyard Barbecued Beans (page 336), Texas Barbecued Brisket (page 318), North Carolina Barbecued Pork (page 326), Pimento Mac and Cheese (page 334), the half grill setup (page 321).

THE HEAT IS ON

BARBECUE & GENDER

In 2021, I attended Barbecue Summer Camp—three days devoted entirely to the art of barbecue—hosted by Texas A&M and Foodways Texas. The meat-filled extravaganza covered everything from handling a pit to understanding beef gradings and exploring the subtleties of cooking with wood. There was one topic that wasn't addressed: the gender discrepancy in the room. Of the 55 camp attendees, I was one of seven women.

The world of grilling and barbecuing has long been a bastion of masculinity. In a scene from *Leave It to Beaver*, the classic sitcom of the late 1950s and early 1960s, Wally Cleaver asks his dad why it is that when the cooking is done inside his mother does it but when it's done outside, his father does it. His father Ward replies, "Well, it's sort of traditional, I guess. You know they say a woman's place is in the home, and as long as she's in the home, she might as well be in the kitchen." When Wally presses more, Ward responds, "Women do alright when they have all the modern conveniences but us men are better at this rugged type of outdoor cooking—sort of a throwback to caveman days."

But how did it become the norm for men to "man" the grill while women keep to the kitchen? In the United States, cooking food over fire on the soil we now call the American South was first done by Indigenous people. As the land was colonized, enslaved men were often the ones who barbecued meat. It was hard, physical work: Typically pits were dug and/or built. This was long before the development of charcoal briquettes, so wood had to be cut and split. This work often went towards celebrations, political events, and other large gatherings, and so the practice of cooking low and slow over fire became synonymous with extra-large cuts of meat and whole animals. Lifting a hog isn't easy work (I host a pig roast every year and can say that smaller pigs are 60 to 80 pounds).

But while not outside, women *were* cooking with fire in early U.S. history. The gas stove wasn't invented until the 1800s, so many women lit logs to power stoves. Furthermore, cooking outside over fire was commonplace for enslaved families who didn't have kitchen access and, sometimes, women were doing that cooking. It is documented that in Arkansas, Marie Jean, an enslaved Black woman, was in charge of a barbecue for a 4th of July celebration in 1840. In his book, *Black Smoke: African Americans and the United States of Barbecue*, Adrian Miller surmises Marie Jean was not the only woman doing this kind of work at the time—she was just one of the few we have documentation of.

The sometimes seemingly intentional exclusion of women from outdoor cooking appears to be the product of more recent history. After World War II, men were encouraged to spend more time at home and less at bars, and the era produced idyllic images of them grilling for their families. According to Dr. Emily Contois in the article "Our Association of Masculinity with Grilling Is Just One More Under-Discussed Facet of Diet Culture" by Michele Ross for Well+Good, "In the years after World War II, as suburban life proliferated—though largely limited to white families—the grill emerged as a home food space for men, where they could simultaneously perform masculinity and familial domesticity." This era also saw the invention of the Weber Kettle Grill, not the first backyard grill, but one that revolutionized grilling by adding a lid, vastly increasing the cooker's versatility.

Digging into this phenomenon more reveals many stereotypical or misogynistic theories. For example, grilling expert Meathead Goldwyn, who leads us to the aforementioned *Leave It to Beaver* scene, writes about the 1950s in his mildly satirical 2022 article, "Man the Grill: Why Don't More Women Grill?": "Since women ruled the kitchen, in fact the entire indoors, the natural division of duties left her there. Not that she minded. The air-conditioned kitchen was her space. She had no interest in the messy grill. Smoke gets in your hair and clothes and you get sweaty. And if you've just paid for a manicure, who wants charcoal under your nails?" In a 2010 *Forbes* article, Meghan Casserly suggests that grilling excites men because it involves fire and some element of danger; it allows men a chance to hang with other men (while women hang in the kitchen); and it doesn't require a lot of cleaning up. Similar arguments cite that men like playing with sharp grilling tools; grilling lets them pretend to help with dinner; and women are scared to cook without the consistency of an oven.

I don't know where these ideas come from, certainly not from real evidence, but I do know that women are doing real work to sear their presence on the scene (with a searing sense of awareness and humor). Chuck Charnichart, Haley Conlin, and Alexis Tovías Morales of Barbs-B-Q in Lockhart, Texas (see page 335), adorn their bright pink menu with hearts. Alison Clem and the late LeAnn Mueller, the women behind La Barbecue in Austin, Texas (see page 324), decorate their menu with a cleaver-toting religious icon dubbed, "Our Lady of Barbecue." Their website proudly states: "Our company is female-owned. That may not sound like a big deal, but in the sausage fest of the BBQ industry, we're proud the future is female." Danielle Bennett, who is a rock star of the barbecue competition circuit (and one of the eight women in the Barbecue Hall of Fame), proudly goes by the nickname Diva Q.

You also have women more quiet about gender, like Tootsie Tomanetz, a trailblazing woman in barbecue who doesn't seem to address it that much. Norma Frances Tomanetz (aka Tootsie) is the 89-year-old pitmaster at Snow's BBQ in Lexington, Texas, which *Texas Monthly* awarded best brisket in 2008 and 2017. She's also a James Beard Award nominee and the focus of an episode of the popular Netflix series *Chef's Table: BBQ*.

Tomanetz started working in 'cue at 31 years old at City Meat Market in Giddings, Texas, where her husband was a butcher. One day, the manager, Hershel Doyle, asked Tootsie to fill in running the pit because he was short-staffed. Despite having no previous experience in barbecuing, Tootsie quickly picked up the craft. She came to co-own a second location of City Meat Market.

Now she works with a pit custom built for her at Snow's. Tootsie's approach to barbecuing is intuitive; she famously uses her hand to gauge the temperature of the pits, managing multiple pits with hundreds of cuts of meat each Saturday (the only day Snow's is open).

Tootsie was one of the seven women in the room at Barbecue Summer Camp. She presented on Friday afternoon so she could have time to get the pit ready for Saturday. When I met her she had a calm, humble demeanor and said, "You know I was named best brisket in Texas"—as if everyone didn't already know. That humility, I would argue, is in and of itself womanly.

For there to be true equity, there can be no rules to owning our identity in the barbecue space. Whether we choose to play up our femininity around the pit or not, women continue to prove their skills. So ladies, pour your charcoal (don't let a man tell you how to do it). Light your fires. Let's get smokin'.

by Morgan Bolling

Grilled Steak Fajitas

Serves 6 ~ Total Time: 1¼ hours, plus 2 hours marinating

The ideal fajitas should be a simple affair featuring tender strips of beef nestled into soft flour tortillas along with some onions and bell peppers. The vegetables should be perfectly softened but not mushy, with an appealing char from the grill. Moving them to a disposable aluminum pan on the cooler side of the grill after searing them gently steams them to finish. Skirt steak is the classic—some say the only—choice for fajitas. A marinade of salty soy sauce, vegetable oil, garlic, and sweet-tangy pineapple juice flavors every crevice, but we also use a trick we learned from Alex Padilla, who was the chef at the Original Ninfa's in Houston back in 2018 (see "Mama Ninfa: The Woman Who Introduced Fajitas to the American Vernacular"): Reserve some marinade to toss with the grilled bell peppers and onion before serving them to boost their flavor. (It's worth noting, this recipe is not the original one cooked by Ninfa Rodriguez Laurenzo, the woman who opened Ninfa's back in 1973. Her family now owns a restaurant called El Tiempo Cantina in Houston that is worth visiting to taste the original.)

Serve the fajitas with pico de gallo, avocado pieces or guacamole, sour cream, and lime wedges. One (6-ounce) can of pineapple juice will yield ¾ cup. We cook the skirt steak between medium and medium-well so that its texture isn't chewy and the steak is easy to eat.

¾	cup pineapple juice
½	cup plus 1 tablespoon vegetable oil, divided
¼	cup soy sauce
3	garlic cloves, minced
2	pounds skirt steak, trimmed and cut crosswise into 6 equal pieces
3	yellow, red, orange, or green bell peppers
1	large red onion, sliced into ½-inch-thick rounds
1¼	teaspoons table salt, divided
1	teaspoon pepper, divided
12	(6-inch) flour tortillas
1	(13 by 9 inch) disposable aluminum pan
1	tablespoon chopped fresh cilantro

1 Whisk pineapple juice, ½ cup oil, soy sauce, and garlic together in bowl. Reserve ¼ cup marinade. Transfer remaining 1¼ cups marinade to 1-gallon zipper-lock bag. Add steak, press out air, seal bag, and turn to distribute marinade. Refrigerate for at least 2 hours or up to 24 hours.

2 Using paring knife, cut around stems of bell peppers and remove cores and seeds. Push toothpick horizontally through each onion round to keep rings intact while grilling. Brush bell peppers and onion evenly with remaining 1 tablespoon oil and season with ½ teaspoon salt and ½ teaspoon pepper. Remove steak from marinade and pat dry with paper towels; discard marinade. Sprinkle steak with remaining ¾ teaspoon salt and remaining ½ teaspoon pepper. Wrap tortillas in aluminum foil; set aside.

3a **For a charcoal grill** Open bottom vent completely. Light large chimney starter filled with charcoal briquettes (6 quarts). When top coals are partially covered with ash, pour evenly over half of grill. Set cooking grate in place, cover, and open lid vent completely. Heat grill until hot, about 5 minutes.

3b **For a gas grill** Turn all burners to high, cover, and heat grill until hot, about 15 minutes. Leave primary burner on high and turn other burner(s) to low.

4 Clean and oil cooking grate. Place bell peppers and onion on hotter side of grill and place tortilla packet on cooler side of grill. Cook (covered if using gas) until vegetables are char-streaked and tender, 8 to 13 minutes, flipping and moving vegetables as needed for even cooking, and until tortillas are warmed through, about 10 minutes, flipping tortillas halfway through cooking.

5 Remove tortillas from grill; keep wrapped and set aside. Transfer vegetables to disposable pan, cover pan tightly with foil, and place on cooler side of grill. (If using gas, cover grill and allow hotter side to reheat for 5 minutes.) Place steak on hotter side of grill and cook (covered if using gas) until charred and meat registers 135 to 140 degrees, 2 to 4 minutes per side. Transfer steak to cutting board and tent with foil. Remove disposable pan from grill.

6 Carefully remove foil from disposable pan (steam may escape). Slice bell peppers into thin strips. Remove toothpicks from onion rounds and separate rings. Return vegetables to disposable pan and toss with cilantro and reserved marinade. Season with salt and pepper to taste. Slice steak thin against grain. Transfer steak and vegetables to serving platter. Serve with tortillas.

The late Mama Ninfa.

Houston Chronicle / *Hearst Newspapers via Getty Images*

MAMA NINFA: THE WOMAN WHO INTRODUCED FAJITAS TO THE AMERICAN VERNACULAR

Ninfa Rodriguez Laurenzo, better known as Mama Ninfa, opened the Original Ninfa's on Navigation Boulevard in Houston, Texas in 1973. In its initial form, Ninfa's was a tiny taco shop. In the years since, Ninfa's has grown into something decidedly larger scale.

Before opening Ninfa's, Laurenzo ran her own tortilla-making business, but when her husband Domenic passed away in 1969 and she was struggling to support their five children, she needed more than just the money the tortilla business earned. To supplement her income, she began selling grilled steak tortillas, a dish that resembled tacos al carbon and was known widely among home cooks. Tacos al carbon translates from Spanish to meat "cooked over coal," and almost always means meat wrapped in a

tortilla. "Fajitas," on the other hand, comes from the word "faja," which means "belt" in Spanish. That's because fajitas are made with a tough, long, narrow cut of beef that resembles a belt, sold as skirt steak. Mexican cowboys (or vaqueros) who ran cattle drives through Texas in the 1930s were partially paid for their work in less-popular cuts of meat—especially the ones that didn't sell well at butcher shops—such as skirt steak. Fajitas may be prepared on a griddle or in a hot skillet, and they are often eaten like a taco, but they don't have to be.

The idea of grilling these specialty cuts remained an underground idea for years, but Mama Ninfa changed all that. With her tacos al carbon, Mama Ninfa introduced grilled skirt steak to Houston's non-vaquero

population. As the taco shop's business picked up, the name of the dish changed to fajitas, and the original dining room was redecorated and expanded into the Tex-Mex mecca it is today. The Original Ninfa's is no longer owned by Mama Ninfa's family, but her legacy lives on in El Tiempo Cantina, a restaurant created by one of her sons.

Before Mama Ninfa passed away in 2001, she had created a successful restaurant operation, been named "Woman Restaurateur of the Year" by the Texas Restaurant Association, received a Humanitarian Award from the Arthritis Foundation, and been inducted into the Texas Women's Hall of Fame. But her most delicious accomplishment? Inspiring the joy that comes to all of us when a platter of sizzling fajitas hits our tables.

Smoked Chicken Wings

Serves 4 to 6 ~ Total Time: 1½ hours, plus 1 hour brining

Smoked chicken wings are a great introduction to smoking on a grill for anyone who is new to the technique. To get juicy, tender meat, we start with a 1-hour brine before the wings hit the grill (gas or charcoal is fine—this isn't big barbecue) to ensure that the meat doesn't dry out. The wings may be relatively quick-cooking, but we give them a barbecue-inspired spice rub of paprika, chili powder, dried oregano, and cayenne for heat and aromatic complexity. We build a two-level fire and start the wings over indirect heat to cook them evenly, and then finish them directly over the coals to sear and crisp the skin. To make them shine—literally—we brush on a tangy-rich savory sauce that gives the char-kissed wings a beautiful sheen.

But there's not just one way to wing. Shalamar Lane is an expat of the South who serves recipes from her Alabama and Texas roots at her LA restaurant My Father's Barbeque, including a boozy dish of smoked wings with Hennessy barbecue sauce. Robyn Lindars, writer of the blog *GrillGirl*, has published a variety of wing recipes, and her Florida Orange Chicken Wings rely upon her own spice blend of orange, coriander, makrut lime, granulated honey, and smoked paprika—a mix she combines with butter and hot sauce. And chef Jiyeon Lee (see "Blending Cultures, Crafting Barbecue") serves smoked wings alongside a spicy, creamy kimchi mayonnaise at Heirloom Market BBQ.

For this recipe, we prefer to buy whole wings and butcher them ourselves because they tend to be larger than wings that come split into flats and drumettes. If you can find only split wings, look for larger ones. Twelve whole wings should ideally equal 3 pounds and will yield 24 pieces (12 drumettes and 12 flats, tips discarded). Do not brine the chicken for longer than 3 hours in step 1 or it will become too salty.

Wings

¼	cup table salt for brining
¼	cup sugar for brining
3	pounds chicken wings, cut at joints, wingtips discarded
2	teaspoons paprika
2	teaspoons chili powder
1¼	teaspoons dried oregano
1¼	teaspoons pepper
1¼	teaspoons garlic powder
1	teaspoon sugar
¼	teaspoon cayenne pepper
2	cups wood chips

Sauce

4	tablespoons unsalted butter
2	tablespoons cider vinegar
2	tablespoons ketchup
¼	teaspoon table salt

1 **For the wings** Dissolve salt and ¼ cup sugar in 2 quarts cold water in large container. Submerge wings in brine, cover, and refrigerate for at least 1 hour or up to 3 hours. Combine paprika, chili powder, oregano, pepper, garlic powder, 1 teaspoon sugar, and cayenne in bowl. Measure out 1 tablespoon spice mixture and set aside.

2 **For the sauce** Melt butter in small saucepan over medium-low heat. Add reserved 1 tablespoon spice mixture and cook until fragrant, about 30 seconds. Carefully add vinegar (mixture will bubble up). Bring to quick simmer, then remove from heat. Whisk in ketchup and salt. Cover and set aside.

3 Remove wings from brine and pat dry with paper towels. Sprinkle wings all over with remaining spice mixture.

4 Just before grilling, soak wood chips in water for 15 minutes, then drain. Using large piece of heavy-duty aluminum foil, wrap soaked chips in 8 by 4½-inch foil packet. (Make sure chips do not poke holes in sides or bottom of packet.) Cut 2 evenly spaced 2-inch slits in top of packet.

5a **For a charcoal grill** Open bottom vent completely. Light large chimney starter mounded with charcoal briquettes (7 quarts). When top coals are partially covered with ash, place wood chip packet on 1 side of grill and pour coals evenly over half of grill, covering wood chip packet. Set cooking grate in place, cover, and open lid vent completely. Heat grill until hot and wood chips are smoking, about 5 minutes.

5b **For a gas grill** Remove cooking grate and place wood chip packet directly on primary burner. Turn all burners to high, cover, and heat grill until hot and wood chips are smoking, about 15 minutes. Leave primary burner on high and turn off other burner(s). (Adjust primary burner [or, if using 3-burner grill, primary burner and second burner] as needed to maintain grill temperature of 400 degrees.)

6 Clean and oil cooking grate. Place wings, fatty side up, on cooler side of grill, arranging drumettes closest to coals (if using charcoal). Cover and cook until wings are darkened in color and meat registers at least 180 degrees, about 40 minutes, flipping wings halfway through cooking.

7a **For a charcoal grill** Slide half of wings to hotter side of grill and cook, uncovered, until charred in spots, 1 to 3 minutes per side. Transfer wings to platter and tent with foil. Repeat with remaining wings.

7b **For a gas grill** Turn all burners to high and cook, uncovered, until wings are charred in spots, 5 to 7 minutes per side. Transfer wings to platter and tent with foil.

8 Reheat sauce over medium heat, about 2 minutes. Toss wings and sauce together in bowl. Serve.

BLENDING CULTURES, CRAFTING BARBECUE

Jiyeon Lee (Chef JiJi) is a woman of many talents and titles. Born and raised in South Korea, she stunned as a model and captivated as a K-pop star. Celebrity and the limelight took a significant toll on Lee and in 1999, the then almost 30-year-old Lee retired from music and moved to Atlanta, where she has broken ground as an award-winning chef on the Southern barbecue scene.

In Atlanta, Lee discovered a passion for culinary arts, a field that was far removed from her initial fame. At 36, she embraced this newfound calling and enrolled in Le Cordon Bleu Atlanta.

Lee worked her way up from intern to acclaimed chef. She eventually met chef Cody Taylor, whom she partnered with— both in marriage and in business. The duo launched Heirloom Market BBQ in 2010, which combines Taylor's Texas-born and Tennessee-raised roots with Lee's Korean heritage. They serve dishes such as gochujang-marinated smoked spare ribs, collard greens with Korean miso, and smoked chicken wings with a kimchi mayo. Heirloom Market BBQ has garnered national acclaim: Taylor and Lee were nominated for the James Beard Award for Best Chef: Southeast in 2020 and 2023, and the restaurant has received a Michelin Bib Gourmand, an award the company gives out to restaurants they think represent the best value for money. Most importantly, the two continue to feed a lot of happy barbecue fans.

by Morgan Bolling

Chef Jiyeon Lee of Heirloom Market BBQ.

Ryan Fleisher

Texas Barbecued Brisket

Serves 12 to 15   ~   Total Time: 6¼ to 8¼ hours, plus 14 hours salting and resting

A proper Texas-style smoked brisket is sublime eating: tender, juicy meat encased in a dark, peppery crust or "bark." Brisket is the holy grail of barbecue because it's not an easy cut to make tender. And so, unsurprisingly, smoking a 10-pound brisket on a charcoal grill takes a little TLC. We've worked out the best practices for bringing brisket to your backyard.

We arrange a C-shaped array of briquettes (known as a charcoal snake; see page 321) in the grill; this setup slowly burns from one end of the C to the other. We top the briquettes with wood chunks, which provide hours of low, smoky heat. We cook the brisket fat side down to insulate the meat against the coals. Wrapping the brisket in aluminum foil toward the end of its cooking time and letting it rest in an insulated cooler for 2 hours ensures ultramoist meat for slicing.

We developed this recipe using a 22-inch Weber kettle charcoal grill. Plan ahead: The brisket must be seasoned at least 12 hours before cooking. We call for a whole beef brisket here, with both the flat and point cuts intact; you may need to special-order this cut. Be sure to read the entire recipe before starting. And while this brisket is so juicy you don't need a sauce, you can serve it with barbecue sauce if you'd like. We admit our Easy Espresso Barbecue Sauce (page 332) is a delicious accompaniment.

1	(10- to 12-pound) whole beef brisket, untrimmed
¼	cup kosher salt
¼	cup pepper
5	(3-inch) wood chunks
1	(13 by 9-inch) disposable aluminum pan

1   With brisket positioned point side up, use sharp knife to trim fat cap to ½- to ¼-inch thickness. Remove excess fat from deep pocket where flat and point are attached. Trim and discard short edge of flat if less than 1 inch thick. Flip brisket and remove any large deposits of fat from underside.

2   Place brisket on rimmed baking sheet. Combine salt and pepper in bowl; sprinkle all over brisket. Cover loosely with plastic wrap and refrigerate for 12 to 24 hours.

3   Open bottom vent completely. Set up charcoal snake: Arrange 60 briquettes, 2 briquettes wide, around perimeter of grill, overlapping slightly so briquettes are touching, leaving 8-inch gap between ends of snake. Place second layer of 60 briquettes, also 2 briquettes wide, on top of first. (Completed snake should be 2 briquettes wide by 2 briquettes high.)

4   Starting 4 inches from 1 end of snake, evenly space wood chunks along length of charcoal snake. Place disposable pan in center of grill so short end of pan runs parallel to gap in snake. Fill pan with 6 cups water. Light chimney starter filled with 10 briquettes (pile briquettes on 1 side of chimney). When coals are partially covered with ash, pour over 1 end of snake. (Make sure lit coals touch only 1 end of snake. Use tongs if necessary to move any coals that touch other end of snake.)

5   Set cooking grate in place. Clean and oil cooking grate. Place brisket, fat side down, directly over water pan, with point end facing gap in snake. Insert temperature probe into side of upper third of point. Cover grill, open lid vent completely, and position lid vent over gap in snake. Cook, undisturbed and without lifting lid, until meat registers 170 degrees, 4 to 5 hours.

6   Place 2 large sheets of aluminum foil on rimmed baking sheet. Remove probe from brisket. Using oven mitts, lift brisket and transfer to center of foil, fat side down. Wrap brisket tightly with first layer of foil, minimizing air pockets between foil and brisket. Rotate brisket 90 degrees and wrap with second sheet of foil. (Use additional foil, if necessary, to completely wrap brisket.) Foil wrap should be airtight. Make small mark on foil with marker to keep track of fat/point side.

7   Remove cooking grate. Starting at still-unlit end of snake, pour 3 quarts unlit briquettes about halfway around perimeter of grill over gap in snake and spent coals. Replace cooking grate. Return foil-wrapped brisket to grill over water pan, fat side down, with point end facing where gap in snake used to be. Reinsert probe into point. Cover grill and continue to cook until meat registers 205 degrees, 1 to 2 hours longer.

8   Remove temperature probe. Transfer foil-wrapped brisket to cooler, point side up. Close cooler and let rest for at least 2 hours or up to 3 hours. Transfer brisket to carving board, unwrap, and position fat side up. Slice flat against grain ¼ inch thick, stopping once you reach base of point. Rotate point 90 degrees and slice point against grain (perpendicular to first cut) ⅜ inch thick. Serve.

DINNER ON THE GROUNDS

Churchgoers across the South eat together for myriad occasions: funerals, weddings, between Sunday worship services. Churches hold fundraisers by selling food, and they serve meals at their homecoming celebrations, an annual occasion when church members who've moved away return to worship and eat. When Southerners think of church, they think of plates piled high with fried chicken, mac and cheese, green beans, and peach cobbler, just as much as they do hymns and hard pews.

The Bible is filled with stories of shared meals that hold sacred meaning, and there are countless examples of fellowship meals throughout church history. But the Southern church supper holds unique significance, especially for women. It is here that women offer, or perhaps show off, their talents to the community.

The Sunday fellowship meal emerged for both practical and communal reasons. Before roads and cars made it easy to travel back and forth between church and home, congregants would come to church with dishes to share between the morning and afternoon services. The shared meal, sometimes called "dinner on the grounds," deepened relationships among those in the church community.

The fellowship meal holds particular significance in the Black church, where it dates back to the 17th century. Sunday was the sole day of rest afforded to the enslaved, and so became a time to prepare and share a feast. On the weeks a clergyperson was in town, which was a rare occasion in America's early days, the enslaved from several plantations came together for a regional service with Holy Communion. This fellowship meal reunified families that had been separated between plantations. It was the closest taste of freedom.

by Kendall Vanderslice

baker and writer exploring the intersection of food, faith, and culture

ALL ABOUT BARBECUE

When the weather's right, you can, of course, cook outdoors anywhere in the world. In the South, that most often means barbecue, noun and verb. Whereas in other parts of the country one might call their back-yard cookout a barbecue (or BBQ), that won't fly in the South. Barbecue requires smoke and meat, and a sense of care far removed from simply throwing burgers and dogs on a grill.

Like many Southern food traditions, barbecue started with Indigenous cooks. According to Natasha Geiling in "The Evolution of American Barbecue" for *Smithsonian Magazine*, Columbus encountered Indigenous tribes cooking food over indirect heat fired by green (freshly cut) wood in the Caribbean. The Spanish explorers called this style of cooking barbacoa, from which the word "barbecue" is derived. As explorers moved North, they continued to witness Native American people cooking this way. In 1540, in what is present-day Mississippi, explorers with Hernando de Soto noted Chickasaw people cooking a feast of pork barbacoa.

As colonists settled the South, barbecue was cooked primarily by enslaved people, who would often cook their own food outside in a pit as well as congregate over barbecue. Plantation owners leaned on enslaved workers to cook barbecue for their community events as well. The events were put on for wealthy white guests, but the person seasoning the meat and firing the pit was most often Black. Men were often enlisted since they were able to lift large cuts of meat and logs. But in his book *Black Smoke*, Adrian Miller highlights Marie Jean (see page 312), a female pitmaster in Arkansas, who may have bought her freedom in the mid 1800s with funds from her cooking, from feeding people and catering events. With her freedom, she kept an inn beloved for its food.

As time goes on, 'cue in the South has evolved. You can find people cooking with fire in diverse ways. And you can find a lot more women overseeing the pits. What they all share is a celebration of the power of cooking over fire. And, if you're not yet well versed in that (or even if you are), here we offer some tips to help you do the same and make barbecue on a backyard charcoal grill. We developed our recipes with a Weber Original Kettle Charcoal Grill, 22-Inch, which is a popular choice.

A Southern Barbecue, *a wood engraving from a sketch by Horace Bradley, published in* Harper's Weekly, *July 1887*

Best Practices for Using a Charcoal Grill

You don't need a barbecue big rig to make big-flavored barbecue at home. You can achieve nicely smoked meats on a charcoal grill, which reaches much hotter temperatures than most gas grills, resulting in great color and char. The smoke from the charcoal and from the sizzling drippings of the food adds flavor and aroma to whatever you cook.

Fire It Up

A chimney starter heats coals evenly and efficiently. Fill the bottom of the chimney starter with two sheets of crumpled newspaper, set it on the lower charcoal grate (make sure the bottom vent is open), and fill the top with charcoal. Allow the charcoal to burn until the top briquettes are partially covered with a thin layer of gray ash. The ash is a sign that the coals are fully lit and ready to be turned out into the grill.

Keep It Clean

To ensure that food will release from the cooking grate with ease, scrape the heated grate clean and then oil it. Clean the inside of the grill lid regularly by scrubbing it with steel wool and water to prevent the carbon buildup from flaking off onto your food.

Dispose of Spent Coals

After grilling, cover the grill and close both the bottom grill vent and top lid vent; let the coals and ash cool for at least 48 hours. We dump cooled coals and ash into a metal bin and pour water over them as a safeguard. The charcoal and ash mixture can then be disposed of in a noncombustible outdoor trash receptacle.

The Half Grill Setup

This is a common setup we use for a charcoal grill when we're cooking food relatively quickly. It creates two cooking zones with a greater difference between heat levels than a two-level fire, with one side intensely hot and the other side comparatively cool.

It's good for bone-in poultry, foods that need both searing and gentle cooking (see Smoked Chicken Wings on page 316), or multicomponent meals that require different heat levels (see Grilled Steak Fajitas on page 314).

To Build It

Distribute the lit coals over half of the grill, piling them in an even layer. Leave the other half of the grill free of coals.

Charcoal Snake: How to Use Your Charcoal Grill for Smoking

You can make truly magnificent barbecue without a smoker; to do so, use a charcoal kettle grill and a charcoal snake, which is a formation of coals in the shape of the letter C.

1   Open the bottom vent completely. This maximizes airflow so that the charcoal and wood chunks burn cleaner, producing better smoke flavor.

2   Arrange 2 rows of briquettes around the perimeter of the charcoal grate, overlapping slightly so the briquettes touch to form a C-shape snake.

3   Top each of those rows with a second layer of briquettes. (The completed arrangement should be 2 briquettes wide by 2 briquettes high.)

4   Place wood chunks at even intervals on top of the charcoal. These will smolder to infuse your food with smoke flavor.

5   Place a disposable aluminum pan in the center, running lengthwise into the gap of the snake. Pour 6 cups of water into the pan. This will keep the temperature more consistent.

6   Light a chimney starter filled with a small amount of briquettes. When the top coals are partially covered with ash, place them over one end of the charcoal snake. Set the cooking grate in place. Cook food covered, leaving the top lid vent completely open.

Flavor Guide to Wood Chips and Chunks

We use wood in two different forms on the grill: chips and chunks. Wood chips can be used on gas grills and charcoal grills, while wood chunks are used with only charcoal grills. Chips are smaller and burn faster than chunks and thus are ideal for contributing flavor to foods that cook more quickly.

There are lots of varieties of wood chips and chunks out there for cooking, and each type provides a uniquely flavored smoke to flavor your food. Here are our tasting notes on some of the most common types.

Fruit (Apple and Cherry)

A lightly sweet, mild smoke. Great for seafood and poultry.

Hickory

A balanced though intense smoke that works with almost any food.

Maple

A relatively mild and tasty smoke on pork and poultry.

Mesquite

A strong smoke that works best with stronger-tasting cuts of beef, pork, lamb, and game.

Oak

A nutty and well-balanced smoke. The traditional choice for many pitmasters.

Essential Equipment

Chimney Starter

Charcoal chimney starters help charcoal light in a controlled manner and are our top choice for charcoal grillers. Look for a roomy charcoal chamber, an insulated handle, and a helper handle to make it easier to precisely distribute the lit coals.

Grill Brush

Cleaning the grill is a small chore with a big payoff: a smooth, gunk-free cooking surface. Short metal bristles are best.

Grill Tongs

You'll need long tongs to safely move food around the grill. We recommend a 16-inch-long set.

Grill Gloves

When you're working over a scorching-hot grill, oven mitts won't cut it. Good gloves keep you safe while allowing you to manipulate tongs or grab a hot cooking grate.

Instant-Read Thermometer

You need to take the finishing temperature of your food—no ifs, ands, or buts. An instant-read thermometer makes that easy, taking just 1 second to measure the temperature.

Probe Thermometer

Probe thermometers tell you when your food is ready without having to lift the grill lid and thus slow down the cooking process. They consist of a probe that's inserted into the food you're cooking and is also connected by a thin wire to a base that sits outside the grill. The base displays the readout so you can monitor the food's temperature. We find this essential for long-smoked foods.

SOUTHERN BARBECUE STYLES

Travel through the South and barbecue will look and taste a little—or a lot—different everywhere.

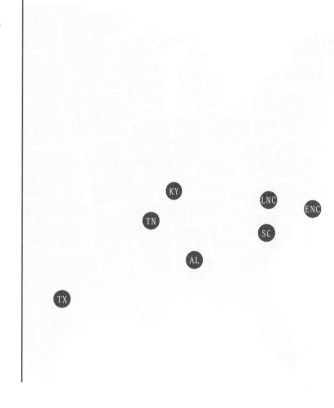 TX Central Texas

Meat(s) of Choice: Brisket, shoulder clod, and beef ribs
Standout Technique: Using indirect heat for next-level brisket
Flavor Notes: Dalmatian rub (aka salt and pepper)
Queens of the Cooker: Tootsie Tomanetz; LeAnn Mueller (1972–2023) and Alison Clem of La Barbecue; Laura Loomis; Chuck Charnichart, Haley Conlin, and Alexis Tovías Morales of Barbs–B–Q; Pat Mares; Kim Dunn; Jess Pryles; Kelli Nevarez

TN Memphis, Tennessee

Meat(s) of Choice: "Wet" and "dry" pork ribs and pork shoulder
Standout Technique: Using a potent dry spice rub and basting the meat during cooking if using sauce
Flavor Notes: Dry spices and an optional thin, sweet barbecue sauce
Queens of the Cooker: Desiree Robinson, Helen Turner

SC Central South Carolina

Meat(s) of Choice: Whole hog, fresh ham, and other pork
Standout Technique: Making barbecue into a barbecue hash
Flavor Notes: Mustard barbecue sauce, nicknamed "Carolina gold," which came from German immigrants in the 18th century (it's worth noting that in South Carolina you can find four styles of barbecue sauce across the state)
Queen of the Cooker: Amanda Riggan

KY Western Kentucky

Meat(s) of Choice: Mutton (sheep)
Standout Technique: Slow-smoking mutton over hickory coals and basting while cooking
Flavor Notes: Black dip BBQ sauce made with Worcestershire sauce
Queen of the Cooker: Suzanne Flint (1968–2024)

ENC Eastern North Carolina

Meat(s) of Choice: Whole hog
Standout Technique: Cooking a whole pig over wood and chopping it finely, serving it with the crispy skin
Flavor Notes: Vinegar barbecue sauce
Queens of the Cooker: Lindsay Bortle, Mrs. Gerri Grady

LNC Lexington, North Carolina

Meat(s) of Choice: Pork shoulder
Standout Technique: Cooking directly over wood, with attention to getting good "outside brown" (aka bark)
Flavor Notes: Vinegar barbecue sauce with just a little tomato
Queens of the Cooker: Elizabeth Karmel, Lyttle Bridges (1916–2008)

AL Alabama

Meat(s) of Choice: Pork and chicken
Standout Technique: Hickory smoking in an open pit
Flavor Notes: White sauce in the north, red sauce in the south
Queens of the Cooker: Myra Grissom Harper, Chequita Walker, Donetta Bethune

BBQ Competitions

Meat(s) of Choice: Ribs and brisket (but varies by competition)
Standout Technique: Showing quality with one bite
Flavor Notes: Varies
Queens of the Cooker: Melissa Cookston, Danielle Bennett (aka Diva Q), Erica Blaire Roby

Texas Smoked Beef Ribs

Serves 6 to 8   ~   Total Time: 6½ to 7¼ hours, plus 30 minutes resting

The best versions of these massive Texas-style smoked beef ribs have a dark, peppery crust and a pink smoke ring surrounding succulent beef. Many barbecue restaurants such as La Barbecue in Austin, Texas (see "LeAnn Mueller's Barbecue Legacy"), serve them only a few days of the week because beef ribs are pricey and don't yield as much profit as brisket or other barbecue. But if you have the means, the ultratender beef is a treat for a special occasion.

This recipe starts at the butcher shop. As with many barbecue cuts, you'll need to special-order the ribs, but it's well worth it. Request two racks of beef plate ribs, each with 1 to 1½ inches of meat on top of the bone to ensure they don't shrink down too much during cooking. To smoke them on a charcoal grill, we use the charcoal snake (see page 321). This C-shaped array of smoldering briquettes provides low, slow, domino-like indirect heat to the meat for upwards of 6 hours. Arranging five wood chunks on top of the charcoal snake sends steady smoke to infuse the meat with flavor. Cook the ribs all the way to 210 degrees to ensure ultratender, juicy beef. We developed this recipe using a 22-inch Weber kettle charcoal grill. We recommend reading the entire recipe before starting.

LEANN MUELLER'S BARBECUE LEGACY

Ali Clem and the late LeAnn Mueller of La Barbecue.

Shanna Hickman / Dish'n Dames

LeAnn Mueller started her professional life as a photographer, moving from her home in Texas to Los Angeles and New York for the perfect shot. But her roots were in barbecue. Her father, Bobby Mueller, had run Louie Mueller Barbecue in Taylor, Texas. It had been ranked as a top barbecue restaurants in Texas for decades and earned him a James Beard America's Classics award. One of the items he was famous for: his beef ribs. In fact, in an article about his passing in *Texas Monthly*, Patricia Sharpe wrote, "No competitor even came close for beef ribs, notoriously hard to do right."

When Bobby Mueller passed away in 2008, LeAnn moved back to Texas. Over the next few years, she worked with her brother to preserve the family legacy, and they opened a barbecue food truck in 2011. When she and her brother had a falling out, she rebranded the truck as La Barbecue, which she ran with her partner, Ali Clem, and legendary pitmaster John Lewis. Over the years, the truck navigated various locales before they secured their first brick-and-mortar spot in an East Cesar Chavez market in Austin in 2017, and then eventually settled into its dedicated building down the street in 2021.

Mueller and Clem continued to serve beef ribs at their restaurant, Friday through Sunday. There is also a whole section of the menu devoted to pickles and another to their housemade sausages, which are so popular they're represented by a cartoon mascot on the menu and on colorful merch that says "Sausage is my safe word."

The two made it a point to shake up the norms of a traditionally macho-male industry with their playful business name, fun cocktails, and a broad selection of champagne you can order alongside the barbecue. They also celebrated who they are. Mueller passed away in June 2023 at the age of 51, but a few days before, among Pride month celebrations, she posted on Instagram, "We are proud to be the *first-ever woman AND lesbian-owned BBQ restaurant in all of Texas*! Since November 2012, we have busted our asses to deliver the best BBQ in the game and keep the legend of Bobby & Trish Mueller alive. 🌭🌭🌭" The restaurant remains open and beloved today, with Clem continuing their work.

by Morgan Bolling

3 tablespoons kosher salt

3 tablespoons pepper

2 (4- to 5-pound) racks beef plate ribs, 1 to 1½ inches of meat on top of bone, trimmed

5 (3-inch) wood chunks

1 (13 by 9-inch) disposable aluminum pan

1 Combine salt and pepper in bowl, then sprinkle ribs all over with salt mixture.

2 Open bottom vent completely. Set up charcoal snake: Arrange 60 briquettes, 2 briquettes wide, around perimeter of grill, overlapping slightly so briquettes are touching, leaving 8-inch gap between ends of snake. Place second layer of 60 briquettes, also 2 briquettes wide, on top of first. (Completed snake should be 2 briquettes wide by 2 briquettes high.)

3 Starting 4 inches from 1 end of snake, evenly space wood chunks on top of snake. Place disposable pan in center of grill so short end of pan runs parallel to gap in snake. Fill pan with 4 cups water. Light chimney starter filled with 15 briquettes (pile briquettes on 1 side of chimney). When coals are partially covered with ash, pour over 1 end of snake. (Make sure lit coals touch only 1 end of snake. Use tongs if necessary to move any coals that touch other end of snake.)

4 Set cooking grate in place. Clean and oil cooking grate. Position ribs next to each other on cooking grate, bone side down, crosswise over disposable pan and gap in snake (they will be off-center; this is OK). Cover grill, position lid vent over gap in snake, and open lid vent completely. Cook undisturbed until rack of ribs overhanging gap in snake registers 210 degrees in meatiest portion, 5½ to 6¼ hours.

5 Transfer ribs to carving board, tent with aluminum foil, and let rest for 30 minutes. Cut ribs between bones and serve.

North Carolina Barbecued Pork

Serves 8 to 10 ～ Total Time: 5¾ to 7¼ hours, plus 19½ hours salting and resting

When you're talking barbecue in North Carolina, you're talking pork. That said, there are two main styles: one based in eastern North Carolina and one from Lexington, a city in the middle-western part of the state. Both styles use low, direct heat and lots of smoke, ideally from smoldering hickory logs. But the pitmasters in the eastern part of the state traditionally cook whole hogs on open pits. In and around Lexington, they usually cook hulking, bone-in pork shoulders—often several at a time—in closed brick pits.

When it comes to serving, in the eastern part of the state you're more likely to get finely chopped 'cue, while in Lexington people can request the (coarser) chop with an option to order extra "outside brown" (aka extra-smoky bark). And while sauces in both areas are tangy, eastern North Carolina sauce should be deeply tangy and spicy. Lexington-style sauce contains ketchup or another tomato product, which makes it redder, sweeter, and a bit thicker. As a nod to each, we suggest different chopping styles and saucing options for our backyard barbecued pork.

We developed this recipe using a 22-inch Weber kettle charcoal grill. Pork butt roast is often labeled Boston butt in the supermarket. Plan ahead: The pork butt must be seasoned at least 18 hours before it is cooked.

3   tablespoons kosher salt

1½   tablespoons pepper

1   (6-pound) bone-in pork butt roast, with ¼-inch fat cap

4   (3-inch) wood chunks

1   (13 by 9-inch) disposable aluminum pan

1   recipe Lexington-Style Barbecue Sauce (page 333) or Eastern North Carolina–Style Barbecue Sauce (page 332)

1   Combine salt and pepper in bowl. Place pork on large sheet of plastic wrap and sprinkle all over with salt mixture. Wrap tightly with plastic and refrigerate for 18 to 24 hours.

2   Open bottom vent completely. Set up charcoal snake: Arrange 60 briquettes, 2 briquettes wide, around perimeter of grill, overlapping slightly so briquettes are touching, leaving 8-inch gap between ends of snake. Place second layer of 60 briquettes, also 2 briquettes wide, on top of first. (Completed snake should be 2 briquettes wide by 2 briquettes high.)

3 Starting 4 inches from 1 end of snake, evenly space wood chunks on top of snake. Place disposable pan in center of grill so short end of pan runs parallel to gap in snake. Fill pan with 4 cups water. Light chimney starter filled with 15 briquettes (pile briquettes on 1 side of chimney). When coals are partially covered with ash, pour over 1 end of snake. (Make sure lit coals touch only 1 end of snake. Use tongs if necessary to move any coals that touch other end of snake.)

4 Set cooking grate in place. Clean and oil cooking grate. Unwrap pork and place, fat side down, over water pan. Insert temperature probe into thickest part of pork. Cover grill, positioning lid vent over gap in snake, and open lid vent completely. Cook undisturbed, without lifting lid, until pork registers 170 degrees, 4 to 5 hours.

5 Place 2 large sheets of aluminum foil on rimmed baking sheet. Remove probe from pork. Using oven mitts, lift pork and transfer to center of 1 sheet of foil, fat side down. Wrap pork tightly with first sheet of foil, minimizing air pockets between foil and pork. Rotate pork 90 degrees and wrap with second sheet of foil. (Use additional foil, if necessary, to completely wrap pork.) Foil wrap should be airtight. Make small mark on foil with marker to keep track of fat side.

6 Remove cooking grate. Starting at still-unlit end of snake, pour 2 quarts unlit briquettes about one-third of way around perimeter of grill over gap in snake and spent coals. Replace cooking grate. Return foil-wrapped pork to grill over water pan, fat side down. Reinsert probe into thickest part of pork. Cover grill and continue to cook until pork registers 200 degrees, 1 to 1½ hours longer. Remove probe. Transfer pork to carving board, fat side up, and let rest in foil for 1½ hours. Remove bone from pork. For Lexington style, chop pork with cleaver into 1-inch pieces. For eastern North Carolina–style, chop pork into ¼-inch pieces. Toss with ⅔ cup sauce. Serve, passing remaining sauce separately.

ON PORK AND JEWISHNESS

From the earliest decades of European and African settlement in the American South, Southern Jews revealed who they were and what they believed through the foods they ate—and the ones they *did not* eat—in a region where treyfe (nonkosher) pork, shellfish, and wild game were at the center of local cuisine.

Pork is forbidden within the ancient Jewish dietary laws of kashrut, which both designates prohibited foods and how kosher—which means "fit" or "proper"—foods should be prepared and eaten. Not all Jews adhere to kashrut, but for those who do, it's a statement of one's commitment to Judaism. Across the South, Jews invented their own regional rules of kashrut.

I grew up in the 1960s and '70s in a Jewish home in Blytheville, Arkansas, where our small synagogue and its families were the heart of my childhood. Fancy Jell-O salad, slow-cooked brisket, noodle kugel, roast chicken, matzoh ball soup, potato latkes, and honey cake were holiday rituals. We also enjoyed the famous vinegar-sauced pork barbecue tradition for which my hometown is well known. When we ate barbecue, it was as a "pig sandwich" in the car with a Cherry Coke at the Kream Kastle drive-in. On weekends we often joined another Jewish family for supper at Blytheville's Dixie Pig restaurant, whose logo featured a winking pig wearing a Confederate cap. We fit in—or thought we did—among white customers who were unfazed by the racially coded symbols that conflated barbecue with the white-controlled Old South.

Today a new generation of Jewish chefs, restaurateurs, delicatessen proprietors, farmers, bagel bakers, artisanal makers, food activists, and consumers are part of a thriving food movement that emphasizes local and seasonal ingredients, environmental sustainability, food equity, and social justice. Wendy Rhein is playing a huge role in moving the dial on this movement. She and her two sons raise chickens, goats, pigs, and sheep on their homestead, Chutzpah Hollow, in southwestern North Carolina. Rhein wanted her boys to connect to the source of their food and to community, and she tapped into her work in Jewish philanthropy to make that happen. This Jewish family raises pigs for their own table and for Rhein's nearby brother. They expect to sell the meat one day in local markets.

The Rheins counter the Jewish taboo against pork with sustainable farming practices, and they ensure that the animals are raised and butchered ethically. Both the success and the challenge of Chutzpah Hollow—the Yiddish word "chutzpah" means extreme self-confidence—are the result of Wendy Rhein's constant reading and study to bravely acquire new skills. She has no lack of plain grit or, more accurately, chutzpah.

Do I eat pork these days? Not so much. But when I do, it is out of respect for cooks, local chefs, farmers, and makers whom I admire. How I understand religious selfhood, my family's eastern European Jewish heritage, and the history of the place where I live constantly shifts as my Jewish South advocates for a more just and inclusive present and future.

by Marcie Cohen Ferris, PhD

writer and scholar of the South—particularly its foodways, material culture, and the Southern Jewish experience—and professor emeritus of American studies at the University of North Carolina at Chapel Hill

Memphis Wet Ribs

Serves 6 to 8 ~ Total Time: 5 to 6 hours, plus 30 minutes resting

Wet or dry? You'd better be prepared to answer that question if you're ordering ribs in Memphis. Memphis dry ribs are just what they sound like—spice-rubbed slow-smoked ribs served dry, meaning without sauce. Wet ribs are sauced, usually both during and after cooking, with a tangy, tomato-based concoction.

Here we go the wet route for succulent ribs that are a delightful mess to eat. A potent spice rub seasons the ribs and also creates a flavorful foundation for the tangy barbecue sauce that's brushed on toward the end of cooking. While the ribs are on the grill, they receive a traditional mop of apple juice and cider vinegar, which keeps them moist as they slowly cook. We developed this recipe using a 22-inch Weber kettle charcoal grill.

Spice Rub

- 2 tablespoons paprika
- 1 tablespoon packed brown sugar
- 1 tablespoon table salt
- 1 teaspoon pepper
- 1 teaspoon onion powder
- 1 teaspoon garlic powder

Barbecue Sauce

- ¾ cup ketchup
- ⅓ cup apple juice
- 2 tablespoons molasses
- 2 tablespoons cider vinegar
- 2 tablespoons Worcestershire sauce
- 1 tablespoon yellow mustard
- 1 teaspoon pepper

Mop

- ¼ cup apple juice
- ¼ cup cider vinegar
- 1½ teaspoons yellow mustard

Ribs

- 2 (2½- to 3-pound) racks St. Louis–style spareribs, trimmed
- 5 (3-inch) wood chunks
- 1 (13 by 9-inch) disposable aluminum pan

1   **For the spice rub** Combine all ingredients in bowl.

2   **For the barbecue sauce** Combine ketchup, apple juice, molasses, vinegar, Worcestershire, mustard, and 2 tablespoons prepared spice rub in medium saucepan and bring to boil over medium heat. Reduce heat to medium-low and simmer until thickened and reduced to 1 cup, about 10 minutes. Off heat, stir in pepper; set aside.

3   **For the mop** Whisk apple juice, vinegar, mustard, and ¼ cup prepared barbecue sauce together in bowl; set aside.

4   **For the ribs** Place ribs on rimmed baking sheet and pat dry with paper towels. Flip ribs meaty side down. Sprinkle bone side of ribs with about one-third of remaining spice mixture. Flip ribs and sprinkle meaty side with remaining spice mixture.

5   Open bottom vent completely. Set up charcoal snake: Arrange 40 briquettes, 2 briquettes wide, around half of perimeter of grill, overlapping slightly so briquettes are touching. Place second layer of 40 briquettes, also 2 briquettes wide, on top of first. (Completed snake should be 2 briquettes wide by 2 briquettes high.)

6   Evenly space wood chunks on top of snake. Place disposable pan in center of grill so short end of pan runs parallel to gap in snake. Fill pan with 6 cups water. Light chimney starter filled with 15 briquettes (pile briquettes on 1 side of chimney). When coals are partially covered with ash, pour over 1 end of snake. (Make sure lit coals touch only 1 end of snake. Use tongs if necessary to move any coals that touch other end of snake.)

7   Set cooking grate in place. Clean and oil cooking grate. Place ribs side by side on grill, meaty side up, lengthwise over water pan. Cover grill, position lid vent over ribs, and open lid vent completely. Cook for 2 hours, basting meaty side of ribs with mop halfway through cooking. Rotate ribs 180 degrees. Brush meaty side of ribs with remaining mop. Cover grill and continue to cook, undisturbed, for 1 hour. Brush meaty side of ribs with half of barbecue sauce and continue to cook, opening lid as little as possible, until tender and fork inserted between ribs meets little resistance, 1 to 2 hours. Transfer ribs meaty side up to clean rimmed baking sheet. Brush meaty side of ribs with remaining sauce. Cover sheet tightly with aluminum foil and let ribs rest for 30 minutes. Serve.

BURNING DOWN BARRIERS IN THE BARBECUE HALL OF FAME

In 2020, Desiree Robinson, cofounder and pitmaster of Memphis's Cozy Corner Restaurant, became the first Black woman inducted into the Barbecue Hall of Fame. She was 83 years old at the time, and she had worked in barbecue for more than 40 years.

Robinson opened Cozy Corner with her late husband, Raymond, in 1977. Raymond initially developed the restaurant's recipes and managed the pits. But Robinson was instrumental in its enduring success, hosting popular local soirées and expanding the menu to include items like Cornish hens, a staple on the menu today. While she worked part time at the restaurant for those first couple of decades, Desiree took over the business when Raymond passed in 2001. She's been running it ever since.

The menu has a few favorites: the aforementioned Cornish hens lacquered with sauce; barbecued bologna that's seared until crispy; pulled pork with a spicy, crisp bark; and her peppery smoked spareribs.

Being named to the Barbecue Hall of Fame is a big deal. For just more than a decade, this accolade has played a critical role in recognizing influential figures in the barbecue world. In addition to being the first Black woman inducted, Robinson was the first *living* Black person inducted; Henry Perry, Christopher B. "Stubb" Stubblefield, and John "Big Daddy" Bishop had been inducted posthumously before her.

According to the *Memphis Flyer*, Desiree is now "semi-retired," and her grandchildren mostly run the business. But she still supports the business as time allows—and eats the delicious food regularly.

by Morgan Bolling

Alabama Smoked Chicken

Serves 4 to 6 ~ Total Time: 2¼ hours

Alabama barbecue tends to focus on pork and chicken smoked over hickory coals. And throughout the state you can find women working over those coals (see page 323), putting their own signature spin on these smoked meats. In northern Alabama you'll find smoked chicken with a creamy white barbecue sauce made with mayonnaise, apple cider vinegar, garlic, black pepper, and other seasonings. Robert Lee Gibson (also known as Big Bob) is credited with inventing this sauce, but many women today serve it with skill. Chef Andrew Zimmern declared Myra Grissom Harper's chicken the best he's had, "Miss Myra's tangy, creamy version is a perfect dipping sauce for the expertly smoked chicken, which certainly tops my list of all time favorite barbecued chicken (just look at that skin!)." Her restaurant, Miss Myra's Pit Bar-B-Q in Birmingham, Alabama, serves smoked chicken (you can order a half chicken or specify white or dark meat) with a choice or white or red barbecue sauce and two sides ranging from turnip greens to deviled eggs.

For our version of smoked chicken we use halved chicken, as is common in Alabama, which makes for a relatively fast cooking time. Coating the chicken in the white barbecue sauce after cooking allows the hot chicken to absorb the sauce and flavors it through and through with a taste of northern Alabama.

1	teaspoon table salt
1	teaspoon pepper
½	teaspoon cayenne pepper
2	(3½- to 4-pound) whole chickens, giblets discarded
2	cups wood chips, soaked in water for 15 minutes and drained
1	(13 by 9-inch) disposable aluminum roasting pan
1	recipe Alabama White Barbecue Sauce (page 333)

1   Combine salt, pepper, and cayenne in small bowl. With 1 chicken breast side down, use kitchen shears to cut along both sides of backbone. Discard backbone and trim any excess fat or skin at neck. Flip chicken over and, using chef's knife, cut through breastbone to separate chicken into halves. Tuck wingtips behind back. Repeat with remaining chicken. Pat chicken dry with paper towels and rub evenly with spice mixture. Using large piece of heavy-duty aluminum foil, wrap soaked chips in 8 by 4½-inch foil packet. (Make sure chips do not poke holes in sides or bottom of packet.) Cut 2 evenly spaced 2-inch slits in top of packet.

2   Open bottom vent halfway and place disposable pan in center of grill. Light large chimney starter filled with charcoal briquettes (6 quarts). When top coals are partially covered with ash, pour into 2 even piles on either side of disposable pan. Place wood chip packet on 1 pile of coals. Set cooking grate in place, cover, and open lid vent halfway. Heat grill until hot and wood chips are smoking, about 5 minutes.

3   Clean and oil cooking grate. Place chicken skin side down in center of grill over disposable pan. Cover, positioning lid vent opposite wood chips, and cook until skin is browned and thighs register 120 degrees, 35 to 45 minutes.

4   Flip chicken skin side up. Cover and continue to cook until skin is deep golden brown and crispy and breasts register 160 degrees and thighs register 175 degrees, 15 to 20 minutes.

5   Transfer chicken to carving board and brush each half with 2 tablespoons sauce. Tent chicken with foil and let rest for 10 minutes. Brush chicken with remaining sauce, carve, and serve.

SAUCE IT

Barbecue is first and foremost about the succulent meat, but sauces are often an essential component. Some styles of barbecue jibe particularly well with certain sauces that reflect regional tastes and traditions. Others are flexible and fun to flavor how you'd like, from sauce you've made yourself. Here we offer our versions of some of the classics.

Easy All-Purpose Barbecue Sauce

Makes about 2½ cups

Total Time: 30 minutes, plus 30 minutes cooling

When you buy bottled barbecue sauce at the store, it's often a version of Kansas City–style sauce. It may not be Southern, and it may ruffle the feathers of a *Southerner*, but, hey, the ubiquitous thick, sticky-sweet, smoky, darkly hued sauce is a familiar taste. This recipe was developed using Frank's RedHot Original Cayenne Pepper Sauce. Grate the onion on the large holes of a box or paddle grater.

2	tablespoons vegetable oil	1½	cups ketchup
½	cup grated onion	¼	cup molasses
1	teaspoon garlic powder	3	tablespoons Worcestershire sauce
1	teaspoon chili powder	3	tablespoons cider vinegar
¼	teaspoon cayenne pepper	2	tablespoons Dijon mustard
		1	teaspoon hot sauce

1   Heat oil in medium saucepan over medium heat until shimmering. Add onion and cook, stirring occasionally, until softened, about 5 minutes. Stir in garlic powder, chili powder, and cayenne and cook until fragrant, about 30 seconds.

2   Stir in ketchup, molasses, Worcestershire, vinegar, mustard, and hot sauce and bring to simmer. Reduce heat to low and cook until flavors meld, about 5 minutes. Let cool completely before serving. (Cooled sauce can be refrigerated for up to 1 week.)

Easy Espresso Barbecue Sauce

Combine 2 tablespoons instant espresso powder and 1 tablespoon hot water in small bowl; let sit for 3 minutes. Stir into onion mixture with ketchup in step 2.

South Carolina Mustard Sauce

Makes about 2½ cups   ~   Total Time: 10 minutes

Mustard barbecue sauce has rightly earned its nickname "Carolina gold." This bracing, vinegary sauce is packed with tang from a heavy dose of yellow mustard mixed with cider vinegar. It's typically found in South Carolina—though it can also be found in Georgia and parts of western North Carolina—so it's made to mingle with pork.

1½	cups yellow mustard	2	teaspoons hot sauce
½	cup cider vinegar	2	teaspoons Worcestershire sauce
6	tablespoons packed brown sugar	1	teaspoon pepper
2	tablespoons ketchup		

Whisk all ingredients together in bowl. (Sauce can be refrigerated for up to 1 week.)

Eastern North Carolina–Style Barbecue Sauce

Makes about 2½ cups   ~   Total Time: 10 minutes

In eastern North Carolina barbecue sauce has a vinegary punch, a bit of spiciness, and plenty of salt. It's thin enough to soak right into finely chopped barbecued pork. Whisking together cider vinegar, hot sauce, salt, black pepper, and red pepper flakes creates a tangy base, while some brown sugar balances the heat. One 12-ounce bottle of Texas Pete Original Hot Sauce will yield more than enough for this recipe.

1½	cups cider vinegar	2	teaspoons kosher salt
1	cup Texas Pete Original Hot Sauce	1	teaspoon pepper
¼	cup packed light brown sugar	1	teaspoon red pepper flakes

Whisk all ingredients together in bowl. (Sauce can be refrigerated for up to 1 week.)

Lexington-Style Barbecue Sauce

Makes about 2½ cups
Total Time: 20 minutes, plus 30 minutes cooling

In Lexington, North Carolina, the sauce gets its tang from plenty of cider vinegar, much like the sauce in eastern North Carolina. But the Lexington sauce is not as fiery as its eastern counterpart. It typically includes ketchup or another tomato product that makes the sauce redder, a touch sweeter, and just a bit thicker.

2	cups cider vinegar	2	teaspoons pepper
1	cup ketchup	1½	teaspoons kosher salt
2	teaspoons granulated garlic	1	teaspoon red pepper flakes

Combine all ingredients in small saucepan and bring to boil over medium-high heat. Reduce heat to medium-low and simmer for 5 minutes. Transfer sauce to bowl and let cool completely. (Sauce can be refrigerated for up to 1 week.)

Alabama White Barbecue Sauce

Makes about 1½ cups   ~   Total Time: 10 minutes

Alabama's signature sauce is white. It has a mayonnaise base, which might surprise those who aren't acquainted with the style. But it makes sense. Mayonnaise is tangy and salty—two elements of a good 'cue sauce. And if you amp it up with vinegar and some spice, you have an appealing sauce that adds some richness to lean meat such as chicken (typical in Alabama; see page 330) or turkey.

¾	cup mayonnaise	½	teaspoon table salt
2	tablespoons cider vinegar	½	teaspoon pepper
2	teaspoons sugar	¼	teaspoon cayenne pepper
½	teaspoon prepared horseradish		

Process all ingredients in blender until smooth, about 1 minute. Refrigerate sauce for at least 1 hour or up to 2 days.

CROWD–PLEASING SIDES

Cookout hostesses take their sides seriously. The concept of "meat and three"—meat and three sides—exists in the Southern lexicon for a reason. A plate of barbecue needs a variety of flavors and textures to feel complete. Southern cookouts are about bounty, and these sides will round out the table nicely.

Pimento Mac and Cheese

Serves 8 to 10
Total Time: 1¼ hours, plus
20 minutes resting

We got the idea to pimento-up our mac and cheese from chef Ashley Christensen (see page 152). She serves a casserole so creamy she goes as far as to call it "pimento mac-n-cheese custard."

We use a bit less béchamel than Christensen so the casserole is easy to serve at a cookout.

- 1   pound elbow macaroni
- ½   teaspoon table salt, plus salt for cooking pasta
- 3   tablespoons unsalted butter
- 2   tablespoons all-purpose flour
- 1   tablespoon dry mustard
- ¾   teaspoon pepper
- 2   cups whole milk
- 2   cups heavy cream
- 1   pound extra-sharp cheddar cheese, shredded (4 cups), divided
- 2   ounces cream cheese
- 2   tablespoons hot sauce
- 1   tablespoon Worcestershire sauce
- 3   (4-ounce) jars pimentos, drained, patted dry, and minced

1   Adjust oven rack to upper-middle position and heat oven to 375 degrees. Bring 4 quarts water to boil in large pot. Add macaroni and 1 tablespoon salt and cook for 5 minutes. Drain macaroni; set aside.

2   Add butter to now-empty pot and melt over medium-high heat. Stir in flour, mustard, pepper, and salt and cook until mixture is fragrant and bubbling, about 30 seconds. Slowly whisk in milk and cream and bring to boil. Reduce heat to medium-low and simmer until sauce is thick enough to coat back of spoon, about 2 minutes, whisking frequently.

3   Remove pot from heat. Add 3 cups cheddar, cream cheese, hot sauce, and Worcestershire to sauce and whisk until cheese is melted. Add pimentos and macaroni and stir until macaroni is thoroughly coated in sauce. Transfer to 13 by 9-inch baking dish and sprinkle with remaining 1 cup cheddar. (Casserole can be wrapped tightly in plastic wrap and refrigerated for up to 24 hours. When ready to serve, remove plastic and bake until heated through, 40 to 45 minutes.) Bake until edges are lightly browned and filling is bubbling, 18 to 20 minutes. Let rest for 20 minutes. Serve.

Green Spaghetti

Serves 6   ~   Total Time: 1 hour

We asked chef Chuck Charnichart (see "The New Smoke in Town: The Women of Barbs-B-Q") to help us develop our version of this creamy, green pepper spaghetti. Knorr brand chicken bouillon is traditional; if you can't find the loose powder, you can crush three bouillon cubes and then measure 2 tablespoons. You can also replace all the bouillon with 2 teaspoons table salt, though the dish will taste less savory. The jalapeño can be seeded or omitted if you desire a milder dish. The sauce will thicken quite a bit as it sits; serve the pasta immediately from the hot pot for the best texture.

2–3	poblano chiles (8½ ounces), stemmed, halved, and seeded
2	teaspoons vegetable oil
2	cups roughly chopped fresh cilantro leaves and stems
8	ounces cream cheese, cut into 8 pieces
1	cup milk
¼	cup sour cream
2	tablespoons chicken bouillon powder
1	jalapeño chile, stemmed and chopped (optional)
1	pound spaghetti
	Table salt for cooking pasta
2	tablespoons unsalted butter

1   Adjust oven rack 6 inches from broiler element and heat broiler. Line rimmed baking sheet with aluminum foil. Brush poblanos all over with oil and arrange skin side up on baking sheet. Broil until skins are spotty brown and beginning to blacken, 4 to 6 minutes. Using tongs, flip poblanos and broil until other side is starting to brown and peppers are softened, 4 to 6 minutes. Let peppers cool slightly, then remove and discard skins.

2   Process skinned poblanos; cilantro; cream cheese; milk; sour cream; chicken bouillon powder; and jalapeño, if using, in blender until smooth, about 1 minute. Set aside.

3   Bring 4 quarts water to boil in large pot. Add pasta and 1 tablespoon salt and cook, stirring often, until al dente. Reserve 1 cup cooking water and drain pasta.

4   Melt butter in now-empty pot over medium heat. Add sauce and bring to simmer, stirring occasionally, until bubbling and slightly thickened, 3 to 5 minutes. Add pasta and cook, tossing constantly with tongs, until pasta is evenly coated with sauce. Adjust consistency with reserved cooking water as needed. Serve immediately.

THE NEW SMOKE IN TOWN: THE WOMEN OF BARBS-B-Q

Opening a new barbecue joint in Texas is bold business. Even more so in Lockhart, a small town known for its handful of highly revered barbecue joints. (Highly revered, as in, Lockhart was declared the state's official barbecue capital in 1999 by the Texas House of Representatives.)

Chuck Charnichart is the latest pitmaster to join Lockhart's host of barbecue bigwigs. At 25 years old, she opened Barbs-B-Q in May 2023, an all-women-owned barbecue joint. Leading Barbs alongside Charnichart are co-owners, close friends, and pitmasters Alexis Tovías Morales and Haley Conlin. Charnichart's hometown—Brownsville, which lies at the southern tip of Texas and borders Mexico—is a motif throughout her cooking. As the child of Mexican immigrants, Charnichart was always more familiar with barbacoa (traditional pit-style cooking from Mexico and the Caribbean) than barbecue.

Charnichart's evolution from making barbacoa to barbecue was one that eventually circled the world. While studying at the University of Texas, Charnichart worked front-of-house at Franklin Barbecue in Austin, run by James Beard Award winner Aaron Franklin. While studying abroad in later years, she worked at a smokeless barbecue shop in Norway, and eventually joined the pits at Goldee's in Fort Worth. There, she perfected her now-famous brisket and hosted a pop-up in 2021, where she served Brownsville-style sides and drinks in the space. That concept planted the seeds for Barbs-B-Q.

The menu at Barbs is classic but filled with Charnichart's spins. The "Molotov" pork ribs are glazed in serrano simple syrup and showered in lime zest for bursts of brightness. In addition to brisket and beef ribs, there are unctuous offerings of smoked turkey with herb butter, fajita sausages, and charro beans topped with queso fresco. Concha and choco puddings round out the dessert offerings.

However, it is Barbs's most popular side, green spaghetti, that best encompasses the innovative yet nostalgic spirit of the menu. The shockingly green noodle dish, coated in a roasted poblano cream sauce, is a traditional Mexican potluck offering. At Barbs, it's a sort of stand-in for mac and cheese. "My whole life, this dish wasn't ever found at any restaurants," Charnichart said. "But it was the side dish at local gatherings; only people in the [Rio Grande] Valley seem to know of it. During Thanksgiving or Christmas, my mom would serve it alongside her slow-cooked brisket. It pairs so well, it just hit me that this is the perfect side."

The joint, and the women behind it, offer both a challenge and an ode to the institution of Texas barbecue—somewhere between darn-good brisket and poblano-forward noodles, Charnichart kicked that door of possibilities wide open.

by Kelly Song

Cook's Country *test cook and journalist*

Strawberry Pretzel Salad

Serves 10 to 12

Total Time: 1 hour, plus 5 hours 20 minutes cooling and chilling

Jell-O salads are an emblem of an era. Food historian Laura Shapiro explains in her book *Perfection Salad: Women and Cooking at the Turn of the Century* that in the early 1900s, with industrial advances such as electric irons and gas stoves, the nature of women's work was changing. Women focused on cleanliness and purity in the kitchen. Jell-O mix was patented in 1897 and was molded into "salads" that were neat and tidy and could be cut so they wouldn't smash other items on the plate. As Shapiro says, "a salad at last in control of itself." This is a delicious salad, consisting of a pretzel crust, a layer of sweetened cream cheese and whipped topping, and a layer of strawberry Jell-O. For a sturdier crust, use (thinner) pretzel sticks not (fatter) rods. Thaw the strawberries in the refrigerator the night before you begin the recipe. You'll puree 2 pounds of the strawberries and slice the remaining 1 pound.

6½	ounces pretzel sticks
2¼	cups (15¾ ounces) sugar, divided
12	tablespoons unsalted butter, melted and cooled
8	ounces cream cheese
1	cup heavy cream
3	pounds (10½ cups) frozen strawberries, thawed, divided
¼	teaspoon table salt
2	tablespoons unflavored gelatin
½	cup cold water

1   Adjust oven rack to middle position and heat oven to 400 degrees. Spray 13 by 9-inch baking pan with vegetable oil spray. Pulse pretzels and ¼ cup sugar in food processor until coarsely ground, about 15 pulses. Add melted butter and pulse until combined, about 10 pulses. Transfer pretzel mixture to prepared pan. Using bottom of dry measuring cup, press crumbs into bottom of pan. Bake until crust is fragrant and beginning to brown, about 10 minutes, rotating pan halfway through baking. Set aside and let it cool slightly, about 20 minutes.

2   Using stand mixer fitted with whisk attachment, whip cream cheese and ½ cup sugar on medium speed until light and fluffy, about 2 minutes. Increase speed to medium-high and, with mixer still running, slowly add cream in steady stream. Continue to whip until soft peaks form, scraping down bowl as needed, about 1 minute longer. Spread whipped cream cheese mixture evenly over cooled crust. Refrigerate until set, about 30 minutes.

3   Meanwhile, process 2 pounds strawberries in now-empty food processor until pureed, about 30 seconds. Strain mixture through fine-mesh strainer set over medium saucepan, using underside of small ladle to push puree through strainer. (You should have 2½ to 3 cups liquid after straining.) Add remaining 1½ cups sugar and salt to strawberry puree in saucepan and cook over medium-high heat, whisking occasionally, until bubbles begin to appear around sides of pan and sugar is dissolved, about 5 minutes; remove from heat.

4   Sprinkle gelatin over water in large bowl and let sit until gelatin softens, about 5 minutes. Whisk strawberry puree into gelatin. Slice remaining 1 pound strawberries and stir into strawberry-gelatin mixture. Refrigerate until gelatin thickens slightly and starts to cling to sides of bowl, about 30 minutes. Carefully pour gelatin mixture evenly over whipped cream cheese layer. Refrigerate salad until gelatin is fully set, at least 4 hours or up to 24 hours. Serve.

Backyard Barbecued Beans

Serves 12 to 16   ~   Total Time: 2½ hours

Barbecued beans are perfect to serve a crowd alongside smoked meats because they're not barbecued at all—they're baked, which means they don't take up valuable space on the grill. A trio of canned beans is enlivened with some pantry flavorings, such as store-bought barbecue sauce fortified by liquid smoke and spicy brown mustard. Ro-Tel Original Diced Tomatoes & Green Chilies offer welcome heat. The beans are meaty from additions of bratwurst and slices of bacon scattered over the top.

Be sure to use a 13 by 9-inch metal baking pan; the volume of the beans is too great for a 13 by 9-inch ceramic baking dish, and it will overflow. We found that Bush's Original Recipe Baked Beans are the most consistent product for this recipe.

½	cup barbecue sauce
½	cup ketchup
½	cup water
2	tablespoons spicy brown mustard
2	tablespoons cider vinegar
1	teaspoon liquid smoke
1	teaspoon granulated garlic
¼	teaspoon cayenne pepper
1¼	pounds bratwurst, casings removed
2	onions, chopped
2	(28-ounce) cans baked beans
2	(15-ounce) cans pinto beans, rinsed
2	(15-ounce) cans cannellini beans, rinsed
1	(10-ounce) can Ro-Tel Original Diced Tomatoes & Green Chilies, drained
6	slices thick-cut bacon, cut into 1-inch pieces

1   Adjust oven rack to middle position and heat oven to 350 degrees. Whisk barbecue sauce, ketchup, water, mustard, vinegar, liquid smoke, granulated garlic, and cayenne together in large bowl; set aside.

2   Cook bratwurst in 12-inch nonstick skillet over medium-high heat, breaking up into small pieces with spoon, until fat begins to render, about 5 minutes. Stir in onions and cook until sausage and onions are well browned, about 15 minutes.

3   Transfer bratwurst mixture to bowl with sauce. Stir in baked beans, pinto beans, cannellini beans, and tomatoes. Transfer bean mixture to 13 by 9-inch baking pan and place pan on rimmed baking sheet. Arrange bacon pieces in single layer over top of beans.

4   Bake until beans are bubbling and bacon is rendered, about 1½ hours. Let cool for 15 minutes. Serve.

To make ahead   At end of step 3, beans can be wrapped in plastic and refrigerated for up to 24 hours. Proceed with recipe from step 4, increasing baking time to 1¾ hours.

Smashed Potato Salad

Serves 8 to 10
Total Time: 50 minutes, plus 2 hours chilling

This Southern potato salad satisfies both those who like their salad chunky and those who like it creamy. Splashing the potatoes with vinegar while they are still hot adds deep flavor before they join the mayo-based dressing. Use the tip of a paring knife to judge the doneness of the potatoes. If the tip inserts easily into the potato pieces, they are done.

3	pounds Yukon Gold potatoes, unpeeled, cut into 1-inch chunks
1	teaspoon table salt, plus salt for cooking potatoes
2	tablespoons distilled white vinegar
1	cup mayonnaise
3	tablespoons yellow mustard
1	teaspoon pepper
¼	teaspoon cayenne pepper
3	hard-cooked large eggs, chopped
3	scallions, sliced thin
½	cup chopped sweet pickles
½	cup finely chopped celery
¼	cup finely chopped onion

1   Combine potatoes, 8 cups water, and 1 tablespoon salt in Dutch oven and bring to boil over high heat. Reduce heat to medium and cook at vigorous simmer until potatoes are tender, 14 to 17 minutes.

2   Drain potatoes in colander. Transfer 3 cups potatoes to large bowl, add 1 tablespoon vinegar, and coarsely mash with potato masher. Transfer remaining potatoes to rimmed baking sheet, drizzle with remaining 1 tablespoon vinegar, and toss gently to combine. Let cool completely, about 15 minutes.

3   Whisk mayonnaise, ½ cup water, mustard, salt, pepper, and cayenne together in bowl. Stir mayonnaise mixture into mashed potatoes. Fold in eggs, scallions, pickles, celery, onion, and remaining potatoes until combined (mixture will be lumpy).

4   Cover and refrigerate until fully chilled, about 2 hours. Season with salt and pepper to taste. Serve.

No.11
FLAVOR,
PRESERVED

Left to right: Refrigerator Pickled Okra (page 351), Grapefruit Arbol Chile Marmalade (page 368),
Dandelion Jelly (page 374), Chow-Chow (page 362), Ají Picante (page 350).

THE TOMATO CLUB GIRLS

In 1913, Sadie Limer, a 16-year-old girl living outside Warrenton, North Carolina (population 807), wrote about her dreams for the future and how she hoped to achieve them: "As my ambition is to be a school-teacher, and knowing that to be a good one, one must be educated, I wanted to get a fairly good education, that is to say, go off to a good high school or college. I also knew it would cost considerable to do so, and I wanted to pay my own tuition, or the greater part if possible. My county agent told me a good way for me to earn some ready money was for me to join the 'Tomato Club,' and I thought so too and joined."

What is a tomato club? For a handful of years in the 1910s, young girls joined tomato clubs across the South to learn how to grow tomatoes, can them, and sell them. Tomato clubs were an outgrowth of the farm demonstration movement, where agricultural scientists wanted to bring their knowledge to the rural communities. But the tomato clubs were different, almost radical, says Elizabeth S. D. Engelhardt, a University of North Carolina scholar who wrote about them in *A Mess of Greens: Southern Gender and Southern Food*.

The purpose of earlier clubs for rural boys and girls, like corn or poultry clubs, was to work independently. With tomato clubs, collective work was required for harvesting, canning, and marketing. A main purpose of the tomato clubs was for girls to make money of their own—what so enticed Sadie Limer to join.

Engelhardt first stumbled upon a mention of Mississippi's tomato clubs in an academic article. (The clubs cropped up there and in Tennessee, Virginia, and the Carolinas.) But Engelhardt found a trove of tomato club records at the state archives in Raleigh, North Carolina. Among those papers were handwritten booklets the girls had to create about their tomato crop: How did they grow them? How much did they harvest? How much did they can? How many did they sell? What were their costs? Their profit? "Tomato clubs are really precious because girls had to tell the story of it," Engelhardt says. "And along the way, they learned all these small business entrepreneurial skills."

The booklets are charming. Some fit in the palm of your hand. Most are notebook size, bound with red or green ribbons, illustrated with color drawings or watercolors of tomatoes. A few even contain photos of the club girls, posing as a group or working over a canning pot. One proud girl had a photo taken of a cluster of 15 large tomatoes grown on one stem for the cover of her booklet. (Engelhardt came across a photo in the archives that was taken outside her own great-great-grandmother's general store in Quebec, North Carolina. Engelhardt's mother recognized relatives in the photo but didn't know their personal tomato club history.)

But tomato clubs were far from a quaint hobby. More than half a million girls joined. They grew and harvested millions of pounds of tomatoes and produced millions of canned goods; many were sold and marketed under individual tomato club labels and sold far and wide, including 65,000 cans from the North Carolina clubs to Cornell and Columbia Universities. That put real money in these girls' pockets.

In 1912, Stella Foster of North Wilkesboro harvested 1,343 pounds of tomatoes, netting a profit of $33.61, or $1,082.21 in today's dollars. Sixteen-year-old Olive Lockhart of Anson County wrote that she joined "for pleasure and profit." A local newspaper described Lockhart as "one of the best known and most successful members of Anson clubs." In 1914, she made $138 in profit, or about $4,300 today. And Bettie Vann Tapscott, a 12-year-old girl from Alamance County, was among the most productive and profitable tomato club girls in the state, according to state records. Tapscott sold hundreds of

canned goods to a cafeteria at University of North Carolina-Chapel Hill. From 1914 to 1915, she netted $266.62, or about $8,200 today.

Perusing these fragile booklets and deciphering the cursive handwriting of these teenage girls from more than a century ago leaves one wanting to know what happened to them. Did they pursue college, start a business, have a career? Local newspaper archives tell us nothing about Foster or Tapscott after their tomato club days, although Lockhart's marriage to a prosperous farmer is noted.

That's what makes the tomato club booklets such treasures, says Virginia Ferris, a special collections librarian at North Carolina State University. "That's what I talk about in classes with students—the silences in archives where we don't have documentation of historically marginalized communities. To have documents like these tomato club booklets written by hand from the perspective of young girls in rural communities is so rare and special. At the same time and what is typical is as they go through life, they kind of disappear from the archives."

But with Sadie Limer, we got lucky. Limer's education and career were better documented than most. She attended Western Carolina Teachers College. And in 1939, at the age of 42, she studied at Columbia University. In the 1960s, she was teaching in Warrenton, where she grew up.

by Andrea Weigl

North Carolina–based food writer, journalist, and documentary film producer

ALL ABOUT THE PRESERVING PANTRY

Whether from the farm stand or the home garden, Southern produce is worth saving. With plenty of warm days per year, the South produces an abundance of especially sweet fruits and vegetables. Cooking them down or pickling them and canning amplifies that sweetness or captures it for less bountiful days.

Key Ingredients for Preserving

Other than fresh fruits and vegetables, there are a few supplemental items you need for home preserving and pickling success. Here's what they are, what they do, and why you need them.

Pectin

There are two basic types of pectin: regular pectin and low-sugar pectin. Regular pectin requires high amounts of sugar and acidity in order to set. In the test kitchen we prefer low-sugar pectin (which is available only in powdered form) as it contains all of the ingredients necessary to form a gel; this allows us to choose a level of sugar based on the preserve and not the pectin. Our favorite pectin is Sure-Jell for Less or No Sugar Needed Recipes; it comes in a bright pink box and is widely available. It's often found in the baking aisle near the gelatin and cornstarch.

Bottled Lemon Juice and Lime Juice

Achieving the proper acidity (pH) level is key for preservation. Without the right pH, boiling water canning is not considered safe. Likewise, without enough acid, unprocessed foods will have a short lifespan, even in the fridge. Acidity also plays a key role in the gelling abilities of pectin; without a consistent pH it can be difficult to predict how a jam or jelly will set. Fresh lemon juice varies too much from lemon to lemon to consistently predict how much it will increase the acidity of a given preserve; bottled lemon (or lime) juice has a tightly controlled pH that is always consistent.

Salt

The additives found in table salt can produce off-flavors and hazy brines and, in fermented pickles, can inhibit the growth of good microbes. Canning salt, often called pickling or preserving salt, is specifically designed for pickle making and doesn't have any iodine or anti-caking agents. This salt also has a very fine grain, which dissolves quickly in water. However, you can swap kosher salt for pickling salt without any adverse effects. If substituting Morton's Kosher Salt for canning salt, increase the measurement by 50 percent (for example, from 1 teaspoon to 1½ teaspoons); if using Diamond Crystal Kosher Salt, increase by 100 percent (from 1 teaspoon to 2 teaspoons).

Sugar

Sugar is a natural preservative. Not only does it add sweetness to jams and jellies, it also enhances the fruits' flavors. When simmered, it makes mixtures thicker. In addition, sugar interacts with natural pectin and encourages it to set. When jams are cooked, sugar bonds with the pectin and provides structure and spreadability. When preserving fruit, a syrup of sugar and water helps the fruit retain its flavor, color, and shape.

Vinegar

In pickle making, vinegar provides not only flavor but also acidity, which helps preserve the pickles and ensure they're safe to eat. Getting pickles to the proper pH is particularly important when canning with boiling water, which is only safe for high-acid foods. The two most common vinegars for pickling are cider vinegar and distilled white vinegar; both are available at a 5 percent acetic acid level, meaning they have a consistent pH. Always use the variety of vinegar called for in the recipe.

Water

Pickles are made using water, vinegar, and salt, so the quality of the water matters. Fluoride and other elements may interfere with the pickling process, and water may contain enough chlorine to delay fermentation. If the water is highly chlorinated, that smell can carry through to the food. Soft tap water or filtered tap water are preferable for pickling. The minerals in hard water can interfere with the formation of acid and might also discolor the pickles. If you have any concerns about your water, use bottled.

Canning Equipment

You can find premade canning kits, but you really don't need a lot of the canning-specific items to preserve like a pro. These are the essential items.

Canning Pot

A large (18- to 21-quart) pot is handy for heating the jars and key for processing the filled jars. We like a pot that has silicone-coated handles for easy gripping and a clear lid so we can monitor what is going on inside.

Funnel

A wide-mouth stainless-steel funnel makes pouring liquids, such as jams and brines, and channeling pieces of fruit into jars easier and tidier. Don't bother with plastic funnels.

Canning Rack

Look for a rack with tall handles that fits inside the pot to keep the jars off the bottom and to make pulling the hot jars out of boiling water easier. Canning pots are often sold with a rack.

Ladle

Transfer cooked foods and pour hot cooking liquid or brine into jars simply and neatly.

Glass Canning Jars

Also known as Mason jars, these are sold with flat metal lids and threaded metal screw rings that hold the lids in place during processing.

Wooden Skewers

Use skewers to release the air bubbles around the inside of each jar once the jars are filled. (We also use them to test produce for doneness.)

Jar Lifter

A canning-specific jar lifter works better than tongs when maneuvering hot filled jars in and out of boiling water because it allows you to grasp the jars firmly.

Timer

Monitoring cooking and processing times is important when preserving.

Pepper Vinegar

Makes about 3 cups　~　Total Time: 15 minutes, plus 20 minutes cooling and 3 weeks infusing

In the South, pepper vinegar is a bracing condiment, equally at home on the family dinner table, at a local diner, or in an upscale restaurant. It's as simple as the name implies, often just peppers, vinegar, sugar, and salt. But the result is so much greater than the sum of its parts: a sharp, spicy condiment that can perk up pulled pork, chili, or grilled meats.

Peppers are indigenous to Central and South America. They reached Europe and then the rest of the world, including West Africa, through colonization. There are hundreds of varieties, each known by a different name according to its region, and all presenting a wide range of heat, from mild to scorchingly hot. They may be preserved minced, sliced, or left whole in oil, vinegar, or pickling brine. Peppers (often cayenne) that are cured in vinegar, which, over time, is suffused with their fiery essence, are especially popular in Cajun, Creole, and soul food restaurants. Preserved vinegar peppers were once an essential part of plantation apothecaries used like medicine to cure ailments from digestive disorders to yellow fever.

Some cooks add garlic, spices, herbs, or even fruit for their own takes on pepper vinegar. For this version, we halve bright red Tabasco chiles (you can also use red Fresno or red jalapeño chiles, or cayenne peppers if you can find them) and pack them into a 1-quart canning jar. We pour a heated mixture of white vinegar, sugar, salt, whole peppercorns, and red pepper flakes over the chiles; let the mixture cool; and then refrigerate it for at least three weeks before serving. Pepper vinegar is spicy. For a milder vinegar, remove the seeds and ribs from the chiles. Serve it with Stewed Collards (page 140) or on top of North Carolina Barbecued Pork (page 326), or use a few dashes to brighten a stew, pork chops, or oysters.

3	cups distilled white vinegar
4	teaspoons sugar
2	teaspoons table salt
1	teaspoon black peppercorns
¼	teaspoon red pepper flakes
6	ounces Tabasco, red Fresno, red jalapeño, or cayenne chiles, halved lengthwise

1 Combine vinegar, sugar, salt, peppercorns, and pepper flakes in medium saucepan and bring to boil over medium-high heat.

2 Place one 1-quart jar under hot running water until heated through, about 1 minute; shake dry. Pack chiles in jar. Pour hot brine into jar, making sure chiles are fully submerged. Let cool completely. Affix jar lid and refrigerate for at least 3 weeks before serving. (Pepper vinegar can be refrigerated for up to 3 months.)

HOT SAUCE

*"Earned all this money but they never take the country out me.
I got hot sauce in my bag, swag."*

Before Beyoncé had hot sauce in her bag, I carried a bottle in the glove compartment of my car on road trips. It's a throwback to my ancestry, migration, and Jim Crow segregation—a time when Black people traveling in the American South carried their own meals, serveware, and condiments because they were unsure where it would be safe to stop for a bite to eat on the road.

That's why, when I first heard the song "Formation" on Queen Bey's *Lemonade* album, I didn't realize that she wasn't really talking about hot pepper sauce. The term also can be a pop culture reference for a weapon. For me, having hot sauce is both a personal preference and a promise that no matter what food I encounter, I'll have a chance to make it taste better.

Popular culture these days presents hot sauce as the ultimate in "dude food," with testosterone as the key ingredient. My cookbook collection tells another story. Southern women have long promoted and produced pepper sauces for home tables.

Mary Randolph included a "Pepper Vinegar" recipe in her iconic 1828 cookbook, *The Virginia House-Wife*. Randolph's formula was simple: Boil a dozen ripe and sliced red (cayenne) peppers in vinegar and strain. Randolph concluded the recipe by enthusiastically noting: "A little of this is excellent in gravy of every kind, and gives a flavour greatly superior to black pepper; it is also very fine when added to each of the various catsups for fish sauce."

Lettice Bryan's *The Kentucky Housewife*, published in 1839, also has a recipe for "Pepper Vinegar." In her version, the red peppers are diced small, steeped in vinegar while jarred for several days, and then boiled and strained to make the sauce. Recipes similar to Bryan's and Randolph's appeared in numerous cookbooks, magazines, and newspapers marketed to women. By the turn of the 20th century, hot sauce recipes had faded from those pages, probably because commercially bottled hot sauces, like Tabasco, were already cheap and ubiquitous.

Yet, over the years, Southern women continued to sing hot sauce's praises. Vertamae Grosvenor, the Gullah Geechee "vibration cook" from South Carolina, praised pepper vinegar as an essential condiment for a pot of Southern greens in her 1996 cookbook *Vertamae Cooks in Americas' Family Kitchen*. Athens, Georgia, native Nicole Taylor has hot sauce recipes in several cookbooks, including her latest, *Watermelon & Redbirds: A Cookbook for Juneteenth and Black Celebrations* published in 2022.

When it comes to the goodness of hot sauce, we're all in the bag.

by Toni Tipton-Martin

Easy Homemade Hot Sauce

Makes about 1 cup ~ Total Time: 20 minutes, plus 4 days fermenting

Here's a recipe for a fermented sauce for anyone who wants to keep something homemade in their bag. We ferment a mix of fiery chiles and sweet red bell peppers in salted water. The briny environment inhibits the growth of mold or harmful pathogens and encourages the growth of a friendly family of lactic acid bacteria, which alters the chiles in delicious ways. After four days of fermentation, the flavor of the chiles transforms from raw and aggressive to tart and fruity with an overarching savory complexity. Tailoring the spiciness of the hot sauce is as easy as removing some or all of the chiles' seeds. Finishing with a glug of olive oil and a bit of sugar further balances and mellows the delicious hot sauce. If you can find Tabasco or cayenne chiles, you can call this Louisiana-style hot sauce. This recipe makes a medium-spicy hot sauce. For a spicier sauce, include all the seeds. For a milder sauce, remove the seeds from the chiles. We recommend wearing rubber gloves when handling the chiles. If you can't find any of the suggested chiles, you can substitute red jalapeño chiles. The leftover brine can be used in marinades, dressings, or cocktails, and on its own as a condiment to spice up soups or braises.

2   tablespoons kosher salt for brining

8   ounces Tabasco, red Fresno, or cayenne chiles, stemmed and halved lengthwise

4   ounces (1 cup) coarsely chopped red bell pepper

1   tablespoon sugar

1   teaspoon kosher salt

2   tablespoons extra-virgin olive oil

1   Whisk 2 cups water and 2 tablespoons salt in 4-cup liquid measuring cup until salt is dissolved. Remove seeds from half of Fresnos. Place Fresnos and bell pepper in 1-quart jar, pressing chiles firmly into bottom of jar.

2   Pour brine into jar with chiles, making sure liquid covers peppers. Fill 1-quart zipper-lock bag with ⅓ cup water, press out air, and seal bag. Place bag of water on top of chiles in jar to keep submerged in brine. Affix jar lid but only partially tighten, leaving lid loose enough to allow air to escape as mixture ferments.

3   Let jar sit at room temperature away from direct sunlight for 4 days. Check container daily, skimming residue from surface and ensuring that chiles remain submerged. (After 2 or 3 days, brine will become cloudy and bubbles will rise to surface when jar is moved.)

4   Drain chiles in fine-mesh strainer, reserving brine for another use, if desired. Process chiles, sugar, and salt in food processor until coarsely pureed, about 1 minute, scraping down sides of bowl as needed. Add oil and pulse until combined, about 2 pulses. Refrigerate hot sauce until ready to use. (Hot sauce can be refrigerated for up to 3 months.)

Q&A: CRYSTAL HARRIS ON MAMA'S SALSA

Crystal Harris is the business owner and creative force behind Mama's Salsa. Harris started the company as a side hustle in 2018 while homeschooling her boys. Mama's Salsa has grown from a small-batch special project to an in-demand staple at markets throughout the Triangle area of North Carolina.

How did you get started?

Well, I would take my boys to our friends' houses, and the moms would ask for authentic Mexican food. So I started making a bunch of salsa and at the end of the playdate I would send home a salsa in a Mason jar. My friends would pay me for that salsa. People loved it. I put it on Facebook and told more people about it that way. It was popular; I remember meeting people in the parking lot at Target to give them salsa. That was spring 2018, and people kept telling each other about it. By summer I had my first farmers' market and that winter I rented a commercial kitchen.

If you started in 2018, was the business affected by the pandemic?

Yes, and of course so was our family. We had a really great year in 2019; business was booming. But I was just making salsa on the weekends and at the farmers' market.

And then obviously 2020 happened. And then my dad got sick and passed away like the first week everything was shutting down.

At the time my husband was working full time with a food truck. That shut down so we were all just home. But the farmers' markets were continuing because they were seen as essential. So we all shifted towards the salsa company and were working with the farmers' markets and different restaurants as hubs for groceries. And my family rallied to help, and our customers rallied around us and kept us busy at one of the hardest times of my life.

I think the low moment was when I lost my dad—my boys and the business are what kept me going during that time. I felt a

commitment to being their mother and I felt a commitment to my customers. That was the lowest I've ever felt in my life. And it was also super high because I could still pull myself out of this terrible situation and I could just keep going through this work as a mother and business owner. And now, I know if I can do that I can do anything.

What's it like to be a mom while running a business?

Everyone asks about balance. I don't know that there will ever be a balance. With each new year, you're just trying to figure it out day by day. It's chaos all the time.

I'm thankful that I do have my husband to help me out. While I'm the more creative one, he's more thoughtful with taxes and organizations. This is totally a family-run business. Whereas it started with me at the forefront, this has become all of us.

This is all Evan [my youngest son] has known. The boys are with us through the highs and the lows. I'm thankful they get to see what it's like to run a business as a family. I also homeschool them. So lots of teaching happens through this business. I love that my boys can see their mom doing this. I think moms are being so much these days. I like them knowing, "My mom can do this, and she can do all the things she wants to do."

What flavors do you sell?

We offer four different flavors; two of them are recipes I grew up eating. Avocado-lime salsa is something we would eat all the time. Another one is a restaurant-style, blended-up pico de gallo, which reminds me of my childhood. I also have a spicy tomatillo salsa, which is a very traditional Mexican recipe, and a smoky chipotle salsa.

Crystal Harris and her family.

What does Southern food mean to you?

I didn't grow up in the South. I grew up in Los Angeles. My husband is from here [North Carolina] and I moved here in 2012. I think I had a lot to learn about Southern food.

What I love about Southern food culture is there's so much to build on. I love being Mexican and combining that with Southern food. There's a lot of overlap. Like cornbread—it is sorta like tortillas. You can find the links between the two.

My boys are being raised as Southern men so they're getting these two cultures. They're getting a mix of the two foods. One of our favorite things I do is make a big bowl of grits and add in our smoky chipotle salsa and add in some cheddar cheese and onions and a fried egg—to me that's just a mix of the two cultures. I think a lot of people are scared to be untraditional. But as my boys grow up, that will be traditional to them.

Quick Tomato Salsa

Makes about 1 cup ~ Total Time: 10 minutes

Since we can't enjoy Harris's salsa without traveling to the source in North Carolina, we offer some punchy recipes of our own. We like the idea of adding this one to Extra-Cheesy Grits (page 179). To ensure that the small amounts of onion, cilantro, and jalapeño in this tomato salsa break down into even pieces and are well distributed, pulse them in a food processor before adding the other ingredients.

¼ small red onion

2 tablespoons minced fresh cilantro

½ small jalapeño chile, seeded and minced

1 (14.5-ounce) can diced tomatoes, drained

2 teaspoons lime juice, plus extra for seasoning

1 small garlic clove, minced

¼ teaspoon table salt

Pinch pepper

Pulse onion, cilantro, and jalapeño in food processor until finely chopped, about 5 pulses, scraping down sides of bowl as needed. Add tomatoes, lime juice, garlic, salt, and pepper and process until smooth, 20 to 30 seconds. Transfer to serving bowl and season with salt and extra lime juice to taste. Serve.

Quick Tomatillo Salsa

Makes about 2 cups ~ Total Time: 35 minutes

A simple, tangy tomatillo-based salsa with jalapeño, cilantro, garlic, and lime juice is great for cutting through rich foods such as Grilled Steak Fajitas (page 314) or Puffy Tacos (page 240)—or just serving with chips. Charring half the tomatillos under the broiler and leaving the other half uncooked produces a moderately tangy and slightly chunky salsa. The salsa comes together easily in the food processor. You can use canned tomatillos in place of the fresh here. We use a 28-ounce can of tomatillos, but they are also available in 26-ounce cans. If you can find only a 26-ounce can, there's no need to buy a second can to make up the extra 2 ounces. For more heat, reserve and add the jalapeño seeds.

1 pound tomatillos, husks and stems removed, rinsed well and dried

1 tablespoon extra-virgin olive oil, divided

1 small white onion, chopped

1 jalapeño chile, stemmed, halved, and seeded

½ cup fresh cilantro leaves

2 tablespoons lime juice

1 garlic clove, minced

¼ teaspoon table salt

Sugar (optional)

1 Adjust oven rack 6 inches from broiler element and heat broiler. Line rimmed baking sheet with aluminum foil. Toss half of tomatillos with 1 teaspoon oil and transfer to prepared sheet. Broil until tomatillos are spotty brown and skins begin to burst, 7 to 10 minutes. Transfer tomatillos to food processor and let cool completely.

2 Halve remaining tomatillos and add to food processor with broiled tomatillos. Add onion, jalapeño, cilantro, lime juice, garlic, and salt. Pulse until slightly chunky, 16 to 18 pulses. Transfer to serving bowl and let stand at room temperature for 15 minutes. Stir in remaining 2 teaspoons oil. Season with salt and sugar, if desired. Serve.

EMBRACING AJÍ PICANTE

Ají picante is a spicy sauce that contains peppers, tomatoes, garlic, onions, cilantro, vinegar, lemon, and water. It is most known as a condiment to complement main dishes in Latin American cuisine and is prepared by blending all the ingredients by hand or in a food processor. The recipe can vary from person to person and region by region. It originates from the Andes Mountains, where the Incas referred to it as uchu. The sauce spread to other countries over time and started to vary based on availability of ingredients. In Colombia, our food is on the milder side, so we use the ají to add spice to and bring out more flavors in our dishes.

When I arrived in the United States from Colombia forty years ago, I rarely saw ají picante. I remember living in Indianapolis and inviting some new friends over for the first time. I served some ají picante with tortilla chips, and they were surprised to learn it wasn't store-bought salsa. When I moved to South Florida just a few years later, I discovered Miami was years ahead of other cities in embracing Latin cuisine and cultures. The special thing about Miami is that it's a melting pot, which has resulted in a fusion cuisine. Miami restaurants build playful and bold menus from the best of Cuban, Colombian, Venezuelan, Peruvian, and Central American food. The staple that I've seen adopted the most from Colombian cuisine is the ají picante. Where Tabasco sauce or salsa had been used in the past, I now see this sauce as the popular choice.

You don't have to take ají picante so seriously. Use whatever pepper you can find and make it as spicy as you'd like. I use a mix of red peppers, which I always have at home, with jalapeños, but you can use any other hot peppers, such as habaneros. For onions, I like to use scallions, but white onions will also do. The key to the sauce is not necessarily the ingredients, but the consistency. It should contain more liquid than other types of salsas. I still use my grandmother's technique of cutting everything by hand, but you can use the food processor and prepare the dish in just minutes.

When I traveled back to Colombia, I was curious to see whether the use of ají picante had changed throughout the years as I've seen it evolve in Miami. I was pleasantly surprised to discover how much more prevalent it was in Colombian cooking, especially in the high-end culinary world. While it had been mostly used at home before, professional chefs are starting to incorporate it to make more creative and bolder dishes. Of course, my family and friends continue to serve it at home. They use this sauce at breakfast to accompany arepas, fritos, or to serve over eggs. For lunch or dinner, we use it to complement beans, soups, seafood, and even meat dishes, but I've learned that this simple and easy-to-make sauce can pair with almost any dish. It is never missing from my kitchen.

by Nadia Domeq

Miami-based recipe developer

Ají Picante

Makes 1½ cups   ~   Total Time: 15 minutes

Ají picante is ubiquitous in Colombia and areas with large populations of Colombian immigrants like Central and South Florida and near Houston and Dallas, Texas. This hot sauce is traditionally served with soups and stews, beans, rice, empanadas, meats, and more. There are countless versions of the sauce; this is Nadia Domeq's. It's tomato-based, with a fiery heat from minced jalapeño that's tempered with fresh vegetables and herbs. Plum tomatoes supply juiciness but hold their shape. Scallions provide a mild allium bite but don't overpower the other flavors, and 2 teaspoons of jalapeño chile provide just the right amount of heat. Thinning the sauce with water allows it to soak into whatever it's topping and infuse the dish with heat and freshness.

2	plum tomatoes, cored and chopped fine
½	red bell pepper, chopped fine
½	cup chopped fresh cilantro
¼	cup water
2	tablespoons distilled white vinegar
2	tablespoons lemon juice
1	tablespoon extra-virgin olive oil
3	scallions, minced
2	garlic cloves, minced
2	teaspoons minced jalapeño chile
1	teaspoon sugar
¼	teaspoon table salt

Combine all ingredients in bowl, stirring to dissolve sugar. Serve. (Salsa can be refrigerated for up to 1 week.)

Refrigerator Pickled Okra

Makes two 1-pint jars   ~   Total Time: 25 minutes, plus 7 days pickling

For anyone intimidated by okra, a pickle is a good place to start. This vegetable actually gets more crisp as it sits in its brine. Pickled okra is delicious in a bloody Mary, sliced on sandwiches or in salads, or as part of a cheese board.

For pickled okra packed with punchy flavor, we create an aromatic brine with a hint of spicy red pepper flakes and whole black peppercorns. Cider vinegar, rounded out with a couple tablespoons of sugar, has an appropriately bright, tart flavor. Packing garlic right into the jars with the okra (rather than steeping it in the brine) provides a sharp, peppery backbone. For a spicier pickle, increase the red pepper flakes to 2 teaspoons. These pickles cannot be processed for long-term storage and should be stored in the refrigerator.

6	garlic cloves, smashed	2	tablespoons sugar
14	ounces fresh okra (4 inches or shorter), stems trimmed	2	tablespoons kosher salt
1½	cups cider vinegar	1	teaspoon red pepper flakes
¾	cup water	1	teaspoon mustard seeds
		1	teaspoon black peppercorns

1   Place two 1-pint jars in large bowl and place under hot running water until heated through, 1 to 2 minutes; shake dry.

2   Add 3 garlic cloves to each hot jar. Tightly pack okra vertically into jars, alternating spears stem side up and stem side down for best fit.

3   Bring vinegar, water, sugar, salt, pepper flakes, mustard seeds, and peppercorns to boil in medium saucepan over medium-high heat; remove from heat. Using funnel and ladle, distribute hot brine over okra to cover. Slide wooden skewer along inside of each jar, pressing slightly on okra, to remove air bubbles, then add extra brine as needed to keep okra covered.

4   Let jars cool completely. Affix jar lids and refrigerate okra for at least 1 week before serving. (Pickled okra can be refrigerated for up to 1 month; okra will become more crisp and flavor will mature over time.)

THE ORIGINS OF OKRA

In this country okra is largely considered inherently Southern, but Dr. Jessica B. Harris points out in her essay "Okra's Deep Roots" for *Garden & Gun* that okra likely originates from the Sahel region of equatorial Africa. It belongs to the same plant family as hibiscus and cotton.

According to Harris, the exact story of how okra made its way across the Atlantic is unclear, but scholars believe this fresh green pod arrived in the Western Hemisphere with enslaved Africans.

Perhaps the first documented mention of the vegetable in the United States is a reference to "un gombeau" in a 1764 handwritten transcription of a deposition with an enslaved woman named Comba in New Orleans (at the time a French colony). Comba was suspected of helping other enslaved people steal a pig and clothes. She was asked if she had given Louis, another enslaved worker, "un gombeau," and she responded that she did. This could have been the first reference to the plant or gumbo, the stew we know today. The word "gombo" means okra in both French and Central Bantu dialect (from a central region of Africa).

While we may not know the exact path, we can confidently say okra runs deep into Southern food culture, finding its way into fry baskets, stew pots, and Mason jars filled with pickle brine.

by Morgan Bolling

Candied Jalapeños

Makes about 1 cup ~ Total Time: 20 minutes, plus 5 hours cooling and chilling

Candied jalapeños, or "Cowboy Candy" as popularized by the Texas cannery WHH Ranch, are sweet-hot slices that add a piquant bite to all kinds of favorite foods. Chop them into chicken or egg salad (see pages 274 and 106), use them as a topping for eggs or sandwiches such as Pickle-Brined Fried Chicken Sandwiches (page 272), place them alongside North Carolina Barbecued Pork (page 326), or serve them as a garnish on a decked-out bloody Mary.

Legend has it that Cowboy Candy was invented in 1922 by Mindie Heironimus, who was just seven years old at the time. When her family's WHH Ranch in San Augustine, Texas, had a surplus of jalapeños, Mindie decided to can them in the same way she did her bread and butter pickles, with sugar and spices. The family liked these spicy-sweet bites so much, they eventually started selling them to the public.

Our version is as easy as heating the sliced fresh chiles in a seasoned simple syrup. A balance of green jalapeños with spicier ripened red ones, and ample sugar with cider vinegar, results in a versatile condiment. Whole coriander seeds contribute complexity and textural contrast. If you can't find red jalapeños, you can substitute Fresno chiles or use twice the amount of green jalapeños. We recommend that you wear rubber gloves while handling the chiles. These jalapeños cannot be processed for long-term storage and should be stored in the refrigerator.

4	green jalapeño chiles, stemmed and sliced ¼ inch thick (about 1 cup)
4	red jalapeño chiles, stemmed and sliced ¼ inch thick (about 1 cup)
¾	cup sugar
¼	cup cider vinegar
¼	cup water
2	teaspoons table salt
1	teaspoon coriander seeds
¼	teaspoon ground turmeric (optional)

1   Combine all ingredients in small saucepan and bring to boil over medium-high heat, stirring to dissolve sugar. Reduce heat to medium and simmer until jalapeños just soften, about 3 minutes. Remove from heat and let cool completely, about 1 hour.

2   Using fork or tongs, transfer jalapeños to 8-ounce jar. Pour syrup over jalapeños to fill jar, leaving ½ inch headspace. Affix jar lid and refrigerate jalapeños for at least 4 hours before serving. (Candied jalapeños can be refrigerated for up to 1 month.)

Quick Pickled Jalapeños

Makes about 1½ cups
Total Time: 40 minutes

This simple pickled jalapeño recipe follows a formula many Tex-Mex chefs use: Heat vinegar, sugar, and salt until the sugar is dissolved, then pour over thinly sliced chiles. Here, distilled white vinegar provides intense tang without overshadowing the flavor of the chiles. If you prefer less heat, halve the jalapeños lengthwise and remove the seeds before slicing. These pickles cannot be processed for long-term storage and should be stored in the refrigerator. Try serving with Texas Breakfast Tacos (page 70) or Chili con Carne (page 203).

1   cup distilled white vinegar

⅓   cup sugar

¼   teaspoon table salt

4   jalapeño chiles, sliced thin

1   Bring vinegar, sugar, and salt to simmer in small saucepan over medium-high heat, stirring occasionally, until sugar dissolves.

2   Place one 1-pint jar under hot running water until heated through, about 1 minute; shake dry. Pack jalapeños in jar. Pour vinegar mixture over jalapeños. Cover loosely and let cool completely, about 30 minutes. Use immediately or affix jar lid and refrigerate jalapeños for up to 1 week.

Quick Pickled Watermelon Rind

Makes about 1 quart ～ Total Time: 25 minutes, plus 2½ hours cooling and pickling

Pickling watermelon rind has been a Southern practice for more than a century. It transforms part of the fruit that typically would be discarded into something delicious. Abby Fisher, the second-known Black woman to write a cookbook, shared lots about preserves and pickles, including a recipe for sweet watermelon rind pickles, in her 1881 cookbook *What Mrs. Fisher Knows About Old Southern Cooking* (see "Abby Fisher: Author, Caterer, Pickle-Maker").

For our version, we use a sweet-salty brine built with cider vinegar, sugar, and salt enhanced with black peppercorns, mustard seeds, and coriander seeds. Adding some cinnamon introduces a lightly warm flavor. Some recipes, including Mrs. Fisher's, cook the rind to give it a softer texture, but for this quick pickle version, we opt to just pour the hot brine over the rind. It still seeps into the rind and results in a snappy, crunchy pickle in just 2 hours.

A 6-pound watermelon will give you more than enough rind. Depending on the size of your jar, you may have extra brine; make sure the rind is fully submerged. You can experiment and add different combinations of spices to the brine. If you want to follow Mrs. Fisher's wisdom, she used fresh ginger and lemon peel. These pickles cannot be processed for long-term storage and should be stored in the refrigerator.

2	pounds watermelon rind	1	teaspoon yellow mustard seeds
1¼	cups cider vinegar	1	teaspoon coriander seeds
1¼	cups sugar		
1½	teaspoons table salt	½	cinnamon stick
1	teaspoon black peppercorns		

1   Using vegetable peeler, remove green skin from watermelon rind; discard. Using spoon, scrape any remaining pink flesh from white rind; discard. Cut rind into 2 by ½-inch strips.

2   Combine vinegar, sugar, salt, peppercorns, mustard seeds, and coriander seeds in small saucepan. Bring to boil over medium-high heat.

3   Place one 1-quart jar under hot running water until heated through, about 1 minute; shake dry. Pack rind and cinnamon stick in jar. Using funnel and ladle, pour hot brine over rind to cover. Let jar cool completely, about 30 minutes.

4   Affix jar lid and refrigerate for at least 2 hours before serving. (Pickles can be refrigerated for up to 1 week.)

ABBY FISHER: AUTHOR, CATERER, PICKLE-MAKER

Abby Fisher, a native of South Carolina, was almost certainly the daughter of an enslaved mother; rarely, persons of African descent were freeborn. Yet in the years following the Civil War and the Emancipation of all enslaved people, the Southerner Abby Fisher made the long journey west to begin her next chapter in California. She arrived in her new home already an accomplished baker, cook, and pickle maker; her "previous condition" did not stop her from leveraging her culinary skills into the career of a San Francisco–based caterer. When she published *What Mrs. Fisher Knows About Old Southern Cooking* in 1881, she was only the second African American woman to have published a work of cookery. And despite her lack of a formal education, Fisher assured her readers that her written instructions in the book would provide them (or even a child) with professional-level expertise.

Fisher must have been urged to divulge her secrets by fans at the California State Fair of 1879, where she took home honors—along with two more at the Mechanic's Institute Fair the following year. Those delectable creations led a who's-who of white San Francisco women to underwrite her cookbook's publication, enabling a generation of California housewives to boast of their superior stove and oven capabilities. Divulging what she knew, Fisher compiled dozens of tempting recipes, from waffles to boiled fish. Readers could acquire still another set of talents prized in those days before electric refrigeration and chain stores: the pickling and conserving of fresh fruits and vegetables, and the production of home remedies. Fisher's "Blackberry Syrup for Dysentery in Children," averred to be an "old plantation remedy," counseled dosages of three teaspoons a day for infants to a half a wine glass thrice daily for adults. Perhaps more frequently, her readers followed her detailed how-tos for watermelon rind pickles, brandy peaches, and other delightful side dishes. Fisher's recipes today may take a bit of modernization, but her chef's star burns brightly into the 21st century.

by Rafia Zafar, PhD

Washington University professor of English, African, and African American studies; writer on food and American identities; and author of Recipes for Respect: African American Means and Meaning

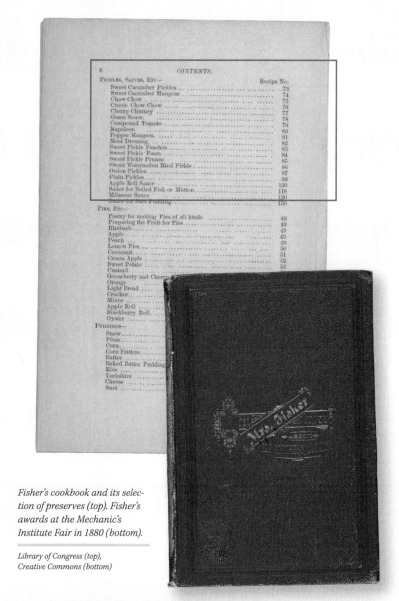

Fisher's cookbook and its selection of preserves (top). Fisher's awards at the Mechanic's Institute Fair in 1880 (bottom).

Library of Congress (top), Creative Commons (bottom)

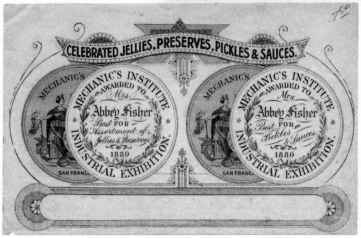

Quick Bread and Butter Pickles

Makes 1 quart ~ Total Time: 20 minutes, plus 3½ hours cooling and chilling

Bread and butter pickles brighten all kinds of meals in the South, sliding into sandwiches and mixing into sauces. These sweet and tangy pickles are typically made from cucumbers, onions, vinegar, sugar, and spices (often black peppercorns, mustard seeds, and turmeric), resulting in a unique flavor. While we have a recipe for canned pickle chips (see page 360), this recipe is quick and fuss-free for pickling novices or those averse to the efforts of traditional pickling projects. To streamline preparation time, we use seasoned rice vinegar, which already contains vinegar, sugar, and salt. We slice the cucumbers into ¼-inch chips using a chef's knife, though a mandoline or cutter for making crinkle cuts can also be used. After 3 hours, these pickles are thoroughly suffused with a lively combination of sweet, sour, and aromatic notes. This formula is transferable to other veggies, so we also offer recipes for quick carrot pickles, fennel pickles, and giardiniera. These pickles cannot be processed for long-term storage and should be stored in the refrigerator.

1¼	cups seasoned rice vinegar
¼	cup water
2	garlic cloves, peeled and halved
½	teaspoon ground turmeric
¼	teaspoon black peppercorns
¼	teaspoon yellow mustard seeds
1	pound pickling cucumbers, sliced crosswise ¼ inch thick
5	sprigs fresh dill

1   Combine vinegar, water, garlic, turmeric, peppercorns, and mustard seeds in small saucepan and bring to boil over medium-high heat.

2   Place one 1-quart jar under hot running water until heated through, about 1 minute; shake dry. Pack cucumbers and dill into hot jar. Using funnel and ladle, pour hot brine over cucumbers to cover. Let jar cool completely, about 30 minutes.

3   Affix jar lid and refrigerate for at least 3 hours before serving. (Pickles can be refrigerated for up to 6 weeks; pickles will soften significantly after 6 weeks.)

Quick Carrot Pickles

Substitute 1 pound carrots, peeled and cut into 4 by ½-inch sticks, for cucumbers and 5 sprigs fresh tarragon for dill. Omit turmeric.

Quick Fennel Pickles

Substitute 1 fennel bulb, stalks discarded, bulb halved, cored, and cut crosswise into ¼-inch-thick slices, for cucumbers. Omit dill and turmeric. Add two 1-inch strips orange zest and ½ teaspoon fennel seeds to saucepan with vinegar.

Quick Giardiniera

Substitute 6 ounces cauliflower, cut into 1-inch florets; 1 celery rib, sliced ¼ inch thick; and 1 carrot, sliced ¼ inch thick, for cucumbers. Omit dill and turmeric. Add ½ teaspoon red pepper flakes to saucepan with vinegar.

ALL ABOUT CANNING

Traditional long-term canning preserves foods at their peak of seasonal freshness: fruits in jams and jellies to all kinds of pickles. The boiling water canning process can seem daunting—since you are dealing with a huge pot of boiling water and multiple glass jars of food—but each step along the way is quite simple. And you can open a jar of freshness in any season. For all of our canned recipes, we instruct you on how to prepare them to simply store in the fridge short-term, but the long-term storing capabilities are what make these recipes seasonal time capsules.

1 Heat the Jars

Many recipes call for sterilizing the jars and lids before filling them; however, the USDA says that this is only necessary when processing jars for less than 10 minutes. We don't sterilize jars in this book because all of our recipes are processed for at least 10 minutes. However, the jars do need to be heated before being filled with hot items or the room-temperature glass may shatter. Jars can either be warmed in the canning pot that will be used for processing or placed under hot running water. As for the lids, they do not need to be heated before using.

2 Fill the Jars

As soon as a preserve has finished cooking, it needs to be portioned into the hot jars. Given that both the preserve and the jars are hot, we find it very helpful to use a wide-mouth canning funnel so you don't make a real mess and possibly burn yourself. A canning funnel works better than a traditional kitchen funnel for this task because the large opening makes filling the jars go quickly (which helps keep the food hot), and the funnel nestles securely into the jar so it's less likely to topple over when full. Because the timing is so important here, we like to have the jars warmed and waiting for the preserve.

3 Measure the Headspace

It is very important to leave some space, known as headspace, between the top of the food and the rim of the jar. If canning larger pieces of fruit or vegetables in liquid, make sure the solids are fully covered by the liquid and then measure the distance between the liquid and the rim of the jar. Each recipe will spell out exactly how much headspace is required (usually between ¼ inch and 1 inch). The headspace leaves room for the food to expand as it heats up during processing. If you have either too much or too little headspace, it can prevent the lid from sealing properly to the jar.

4 Release the Air Bubbles

After filling the jars and measuring the headspace, use a wooden skewer to remove any air bubbles trapped in the jar. For thick preserves, draw the skewer upward to release the bubbles. For larger pieces of fruit or vegetables in liquid, press the skewer against the food to release the air bubbles. If left undisturbed, the air bubbles will collect at the top of the jar during processing and alter the headspace, which can prevent the jar from sealing properly. Once the air bubbles have been removed, be sure to add extra jam or liquid as needed so that the headspace measurement is correct.

5 Add the Lids and Rings

Before adding the lids and rings, it is important to wipe the rim of the jar clean of any drips. Once clean, place the lids on top and screw on the rings until just fingertip-tight. Do not overtighten the rings, or you will prevent any air from escaping the jars during processing, which is a key part of the canning process. Note that the lids cannot be reused. The rings, however, can be used several times as long as they are in good shape.

6 Process the Jars

Using a jar lifter, lower the hot, filled jars into the rack inside the pot of boiling water. Make sure the jars are covered by at least 1 inch of water; if necessary add more water. Bring the water back to a boil and then process (boil) the jars for the amount of time prescribed in each recipe. Be sure to start the timer only after the water has returned to a boil. Processing times will vary based on the size of the jars, your altitude, and the type of food inside the jars. Smaller jars and lower elevations have shorter processing times than larger jars and higher elevations. The USDA has determined safe processing times for all different types of food, which we follow in our recipes.

7 Let the Jars Seal Themselves

After the processing time is up, turn off the heat and let the jars sit in the hot water for 5 minutes. This allows the boiling-hot food inside the jars to settle down and starts the lid-sealing process. After 5 minutes, remove the jars from the pot and allow them to cool at room temperature for 24 hours. As the food cools, it contracts, which makes a small vacuum form inside the jar. The pull of this vacuum pops the flexible metal lid inward, an indication that the jar has been hermetically sealed and oxygen can no longer pass through. To test the seal, press on the lid with your finger; a sealed lid will feel firm, while an unsealed lid will flex under the pressure and make a small popping sound.

What About Botulism?

Food-borne botulism is a rare but serious illness, and most cases are due to improperly home-canned foods. Luckily, avoiding botulism is very easy if you follow our recipes exactly. The processing times given in our recipes are derived from the USDA Complete Guide to Home Canning; these times are long enough to neutralize any dangerous toxins inside the jars.

We measure the pH of every recipe and have been careful to stay well below the minimum level (pH of 4.6) for food safety and botulism in canned goods. The pH for your batches at home will be the same as long as you use bottled lemon or lime juice and don't substitute other types of vinegar.

Be sure to work cleanly. Thoroughly wash the food, jars, rings and lids, counter, sink, and your hands before starting a home-canning project to reduce the possibility of contamination.

Lastly, when in doubt, throw it out. Always discard food from jars that have lost their seal during storage, as it is a sign that bacteria, mold, or other toxins might be growing inside the jar. Also, if a jar is still sealed but the food inside looks or smells off when you open it, you should discard it.

Dill Pickle Chips

Makes four 1-pint jars ~ Total Time: 1 hour, plus 27 hours salting and cooling

Pickles add balance to a Southern plate. The salty-tangy bites counter the richness of iconic Southern foods such as barbecue and fried chicken.

This recipe makes pickle chips that are tart and full of unmistakable dill flavor, the result of a combination of dill seed and fresh dill. Mustard seeds and garlic add heat, while a little sugar balances the acidity of the cider vinegar.

To preserve the crunch, we salt the cucumbers for several hours to draw out water and then pack the raw slices into our jars, along with a bit of Ball Pickle Crisp (see "Keep 'Em Crisp"), before covering them with hot brine. We process the cucumber slices using a low-temperature pasteurization method, maintaining them in a hot-water bath at 180 to 185 degrees for 30 minutes to produce crisp pickles. To double the recipe, double all the ingredients and use a larger pot when making the brine; the processing time will remain the same.

2½	pounds pickling cucumbers, ends trimmed, sliced ¼ inch thick
2	tablespoons canning and pickling salt
2	cups chopped fresh dill plus 4 large sprigs
3	cups cider vinegar
3	cups water
¼	cup sugar
1	tablespoon yellow mustard seeds
2	teaspoons dill seeds
½	teaspoon Ball Pickle Crisp
4	garlic cloves, peeled and quartered

Dill Pickle Spears

After trimming both ends from cucumbers, quarter cucumbers lengthwise and cut into 4-inch-long spears. Pack cucumber spears vertically into jars; salting and processing times will remain the same.

KEEP 'EM CRISP

The fresh snap of a homemade pickle is so satisfying; to keep vinegar-based pickles—such as Dill Pickle Chips—crisp, we find it beneficial to add Ball Pickle Crisp, which is simply a granulated form of calcium chloride. It reinforces the naturally occurring pectin in vegetables and helps keep pickles crunchy after being processed and stored for months in brine.

1   Toss cucumbers with salt in bowl and refrigerate for 3 hours. Drain cucumbers in colander (do not rinse), then pat dry with paper towels.

2   Bundle chopped dill in cheesecloth and secure with kitchen twine. Bring dill sachet, vinegar, water, sugar, mustard seeds, and dill seeds to boil in large saucepan over medium-high heat. Cover, remove from heat, and let steep for 15 minutes; discard sachet.

3   Meanwhile, set canning rack in canning pot, place four 1-pint jars in rack, and add water to cover by 1 inch. Bring to simmer over medium-high heat, then turn off heat and cover to keep hot.

4   Place dish towel flat on counter. Using jar lifter, remove jars from pot, draining water back into pot. Place jars upside down on towel and let dry for 1 minute. Add ⅛ teaspoon Pickle Crisp to each hot jar, then pack tightly with dill sprigs, garlic, and drained cucumbers.

5   Return brine to brief boil. Using funnel and ladle, pour hot brine over cucumbers to cover, distributing spices evenly and leaving ½ inch headspace. Slide wooden skewer along inside of jar, pressing slightly on vegetables to remove air bubbles, and add extra brine as needed.

6a   **For short-term storage** Let jars cool completely, cover with lids, and refrigerate for 24 hours before serving. (Pickles can be refrigerated for up to 3 months; flavor will continue to mature over time.)

6b   **For long-term storage** While jars are warm, wipe rims clean, add lids, and screw on rings until fingertip-tight; do not overtighten. Before processing jars, heat water in canning pot to temperature between 120 and 140 degrees. Lower jars into water, bring water to 180 to 185 degrees, then cook for 30 minutes, adjusting heat as needed to maintain water between 180 and 185 degrees. Remove jars from pot and let cool for 24 hours. Remove rings, check seals, and clean rims. (Sealed jars can be stored in a cool, dark place for up to 1 year.)

Chow-Chow

Makes four 1-cup jars ~ Total Time: 1 hour, plus 3 hours salting

Playfully named chow-chow is a flavorful pickled sweet green tomato relish that's perfect for those who are serious about saving and savoring every bit of the harvest. While Southern versions typically include green tomato and cabbage, chow-chow can be enhanced with a medley of regional and seasonal vegetables

You can find recipes called chow-chow in cookbooks as far back as Marion Cabell Tyree's 1878 book *Housekeeping in Old Virginia*. But there are versions of a similar (and possibly the same) pickle in earlier Southern cookbooks with different names: "piccalilli" (probably inspired by a British condiment with the same name), "Indian pickles," or "yellow pickles." Some propose the name chow-chow was derived from the French term "chou" for cabbage, a common ingredient in chow-chow thanks to the French-speaking Acadian settlers in Louisiana. Others trace the origins of chow-chow to piquant sauces brought over by Chinese railroad workers in the 19th century.

For this version, jalapeño and cayenne provide heat. Bell peppers give a mild fruitiness, and the cabbage lends crispness. Using a food processor creates the perfect size pieces. Salting the vegetables for 3 hours pulls out any excess moisture. Adding them to the brine off heat keeps the cabbage crisp and the peppers and tomatoes firm. To double the recipe, double all of the ingredients and pulse the vegetables in six batches. Increase the simmering time in step 3 to about 8 minutes. Chow-chow is delicious added to Bacon, Lettuce, and Fried Green Tomato Sandwiches (page 267), or try swapping it in for the pickles in our Smashed Potato Salad (page 337).

3	green tomatoes, cored and chopped coarse
1	cup coarsely chopped green cabbage
1	cup coarsely chopped green bell pepper
½	cup coarsely chopped red bell pepper
½	cup coarsely chopped onion
1	jalapeño chile, stemmed, seeded, and chopped
1½	tablespoons canning and pickling salt
½	cup distilled white vinegar
½	cup sugar
1¼	teaspoons yellow mustard seeds
½	teaspoon celery seeds
¼	teaspoon ground turmeric
¼	teaspoon cayenne pepper

1   Combine tomatoes, cabbage, bell peppers, onion, and jalapeño in bowl. Working in 3 batches, pulse vegetables in food processor until pieces measure ¼ to ½ inch, 4 to 6 pulses; transfer to separate bowl. Stir in salt, cover, and refrigerate for 3 hours.

2   Set canning rack in canning pot, place four 1-cup jars in rack, and add water to cover by 1 inch. Bring to simmer over medium-high heat, then turn off heat and cover to keep hot.

3   Transfer vegetables to colander and let drain for 20 minutes. Bring vinegar, sugar, mustard seeds, celery seeds, turmeric, and cayenne to boil in large saucepan over high heat. Reduce to simmer and cook until slightly thickened, about 5 minutes. Off heat, stir in drained vegetables.

4   Place dish towel flat on counter. Using jar lifter, remove jars from pot, draining water back into pot. Place jars upside down on towel and let dry for 1 minute. Using funnel and ladle, portion relish into hot jars, leaving ½ inch headspace. Slide wooden skewer along inside of jar, pressing slightly on relish to remove air bubbles.

5a   **For short-term storage** Let jars cool completely. Cover with lids and refrigerate until ready to serve. (Relish can be refrigerated for up to 6 months.)

5b   **For long-term storage** While jars are hot, wipe rims clean, add lids, and screw on rings until fingertip-tight; do not overtighten. Return pot of water with canning rack to boil. Lower jars into water, cover, bring water back to boil, then start timer. Cooking time will depend on your altitude: Boil 10 minutes for up to 1,000 feet, 15 minutes for 1,001 to 3,000 feet, 20 minutes for 3,001 to 6,000 feet, and 25 minutes for 6,001 to 8,000 feet. Turn off heat and let jars sit in pot for 5 minutes. Remove jars from pot and let cool for 24 hours. Remove rings, check seals, and clean rims. (Sealed jars can be stored in cool, dark place for up to 1 year.)

A CAN-DO ATTITUDE: THE FEMALE AGENTS WHO BROUGHT CANNING INTO COMMUNITIES

For several decades in the early 20th century, the knowledge required to learn home canning practices was brought directly into American homes and communities by a nationwide cadre of women. The Victory Gardens that citizens were encouraged to grow during World War I, so as to reduce the need for food rationing (see page 135), resulted in a bounty of produce needing preservation.

At the time, however, home canning was not commonly employed, particularly those practices deemed "safe," such as two-piece lid enclosures and the need to pressure can low-acid foods. Enter the U.S. government. Through the creation of the Smith-Lever Act of 1914, officials at the USDA founded a national Cooperative Extension Service, offering outreach programs nationwide. The stated intention of this initiative was to educate Americans, especially those living in rural settings, about innovations in agricultural practices and technology as they related to home and farm life. This is how home demonstrations, also known as home demonstration clubs and homemaker clubs, came to be. These programs,

Women working together to can food in an industrial kitchen during World War I.

Library of Congress

which were racially segregated, proved to be quite popular. By World War II, home demonstration clubs had 55,185 total members in 2175 clubs, of which 12,952 members were African American in 587 home demonstration clubs (according to "Green 'N' Growing: The History of Home Demonstration and 4-H Youth Development in North Carolina," a website of the Special Collections Research Center at the NCSU Libraries).

Federally employed and appointed agents, all of them women, worked with individual state agencies to spread "expert" information on home economics and "homemaker" skills, chief among them home canning. These skills were taught through community meetings, as well as in community members' homes. A USDA booklet from 1951 declared the objective of the home demonstrator agent as such: "To give rural people, in a form in which they can use it at a time when they need it, information that will enable them to become better citizens in a democracy."

Attendees of these programs not only learned new information on food preservation and more, they used their newly acquired skills to produce and sell goods to generate income and personal empowerment. As professor, historian, and author Marcie Cohen Ferris writes in *The Edible South*, "Producing and selling these goods not

only connected rural women to social and economic networks that stretched far beyond their farms, but also shifted how they thought about themselves."

Furthermore, Ferris relays how "female extension agents strengthened their constituents' sense of self-worth by recognizing their contributions to the household economy." Money garnered by women from the items they sold at female extension agent–organized "curb markets" especially by women of color, was used to "buy special treats for themselves and their families, and, not infrequently, to pay rents and mortgages and buy needed farm equipment."

Home demonstration clubs became beloved spaces where women could develop new skills while at the same time socialize and, later, as the clubs evolved, engage in community outreach, including offering services for the elderly and infirm in local communities, as well as fundraising for charities. By the 1960s, with more mechanized food production, the need for the clubs waned—along with government funding—but the skills and community stayed.

by Ashley English

food and agricultural writer and 11-time cookbook author dedicated to a self-sustaining life

Apple Butter

Makes two 1-cup jars ~ Total Time: 1½ hours

Even though it takes some time, making apple butter outdoors and in large quantities is a ritual that persists throughout Appalachia and much of the South. Families gather in their backyards to process the season's bounty, while churches and schools come together to make this deeply concentrated spreadable sauce for fundraising. Festivals, such as the annual Apple Butter Festival in Berkeley Springs, West Virginia, are dedicated specifically to the craft.

In her article "Peel, Chop and Stir for Hours: How Appalachia's Beloved Community Apple-Butter Parties Live On" for the *Washington Post*, Jane Black details how these annual events can start in the morning with an assembly line of peeling,

coring, and chopping apples into "snits" before tossing them into buckets. (Sometimes kids aren't invited since the drinking can begin early.)

Apple butter–making began as a practical way to preserve the abundance of apples found in the mountains year-round. With over 600 varieties still present in the region, the debate over which apple makes the best butter is a reflection of the area's geographic diversity and individualism. There's also debate over whether to add sugar or not. And some families tip in a package of Red Hot candies for a nostalgic addition of cinnamon flavor.

For our version we opt for two apple varieties available at most grocery stores:

McIntosh and Granny Smith. McIntosh are prized for their sweet flavor, and Granny Smiths add some complexity. But you could try using a mix of sweet and tart apples that are grown near you. While there is debate among recipe writers, we found cooking the apples with the skins provides more flavor. Plus the apples soften enough that the flesh separates from the skins when passed through a food mill or mesh strainer. Many recipes call for water, but using apple cider and pungent Calvados doubles down on apple flavor. If you want, you can add some Red Hots (or a pinch of cinnamon) during the last 20 minutes of cooking to get that cinnamon infusion.

1½ pounds McIntosh apples, cored, quartered, and cut into 1-inch pieces

1 pound Granny Smith apples, cored, quartered, and cut into 1-inch pieces

⅔ cup apple cider

⅔ cup Calvados or applejack

½ cup granulated sugar

⅓ cup packed light brown sugar

2 tablespoons bottled lemon juice

¼ teaspoon table salt

1 Bring apples, cider, and Calvados to boil in large saucepan over medium-high heat. Reduce heat to medium-low, cover, and simmer, stirring occasionally, until apples are very soft, about 30 minutes.

2 Working in batches, process mixture through food mill fitted with medium disk set over bowl; alternatively, use rubber spatula to work mixture through fine-mesh strainer set over bowl. Return puree to clean saucepan.

3 Stir in granulated sugar, brown sugar, lemon juice, and salt. Cook over low heat, stirring occasionally, until mixture is browned, thickened, and rubber spatula leaves distinct trail when dragged across bottom of pot, 45 minutes to 1 hour.

4 Let apple butter cool slightly. Using funnel and spoon, portion apple butter into two 1-cup jars.

5a **For short-term storage** Let apple butter cool completely. Cover with lids and refrigerate until ready to serve. (Apple butter can be refrigerated for up to 1 month.)

5b **For long-term storage** Wipe jar rims clean, add lids, and screw on rings until fingertip-tight; do not overtighten. Bring canning pot of water with canning rack to boil. Lower jars into water, cover, bring water back to boil, then start timer. Cooking time will depend on your altitude: Boil 10 minutes for up to 1,000 feet, 15 minutes for 1,001 to 3,000 feet, 20 minutes for 3,001 to 6,000 feet, or 25 minutes for 6,001 to 8,000 feet. Turn off heat and let jars sit in pot for 5 minutes. Remove jars from pot and let cool for 24 hours. Remove rings, check seals, and clean rims. (Sealed jars can be stored in cool, dark place for up to 1 year.)

APPLES IN APPALACHIA

For more than 250 years, apples grew throughout the South; varieties originated in Mississippi and coastal North Carolina. Mobile, Alabama, exported apples to Northern states. The most important 19th-century fruit nurseries in the South were outside Columbia, South Carolina, and Augusta, Georgia. Southerners enjoyed hundreds of varieties all year, from Carolina Red June, an early summer variety, to Ralls Janet that ripened in November and kept in a root cellar until May.

Then, in less than the lifetime of a tree, Southerners lost many of their apples. In the early 20th century, a changing economy encouraged folks to move from farms to factories and to plant more profitable soybeans instead of apples. Orchards shrank; varieties disappeared. The rich harvest of apples grown in the South diminished from almost 2,000 varieties to a few hundred. Everywhere except in the southern Appalachians.

In the Appalachians apples were a quotidian fruit, entwined with people and places. Dried apples had once functioned as currency in remote mountain valleys like Rock Castle in Patrick County, Virginia. "Stillhouse" apples like Parmar and Hewe's Crab went to distilleries. Limbertwigs headed to the cider mill. Fried apples showed up on breakfast plates alongside applewood-cured sausage. Appalachian cooks stuffed dried apples into hand pies made flaky with leaf lard. Sunday dinner, the midday meal, included a spoonful of applesauce alongside a slice of silky pink ham. Appalachian kitchens had a jar of cider vinegar to douse beans and add a "whang" (Appalachian slang for a sort of tang) to potato salad and deviled eggs.

Through industrialization, Appalachian apple trees endured. Today this rich apple tradition persists. Home cooks may make apple butter in slow cookers but church fundraisers keep up the tradition of apple butter cooked in iron pots over a fire. Magnum Bonums and Grimes Goldens still populate farm stands, and wild seedling trees line steep mountain roads.

A few miles from our farm in southwest Virginia, an ancient apple tree rests beside a crumbling farmhouse, protected from cattle by a barbed wire fence. The family's modern brick ranch sits on the hill just above this treasured tree, a family apple with no formal name. From my office window I can see a copse of wild seedling apples, scraggly trees with drooping limbs and bear claw scars halfway up the trunks. Today two strands of apple history, those tamed and named, and their wild cousins, flourish in the Appalachians.

by Diane Flynt

founder of Foggy Ridge Cider in the Virginia Blue Ridge Mountains and author of Wild, Tamed, Lost, Revived: The Surprising Story of Apples in the South

Preserved Peaches in Syrup

Makes four 1-pint jars   ~   Total Time: 1 hour

Don't equate these preserved peaches with canned peaches at the grocery store; these are tender, with a balanced sweetness that allows the summer fruit flavor to shine. For pure peach flavor, use just sugar and water for the syrup. Or add cinnamon, ginger, and vanilla to introduce warm flavor (remove the flavorings before jarring the peaches). Try using these peaches in our recipe for Peach and Burrata Salad (page 130) or just snack on them plain. After eating the peaches, the leftover syrup can be combined with seltzer for a DIY soda. Yellow peaches are a must here; white peaches, which do not have enough natural acidity, are not a safe substitute in this recipe. In step 4, you can peel firmer peaches with a serrated vegetable peeler. In step 7, it's important to pack the peaches into the jars while they're hot.

3   pounds ripe but firm yellow freestone peaches

2   cups sugar

2   cinnamon sticks; 1 (6-inch) piece ginger, peeled and sliced into ¼-inch-thick rounds; and/or 1 vanilla bean, halved (optional)

1   Set canning rack in large pot, place four 1-pint jars in rack, and add water to cover by 1 inch. Cover pot and bring to simmer over high heat, then turn off heat and cover to keep hot.

2   Meanwhile, bring 3 quarts water to boil in Dutch oven. Fill large bowl halfway with ice and water. Score small X at base of each peach with paring knife.

3   Lower peaches into boiling water with slotted spoon. Cook until skins loosen at base of peaches, about 1 minute. (Firmer peaches may need up to 3 minutes.) Using slotted spoon, immediately transfer peaches to ice bath and let cool for about 1 minute; discard water in Dutch oven.

4   Starting at X on base of each peach, use paring knife to remove strips of loosened skin. Cut each peach in half through stem and remove pit. Cut each half in half.

5   In now-empty Dutch oven, bring 3 cups water; sugar; and flavoring, if using, to boil over high heat, stirring to dissolve sugar. Add peaches, return to boil, then immediately remove pot from heat. Let peaches sit in syrup for 3 minutes. Discard flavoring, if using.

6   Meanwhile, place dish towel flat on counter. Using jar lifter, remove jars from pot, draining water back into pot. Place jars upside down on towel and let dry for 1 minute.

7   Using slotted spoon, gently pack peaches into jars. Using funnel and ladle, pour hot syrup over peaches to cover, leaving 1 inch headspace at tops of jars. Slide wooden skewer along inside of jars, pressing slightly against peaches to remove air bubbles. Add extra syrup as needed.

8a   **For short-term storage**   Let jars cool completely. Cover with lids and refrigerate until ready to serve. (Peaches can be refrigerated for up to 1 week.)

8b   **For long-term storage**   While jars are hot, wipe rims clean, add lids, and screw on rings until fingertip-tight; do not overtighten. Return pot of water with canning rack to boil. Lower jars into water, cover, bring water back to boil, then start timer. Cooking time will depend on your altitude: Boil 20 minutes for up to 1,000 feet, 25 minutes for 1,001 to 3,000 feet, 30 minutes for 3,001 to 6,000 feet, and 35 minutes for 6,001 to 8,000 feet. Turn off heat and let jars sit in pot for 5 minutes. Remove jars from pot and let cool for 24 hours. Remove rings, check seals, and clean rims. (Sealed jars can be stored in a cool, dark place for up to 1 year.)

A PEACH BY ANY OTHER NAME

Despite being so iconically Southern, peaches, as Kelly Alexander explains in her book of the same name, were growing wild in China more than 3000 years ago. It's thought that peaches came to the South in a circuitous trade route through a port in Florida. And for a while this sweet fruit proliferated in the South—to the extreme. In naturalist John Larson's 1709 book, *A New Voyage to Carolina*, he warns to weed out peach trees, "otherwise they make our Land a Wilderness of Peach-Trees."

Cooks would use them; you can find recipes in Southern cookbooks from the early 1800s for everything from peach cobbler and peach marmalade to peach cordials and more. But peaches weren't a serious moneymaker for farmers.

That changed in the 1870s when Georgia farmer Samuel Rumph cross-pollinated two peach varieties and named them after his wife Clara Elberta Moore; this gave way to the fruitful Elberta peach trees. This tree was able to produce a high load of juicy, freestone peaches that were excellent for eating fresh or canning. It made shipping peaches outside the state a worthwhile endeavor and turned peaches into a cash crop for the Georgia economy, eventually becoming more profitable than cotton.

In the 1920s, farmers and marketers took advantage of this, driving home the idea that Georgia was the state to procure peaches from. There were massive festivals and pageants to celebrate the fuzzy fruit. In his article "Peaches Are a Minor Part of Georgia's Economy, but They're Central to Its Mythology" for the Conversation, William Thomas Okie talks about how the elaborate pageants sold the state pride: "[They] told a story of the peach, personified as a young maiden and searching the world for a husband and a home: from China, to Persia, to Spain, to Mexico, and finally to Georgia, her true and eternal home."

Today, more peaches are produced in California than any other state (Georgia actually comes in at a distant third, also behind South Carolina). But the state keeps the nickname "The Peach State." This blushed golden fruit has been its state fruit since 1995.

by Morgan Bolling

Grapefruit–Arbol Chile Marmalade

Makes four 1-cup jars   ~   Total Time: 3 hours, plus 17 hours cooling and chilling

Stephanie McClenny, owner of Confituras, a preserves company based out of Austin, Texas, didn't grow up in the South. She lived in Kenya, Tunisia, and Uganda, where her dad held foreign-service posts, all before she turned four. She then moved to Orange County, California, and didn't land in the South until she was 21, when the music scene in Austin pulled her in.

While supporting an elderly couple for work, she started getting passionate about the ingredients she sourced and the foods she cooked for them. When she went on to be an elementary school nurse, she would leave the school in the afternoon and spend the rest of her night cooking. By 2008 she was writing a regular food blog called Cosmic Cowgirl, and in 2010 she started Confituras.

McClenny prides herself on using local Texas produce for both quality and sustainability. She challenges herself and her team to make only jams with produce that is in season. And she has managed to do all of this while creating some really intriguing flavor combinations, such as fig with bay and honey; blueberry lavender; and strawberry, balsamic, and black pepper. We were inspired by one of her flavor combinations, Backyard Grapefruit and Chile de Arbol Jam, to add arbol chiles to a recipe for grapefruit marmalade. The warm chile flavor adds spicy nuance and balance to the delightfully bittersweet flavor of grapefruit.

Any grapefruit variety can be used; the flavor and color of the marmalade will vary only slightly. McClenny has made a variety of grapefruit preserves using this cold-weather fruit, including grapefruit–rose water jelly. So once you get this one down, feel free to play around with other creative ideas.

4	cups water	2	dried arbol chiles, sliced thin
2	grapefruits (12 ounces each), scrubbed	3½	cups sugar
1	lemon, scrubbed		

1   Bring water, grapefruits, lemon, and chiles to boil in large saucepan over high heat. Reduce heat to low and cover pot with heavy-duty aluminum foil and lid. Simmer gently until fruit is easily pierced with skewer, about 1½ hours, turning grapefruits over halfway through cooking. Off heat, let mixture cool, covered, for at least 5 hours or up to 24 hours.

2   Set canning rack in canning pot, place four 1-cup jars in rack, and add water to cover by 1 inch. Bring to simmer over medium-high heat, then turn off heat and cover to keep hot. Place 2 small plates in freezer to chill.

3   Transfer grapefruits and lemon to cutting board; cut grapefruits into 8 pieces each and lemon into quarters. Using paring knife, scrape pulp with most of pith from peels; reserve pulp and peels separately. Return pulp to pot with liquid, mash lightly with potato masher, bring to simmer over medium heat, and cook for 10 minutes. Meanwhile, slice peels into thin strips, then cut crosswise into ¼-inch pieces.

4   Strain liquid through fine-mesh strainer into Dutch oven, pressing firmly on solids; discard solids. Stir in chopped peels and sugar. Bring to vigorous boil over medium-high heat, stirring and adjusting heat as needed, until thickened and registers 220 to 222 degrees, 15 to 25 minutes. Remove pot from heat.

5   To test consistency, place 1 teaspoon marmalade on chilled plate and freeze for 2 minutes. Gently push cooled marmalade with your finger; marmalade should wrinkle around edges when set. If runny, return pot to heat and simmer for 1 to 3 minutes longer before retesting. Skim any foam from surface of marmalade using large spoon.

6   Place dish towel flat on counter. Using jar lifter, remove jars from pot, draining water back into pot. Place jars upside down on towel and let dry for 1 minute. Using funnel and ladle, portion hot marmalade into hot jars, leaving ¼ inch headspace. Slide wooden skewer along inside edge of jar and drag upward to remove air bubbles.

7a   **For short-term storage** Let marmalade cool completely, cover, and refrigerate until marmalade is set, 12 to 24 hours. (Marmalade can be refrigerated for up to 3 months).

7b   **For long-term storage** While jars are hot, wipe rims clean, add lids, and screw on rings until fingertip-tight; do not overtighten. Return pot of water with canning rack to boil. Lower jars into water, cover, bring water back to boil, then start timer. Cooking time will depend on your altitude: Boil 10 minutes for up to 1,000 feet, 15 minutes for 1,001 to 3,000 feet, 20 minutes for 3,001 to 6,000 feet, or 25 minutes for 6,001 to 8,000 feet. Turn off heat and let jars sit in pot for 5 minutes. Remove jars from pot and let cool for 24 hours. Remove rings, check seals, and clean rims. (Sealed jars can be stored in a cool, dark place for up to 1 year.)

YOUR HEART IS YOUR HOME

A Ford in the driveway.
A Ford in the White House.
Shag carpet.
Shag haircut.
Bee Gees on the radio.
Fast food is new! My mom's cooking is old-fashioned!
1970s, small-town girl in a ranch house on a hill in North Georgia, mind racing.

About my mother's cooking.

She had five or so meals in her repertoire. (There was no *NYT* Cooking app!) All included a side of vegetables from our garden behind the house. There were casseroles, burgers, country-fried steak, fried chicken, pot roast on Sundays and, when we were feeling extra-international, spaghetti and meat sauce. If money was tight, we ate breakfast for dinner or fried bologna and cheese sandwiches. I devoured most of it. Still, in my head I constantly counted the days until I could fly free and devour all the experiences of the wider world.

Fast-forward a lifetime: Wanderlust and curiosity are still my strong suits. I recently wrote my first children's book, *Your Heart Is Your Home: A Guide for Those Who Decide to Roam*, intended to be a loving little pep session for kids (of all ages) about taking pride in where you're from but also loving and exploring our big wonderful world.

"If one day you leave home, because there's a world to roam, here's what to pack in your luggage or sack … Pack your imagination, some hope, and then pen us a letter. Tell us how others are making the world better."

History has shown that the pendulum of human behavior swings. These days, in the United States, it feels like that pendulum is to the extreme right, with a large part of our country trapped in fear-based thinking, rejecting those who don't look, live, or eat like them. I worry about our children not being taught to love the world. I worry about an entire generation of kids learning to reject foods and folks and faraway lands simply because they're unfamiliar.

"Load up the foods you've loved since birth, but make room for new tastes across this great earth … Whether you travel the globe or stay the local route, if you keep your mind right, you can figure it out."

A few simple lines from a children's book won't change the world, but I know that change is possible. Let's feed our children good foods from around the globe. Let's also serve up more learning and love and hope and open-mindedness, so that from an early age, kids can dream (obsess even) about flying free.

by Kyle Tibbs Jones

co-founder and editorial and communications director at the Bitter Southerner, *host of* BATCH *podcast, and author of the children's book* Your Heart Is Your Home

Red Pepper Jelly

Makes four 1-cup jars ~ Total Time: 30 minutes, plus 12 hours 20 minutes cooling and chilling

Pepper jelly, a spicy-sweet spread made from lots of red bell peppers and some chiles, was popularized in Lake Jackson, Texas, during the 1970s. Some older siblings include Caribbean pepper sauces and "hot pepper jelly" that often rely on Scotch bonnet peppers for intense heat, as well as Thai and Malaysian sweet chile sauces. The timelessly delicious pairing of sweet and heat is globally resonant.

For our recipe, habanero chiles offer lingering, full-bodied flavor and spiciness to offset the sweetness of red bell peppers. Do not substitute other types of vinegar for the distilled white vinegar. To make this jelly spicier, reserve and add the chile seeds. Do not substitute other brands of low-sugar pectin for the Sure-Jell.

3½ cups sugar, divided

¼ cup Sure-Jell for Less or No Sugar Needed Recipes

1 pound red bell peppers, stemmed, seeded, and cut into 1-inch pieces

3 habanero chiles, halved, stemmed, and seeded

¼ cup water

2 cups distilled white vinegar

1 Set canning rack in canning pot, place four 1-cup jars in rack, and add water to cover by 1 inch. Bring to simmer over medium-high heat, then turn off heat and cover to keep hot.

2 Whisk ¼ cup sugar and Sure-Jell together in bowl; set aside. Pulse bell peppers and habaneros in food processor until finely chopped, 12 to 15 pulses, scraping down bowl as necessary. Transfer bell pepper mixture to Dutch oven and stir in water. Cover and cook over medium heat until peppers have softened, 10 to 15 minutes. Uncover and simmer until water has evaporated, about 1 minute.

3 Add vinegar and Sure-Jell mixture to pot and bring to boil, whisking constantly. Add remaining 3¼ cups sugar and bring to vigorous boil, whisking constantly. Once boiling, cook for 1 minute, whisking constantly. Remove pot from heat and skim foam from surface using large spoon.

4 Place dish towel flat on counter. Using jar lifter, remove jars from pot, draining water back into pot. Place jars upside down on towel and let dry for 1 minute. Using funnel and ladle, portion hot jelly into hot jars, leaving ¼ inch headspace.

5a **For short-term storage** Let jelly cool completely, cover, and refrigerate until set, 12 to 24 hours. Stir to redistribute peppers before serving. (Jelly can be refrigerated for up to 4 months.)

5b **For long-term storage** While jars are hot, wipe rims clean, add lids, and screw on rings until fingertip-tight; do not overtighten. Return pot of water with canning rack to boil. Lower jars into water, cover, bring water back to boil, then start timer. Cooking time will depend on your altitude: Boil 10 minutes for up to 1,000 feet, 15 minutes for 1,001 to 3,000 feet, 20 minutes for 3,001 to 6,000 feet, or 25 minutes for 6,001 to 8,000 feet. Turn off heat and let jars sit in pot for 5 minutes. Remove jars from pot and let cool for 24 hours. Remove rings, check seals, and clean rims. (Sealed jars can be stored in cool, dark place for up to 1 year.)

Homemade Peanut Butter

Makes about 1 cup ～ Total Time: 10 minutes, plus 20 minutes cooling

Making your own peanut butter is empowering; you control the ingredients and the final texture. It's also fun, less expensive than buying prepared peanut butter, and easy—all it takes is a food processor, some dry-roasted peanuts, and salt to make a nostalgic spread, just as delicious eaten out of the jar as spread on saltine crackers for DIY Nabs (see "In the Know About Nabs").

After about 30 seconds of processing, the peanuts will have the texture of coarse, wet sand. After about 1 minute, all the peanuts will have been broken up, and a ball will form. Keep processing—after 1½ minutes, a paste will form. By the 3-minute mark, you'll have spreadable peanut butter. Process for 1 more minute to yield smooth peanut butter worth making at home. If you can find only salted dry-roasted peanuts, omit the salt and season to taste before serving. Up to a point, a little liquid thickens nut butters, so you can add some, little by little, and continue to process if needed to reach the desired consistency.

    2   cups dry-roasted peanuts
    ½   teaspoon table salt

1   Process peanuts and salt in food processor until smooth, about 4 minutes (mixture will initially form clumps but will eventually thin out), scraping down sides and bottom of bowl as needed.

2   Transfer to 1-cup jar and let cool completely, about 20 minutes, before serving. (Peanut butter can be stored at room temperature for up to 2 months. Stir to incorporate any oil that has separated before serving.)

Chocolate Peanut Butter

Substitute ⅔ cup milk chocolate chips for ½ cup peanuts. Increase cooling time to 1 hour to allow peanut butter to thicken. If peanut butter is thinner than desired after cooling, thicken by stirring in water, 1 teaspoon at a time, until desired consistency is reached.

Chunky Peanut Butter

Reserve ½ cup peanuts. Process remaining 1½ cups peanuts with salt until smooth. Add reserved ½ cup peanuts and pulse until broken into ¼-inch pieces, 6 to 8 pulses.

Honey Peanut Butter

Process 3 tablespoons honey and 2 tablespoons peanut or vegetable oil with peanuts and salt.

Maple–Pumpkin Spice Peanut Butter

Process ¼ cup peanut or vegetable oil, 2 tablespoons maple syrup, and 1½ teaspoons pumpkin pie spice with peanuts and salt.

IN THE KNOW ABOUT NABS

Most Southerners know what a Nab is, even if they don't know that name. It's a regional distinction, most common in the Carolinas, for peanut butter sandwich crackers. Some people use the name to refer to any square sandwich crackers, while others reserve it for the best of the lot, the orange crackers stuffed with peanut butter.

The idea was originally developed in Charlotte, North Carolina, in 1915. Philip Lance was a food distributor working in the area, and due to a business snafu 500 pounds of peanuts were shipped to him. Not wanting to waste any, he roasted these peanuts at home and sold them by the bag around Charlotte. His wife, Mary, and their two daughters took the business up a notch and ground the peanuts into peanut butter, spread it on saltine crackers, and began selling the sandwiches in packages.

The business was called Lance Inc. It was primarily a candy company through World War II, but the crackers were so successful they shifted the business. Today, they sell a variety of sandwich crackers including ToastChee, the name by which their peanut butter crackers are known.

The name Nabs didn't come about until the late 1920s. Nabisco (the American snack company) saw how popular these peanut butter crackers were and opened a bakery selling a sleeve of sealed peanut butter snack crackers for five cents in 1924. They went on to shorten the name to Nab in 1928. With two products so similar in Charlotte, people adopted this shorter name to cover all of them.

by Morgan Bolling

Scuppernong Jelly

Makes two 1-cup jars ～ Total Time: 1 hour, plus 38 hours straining, cooling, and chilling

These special grapes are only seasonally available, and it's common to preserve them. The supersweet flesh and juice combined with the sour skin of scuppernongs makes for a beautifully flavored jelly, perfect for an elegant cheese board. Red muscadine or Concord grapes can be substituted for the scuppernong grapes. It is common for small tartrate crystals to form in grape juice; chilling the juice in step 3 encourages the crystals to grow, thus making it easier to strain them out. This jelly cannot be processed for long-term storage and should be stored in the refrigerator.

2	pounds scuppernong grapes, stemmed and washed
¾	cup water
1	cup sugar, divided
1	tablespoon Sure-Jell for Less or No Sugar Needed Recipes

1 Bring grapes and water to boil in large saucepan over medium-high heat. Reduce heat to medium, cover, and simmer, crushing grapes occasionally with potato masher, until grape pulp has started to soften and is separated from skins, 5 to 7 minutes.

2 Working in batches, strain mashed grapes through fine-mesh strainer into large bowl, pressing on solids to extract as much liquid as possible; discard solids. Clean strainer.

3 Moisten and wring dry triple layer of cheesecloth. Line now-empty strainer with prepared cheesecloth and set in separate bowl. Pour juice into strainer and let sit, without disturbing, for 1 hour. Cover juice and refrigerate for at least 24 hours or up to 48 hours. Discard solids left in cheesecloth and rinse cheesecloth well; set aside.

4 After refrigeratng juice, moisten and wring dry reserved cheesecloth. Line fine-mesh strainer with prepared cheesecloth and set in separate bowl. Strain juice again, then measure out 1¾ cups juice. (Reserve extra juice for another use; add water to juice as needed to equal 1¾ cups.)

5 Combine ¼ cup sugar and Sure-Jell in small bowl. Bring juice to boil in large saucepan over high heat. Whisk in Sure-Jell mixture and return to boil. Whisk in remaining ¾ cup sugar and bring to rolling boil. Once mixture is boiling and foam begins to climb toward top of saucepan, continue to cook, whisking constantly, for 1 minute. Off heat, skim any foam from surface using large spoon.

6 Place two 1-cup jars under hot running water until heated through, about 1 minute; shake dry. Using funnel and ladle, portion hot jelly into hot jars, leaving at least ¼ inch headspace. Remove any further foam from surface of jelly using teaspoon.

7 Let jelly cool completely, about 1 hour. Affix jar lid and refrigerate until jelly is set, about 12 hours. (Jelly can be refrigerated for up to 3 months.)

THE MOTHER VINE

North Carolina's state fruit, scuppernongs, are a type of juicy, superlatively sweet grape known for their golden-green skin, distinct aroma, and late-summer arrival. They're hard to find outside of warm summer months and are known to be a farmers' market delicacy when available.

The grapes are named after the Scuppernong River, near Albemarle Sound, where they were initially found growing in the wild before 17th-century cultivation. "Scuppernong" comes from the Algonquin word ascopa, the sweet bay tree indigenous to the Southeastern United States.

Scuppernongs are a type of muscadine, a broader term for red or golden sweet grapes found in the South. In Roanoke Island, North Carolina, there is a plant known by residents as the "Mother Vine" that at one point spanned almost an acre of land. It's thought that the Mother Vine gave birth to the first bronze muscadines, from which scuppernongs eventually evolved. In 1584, two explorers landing on the North Carolina coast wrote that the land was "so full of grapes as the very beating and surge of the seas overflowed them . . . in all the world, the like abundance is not to be found." Some believe that the Mother Vine was planted by the Croatan Indians or early settlers from England and that its vines are the same these explorers wrote about.

A more colorful piece of folklore ties the sweetness of the Mother Vine grapes to a woman named Virginia. The story goes that this very kind woman was put under a curse by a sorcerer whose love she rejected; he turned her into a white doe. Two men, one Virginia's true love and one a warrior, tracked down the deer. They reached her at the same time and both fired arrows—one magical arrow from her lover, shot in an attempt to save her from the curse, and the other arrow from the warrior (not knowing she was indeed a woman) shot to kill the prized deer. She died from that arrow and was buried in a spot in coastal North Carolina. A new vine with extraordinarily sweet but blood-red grapes sprouted near the pool where Virginia died.

Today the Mother Vine resides on a piece of land owned by a couple, Jack and Estelle Wilson. Over their nearly 70 years owning this land, they've had a changing relationship with the vine. At one point, they uprooted about half the vine that encompassed much of their property. But now, they take care of it. In a piece called, "The Keepers of the Mother Vine" for North Carolina's *Our State* magazine, Estelle says, "We might own the land … but the vine belongs to all people." This centuries-old vine is a still-living testament to the deep-rooted viticulture in the region, and a symbol of the enduring appeal of scuppernongs.

Scuppernong wine, a Southern delicacy, is made from these late-summer grape harvests; Harper Lee mentioned it in her 1960 masterpiece, *To Kill a Mockingbird*. Dublin Winery in North Carolina makes Mothervine Wine using grapes harvested off clippings replanted from this old vine. Beyond wine, scuppernongs are used to create jellies, jams, and preserves and have a devout following during their limited growing season.

by Morgan Bolling

Dandelion Jelly

Makes two 1-cup jars
Total Time: 1 hour, plus 13 hours cooling and chilling

Dandelions are not often considered for cooking, but some know that these weeds are a culinary gem. Older recipes (and home remedies) abound: You can sauté dandelion greens, steep the flowers in tea, use them to make wine, or cook them with sugar before setting the mixture with pectin to make a golden jelly that has a floral flavor, not far from honey.

This jelly is delicious smeared on pancakes or biscuits, or served with cheese. While fresh petals are often used for this recipe, they are highly seasonal and can be hard to source naturally. So we developed this recipe with dried dandelion flowers. Lemon juice and zest make the dandelion flavor pop. Food-safe dried dandelion flowers can be purchased at specialty tea shops, health stores, or online. Dried dandelion flowers can include both green parts, white fuzzy parts, and the yellow petals. All of these can be used to steep the dandelion liquid. This jelly cannot be processed for long-term storage and should be stored in the refrigerator.

¼ cup dried dandelion flowers

1 (2-inch) strip lemon zest plus
1 teaspoon juice

1½ cups boiling water

1 cup sugar, divided

5 teaspoons Sure-Jell for Less or
No Sugar Needed Recipes

1 Steep dandelion flowers and lemon zest in boiling water in bowl for 10 minutes. Strain infusion through fine-mesh strainer into small saucepan, pressing on solids to extract as much liquid as possible; discard solids.

2 Combine ¼ cup sugar and Sure-Jell in small bowl. Bring dandelion infusion to boil over medium-high heat. Whisk in Sure-Jell mixture and return to boil. Whisk in lemon juice and remaining ¾ cup sugar and bring to rolling boil. Once mixture is boiling and foam begins to climb toward top of saucepan, continue to cook, whisking constantly, for 1 minute. Off heat, skim any foam from surface of jelly using large spoon.

3 Place two 1-cup jars under hot running water until heated through, about 1 minute; shake dry. Using funnel and ladle, portion hot jelly into hot jars, leaving at least ¼ inch headspace. Remove any further foam from surface of jelly using teaspoon.

4 Let jelly cool completely, about 1 hour. Affix jar lid and refrigerate until jelly is set, about 12 hours. (Jelly can be refrigerated for up to 3 months.)

SOUTHERN FOLK HERBALISM

While folk medicines vary across the globe, the tradition in the Southern United States relies on a combination of indigenous plants (including American ginseng, goldenrod, and echinacea) and domesticated herbs (such as mint, yarrow, elderflower, and licorice) used together with an assemblage of methods. In the article "A History of Southern and Appalachian Folk Medicine" in the *Journal of the American Herbalists Guild*, Southern herbalist Phyllis D. Light describes how "Old World" European humoral medicine and reliance on ritual "joined with Native American herbal practices to form the unmistakable foundations of Southern Folk Medicine." Light began her own studies with her Creek/Cherokee grandmother and Appalachian elders and founded and directs the Appalachian Center for Natural Health.

Another major influence on Southern herbalism came with the slave trade, as enslaved Africans carried the oral traditions of their various herbal practices with them on their perilous journeys from North and West Africa. Later waves of Irish and Scots-Irish immigrants lent additional layers to the cultural melting pot that evolved into what is known as Southern Folk Herbalism today.

While men and women practice various types of herbalism, historically, women were the "pharmacists, cultivating healing herbs and exchanging secrets of their uses," argues scholars Barbara Ehrenreich and Deirdre English in their book *Witches, Midwives and Nurses: A History of Women Healers*. For many generations, the rural South—and especially southern Appalachia—was cut off from doctors' offices. Local herbalists, sometimes known as granny women or granny witches, were indispensable in these remote communities.

Cultural connection was crucial for the health of marginalized communities, especially Black Southerners. According to Leah Penniman, agricultural educator and author of *Farming While Black: Soul Fire Farm's Practical Guide to Liberation on the Land*, "By the mid-18th century, both Virginia and South Carolina made it a capital offense for enslaved people to teach or learn about herbal medicine and prohibited us from working in apothecaries." While more renowned for her abolitionist work, Harriet Tubman was also notable for her use of herbalism for food and medicine. Emma Dupree, born in Pitt County, North Carolina, in 1897, was the daughter of formerly enslaved parents and was known as "that little medicine thing" for her "garden-grown pharmacy."

Today, Southerners continue to practice folk herbalism, also sometimes called root work and kitchen witchery. This includes the BIPOC collective Harriet's Apothecary, which offers educational resources for community healing. Southern folk herbalist Lauren Haynes, based in Chattanooga, Tennessee, first started her company, Wooden Spoon Herbs, at a farmers' market. Her products are now available at Whole Foods Markets across the nation. And Gullah chef Sallie Ann Robinson prioritizes the use of herbs and folk plants in her traditional cooking. Her cookbook *Cooking the Gullah Way, Morning, Noon, and Night* includes an entire chapter on "Gullah Folk Beliefs and Home Remedies," highlighting the ways that food and medicine can be one and the same.

by KC Hysmith

No.12

EVERYDAY TREATS

Left to right: Stuffed Red Velvet Cookies (page 408), Pralines (page 404), Peach Dumplings (page 383), food activist Georgia Gilmore (see page 419), Rich Vanilla Ice Cream (page 396).

ON OUR OWN TERMS

HOW COTTAGE BAKERS HAVE RECLAIMED AND TRANSFORMED THE DOMESTIC SPACE

Grace Garay sets her alarm anywhere between midnight and 2 a.m. That's when she rises to bake for customers who will line up in front of her Orlando home on Saturday to pick up their much-anticipated pastry orders from Nomad Bakehouse. Garay lives in the periwinkle-colored house with her mother, Miriam Zaldivar McCullough, and operates Nomad, her cottage baking business, from the same address. In a typical weekend, Nomad Bakehouse produces 450–500 pastries and 80 loaves of naturally leavened sourdough bread from the micro-bakery space. By morning, Garay has filled speed racks with delectables made with whole-grain flours and local produce, flaky layers of laminated pastry, tall biscuits, golden brioche buns, and cookies the size of your head.

Garay is a first-generation American with Puerto Rican and Honduran roots. Her mother came to the United States in the 1980s, traversing Mexico in search of a better life. Common to the immigrant experience, Garay's mother worked tirelessly to provide for her family without the luxury of choosing her own path. She simply worked. That ethic suffused Garay's mindset with an ideal she's carried into her own life.

"We're women and we're capable of doing anything we need to do," she says. On visits to Honduras, Garay saw women setting makeshift tables on their patios and calling it a restaurant, rolling up their sleeves to get the work done while creating community, a natural extension of Honduran culture. Though Garay was classically trained with years of experience in high-volume bakeries, restaurants, and hotels all around the United States (hence, the nomad in Nomad Bakehouse), the industry wore on her. Its people and systems amounted to abusive work environments, thankless long hours, and a bottom line focus that lodged in her work-weary body. She sought a better way. Inspired by a connection to whole-grain flours and spurred by necessity, Garay carved a new path.

"Cottage allows you to build something entirely different," she says. In its earliest references, cottage referred to "a variety of commercial activity or trade, which is carried out partly or wholly in people's homes."

From the Nomad website: "When the Covid Pandemic threatened our food supply, I was presented with the opportunity to feed my community on my own terms and from within my own home, with ingredients I respected."

* * * * * *

In Atlanta, Georgia, the line for Osono Bread snakes across the concrete lot minutes after the Grant Park Farmers Market's opening bell. Beneath the market tent are Betsy Gonzales and her sister, Taylor Gonzales, displaying wooden planks lined with loaves of naturally leavened bread—Pullman loaves and multigrain loaves, milk bread and oat porridge boules. In the pastry case are cardamom buns and crumb cakes and Osono's legendary brioche doughnuts in flavors such as ube, crème brûlée, pistachio, and horchata.

Betsy Gonzales is a first-generation American. Her mother, Eldi, emigrated from Guatemala in the 1980s, a single mother to two young girls. Gonzales attributes her entrepreneurial spirit to her mother, having witnessed the importance of autonomy and independence from a young age. "When you are a first generation child, you know what your parents are doing, and the sacrifices they make," says Gonzales.

When baking came to the fore, Gonzales couldn't afford the traditional culinary route, something not uncommon for women of color, who often face barriers to launching businesses and equitable access to economic opportunity. Gonzales, instead of going through formal schooling, took a job at Little Tart Bakeshop in Atlanta before creating her own immersion program: Using the powers of Instagram, she reached out to bakers in Europe and asked if she could travel to learn from them. What she found in Europe were small teams of one to three people producing high-quality, naturally leavened bread and pastries at scale. She returned home ready to bake, planting the seeds of Osono from her home oven while working her Little Tart bakery job. Slowly, she outfitted her home with professional equipment. By 2018, she developed a bread subscription service. A year later, she established a relationship with local farmer Brent Hall of Freewheel Farm to sell directly to consumers, and in 2020, when she was furloughed from her job due to the COVID-19 pandemic, Osono Bread launched into markets full-time, garnering press and accolades across city papers and beyond.

For Gonzales, cottage baking fosters introspection: What values matter to me? How can I share with my community? More than that, the bakery is a space to reclaim her power and autonomy as a brown, queer woman: "My experience has always been something I have to prove. Engaging in this model has allowed me to play in this space. I do everything a typical baker does, I'm just not zoned commercial. As a first-generation American, why wouldn't I want to do this?"

* * * * * *

Across the long arc of history are the twin threads of nourishment and survival woven together by women's work in the kitchen. For centuries, the domestic space, and the food and care work performed there, was the heart of a woman's world, and a place that was historically invisible and devalued, even as it sustained whole villages and fueled political movements.

For immigrant women, this space is a means of survival and resourcefulness when economic and social barriers muddy the prescribed path. So many find a way, whether it's making injera from home, selling tamales out of the back of a truck, or dishing out plates from the garage or backyard; the list goes on, and it is work women have been doing ever since the first fire was stoked.

In cottage bakeries all over the South, bakers are changing the paradigm of what it means to work from home, bringing the artisanal into the domestic space, bucking industry norms, and reclaiming their power and connection to local food systems. If ever there was a space worth reimagining, the kitchen is it.

by Keia Mastrianni

writer, cookbook author, baker, and photographer based in western North Carolina

Peach Cobbler

Serves 8   ~   Total Time: 1¾ hours, plus 30 minutes cooling

Peach cobbler is the epitome of summer desserts, with peaches that bubble to sticky sweetness under a baked topping. The first published mention of cobbler (at the time spelled "cobler") was likely in 1839, in Lettice Bryan's *The Kentucky Housewife*. According to Bryan, "A peach pot-pie, or cobler as it is often termed, should be made of clingstone peaches, that are very ripe, and then pared and sliced from the stones." She finished the recipe with, "Eat it warm or cold. Although it is not a fashionable pie for company, it is very excellent for family use, with cold sweet milk."

In more recent times, in 2015, the Louisiana Legislature issued a resolution that recognized the state's "official meal." The meal, the resolution says, is based on the "proud cuisines birthed from the mix of ethnic heritages and identities" of North Louisiana. The menu was created by private chef Hardette Harris. Peach cobbler made the list. It is a timeless dessert.

Our homey version calls for baking the peaches first; when the dough is added, the now-hot peaches cook the buttermilk biscuits from the bottom, so the topping isn't too doughy. Adding lemon juice brightens the peach flavor, and using a relatively low amount of sugar compared to other recipes allows the fruitiness to shine. Brushing the biscuits with melted butter as soon as they come out of the oven adds extra richness and a light crunch.

Look for the best peaches you can find. In a pinch you can substitute 2½ pounds of thawed and drained frozen peaches for fresh; if the peaches are still cold when you assemble the filling, you may have to increase the baking time in step 3 to 40 minutes.

Biscuit Topping

1½	cups (7½ ounces) all-purpose flour
5	teaspoons sugar, divided
1½	teaspoons baking powder
½	teaspoon baking soda
½	teaspoon table salt
¾	cup buttermilk
6	tablespoons unsalted butter, melted, plus 1 tablespoon unsalted butter

Filling

¾	cup (5¼ ounces) sugar
1	tablespoon cornstarch
	Pinch table salt
3	pounds peaches, peeled, halved, pitted, and cut into ½-inch-thick wedges
1	tablespoon lemon juice

1   Adjust oven rack to middle position and heat oven to 375 degrees. Line rimmed baking sheet with parchment paper.

2   **For the biscuit topping** Whisk flour, 1 tablespoon sugar, baking powder, baking soda, and salt together in large bowl; set aside. Stir buttermilk and melted butter together in 2-cup liquid measuring cup (butter will clump; this is OK); set aside.

3   **For the filling** Combine sugar, cornstarch, and salt in large bowl. Add peaches and lemon juice and mix gently with rubber spatula to combine. Transfer peach mixture to 8-inch square baking pan or dish. Place pan on prepared sheet and bake until filling is hot and starting to bubble around edges, about 30 minutes. Transfer sheet to wire rack and gently stir peach mixture. Increase oven temperature to 475 degrees.

4   Once oven reaches 475 degrees, add buttermilk mixture to flour mixture and stir with rubber spatula until just incorporated. Using greased ¼-cup dry measuring cup, drop 9 scant scoops of dough, evenly spaced, onto hot peach filling. Sprinkle tops with remaining 2 teaspoons sugar.

5   Bake until biscuits are golden brown and toothpick inserted in center biscuit comes out clean, 12 to 14 minutes. Melt remaining 1 tablespoon butter and brush over biscuits. Let cobbler cool on wire rack for at least 30 minutes before serving.

WELCOME HOME COBBLER

In the aftermath of World War II, as troops began demobilizing in 1945 and 1946, millions of men and 350,000 women were returning home to the United States. And families welcomed them with heartfelt meals. In *The American Plate: A Culinary History in 100 Bites*, author Libby H. O'Connell says, "Generally, mothers, wives, and other women prepared the new veterans' favorite dishes, as at-home food preparation was even more gender-based than it is today." Even though rationing was in effect for more than a year after the war ended, these women found ways to make the meals comforting and representative of the food from the veteran's culinary heritage, O'Connell explains. Such feasts spanned across ethnic and racial lines.

by Morgan Bolling

A GLOSSARY OF FRUIT DESSERTS

Dessert is usually not optional in the South, so having something sweet—and not necessarily fussy—after lunch or dinner or in between is customary. In the hot summer months, tossing juicy, ripe local fruit in a casserole with a topping and baking is commonplace. Fruit desserts are fancy-free affairs but overloaded with appeal. The next best thing to the taste of a crumble, grunt, or sonker is its quirky moniker, which can change depending on where you are in the South. Each of these desserts has a sweetened topping that can be anything from a pastry or biscuit dough to a pancake-like batter to a streusel. And with such nuanced differences, no one can seem to agree on what to call them. One cook's cobbler is another cook's buckle.

Here's a handful of our favorite fruit desserts and their characteristics as we have defined them over the years.

Betty: Sweetened fruit baked with layers of bread crumbs and butter.

Buckle: Thick cake batter poured over fruit. Buckle sometimes resembles a streusel-topped coffee cake.

Cobbler: Biscuit dough dolloped over fruit to resemble cobblestones. But step lightly when using the name. On some places, a cobbler can be topped with batter; it can be a rectangular, double-crust fruit pie; or it can be the same as a Betty.

Crisp/Crumble: Fruit baked under a crunchy, streusel-like topping. Crisps often contain oats; crumbles are often oat-free.

Pandowdy: Fruit with pie dough or bread pressed into it as it bakes.

Sonker: Syrupy cooked fruit baked under a pancake batter.

Simple Blueberry Cobbler

Serves 8 to 10   ~   Total Time: 1 hour

We've found recipes referring to this style of cobbler—which features a pancake-like batter swaddling a hefty amount of fruit—as "Texas-style," but recipes for cobbler from Texas are as diverse as the people in that state. This version isn't layered: The whole thing becomes a dense, sweet, cakey cobbler that you can get into the oven in minutes. It's an anytime dessert, when blueberries are around.

For middle-of-the-week ease, we minimize the ingredient list (self-rising flour for flour and leavener, and sweetened condensed milk for liquid and sugar). A final sprinkling of sugar gives the finished cobbler a gorgeous browned crust. Serve with vanilla ice cream.

1	(14-ounce) can sweetened condensed milk	8	tablespoons unsalted butter, melted
1¼	cups (6 ounces) self-rising flour	10	ounces (2 cups) blueberries
½	cup whole milk	¼	cup (1¾ ounces) sugar

1   Adjust oven rack to middle position and heat oven to 350 degrees. Grease 13 by 9-inch baking dish. Whisk condensed milk, flour, milk, and melted butter together in bowl. Pour batter into prepared baking dish. Sprinkle blueberries and sugar evenly over surface.

2   Bake until deep golden brown and toothpick inserted in center comes out clean, about 35 minutes. Transfer cobbler to wire rack; let cool for 10 minutes. Serve warm.

Peach Dumplings

Serves 6 to 8 ~ Total Time: 2¼ hours

You may know apple dumplings as almost-whole fruit steaming within a dumpling wrapper of buttery pastry. Old-fashioned peach dumplings in the South are kind of like this and kind of like peach cobbler. They're made by wrapping peach halves or slices in pastry dough and baking or boiling the dumplings in a sweetened syrup. Many recipes tucked in community cookbooks (or online) call for using store-bought crescent dough and lemon-lime soda as a makeshift syrup. These tricks nod to cooks' ingenuity in using convenience products when they became mainstream.

For a version that comes together almost as quickly, this recipe starts with two large ripe peaches cut into wedges (frozen sliced peaches work just as well). The dough is meant to be more fluffy than flaky; baking powder gives it lightness and keeps the dumpling fluffy even after simmering in a sweet sauce. Blending a couple of peach slices and ½ cup of concentrated peach preserves into the sauce amplifies the flavors and makes it thicker and more luscious. We developed this recipe using a metal baking pan. If using a glass or ceramic baking dish, increase the baking time by 10 minutes in step 6. Serve with vanilla ice cream or whipped cream, if desired.

Dough

1½ cups (7½ ounces) all-purpose flour
1 tablespoon sugar
2 teaspoons baking powder
¾ teaspoon table salt
½ cup whole milk
2 tablespoons unsalted butter, melted

Peaches and Sauce

2 large fresh peaches, peeled, halved, pitted, and each half cut into 4 equal wedges, or 10 ounces frozen sliced peaches, divided
¾ cup water
6 tablespoons unsalted butter, cut into 6 pieces
⅓ cup (2⅓ ounces) plus 1 teaspoon sugar, divided
Pinch table salt
½ cup peach preserves
1 tablespoon lemon juice
¼ teaspoon ground cinnamon

1 **For the dough** Adjust oven rack to middle position and heat oven to 350 degrees. Combine flour, sugar, baking powder, and salt in large bowl. Combine milk and melted butter in second bowl (butter may form clumps). Using rubber spatula, stir milk mixture into flour mixture until just incorporated. Turn dough onto lightly floured counter and knead until no streaks of flour remain, about 1 minute. Return dough to large bowl, cover with plastic wrap, and set aside.

2 **For the peaches and sauce** Set aside 12 peach slices. (If using frozen peaches, select 12 largest slices and return to freezer until ready to use.)

3 Combine water, butter, ⅓ cup sugar, salt, and remaining 4 peach slices in medium saucepan. Bring to simmer over medium-high heat and cook, stirring occasionally, until butter is melted and sugar is dissolved (and frozen peaches are thawed). Remove from heat and let cool for 5 minutes. Transfer peach mixture to blender, add peach preserves and lemon juice, and process until smooth, about 30 seconds. Set aside peach sauce.

4 Roll dough into 12-inch square, about ⅛ inch thick. Using pizza cutter or chef's knife, trim away and discard outer ½-inch edges of dough to make neat square. Cut dough in half. Working with 1 dough half at a time, cut crosswise into 3 equal rectangles, then cut each rectangle diagonally to create triangles. Repeat with second dough half. (You should have 12 triangles.)

5 Working with 1 dough triangle at a time, place 1 reserved peach slice on wide end of triangle. Roll dough around peach slice and transfer dumpling, seam side down, to 8-inch square baking pan. Repeat with remaining dough triangles and peach slices, staggering dumplings in 3 rows of 4 (dumplings will touch; this is OK).

6 Pour peach sauce over dumplings in pan. Combine cinnamon and remaining 1 teaspoon sugar in small bowl. Sprinkle dumplings with cinnamon sugar. Bake until dumplings are golden on top and syrup is bubbling in center of pan, about 45 minutes. Let cool for 10 minutes before serving.

Apple Pandowdy

Serves 6 ~ Total Time: 1¾ hours,
plus 1 hour 50 minutes chilling and cooling

Right after World War II, Americans needed a dose of sugar—and singer Dinah Shore gave it to them. Her inescapable "Shoo-Fly Pie and Apple Pan Dowdy" was a top-10 hit in 1946, inspiring covers from Guy Lombardo and Ella Fitzgerald. Shore was hardly alone in singing about food: Eileen Barton crooned "If I Knew You Were Comin' I'd've Baked a Cake," and Doris Day served up "Tacos, Enchiladas, and Beans."

Dinah Shore (née Frances "Fanny" Rose Shore) was born in Winchester, Tennessee, to Russian Jewish shop-keepers Anna (Stein) and Solomon Shore. She stayed in Tennessee until after she graduated from Vanderbilt University.

Shore's hit presaged more than just decades of musical success—she became a celebrated cook, too, with influences from her Southern roots and her immigrant parents. Dinner at Shore's Beverly Hills home was among the most coveted invitations in town, inspiring celebrity cooking segments with Frank Sinatra and Ann-Margret on her 1970s talk show, *Dinah's Place*, and three best-selling cookbooks—including, of course, *Someone's in the Kitchen with Dinah*.

While apple pandowdy is typically considered a Northern dessert, we wanted to include a recipe in honor of Shore (and also because it's delicious). Pandowdy is similar to skillet apple pie, except that during baking the crust is pressed or slashed so the juices from the filling flood over the top and caramelize as the dessert continues to bake. Yes, you purposely mess up the top, leaving a dowdy-looking result. To avoid smothered, mushy apples from pressing into the crust, we cut the all-butter dough (with a little sour cream for a slight tang) into squares and casually arrange them to overlap on top. The partial coverage promotes ventilation, allowing the apples to keep their shape and not overcook. Do not use store-bought pie crust in this recipe; it yields gummy results.

Dinah Shore leading a public cooking demonstration in 1983.

Bob Riha Jr. / Getty Images

Pie Dough

- 3 tablespoons ice water
- 1 tablespoon sour cream
- ⅔ cup (3⅓ ounces) all-purpose flour
- 1 teaspoon granulated sugar
- ½ teaspoon table salt
- 6 tablespoons unsalted butter, cut into ¼-inch pieces and frozen for 15 minutes

Filling

- 2½ pounds Golden Delicious apples, peeled, cored, halved, and cut into ½-inch-thick wedges
- ¼ cup packed (1¾ ounces) light brown sugar
- ½ teaspoon ground cinnamon
- ¼ teaspoon table salt
- 3 tablespoons unsalted butter
- ¾ cup apple cider
- 1 tablespoon cornstarch
- 2 teaspoons lemon juice

Topping

- 1 tablespoon granulated sugar
- ¼ teaspoon ground cinnamon
- 1 large egg, lightly beaten
  Vanilla ice cream

1 **For the pie dough** Combine ice water and sour cream in bowl. Process flour, sugar, and salt in food processor until combined, about 3 seconds. Add butter and pulse until size of large peas, 6 to 8 pulses. Add sour cream mixture and pulse until dough forms large clumps and no dry flour remains, 3 to 6 pulses, scraping down sides of bowl as needed.

2 Form dough into 4-inch disk, wrap tightly in plastic wrap, and refrigerate for 1 hour. (Wrapped dough can be refrigerated for up to 2 days or frozen for up to 1 month. If frozen, let dough thaw completely on counter before rolling.)

3 Adjust oven rack to middle position and heat oven to 400 degrees. Line rimmed baking sheet with parchment paper. Let chilled dough sit on counter to soften slightly, about 5 minutes, before rolling. Roll dough into 10-inch circle on lightly floured counter. Using pizza cutter, cut dough into four 2½-inch-wide strips, then make four 2½-inch-wide perpendicular cuts to form squares. (Pieces around edges of dough will be smaller.) Transfer dough pieces to prepared sheet, cover with plastic, and refrigerate until firm, at least 30 minutes.

4 **For the filling** Toss apples, sugar, cinnamon, and salt together in large bowl. Melt butter in 10-inch ovensafe skillet over medium heat. Add apple mixture, cover, and cook until apples become slightly pliable and release their juice, about 10 minutes, stirring occasionally.

5 Whisk cider, cornstarch, and lemon juice in bowl until no lumps remain; add to skillet. Bring to simmer and cook, uncovered, stirring occasionally, until sauce is thickened, about 2 minutes. Off heat, press lightly on apples to form even layer.

6 **For the topping** Combine sugar and cinnamon in small bowl. Working quickly, shingle dough pieces over filling until mostly covered, overlapping as needed. Brush dough pieces with egg and sprinkle with cinnamon sugar.

7 Bake until crust is slightly puffed and beginning to brown, about 15 minutes. Remove skillet from oven. Using back of large spoon, press down in center of crust until juices come up over top of crust. Repeat four more times around skillet. Make sure all apples are submerged and return skillet to oven. Continue to bake until crust is golden brown, about 15 minutes longer.

8 Transfer skillet to wire rack and let cool for at least 20 minutes. Serve with ice cream, drizzling extra sauce over top.

Strawberry Sonker

Serves 6 ~ Total Time: 2 hours

Not quite a pie and not quite a cobbler, sonker is a juicy, fruit-filled, deep-dish dessert rarely found outside Surry County, North Carolina. In fact, it's almost exclusively baked in the town of Mount Airy, which sits in the shadows of the Blue Ridge Mountains. Historically, a pan of sonker was made to gather local produce (ranging from wild blackberries to backyard peaches to sweet potatoes) into a deep, shareable dish—a type of bread pan that was some 3-4 inches deep, and is "unknown in modern kitchens," Beth Tartan explains in *North Carolina and Old Salem Cookery*. It was large enough to feed a farmful of workers and transportable enough to bring to church supper. Beyond those details, it's hard to pin down what a sonker really is. Food journalist Kim Severson (see page 423) emphasizes in her article "Sonkers, Grunts, Slumps and Crumbles" for the *New York Times*, "The dessert is baked nowhere else in the nation. But … as with so many country recipes, definitive answers are as elusive as that white whale."

There's a hazy separation between pies, cobblers, Bettys, and crisps (see page 382), and a sonker is simultaneously akin to all of these fruity topped desserts. Some say a sonker is deeper than a cobbler and juicier, or that the topping is more like a pancake than a biscuit. Others say that serving sonker with a sugary gravy or dip (made of sugar, water, and cornstarch) keeps it in its own lane. This unique dessert is celebrated at the annual Mount Airy Sonker Festival, where bluegrass music, flat-foot dancing, and a host of sonkers reign over the region for one autumn afternoon.

For our version, we were intrigued by the "lazy" sonker, a subset of the dessert in which the fruit is cooked into a sweet stew and topped with a pancake batter that bakes into a distinct, lightly crisp layer of cake. Stewing the fruit (in this case strawberries, blueberries, or peaches) directly in a baking dish reduces them to create a level surface to hold a light batter. How does the batter stay on top of the fruit? Using extra melted butter in place of some of the milk helps keep the batter in a flat layer, similar to the way oil rises above vinegar in a dressing.

You can use frozen strawberries in this recipe, there's no need to let them thaw. In steps 2 and 3, be sure to stir the strawberry filling as directed, scraping the bottom of the dish to incorporate the cornstarch so that it evenly and thoroughly thickens the mixture. In step 3, add the butter to the batter while it is still hot so it remains pourable, and be sure to mix the batter only right before pouring it over the filling.

2	pounds fresh strawberries, hulled (6½ cups)
1	cup (7 ounces) sugar, divided
½	teaspoon table salt, divided
¼	cup water
3	tablespoons cornstarch
1	cup (5 ounces) all-purpose flour
1	teaspoon baking powder
½	cup whole milk
8	tablespoons unsalted butter, melted and hot
¼	teaspoon vanilla extract

1   Adjust oven rack to middle position and heat oven to 350 degrees. Line rimmed baking sheet with parchment paper. Combine strawberries, ¼ cup sugar, and ¼ teaspoon salt in bowl. Whisk water and cornstarch together in second bowl; add to strawberry mixture and toss until strawberries are evenly coated.

2   Transfer strawberry mixture to 8-inch square baking dish and place dish on prepared sheet. Bake until filling is bubbling around sides of dish, 35 to 40 minutes, stirring and scraping bottom of dish with rubber spatula halfway through baking.

3   Remove sheet from oven and stir filling, being sure to scrape bottom and corners of dish with rubber spatula. Whisk flour, baking powder, remaining ¾ cup sugar, and remaining ¼ teaspoon salt together in bowl. Whisk in milk, hot melted butter, and vanilla until smooth. Pour batter evenly over filling.

4   Bake until surface is golden brown and toothpick inserted in center comes out with no crumbs attached, 35 to 40 minutes, rotating dish halfway through baking. Let sonker cool on wire rack for 15 minutes. Serve.

Blueberry Sonker

Substitute 2 pounds (6½ cups) fresh blueberries for strawberries.

Peach Sonker

Substitute 2½ pounds peaches, peeled, halved, pitted, and cut into ½-inch-thick wedges, for strawberries.

FLOUR RATIONS AND RIOT

During the American Civil War, both the Union and the Confederacy were faced with food rations, especially on staples such as meat, coffee, flour, and sugar. By the mid-1860s, food prices in the South had inflated to nearly ten times higher than they were at the beginning of the war. As a result, wealthy individuals and merchants hoarded basic food-stuff, cutting off access to the poorest classes and limiting it for many others. In response to these oppressive conditions, large groups of mostly white Southern women organized protests in order to regain access to food.

One of the largest and most destructive of these protests was the Richmond Bread Riot, which occurred in the Confederate capital of Richmond, Virginia, on April 2, 1863. A group of 5,000 people, made up of workers from the Confederate ordnance establishment (munitions factories) and wives of local ironworks laborers, gathered to discuss food shortages and resolved to seek a peaceful meeting with the governor. Denied a meeting, the women looted shops in protest. The Richmond Bread Riot became infamous for the involvement of the president of the Confederacy, Jefferson Davis, who spoke to the crowd before they dispersed with their seized bread. The women continued to protest but were threatened with violence by the City Battalion. News reports of the riot further complicated the situation by casting pro-testers as lower-class citizens or even relocated "Yankees" who were not actually starving. These divisions only served to deepen the fractures between the classes throughout the American South, hastening the defeat of the Confederacy.

Protests were held throughout the South. In March 1863, dozens of soldiers' wives gathered to protest the price of flour in Salisbury, North Carolina. They went directly to store owners' homes and businesses and demanded lower prices; when denied, they threatened to take the flour by force. Later in September, after the U.S. Navy blockaded Mobile Bay, Alabama, women marched against scarce and expensive food supplies. Smaller but still powerful riots occurred in several cities in Georgia. While these protests did not change the outcome of the war, they were important opportunities for women's agency in Southern food history.

by KC Hysmith

Strawberry Cornmeal Shortcakes

Serves 8   ~   Total Time: 1¼ hours

The English put the "short" (a word that describes the crumbly quality of fat-enriched doughs) in the name shortcake, but the fruit-and-pastry dessert is all-American. According to the article "The Long and Short of the Classic Shortcake" in the *Chicago Tribune*, fruit shortcakes were all the rage in the 1800s, featuring such fruits as bananas and raspberries in addition to the still-beloved strawberries.

But it's possible that shortcakes' origins are much older. According to Maria Zizka's story and recipe for PBS, "Local and Seasonal: Strawberry Shortcake," Native Americans mashed strawberries with cornmeal and cooked them into a cake that may have later evolved into strawberry shortcakes. That said, the first known published recipe for something similar to what we think of as strawberry shortcakes today was found in 1847 in Philadelphia cookbook *Miss Leslie's Lady's New Receipt-Book*—crisp round cakes, split and stuffed with icing and strawberries. It wasn't long until Southern cookbooks started including them. Tennessee-born Malinda Russell published a recipe in her 1866 cookbook *A Domestic Cook Book*, the first known U.S. cookbook published by a Black woman. Her recipe is as short as the cakes: She makes cream biscuits, fills the warm biscuits with crushed berries stirred "thick with white sugar," and pours sweet cream over them.

The simple recipe's versatility has made it a canvas for modern chefs. Chef Vivian Howard (see page 206) makes a version of strawberry shortcake with basil whipped cream tucked between coconut cornbread cakes on her PBS Show *A Chef's Life*. James Beard Award–nominated author Jerrelle Guy offers a version with the timeless Italian combination of strawberries and balsamic vinegar on an olive oil biscuit in her book, *Black Girl Baking: Wholesome Recipes Inspired by a Soulful Upbringing*. And Maria Zizka's version incorporates a touch of rose water.

Our recipe brings cornmeal back into the picture. Cornmeal in the biscuits adds a sweet, nutty flavor and a delicate crunch that offsets the tender berries and plush cream filling. Tossing sliced strawberries with sugar and letting them sit releases their juice for a sweet syrup to soak into the biscuits. Because the sweetness level of strawberries can vary, taste the berries and add up to 2 tablespoons of extra sugar if needed. While the shortcakes are best served warm, the cooled cakes can be stored in a zipper-lock bag at room temperature for 24 hours. They will lose some of their crispness, but you can bring it back by warming the biscuits in a 300-degree oven for 10 minutes. If you'd like to follow Howard's or Guy's lead, you can sprinkle in some coconut or drizzle the berries with balsamic glaze.

Strawberries

- 2 pounds strawberries, hulled and sliced thin (5 cups)
- ¼ cup (1¾ ounces) sugar, plus extra as needed
- 2 teaspoons lemon juice
- ⅛ teaspoon table salt

Shortcakes

- 1½ cups (7½ ounces) all-purpose flour
- ½ cup (2½ ounces) stone-ground cornmeal
- ¼ cup (1¾ ounces) plus 1 tablespoon sugar, divided
- 2 teaspoons baking powder
- ½ teaspoon baking soda
- ¾ teaspoon table salt
- ⅔ cup buttermilk, chilled
- 1 large egg
- 8 tablespoons unsalted butter, melted and cooled

Whipped Cream

- 1½ cups heavy cream, chilled
- 4 teaspoons sugar
- 1 teaspoon vanilla extract

1 **For the strawberries** Gently toss all ingredients together in bowl and refrigerate for at least 30 minutes or up to 1 hour. Taste strawberry mixture for sweetness and add extra sugar if needed.

2 **For the shortcakes** Meanwhile, adjust oven rack to middle position and heat oven to 425 degrees. Line rimmed baking sheet with parchment paper. Whisk flour, cornmeal, ¼ cup sugar, baking powder, baking soda, and salt together in large bowl. Whisk buttermilk and egg in separate bowl until combined; add melted butter and stir until butter forms clumps.

3 Add buttermilk mixture to flour mixture and stir with rubber spatula until just incorporated. Lightly spray ⅓-cup dry measuring cup with vegetable oil spray. Stagger 8 level portions of batter on prepared sheet, about 1½ inches apart. Sprinkle tops with remaining 1 tablespoon sugar. Bake until shortcakes are golden brown, about 14 minutes, rotating sheet halfway through baking. Transfer shortcakes to wire rack and let cool for at least 10 minutes.

4 **For the whipped cream** Using stand mixer fitted with whisk attachment, whip cream, sugar, and vanilla on medium-low speed until foamy, about 1 minute. Increase speed to high and whip until stiff peaks form, 1 to 3 minutes.

5 Split each shortcake in half horizontally. Spoon ½ cup strawberry mixture over each shortcake bottom, followed by ⅓ cup whipped cream; top with shortcake tops. Serve, passing any remaining whipped cream separately.

Chocolate Éclair Cake

Serves 15 ~ Total Time: 1 hour, plus 8 hours chilling

Despite its name, chocolate éclair cake is neither an outsize éclair nor a baked cake; it more closely resembles an easy classic icebox cake. Cookies are layered with a creamy filling; they rest in the refrigerator until the cookies absorb the moisture from the filling and transform into a sliceable, cake-like layer. Recipes for icebox cakes started showing up in the 1920s and '30s with the advent of the modern-day refrigerator. The most famous recipe involved Nabisco chocolate wafers, and the company printed the recipe on the back of the wafer boxes. This version layers the cookies (usually graham crackers) with pudding; after it's slicked with a ganache-like topping, it tastes like a fancy éclair.

Recipes in community cookbooks mention that this dessert is ideal for a tailgate, barbecue, or church supper, or even as a quick birthday cake. Most of them call for making the creamy mixture with pudding mix and Cool Whip (essentially a double for Bavarian cream, an elegant filling made from folding stabilized whipped cream into an egg-based custard) and topping the cake with canned chocolate frosting. And while we love the Southern classic (see "Baking with Love"), here we offer a version with a simple homemade pudding and chocolate ganache. Six ounces of finely chopped semisweet chocolate can be used in place of the chips.

1¼	cups (8¾ ounces) sugar
6	tablespoons cornstarch
1	teaspoon table salt
5	cups whole milk
4	tablespoons unsalted butter, cut into 4 pieces
5	teaspoons vanilla extract
1¼	teaspoons unflavored gelatin
2	tablespoons water
2¾	cups heavy cream, chilled, divided
14	ounces graham crackers
1	cup (6 ounces) semisweet chocolate chips
5	tablespoons light corn syrup

1 Combine sugar, cornstarch, and salt in large saucepan. Whisk milk into sugar mixture until smooth and bring to boil over medium-high heat, scraping bottom of pan with heatproof rubber spatula. Immediately reduce heat to medium-low and cook, continuing to scrape bottom, until thickened and large bubbles appear on surface, 4 to 6 minutes. Off heat, whisk in butter and vanilla. Transfer pudding to large bowl and place plastic wrap directly on surface of pudding. Refrigerate until cool, about 2 hours.

2 Sprinkle gelatin over water in bowl and let sit until gelatin softens, about 5 minutes. Microwave until mixture is bubbling around edges and gelatin dissolves, 15 to 30 seconds. Using stand mixer fitted with whisk attachment, whip 2 cups cream on medium-low speed until foamy, about 1 minute. Increase speed to high and whip until soft peaks form, 1 to 3 minutes. Add gelatin mixture and whip until stiff peaks form, about 1 minute.

3 Whisk one-third of whipped cream into chilled pudding, then gently fold in remaining whipped cream, 1 scoop at a time, until combined. Cover bottom of 13 by 9-inch baking dish with layer of graham crackers, breaking crackers as necessary to fit. Top with half of pudding–whipped cream mixture (about 5½ cups) and another layer of graham crackers. Repeat with remaining pudding–whipped cream mixture and remaining graham crackers.

4 Combine chocolate chips, corn syrup, and remaining ¾ cup cream in bowl and microwave on 50 percent power, stirring occasionally, until smooth, 1 to 2 minutes. Let glaze cool completely, about 10 minutes. Spread glaze over top and refrigerate cake for at least 6 hours or up to 2 days before slicing and serving.

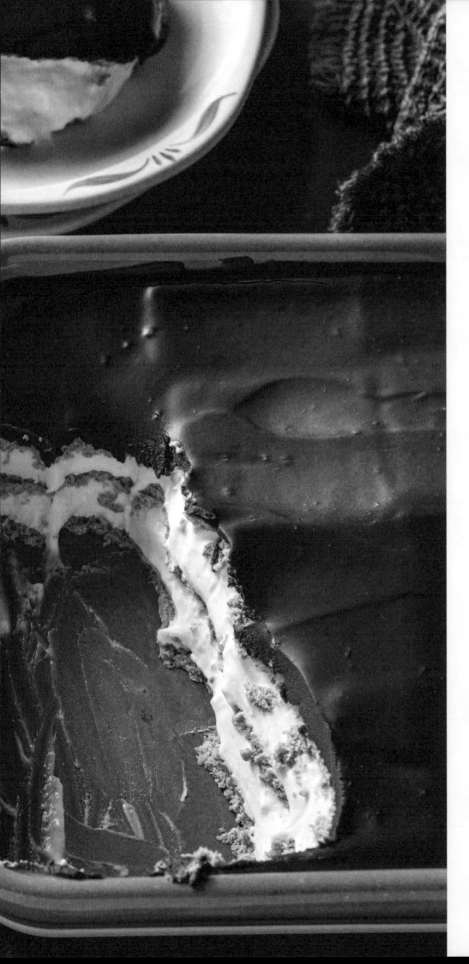

BAKING WITH LOVE

Chocolate éclair cake is a recipe I learned how to make in 2009 from Sandy Smith, the mother of my at-the-time boyfriend, Troy. She made the best éclair cake in Deep Run, North Carolina (and, honestly, in the surrounding towns too).

Like many Southern women she followed a quick formula: two (3.4-ounce) packages of pudding mix with 3 cups of milk (if you followed the package directions, you'd use more milk—this lower ratio is key). Whisk those together and let them sit for 5 minutes, until the mixture looks thick, then fold in an 8-ounce container of Cool Whip. Next, layer this pudding mixture between graham crackers in a 13 by 9-inch pan (three layers of graham crackers and two layers of pudding). Finally, heat a container of Duncan Hines chocolate frosting in the microwave until it's pourable, and drizzle that over top the last layer of graham crackers. You want to smear it out so you have just enough chocolate coating the whole cake, which you let sit in the fridge until the chocolate firms up.

Like many mothers' recipes, this was one I could never make quite as good as she did. Unsure why mine wasn't turning out the same, I watched her make it multiple times, I took notes, I even tried weighing ingredients precisely. Troy and I joked about it: Was she slipping in any secret ingredients? The secret ingredient, I learned, was baking with a mother's love. It really can make food taste different.

Try your hand at our scratch-made recipe or follow the formula Mrs. Smith taught me. Either way you'll have a delicious sweet dessert worthy of a picnic, a potluck, or even a birthday for an ex-boyfriend you still like.

by Morgan Bolling

New Orleans Bourbon Bread Pudding

Serves 8 to 10   ~   Total Time: 2¾ hours, plus 30 minutes cooling

Annie Laura Squalls was the pastry chef at Louisiana's Pontchartrain Hotel for more than two decades. Her baked goods were legendary. We learned a trick from her old-fashioned bread pudding recipe, which was made with stale regular bread that she toasted in the oven to dry it out and then buttered before mixing with a rich custard. Here we offer a recipe that builds on that technique, one with a rich, scoopable custard that envelops the bread with a balance of sweetness and warm spiciness (from cinnamon and nutmeg). To really ensure the pudding isn't soggy, this recipe calls for toasting the bread rather than simply staling it. Crusty baguettes are found all over New Orleans; we tear one into ragged pieces to give the pudding a rustic look. A mixture of 3 parts cream to 1 part milk makes a rich custard that doesn't curdle. Sprinkling cinnamon, sugar, and butter on top of the pudding in the final 20 minutes of baking results in a delightful caramelized topping.

We also took a cue from a recipe in Kelly Fields's cookbook *The Good Book of Southern Baking: A Revival of Biscuits, Cakes, and Cornbread* that substitutes some of the torn bread with panko bread crumbs. "This version has the same flavor as the original recipe," she says, "but a phenomenally smooth texture." We tried using some panko in our version and agree; while it may not be typical, it contributes to a rich, dense texture. To try this yourself, substitute 4 cups of panko (do not toast) for 4 cups of the torn baguette. This bread pudding is great on its own, but for a little more richness and kick, drizzle Bourbon Sauce (recipe follows) over individual servings.

1	(18- to 20-inch) baguette, torn into 1-inch pieces (10 cups)
1	cup golden raisins
¾	cup bourbon, divided
8	large egg yolks
1½	cups packed (10½ ounces) light brown sugar
3	cups heavy cream
1	cup whole milk
1	tablespoon vanilla extract
1½	teaspoons ground cinnamon, divided
¼	teaspoon ground nutmeg
¼	teaspoon table salt
3	tablespoons granulated sugar
6	tablespoons unsalted butter, cut into 6 pieces and chilled

1   Adjust oven rack to middle position and heat oven to 450 degrees. Arrange bread in single layer on rimmed baking sheet and bake until crisp and browned, about 12 minutes, turning pieces over and rotating sheet halfway through baking. Let bread cool. Reduce oven temperature to 300 degrees.

2   Meanwhile, bring raisins and ½ cup bourbon to simmer in small saucepan over medium-high heat, 2 to 3 minutes. Strain mixture, reserving bourbon and raisins separately.

3   Grease 13 by 9-inch broiler-safe baking dish. Whisk egg yolks, brown sugar, cream, milk, vanilla, 1 teaspoon cinnamon, nutmeg, and salt together in large bowl. Whisk in reserved bourbon plus remaining ¼ cup bourbon. Add toasted bread and toss until evenly coated. Let mixture sit until bread begins to absorb custard, about 30 minutes, tossing occasionally. If most of bread is still hard, continue to soak for 15 to 20 minutes.

4   Pour half of bread mixture into prepared baking dish and sprinkle with half of raisins. Pour remaining bread mixture into dish and sprinkle with remaining raisins. Cover with aluminum foil and bake for 45 minutes.

5   Meanwhile, mix granulated sugar and remaining ½ teaspoon cinnamon in small bowl. Using your fingers, cut butter into sugar mixture until size of small peas. Remove foil from pudding, sprinkle with butter mixture, and bake, uncovered, until custard is just set, 20 to 25 minutes. Remove pudding from oven and heat broiler.

6   Once broiler is heated, broil pudding until top forms golden crust, about 2 minutes. Transfer to wire rack and cool for at least 30 minutes or up to 2 hours before serving.

Bourbon Sauce

Makes about 1 cup
Total Time: 15 minutes

Bourbon or rum sauce is drizzled over portions of bread pudding in New Orleans. It's potent stuff, so just a tablespoon per serving is enough. Leftover sauce is good over ice cream—for adults only.

1½	teaspoons cornstarch
¼	cup bourbon, divided
¾	cup heavy cream
2	tablespoons sugar
	Pinch table salt
2	teaspoons unsalted butter, cut into small pieces

Whisk cornstarch and 2 tablespoons bourbon in small bowl until well combined. Heat cream and sugar in small saucepan over medium heat until sugar dissolves. Whisk in cornstarch mixture and bring to boil. Reduce heat to low and cook until sauce thickens, 3 to 5 minutes. Off heat, stir in salt, butter, and remaining 2 tablespoons bourbon. Serve. (Sauce can be refrigerated for up to 5 days; reheat on stovetop.)

Huguenot Torte

Serves 4 to 6 ~ Total Time: 1¼ hours, plus 30 minutes cooling

A favorite dessert of President Harry Truman's, often made by First Lady Bess Truman, was something called Ozark pudding—but it's not actually a pudding. It's more akin to an apple- and pecan-laden cake with a sweet, crusty macaroon topping. And while the Missouri-born Trumans called it Ozark pudding, it goes by another name in the South, especially in South Carolina: Huguenot torte.

A recipe for Huguenot torte was published in 1950 in *Charleston Receipts*, a Junior League cookbook that is both iconic and complicated (see "Charleston Receipts"). Culinary historian John Martin Taylor tracked down the recipe author, Evelyn Anderson Florance, a chef from Charleston. He discovered that she had added it to the menu of the Huguenot Tavern in the 1940s. Her introduction to this dessert was actually on a trip to Texas in the 1930s, more than a decade before Truman became president. The dessert left such an impression that she recreated it with her own touches and renamed it the Huguenot torte, in tribute to the tavern, in her submission to *Charleston Receipts*.

In the Mississippi newspaper the *Hattiesburg American*, historian John Egerton, however, suggests that the history is older. He points to Atlanta culinary icon Henrietta Dull; her apple torte appeared in her 1928 cookbook *Southern Cooking* and may have inspired later versions of Huguenot torte/Ozark pudding given its identical ingredient list. Regardless of its origin, regardless of what you call it, this recipe is quick to stir together and yields a delicious dessert with a delightful mix of textures. Using Granny Smith apples lends brightness, and toasting pecans brings out their nutty flavors. Sprinkling the dessert with sugar before baking gives it the signature crackly, crisp topping. We suggest serving it warm with vanilla ice cream.

CHARLESTON RECEIPTS

Published in 1950, *Charleston Receipts* is America's oldest Junior League cookbook still in print. Considered an essential text in many Lowcountry kitchens, as well as a treasury of Charleston and Southern food history, this cookbook also demonstrates the diverse cultural makeup of a town and a region marked by global trade, civil war, plantation culture, and even climate change. While there's no denying the cookbook's popularity, it is an artifact that is frozen in time, offering a narrow view of how Charlestonians cooked and ate. Tucked between classic Southern dishes such as gumbo and green tomato pickle, early editions of the cookbook feature recipes with racist descriptions and idyllic rhetoric about slavery. Gullah verses scattered throughout the cookbook nod to Charleston's historic African American community, while simultaneously creating a distinction between "the help" who prepared the food and the white women who took credit for it. The images, sketched by Charleston artists, largely depict the privileged social classes, further reinforcing the romanticized view of the cookbook and its so-called "table call of the South." Forty years later, the group published *Charleston Receipts Repeats*, "a collection of recipes that celebrates an abundance of fresh seafood and game, garden-grown vegetables, and succulent fruits while keeping efficiency in mind." All of the symbols of elitism, including the following introduction to the baking chapter, were removed.

CAKES

"No Ma'am', I ain' fuh measure. I jes' jedge by my own repinion. I teck muh flour en' muh brown sugah, en' two-t'ree glub uh muhlassis." "What do you mean by glub?" "You know de soun' muhlassis meck w'en 'e come fum de jug? Glub! Glub!"

Whenever I boil or brew or bake,
How hard I try! What pains I take!
There isn't a step I don't discuss.
My measuring is meticulous.
And what's the result of the fuss and fiddle?
My cake sinks heavily in the middle!
Then old Maria follows me
With a hand that's deft and a smile of glee.
With a touch as light as an angel's kiss,
She stirs in a little of that or this,
With lavish seasoning "to taste"
And calm indifference to waste.
Though her method is all a grave mistake,
The result is always a *super*-cake!

by KC Hysmith and
Toni Tipton-Martin

½	cup (2½ ounces) all-purpose flour	1½	cups pecans, toasted and chopped
2	teaspoons baking powder	2	cups (14 ounces) plus 1 teaspoon sugar, divided
½	teaspoon table salt	4	large eggs
2	Granny Smith apples, peeled, cored, halved, and cut into ½-inch pieces	1	tablespoon vanilla extract

1   Adjust oven rack to middle position and heat oven to 350 degrees. Grease and flour 8-inch square baking pan.

2   Whisk flour, baking powder, and salt together in large bowl. Stir in apples and pecans. Whisk 2 cups sugar, eggs, and vanilla together in separate bowl until pale yellow, about 1 minute. Stir sugar mixture into flour mixture until thoroughly combined. Scrape batter into prepared pan and sprinkle with remaining 1 teaspoon sugar.

3   Bake until golden brown and toothpick inserted in center of pudding comes out with few crumbs attached, 45 to 50 minutes. Transfer to wire rack and let cool for 30 minutes before serving.

SARTORIAL PANTRY

The ingenuity of Southern women extends far beyond the kitchen, but it so often relates to food. From the late-19th through the mid-20th centuries, the practice of making clothing for all ages from sacks used for flour, sugar, and other foods was common throughout the United States, but especially in rural regions. These sacks were often made from durable raw cotton sourced from mills in the South.

Due to limited access to markets and the need for eating filling meals multiple times a day, rural house- and farmwives bought large quantities of flour and sugar for their kitchens. They then turned this steady supply of food sacks into dresses and other functional items such as towels, rags, and diapers. A 100-pound bag of flour provided just over one yard of material; three to four sacks made an adult woman's dress.

Realizing the importance of these sacks to the sartorial needs of the rural housewife, a man named Asa T. Bales of Missouri filed a patent for pattern-printed cotton flour sacks in 1924. Bales worked for the George P. Plant Milling Company in St. Louis, which used his patent to produce Gingham Girl flour packaged in red-and-white checkered dress-quality cotton. Other manufacturers followed suit with their own patterns and designs and even preprinted cut-outs for children's clothes. Flour mill logos were rendered in water-soluble inks that would disappear after washing.

During World War II, higher-quality fabrics (such as silk) were rationed and textile manufacturers focused on other materials for war efforts, but flour sacks were categorized for agricultural and industrial uses and remained readily available. After the war, many food and feed manufacturers switched to cheaper paper packaging and the flour sack dress slowly became fashion of the past.

by KC Hysmith

Rich Vanilla Ice Cream

Serves 8 (Makes about 1 quart)   ~   Total Time: 1 hour, plus 7 hours 20 minutes chilling

Alongside her many recipes for ice cream in *The Virginia House-Wife*, Mary Randolph writes, "When ice creams are not put into shapes, they should always be served in glass with handles." Today, shaped ice cream is a kind of confection you're likely to get on a stick out of an ice cream truck, but in the 1800s, it was in vogue to freeze ice cream in intricate animal, fruit, boat, or witch shaped molds at home. According to Emily Wishingrad for the *Smithsonian Magazine*, "In addition to being molded into various shapes, the ice creams were flavored with ingredients to match the coloring of the objects they were meant to imitate (an ice cream made to look like an artichoke could be flavored with pistachio for its green hue, for example)."

Cynthia Wong (see "Fried Chicken or Ice Cream: That is the Question" on page 398) is still making intricate art of shaping ice cream today with her elaborate and ultrarealistic food dupes—decorated ice creams that look just like fried chicken, fresh-picked peaches, shellfish, hot dogs, and more.

No matter how you serve ice cream, it's important that it's thick, rich, and luxuriously creamy. This recipe for vanilla ice cream made with a traditional custard base is a bit of a project, but one with an elegant payoff. The quicker the ice cream freezes, the smoother, creamier, and less perceptibly icy the results. So we supplement the sugar with corn syrup, which ensures a faster freezing time, and we use a superchilling method for the base, freezing a small amount separately and then adding it back into the rest before churning.

6	large egg yolks
½	cup plus 2 tablespoons (4⅓ ounces) sugar, divided
1	vanilla bean
1¾	cups heavy cream
1¼	cups whole milk
⅓	cup light corn syrup
¼	teaspoon table salt

1   Place 8½ by 4½-inch loaf pan in freezer. Set fine-mesh strainer in large bowl. Whisk egg yolks and ¼ cup sugar in second large bowl until smooth, about 30 seconds.

2   Cut vanilla bean in half lengthwise. Using tip of paring knife, scrape out seeds. Combine vanilla bean and seeds, cream, milk, corn syrup, salt, and remaining 6 tablespoons sugar in medium saucepan. Heat over medium-high heat, stirring occasionally, until mixture registers 175 degrees, 5 to 10 minutes. Off heat, slowly whisk heated cream mixture into yolk mixture.

3   Return mixture to saucepan and cook over medium-low heat, stirring constantly, until mixture thickens and registers 180 degrees, about 4 minutes. Immediately pour custard through prepared strainer and let cool until no longer steaming, about 20 minutes, stirring occasionally. Cover and refrigerate until well chilled, at least 2 hours or up to 24 hours.

4   Transfer custard to ice cream maker and churn until mixture resembles thick soft-serve ice cream and registers about 21 degrees, 15 to 25 minutes. Transfer ice cream to chilled loaf pan and press plastic wrap onto surface. Freeze until firm, at least 3 hours. Serve.

A ripe pawpaw fruit on its tree.

Gajus / Shutterstocks

AMERICA'S FORGOTTEN FRUIT

Pawpaws—sometimes referred to as "America's forgotten fruit"—are the largest fruit indigenous to North America. These green-skinned peanut-shaped fruits range from 3 to 6 inches long. Their interiors vary from a soft yellow to a golden or light orange hue. Each pawpaw contains several large lima bean–size seeds. This fruit grows in hanging clusters that resemble a "hand" of bananas. Some people refer to papayas as pawpaws (or papaws), but they are not the same fruit.

A member of the custard-apple family, pawpaws have creamy, rich, and custardy flesh that's highly aromatic and lacks tartness and acidity. They have notes of banana, mango, and pineapple and vary in flavor depending on the variety and growing location. Underripe pawpaws are generally quite mild, but like bananas, they intensify in flavor as they ripen.

Pawpaws are primarily found in the eastern half of the United States, roughly from Missouri to Maryland. Most local supermarkets in that region don't sell pawpaws because they're in short supply and spoil quickly; you're more likely to find them at farmers' markets when they're in season. Depending on their latitude, pawpaws can be harvested from late July to October, when the trees' big green leaves begin to turn golden, which indicates that the fruit is ripe. Pawpaws must be picked when ripe (unripe pawpaws will not ripen off the tree). There are a few small processing plants in the growing regions where locals can process their pawpaws, allowing people to order packaged pulp online, but they sell out quickly.

Pawpaw Ice Cream

Omit vanilla bean. Reduce milk to 1 cup. Whisk 1 cup mashed pawpaw pulp into chilled custard at beginning of step 4 before churning ice cream.

HOW TO PREP A PAWPAW

Once you remove a pawpaw's seeds, it's easy to scoop out the flesh.

1   Using chef's knife, halve pawpaw lengthwise and pull apart with your hands.

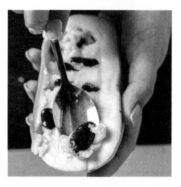

2   Using spoon, remove seeds from pawpaw halves.

3   Scoop seeded pawpaw flesh out of skins and into large bowl.

4   Evenly mash pawpaw into coarse pulp with potato masher.

FRIED CHICKEN OR ICE CREAM: THAT IS THE QUESTION

For Cynthia Wong, head of Life Raft Treats (an ice cream truck in Charleston, South Carolina), making dessert was always a form of play. At a young age, she shaped Play-Doh into loaves of bread. Her mother's parenting strategy was to allow her to bake if she behaved. Her idea of summer fun was picking strawberries in her backyard for sweet creations.

Now, after a decades-long career as a James Beard Award–nominated pastry chef, Wong has returned to the kind of dessert-making she loves best. The transition occurred when Wong was feeling stuck: "I got to the point where I couldn't handle how serious food was anymore." Wong, who grew up in a Burmese-Chinese family in Alabama, says that being an Asian woman chef in the South means she doesn't fit into a box—and her food didn't have to either.

That's when her idea for Life Raft came floating in: What's more fun than ice cream? At first, her business began with just scoops and pints. But Wong, who "always loved novelties more than ice cream, like a bar with a crunchy shell," found herself yearning for more. As a child (and an adult), she was also "completely obsessed" with Japanese fake food. One day, during a nap-induced dream, she put two and two together and the sum was ice cream in the shape of fried chicken.

The idea was lively, funny, and a little ridiculous—everything Wong thought food should be. The Not Fried Chicken was "a product of being raised in the South," Wong said, and it conjured memories of going to KFC with her father on the weekend and of eating her mother's homemade Burmese-style fried chicken. "Everyone on earth eats fried chicken," she said.

And everyone in Charleston eats fried chicken–shaped ice cream. Long lines snake outside of her mint green food truck (which, inspired by her adoration of mint chocolate chip ice cream, she snagged at a postal vehicle auction). She hands out one "chicken" drumstick after another, composed of waffle-flavored ice cream, a chocolate-covered cookie "bone," and a craggy coating of white chocolate and corn flakes.

Her creations don't stop there. There are sorbet bombes in the shape of perfect fruit (complete with fuzzy peach skin). And Wong's signature ice cream sandwich looks exactly like a hoagie—"lettuce," "roast beef," and all. For weddings, her team fashions "seafood" towers, complete with ice cream oysters, shrimp, and other shellfish delights.

Cynthia Wong serving (top) her Not Fried Chicken (bottom).

Peter Frank Edwards / Redux 2019 (top)

Wong says the key to creating all of these unique shapes is using a blast freezer, which locks each component into place at −40 degrees. Her 10-person team creates each shape by hand, using molds for custom designs or simply hand-piping each creation.

And Wong's ice cream flavors are as sophisticated as her designs. Whether they incorporate homemade marmalade from her backyard fruit trees, or use local dairy that "came out of the cow three days ago," Wong says her creations will always stay true to flavor.

by Kelly Song

Cook's Country *test cook and journalist*

ALL ABOUT CANDYMAKING

Southerners have a sweet tooth: Their passion for candymaking and a robust roster of classic candy recipes support it. Candy requires some attention, but it's a fun and satisfying home project that yields a treat to fill your crystal bowls or to gift to friends and family.

Having an accurate, fast instant-read thermometer (rather than a slow-moving clip-on candy thermometer) is key when it comes to making candy. Before you start cooking, we recommend you calibrate your thermometer using ice water (which should register 32 degrees) and/or boiling water (which should register 212 degrees).

Cooking Sugar

Many candies begin with cooking sugar and water (and sometimes additions of corn syrup and other sugars for flavor) in a heavy-duty pot on the stove. (Use a large saucepan with tall enough sides to contain bubbles and bursts.) Each recipe calls for cooking the sugar to a particular temperature, which determines its outcome, whether it's a light syrup or a golden caramel.

There are some details that may seem very minor but actually make cooking with sugar so much more successful (and safe).

1 Pour the Sugar into the Center of the Pan

Carefully add the sugar to the center of the pan, taking care not to get any on the sides of the pot. This prevents crystallization, which will give you grainy candy.

2 Cook Without Stirring

There's no need to stir sugar while it's cooking and, in fact, it can be a detriment if it causes the sugar syrup to splash onto the sides of the pan and crystallize.

3 Take the Temperature

To determine the doneness of sugar syrup, we use an instant-read thermometer. To ensure an accurate reading, swirl the syrup to even out hot spots and then tilt the pot so the syrup pools 1 to 2 inches deep. Move the thermometer back and forth for about 5 seconds before taking a reading.

Bourbon Balls

Makes about 24 balls ~ Total Time: 25 minutes, plus 1 hour chilling

There are two main types of bourbon balls—one is more akin to the version sold by Rebecca Ruth (see "From Classroom to Candy Store"), with a creamy, boozy spiked filling enrobed in chocolate. The other type of bourbon ball is a no-bake cookie; it's a more approachable take for home cooks since it doesn't require as much candymaking prowess. That's what we offer here: It comes together quickly using crushed vanilla wafers, toasted pecans, confectioners' sugar, and bourbon. Both types are delicious, but this one is faster to assemble and doesn't require tempering chocolate.

Light corn syrup binds the cookie mixture, while unsweetened cocoa powder adds rich chocolate flavor. Either Dutch-processed or natural cocoa powder can be used. Rolling the balls in granulated sugar adds a glistening finish, and refrigerating firms up the balls.

2½ cups (6 ounces) vanilla wafers

1 cup pecans, toasted

½ cup (2 ounces) confectioners' sugar

6 tablespoons bourbon

3 tablespoons light corn syrup

1½ tablespoons unsweetened cocoa powder

½ cup (3½ ounces) granulated sugar

1 Process vanilla wafers and pecans in food processor until finely ground, about 15 seconds. Transfer to large bowl. Stir in confectioners' sugar, bourbon, corn syrup, and cocoa.

2 Spread granulated sugar in shallow dish. Working with 1 heaping tablespoon dough at a time, shape mixture into 1-inch balls; roll in sugar. Transfer balls to plate and refrigerate until firm, at least 1 hour. Serve. (Bourbon balls can be refrigerated in airtight container for up to 1 week.)

FROM CLASSROOM TO CANDY STORE

The state of Kentucky houses nearly twice as many bourbon barrels as its human population. During its rise to becoming the state's top spirit, bourbon shaped many elements of Kentucky's cuisine, including its sweets. Rebecca Ruth is a candy business that infuses candy with bourbon to create bourbon balls.

Rebecca Gooch and Ruth Hanly (later Ruth Hanly Booe) met as part-time Kentucky school teachers. The two made candy to give away as presents. But in 1919 they permanently swapped the chalkboards for candy molds and started Rebecca Ruth Candy in Frankfort, Kentucky. In a period when women were seldom encouraged, and definitely not expected, to found and run a business, the two intentionally chose a name that highlighted the fact that it was run by two women.

The path wasn't totally sweet. Ruth left the business after getting married and having a child but returned to Frankfort after being widowed. Not long after, Rebecca married and sold her shares to Ruth. Ruth found herself in the throes of running a candy company solo while navigating single motherhood. All of this coincided with the onset of the Great Depression, which made chocolate a luxury few could afford. Banks were less willing to provide loans, especially to a single mother running what they may have perceived as a superfluous business.

Despite the adversity, Ruth kept her business afloat through 1936, when Eleanor Hume Offutt (a Kentucky dignitary) suggested adding bourbon to Ruth's chocolates. It took two years to perfect the recipe, but the resulting bourbon balls—a creamy whiskey center enrobed in chocolate—took off. In the book *A Culinary History of Kentucky: Burgoo, Beer Cheese and Goetta*, Fiona Young-Brown says, "By the time World War II rolled around, even rationing could not stop Rebecca Ruth. Loyal customers saved their sugar rations to share with Ruth."

Ruth passed away in 1973, but you can still order Rebecca Ruth's bourbon balls, the delicious product of turning life's lemons into a unique blend of whiskey and chocolate.

by Morgan Bolling

Ruth Hanly Booe hand-stretching candy.

Rebecca Ruth Candy Inc.

Sea Foam Candy

Makes about 3 dozen candies ~ Total Time: 1¼ hours, plus 2 hours 10 minutes cooling

Sea foam candy is a take on the Southern classic candy divinity. Divinity is a soft, snow-white, nougat-like treat studded with buttery pecans. Recipes from early 20th-century Southern United States have a texture and taste similar to early recipes in the Middle East and then Europe. The rise of divinity in the United States paralleled the growing popularity of corn syrup. Some claim that it was corn syrup makers who invented divinity as a way to market their product. And the name? Legend has it someone initially tasted it and said it was "divine."

Also divine, sea foam candy replaces some of the white sugar with brown sugar so it has a deeper caramelized flavor. And the naming of this cousin to divinity is a bit more obvious—its marshmallowy texture mirrors that of the foam that forms when the sea hits the shore.

Roughly equal parts of white and brown sugar provide this sea foam candy recipe with the right sweetness and rich flavor. Toasting the pecans adds a deep nutty flavor. And finally, a splash of white vinegar cuts the sweetness. Many cookbooks caution not to make sea foam candy on a humid day, and this recipe is no exception, as it will not set up properly in hot or humid conditions. You will need an instant-read thermometer. You can use a 1¾-inch ice cream scoop to portion the sea foam candy in step 4.

3	cups (12 ounces) pecan halves
¾	cup water
1¾	cups (12¼ ounces) granulated sugar
1½	cups packed (10½ ounces) light brown sugar
1	cup light corn syrup
3	large egg whites
⅛	teaspoon table salt
1	teaspoon vanilla extract
1½	teaspoons distilled white vinegar

1 Adjust oven rack to middle position and heat oven to 350 degrees. Spread nuts in single layer on rimmed baking sheet. Toast nuts until fragrant and lightly browned, 10 to 12 minutes, stirring once or twice. Let nuts cool completely. Select 40 pecan halves for garnish and set aside; coarsely chop remaining nuts. Place chopped nuts in fine-mesh strainer and shake to remove dust; set chopped nuts aside. Line 2 rimmed baking sheets with parchment paper.

2 Pour water into 2- to 3-quart heavy-bottomed saucepan; add granulated sugar, brown sugar, and corn syrup to center of saucepan, taking care to keep sugar granules from coating sides of pot. Bring mixture to boil over high heat without stirring; reduce heat to medium and cook, without stirring, until syrup registers 255 degrees, about 14 minutes.

3 Meanwhile, fit stand mixer with whisk attachment and beat egg whites at high speed until mixture forms stiff peaks when whisk is lifted, about 1 minute. When hot syrup is ready, with mixer running at medium speed, pour into egg whites in slow, steady stream; add salt. Increase speed to high and continue to beat until mixture loses its sheen and holds medium-stiff peaks when whisk is lifted, 15 to 25 minutes. (Begin checking as soon as thin threads of mixture start to pull away from sides of bowl.) Add vanilla, vinegar, and chopped nuts; beat on medium speed until just combined, about 10 seconds.

4 Working quickly, drop rounded tablespoons of mixture onto prepared baking sheets. Garnish each round with pecan half, pressing gently to adhere. Let stand at room temperature until firm, 2 to 4 hours. Peel candies off parchment and transfer to airtight container, sliding fresh sheets of parchment paper between layers of candies. (Sea foam candy can be stored at room temperature for up to 1 week.)

THE PRALINIÈRES OF NEW ORLEANS

Louisiana-style pralines, developed as an adaptation of the classic French candy by the same name, first took root in New Orleans cuisine late in the 18th century. Enslaved and free Black women created the confections using butter, milk, sugar, and—in place of the almonds favored in France—pecans.

By the end of the Civil War, pralines were a popular street food in the French Quarter, where vendors—almost always Black women—sold the candy to locals and visitors alike. Speaking a French-Creole patois, many of the vendors dressed themselves in stereotypical "mammy" costumes as a marketing tool. They'd step into full skirts, wrap aprons around their waists, and tie headwraps, or tignons, around their heads before hitting the streets to sell their goods.

Over the next decades, and well into the twentieth century, many of these pralinières built successful small businesses. As scholar Chanda Nunez writes in a 2011 research study for the University of New Orleans, pralines were a simple sweet treat for customers, but also for the vendors: "The candy represented a path to economic freedom and additional income."

With nicknames including Tante Marie, Praline Zizi, and Zabet, pralinières were celebrated for their confections at the same time as they were continually discriminated against. But with tourists and high-ranking government officials as customers, many were successful enough to pass their businesses down to subsequent generations. Today, the mammy caricature has mostly been subsumed, and the praline trade has mostly moved into brick-and-mortar tourist shops that line the streets of New Orleans.

Pralines

Makes about 16 pralines   ~   Total Time: 45 minutes, plus 1 hour cooling

This famous New Orleans candy is made of boiled sugar enriched with butter and milk and laden with pecans. It's cooked to a melt-in-your-mouth texture that is set but crumbly, not crack-your-teeth hard. Using evaporated milk—milk with 60 percent of the water removed—reduces the time it takes to boil the moisture out of the mixture. Achieving the pralines' signature texture comes down to temperature (cooking the mixture to about 237 degrees) and agitation (stirring a lot before and after the pecans are added allows the pralines to set up once cooled).

When portioning the candies, keep the pot over low heat and use a long-handled spoon. You will need an instant-read thermometer. You may end up with fewer than 16 pralines. A 12-ounce can of evaporated milk is about 3 inches in diameter; you can use it to draw the circles. The pralines are also delicious crumbled over ice cream.

1	cup (7 ounces) granulated sugar	6	tablespoons unsalted butter, cut into 6 pieces
1	cup packed (7 ounces) light brown sugar	½	teaspoon table salt
¾	cup evaporated milk	1½	cups pecans, chopped

1   Using pencil, draw 8 evenly spaced 3-inch circles, in 2 rows of 4, on each of two 16 by 12-inch sheets of parchment paper. Line 2 rimmed baking sheets with marked parchment, marked side down.

2   Combine granulated sugar, brown sugar, evaporated milk, butter, and salt in large saucepan. Bring to boil over medium-high heat, stirring frequently with long-handled metal spoon. Once boiling, reduce heat to medium and continue to boil, stirring frequently and making sure to scrape corners of saucepan, until mixture registers 236 to 238 degrees, 9 to 13 minutes longer. (To take temperature, tilt saucepan so sugar mixture pools to 1 side.)

3   Reduce heat to low and stir in pecans. Stir constantly over low heat for 3 minutes (mixture will thicken slightly and lighten in color).

4   Keep saucepan over low heat. Working quickly, spoon approximate 2-tablespoon portions of praline mixture onto each parchment circle and immediately spread with spoon so mixture fills out circle (use dinner spoon to help scrape mixture from long-handled spoon if necessary).

5   Let sit until firm, at least 1 hour. (Be careful when moving sheets; underside will be hot after portioning pralines.) Serve. (Pralines can be stored at room temperature for up to 3 days or frozen for up to 1 month.)

Peanut Brittle

Makes about 1½ pounds brittle   ~   Total Time: 40 minutes, plus 1 hour cooling

According to a Southern legend, brittle was invented by a woman around 1890, but not on purpose. Story goes she was making taffy but accidentally used baking soda in place of cream of tartar. Not wanting to be wasteful, she kept cooking the mixture and the result was a crunchy, hard, and deliciously sweet brittle candy.

However peanut brittle came to be, this irresistible candy is one we are happy to have. At its best, peanut brittle strikes a balance of butterscotch notes and nut flavor and is crunchy but not tooth-breaking. It's great for gifting, snacking on, or just anytime you want to satisfy a sweet craving. You will need an instant-read thermometer.

1	teaspoon baking soda
1	teaspoon kosher salt
½	cup water
6	tablespoons unsalted butter
1½	cups (10½ ounces) sugar
1¼	cups corn syrup
2	cups dry-roasted peanuts
1	teaspoon flake sea salt

1   Adjust oven rack to middle position and heat oven to 350 degrees. Grease rimmed baking sheet, line baking sheet with parchment paper, and grease parchment. Combine baking soda and kosher salt in small bowl; set aside.

2   Combine water and butter in large saucepan and cook over medium-high heat until butter is melted. Pour sugar and corn syrup into center of saucepan, taking care not to let sugar granules touch sides of pan.

Gently stir until all sugar is moistened. Bring to boil and cook, without stirring, until syrup has faint golden color and registers 300 degrees, 10 to 15 minutes.

3   Meanwhile, line second rimmed baking sheet with parchment. Add peanuts in single layer and bake until lightly toasted, about 5 minutes. Keep peanuts warm.

4   Reduce heat to medium-low and continue to cook, gently swirling pan, until syrup is amber-colored and registers 325 degrees, 4 to 6 minutes. Using parchment as sling, add peanuts and stir until combined. Off heat, stir in baking soda mixture. Working quickly, transfer mixture to greased and lined baking sheet and smooth into even layer with greased rubber spatula. Sprinkle with flake sea salt. Let cool completely, about 1 hour. Break brittle into rough squares and serve.

Chocolate-Marshmallow Sandwich Cookies

Makes 12 sandwich cookies ~ Total Time: 2 hours, plus 20 minutes chilling

Few treats have a following as great as the MoonPie, a construction of marshmallow layered between two graham cookies, fully coated in a thin layer of chocolate. People below the Mason-Dixon line know they are delicious paired with an RC Cola.

Every year the town of Bell Buckle, Tennessee, hosts an RC Cola–MoonPie Festival during which they crown a RC King and a MoonPie Queen. The outdoor retail chain Bass Pro Shops has hosted multiple MoonPie eating contests. And Mobile, Alabama, rings in the New Year by dropping a 600-pound electric moon pie. The MoonPie is iconic. Another Southern food icon, Mildred Council (more commonly referred to as Mama Dip; see page 23), wrote an ode to moon pies in *Southern Cultures* magazine. She talks about getting them at country stores in Bynum and Carrboro, North Carolina, when she was a child. She ends the piece with, "I love a Moon Pie. I would eat one now if I had it." And the MoonPie continues to stand as an icon for younger generations nationwide; the company's X account is well known for its posts featuring the unmistakable sass of a millennial Southerner.

The Chattanooga Bakery in Chattanooga, Tennessee, has been producing this popular packaged treat since 1917. We love MoonPies so much that we wanted to offer a recipe to make them at home. We use an equal amount of all-purpose and graham flours to give the cookies a slightly coarse texture and toasty flavor. Graham flour, also known as stone-ground whole-wheat flour, is coarser and less processed than conventional whole-wheat flour. Once the cookies cool, we sandwich homemade marshmallow

between them, working quickly while the marshmallow is still warm and malleable. To ensure even distribution, we apply gentle pressure and a light twisting motion. After dipping the sandwiches in chocolate and smoothing them out, the moon pies look celestially shiny, and delicious.

Cookies

1¼ cups (6¼ ounces) all-purpose flour

1 cup plus 2 tablespoons (6¼ ounces) graham flour

¾ cup (5¼ ounces) sugar

1 teaspoon baking powder

1 teaspoon baking soda

¾ teaspoon table salt

¼ teaspoon ground cinnamon

12 tablespoons unsalted butter, melted and cooled

5 tablespoons water

2 tablespoons molasses

1 teaspoon vanilla extract

Filling

6 tablespoons water, divided

2 teaspoons unflavored gelatin

¼ cup light corn syrup

⅔ cup (4⅔ ounces) sugar

⅛ teaspoon table salt

1 teaspoon vanilla extract

Coating

12 ounces bittersweet chocolate (9 ounces chopped fine, 3 ounces grated)

1 tablespoon coconut oil

1 **For the cookies** Adjust oven rack to middle position and heat oven to 350 degrees. Line 2 rimmed baking sheets with parchment paper. Whisk all-purpose flour, graham flour, sugar, baking powder, baking soda, salt, and cinnamon together in bowl of stand mixer. Add melted butter, water, molasses, and vanilla. Using paddle attachment, mix until dough comes together, about 20 seconds.

2 Transfer dough to counter and divide into 2 equal pieces. Working with 1 piece of dough at a time (keep remaining piece covered with plastic wrap), roll into 12-inch circle, ⅛ inch thick, between 2 large sheets of parchment. Remove top piece of parchment. Using 3-inch round cookie cutter, cut dough into 8 rounds; carefully transfer rounds to prepared sheets, spacing ½ inch apart. Gently reroll scraps into 8-inch circle, ⅛ inch thick, then cut into 4 rounds and transfer to sheets.

3 Bake cookies, 1 sheet at a time, until edges are set, about 10 minutes, rotating sheet halfway through baking. Transfer sheet to wire rack and let cookies cool completely. (Cookies can be stored at room temperature for up to 1 day.)

4 **For the filling** Whisk 3 tablespoons water and gelatin together in clean, dry mixer bowl fitted with whisk attachment. Let sit until very firm, about 5 minutes.

5 Meanwhile, combine corn syrup and remaining 3 tablespoons water in small saucepan. Pour sugar and salt into center of saucepan (do not let sugar hit saucepan

sides). Bring to boil over medium-high heat and cook, gently swirling saucepan, until sugar has dissolved completely and mixture registers 240 degrees, 4 to 6 minutes.

6   Turn mixer speed to low and carefully pour hot syrup into gelatin mixture, avoiding whisk and sides of bowl. Gradually increase speed to high and whip until mixture is very thick and stiff and coats whisk, about 7 minutes, scraping down bowl as needed. Add vanilla and mix until incorporated, about 15 seconds.

7   To assemble, place 12 cookies upside down on counter. Working quickly with 1 cookie at a time, place 2 tablespoons marshmallow filling in center of cookie and spread evenly with back of spoon. Place second cookie on top of filling, right side up, and gently press and twist until filling is even with edges of cookies. Let sit for 15 minutes, until filling is set.

8   **For the coating** Line baking sheet with clean sheet of parchment. Microwave finely chopped chocolate in medium bowl at 50 percent power, stirring often, until about two-thirds melted, 2 to 4 minutes. (Melted chocolate should not be much warmer than body temperature; check by holding bowl in palm of your hand.) Add grated chocolate and coconut oil and stir until smooth, returning to microwave for no more than 5 seconds at a time to finish melting if necessary.

9   Rotate filling-exposed side of 1 sandwich cookie in chocolate until filling and cookie edges are fully covered. Place sandwich cookie in chocolate and, using 2 forks, gently flip to fully coat all sides. Lift cookie out of chocolate with fork. Using offset spatula, spread chocolate on top of cookie into thin, even layer, allowing excess to run of sides. Tap fork against edge of bowl, then wipe underside of fork on edge of bowl to remove excess chocolate from bottom of cookie. Use second fork to slide sandwich cookie onto prepared sheet. Repeat with remaining sandwich cookies, returning chocolate to microwave for no more than 5 seconds at a time if it becomes too firm.

10   Refrigerate sandwich cookies until chocolate is set, about 20 minutes, before serving. (Sandwich cookies can be stored at room temperature for up to 2 days.)

Stuffed Red Velvet Cookies

Makes 12 cookies ~ Total Time: 1 hour, plus 4 hours chilling and cooling

This recipe is inspired by the stuffed cookies from baker and chef Adrian Lipscombe. We adapted Lipscombe's bakeshop recipe for the home cook. To ensure a neat, sturdy stuffed cookie, we made a relatively stiff cream cheese filling, keeping the ratio of sugar to cream cheese and softened butter low, and freezing it in disks to make it easy to wrap dough around. Vibrant lemon zest; finely chopped pecans; and creamy, sweet white chocolate chips enhance the flavor of the cookie dough and complement the classic red velvet and tangy cream cheese. Adding a bit of whole-wheat flour to the dough contributes more structure, making it easier to shape when raw and less fragile after fully baked and cooled (the flavor is pleasantly nutty too). You can use either Dutch-processed or natural cocoa powder and liquid or gel food coloring in this recipe. You can substitute an additional ½ cup of white chocolate chips for the pecans if you prefer.

Filling

½ cup (2 ounces) confectioners' sugar

4 ounces cream cheese, softened

2 tablespoons unsalted butter, softened

Pinch table salt

⅛ teaspoon vanilla extract

Cookies

2⅔ cups (13⅓ ounces) all-purpose flour

⅔ cup (3⅔ ounces) whole-wheat flour

1 tablespoon unsweetened cocoa powder

1¼ teaspoons table salt

1 teaspoon baking soda

16 tablespoons unsalted butter, melted

1 cup packed (7 ounces) light brown sugar

½ cup (3½ ounces) granulated sugar

2 large eggs

1½ teaspoons grated lemon zest

2 teaspoons vanilla extract

1 tablespoon red food coloring

1 cup (6 ounces) white chocolate chips

½ cup fincly chopped pecans

1 **For the filling** Using stand mixer fitted with paddle, beat all ingredients on low speed until sugar is mostly moistened, about 1 minute. Increase speed to medium-high and beat until fluffy and smooth, 2 to 3 minutes, scraping down bowl as needed.

2 Line rimmed baking sheet or large, flat plate with parchment paper. Using tablespoon measure and small spoon (or #60 scoop), divide filling into 12 equal portions on prepared sheet. Use back of spoon to lightly flatten each portion into rough disk shape (no greater than 1½ inches in diameter). Freeze until solid, at least 2 hours. (Filling can be frozen for up to 1 week.)

3 **For the cookies** Adjust oven rack to middle position and heat oven to 425 degrees. Line 2 rimmed baking sheets with parchment paper. Whisk all-purpose flour, whole-wheat flour, cocoa, salt, and baking soda together in large bowl.

4 Whisk melted butter, brown sugar, and granulated sugar in second large bowl until smooth. Whisk in eggs, lemon zest, vanilla, and food coloring until smooth and creamy, about 30 seconds. Stir in half of flour mixture with rubber spatula or wooden spoon. Stir in chocolate chips, pecans, and remaining flour mixture. (Mixture will be stiff; once dough begins to stiffen, you can mix with your hands until dough is evenly combined.)

5 Divide dough into 12 equal portions (about 3½ ounces or ⅓ cup each). Flatten each dough portion into disk shape, about 3 inches in diameter. Working quickly, place 1 disk of frozen filling in center of each dough disk. Wrap edges of dough up and around filling, seal dough, and shape into smooth disk shape (about 3½ inches in diameter and ½ inch thick), taking care to ensure filling remains in center of each cookie. Space cookies evenly on prepared sheets, 6 cookies per sheet.

6 Bake cookies, 1 sheet at a time, until edges of cookies are beginning to puff and crack, 7 to 8 minutes. Let cookies cool completely on sheets, about 2 hours. Serve.

Q&A: ADRIAN LIPSCOMBE ON REVITALIZATION (AND COOKIES)

*A portrait of
Adrian Lipscombe.*

Dahli Durley

This recipe is inspired by the stuffed cookies that Toni Tipton-Martin received as a gift from baker and chef Adrian Lipscombe. We ordered some from Lipscombe's bakeshop in Wisconsin (which has since closed) and worked with her to adapt her recipe for these memorable treats for the home cook. In our exchange, Lipscombe, who is not only a baker but also a mother of four and a city planner, goes on to share a bit about her Texas roots; her family's deep and abiding relationship with food, including their Juneteenth feast traditions; how she became the chef-owner of the café; and what she is up to now that she's moved back to Texas.

What are the roots of this recipe for you? We're used to seeing red velvet cake, but how did it become a cookie?
Cookies are one dessert that everyone knows. I love taking recipes and making them even more extravagant. Red velvet cake is one of my favorite desserts, and finding a way to make it a cookie that tasted just as good was key. I did not want to put icing on the outside of the cookie; I wanted to find a way to stuff the cookie with icing.

You're a native of Texas. Can you tell us more about how your roots led you to become passionate about food?
I am originally from San Antonio and am a sixth-generation Texan. My family is from what is known as Central Texas and the Hill Country. My passion for food comes from my elders, who used food, as many families do, as our bridge to bring us together. Many of my family members are nicknamed after food. I even have an Aunt Cookie.

My Nana is the family member who cooked for every occasion and for everyone, especially desserts. You could always guarantee there would be a cake or cookies at her house, and you would definitely be leaving with a to-go dessert, wrapped in foil. She has fed every single family member cinnamon rolls, pound cakes, cookies, and more. She was also the editor of the church cookbooks and an avid cookbook collector. I spent many summers in front of her bookcases looking at cookbooks and listening to her talk to friends and sisters about recipes. My grandfather was a sous chef in his youth and Great Aunt Jo went to culinary school and made wedding cakes for over 30 years.

Our family never wrote down recipes; we learned by watching when we were young and participating when we got older. It was said that as you became an adult, if you forgot a recipe or an ingredient, it must be time for you to come home and cook it with your elders.

La Crosse, Wisconsin, is a long way from Texas. What drew you there? How did you become chef-owner of Uptowne Cafe and Bakery?
Moving to the Midwest was never in my plans. Before moving I was already operating a wholesale bakery in Austin, going to school, and working a full-time job. I was in a chapter where I had theories about revitalization and was ready for a change.

I was working on a city planning project about revitalization, and in the La Crosse area, there was a vacant restaurant. It was very serendipitous how things worked out, being able to work with the landlord and the community to open a restaurant. I was able to create a community impact space to revitalize the community, provide amazing opportunities for the community to come together, and shape an amazing farm-to-table restaurant that allowed me to tell my story through food.

As you transition back to Austin, what's next for you?
I am very happy to be back home, and baking will always be part of my plans. I hope to focus on telling the story of Black Texas chefs, advocate for farmers, and maybe open another restaurant. Also, making amazing cookies with a twist is a must for me.

Red foods are traditional for Juneteenth celebrations. What are your thoughts on making these cookies for Juneteenth?
I love the idea of the red velvet cookie joining a Juneteenth celebration table. Even before Juneteenth was a national holiday, I always took time off to be with my family. Our reunions centered on Juneteenth. Being from this part of Texas, there are certain foods you would see that would show the cultural diversity of Black and [Latin] culture in our food. The food that surrounds our table varies from fruit, red drink or red punch, assorted tamales, rice and beans, pan dulce, carne asada, and fajitas with freshly made tortillas, salsa, pico, tortilla chips, and guacamole. And there's smoked barbecue: hot guts (aka sausage), brisket, and beef ribs. There's smoked chicken, fried chicken, pound cakes, potato salad, macaroni, pies, and of course cookies.

Moravian Cookies

Makes about 60 cookies   ~   Total Time: 1½ hours, plus 1 hour 25 minutes chilling and cooling

Winston-Salem, North Carolina, has one of the largest Moravian populations in the United States, and local businesses uphold the Moravian baking heritage. Bakeries such as Dewey's, Winkler, and Wilkerson sell buns, sugar cakes, Moravian chicken pies, and their renowned spice cookies. Evolving from the German lebkuchen cookie (through the relocation of many Moravians from today's Czech Republic to Germany, and then the United States), this cookie merges a rich spice mix with distinctive baking methods, resulting in a crispy, wafer-thin treat.

Many recipes use a large amount of molasses and chill the resulting sticky dough to make it more workable. This one swaps in a little brown sugar for some of the wet molasses and comes together with cold butter in the food processor. It's important to roll this dough incredibly thin, so be sure to give it the full hour (or longer) to chill in step 2. Take care not to overbake these cookies, or they will taste slightly bitter.

1¾ cups (8¾ ounces) all-purpose flour

¼ cup packed (1¾ ounces) light brown sugar

2 teaspoons ground ginger

1 teaspoon ground cinnamon

½ teaspoon ground allspice

½ teaspoon baking soda

⅜ teaspoon table salt

¼ teaspoon ground cloves

6 tablespoons unsalted butter, cut into ½-inch cubes and chilled

6 tablespoons molasses

1 Process flour, sugar, ginger, cinnamon, allspice, baking soda, salt, and cloves in food processor until combined, about 5 seconds. Scatter butter over top and process until sandy, about 30 seconds. Add molasses and process until dough forms, about 1 minute longer. Divide dough into 3 pieces, form each piece into disk, wrap disks in plastic wrap, and refrigerate for 1 hour.

2 Adjust oven rack to middle position and heat oven to 300 degrees. Line 2 baking sheets with parchment paper.

3 Roll 1 disk of dough ⅟₁₆ inch thick between 2 pieces of parchment, gathering and rerolling scraps once and rechilling dough if it becomes sticky. Using 2½-inch fluted round cutter, cut dough into rounds; space rounds ½ inch apart on prepared sheets. Bake, 1 sheet at a time, until cookies are firm when pressed gently and edges are just beginning to color, about 10 minutes, rotating sheet halfway through baking. Let cookies cool on sheet for 5 minutes, then slide cookies, still on parchment, onto wire rack. Repeat with remaining dough. Let cookies cool completely before serving. (Cookies can be stored at room temperature for up to 3 days.)

THE LEGACY OF MRS. HANES: FROM FAMILY TRADITION TO COOKIE EMPIRE

Evva Hanes at Mrs. Hanes' Moravian Cookies.

Peter Frank Edwards / Redux 2019

Evva Hanes of Clemmons, North Carolina, transformed a long-standing Moravian cookie tradition she observed from her mother into a thriving family venture, Mrs. Hanes' Moravian Cookies.

A Protestant religious group, the Moravians escaped persecution in their home Czech Republic by relocating to Germany. Before the American Revolution, Moravian missionaries settled in Pennsylvania. Beyond religion, they introduced a ginger cookie recipe called lebkuchen. In the mid-1700s, members moved to found a religious commune in what's now Winston-Salem, North Carolina. Their baking legacy has endured for centuries.

Born the youngest of seven, Evva Caroline Foltz watched her mother, Bertha Foltz, craft hundreds of these thin, spiced cookies to bolster the family's modest dairy income. Bertha innovated with a crispy vanilla variant, extending sales beyond the Christmas season. By the age of 20, Evva inherited and expanded the venture, diversifying with flavors such as lemon and black walnut. She married Travis Hanes and transformed her kitchen endeavor into a larger-scale operation beside their residence. By 2010, their popularity skyrocketed with an endorsement from Oprah Winfrey. In her tribute to Evva in the *New York Times*, Kim Severson reported that Mrs. Hanes' Moravian Cookies sold about 10 million cookies or $2 million worth of cookies per year.

Evva's influence survives in the Friedberg Moravian Church, on the road where she was both born and passed away in 2023, and in her beloved cookies.

by Morgan Bolling

Cowboy Cookies

Makes 16 cookies ~ Total Time: 1¼ hours, plus 20 minutes cooling

Along with a rise in popularity of TV westerns and movies that characterized the 1950s Cold War era came a cookie that captured Americans' escapist Wild West nostalgia. Cowboy cookies, packed with rolled oats, chocolate chips, toasted nuts, and flakes of coconut, are perfect for tucking into your saddlebag to enjoy at high noon—or into your lunch tote for an afternoon snack.

Since these cookies are jam-packed with mix-ins, making them is a fine balancing act. The coconut and oats absorb moisture, which can lead to a tough cookie. Adding lots of melted butter helps keep them tender and chewy. Staggering ¼-cup portions of dough onto the baking sheets yields oversize cookies with enough room to spread. Finally, it's important to deliberately underbake them to ensure these cookies have a perfectly crisp exterior and soft chew once cooled.

We prefer old-fashioned rolled oats in this recipe, but you can use quick or instant oats in a pinch. Do not use thick-cut oats here; the cookies will spread too much. These cookies are big and benefit from the extra space provided by a rimless cookie sheet if you have one.

1¼ cups (6¼ ounces) all-purpose flour

¾ teaspoon baking powder

½ teaspoon baking soda

½ teaspoon table salt

1½ cups packed (10½ ounces) light brown sugar

12 tablespoons unsalted butter, melted and cooled

1 large egg plus 1 large yolk

1 teaspoon vanilla extract

1¼ cups (3¾ ounces) old-fashioned rolled oats

1 cup pecans, toasted and chopped coarse

1 cup (3 ounces) sweetened shredded coconut

⅔ cup (4 ounces) semisweet chocolate chips

1 Adjust oven rack to middle position and heat oven to 350 degrees. Line 2 rimless cookie sheets with parchment paper. Whisk flour, baking powder, baking soda, and salt together in bowl.

2 Whisk sugar, melted butter, egg and yolk, and vanilla in large bowl until combined. Stir in flour mixture until no dry streaks remain. Stir in oats, pecans, coconut, and chocolate chips until fully combined (mixture will be sticky).

3 Lightly spray ¼-cup dry measuring cup with vegetable oil spray. Using measuring cup, drop level portions of dough onto prepared sheets, staggering 8 portions per sheet and spacing them about 2½ inches apart. Divide any remaining dough among portions.

4 Bake cookies, 1 sheet at a time, until edges are browned and set and centers are puffed with pale, raw spots, 15 to 17 minutes, rotating sheet halfway through baking. Do not overbake.

5 Let cookies cool on sheet for 5 minutes, then transfer to wire rack and let cool completely before serving. (Cookies can be stored at room temperature for up to 3 days.)

THE FIRST LADY BAKE-OFF

A baking contest that felt like a relic of the 1950s, *Family Circle* magazine's presidential cookie competition began in 1992 with the soon-to-be first lady Hillary Clinton.

The magazine launched the program after Hillary Clinton commented during Bill Clinton's first presidential campaign, "You know, I suppose I could've stayed home and baked cookies and had teas, but what I decided to do was to fulfill my profession, which I pursued before my husband was in public life." Many reacted with anger toward what they viewed as a disparagement of the housewife. And in a smart PR move, *Family Circle* began their cookie bake-off, pushing Hillary Clinton and Barbara Bush to submit recipes to appeal to the American public.

Debbie Walsh, director of the Center for American Women and Politics at Rutgers University, told NPR's *All Things Considered* in 2016, "It felt almost as though [Hillary Clinton] had stepped outside the bounds of what was seen as the traditional role of first lady, potential first lady. And therefore, she had to pay a price. And the price she paid was then being placed in the midst of a cookie bake-off." As Walsh noted, it's important to call out (for all of us bakers out there) that being a high-achieving woman and baking are not mutually exclusive, and that people who choose to stay at home with families do much more than bake cookies and drink tea.

The baking contest, which lasted until 2016, was known to have a pretty solid track record of the winning cookie lining up with whose spouse ultimately won the presidential seat (five out of seven). Even in 2012, Amy Walter wrote for the piece "Working Moms, First Ladies, and Recalling Hillary Clinton's 'Baking Cookies' Comment" for ABC News, "It is remarkable that [20] years after Clinton's 'cookie' remarks, the issue of the role of women in the workplace and home is as raw and polarizing as ever. At the end of the day, while the issue of women's roles in society have evolved, the role of the first lady does remain trapped in stereotypes that are tougher to break."

In a twist during the final contest, Bill Clinton, not Hillary, provided a recipe since Hillary was the first female nominee of a major party. But rather than create his own, he submitted Hillary's recipe. The only person to win the contest twice other than Hillary Clinton herself was Laura Bush with her cowboy cookie recipe. We love these cookies, nutty-rich and chockablock with mix-ins, so we've perfected our own version, which we think could win any contest.

by Morgan Bolling

Q&A: DANIELLA SENIOR ON COFFEE, COOKIES, AND SERVING WOMEN

Daniella Senior grew up in Santo Domingo, Dominican Republic, and started her first dessert catering business at the young age of 13 years old. At 18, she went to culinary school in New York before moving to Washington, D.C., and eventually opening Colada Shop, a D.C.-based restaurant and café group serving Cuban food, coffee, and cocktails. Senior learned to cook Cuban food from her grandma, who was of Cuban descent. We interviewed her about her transnational food and beverage experience and being a woman business owner.

What motivated you to start Colada Shop?
Juan, one of my business partners, and I both have a very strong passion for the beverage sector. We started a consultancy and a lot of our clients were in Miami. Personally I couldn't wait to land because I really wanted a guava pastelito and a strong coffee. I missed those flavors and they weren't available [elsewhere in the United States]. Also, I was working in a lot of cafés and I honestly found a huge lack of identity within them: They all kind of looked the same; they served pretty much the same products. And some of them were kind of pretentious when it came to the coffee component. I just wanted warmth and happiness and hospitality. So out of [those feelings] Colada Shop was born.

Has being a woman impacted how you run your business?
One hundred percent; it definitely has. For me I knew I wanted a family; I knew I wanted stability. I just didn't really find how I was going to merge both things. We've taken that very much into account in building Colada Shop with our hiring practices and making sure that we have supportive policies towards women, including single mothers. We have flexible scheduling, which is one of the things that has allowed us to retain a lot of our team; we work with our team on their schedules, which allows them to pick up their kids after school or from daycare and then come back. It's also reflected in the benefits we provide.

Do you have advice for anyone starting a similarly equitable business?
It's a difficult task, especially when you're starting off. I don't think that the laws are conducive to supporting small businesses in this way, so you have to be very intentional in your budgeting but also in your messaging. When employees have an understanding that you're really bending backwards to make sure they have the right structure, then it creates a culture where they're really taking care of the business and driving the business as well.

Now tell us about these cookies.
I am excited to share this recipe because the guava, the saltiness, the oats—it creates a kind of sweet-salty cookie that you want to keep nibbling. It is one of our favorite recipes, and we've seen a lot of success with our guests. They're a merge of flavors I grew up with and a quintessential American cookie. I've basically been in the United States for the same amount of time that I've been out of it, so it feels like this cookie represents a crossroads of where I am in my life.

Oat Guava Cookies

Makes 24 cookies ~ Total Time: 1½ hours

This is Daniella Senior's recipe from Colada Shop in Washington, D.C. Guava paste is a thick mixture of guava, sugar, and often pectin or other stabilizers and/or flavorings. It can be found in many large grocery stores or ordered online. We suggest chilling the guava paste to make it firmer, which makes it easier to cut and less prone to breaking apart when mixed into the dough. These cookies are big and benefit from the extra space provided by rimless cookie sheets. If you don't have three cookie sheets, you can reuse one or two cookie sheets; cool in between batches.

3⅓	cups (10 ounces) old-fashioned rolled oats	1	cup packed (7 ounces) light brown sugar
1½	cups (7½ ounces) all-purpose flour	¾	cup (5¼ ounces) granulated sugar, divided
1	teaspoon ground cinnamon	2	large eggs
½	teaspoon table salt	1½	teaspoons vanilla extract
½	teaspoon baking powder	½	cup (1½ ounces) shredded sweetened coconut, toasted
½	teaspoon baking soda	8	ounces guava paste, chilled and cut into ½-inch pieces (1 cup)
16	tablespoons unsalted butter, softened		

1   Adjust oven rack to middle position and heat oven to 350 degrees. Line 3 rimless baking sheets with parchment paper. Whisk oats, flour, cinnamon, salt, baking powder, and baking soda together in large bowl.

2   Using stand mixer fitted with paddle, beat butter, brown sugar, and ½ cup granulated sugar together on medium-high speed until light and fluffy, about 3 minutes. Reduce speed to low, add eggs and vanilla, and mix until combined, scraping down sides of bowl as needed. Slowly add flour mixture and mix until just combined, scraping down bowl as needed. Add coconut and mix until just combined.

3   Stir guava paste and remaining ¼ cup granulated sugar together in separate bowl until guava paste is coated in sugar. Stir guava mixture into cookie dough with rubber spatula until just incorporated. Divide dough into 24 portions (about 2⅓ ounces or 1 heaping ¼ cup each). Shape portions into balls. Place dough balls on prepared sheets, 8 balls per sheet, staggering portions and spacing them about 2½ inches apart. Using your hand, flatten balls to ¾-inch thickness.

4   Bake cookies, 1 sheet at a time, until edges are browned and set and centers are puffed with some pale, raw spots, 15 to 18 minutes, rotating sheet halfway through baking. Do not overbake. Let cookies cool on sheet for 5 minutes. Using spatula, transfer cookies to wire rack and let cool for 10 minutes before serving.

APPALACHIAN GINGERBREAD

A TIME-HONORED TRADITION

Malinda Russell's *A Domestic Cook Book*, published in 1866, is celebrated as the first cookbook by an African American author, but it has another distinction as the earliest known published collection of recipes from the southern Appalachians. As such, it stands as a document to the Southern mountaineers' love of gingerbread.

Amelia Simmons's 1796 cookbook, *American Cookery*, the first published in the United States, has four gingerbread recipes. Mary Randolph's *The Virginia House-Wife*, which Russell identifies as a primary source of her culinary education, has three, and Abby Fisher's 1881 book *What Mrs. Fisher Knows About Old Southern Cooking* has one for cake and one for cookies. But Russell's book, which records recipes that she made and served and sold at her Chuckey Mountain, Tennessee boardinghouse and later at her bakery, contains 10 different gingerbread recipes, two for snaps, one for ginger nuts, and one for ginger pudding.

That love of gingerbread is still celebrated every fall in the Kentucky mountains at the annual Knott County Gingerbread Festival, commemorating not only the sweet and its makers but also an old-time political tradition in which competing candidates would hire the best local gingerbread makers to hand out treats at the polls, hoping to win votes.

One logical explanation for the preponderance of ginger in the sweets made by Russell and other mountain bakers is the regional presence of black pepper and orange "wild ginger," a native plant that grows at high temperate elevations and was plentiful in the Appalachian mountains. It was foraged, dried, and ground by early settlers and used to flavor both food and drinks and would have been widely available when imported spices weren't.

But I like to think there's an additional reason for our love of dark, rich gingerbread: a flavor preference I call "Appalachian umami." That meaty umami resonance is present in the signature foods of the region—country ham, sock sausage, dried apple stack cake, shuck beans—but along with it comes a tangy accent that my mama liked to say "has a whang to it." Gingerbread's blend of deep butteriness with browned sugariness, underscored by a spicy bite of "whang," is the epitome.

And that intense tango of tastes is no doubt why I first fell in love with the Not-Afraid-of-Flavor Gingerbread recipe from the late pastry chef Karen Barker of Durham, North Carolina. Barker elevated a simple gingerbread with the addition of coffee (umami), black pepper and orange juice ("whang"), and plenty of ginger. But keeping to my heritage of mountain-larder-improv, I started adding and substituting the likes of cocoa and sorghum syrup (more umami) and marmalade (a bit more "whang").

The result is this Gingerbread Snack Cake, which can be gussied up for company, served on a plate with whipped cream. But if you want to do it the way grandmas and mamas have for centuries, just leave it in the pan on the counter with a knife and let anybody have some anytime they get a craving.

by Ronni Lundy

James Beard Award–winning author, and food and culture writer with 40 years of experience writing about southern Appalachia

Gingerbread Snack Cake

Serves 10 to 12 ~ Total Time: 1½ hours, plus 3 hours cooling

This tender, gingery snack cake is big on flavor and low on fuss. It starts with Karen Barker's Not-Afraid-of-Flavor Gingerbread recipe (see "Appalachian Gingerbread: A Time-Honored Tradition") and adds other flavors, including cocoa and orange marmalade. Sweet sorghum syrup gives a buttery resonance plain molasses cannot. The surprising additions of brewed coffee and black pepper layer in subtle bitterness and spiciness that balance the cake's sweetness.

If you can't find sorghum syrup, you can substitute molasses—just make sure it's not blackstrap. We like the complexity of a bitter orange marmalade, such as the one made by Bonne Maman, in this snack cake; do not substitute a sweet marmalade. Dust with confectioners' sugar before cutting, if desired.

2¼	cups (11¼ ounces) all-purpose flour
1	teaspoon baking soda
1	teaspoon ground ginger
1	teaspoon ground cinnamon
½	teaspoon unsweetened cocoa powder
½	teaspoon table salt
½	teaspoon pepper
½	cup buttermilk
½	cup room-temperature brewed coffee
¼	cup orange marmalade
8	tablespoons unsalted butter, softened
1	cup (7 ounces) sugar
3	large eggs
2	tablespoons finely chopped crystallized ginger
1	cup sweet sorghum syrup
½	cup vegetable oil

1   Adjust oven rack to middle position and heat oven to 350 degrees. Grease and flour 13 by 9-inch baking pan. Whisk flour, baking soda, ground ginger, cinnamon, cocoa, salt, and pepper together in bowl. Whisk buttermilk, coffee, and marmalade in second bowl until smooth.

2   Using stand mixer fitted with paddle, beat butter and sugar on medium-high speed until pale and fluffy, about 3 minutes. Add eggs and crystallized ginger and beat until smooth. Add sorghum syrup and oil and beat until uniform.

3   Reduce speed to low and add flour mixture in 3 additions, scraping down bowl as needed, and mix until just combined. Add buttermilk mixture and mix until smooth. Give batter final stir by hand. Pour batter into prepared pan and smooth top with rubber spatula. Bake until toothpick inserted in center comes out clean, 40 to 45 minutes (cake will spring back when touched and sides will begin to come away from pan).

4   Transfer pan to wire rack and let cake cool completely, about 3 hours. Cut into squares and serve.

SORGHUM SYRUP

Molasses, a typical gingerbread ingredient, is a dark syrup that is a by-product of the process of making sugar from sugarcane. Sorghum syrup, or sorghum molasses as it's often called, is an elixir made directly from the process of extracting and then heating the juice from sorghum cane. It has a more complex and nuanced flavor than plain molasses, and it ratchets up the flavor profile of any recipe it's added to.

If you're familiar with sorghum grain, we are talking about the same plant, but only specific varieties of the plant have a sugary juice that can be extracted to make the syrup. While sorghum grain was brought to the United States from Africa in the 1600s, these specific sorghum cane plants were imported in the 1800s to be cultivated as an alternative to cane sugar, since sorghum cane grows in temperate to colder climates. But while the syrup is delicious, it doesn't crystallize well the way sugar syrup does, and when beet sugar was discovered later in that century, the commercial processing of sorghum syrup was largely abandoned. Small farmers still grew and processed the syrup for their own use, though, particularly in the southern Appalachians, where it is beloved for its rich flavor.

In the mountains, you can still find folks who might refer to what their family grew as sugarcane when it was, in fact, sorghum (sugarcane won't thrive in mountain climates). While it used to be a product you could find only in certain regions, sorghum syrup is now available in specialty food stores and by mail order from a number of producers. Like wine, sorghum syrups are distinguished by the variety of cane, their terroir, and the techniques of the maker, so you may want to sample more than one. To fall in love with sorghum syrup, use a fork to mix 2 tablespoons of it with 1 tablespoon of softened butter and then slather that on a warm biscuit: messily divine.

Pound Cake

Serves 8 ~ Total Time: 1½ hours, plus 2 hours 10 minutes cooling

Rich, buttery, elegant pound cake wasn't a Southern invention. In her book *American Cake: From Colonial Gingerbread to Classic Layer, the Stories and Recipes Behind More Than 125 of Our Best-Loved Cakes*, Anne Byrn explains that pound cake likely came to the United States from England. The first known stateside recipe is from 1754 from Wicomico Church in Virginia (the church submitted the saved recipe to Helen Bullock's 1938 *The Williamsburg Art of Cookery* compilation). It's thought that this cake, which got its name because it was made with a pound each of butter, sugar, flour, and eggs, was made throughout the early colonies. It appeared in such iconic Southern cookbooks as Amelia Simmons's *American Cookery* (1796), Mary Randolph's *The Virginia House-Wife* (1824), and Abby Fisher's *What Mrs. Fisher Knows About Old Southern Cooking* (1881). Fisher's book features a "gold" and a "silver" version of the cake, which call for egg yolks and beaten egg whites, respectively.

Many pound cakes get their height from the leavening effects of creaming butter and sugar until light and fluffy. The butter holds small air pockets that create a tender, tight crumb in the cake when baked. But Kate Williams points out in her article, "How Pound Cake Became a Southern Classic" for Southern Kitchen, that these early recipes were published before electric mixers were available. Creaming butter and sugar with a wooden spoon and muscle enough to leaven a cake would take extreme work and skill. So Fisher's silver version, and many others from that time, incorporated yeast and whipped egg whites, likely to add leavening power.

By the time Georgia Gilmore was baking pound cakes (see "Feeding the Fight"), yeast and egg whites were less common. And making pound cakes required, as it does today, a lot of finesse. For many recipes, the ingredients have to be at certain temperatures (namely, softened butter) before baking to achieve the proper final texture. But for our version, we employ an untraditional method: We incorporate hot melted butter in the food processor. The fast-moving blade and the melted butter cause the liquid ingredients to quickly emulsify before they have a chance to curdle. Sifting the dry ingredients over the emulsified egg mixture in three additions ensures that no pockets of flour mar the finished cake.

1½	cups (6 ounces) cake flour
1	teaspoon baking powder
½	teaspoon table salt
1¼	cups (8¾ ounces) sugar
4	large eggs, room temperature
1½	teaspoons vanilla extract
16	tablespoons unsalted butter, melted and hot

1 Adjust oven rack to middle position and heat oven to 350 degrees. Grease and flour 8½ by 4½-inch loaf pan. Whisk flour, baking powder, and salt together in bowl.

2 Process sugar, eggs, and vanilla in food processor until combined, about 10 seconds. With processor running, add hot melted butter in steady stream until incorporated. Transfer to large bowl.

3 Sift flour mixture over egg mixture in 3 additions, whisking to combine after each addition until few streaks of flour remain. Continue to whisk batter gently until almost no lumps remain (do not overmix).

4 Transfer batter to prepared pan and smooth top with rubber spatula. Gently tap pan on counter to settle batter. Bake until toothpick inserted in center comes out with few crumbs attached, 50 minutes to 1 hour, rotating pan halfway through baking.

5 Let cake cool in pan on wire rack for 10 minutes. Run thin knife around edge of pan, remove cake from pan, and let cool completely on rack, about 2 hours. Serve. (Cake can be stored at room temperature for up to 3 days or frozen for up to 1 month; defrost cake at room temperature.)

Almond Cake

Add 1 teaspoon almond extract and ¼ cup slivered almonds to food processor with sugar, eggs, and vanilla. Sprinkle 2 tablespoons slivered almonds over cake before baking.

Ginger Cake

Add 3 tablespoons minced crystallized ginger, 1½ teaspoons ground ginger, and ½ teaspoon ground mace to food processor with sugar, eggs, and vanilla.

Lemon Cake

Add 2 tablespoons grated lemon zest (2 lemons) and 2 teaspoons juice to food processor with sugar, eggs, and vanilla.

FEEDING THE FIGHT

Georgia Gilmore proved that a hearty meal can power any honest effort, including an entire civil rights movement.

Gilmore, a Black food activist born in 1920 in Montgomery, Alabama, was best known for leading the Club from Nowhere during the Montgomery bus boycott. The group, named after its anonymous membership of both Black and white women, is credited for feeding and funding the boycott through their homemade meals and widespread fundraising efforts.

Prior to the resistance, Gilmore worked as a cook at the National Lunch Company. She lost her job in 1965, however, as a result of testifying in defense of Martin Luther King Jr. after he was indicted. Following Gilmore's dismissal, King and other resistance leaders pooled funds to help Gilmore start a home restaurant, which became a central hub for boycotters to eat, congregate,

and strategize. At Gilmore's counter often sat King himself, who famously loved her pork chops, and who brought in diners such as Lyndon B. Johnson and Robert F. Kennedy.

Gilmore was a key member of resistance meetings from day one. There, she rallied cooks, maids, and service workers to form the Club from Nowhere. The club's efforts started small, selling fried chicken sandwiches in the church parking lot of group meetings. Once they gained traction, the women branched out to providing full dinners (including pork chops, chicken dinners, lima beans, fried fish, and greens) and baked goods such as pies and cakes, including her famous pound cake. The group sold these meals to boycotters across Montgomery, stationing themselves at beauty parlors, laundromats, rallies, mass meetings, and their own homes.

Hundreds of dollars were raised each week by food sales, which were donated to

the Montgomery Improvement Association (the leading resistance group of the movement). The funds helped pay for alternative transportation during the 381-day bus boycott, which relied on a carpool system of more than 300 cars, trucks, and wagons. The Club from Nowhere's funds supported the gas, insurance, and vehicle repairs necessary to transport Black workers across town.

In a 1986 interview for the documentary *Eyes on the Prize: America's Civil Rights Years (1954–1965)*, Gilmore credited the women of the club as the reason for the boycott's success: "You see, they were maids and cooks. And they was the one that really and truly kept the bus running."

by Kelly Song

Cook's Country *test cook and journalist*

No.13
CELEBRATION
SWEETS

Left to right: Chocolate Soufflés (page 426), Bananas Foster (page 425), Chocolate-Lemon Doberge Cake (page 442), Brûléed Buttermilk Pie (page 464).

CAKE
PIE
VS.

WHY HOLDING TIGHT TO A RECIPE IS POWER

If you've lived in the South, odds are you've met an older woman who will not give you a recipe. The more you try to convince her that the secret to her pound cake is safe with you, the tighter she holds on.

Intellectual property in the form of a recipe is not to be taken lightly. It's power.

She might hint that the secret is a little lemon zest, or even walk through the whole thing with the niece that drives her to church. If she has a little money and a sense of humor, she might even get it engraved on her tombstone.

But more likely than not, it dies with her.

Even the best chefs have this problem. Charlie Mitchell, the first Black chef in New York to pull down a Michelin star, can't get his grandmother to reveal the secret to her sweet potato pie. "I can make it, but it is never exactly like hers," he told a magazine writer. "I haven't figured out why yet." She keeps dangling it like stick bait. Come back to Georgia, she says, and I'll teach you.

A recipe's power as cultural currency becomes crystal clear when you go to a school fundraiser or church supper in a new town and offer to bring your lemon bars. "You'll need to bring something else," the organizers will say. "Sarah has lemon bars."

Recipe hoarding, by and large, is a gendered pursuit. Especially among older generations, men hold a disproportionate amount of power. But a woman with the only key to a beloved family recipe in her pocket or a queen so good at lemon bars that no one would dream of trying to push her from the throne? That's a certain kind of power too.

I didn't fully understand the complex, intertwined relationship among Southern women, power, and cooking until someone recently reminded me that in 2013, I stood on a stage debating whether cake or pie was superior with the brilliant food journalist Kat Kinsman.

The event was part of an annual symposium arranged by the Southern Foodways Alliance, an important organization run for years by one man.

More often than not, the stars of the annual symposium were men. The stories that sprang from the event were told by so many men that Kathleen Purvis, a storied food editor from North Carolina and a regular at the event, declared once that men are the carpetbaggers of Southern food writing.

The theme the year I was invited to defend cake was "Women at Work," an examination of the role of women in Southern foodways. It was an attempt at counterprogramming coated in Gen X irony. There was a decidedly '50s housewife vibe built into the staging. The food scholar Marcie Cohen Ferris delivered a keynote from a podium set-dressed like a stove. Kat and I were encouraged to walk on stage dressed as cartoonish versions of Southern ladies.

I made a joke about it in my opening salvo: "Like family and church, cake is one of the pillars of Southern culture. Cake's position as the cultural currency for Southern women is of such importance that I have worn a dress. It is the first time I have been in a dress in more than 20 years."

At the time, the whole thing seemed funny and clever. Now it makes me cringe. The #MeToo movement hadn't yet reminded us how blind we can be to the sexism that swirls all around us, and the racial reckoning marked by Black Lives Matter had yet to reach the leadership of the alliance.

Still, I stand by our respective arguments for which is the most important Southern baked good.

"When you bake a pie, you are in the kitchen in the company of ghosts," Kat offered. "If you are crafting a crust, it's most likely because at some point in your life, someone thought well enough of you to stand beside you at a counter and gift the muscle memory from her hands to yours."

I countered that the cake is the sweet, tangible talisman of the South. It's connection, tradition, mother, and love. Kat called cake Carrie Underwood. Pie, she said, is June Carter Cash. I said pies are folk art and cakes are masterpieces. One has a wedding cake, not a wedding pie. And they don't try to break you out of prison with a pie.

We ended in a tie, because, really, life needs fewer winners and losers and more cooperation. But I think Kat won. "As we all know," she said from the stage, "in the South, there is perhaps no currency more vaunted and valuable than having a recipe with an ingredient that no one else can figure out."

by Kim Severson

national food correspondent for the New York Times, *Pulitzer Prize recipient, and four-time James Beard Award winner*

Bourbon Butterscotch Pudding

Serves 8 ~ Total Time: 50 minutes, plus 3 hours chilling

Acclaimed pastry chef Lisa Donovan (see "Sweetly Paying It Forward") has left her mark on Southern food culture not just with her baking prowess but also with her powerful pen and relentless advocacy.

In her evocative memoir, *Our Lady of Perpetual Hunger*, Donovan recounts leaving an abusive relationship, making a name for herself in the food world, and her experiences with sexism in that world and in restaurant kitchens. The candor was well received; Donovan won the 2021 M.F.K. Fisher Prize for her memoir.

Donovan is also co-creator of Southern Restaurants for Racial Justice, which raises funds to support Black food-industry start-ups and secure legacy businesses.

As for the pastry, in an article for *Food & Wine* titled "My Notebooks Tell the Story of How I Became a Chef," Donovan defines her style as "simple cakes and pies and puddings, with salty crunch and beautiful buttermilk cream; simple, simple, simple, but with articulated flavors." Simple, however, doesn't mean easy. "The tricky thing about simplicity is that you really have to know your shit. There is nowhere to hide when you partner with simple."

Her recipe for bourbon butterscotch pudding is simple with an impactful (and adult) spin. Here we provide our take, adding a glug of bourbon to our classic butterscotch pudding. As Donovan said in the article "A Grown-Up Pudding Cup" in *Garden & Gun*, "The trick is not being scared of really introducing some booze." Play around with adding (or taking away) a tablespoon or two to your taste.

When taking the temperature of the caramel in step 1, tilt the saucepan and move the thermometer back and forth to equalize hot and cool spots. It's important to use an immersion blender or whisk vigorously in step 2 in order to fully emulsify the butter and get a silky-smooth pudding at the end of cooking. If you like, follow Donovan's lead by topping servings of the pudding with lightly sweetened whipped cream and something crunchy, such as salted peanuts, cocoa nibs, crushed-up brittle or toffee, or some flaked sea salt.

SWEETLY PAYING IT FORWARD

We'd walk down three flights of stairs, slowly because he was just five and she was just one. Her on my hip, him holding my hand, one faded teal step, two, then three— we took this walk every morning to get him to school and then again every afternoon to come home. There were some days, usually after I'd worked a 4 p.m. to 3 a.m. shift as a waitress to wealthy college students, when I had a little cash in my pocket that we'd wander across Belmont Boulevard to a market with a lunch-line-style buffet to see what we might find with our quarters, to make something nice out of days that were increasingly feeling like a burden for my small, young family. When you owe everyone a buck and a dime, what's four dollars for a spring roll and a mango sticky rice to share between the three of you?

The first few times, in 2005, that we staggered into her restaurant, called the International Market, she just kindly smiled and sized us up. I, too, now have the same gaze when I see a young mother doing the standard, occasionally desperate, acrobatics of it all. She clocked our regular order after our third or fourth time. She also clocked me counting quarters and paying with sticky dollar bills that still reeked of Red Bull and hot sauce. After some time, we never paid for mango sticky rice again. She let me pay for the spring roll because, I'm quite certain, she knew that it was important for me to do so as their mother.

I would learn, far too late when the restaurant was closing, shortly after her death in 2018, that her name was Patti Myint, and that she had been cooking and serving Nashville in that simple but remarkable market since 1975.

This was also the year I started selling pastries out of my apartment baking while the kids slept, delivering before my shifts. I started bringing her a gift of hand pies as a thank-you between two mothers. It was small, but this exchange became a huge part of how I learned to exist in this world. Give as much as you can, recognize that the struggle and the beauty of life are all happening simultaneously for everyone, and pay whatever you can forward, quietly, even (and especially) if through a gift of rice with coconut milk and sliced mango.

by Lisa Donovan

chef and James Beard Award–winning writer whose memoir, Our Lady of Perpetual Hunger, *earned her a Les Dames d'Escoffier International M.F.K. Fisher Prize*

12	tablespoons unsalted butter, cut into ½-inch pieces	1	teaspoon lemon juice
½	cup (3½ ounces) granulated sugar	¾	teaspoon table salt
		1	cup heavy cream, divided
½	cup packed (3½ ounces) dark brown sugar	2	cups whole milk, divided
		¼	cup bourbon
¼	cup water	4	large egg yolks
2	tablespoons light corn syrup	¼	cup cornstarch
		2	teaspoons vanilla extract

1   Bring butter, granulated sugar, brown sugar, water, corn syrup, lemon juice, and salt to boil in large saucepan over medium heat, stirring occasionally to dissolve sugar and melt butter. Once mixture is at full rolling boil, cook, stirring occasionally, for 5 minutes (caramel will register about 240 degrees). Immediately reduce heat to medium-low and simmer gently (caramel should maintain steady stream of lazy bubbles; if not, adjust heat accordingly), stirring frequently, until mixture is color of dark peanut butter, 12 to 16 minutes (caramel will register about 300 degrees and should have slight burnt smell).

2   Off heat, carefully pour ¼ cup cream into caramel mixture and swirl to incorporate (mixture will bubble and steam); let bubbling subside. Submerge immersion blender in mixture and process for 30 seconds. (Alternatively, whisk mixture vigorously, scraping corners of saucepan, for 45 seconds.) Return saucepan to medium heat and gradually whisk in remaining ¾ cup cream until smooth. Whisk in 1¾ cups milk and bourbon until mixture is smooth, making sure to scrape corners and sides of saucepan to remove any remaining bits of caramel. Remove from heat.

3   Meanwhile, microwave remaining ¼ cup milk until simmering, 30 to 45 seconds. Whisk egg yolks and cornstarch in large bowl until smooth. Gradually whisk in hot milk until smooth; set aside (do not refrigerate).

4   Return saucepan to medium-high heat and bring mixture to full rolling boil, whisking frequently. Once mixture is boiling rapidly and beginning to climb toward top of saucepan, immediately pour into bowl with yolk mixture in 1 motion (do not add gradually). Whisk thoroughly for 10 to 15 seconds (mixture will thicken after few seconds). Whisk in vanilla. Spray piece of parchment paper with vegetable oil spray and press on surface of pudding.

5   Refrigerate until cold and set, at least 3 hours or up to 3 days. Whisk pudding until smooth before serving.

Bananas Foster

Serves 4   ~   Total Time: 20 minutes

Invented during the 1950s at Brennan's (see page 76), one of New Orleans's most storied restaurants, bananas Foster is a dessert and a magic show: A rum sauce is ignited around pieces of banana, often tableside, and the flambéed fruit is served over ice cream and quickly devoured.

In her memoir, *Miss Ella of Commander's Palace*, Ella Brennan recounts being tasked with coming up with the dessert for Richard Foster, the New Orleans Crime Commission chairman. A little frazzled, she grabbed the bananas and added a flambé inspired by baked Alaska. Today the dish is on their menu with the title "World Famous Bananas Foster." Following the Brennan's formula, we call for rum in our recipe for a little complexity. Cinnamon and lemon juice add some nuance to the sauce. For ease, we opted to forgo the flambéing step in this recipe. Cooking the bananas cut side down gives them a little color, and gold rum adds some of the caramel flavor you would get from a flambé. Look for yellow bananas with very few spots; overly ripe bananas will fall apart during cooking.

½	cup packed (3½ ounces) dark brown sugar	3	ripe bananas peeled, halved crosswise, then halved lengthwise
¼	cup plus 2 teaspoons gold rum, divided	4	tablespoons unsalted butter, cut into 4 pieces
2	tablespoons water		
1	cinnamon stick	1	teaspoon lemon juice
¼	teaspoon table salt		Vanilla ice cream

1   Combine sugar, ¼ cup rum, water, cinnamon stick, and salt in 12-inch skillet. Cook over medium heat, whisking frequently, until sugar is dissolved, 1 to 2 minutes. Add bananas, cut side down, to skillet and cook until glossy and golden on bottom, 1 to 1½ minutes. Flip bananas and continue to cook until tender but not mushy, 1 to 1½ minutes longer. Using tongs, transfer bananas to rimmed serving dish, leaving sauce in skillet.

2   Off heat, discard cinnamon stick. Whisk butter into sauce, 1 piece at a time, until incorporated. Whisk in lemon juice and remaining 2 teaspoons rum. Pour sauce over bananas. Serve with vanilla ice cream.

Chocolate Soufflés

Serves 8 ~ Total Time: 1 hour, plus 3 hours freezing

You can source Edna Lewis's famous recipes for chocolate soufflé online or in books, so you can try those ethereal treats. Here we're offering a recipe that you can make ahead by freezing and then baking. This ensures perfect soufflés on your first try.

1	tablespoon unsalted butter, softened, plus 4 tablespoons cut into ½-inch pieces
1	tablespoon plus ⅓ cup (2⅓ ounces) granulated sugar, divided
8	ounces bittersweet or semisweet chocolate, chopped
1	tablespoon orange-flavored liqueur, such as Grand Marnier
½	teaspoon vanilla extract
⅛	teaspoon table salt
2	tablespoons water
6	large eggs, separated, plus 2 large whites
2	tablespoons confectioners' sugar
¼	teaspoon cream of tartar

1 Grease eight 8-ounce ramekins with softened butter, then coat evenly with 1 tablespoon granulated sugar; refrigerate until ready to use. Microwave chocolate and remaining 4 tablespoons butter in large bowl at 50 percent power, stirring occasionally, until smooth, 2 to 4 minutes. Stir in orange liqueur, vanilla, and salt; set aside.

2 Bring remaining ⅓ cup granulated sugar and water to boil in small saucepan, then reduce heat to medium and simmer until sugar dissolves. Add egg yolks to stand mixer fitted with paddle; with mixer running, slowly add sugar syrup and beat on medium speed until mixture triples in volume, about 3 minutes. Fold into chocolate mixture.

3 Using clean, dry mixer bowl and whisk attachment, whip egg whites, confectioners' sugar, and cream of tartar on medium-low speed until foamy, about 1 minute. Increase speed to medium-high and whip until stiff peaks form, 3 to 4 minutes. Using rubber spatula, vigorously stir one-quarter of whipped whites into chocolate mixture. Gently fold remaining whites into chocolate mixture until just incorporated.

4 Fill each chilled ramekin almost to rim, wiping each rim clean. Cover each ramekin tightly with plastic wrap and freeze until firm, at least 3 hours or up to 1 month. (Do not thaw before baking.) To serve, adjust oven rack to middle position, heat oven to 400 degrees, and bake soufflés until fragrant, fully risen, and exterior is set but interior is still a bit loose and creamy, 16 to 18 minutes.

EDNA LEWIS'S SOUFFLÉ(S)

People don't often think of light, airy chocolate soufflé as inherently Southern. But for one Southern icon, Edna Lewis, the dish helped build her signature style.

Lewis was born in Freetown, Virginia, in 1916 and moved to New York in her early 30s. There, she had stints working as a seamstress and writing for a political newspaper. Meanwhile she began throwing dinner parties with a friend and antique dealer, John Nicholson.

In 1948 Nicholson opened Café Nicholson on the Upper East Side, a place he originally imagined as a bakery. But, according to a *New York Times* obituary, Lewis convinced him to make it a full-fledged restaurant. Nicholson hired her as the chef, giving her a fifty-fifty stake in the restaurant. The restaurant was eclectic with decorations he described as "fin de siècle Caribbean of Cuba style," meaning diverse, eccentric, and a bit romantic. Lewis shopped in basements to decorate the restaurant that became a gathering place for creatives. Even though this was in New York, it became a place for Lewis to hone the cooking she learned in the South and develop her culinary voice.

One of the signature menu items: Lewis's chocolate soufflé. You can find her recipe for this version in a December 1979 issue of the *New York Times*. The *Times* noted the recipe produces something with the texture of a "kind of soufflé-pudding," while the *New York Herald Tribune* described this soufflé as "light as a dandelion seed in a high wind."

This wasn't the only time Lewis had been famous for her chocolate soufflé. She spent a year as a guest chef at the Fearrington House in North Carolina (see page 106) in the 1980s. She worked with owners Jenny and R.B. Fitch to build a menu that combined Southern hospitality with their love of French food. That chocolate soufflé graced the cover of *Gourmet* magazine in the '80s and is still on the menu today.

The recipes from Café Nicholson and the Fearrington House are a little different. The Café Nicholson recipe has egg yolks, while the version from Fearrington uses all whites and has more chocolate. Did she change her recipe or is that just how they've been printed? No matter, Edna Lewis's tale of two soufflés is a sweet reminder that whether in the South or North, great cooking (and some chocolate) can elevate a menu.

by Morgan Bolling

ALL ABOUT LAYER CAKES

What signals a party more than a towering cake, standing tall on a pedestal, with swirls of frosting wrapping fluffy, buttery layers? The South is home to some of the most elaborate cakes, many with fascinating histories on their rise to stardom. But don't let the shine scare you: No matter how towering the cake, there are some universal steps for ensuring success, such as dividing the batter evenly among the pans so the layers bake at the same rate and have the same height. Other key factors, such as the type of flour and the mixing method, depend on the desired outcome. Cake flour, which has a low protein content, will deliver cake layers with a delicate, fine crumb, whereas all-purpose flour gives cake more structure. Creaming the butter and sugar results in a fluffy crumb and layers with good height, but sometimes another approach is best: reverse creaming. This technique of mixing butter into the dry ingredients creates a sturdy cake with an ultrafine, downy crumb. We turn to both techniques in this book. Here's a primer on making your cake the belle of the ball.

Cake Equipment

Digital Scale
Weighing dry ingredients ensures consistent results. We prefer digital scales for their readability and precision. Look for one that has a large weight range and that can be zeroed.

Stand Mixer
A stand mixer, with its hands-free operation, numerous attachments, and strong mixing arm, is a worthwhile investment if you plan on baking cakes regularly (KitchenAid is the gold standard). Heft matters, as does a strong motor that doesn't give out when whipping for a long period of time.

Rimmed Baking Sheet
Baking sheets aren't just for cookies. Bake thin cake layers for wide-screen sheet cakes such as Texas Chocolate Sheet Cake (page 450) on a sturdy stainless-steel half sheet pan.

8- and 9-inch Round Cake Pans
We have two requirements for a cake pan: sides that are at least two inches tall and a light color. Tall sides reduce the risk of batter rising up over the edge of the pan, while a light finish produces evenly baked, taller, and more level cakes with a tender crust. (By contrast, a darker pan produces a darker cake, as dark-colored pans absorb heat more efficiently than light-colored ones. Darker pans also tend to cause cakes to dome.)

Cooling Rack
A good wire rack allows air to circulate all around the cake as it cools. We like a stainless steel grid rack that can fit inside a rimmed baking sheet (helpful for glazing cake—or elevating fried chicken).

Cardboard Rounds
Cardboard rounds—which you can buy online or in craft stores—are simple but immensely helpful: They're great for moving cake layers, building cakes, lifting and transporting cakes, and serving cakes.

Offset Spatula
For frosting a cake, there's no better tool than an offset spatula. The long, narrow blade is ideal for scooping and spreading frosting.

Piping Sets
Floppy cloth pastry bags can stain or hold on to smells. Canvas bags tend to be too stiff. We prefer plastic bags; they're easy to handle for neat cake decorating and effortless to clean. In addition, we consider six different tips essential to cover a range of decorating needs: #4 round, #12 round, #70 round, #103 petal, #2D large closed star, and #1M open star. You'll also want four couplers—plastic nozzles that attach the tip to the bag.

Cake Stand
While you can frost and decorate cakes on any surface, it's much easier to get smooth coatings on a rotating cake stand.

Preparing Cake Pans

If you want to remove cakes from pans to build a layer cake, you'll need to line the pans; otherwise, the cake could stick and break into pieces as you attempt to remove it.

Creating Cake Layers

Sometimes cakes are two-layer affairs (one layer per cake pan) and sometimes they reach greater heights. If we're making a four-layer cake, it usually means we're slicing standard layers in half. The task seems daunting, but if you follow these instructions, you'll achieve thin, even layers without stress.

1   Place cake pan on sheet of parchment paper and trace around bottom of pan. Cut out parchment circle.

2   Evenly spray bottom and sides of pan with vegetable oil spray or rub with butter.

3   Fit parchment into pan, grease parchment, and then sprinkle with several table-spoons of flour. Shake and rotate pan to coat it evenly, then shake out excess.

1   Measure height of cake. Using paring knife, mark midpoint at several places around sides of cake.

2   Using marks as guide, cut horizontal line around sides of layer.

3   Following scored line, run knife around cake several times, cutting inward. Once knife is inside cake, use back-and-forth motion.

4   Once knife cuts through cake, separate layers and gently insert your fingers between them. Lift top layer and place it on counter.

Frosting a Layer Cake

These frosting steps are for a two-layer cake, but the technique is transferable to more layers.

1 Keep the Platter Clean

Cover the edges of the cake stand or platter with four strips of parchment paper. The strips ensure that extra frosting doesn't end up on the platter. Once the cake is frosted, you can slide out and discard the parchment for a neat presentation.

2 Frost the First Layer

You may want to anchor your cake by dolloping a small amount of frosting in the center of the cake stand and then placing a cake layer on top. Dollop the correct portion of frosting in the center of the cake layer. Using an offset spatula, spread the frosting evenly from the center to the edge of the cake. (The recipe may instruct you to leave a border.)

3 Frost the Top

Place the second layer on top, making sure it's aligned with the first layer. As you place the top layer, don't push down on it or you risk squeezing the frosting out the sides of the cake, but do press gently to make sure it adheres. Spread frosting evenly over the top layer, pushing it over the edge of the cake.

4 Frost the Sides

Gather several tablespoons of frosting with the tip of an offset spatula. Gently smear frosting onto the sides of the cake. Once covered, gently run the edge of the spatula around the sides of the cake to smooth out bumps and tidy areas where the frosting on the top and sides merge. Remove the strips of parchment before serving.

When's the Cake Done?

The amount of time it will take for a cake to bake depends on many factors, such as the temperature of the oven and the depth of the batter. But don't rely on the recipe's time alone: A near foolproof way to test doneness is with the classic toothpick test. Most butter cakes are finished baking when a toothpick inserted in the center of the cake comes out clean. For moister chocolate cakes, the toothpick should come out with a few crumbs attached to ensure the cake isn't dry.

Cooling with Care

The majority of cakes need just a little cooling time in the pan—about 10 minutes—to set up, after which they should be removed from the pan so that the residual heat doesn't overbake them. Cool cakes on a wire cooling rack. When you remove a cake from a pan, be sure to remove the parchment before reinverting the cake. If you're storing cooled cake layers at room temperature before building your layer cake, wrap them well in plastic wrap. If you opt to freeze them, wrap them in plastic followed by a layer of aluminum foil. You can freeze layers for up to one month; defrost wrapped cakes at room temperature.

Caramel Cake

Serves 8 ~ Total Time: 1¾ hours, plus 1 hour cooling

The name caramel cake doesn't actually describe the cake itself but rather the thick, toffee-flavored icing that forms a crystalline crust on top of the rich, buttery yellow cake beneath. We're in awe of the lengths some go to achieve the grandest frosting, such as Maya Angelou in her recipe inspired by her grandmother's soul-healing cake (see "Momma and Maya's Caramel Cake"). In *My Mother's Southern Desserts: More Than 180 Treasured Family Recipes for Holiday and Everyday Celebrations*, the acclaimed *Food & Wine* editor James Villas also notes the treasured status of caramel cake. He says that Paw Paw's Birthday Caramel Cake with Caramel Frosting "has been in our family for at least four generations, and Mother has already handed down the recipe to my young niece." The traditional process involves boiling brown sugar, butter, milk and vanilla, then beating it quickly before it hardens. We whip our frosting in a stand mixer and stir in confectioners' sugar and extra softened butter to keep the frosting soft and spreadable for people who aren't as quick with their decorating skills. But this frosting still hardens over time. And if the frosting does begin to stiffen while you are working, you can microwave it for about 10 seconds (or until it returns to a spreadable consistency).

Cake

- ½ cup buttermilk, room temperature
- 4 large eggs, room temperature
- 2 teaspoons vanilla extract
- 2¼ cups (11¼ ounces) all-purpose flour
- 1½ cups (10½ ounces) granulated sugar
- 1½ teaspoons baking powder
- ½ teaspoon baking soda
- ¾ teaspoon table salt
- 16 tablespoons unsalted butter, cut into 16 pieces and softened

Frosting

- 2 cups packed (14 ounces) dark brown sugar
- 12 tablespoons unsalted butter, cut into 12 pieces and softened, divided
- ½ teaspoon table salt
- ½ cup heavy cream
- 1 teaspoon vanilla extract
- 2½ cups (10 ounces) confectioners' sugar, sifted

1 **For the cake** Adjust oven rack to middle position and heat oven to 350 degrees. Grease two 9-inch round cake pans, line with parchment paper, grease parchment, and flour pans. Whisk buttermilk, eggs, and vanilla together in 4-cup liquid measuring cup. Using stand mixer fitted with paddle, mix flour, sugar, baking powder, baking soda, and salt on medium-low speed until combined, about 15 seconds. Add butter, 1 piece at a time, and beat until only pea-size pieces remain. Add half of buttermilk mixture, increase speed to medium-high, and beat until light and fluffy, about 2 minutes. Slowly add remaining buttermilk mixture and beat until incorporated, about 15 seconds. Give batter final stir by hand.

2 Divide batter evenly between prepared pans and bake until golden and toothpick inserted in center comes out clean, 20 to 25 minutes, rotating pans halfway through baking. Let cakes cool in pans on wire rack for 10 minutes. Remove cakes from pans and let cool completely on rack, at least 1 hour.

3 **For the frosting** Heat brown sugar, 8 tablespoons butter, and salt in large saucepan over medium heat until small bubbles appear around perimeter of pan, 4 to 8 minutes. Whisk in cream and cook until ring of bubbles reappears, about 1 minute. Off heat, whisk in vanilla.

4 Transfer hot frosting mixture to clean, dry stand mixer bowl; fit mixer with paddle and gradually mix in confectioners' sugar on low speed until incorporated. Increase speed to medium-low and beat until frosting is pale brown and just warm, 3 to 5 minutes. Add remaining 4 tablespoons butter, 1 piece at a time, and beat until light and fluffy, 1 to 2 minutes.

5 Place 1 cake round on platter. Spread ¾ cup frosting over cake, then top with second cake round. Spread remaining frosting evenly over top and sides of cake. Serve.

MOMMA AND MAYA'S CARAMEL CAKE

Maya Angelou, writer, poet, and cookbook author, writes about her grandmother's caramel cake in her cookbook, *Hallelujah! The Welcome Table: A Lifetime of Memories with Recipes*. The book is a mix of life stories and recipes, and the story tied to caramel cake involves her grandmother, Annie Henderson, whom Angelou called Momma.

Angelou writes about a period of her childhood when she became mute (except for speaking to her brother) after being assaulted—the story behind her famous memoir, "I Know Why the Caged Bird Sings." A teacher reprimanded Maya for staying silent, at first with words and then by slapping her in front of the class. Maya ran to her grandmother's store with her brother following a throw behind. And Momma, after calming her down, walked Maya back to school and slapped the teacher in front of the classroom before declaring, "Now, Sister, nobody has the right to hit nobody in the face. So I am wrong this time, but I'm teaching you a lesson." Momma then turned to Maya and told her to sit back down and receive her lesson. It was the only time Maya saw her grandmother get physical. That afternoon, when Maya returned home, there was a gorgeous caramel cake, "looking like paradise, oozing sweetness," waiting for her on the counter. Her uncle explained, "This cake can't pay you for being slapped in the face. Momma made it just to tell you how much we love you and how precious you are."

Momma was born to freed slaves in 1877. To support her children, she would sell freshly fried meat pies to workers at the local cotton gin and lumber mill, and she went on to open a store in Stamps, Arkansas, where she became a community leader. Momma raised Maya and her brother for a large part of their childhood. Maya revered Momma's cooking. She explains how her grandmother didn't have access to brown sugar, so for the caramel cake, she made homemade caramel through a laborious process that resulted in a grand cake: "Making her caramel cake took four to five hours, but the result was worthy of the labor. The salty sweetness of the caramel frosting along with the richness of the batter made the dessert soften and liquefy on the tongue and slip quietly down the throat almost without notice. Save that it left a memory of heaven itself in the mouth."

Maya Angelou's recipe for caramel cake calls for soaking a yellow cake with a caramel syrup and coating it in a caramel frosting made with browned butter. It yields a divine slice.

by Morgan Bolling

Smith Island Cake

Serves 10 to 12   ~   Total Time: 2¼ hours, plus 3 hours chilling and cooling

Smith Island, Maryland, may be a small place (with a population of less than 300 people), but it boasts a cake with a reputation so grand that it's the official state dessert: Smith Island cake. Born in the early 1900s, this impressive dessert features multiple thin layers of buttery yellow cake sleekly separated with a shiny, rich, fudgy frosting.

This island in the Chesapeake Bay historically was sustained by the fishing industry. According to the Smith Island Baking Company, when fishermen embarked on extended voyages, their wives gave them this layered cake as a sweet send-off. We spoke to Elaine Eff, a Maryland folklorist who helped create the Smith Island Visitor's Center (now the Smith Island Cultural Center), and she theorized this cake was a good fit because the dense, sugary layers provided a vital energy boost, and the high ratio of chocolate frosting to yellow cake kept the dessert moist over extended periods of time. She also noted that on the island, it is so ubiquitous it's just called "cake."

One other reason for the multiple thin layers, Eff explained, was timing. Smith Island didn't get electricity until the 1950s, which meant the island women had to bake using a metal box called a cooker over a wood stove. It was sort of a precursor to a toaster oven with a relatively small amount of space. With such a set-up, thin cake layers were more forgiving than thick layers, which could be prone to uneven baking.

This layered creation may have been an inventive solution to constraints of the era, but it's also uniquely delicious, and locals are deeply proud of it. Eff remembered the determination that went into naming the cake the state dessert. She said, "It was an absolute miracle that this became the state dessert." Mary Ada Marshall brought cakes from her home on the island to the mainland and went from one elected official to another, dropping off cakes and campaigning for their recognition. The determination paid off, and in 2008 the cake became the official state dessert of Maryland, a significant honor for the island.

The population of Smith Island is shrinking, and with water rising, so is the physical space. "One of the things that will probably outlive the island is the Smith Island cake. That breaks my heart," Eff says.

To make all those beautiful layers in our homage to this special cake, we call for baking yellow cake batter in eight portions, spreading a thin layer of the batter in two cake pans at a time and baking the layers in four intervals for about 10 minutes each. Many recipes for the ganache-like frosting include milk, but heavy cream gives the frosting extra body for supporting the cake's many layers. You may have extra batter after baking all of the cake layers. Be sure to let the cake pans cool completely before filling with more batter.

Frosting

10	ounces bittersweet chocolate, chopped
1	cup heavy cream
1	cup (7 ounces) sugar
¼	teaspoon table salt
1	teaspoon vanilla extract
8	tablespoons unsalted butter, softened

Cake

2½	cups (10 ounces) cake flour
1¼	teaspoons baking powder
¼	teaspoon baking soda
¾	teaspoon table salt
1¾	cups (12¼ ounces) sugar, divided
1	cup buttermilk, room temperature
10	tablespoons unsalted butter, melted and cooled
3	large eggs, separated, plus 3 large yolks, room temperature
3	tablespoons vegetable oil
2	teaspoons vanilla extract
	Pinch cream of tartar

1 **For the frosting** Place chocolate in large bowl. Heat cream, sugar, and salt in small saucepan over medium-low heat, stirring occasionally, until sugar dissolves and mixture begins to simmer. Pour hot cream mixture over chocolate and whisk until smooth. Whisk in vanilla and butter until glossy. Cover and refrigerate until frosting is firm but still spreadable, about 1 hour.

2 **For the cake** Adjust oven rack to middle position and heat oven to 350 degrees. Generously grease two 9-inch round cake pans, line with parchment paper, grease parchment, and flour pans. Whisk flour, baking powder, baking soda, salt, and 1½ cups sugar together in bowl. Whisk buttermilk, melted butter, egg yolks, oil, and vanilla together in second bowl.

3 Using stand mixer fitted with whisk attachment, whip egg whites and cream of tartar on medium-low speed until foamy, about 1 minute. Increase speed to medium-high and whip whites to soft billowy mounds, about 1 minute. Gradually add remaining ¼ cup sugar and whip until glossy, stiff peaks form, 2 to 3 minutes; transfer to third bowl.

4 Add flour mixture to now-empty mixer bowl and mix on low speed, gradually adding buttermilk mixture and mixing until almost incorporated (a few streaks of dry flour will remain), about 15 seconds. Scrape down bowl, then mix on medium-low speed until smooth and fully incorporated, 10 to 15 seconds.

5 Using rubber spatula, stir one-third of whites into batter. Gently fold remaining whites into batter until no white streaks remain. Spread about ⅔ cup batter in even layer in each prepared pan. Bake until edges are golden brown and cake springs back when touched, 10 to 14 minutes. Let cakes cool in pans on wire rack for 5 minutes. Run thin knife around edge of pans, remove cakes from pans, discarding parchment, and let cool completely on rack. Let pans cool completely, reline pans with parchment, grease parchment, and flour pans. Repeat process 3 times for a total of 8 layers.

6 Line edges of cake platter with 4 strips of parchment to keep platter clean. Place 1 cake layer on platter. Spread ¼ cup frosting evenly over top, right to edge of cake. (If frosting is too stiff, let stand at room temperature for 5 minutes, then stir to soften.) Repeat with 6 more cake layers, spreading ¼ cup frosting evenly over each layer. Top with remaining cake layer and spread remaining frosting evenly over top and sides of cake. To smooth frosting, run edge of offset spatula around cake sides and over top. Carefully remove parchment strips before serving.

Apple Stack Cake

Serves 10 to 12 ~ Total Time: 2¼ hours, plus 29 hours cooling and softening

Appalachian stack cakes were born of necessity. During tough times, resourceful Appalachian cooks, unable to spare eggs and butter for conventional cake, baked up thin, crisp, spiced rounds, filled them with various fruit mixtures, and left them to "ripen." After a couple of days, the filling moistened the sturdy layers, yielding a soft, fruity cake with robust flavor.

In Appalachian folklore the stack is a wedding cake; women in the town would each bake a single layer of cake and then bring it to the wedding reception to stack together, with layers sandwiching apple filling. The towering cake would be big enough to feed the wedding guests—particularly fitting if the bride was popular. In her article for *Southern Living*, "Why Apple Stack Cake Is a Special-Occasion Dessert," Ronni Lundy says this is likely just legend: Assuming everyone had different shaped pans, stacking the cake would be difficult. Plus, this cake only achieves the right texture after a day or more, once the filling softens the cookie-like layers; that can't happen within the course of a wedding reception.

Apple stack cake was more likely a Thanksgiving or Christmas dessert, especially considering the work involved. Like cakes made by modern chefs, this recipe is enriched with some eggs and butter. It has hearty, cookie-like layers but also a rich taste. Allowing the stack cake to sit is vital, as it allows the layers to soak up moisture from the homemade apple butter. We like to serve this cake at room temperature, but if you don't have the time to let it sit out of the refrigerator, it is still delicious cold.

Filling

3	(6-ounce) bags dried apples
1	cup packed (7 ounces) light brown sugar
1½	teaspoons ground cinnamon
½	teaspoon ground cloves
½	teaspoon ground allspice

Layers

6	cups (30 ounces) all-purpose flour
1	tablespoon baking powder
1	teaspoon baking soda
¼	teaspoon table salt
½	cup buttermilk
2	large eggs
1	teaspoon vanilla extract
16	tablespoons unsalted butter, softened
1	cup (7 ounces) granulated sugar
1	cup packed (7 ounces) light brown sugar
	Confectioners' sugar for dusting

1 **For the filling** Place apples in medium saucepan and add water to cover. Bring to boil over high heat. Reduce heat to medium-low and simmer until apples are completely softened, about 10 minutes. Drain apples and let cool until just warm, about 15 minutes. Puree apples in food processor until they form a chunky paste. Transfer to bowl and stir in sugar, cinnamon, cloves, and allspice. (Filling can be refrigerated for up to 2 days.)

2 **For the layers** Adjust oven racks to upper-middle and lower-middle positions and heat oven to 350 degrees. Spray 2 rimmed baking sheets with vegetable oil spray. Whisk flour, baking powder, baking soda, and salt together in medium bowl. Whisk buttermilk, eggs, and vanilla together in 4-cup liquid measuring cup.

3 Using stand mixer fitted with paddle, beat butter, granulated sugar, and brown sugar on medium-high speed until light and fluffy, about 2 minutes, scraping down bowl as needed. Reduce speed to medium-low and add flour mixture in 3 additions, alternating with buttermilk mixture in 2 additions, scraping down bowl as needed. Give dough final stir by hand. (Dough will be thick.)

4 Divide dough into 8 equal portions. Roll 2 portions of dough (keep remaining portions covered) into 10-inch circle about ¼ inch thick. Using 9-inch cake pan as template, trim away excess dough to form 2 perfectly round 9-inch disks. Transfer disks to prepared baking sheets and bake until golden brown, 10 to 12 minutes, switching and rotating sheets halfway through baking. Transfer disks to wire rack. Repeat rolling and baking with remaining dough portions, letting baking sheets cool completely between batches. Let disks cool for at least 1 hour. (Layers can be wrapped tightly in plastic and stored at room temperature for up to 2 days.)

5 Place 1 layer on serving plate and spread with 1 cup filling. Repeat 6 times. Top with final layer, wrap tightly in plastic, and refrigerate until layers soften, at least 24 hours or up to 2 days. Let cake sit at room temperature for at least 4 hours. (If you're short on time, cake can also be served cold from refrigerator.) Unwrap cake. Dust with confectioners' sugar. Serve.

Blackberry Jam Cake

Serves 10 to 12 ~ Total Time: 2 hours, plus 3½ hours cooling and chilling

Jam cake is a moist, dense cake that gets its signature texture from jam stirred into the batter. The rich cake layers alternate with a boiled milk frosting, and the result is a very moist cake that keeps well. Outfitted with warm spices, the cake is typically served at Christmas. Some Kentuckians lay claim to the cake, but according to Damaris Phillips in the article "Why Old-Fashioned Kentucky Jam Cake Tastes Like Home" for *Southern Living*, the recipe came to Kentucky and other Appalachian states from German immigrants who first settled in Pennsylvania before moving south.

For this version, we toast cinnamon, allspice, and cloves to give the cake an aromatic quality without masking the star ingredient: a generous scoop of blackberry jam. Many cooks swear by making a homemade jam for this cake, but we turn to store-bought for ease. Thinning the jam in the microwave and adding a little water to the batter made the layers light and fluffy.

A boiled frosting—one made by cooking a milk-and-flour paste and then beating butter into it until it's silky and custardy—with notes of caramel complements the lightly spiced blackberry cake. Spreading an extra layer of jam on the first cake layer after frosting reinforces the bright blackberry flavor. Plan ahead, as the frosting needs time to cool.

Cake

2	teaspoons ground cinnamon
¼	teaspoon ground allspice
⅛	teaspoon ground cloves
¾	cup seedless blackberry jam
1	cup buttermilk, room temperature
3	tablespoons water
1	teaspoon vanilla extract
3	cups (15 ounces) all-purpose flour
1	tablespoon baking powder
¾	teaspoon table salt
20	tablespoons (2½ sticks) unsalted butter, softened
1⅓	cups (9⅓ ounces) granulated sugar
½	cup packed (3½ ounces) light brown sugar
4	large eggs, room temperature

Frosting

1½	cups packed (10½ ounces) dark brown sugar
¼	cup (1¼ ounces) all-purpose flour
3	tablespoons cornstarch
½	teaspoon table salt
¼	teaspoon baking soda
1½	cups whole milk
2	teaspoons vanilla extract
24	tablespoons (3 sticks) unsalted butter, cut into 24 pieces and softened
¼	cup seedless blackberry jam
1½	cups walnuts, toasted and chopped (optional)

1 **For the cake** Adjust oven rack to lower-middle position and heat oven to 350 degrees. Grease two 9-inch round cake pans, line with parchment paper, grease parchment, and flour pans. Heat cinnamon, allspice, and cloves in small skillet over medium heat until fragrant, about 1 minute; set aside. Microwave jam in bowl until thin enough to pour, 35 to 45 seconds, stirring halfway through microwaving.

2 Whisk buttermilk, water, and vanilla into jam. Whisk flour, baking powder, salt, and toasted spices together in large bowl. Using stand mixer fitted with paddle, beat butter, granulated sugar, and brown sugar on medium-high speed until light and fluffy, about 2 minutes. Reduce speed to medium-low and add eggs, one at a time, until incorporated. Add flour mixture in 3 additions, alternating with jam mixture in 2 additions, stopping occasionally to scrape down bowl.

3 Divide batter evenly between prepared pans and smooth tops with rubber spatula. Gently tap pans on counter to release air bubbles. Bake until deep golden brown and toothpick inserted in center comes out clean, 35 to 40 minutes, rotating pans halfway through baking. Let cakes cool in pans on wire rack for 10 minutes. Remove cakes from pans, discarding parchment, and let cool completely on rack, at least 1 hour.

> continued

4 **For the frosting** Meanwhile whisk sugar, flour, cornstarch, salt, and baking soda together in bowl. Slowly whisk in milk until smooth. Strain mixture through fine-mesh strainer into medium saucepan. Cook over medium heat, whisking constantly, until mixture boils and is very thick, 5 to 7 minutes. Transfer milk mixture to clean bowl and let cool completely, about 2 hours.

5 Using stand mixer fitted with whisk attachment, mix cooled milk mixture and vanilla on low speed until combined, about 30 seconds. Add butter, 1 piece at a time, and whip until incorporated, about 2 minutes. Increase speed to medium-high and whip until frosting is light and fluffy, about 5 minutes. Let sit at room temperature until stiff, about 1 hour.

6 Whisk jam in bowl until smooth. Line edges of cake platter with 4 strips of parchment to keep platter clean. Place 1 cake layer on platter. Spread 1½ cups frosting evenly over top, right to edge of cake. Spread jam over frosting, leaving ½-inch border. Top with remaining cake layer and spread remaining frosting evenly over top and sides of cake. Press walnuts, if using, onto sides of cake. Refrigerate cake until set, about 30 minutes. Carefully remove parchment strips before serving. (Frosted cake can be refrigerated for up to 24 hours; bring to room temperature before serving.)

FROM BLACKBERRIES TO JAM CAKE

When I was a girl, our blackberries came from the graveyard. We donned long sleeves, thick britches in the sweltering July heat. In praise of our bloodline, we took up pails and buckets, risked the prick of the brambles, the itch of poison ivy, and chiggers for the jeweled globes of fruit. My grandparents spoke the names of our kin, pointed out their graves, then grew quiet. Even the cows and horses bowed their heads. The only sound was the plunk of berries hitting the bucket or the caw of a crow in the pine-lined sky. The whole Earth seemed to grow silent in reverence.

Author Crystal Wilkinson

Andrew Cenci / the New York Times / Redux

We stood in the blackberry patch, picked berries, and prayed for: Henry Adams, James Jones, Jim Kit, for Esther, Herlon, Betty Burdett, Frank Wilhite, Andrew, Betty Napier, for Bolden, Delilah, Enoch, Fannie, Green, Isabel, James Thomas, Jesse D., Jessie P., for Big Joe, Judy, Jula, Lillie, Mack, Mary Thomas, Melinda Jenkins, Patrick, Paul, Walter, Lucy, and the others. We ate warm blackberries in the sun before we took the rest home to be washed, canned, or frozen. All summer we ate blackberry soup, devoured cobbler.

In winter, before Christmas, Granny rose early, headed to the cellar, retrieved a jar of blackberries. She took up her saucepan and sugar. She made jam. She pulled her mixing bowl from the cupboard, creamed butter and sugar. Added the eggs one at a time. Sprinkled cloves, cinnamon, and added pecans, raisins, and peach preserves. She added baking soda to buttermilk, told me to always remember that it's baking soda, not powder. She sifted flour. Stirred in the jam and I watched the mix turn from purple to lavender before she poured it into her cake pan. When the cake was done we bowed our heads in prayer before we ate on Christmas day.

Years later, a week before Christmas, I grease my Bundt pan, heat my oven to 350 degrees. I take up my grandmother's yellow mixing bowl. I sift flour. I cream butter and sugar. I take out frozen berries and make jam. A pensive glow floated across my grandmother's face while she baked as if there was always something greater at work beyond the small kitchen we stood in. In the dim lighting of my own kitchen, a flicker of memory is all I need to lead me back to my people. Some things never leave you. A strand of loose hair she pressed behind her ear, the way she smelled, the sigh she made when she grew tired. I remember her hands, the way her wrist turned when she stirred the batter. The dim light sparkles in my own kitchen, my wrist turns, the deep purple jam turns lavender in my grandmother's yellow mixing bowl. I sprinkle cloves and cinnamon, bake jam cake in her honor.

by Crystal Wilkinson

award-winning author of the culinary memoir Praisesong for the Kitchen Ghosts: Stories and Recipes from Five Generations of Black Country Cooks, *as well as a collection of poems and three works of fiction*

Lady Baltimore Cake

Serves 10 to 12
Total Time: 2 hours, plus
2 hours 10 minutes cooling

Statuesque Lady Baltimore cake is dressed to impress, with three layers of tender white cake, stripes of dried fruit and nut filling, and mounds of sticky meringue-like icing. The cake became popular after it played an important role in the 1906 romance novel *Lady Baltimore* by Owen Wister (set in Charleston, South Carolina). The book became a best seller, and bakers started making Lady Baltimore cakes based on Wister's description. Over a hundred years later, Lady Baltimore cake is still popular in the South, especially around Christmas.

This cake's filling consists of plenty of ground dried fruit, pecans, and bourbon. Using a mixture of fruits gives the filling a vibrant flavor. Combining the sticky, nutty mixture with some frosting makes it easier to spread. Sandwiching that between tender white layer cake and swaddling the whole thing in a sweet seven-minute frosting results in a cake that would be worthy of taking a leading role in another best-selling book.

> continued

Cake

1	cup whole milk, room temperature
6	large egg whites, room temperature
2	teaspoons vanilla extract
2¼	cups (9 ounces) cake flour
1¾	cups (12¼ ounces) granulated sugar
2	teaspoons baking powder
1	teaspoon table salt
12	tablespoons unsalted butter, cut into 12 pieces and softened but still cool

Sugared Pecans

2	cups pecans
2	tablespoons granulated sugar
¼	teaspoon table salt
1	tablespoon bourbon, rum, or water
1	tablespoon unsalted butter
2	teaspoons vanilla extract
1	teaspoon packed light brown sugar

Frosting

1¾	cups (12¼ ounces) granulated sugar
3	large egg whites
7	tablespoons cold water
5	teaspoons light corn syrup
¼	teaspoon cream of tartar
	Pinch table salt
1¼	teaspoons vanilla extract
1	cup dried mixed fruits (any combination of cherries, dates, figs, pineapple, and raisins)
¼	cup pecans, toasted
2	tablespoons bourbon, rum, or water

1   **For the cake** Adjust oven rack to middle position and heat oven to 350 degrees. Grease three 8-inch round cake pans, line with parchment paper, grease parchment, and flour pans. Whisk milk, egg whites, and vanilla together in bowl.

2   Using stand mixer fitted with paddle, mix flour, sugar, baking powder, and salt on low speed until combined, about 5 seconds. Add butter, 1 piece at a time, until only pea-size pieces remain, about 1 minute. Add half of milk mixture, increase speed to medium-high, and beat until light and fluffy, about 30 seconds. Reduce speed to medium-low, add remaining milk mixture, and mix until incorporated, about 15 seconds (batter may look curdled). Give batter final stir by hand.

3   Divide batter evenly among prepared pans and smooth tops with rubber spatula. Gently tap pans on counter to release air bubbles. Bake until toothpick inserted in center comes out clean, 18 to 22 minutes, switching and rotating pans halfway through baking. Let cakes cool in pans on wire rack for 10 minutes. Remove cakes from pans, discarding parchment, and let cool completely on rack, about 2 hours.

4   **For the sugared pecans** While cakes cool, spread pecans in even layer on rimmed baking sheet and toast in oven, tossing occasionally, until fragrant and deepened in color, 6 to 8 minutes. While pecans are toasting, stir granulated sugar and salt together in bowl.

5   Bring bourbon, butter, vanilla, and brown sugar to boil in medium saucepan over medium-high heat, whisking constantly. Stir in pecans and cook, stirring constantly, until pecans are shiny and almost all liquid has evaporated, about 1½ minutes.

6   Toss pecans in bowl with sugar-salt mixture, return to sheet, and let cool completely; set aside.

7   **For the frosting** Combine sugar, egg whites, cold water, corn syrup, cream of tartar, and salt in bowl of stand mixer. Set bowl over saucepan filled with 1 inch barely simmering water, making sure that water does not touch bottom of bowl. Cook, whisking constantly, until mixture registers 160 degrees, 5 to 10 minutes.

8   Remove bowl from heat and transfer to stand mixer fitted with whisk attachment. Whip warm egg white mixture on medium speed until soft peaks form, about 5 minutes. Add vanilla, increase speed to medium-high, and continue to whip until mixture has cooled completely and stiff peaks form, 5 to 7 minutes.

9   Process dried fruits and pecans in food processor until finely chopped, 20 to 30 seconds. Transfer to bowl and mix in bourbon. Stir in 2 cups frosting.

10   Line edges of cake platter with 4 strips of parchment paper to keep platter clean. Place 1 cake layer on platter. Spread half of dried fruit mixture evenly over top. Repeat with 1 more cake layer, pressing lightly to adhere, and remaining dried fruit mixture. Top with remaining cake layer, pressing lightly to adhere. Spread frosting evenly over top and sides of cake, using back of spoon to create attractive swirls and peaks in icing. Decorate with sugared pecans. Carefully remove parchment strips before serving.

BAKING IN SOUTHERN LITERATURE

The United States boasts an abundance of delicious food and wonderful stories, but no region puts these two beloved entities together with more creativity and energy than the South. From poets and playwrights to short-story writers and novelists, the South is home to countless authors and their literary works in which food and cooking play a meaningful role. Southern literature abounds with characters who are cooking, eating, and talking about food. The most memorable of these food-centered literary creations involve baking, and the finest of these center on cakes.

In *To Kill a Mockingbird*, published in 1960, author Harper Lee references Lane cake, not once but twice. Scout Finch notes that her neighbor, Miss Maudie Atkinson, has baked her famous Lane cake to welcome Aunt Alexandra to the Finches' home; later Miss Maudie promises to make another just as long as she can do so without revealing her secret recipe to an inquisitive and competitive neighbor. The recipe for this four-layer showstopper of a celebration cake first appeared in a cookbook self-published by Emma Rylander Lane in 1898. The cake has a luscious filling studded with pecans, raisins, and shredded coconut, and is traditionally spiked with a prodigious amount of whiskey, which Scout refers to as "shinny."

Just a few years earlier, in 1956, Truman Capote put the baking of cakes at the heart of his beautiful and moving short story *A Christmas Memory*. Set in the 1930s and first published in *Mademoiselle*, the tale follows two cousins, a seven-year-old boy and an elderly spinster, who collaborate on making 30 fruitcakes each November as gifts for people they appreciate and admire. We follow them in acquiring precious ingredients, first using their Fruitcake Fund to purchase raisins and bootleg whiskey, and then foraging for windfall pecans, which they crack by the fire.

The queen of stirring Southern kitchen life into writing is Eudora Welty, whose novels, short stories, and essays illuminate 20th-century literature with women's lives at the center. In her 1946 novel, *Delta Wedding*, Welty focuses us on Ellen, who is making Mashula's Coconut Cake using a treasured family recipe. While cooking, she visits with her just-arrived nine-year-old niece, Laura, and quietly mulls over the family dramas swirling around the upcoming wedding of her daughter. Her actions are so carefully detailed that a Welty scholar, Dr. Anne Romines, wrote about the role of this baking sequence in the novel, and later created a beautiful cake recipe based on the details given in the story—separating the dozen guinea eggs, grating lemon rind, pounding blanched almonds with rose water in a mortar for the luscious filling.

In addition to these three verbal celebrations of Southern baking, consider spending time with *A Good Meal Is Hard to Find*, by Amy C. Evans (see page 219), a painter, and Martha Hall Foose (see page 477), a chef and writer. This unique collection of whimsical characters, beautiful images, and timeless recipes is a charming love letter to Southern cooking and comfort food. Evans, who is known as much for capturing oral stories as for her paintings of vintage objects, creates a cast of strong, sometimes quirky women who span generations—"women who raised us and fed us and told us stories and were glad when they finally got to sit down and put their feet up for a spell." Over hefty slices of pink strawberry cake and glugs of bourbon, she conspires with Foose to write vignettes and recipes to match the people (and paintings): Francine's Milk and Honey Cake, Lena's Coffee Shortbread, and Flannery's Gracious Coffee Fudge Cake are just a few of the Anytime Sweets that will get you baking.

by Nancie McDermott

native North Carolina food writer, cooking teacher, and author of many cookbooks

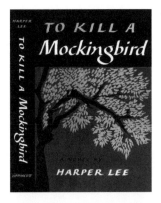

HarperCollins Publishers (Top)
Penguin Random House (Bottom)

Chocolate-Lemon Doberge Cake

Serves 10 to 12 ~ Total Time: 2 hours, plus 5½ hours cooling

The celebratory, showstopping doberge cake from New Orleans holds almost as many stories as it does layers of sponge cake. Pronounced "doe-bash" by locals, the cake makes an appearance most often at birthday events and is a symbol of extravagant celebration.

The doberge cake was created in 1933 by Beulah Ledner, a New Orleans native and daughter of German immigrants. Like her parents, Ledner ran a bakery, and was always drawn to the stunning dobos torte from Hungary. While she loved the richness of the torte—a five-layer vanilla cake soaked in caramel, frosted with chocolate buttercream, and topped with hard caramel (designed to ship long distances without spoiling)—Ledner found the dessert too dense for the New Orleans heat and humidity. She concocted a lighter, fluffier cousin, opting for eight layers of yellow butter cake, chocolate custard filling, buttercream, and a fondant coating. To please the neighborhood, Beulah gave its name a French flair, the title "doberge" evolving from the French word "d'auberge," meaning "country inn."

Ledner's bakery was eventually bought by Joe Gambino in 1946, and Joe Gambino's Bakery remains the main purveyor of doberge cakes today. In addition to the original chocolate flavor, Gambino also serves lemon and caramel variations, with their most popular cake being a "half-half" version featuring both lemon and chocolate (the flavors are split directly down the middle, so that it can be shared among guests with different preferences).

We wanted to offer a recipe for a doberge cake that—despite looking lavish—is achievable for a home cook in search of a rewarding project. Rather than making the difficult choice between chocolate and lemon, we use both. This is something we learned from chef Kelly Fields, who created a doberge cake with alternating layers of filling—here, we opt for a light chocolate custard and a punchy, floral lemon curd. We seal the entire cake with a zingy lemon buttercream, and coat that with a shiny, pourable chocolate ganache. We recommend using a cake turntable to ensure filling layers are level and frosting is smooth, for a cleaner presentation and to prevent the cake from tilting.

Cake

4	large eggs plus 2 large yolks
½	cup buttermilk
1	tablespoon vanilla extract
2¼	cups (9 ounces) cake flour
1¾	cups (12¼ ounces) granulated sugar
1¼	teaspoons baking powder
¼	teaspoon baking soda
½	teaspoon table salt
8	tablespoons unsalted butter, softened
½	cup vegetable oil

Pudding

2	tablespoons granulated sugar
1½	tablespoons Dutch-processed cocoa powder
1½	tablespoons cornstarch
⅛	teaspoon table salt
⅔	cup whole milk
¼	cup heavy cream
2	ounces bittersweet chocolate, chopped fine

Syrup

⅓	cup (2⅓ ounces) granulated sugar
⅓	cup water

Buttercream

20	tablespoons (2½ sticks) unsalted butter, softened
2½	cups (10 ounces) confectioners' sugar
⅛	teaspoon table salt
2	tablespoons heavy cream
1	tablespoon grated lemon zest plus ¼ cup juice (2 lemons)

Ganache

8	ounces bittersweet chocolate, chopped fine
1	cup plus 2 tablespoons heavy cream
1	tablespoon corn syrup
⅛	teaspoon table salt
⅔	cup lemon curd, jarred or homemade

1   **For the cake** Adjust oven rack to middle position and heat oven to 350 degrees. Grease three 8-inch round cake pans, line with parchment paper, grease parchment, and flour pans. Combine eggs and yolks, buttermilk, and vanilla in 2-cup liquid measuring cup and beat with fork until smooth.

2   Combine flour, sugar, baking powder, baking soda, and salt in bowl of stand mixer. Fit mixer with paddle and mix on low speed until combined, about 20 seconds. Add butter and oil and mix on low speed until combined, about 30 seconds. Increase speed to medium and beat until lightened, about 1 minute. Reduce speed to low and, with mixer running, slowly add egg mixture. When mixture is fully incorporated, stop mixer and scrape down bowl and paddle thoroughly. Beat on medium-high speed until batter is pale, smooth, and thick, about 3 minutes. Divide batter evenly among prepared pans and smooth tops. Gently tap pans on counter to release air bubbles.

3   Bake cakes until toothpick inserted in center comes out with few crumbs attached, 20 to 25 minutes, switching and rotating pans halfway through baking. Let cakes cool in pans on wire rack for 15 minutes. Remove cakes from pans, discarding parchment, and let cool completely on rack, about 2 hours. (Cooled layers can be wrapped tightly with plastic and stored at room temperature for up to 24 hours).

4   **For the pudding** Meanwhile, whisk sugar, cocoa, cornstarch, and salt together in large saucepan. Whisk in milk and cream until smooth. Cook over medium heat, whisking constantly, until mixture is thickened and bubbling over entire surface, 3 to 5 minutes. Off heat, whisk in chocolate until melted and fully incorporated.

5   Transfer pudding to large bowl. Place plastic wrap directly on surface of pudding and refrigerate until well chilled, at least 2 hours. (Pudding can be refrigerated in airtight container for up to 3 days.)

6   **For the syrup** Bring sugar and water to boil in small saucepan over high heat and stir until sugar is dissolved, about 1 minute. Let cool completely, about 30 minutes.

7   **For the buttercream** Using clean, dry mixer bowl and whisk attachment, whip butter in stand mixer on medium-high speed until smooth, about 20 seconds. Add sugar and salt and mix on medium-low speed until most of sugar is moistened, about 45 seconds. Scrape down bowl; add cream and whip on medium-high speed until light and fluffy, about 4 minutes, scraping down bowl as needed. Add lemon zest and juice and whip until incorporated, about 30 seconds. (Frosting can be refrigerated for up to 2 days. If refrigerated, let stand at room temperature for 30 minutes before using).

8   Transfer fully cooled cakes to cutting board. Using long serrated knife, cut 1 horizontal line around sides of each layer; then, following scored lines, cut each layer into 2 even layers. Place 1 cake layer on 8-inch cardboard round, cut side up. Using pastry brush, gently dab syrup onto cake until evenly moistened, about 1½ tablespoons. Spread ⅓ cup chocolate pudding evenly over top, leaving ¼-inch border around edge of cake. Top with second cake layer (cut side up). Repeat brushing with syrup and spread ⅓ cup lemon curd over top, leaving ¼-inch border. Repeat with three more layers, alternating pudding and lemon curd and ending with layer of pudding. Place remaining cake layer cut side down over pudding.

9   Using offset spatula, spread all of buttercream evenly over sides and top of cake. Refrigerate cake for 1 hour.

10   **For the ganache** Place chocolate in 4-cup liquid measuring cup or bowl. Bring cream, corn syrup, and salt to simmer in small saucepan over medium heat, 1 to 2 minutes. Pour cream mixture over chocolate and let stand for 1 minute. Whisk mixture until thick and smooth.

11   Remove cake on cardboard round from refrigerator and place on wire rack set in parchment paper–lined rimmed baking sheet. Working quickly, pour ganache over top of chilled cake (starting in center of cake), letting ganache drip down and coat sides of cake (allow excess ganache to puddle onto baking sheet). Refrigerate cake on rack until ganache is set, about 20 minutes. Using large spatula(s), transfer cake on cardboard round to platter or large cutting board and serve. (Wrap leftover cake in plastic and refrigerate; bring to room temperature before serving.)

Coconut Layer Cake

Serves 10 to 12   ~   Total Time: 2 hours, plus 2 hours cooling

Sitting tall on a pedestal under a glass dome, spread with clouds of luscious white frosting and topped with a deep drift of downy coconut, coconut cake is an iconic Southern dessert. While this image is universally evocative, there are a few well-known ways that folks personalize this beloved cake in the South.

Cheryl Day, cookbook author, baker, and co-founder of Southern Restaurants for Racial Justice, adds just ¼ teaspoon of ground cardamom to her cake batter, which imparts a very delicate but delightful floral note. She also soaks each cake layer with a mixture of coconut milk and vanilla so the cake stays extra moist.

Dolester Miles, the pastry chef who earned a James Beard Award in 2018 for her baking at Frank Stitt's Highlands Bar and Grill in Birmingham, Alabama, makes every layer of her coconut cake grand. She grinds toasted pecans and coconut until fine before mixing them into the cake batter. She then creates a custardy filling by cooking egg yolks, sweetened condensed milk, butter, cream of coconut, and plenty of shredded coconut. After spreading the filling between the coconut- and pecan-flecked cake layers, she tops the whole thing off with coconut whipped cream and a sprinkling of toasted coconut.

Robert Carter, formerly of Peninsula Grill in Charleston, South Carolina, made a 12-pound, $270 coconut cake based on his grandmother's recipe. He layered coconut-infused pound cake with coconut buttercream, creating a celebrated 12-layer tower.

What was most important to us in honoring this Southern queen was infusing it with coconut flavor throughout. Using cream of coconut and coconut extract in the rich, moist cake delivers, as does a fluffy egg white–based buttercream flavored with more coconut extract and cream of coconut. For us, the coating of toasted shredded coconut is requisite and provides textural interest and a final dose of flavor. Be sure to use cream of coconut (such as Coco López) and not coconut milk here. One 15-ounce can of cream of coconut is enough for both the cake and the frosting.

Cake

1	large egg plus 5 large whites
¾	cup cream of coconut
¼	cup water
1	teaspoon coconut extract
1	teaspoon vanilla extract
2¼	cups (9 ounces) cake flour
1	cup (7 ounces) sugar
1	tablespoon baking powder
¾	teaspoon table salt
12	tablespoons unsalted butter, cut into 12 pieces and softened
2	cups (6 ounces) sweetened shredded coconut

Frosting

4	large egg whites
1	cup (7 ounces) sugar
	Pinch table salt
1	pound (4 sticks) unsalted butter, each stick cut into 6 pieces and softened
¼	cup cream of coconut
1	teaspoon coconut extract
1	teaspoon vanilla extract

1 **For the cake** Adjust oven rack to lower-middle position and heat oven to 325 degrees. Grease two 9-inch round cake pans, line with parchment paper, grease parchment, and flour pans. Whisk egg and whites together in 4-cup liquid measuring cup. Whisk in cream of coconut, water, coconut extract, and vanilla.

2 Using stand mixer fitted with paddle, mix flour, sugar, baking powder, and salt on low speed until combined. Add butter, 1 piece at a time, until only pea-size pieces remain, about 1 minute. Add half of egg mixture, increase speed to medium-high, and beat until light and fluffy, about 1 minute. Reduce speed to medium-low, add remaining egg mixture, and beat until incorporated, about 30 seconds. Give batter final stir by hand.

3 Divide batter evenly between prepared pans and smooth tops with rubber spatula. Gently tap pans on counter to release air bubbles. Bake until toothpick inserted in center comes out clean, about 30 minutes, rotating pans halfway through baking.

4 Let cakes cool in pans on wire rack for 10 minutes. Remove cakes from pans, discarding parchment, and let cool completely on rack, about 2 hours. (Cake layers can be wrapped tightly in plastic wrap and stored at room temperature for up to 24 hours or wrapped in additional layer of aluminum foil and frozen for up to 1 month; defrost cakes at room temperature.) Meanwhile, spread shredded coconut on rimmed baking sheet and toast in oven until shreds are mix of golden brown and white, 15 to 20 minutes, stirring 2 or 3 times; let cool.

5 **For the frosting** Combine egg whites, sugar, and salt in bowl of stand mixer and set over medium saucepan filled with 1 inch barely simmering water, making sure that water does not touch bottom of bowl. Cook, whisking constantly, until mixture is opaque and registers 120 degrees, about 2 minutes.

6 Remove bowl from heat and transfer to stand mixer fitted with whisk attachment. Whip egg white mixture on high speed until glossy, sticky, and barely warm (80 degrees), about 7 minutes. Reduce speed to medium high and whip in butter, 1 piece at a time, followed by cream of coconut, coconut extract, and vanilla, scraping down bowl as needed. Continue to whip until combined, about 1 minute.

7 Using long serrated knife, cut 1 horizontal line around sides of each layer; then, following scored lines, cut each layer into 2 even layers.

8 Line edges of cake platter with 4 strips of parchment to keep platter clean. Place 1 cake layer on platter. Spread ¾ cup frosting evenly over top, right to edge of cake. Repeat with 2 more cake layers, pressing lightly to adhere and spreading ¾ cup frosting evenly over each layer. Top with remaining cake layer and spread remaining frosting evenly over top and sides of cake. Sprinkle top of cake evenly with toasted coconut, then gently press remaining toasted coconut onto sides. Carefully remove parchment strips before serving. (Cake can be refrigerated for up to 24 hours; bring to room temperature before serving.)

A PIECE OF CAKEWALK HISTORY

Anyway you slice it, the cakewalk has a complex history. The phrase, first used in print in the 1860s, refers to a type of dance, a style of music, a carnival game, and a colloquial saying.

Most commonly, cakewalk refers to a dance contest where the winner earns a cake as a prize. Historians trace the origins of the dance, including its circular or linear path, jumps, and processional steps, to the dancing culture developed by enslaved and later emancipated African Americans in the South. Testimonies and oral histories from formerly enslaved people describe the cakewalk as both an evolution of traditional African dances and mimicry of the formal European dances practiced by white slaveholders.

After a demonstration of the cakewalk at the 1876 Centennial Exposition in Philadelphia, the dance was appropriated by male performers wearing blackface in minstrel shows. This display transported the cakewalk out of the South and onto a national stage, spurring the creation of numerous cakewalk-themed ragtime songs as well as a musical comedy called *Clorindy*, or *The Origin of the Cake Walk*, which opened on Broadway in New York in 1898. The style of dance, along with its racialized appropriation, soon swept the globe, finding popularity across Europe and South America. These global iterations rarely included cake prizes for the dancers.

While the minstrel version of the cakewalk is indecorous today, a dance-less game of chance known as a cakewalk is often played at modern-day carnivals and fundraising events. Similar to musical chairs, participants walk around numbered spots or chairs in time to music. Once the music stops, a number is drawn at random and the participant standing or sitting on that number wins a cake. And as early as the 1860s, the phrase "cakewalk" was used to refer to something that was easy, or "a piece of cake."

by KC Hysmith

Hummingbird Cake

Serves 10 to 12 ~ Total Time: 2 hours, plus 3 hours 20 minutes cooling and chilling

The recipe for this irresistible spice layer cake, packed with bananas, pineapple, and pecans and covered with a rich, tangy cream cheese frosting, was famously submitted to *Southern Living* in 1978 by Mrs. L.H. Wiggins of Greensboro, North Carolina. It has since become the magazine's most popular recipe, gaining a reputation as a Southern classic. Yet both the cake's name and its tropical fruits point to its origin outside of the American South, in Jamaica, where a particularly gorgeous variety of long-tailed hummingbird (also known as the doctor bird) is the national bird.

According to a 1969 story in the *Daily Gleaner* newspaper, representatives from Air Jamaica held press conferences in New York and Miami, showcasing Jamaican food and fashion as a way to publicize their new American flight schedule. "Press kits presented included a Jamaican menu modified for American kitchens, and featured recipes like the doctor bird cake, made with bananas," it reads. Other such recipes for a spiced, unfrosted tube cake that included pineapple and banana known as doctor bird cake, Jamaican cake, cake that doesn't last, or, of course, hummingbird cake existed at least a decade before Mrs. Wiggins's submission. That said, if it was Wiggins's own decision to transform the cake into the layered, frosted icon we know today, then Southerners everywhere owe her a debt of gratitude.

To prevent an overly dense cake, we include a relatively moderate amount of oil and plenty of leavener to lighten our cake's crumb. Chunks of banana weigh down the cake; mashing the bananas is a better approach and distributes banana flavor evenly throughout the layers. To boost pineapple flavor, we more than double the amount of fruit from what's typical, boiling down the juices to concentrate their flavor and eliminate extra moisture. Finished with a rich cream cheese frosting and a sprinkling of chopped toasted pecans, this retro cake is stunning and delicious. Toast a total of 2 cups of pecans to divide between the cake and the frosting.

Cake

- 2 (8-ounce) cans crushed pineapple in juice
- 3 cups (15 ounces) all-purpose flour
- 2 teaspoons baking powder
- 1 teaspoon baking soda
- 1 teaspoon ground cinnamon
- 1 teaspoon table salt
- 2 cups (14 ounces) granulated sugar
- 3 large eggs
- 1 cup vegetable oil
- 4 very ripe large bananas, peeled and mashed (2 cups)
- 1½ cups pecans, toasted and chopped
- 2 teaspoons vanilla extract

Frosting

- 20 tablespoons (2½ sticks) unsalted butter, softened
- 5 cups (20 ounces) confectioners' sugar
- 2½ teaspoons vanilla extract
- ½ teaspoon table salt
- 1¼ pounds cream cheese, cut into 20 pieces and chilled
- ½ cup pecans, toasted and chopped

1 **For the cake** Adjust oven rack to middle position and heat oven to 350 degrees. Grease two 9-inch round cake pans, line with parchment paper, grease parchment, and flour pans. Drain pineapple in fine-mesh strainer set over bowl, pressing to extract juice; set aside solids. Pour juice into small saucepan and cook over medium heat until reduced to ⅓ cup, about 5 minutes.

2 Whisk flour, baking powder, baking soda, cinnamon, and salt together in bowl. Whisk sugar and eggs together in large bowl; whisk in oil. Stir bananas, pecans, vanilla, reserved pineapple solids, and reduced juice into sugar-egg mixture. Stir in flour mixture until just combined.

3 Divide batter evenly between prepared pans and smooth tops with rubber spatula. Bake until dark golden brown on top and toothpick inserted in center comes out clean, 50 to 55 minutes, rotating pans halfway through baking. Let cakes cool in pans on wire rack for 20 minutes. Remove cakes from pans, discarding parchment, and let cool completely on rack, about 2 hours.

4 **For the frosting** Using stand mixer fitted with paddle, beat butter, sugar, vanilla, and salt on low speed until smooth; continue to mix for 2 minutes, scraping down bowl as needed. Increase speed to medium-low, add cream cheese, 1 piece at a time, and mix until smooth; continue to mix for 2 minutes.

5 Line edges of cake platter with 4 strips of parchment to keep platter clean. Place 1 cake layer on platter. Spread 2 cups frosting evenly over top, right to edge of cake. Top with remaining cake layer, press lightly to adhere, then spread 2 cups frosting evenly over top. Spread remaining frosting evenly over sides of cake. To smooth frosting, run edge of offset spatula around cake sides and over top. Sprinkle top of cake with pecans. Carefully remove parchment strips. Refrigerate cake for at least 1 hour or up to 2 days before serving.

Porter Plum Pudding Layer Cake

Serves 12 to 16 ~ Total Time: 2 hours, plus 11 hours soaking, cooling, and chilling

To honor Eliza Seymour Lee's historic porter plum pudding (see "Eliza's Pudding"), we created a resplendent layer cake for the contemporary table with flavors of Lee's recipe—dried fruits, porter, nutmeg, citrus, brown sugar, and ginger. Moist cake layers get even more flavor from a brush of porter syrup. We reserve some of the syrup to create a caramel-like sauce for decorating. Tangy cream cheese frosting is the perfect counterpoint to the fruity spiced cake. You can use traditional or nonalcoholic porter beer in this recipe. You can use a single variety of raisins if you prefer. Do not substitute liquid buttermilk for the buttermilk powder. To ensure the proper consistency for the frosting, use cream cheese and butter that's softened but still somewhat firm (about 65 degrees).

ELIZA'S PUDDING

My fascination with my great-great-great-grandmother Eliza Seymour Lee (1800–1874) began at an early age when I realized we walked the same streets and neighborhoods of downtown Charleston. I felt a bond with Eliza because even as a child I knew I wanted to be, like her, a chef.

Today Eliza Seymour Lee is remembered in Charleston as a caterer, pastry chef, and restaurateur, but her legacy has so many dimensions. I've been driven throughout my life to share her stories and recipes.

Eliza was the daughter of the chef Sally Seymour, the enslaved mistress of Charleston planter Thomas Martin. Eliza learned everything about cooking alongside other enslaved people who were being trained by her mother. She excelled in the French style of the culinary arts, specifically baking and cooking meats. Following Sally's death, Eliza was manumitted—released from slavery—and she inherited her mother's businesses and property. Soon Eliza was considered to be one of the most successful businesswomen in Charleston, an extraordinary position for a free woman of color in the prewar South. She was hired to cater private functions for the planter aristocracy when dignataries were visiting the city. Her passion for perfection made her famous.

One of Eliza's most celebrated recipes was her plum pudding, a dense dessert made with dried fruit, though not plums—as with its cousins figgy pudding and Christmas pudding, the word "plum" refers to dried fruits like raisins, currants, cherries, and dates. Eliza's recipe calls for adding a bottle of boiled porter to a chopped-up "four-penny" loaf of stale bread, followed by beaten eggs and a mixture of flour, ginger, nutmeg, and salt. Finally, dried fruits—raisins, currants, and citron—go in, plus brown sugar. She would then wrap the mixture in a towel and boil it for 5 hours.

In researching other plum pudding recipes from the period, I found that Eliza's addition of ginger was unique. Perhaps this was a connection to her husband's birthplace, Barbados, an important grower and exporter of ginger, making Eliza's recipe an expression of the culinary diaspora, woven from many diverse heritages.

by Robin Lee Griffith

chef, food stylist, and food TV and hospitality professional

Cake

1½	cups porter beer
¾	cup (3¾ ounces) raisins
¾	cup (3¾ ounces) golden raisins
¾	cup (3¾ ounces) dried currants
1¾	cups (8¾ ounces) all-purpose flour
2	teaspoons baking powder
1	teaspoon baking soda
2	teaspoons ground ginger
1	teaspoon ground nutmeg
1	teaspoon table salt
1¼	cups packed (8¾ ounces) plus ⅔ cup packed (4⅔ ounces) light brown sugar, divided
¾	cup vegetable oil
3	large eggs
1	tablespoon vanilla extract
2	teaspoons grated lemon zest
2	tablespoons unsalted butter, chilled and cut into 2 pieces

Frosting

16	tablespoons unsalted butter, softened
3	cups (12 ounces) confectioners' sugar
⅓	cup buttermilk powder
2	teaspoons vanilla extract
¼	teaspoon salt
12	ounces cream cheese, chilled and cut into 12 pieces

1 **For the cake** Combine porter, raisins, golden raisins, and currants in bowl. Cover and let sit until fruit is plump, at least 8 hours or up to 24 hours. Drain fruit in fine-mesh strainer set over bowl, gently tossing fruit to release liquid; reserve fruit and ⅔ cup porter and discard any extra porter.

2 Adjust oven rack to middle position and heat oven to 350 degrees. Grease three 8-inch round cake pans, line with parchment paper, and grease parchment. Whisk flour, baking powder, baking soda, ginger, nutmeg, and salt together in bowl.

3 Whisk 1¼ cups sugar, oil, eggs, vanilla, and lemon zest in large bowl until smooth. Stir in drained fruit. Fold in flour mixture until just combined. Divide batter evenly among prepared pans and smooth tops with rubber spatula. Bake until cakes are golden brown and skewer inserted in center comes out clean, 25 to 28 minutes, switching and rotating pans halfway through baking. Let cakes cool in pans on wire racks for 5 minutes. Invert cakes onto wire racks, discarding parchment. Using skewer, poke 30 holes in each cake layer.

4 Bring reserved ⅔ cup porter and remaining ⅔ cup sugar to simmer in large saucepan over high heat. Reduce heat to medium-low and simmer until syrup is thick, frothy, and reduced to ⅔ to ¾ cup, 5 to 10 minutes, adjusting heat as needed to maintain active simmer without allowing syrup to froth over. Off heat, after frothing subsides, measure out ¼ cup syrup and brush over warm cakes. Let cakes cool completely on rack, about 2 hours.

5 Meanwhile, return remaining syrup to simmer over medium-low heat. Off heat, whisk in chilled butter until smooth. Transfer syrup to bowl and set aside to cool completely.

6 **For the frosting** Using stand mixer fitted with paddle, beat butter, sugar, buttermilk powder, vanilla, and salt on low speed until smooth, 2 to 3 minutes, scraping down bowl as needed. Increase speed to medium-low; add cream cheese, 1 piece at a time; and mix until smooth, 2 to 4 minutes.

7 Place 1 cake layer on cake platter, syrup side up. Spread 1 cup frosting evenly over top, to edges of cake. Repeat with remaining layers, spreading 1 cup frosting evenly over each. Spread thin layer of frosting evenly over sides of cake, scraping sides with edge of offset spatula to create sheer veil of frosting. (Cake sides should still be visible.) Decorate top of cake with remaining frosting as desired. Chill cake until frosting is set, at least 1 hour.

8 Stir cooled porter syrup to loosen, then decorate cake with syrup as desired. (Microwave syrup as needed, for a few seconds at a time, if it is too thick to loosen by stirring.) Serve cake with any remaining porter syrup or reserve syrup for another use. (Cake can be refrigerated for up to 24 hours.)

Texas Chocolate Sheet Cake

Serves 12 to 15 ~ Total Time: 1 hour, plus 2 hours cooling and chilling

This chocolate cake is short in stature but has a Texas-sized wingspan. Many define this pecan-topped cake by the chocolate icing that comes together on the stovetop. Once the icing is poured over the cake, some soaks in, yielding multiple textures: a rich, brownie-like bottom layer of cake, a fudgy middle layer, and a sweet chocolate icing. The whole thing is topped off with toasted chopped pecans for welcome crunch among all that fudge.

This cake has several names. Outside of Texas, it's often referred to as Texas sheet cake. When you're in Texas, you may hear brownie sheet cake, chocolate sheet brownies, brownie cake, chocolate sheet cake, or chocolate sheath cake. Some older recipes from Texas are just called chocolate cake—that's how iconic it is in the Lone Star State.

Some believe Lady Bird Johnson popularized the cake, but historians haven't backed that up. Others link its rise to a recipe for a delicious German chocolate cake featured in a 1950s Dallas newspaper that was much passed along. As Joy Wilson, also known as Joy th Baker, says on her website, "Texas Sheet Cake is one of those recipes that, because of its ease and deliciousness (thank you pecans and chocolate), just got around through recipe cards and church cookbooks and imprinted itself into so many of our family recipe arsenals."

Whatever you choose to call it, this many-serving cake is one your friends will thank you for if you bring it to a party. While this approach breaks from many recipes, we like to pour the icing on the cake while it's still warm to allow it to soak into the cake and achieve a really nice fudgy layer between the cake and icing.

Cake

2	cups (10 ounces) all-purpose flour
2	cups (14 ounces) granulated sugar
½	teaspoon baking soda
½	teaspoon table salt
2	large eggs plus 2 large yolks
¼	cup sour cream
2	teaspoons vanilla extract
8	ounces semisweet chocolate, chopped
¾	cup vegetable oil
¾	cup water
½	cup (1½ ounces) unsweetened cocoa powder
4	tablespoons unsalted butter

Icing

8	tablespoons unsalted butter
½	cup heavy cream
½	cup (1½ ounces) unsweetened cocoa powder
1	tablespoon light corn syrup
3	cups (12 ounces) confectioners' sugar
1	tablespoon vanilla extract
1	cup pecans, toasted and chopped

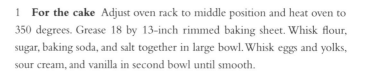

1 **For the cake** Adjust oven rack to middle position and heat oven to 350 degrees. Grease 18 by 13-inch rimmed baking sheet. Whisk flour, sugar, baking soda, and salt together in large bowl. Whisk eggs and yolks, sour cream, and vanilla in second bowl until smooth.

2 Heat chocolate, oil, water, cocoa, and butter in large saucepan over medium heat, stirring occasionally, until smooth, 3 to 5 minutes. Whisk chocolate mixture into flour mixture until incorporated. Whisk egg mixture into batter. Transfer batter to prepared sheet. Bake until toothpick inserted in center comes out clean, 18 to 20 minutes, rotating sheet halfway through baking. Transfer sheet to wire rack.

3 **For the icing** About 5 minutes before cake is done baking, heat butter, cream, cocoa, and corn syrup in large saucepan over medium heat, stirring occasionally, until smooth, about 4 minutes. Off heat, whisk in sugar and vanilla. Spread warm icing evenly over hot cake and sprinkle with pecans. Let cake cool completely in pan on wire rack, about 1 hour, then refrigerate until icing is set, about 1 hour longer. Serve.

SCRATCH CAKES VERSUS CAKE MIX

"Scratch cakes"—cakes baked from scratch—are what Granny Willie Mae baked in her Louisiana kitchen. Decades ago, long before she had the help of modern technology with its electric mixers, Granny would beat the softened butter and sugar together with a hand crank mixer until they were sufficiently creamed: light and fluffy.

Cake making was not the seamless process we have today: Connect the paddle attachment to a stand mixer and let the motor do the work. The scratch cakes of the early 20th century were a true labor of love. These kitchen tasks required a baker's undivided attention, and even some physicality. While many home bakers today dally around the kitchen on a leisurely afternoon and order takeout while baking, Granny and her contemporaries still had to cook. Granny cooked every meal for her family of ten—and also for the white family she worked for as a domestic. If she needed eggs for a cake, she went outside to the chicken coop to gather them.

The convenience that boxed cake mix offered women like her during this time was significant. Cake mix has been around since the 1930s when Granny was just a girl. World War II meant the tasks required of women in this country stretched beyond the homes and fields and into industry sectors that were previously dominated by men. Women were still required to cook; they just had less time to do so. The popularity of convenience foods skyrocketed.

My Granny didn't use cake mixes, but plenty of her friends and relatives did—as do mine. And home bakers have been "doctoring up" cake mixes the entire time. Cake mix didn't stifle the innovation of home bakers—it unleashed it! The barrier of entry to cake making was reduced from experienced baker to curious novice. Anyone can follow the simple directions on the back of a cake box: Add ingredients. Stir. Bake! The creativity came from adding something extra: pudding mix and buttermilk, or sour cream and another egg. Plus, using cake mix means you have a little extra time for other components of the cake—homemade frostings and fillings.

Choosing between cake mix and scratch cakes is a matter of preference. Many home bakers flip-flop between the two depending on the type of cake they are making, or the amount of energy they want to invest into the cake.

by Vallery Lomas

winner of The Great American Baking Show *and author of the cookbook* Life is What You Bake It: Recipes, Stories, and Inspiration to Bake Your Way to the Top

BAKE THE KING OF CAKES

New Orleans is a city of people with passionate opinions, especially concerning food. The easiest way to start an argument among New Orleanians is to pronounce as fact your opinion on, say, the best way to boil crawfish or how dark to take your roux for a certain dish—you'll barely need to pause before your sparring partner interjects to inform you that you are wrong and that the way their grandma prepared it is actually correct.

King cake, the reigning dessert of Mardi Gras, is no exception. This celebratory circle of dough has achieved near mythic status in Louisiana, and where to get the best one is the subject of intense debate. I'm here to pronounce my own strong opinion—the very best king cake is the one you make yourself. Many folks will tell you the best king cake was from McKenzie's, a local bakery chain that, in the New Orleans colloquialism, "ain't dere no more." Though now shuttered, the bakery also famously originated the tradition of including a baby figurine, meant to represent the infant Jesus, in the king cake.

These babies were once made of porcelain and are now typically plastic, though other charms are deployed as well—in the past, folks might use an almond or a dried bean. The guest who receives the baby is responsible for bringing the king cake to the next gathering. In your average Louisiana workplace, this means you'll likely have the chance to enjoy king cake every single workday through the Mardi Gras season.

In its simplest form, king cake is a soft bread filled with a ribbon of cinnamon sugar and topped with a sweet glaze and brightly colored sanding sugar representing the colors of Mardi Gras. I wanted my own king cake to feature an elegant ring of dough and have a strong pop of cinnamon flavor with a more moderate overall sweetness. The version published here is traditional, with a few modern tweaks to make it easier to make and enjoy.

Begin with a simplified enriched bread dough (this one's got melted butter). Chill the dough, divide it in two, and fill each half with a lush cinnamon spread before braiding the two pieces together—working with cold dough makes this assembly a breeze. The filling includes gingersnap crumbs, which help lock the buttery spiced filling into place so that each slice features a distinct swirl. This is a great opportunity to use the very best cinnamon you have; an excellent, fresh cinnamon will really shine in this recipe.

Next, place the braided ring of dough in a round cake pan to rise and bake. King cakes are often baked free-form on a sheet tray rather than baked in a pan. I prefer the latter—having the support of the sides of a round cake pan allows you to use a more tender dough and still get a great rise and shape without the filling leaking out and scorching the bottom. Last, use sour cream in the glaze to cut the sweetness and add a bit of tang.

These breaks from king cake convention might stir up a debate here in New Orleans, but I think you'll find the result well worth it. If you include a charm with your king cake, don't forget to remind your guests to expect it—especially so that they can plan to bring the king cake to the next party.

by Bronwen Wyatt

pastry chef and owner of boutique cake studio Bayou Saint Cake

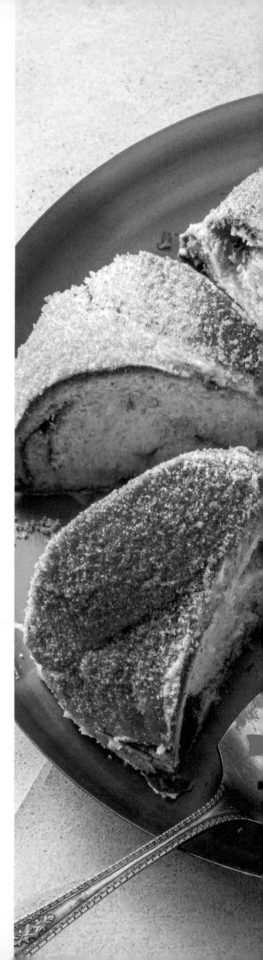

King Cake

Serves 8 ~ Total Time: 2½ hours, plus 3 hours 50 minutes to
4 hours 20 minutes chilling, rising, and cooling

A round baked good containing a symbolic trinket, eaten in celebration of the holiday of Epiphany, is found across the Catholic diaspora. Epiphany marks the three kings' visit to baby Jesus. It's generally agreed that New Orleans inherited the king cake from France and Spain. In francophone cultures, you might enjoy a galette des rois, a confection of puff pastry and almond frangipane, while in Spain the rosca de reyes consists of brioche topped with dried fruit. In New Orleans, this has morphed into a circle of sweet bread, often flavored with cinnamon and topped with purple, green, and gold sanding sugar. The colors represent justice, faith, and power (though that may be a New Orleans legend in its own right).

In Louisiana, king cake is eaten between January 6, the feast of Epiphany, and the day before Lent, Mardi Gras. In recent years, local bakers have competed to develop increasingly innovative king cake flavors, and you'll find them now filled with anything from praline to chocolate to strawberry. There are even savory versions such as those filled with boudin.

This version from pastry chef Bronwen Wyatt (see "Bake the King of Cakes") is tall and fluffy. You'll need about 10 gingersnap cookies to yield ½ cup of crumbs. To make the crumbs, pulse the cookies in a food processor or place them in a zipper-lock bag and crush them with a rolling pin. You can substitute graham crackers or Biscoff cookie crumbs for the gingersnap crumbs. This recipe was developed using a light-colored cake pan; if your pan is dark, begin checking for doneness at about 35 minutes (before tenting it with foil). Be sure to advise your guests if you hide an (inedible) baby under your cake.

Cake

2½	cups (12½ ounces) all-purpose flour
¼	cup (1¾ ounces) granulated sugar
2¼	teaspoons instant or rapid-rise yeast
¾	teaspoon table salt
⅓	cup plus 1 tablespoon water, divided
3	large eggs, divided
3	tablespoons whole milk
3	tablespoons unsalted butter, melted
2	teaspoons vanilla extract
	Vegetable oil spray
	Purple, green, and yellow colored sanding sugars
1	king cake baby, dried bean, or almond (optional)

Filling

8	tablespoons unsalted butter, softened
½	cup (2 ounces) gingersnap crumbs
½	cup (3½ ounces) granulated sugar
¼	cup packed (1¾ ounces) brown sugar
2	teaspoons ground cinnamon
1	teaspoon vanilla extract
⅛	teaspoon table salt

Glaze

3	cups (12 ounces) confectioners' sugar
½	cup sour cream
1	teaspoon vanilla extract
	Pinch table salt

> continued

1 **For the cake** Whisk flour, sugar, yeast, and salt together in bowl of stand mixer. Whisk ⅓ cup water, 2 eggs, milk, melted butter, and vanilla together in 2-cup liquid measuring cup. Make well in flour mixture and add water mixture to well. Fit mixer with paddle and mix on low speed until ingredients are just combined, about 30 seconds. Increase speed to medium-high and mix until dough forms stretchy, web-like strands on sides of bowl, about 5 minutes, scraping down sides of bowl half-way through mixing (dough will be soft and sticky). Transfer dough to lightly greased large bowl and coat dough lightly with oil spray. Cover with plastic wrap and refrigerate for at least 2 hours or up to 24 hours.

2 **For the filling** Using clean stand mixer bowl and paddle, beat all ingredients on medium speed until well combined, about 1 minute. (Filling can be refrigerated for up to 2 days; let filling sit at room temperature until softened, at least 15 minutes, before spreading onto dough in step 5.)

3 **For the glaze** Whisk all ingredients together in bowl until smooth. Refrigerate until ready to use. (Glaze can be refrigerated for up to 2 days.)

4 Grease 9-inch round cake pan, line with parchment paper, and grease parchment. Working quickly, transfer dough to lightly floured counter and divide into 2 equal portions (about 12 ounces each). Lightly flour dough portions. Roll each portion into 12 by 4-inch rectangle with long edge parallel to counter edge.

5 Using offset spatula, spread half of filling over 1 dough rectangle, leaving ¾-inch border at long edge of dough opposite counter edge. Beginning with long edge nearest you, roll dough away from you into even log, pushing in ends to create even thickness. Pinch seam to seal and roll log seam side down. Repeat with second dough rectangle and remaining filling.

6 Place dough logs next to each other, perpendicular to counter edge. Cross left log tightly over right log. Continue twisting, 3 times total, to wrap dough logs around each other. Carefully transfer shaped dough to prepared pan, forming ring in pan, and pinch both ends together to seal. Cover pan loosely with plastic wrap and let rise at room temperature until doubled in size, 1 to 1½ hours.

7 Adjust oven rack to middle position and heat oven to 350 degrees. Whisk remaining 1 egg and remaining 1 tablespoon water together in small bowl. Brush dough evenly with egg wash. Bake until cake is glossy and deep golden brown, about 35 minutes. Tent cake with aluminum foil and continue to bake until center of cake registers 200 to 210 degrees, 15 to 20 minutes longer.

8 Transfer cake to wire rack set in rimmed baking sheet and let rest until cool enough to handle, about 20 minutes. Run paring knife around edges of pan. Carefully remove cake from pan and transfer to rack, rounded side up, discarding parchment. Pour glaze evenly over cake and let sit until glaze stops running but is still wet, about 5 minutes. Sprinkle with colored sugars, alternating colors in pinwheel pattern around cake. Let cake cool until just warm, about 30 minutes.

9 Transfer cake to serving platter. Hide king cake baby underneath cake, if using. Serve.

SHAPING KING CAKE

1 Spread half of filling over 1 dough rectangle, leaving ¾-inch border at long edge of dough opposite counter edge.

2 Roll dough away from you, pushing in ends to create even thickness. Pinch seams to seal and roll log seam side down.

3 Place dough logs next to each other and cross left log tightly over right log. Continue twisting, 3 times total.

4 Carefully transfer shaped dough to prepared pan, forming ring in pan; pinch both ends together to seal.

ALL ABOUT PIES

Pies are welcoming desserts. They have delicious fillings encased in lovingly made pastry. They can hold tender seasonal fruits or custards flavored by your imagination. If a Southerner offers you a piece of pie, they're offering you a piece of their heart (and hard work). With a little instruction, we'll try to make the work a little less hard—and very rewarding.

Pie Equipment

Digital Scale

Yes, this again. Weighing dry ingredients is especially important for pie dough.

Food Processor

Sorry, Grandma: We never make pie dough by hand anymore, and we don't recommend it. A food processor cuts ingredients into flour evenly so you're less likely to overwork your dough, and it does so efficiently so everything stays cold. Look for a workbowl that has a capacity of at least 11 cups.

Rolling Pin

There are many styles of rolling pins, but we like the classic French-style wood pins without handles. They come straight and tapered. We tend to reach for straight pins, which make achieving even dough thickness and rolling out larger disks easy. A slightly textured surface results in less sticking.

Bench Scraper

This basic tool is handy for moving pie dough, lifting dough while you roll it, marking dough at intervals, and cutting dough into pieces.

Kitchen Shears

Once pie dough is placed in the pie plate, we trim the edge so the overhang isn't too thick and doughy when folded over.

Pastry Brush

We use a pastry brush to paint crusts with water or egg wash before they enter the oven.

Small Offset Spatula

Smoothing pie surfaces or decorating with whipped cream is a lot easier (and neater) with a mini offset spatula.

Instant-Read Thermometer

In the dessert realm, thermometers aren't just for candy making. They also take the temperature of a pastry cream or fruit curd, or judge the doneness of custard-based pies. A digital instant-read thermometer—rather than a slow-registering stick candy thermometer—will provide you with an accurate reading almost immediately; this is especially important with egg-based fillings, which can quickly overcook into a curdled mess.

Pie Plate

A pie plate is one of the most important items for perfect pie baking. While Pyrex and good ceramic dishes stand the test of time, we also like golden-hued metal plates, which bake crusts beautifully without overbrowning; even bottom crusts emerge crisp and flaky. We prefer plates without a fluted lip, which allows for maximum crust-crimping flexibility.

Ceramic Pie Weights

There are innovative substitutes for pie weights on the market, and many home bakers use dried beans or rice or sugar or coins. But we have our best success with classic pie weights.

Pie Carrier

Pies are for sharing. Traveling with a delicate pie can feel like tempting fate, but a good pie carrier can make the task easier and more secure.

Pie Server

Surprisingly, serving up a slice of pie isn't always the easiest part of pie baking. You can use a knife, but a pie server—essentially a pointed spatula—is specifically designed to cut, remove, and transport pie slices and helps produce picturesque, intact pieces.

Making Pie Crust

For many, making pie crust is the most challenging part of baking pie. For Southerners, however, the motions are often muscle memory. Many use their hands to rub fat into flour, just like their mothers and grandmothers did before them; some might use two knives to instinctively cut through ingredients. Lard—what households once always kept on hand—is a popular choice for the fat for its savory richness and the distinct short texture it provides. Some use shortening and others use butter for flavor and flakiness.

This pie crust is for those who might not have Southern hands or who might not be expert pie bakers, but it tastes as good as any. It's a multipurpose all-butter pie dough, with an exceptionally rich, full flavor—one bite, and you know it's butter. The sour cream in this dough provides acid, which inhibits gluten development, making the dough easy to roll and the baked crust tender. It starts in the food processor for ease and is finished in a bowl with a spatula.

Double-Crust Pie Dough

Makes one 9-inch double crust
Total Time: 35 minutes, plus 1 hour chilling

6	tablespoons ice water
¼	cup sour cream
2½	cups (12½ ounces) all-purpose flour
1	tablespoon sugar
1¼	teaspoons table salt
16	tablespoons unsalted butter, cut into ½-inch pieces and frozen for 15 minutes

1 Whisk ice water and sour cream in bowl. Process flour, sugar, and salt in food processor until combined, about 5 seconds. Scatter butter over top and pulse until butter pieces are no larger than peas, about 10 pulses. Add sour cream mixture and pulse until dough forms clumps and no dry flour remains, about 15 pulses, scraping down sides of bowl as needed. (Dough will be loose and have texture of wet sand.)

2 Transfer dough to counter and knead briefly until dough comes together. Divide dough in half. Place each dough half onto sheet of plastic wrap and form into 4-inch disk. Wrap tightly in plastic and refrigerate for 1 hour. (Wrapped dough can be refrigerated for up to 2 days or frozen for up to 1 month. If frozen, let dough thaw completely on counter before rolling.)

Single-Crust Pie Dough

Makes one 9-inch single crust
Total Time: 35 minutes, plus 1 hour chilling

¼	cup ice water
4	teaspoons sour cream
1¼	cups (6¼ ounces) all-purpose flour
1½	teaspoons sugar
½	teaspoon table salt
8	tablespoons unsalted butter, cut into ¼-inch pieces and frozen for 15 minutes

1 Whisk ice water and sour cream in bowl. Process flour, sugar, and salt in food processor until combined, about 5 seconds. Scatter butter over top and pulse until butter pieces are no larger than peas, about 10 pulses. Add sour cream mixture and pulse until dough forms clumps and no dry flour remains, about 12 pulses, scraping down sides of bowl as needed. (Dough will be loose and have texture of wet sand.)

2 Transfer dough to counter and knead briefly until dough comes together. Place dough on sheet of plastic wrap and form into 4-inch disk. Wrap tightly in plastic and refrigerate for 1 hour. (Wrapped dough can be refrigerated for up to 2 days or frozen for up to 1 month. If frozen, let dough thaw completely on counter before rolling.)

Shaping Single-Crust Pie Dough

Once you know how to make pie dough, fitting the dough into the plate is simple.

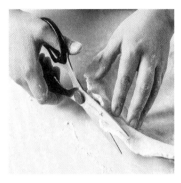

1   Trim overhang to ½ inch beyond lip of plate.

2   Tuck overhang under itself; folded edge should be flush with edge of plate.

3   Crimp dough evenly around edge of plate.

Making a Lattice-Top Crust

A lattice top doesn't just make fruit pies like Fresh Peach Pie (page 460) look good, but it also helps the right amount of moisture escape for the perfect filling. Here is how to do it. If you like, you can use a fluted cutter to give the strips a wavy edge.

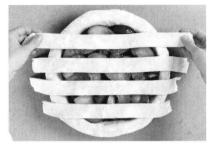

1   Space 4 dough strips evenly across top of pie, parallel to counter edge.

2   Fold back first and third strips almost completely. Lay 1 strip across pie, perpendicular to second and fourth strips, keeping it snug to folded edges of dough strips.

3   Unfold first and third strips over top of perpendicular strip.

4   Fold back second and fourth strips and add second perpendicular strip, keeping it snug to folded edge. Unfold second and fourth strips over top.

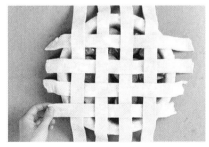

5   Repeat weaving remaining strips evenly across pie, alternating between folding back first and third strips and second and fourth strips to create lattice pattern.

Aunt Jule's Pie

Serves 8 ~ Total Time: 2 hours, plus 4½ hours chilling and cooling

In the *Cook's Country* archives, we used to have a recipe for Jefferson Davis Pie. We learned that this pie, named after the Confederate general, was most likely invented by, and should have been attributed to, an enslaved woman, Aunt Jule. So we asked baker and activist Arley Bell to redevelop our old pie recipe (see "Q&A: Arley Bell on Arley Cakes and Developing Aunt Jule's Pie"). And we've named it after the woman who deserves the credit. Per a suggestion from Arley Bell's husband, we love serving this pie with Bourbon Whipped Cream (page 463) made with Uncle Nearest Bourbon (see "Women in Distilling" on page 493).

1	recipe Single-Crust Pie Dough (page 456)
8	tablespoons unsalted butter
½	cup golden raisins
½	cup pitted dates
½	cup pecans, toasted and roughly chopped
¾	teaspoon table salt, divided
1	cup packed (7 ounces) light brown sugar
3	tablespoons all-purpose flour
½	teaspoon ground nutmeg
¼	teaspoon ground allspice
5	large egg yolks
1¼	cups heavy cream
1	teaspoon cider vinegar

1   Roll dough into 12-inch circle on floured counter. Loosely roll dough around rolling pin and gently unroll it onto 9-inch pie plate, letting excess dough hang over edge. Ease dough into plate by gently lifting edge of dough with your hand while pressing into plate bottom with your other hand.

2   Trim overhang to ½ inch beyond lip of plate. Tuck overhang under itself; folded edge should be flush with edge of plate. Crimp dough evenly around edge of plate. Wrap dough-lined plate loosely in plastic wrap and refrigerate until firm, about 30 minutes. Adjust oven rack to bottom position and heat oven to 325 degrees.

3   Melt butter in 8-inch skillet over medium heat. Cook, swirling skillet constantly, until solids turn color of milk chocolate and have toasty aroma, 3 to 5 minutes. Immediately remove skillet from heat and scrape browned butter into small heatproof bowl; set aside to cool.

4   Combine raisins, dates, pecans, and ¼ teaspoon salt in food processor and process until finely ground, about 30 seconds.

5   Combine brown sugar, flour, nutmeg, allspice, and remaining ½ teaspoon salt in large bowl. Add browned butter and whisk until fully combined. Whisk in egg yolks until fully combined. Whisk in cream and vinegar.

6   Press nut and fruit mixture into bottom of chilled pie crust. Pour custard over top. Transfer to oven and bake until center of pie registers 185 to 190 degrees and is set (filling will jiggle slightly when pie is shaken), about 1 hour. Let pie cool on wire rack until set, at least 4 hours. Serve.

Q&A: ARLEY BELL ON ARLEY CAKES AND DEVELOPING AUNT JULE'S PIE

Arley Bell is a baker and the owner of Arley Cakes, the cake-and-more business she started in 2016 that has grown into its strong mission statement: Sweet treats with a focus on social justice and a more equitable world. At first the business was a side gig for Bell fulfilling baked good orders for holidays and birthdays, but events in 2017 drove her to, as she says, "make the things I care about so much a more central part of the work I was doing." After neo-Nazi James Fields ran his car into a crowd peacefully protesting the Unite the Right Rally in Charlottesville, Virginia, Bell took out her pastry bag and started writing political messages on her cakes, things like "Black Lives Matter" and "Justice for Breonna [Taylor]," and names of other victims of police brutality. People could donate to a relevant cause in exchange for a baked good. In 2020, Bell left her full-time job to focus on Arley Cakes. She spent her time taking private orders, doing online advocacy work, hosting fundraisers, and pointing people toward action items. In 2023, Bell had a baby and, like many women, her work time shifted. She is now doing mostly wholesale orders, and she's thinking about the world from a new perspective: She wants to help build a world that is better for her daughter, Eliza.

We asked Bell to do a bold task for us: Redevelop a pie recipe from our archives that was problematic. The pie, a custard pie with dried fruit, nuts, and spices, was a delicious dessert but was named Jefferson Davis Pie after the president of the Confederate States. Like many desserts of the time, the pie didn't get its name from its inventor but rather from a male icon of the time. Some sources point to an enslaved woman: Aunt Jule Ann (some sources say Mary Ann or Julie Ann), who was enslaved by the Warren family. A 1926 article in the *Kansas City Star* says about the pie, "One Sunday, when there were distinguished guests at the Warren's, Aunt Jule Ann served a new kind of pie—so toothsome, so delicious, that there was a general desire to know how it was made."

The origin story gets shaky: Some sources say Aunt Jule was a Confederate sympathizer and so named the pie Jeff Davis herself. Others say it was named that because the Warren family were fans of Jefferson Davis. And some say that Jeff Davis ate and loved this pie. While we cannot say definitively how this pie came to be, we want to give credit back to the likely inventor of it. So we asked Arley Bell to take a spin, updating our old recipe for a more modern audience and renaming it after Aunt Jule. We interviewed Bell about the pie.

Had you ever heard of this pie before we connected?
No, I had not. But it's familiar; the base of it is like a chess pie. I had never seen a chess pie with dried fruit and nuts. And hadn't heard the mythology associated with the pie. That said, I did grow up in New Jersey, so my elementary years were shaped by that. The way I was taught about the Civil War was shaped by that, so I came in with some context for Jefferson Davis.

Can you talk about the process of redeveloping this pie and how you went about that?
I lived in Charlottesville a while and went to UVA. There are lots of things attributed to Thomas Jefferson that were his slaves' accomplishments. It's definitely a familiar tale, an old Southern slave-owning white man getting the credit. And it's worth noting, it's hard to be definitive. It seems like she [Aunt Jule] wasn't Jefferson Davis's slave. It was interesting looking at recipes and writings and to see who mentioned Aunt Jule and who didn't at all.

And can you talk about the flavor choices?
The concept of the pie was honestly a little weird to me. My husband was super-pumped about it since he loves raisins. That said, I did like the older *Cook's Country* recipe way more than I anticipated. The layer of nuts and fruits on the bottom bakes really well so it is more like a soft, gooey Fig Newton filling but more smooth.

How did making this pie connect to some of your work and mission?
This is part of the problem, that racist white men have been able to rewrite history in a way that erases people. And I feel like this pie project reclaimed that history in a way that is joyful to me. I like that it is addressing a problem but doing it in a way that is a celebration—it's a pie. We're baking a pie to just enjoy. And we're calling it Aunt Jule's pie. But the political stuff, a lot of it can be really heavy, those things are important. It's not just like things should be fun all the time. But a pie is a really joyful way to talk about and address this issue.

Fresh Peach Pie

Serves 8 ~ Total Time: 2½ hours, plus 5 hours resting and chilling

Eaten out of hand, a juicy peach is one of summer's greatest pleasures. Belinda Smith-Sullivan, chef, food writer, spice entrepreneur, and author, sure thinks so. In her cookbook, aptly titled Just Peachy, she shares interesting peach facts, seasonal varietals, American peach festivals, plus recipes for all things peach—including a delicious old-fashioned peach pie. Ours is a straightforward version that you can customize by adding blackberries, stirring in almond extract, or orange zest or other flavors as you desire. If your peaches are too soft to withstand the pressure of a peeler, cut a shallow X in the bottom of the fruit, blanch them in a pot of simmering water for 15 seconds, and then shock them in a bowl of ice water before peeling. For fruit pectin we recommend both Sure-Jell for Less or No Sugar Needed Recipes and Ball RealFruit Low or No-Sugar Needed Pectin.

1   recipe Double-Crust Pie Dough
     (page 456)

3   pounds ripe but firm peaches, peeled,
     halved, pitted, and cut into 1-inch pieces

½   cup (3½ ounces) plus 2 tablespoons
     sugar, divided

1   teaspoon grated lemon zest plus
     1 tablespoon juice

⅛   teaspoon table salt

2   tablespoons low- or no-sugar-needed
     fruit pectin

¼   teaspoon ground cinnamon
     Pinch ground nutmeg

1   tablespoon cornstarch

1   large egg, lightly beaten with
     1 tablespoon water

1   Roll 1 disk of dough into 12-inch circle on floured counter. Loosely roll dough around rolling pin and gently unroll it onto 9-inch pie plate, letting excess dough hang over edge. Ease dough into plate by gently lifting edge of dough with your hand while pressing into plate bottom with your other hand. Leave any dough that overhangs plate in place. Wrap dough-lined plate loosely in plastic wrap and refrigerate until firm, about 30 minutes. Roll other piece of dough into 13 by 10½-inch rectangle on floured counter, then transfer to parchment paper–lined rimmed baking sheet; cover loosely with plastic and refrigerate until firm, about 30 minutes.

2   Using pizza wheel, fluted pastry wheel, or paring knife, trim ¼ inch dough from long sides of rectangle, then cut lengthwise into eight 1¼-inch-wide strips. Cover loosely with plastic and refrigerate until firm, about 30 minutes. Adjust oven rack to middle position and heat oven to 400 degrees.

3   Meanwhile, toss peaches, ½ cup sugar, lemon zest and juice, and salt in bowl and let sit for at least 30 minutes or up to 1 hour. Combine pectin, cinnamon, nutmeg, and remaining 2 tablespoons sugar in small bowl; set aside. Measure out 1 cup peach pieces and mash with fork to coarse paste. Drain remaining peach pieces through colander set in bowl, reserving ½ cup peach juice. Return peach pieces to now-empty bowl and toss with cornstarch.

4   Whisk reserved peach juice and pectin mixture together in 12-inch skillet. Cook over medium heat, stirring occasionally, until thickened slightly and pectin is dissolved (liquid should become less cloudy), 3 to 5 minutes. Transfer peach-pectin mixture and peach paste to bowl with peach pieces and stir to combine. Spread peach mixture into dough-lined plate.

5   Remove dough strips from refrigerator; if too stiff to be workable, let sit at room temperature until softened slightly but still very cold. Space 4 strips evenly across top of pie, parallel to counter edge. Fold back first and third strips almost completely. Lay 1 strip across pie, perpendicular to second and fourth strips, keeping it snug to folded edges of dough strips, then unfold first and third strips over top. Fold back second and fourth strips and add second perpendicular strip, keeping it snug to folded edge. Unfold second and fourth strips over top. Repeat weaving remaining strips evenly across pie, alternating between folding back first and third strips and second and fourth strips to create lattice pattern. Shift strips as needed so they are evenly spaced over top of pie. (If dough becomes too soft to work with, refrigerate pie and dough strips until firm.)

6   Trim overhang to ½ inch beyond lip of plate. Pinch edges of bottom crust and lattice strips together firmly to seal. Tuck overhang under itself; folded edge should be flush with edge of plate. Crimp dough evenly around edge of plate. (If dough is very soft, refrigerate for 10 minutes before baking.) Brush surface with egg wash.

7   Place pie on aluminum foil–lined rimmed baking sheet and bake until crust is light golden, 20 to 25 minutes. Reduce oven temperature to 350 degrees, rotate sheet, and continue to bake until juices are bubbling and crust is deep golden brown, 30 to 50 minutes longer. Let pie cool on wire rack until filling has set, about 4 hours. Serve.

Thoroughbred Pie

Serves 8 ~ Total Time: 2¼ hours, plus 4½ hours cooling and chilling

The original recipe for Derby Pie—the chocolate-walnut-bourbon pie served at Kentucky Derby parties—is the closely guarded secret of the Kern family of Prospect, Kentucky. Husband and wife Walter and Leaudra Kern developed the recipe with their son, George. According to the family's website, each family member had a different name they wanted to call the pie, so they wrote all of them on slips of paper and put them in a hat. "Derby Pie" was the name they drew. The sweet, custardy, chocolate and nut–packed pie was so good they had it trademarked, Derby-Pie®. And they protect the proprietary recipe behind closed doors—literally. People who work in other areas of the company such as packaging are required to stay away from the mixing room when the pies are being put together.

Nowadays you will see pies inspired by this famous one with similar (but legal) names: Kentucky chocolate walnut pie, pegasus pie (a nod to the Kentucky Derby's Pegasus Parade), winner's circle pie, run for the roses pie, Kentucky Oaks pie, and the one we used: thoroughbred pie.

To create a version worthy of this elusive delicacy, we did some culinary detective work and ordered a pie straight from the Kern kitchen. Inspired by its texture and flavor, we use a combination of brown and white sugars, and employ cornstarch for thickening. A hit of bourbon is a nod to the Derby, and the booze also balances the sweetness. To make it our own, we incorporate browned butter, which adds depth and pairs well with the toasted walnuts. After parbaking the shell, we sprinkle the bottom with bittersweet chocolate and spread it into an even layer once it melts. Though we'll never have the original Derby-Pie® recipe, we think this one is worthy of a Triple Crown. We love serving it with our Bourbon Whipped Cream.

1	recipe Single-Crust Pie Dough (page 456)	½	cup packed (3½ ounces) light brown sugar
3	ounces bittersweet chocolate, chopped fine	2	tablespoons cornstarch
8	tablespoons unsalted butter, cut into 8 pieces	½	teaspoon table salt
3	tablespoons bourbon	2	large eggs plus 1 large yolk, lightly beaten
¾	cup (5¼ ounces) granulated sugar	1	teaspoon vanilla extract
		1½	cups walnuts, toasted and chopped

1 Roll dough into 12-inch circle on floured counter. Loosely roll dough around rolling pin and gently unroll it onto 9-inch pie plate, letting excess dough hang over edge. Ease dough into plate by gently lifting edge of dough with your hand while pressing into plate bottom with your other hand.

2 Trim overhang to ½ inch beyond lip of plate. Tuck overhang under itself; folded edge should be flush with edge of plate. Crimp dough evenly around edge of plate. Wrap dough-lined plate loosely in plastic wrap and refrigerate until firm, about 30 minutes. Adjust oven racks to middle and lower-middle positions and heat oven to 350 degrees.

3 Line chilled pie shell with double layer of aluminum foil, covering edges to prevent burning, and fill with pie weights. Bake on foil-lined rimmed baking sheet on upper rack until edges are set and just beginning to turn golden, 25 to 30 minutes, rotating sheet halfway through baking. Remove foil and weights, rotate sheet, and continue to bake crust until golden brown and crisp, 10 to 15 minutes longer. Transfer sheet to wire rack. Sprinkle chocolate evenly over hot pie crust and let sit until softened, about 5 minutes; smooth into even layer. Decrease oven temperature to 325 degrees.

4 Melt butter in small saucepan over medium-low heat. Cook, stirring constantly, until butter is nutty brown, 5 to 7 minutes. Off heat, slowly stir in bourbon (mixture will bubble vigorously). Let mixture cool for 5 minutes.

5 Whisk granulated sugar, brown sugar, cornstarch, and salt in large bowl until combined. Whisk in eggs and yolk and vanilla until smooth. Slowly whisk in butter mixture until incorporated. Stir in walnuts. With pie still on sheet, pour mixture into chocolate-lined crust. Bake on lower rack until filling is puffed and center jiggles slightly when pie is gently shaken, 35 to 40 minutes, rotating sheet halfway through baking. Let pie cool completely on wire rack, about 4 hours. Serve.

Bourbon Whipped Cream

Makes about 2 cups

For the most efficient whipping, make sure your heavy cream is as cold as possible.

- 1   cup heavy cream, chilled
- 2   tablespoons bourbon
- 1½ tablespoons light brown sugar
- ½   teaspoon vanilla extract

Using stand mixer fitted with whisk, mix all ingredients together on medium-low speed until foamy, about 1 minute. Increase speed to high and whip until stiff peaks form, 1 to 3 minutes. (Whipped cream can be refrigerated for up to 4 hours.)

BAKING AS A FORM OF SOCIAL JUSTICE

If the personal is political, there's nothing more political than a Southern woman's baking. Generations of Southern women have used their cooking and baking abilities to further the efforts of social causes from civil rights to reproductive justice.

Some women baked to advance issues in their community. Georgia Gilmore (see "Feeding the Fight" on page 419) supported the Montgomery bus boycott through her fundraising organization the Club from Nowhere. Today, Southern bakers are continuing the tradition.

Arley Bell (see "Q&A: Arley Bell on Arley Cakes and Developing Aunt Jule's Pie" on page 459) of Richmond, Virginia, and Becca Rea-Tucker of Austin, Texas, use their baking to support social justice causes including Black Lives Matter, abortion access, trans rights, and immigration issues. Bell and Rea-Tucker each work out of their home bakeries, raising money through bake sales and fundraisers. They share images of baked goods piped with explicit calls to action in frosting or pie crusts with cut-out messages on their respective social media platforms.

The digital age has led to an influx of Southern bakers using their baked goods for social justice. Bakers Against Racism, founded by several D.C.-based pastry chefs as a digital community for activism and baking after the murder of George Floyd in 2020, developed into a global grassroots network that uses digital bake sales to fund numerous social causes. Dubbed the "unofficial world's largest bake sale," BAR has raised over $2.5 million dollars worldwide.

While countless Southerners use food as a form of social justice, the act of baking carries additional significance for Southern women who were often stewards of baking-specific skill sets that were shared woman to woman.

by KC Hysmith

Brûléed Buttermilk Pie

Serves 8 ~ Total Time: 2¼ hours, plus 3½ hours cooling and chilling

Buttermilk pies have a creamy texture, a tangy-sweet flavor from buttermilk, and a browned top. Jerrelle Guy, author of *Black Girl Baking,* adds a brûléed top to her version. The inspiration? A miscommunication. One time her aunt recounted her pie recipe on the phone, but something got lost; when Guy baked the pie, margarine pooled on top and the sugar and eggs were scorched. However, what seemed like a mistake reminded Guy of a delicious crème brûlée, so she added the concept of a crunchy, caramelized top to her own recipe.

As Guy writes in the introduction of her book, baking with her senses has brought successes and failures. "My grandmother was a resilient baker—resourceful, intuitive and smart and the thing that just recently dawned on me is that she never used a kitchen scale. Yet every Sunday her biscuits were spot-on." Guy didn't buy a scale until she turned baking into a business. For her, like for so many Southern women bakers, baking is a divine feeling.

To try our hand at pie brûlée, we chill the pie, add a topping of sugar, and torch that until it's beautifully caramelized. Use commercial cultured buttermilk (avoid nonfat), as some locally produced, artisanal buttermilks that we tested were prone to curdling during baking.

1	recipe Single-Crust Pie Dough (page 456)
1	cup (7 ounces) sugar, divided
1	tablespoon cornstarch
¾	teaspoon table salt
2	large eggs plus 5 large yolks
1¾	cups buttermilk
¼	cup heavy cream
4	tablespoons unsalted butter, melted and cooled
2	teaspoons distilled white vinegar
1½	teaspoons vanilla extract

1 Roll dough into 12-inch circle on floured counter. Loosely roll dough around rolling pin and gently unroll it onto 9-inch pie plate, letting excess dough hang over edge. Ease dough into plate by gently lifting edge of dough with your hand while pressing into plate bottom with your other hand.

2 Trim overhang to ½ inch beyond lip of plate. Tuck overhang under itself; folded edge should be flush with edge of plate. Crimp dough evenly around edge of plate. Wrap dough-lined plate loosely in plastic and freeze until dough is firm, about 15 minutes.

3 Meanwhile, adjust oven rack to middle position and heat oven to 350 degrees. Whisk ¾ cup sugar, cornstarch, and salt together in large bowl. Whisk eggs and yolks into sugar mixture until well combined. Whisk buttermilk, cream, melted butter, vinegar, and vanilla into sugar-egg mixture until incorporated; set aside.

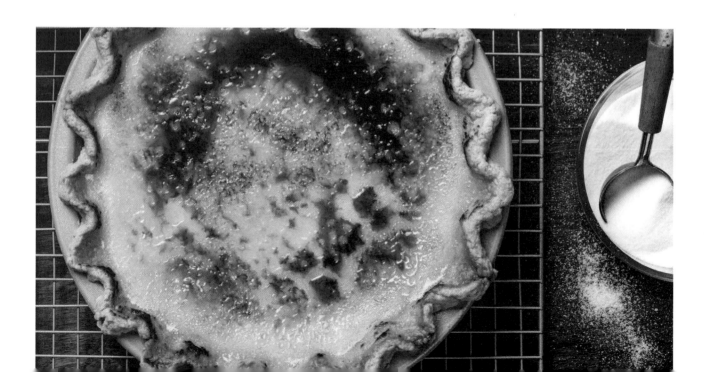

Lemon Chess Pie

Serves 8 ~ Total Time: 2 hours, plus 4½ hours chilling and cooling

4 Place chilled pie shell on aluminum foil–lined rimmed baking sheet. Line shell with double layer of foil, covering edges to prevent burning, and fill with pie weights. Bake until edges are light golden brown, 30 to 40 minutes. Remove foil and weights, rotate sheet, and reduce oven temperature to 300 degrees. Bake until crust bottom dries out and turns light golden brown, 20 to 25 minutes longer. (If crust begins to puff, pierce gently with tip of paring knife.) (Crust must still be warm when filling is added.)

5 Whisk buttermilk mixture to recombine and, with pie still on sheet, carefully pour into hot crust. Bake until filling in center of pie registers 180 degrees, about 40 minutes (filling will jiggle slightly when pie is shaken; pie will set as it cools). Let pie cool on wire rack for 30 minutes. Refrigerate for at least 3 hours or up to 24 hours.

6 Just before serving, remove pie from refrigerator; gently dab surface with paper towels as needed to absorb any condensation. Sprinkle pie evenly with 2 tablespoons sugar (tilting and tapping dish to evenly distribute sugar). Ignite torch; holding flame 4 to 5 inches from surface of pie, sweep flame over surface to melt sugar (sugar should look transparent but not caramelized). Sprinkle pie evenly with remaining 2 tablespoons sugar. Ignite torch; holding flame 1 to 2 inches from surface, slowly move flame over pie, starting from edges and moving into center, to evenly caramelize sugar. Let sit until sugar is set, about 1 minute. Serve.

Dating back to the 1800s, chess pie is a cousin to buttermilk, vinegar, custard, and translucent pies. It's made from ingredients cooks had in their pantry, namely lots of eggs, sugar, butter, sometimes milk or cream, and a little flour or cornmeal.

As Rebecca Sharpless (page 7) writes in her book *Grain and Fire*, "One of the great mysteries of Southern baking is chess pie"; no one knows exactly how it came to be. Some say it was derived from a cheese pie. The late Southern chef Phila Hach theorizes the name may come from chestnut flour, which could have been used as a thickener before now-standard cornmeal. Other tales point to the name coming from the cold "chest" that pies would have been stored in. And there's another theory yet that the name came from a waitress, plantation owner, or enslaved cook who, when asked what she was making, replied, "just pie," and it was misheard as "chess pie."

However it got its name, chess pie comes together quickly, and it's pretty sweet. All sorts of chess pie variations exist: everything from the more common lemon and chocolate to salted honey or browned butter.

This chess pie nicely balances the sweet with tangy. Five eggs set the filling while 3 tablespoons of lemon juice and 1 tablespoon of zest contribute tartness. Regular yellow cornmeal (not stone ground) works best here. Make the filling before baking the shell so the cornmeal has time to soften.

1 recipe Single-Crust Pie Dough (page 456)

5 large eggs

1¾ cups (12¼ ounces) plus 1 teaspoon sugar, divided

2 tablespoons cornmeal

1 tablespoon grated lemon zest plus 3 tablespoons juice

¼ teaspoon table salt

8 tablespoons unsalted butter, melted and cooled

1 Roll dough into 12-inch circle on floured counter. Loosely roll dough around rolling pin and gently unroll it onto 9-inch pie plate, letting excess dough hang over edge. Ease dough into plate by gently lifting edge of dough with your hand while pressing into plate bottom with your other hand.

2 Trim overhang to ½ inch beyond lip of plate. Tuck overhang under itself; folded edge should be flush with edge of plate. Crimp dough evenly around edge of plate. Wrap dough-lined plate loosely in plastic wrap and refrigerate until firm, about 30 minutes. Adjust oven rack to middle position and heat oven to 350 degrees.

3 Whisk eggs in bowl until smooth. Slowly whisk in 1¾ cups sugar, cornmeal, lemon zest and juice, and salt until combined. Whisk in melted butter.

4 Line chilled pie shell with double layer of aluminum foil, covering edges to prevent burning, and fill with pie weights. Bake on foil-lined rimmed baking sheet until edges are set and just beginning to turn golden, 25 to 30 minutes, rotating sheet halfway through baking. Remove foil and weights. (Crust must still be warm when filling is added.) Whisk filling to recombine and, with pie still on sheet, carefully pour into hot crust. Bake until surface is light brown and center jiggles slightly, 35 to 40 minutes. Sprinkle with remaining 1 teaspoon sugar. Let cool completely on wire rack, about 4 hours. Serve.

French Silk Chocolate Pie

Serves 8   ~   Total Time: 1¼ hours, plus 4 hours chilling and cooling

Don't let the name fool you: The recipe for French silk pie—a retro pie that's lighter and less dense than chocolate cream pie (the filling literally melts in your mouth) but silky-smooth and packed with richness—was born in America. This icebox pie was created by a Maryland woman, Betty Cooper, in 1951 for the third annual Pillsbury Bake-Off.

Cooper's original recipe called for whipping butter, sugar, three squares of melted-and-cooled unsweetened chocolate, and raw eggs until the mixture was light and fluffy. She chilled the filling in a pie crust until it was firm—no baking required.

For our version, we call to cook the eggs with sugar on the stovetop—whipping them in the process—until the mixture is light and thick. This adds density and avoids any concerns of using raw eggs. Incorporating a stick of softened butter gives the pie a silky-smooth texture. Using bittersweet chocolate in the filling boosts chocolate flavor better than milder varieties can. And folding whipped cream into the filling before spooning it into the pie shell lightens the filling to airy, silky perfection. We like to serve this pie with more whipped cream and chocolate curls.

ICEBOX PIES

Icebox pies date back to the early 1800s in the American South, and they get their name from the iceboxes where they were traditionally kept cool. They feature cool, creamy fillings that range from simple (tart, bracing citrus) to decadent (rich chocolate). They can have a classic flaky pie crust or an easy crumb crust made from cookies or graham crackers. Although they're traditionally made with egg whites, we have taken a couple routes to thickening our icebox fillings to the perfect, sliceable consistency. In these desserts, you need to turn on the oven only to bake the crust.

1   recipe Single-Crust Pie Dough (page 456)

1   cup heavy cream, chilled

3   large eggs

¾   cup (5¼ ounces) sugar

2   tablespoons water

8   ounces bittersweet chocolate, melted and cooled

1   tablespoon vanilla extract

8   tablespoons unsalted butter, cut into ½-inch pieces and softened

1   Roll dough into 12-inch circle on floured counter. Loosely roll dough around rolling pin and gently unroll it onto 9-inch pie plate, letting excess dough hang over edge. Ease dough into plate by gently lifting edge of dough with your hand while pressing into plate bottom with your other hand.

2   Trim overhang to ½ inch beyond lip of plate. Tuck overhang under itself; folded edge should be flush with edge of plate. Crimp dough evenly around edge of plate. Wrap dough-lined plate loosely in plastic wrap and refrigerate until firm, about 30 minutes. Adjust oven rack to middle position and heat oven to 350 degrees.

3   Line chilled pie shell with double layer of aluminum foil, covering edges to prevent burning, and fill with pie weights. Bake on foil-lined rimmed baking sheet until edges are set and just beginning to turn golden, 25 to 30 minutes, rotating sheet halfway through baking. Remove foil and weights, rotate sheet, and continue to bake crust until golden brown and crisp, 10 to 15 minutes longer. Transfer sheet to wire rack and let cool completely, about 30 minutes.

4   Using handheld mixer set at medium-high speed, whip cream to stiff peaks, 2 to 3 minutes. Refrigerate until ready to use.

5   Combine eggs, sugar, and water in large heatproof bowl set over saucepan filled with 1 inch barely simmering water, making sure that water does not touch bottom of bowl. Using handheld mixer on medium speed, beat until egg mixture is thickened and registers 160 degrees, 7 to 10 minutes. Remove bowl from heat and continue to beat until egg mixture is fluffy and cooled completely, about 8 minutes.

6   Add chocolate and vanilla to egg mixture and beat until incorporated. Beat in butter, few pieces at a time, until incorporated. Using rubber spatula, fold in refrigerated whipped cream until no white streaks remain. Transfer filling to cooled crust, smoothing top with spatula. Refrigerate, uncovered, until set, at least 3 hours. Serve.

REALLY GOOD KEY LIME PIE

The origin of key lime pie is a subject of intense debate. One story goes that in the late 1800s, fishermen in southern Florida would put together makeshift meals on their skiffs by soaking stale Cuban bread with easy-to-store canned condensed milk and wild turtle or bird eggs. They squeezed juice from local key limes so that the acidity would both "cook" the eggs and add flavor. Observing these men, a local cook known as Aunt Sally was inspired to turn their creation into a tangy pie.

Another theory says key lime pie was born in the 1930s as an adaptation of a recipe called Magic Lemon Cream Pie created by the Borden condensed milk company. This icebox pie recipe calls for combining egg yolks, sweetened condensed milk, and lemon juice into a no-cook custard that gets topped with meringue. It looks strikingly similar to most modern key lime pie recipes but uses a different citrus.

However and wherever key lime pie was born, the pie has become a point of pride in Florida, where it's the official state pie. But even within the Sunshine State, the dessert inspires heated opinions. In the 1960s, state representative Bernie Papy Jr. called to impose a $100 fine on anyone calling the dessert "key lime pie" without using real key limes. And while no one has pushed this legislation, many believe that green food coloring ruins the pie. A graham cracker crust and a whipped cream topping are common elements, but plenty of Floridians adamantly defend a traditional pastry crust and/or a meringue top. My recipe may not adhere to everyone's definition, but it does have a soft yet set filling that straddles the fine line between sweet and tart.

by Lindsay Autry

culinary instructor, recipe developer, and media professional

Key Lime Pie

Serves 8 ~ Total Time: 1¾ hours, plus 5 hours cooling and chilling

This recipe for key lime pie started with what many think of as the go-to: the recipe on the back of the bottle of Nellie & Joe's Famous Key West Lime Juice. Increasing amounts and adding heavy cream make an impressively tall slice of pie that's extra-luscious. Mixing some pretzels into the graham cracker crust contributes a buttery saltiness that balances the sweet-tart filling. A pillowy meringue topping adds a contrasting texture. Be sure to zest the limes to get the 2 teaspoons of zest needed for the garnish before juicing them. You'll need to buy two 14-ounce cans of sweetened condensed milk to yield the 1½ cups for this recipe. We call for Persian limes in this recipe, but if you'd prefer to use key lime juice you'll need to squeeze about 18 key limes to get ¾ cup of juice.

Crust

- 6 ounces graham crackers, broken into 1-inch pieces (about 11 crackers)
- 2 ounces mini pretzel twists (about 35 twists)
- ¼ cup packed (1¾ ounces) light brown sugar
- ¼ teaspoon table salt
- 8 tablespoons unsalted butter, melted

Filling

- 1½ cups sweetened condensed milk
- ¾ cup lime juice (6 limes)
- 6 tablespoons heavy cream
- 4 large egg yolks
- ⅛ teaspoon table salt

Meringue

- 2 large egg whites
- ¼ teaspoon table salt
- ¼ teaspoon cream of tartar
- ½ cup (3½ ounces) granulated sugar
- ¼ cup water
- 1 tablespoon vanilla extract
- 2 teaspoons grated lime zest

1 **For the crust** Adjust oven rack to middle position and heat oven to 350 degrees. Process cracker pieces, pretzels, sugar, and salt in food processor until finely ground, about 30 seconds. Add melted butter and pulse until combined, about 8 pulses.

2 Transfer cracker mixture to 9-inch pie plate. Using bottom of dry measuring cup, press crumbs firmly into bottom and up sides of plate. Place plate on rimmed baking sheet and bake until crust is fragrant and set, about 17 minutes. Transfer sheet to wire rack.

3 **For the filling** Whisk all ingredients in bowl until fully combined. With pie plate still on sheet, carefully pour filling into crust (crust needn't be completely cooled). Transfer sheet to oven and bake pie until edge of filling is set but center still jiggles slightly when shaken, about 30 minutes.

4 Place pie on wire rack and let cool completely, about 1 hour. Refrigerate uncovered until fully chilled, at least 4 hours, or cover with greased plastic wrap and refrigerate for up to 24 hours.

5 **For the meringue** Using stand mixer fitted with whisk attachment, whip egg whites, salt, and cream of tartar on medium-high speed until soft peaks form, 2 to 4 minutes.

6 Combine sugar and water in small saucepan. Bring to rolling boil over medium-high heat and cook until syrup registers 240 degrees, 1 to 3 minutes.

7 Working quickly, turn mixer to medium speed. With mixer running, slowly and carefully pour hot syrup into egg white mixture (avoid pouring syrup onto whisk, if possible). Add vanilla. Increase speed to medium-high and whip until shiny, stiff peaks form, about 2 minutes.

8 Spread meringue over pie filling, leaving 1-inch border around pie. Working gently, use spatula or spoon to create swirls and cowlicks over surface of meringue. Sprinkle meringue with lime zest. Slice pie into wedges with wet knife, wiping knife clean between slices. Serve.

Banana Pudding Pie

Serves 8 ~ Total Time: 1¼ hours, plus 4 hours chilling

Buxton Hall Barbecue in Asheville, North Carolina, was known for their whole hog barbecue. But even non–meat eaters would go to this spot to try the banana pudding pie. This pie was invented by former pastry chef Ashley Capps.

As a child, Capps was fond of her mother's meringue-topped banana pudding. Transforming the childhood dessert into a pie fit for a restaurant was "a combination of technique and nostalgia," a blending of her "inner child and Southern roots."

We visited her in 2019 and watched her build the pie with a mesmerizing confidence, carefully forming the crumb crust into the corner of the pie plate, the "neck" of the pie, so the slices stay sturdy. She stirred the pudding with a spatula, not a whisk, so the custard wouldn't curdle in the corners of the pot. She insisted that cooking the egg whites to 168 degrees is the key to a stable meringue, "although the textbooks disagree."

While she worked, she talked about the arc of a culinary career: the struggle of learning the process and techniques; the discipline of repetition; and, after sufficient growth and self-awareness, the feeling of fulfillment from making the same thing as close to perfect every time. Her passion for the process

is evident, as is her creativity. Speaking of how she started making this pie, she explains, "When I have an idea, it's not gonna leave me until I try it."

The banana pudding pie was a hit on the Buxton Hall menu from day one. And even though Capps left the restaurant on good terms to pursue other opportunities, the pie remained.

Here is our take on Capps's pie. For a sturdy crust, we use ground Nilla Wafers (a vanilla-y standard of puddings) plus additional flour. Some gelatin firms the pudding layer just enough to get clean slices. A pinch each of ground cinnamon and allspice makes the perfect backdrop for sliced fresh bananas. We top it all off with a cooked meringue, swapping in some brown sugar for added caramel undertones. Browning the meringue topping adds a slight toasty bitterness that perfectly offsets the sweet pudding underneath. Peel and slice the bananas just before using to help prevent browning. Chilling the topped pie for longer than 4 hours may cause the top to deflate. But don't worry; it will still be delicious. If broiling the topping, be sure to use a broiler-safe pie plate for this recipe.

Crust

4	cups (8⅓ ounces) vanilla wafers	
3	tablespoons packed light brown sugar	
1	tablespoon all-purpose flour	
¼	teaspoon table salt	
6	tablespoons unsalted butter, melted	

Filling

2	teaspoons unflavored gelatin
1¾	cups half-and-half, divided
¾	cup (5¼ ounces) granulated sugar
5	large egg yolks
2	tablespoons all-purpose flour
¼	teaspoon table salt
	Pinch ground cinnamon
	Pinch ground allspice
2	tablespoons unsalted butter, cut into 2 pieces and chilled
1	tablespoon vanilla extract
2	ripe bananas, peeled and sliced ¼ inch thick (1½ cups)

Meringue

⅓	cup (2⅓ ounces) granulated sugar
⅓	cup packed (2⅓ ounces) light brown sugar
4	large egg whites
¼	teaspoon cream of tartar
⅛	teaspoon table salt

1 **For the crust** Adjust oven rack 8 inches from broiler element and heat oven to 325 degrees. Pulse cookies, sugar, flour, and salt in food processor until finely ground, about 10 pulses. Add melted butter and pulse until combined, about 8 pulses, scraping down sides of bowl as needed. Transfer mixture to 9-inch pie plate (it will seem like a lot of crumbs).

2 Using your hands, press crumbs firmly up sides of plate, building walls about ¼ inch thick and leveling top edge. Press remaining crumbs into even layer on bottom of plate, firmly pressing crumbs into corners of plate. Place plate on rimmed baking sheet and bake until crust is fragrant and beginning to darken at edges, 18 to 20 minutes. Transfer plate to wire rack.

3 **For the filling** Meanwhile, sprinkle gelatin over ½ cup half-and-half in small bowl and let mixture sit until gelatin softens, about 5 minutes. Whisk sugar, egg yolks, flour, salt, cinnamon, allspice, and remaining 1¼ cups half-and-half in large saucepan until fully combined. Cook over medium heat, whisking constantly and scraping corners of saucepan, until mixture thickens, bubbles burst across entire surface, and mixture registers 180 degrees in several places, 5 to 7 minutes. Off heat, whisk in butter, vanilla, and gelatin mixture until combined.

4 Stir bananas into hot filling. Pour filling into crust (crust needn't be completely cooled). Press parchment paper directly onto surface of filling and refrigerate until set, at least 4 hours or up to 24 hours.

5 **For the meringue** Whisk all ingredients together in bowl of stand mixer. Place bowl over saucepan filled with 1 inch barely simmering water, making sure water does not touch bottom of bowl. Whisking gently but constantly, cook until mixture registers 160 to 165 degrees, 5 to 8 minutes. Remove bowl from heat and transfer to stand mixer fitted with whisk attachment. Whip mixture on high speed until meringue forms stiff peaks and is smooth and creamy, 2 to 3 minutes.

6 Gently peel off parchment from filling (if any filling sticks to parchment, scrape off and smooth back over surface of pie). Spread meringue over filling, making sure meringue touches edges of crust. Working gently, use spatula or spoon to create swirls over surface.

7a **For a broiler** Heat broiler. Broil until meringue is well browned, 1 to 2 minutes, rotating plate as needed for even browning.

7b **For a torch** Ignite torch; continuously sweep flame about 2 inches above meringue until well browned.

8 Slice pie into wedges with wet knife, wiping knife clean between slices. Serve immediately. (Topped pie can be refrigerated for up to 4 hours.)

No. 14

SOUTHERN SIPPERS

Left to right: Coquito (page 507); Joy Perrine, the Bad Girl of Bourbon (see page 488);
Plum Reviver (page 493); Southern Milk Punch and Clarified Milk Punch (page 499);
Leah Wong Ashburn, CEO of Highland Brewing Company (see page 503).

Joy Perrine: Amy C. Evans / Southern Foodways Alliance; Leah Wong Ashburn: Highland Brewing

CAN I FIX YOU A DRINK?

WHEN SOUTHERN WOMEN HOST, NO ONE GOES THIRSTY

"Bartending is about hospitality. Women care about other people's experiences."

– Dr. Nicola Nice, sociologist, brand strategist, and founder of Pomp and Whimsy, a beverage brand dedicated to the spirit known as Mother Gin

Welcome to the South. It's hot. It's probably humid. And chances are, you're thirsty. Drinks matter here—as refreshment, as ritual, as social lubricant, as big business, and perhaps most of all, as expressions of hospitality.

For centuries, Southern men have made names for themselves as distillers, brewers, mixologists, and more. But it's the Southern hostesses—often unnamed, unheralded, or unseen—who are the real heroines of this story. When someone presses a drink into your hand, it's more than a promise to slake your thirst. It's an act of care and a show of generosity. Southern women know this, and they wield the position of hostess with both selflessness and power.

It's a fraught image, the Southern woman as hostess. The term itself might conjure up an image of a well-off, well-dressed woman, probably white, who flits among her guests while unseen domestic workers, probably nonwhite, do the cooking and cleaning. That trope is, of course, grounded in ugly historical reality. And it persists today, when women of color disproportionately occupy low-paying service roles.

Across the South, though, women have always supplied the ingenuity, creativity, and hard work that fuels the region's reputation for hospitality. They've practiced this art in private and public settings and among family, friends, and strangers. Traditional models of female entrepreneurship in the region have been limited to boarding houses, tea rooms, and catering businesses.

At home, refreshment might have come in the form of freshly brewed iced tea, topped with a sprig of home-grown mint, for a daytime gathering of a bridge club; a round of Bloody Marys before Thanksgiving lunch; martinis stirred for a husband after a long day at the office; or mixed drinks offered to their guests at a cocktail or formal dinner party. But feminist historians are turning the spotlight on other notable hostesses who hid a "booming underground alcohol market" from male dominance all across the globe, and that includes bootleggers and rum runners in the American South. We can raise a glass to that!

The opportunities for women to earn a living in bars and other public drinking places were certainly limited, as Mallory O'Meara explains in her provocative book *Girly Drinks: A World History of Women and Alcohol*. But, "Women always found a way to secretly brew, distill, sell or drink in pulquerias, shebeens, hidden dramshops, or their own kitchens."

In 1904, housewives learned to make cocktails from the first cocktail book written by a woman, Mae E. Southworth, entitled *One Hundred and One Beverages*. It was a recipe collection that "expected that a woman be able to make a cocktail, just as she could cook a roast or bake a pie." When Prohibition pushed drinking alcohol into private spaces, namely the home, women enacted their hostessing skills operating secret rooms and private clubs called speakeasies where they welcomed guests with entertainment and the opportunity to socialize, while enjoying illicit booze supplied by female smugglers. During World War II, female bartending moved out into the open when women, symbolized by Bessie the Bartender (like her counterpart Rosie the Riveter), left their homes to fill jobs left by men that kept the American economy running. And in the mid-1950s, Marge Samuels, a woman with a chemistry degree, an artistic flair, and a genius for marketing, designed a new look for whiskey bottles that "changed the whiskey marketing game forever": the red wax covering on the top of the bottle that drips down the side and identifies one of the South's most beloved brands, Maker's Mark.

The list of achievements goes on.

All of this is to say that women have been and continue to be a major influence on American hospitality, offering to "fix you a drink" no matter who you are, whether we're talking about Nicole Stipp and Kaitlyn Soligan's Trouble Bar in Louisville, Kentucky, whose mission is inclusivity, or Julie Mabry's Pearl Bar, a welcoming safe space for lesbians and queer folks in Houston, Texas.

In the 21st century, we celebrate a broader interpretation of the hostess and her place at the Southern table. Today, a Southern hostess could be serving soft drinks at her daughter's quinceañera. She could be pouring the wine at a Passover seder. She could be mixing drinks at the cocktail bar she owns. She could be your restaurant sommelier or wine educator.

O'Meara sums it up like this: "Despite the constraints of a patriarchal society, women were [and still are] a major influence on the modern world's alcohol culture, from South African beer halls to American beer cans."

Cheers!

by Sara Camp Milam and Toni Tipton-Martin

Camp Milam: managing editor for the Southern Foodways Alliance, including Gravy *quarterly and* Gravy *podcast, and co-author, with Jerry Slater, of* The Southern Foodways Alliance Guide to Cocktails

Lemonade

Serves 6 to 8   ~   Total Time: 15 minutes, plus 1 hour chilling

Mikaila Ulmer of Me & the Bees Lemonade.

Jacob Ulmer

Mikaila Ulmer of Austin, Texas, was running her multimillion dollar company Me & the Bees Lemonade before she turned 19. Why "the bees"? Ulmer was inspired by startling back-to-back bee stings she got when she was four. Fear after those fateful stings turned into fascination once Ulmer started learning about bees and their contributions to the ecosystem—and that fascination turned into a business. Like many kids, Ulmer opened a lemonade stand; unlike many kids, she grew it into a full-blown national wholesale company, one that received funding from Whole Foods Market and from the entrepreneur competition show *Shark Tank*. Also, unlike many lemonade stands, this one benefits those bees Ulmer's so thankful for; a percentage of her lemonade sales goes to organizations working to save honeybees. "Buy a Bottle . . . Save a Bee" is her motto.

Ulmer's recipe is adapted from her great-grandmother's flax seed (a health aid) lemonade except, inspired by one of bees' many gifts, she uses flavorful honey in place of some of the sugar. You should seek out Me & the Bees Lemonade in stores or order it online to get a true taste of Ulmer's drink (and to benefit the bees). But if you want to make a big batch of your own for a party, we offer this crowd-pleasing version. Muddling lemon slices with granulated sugar extracts the oils in the peels for deep flavor and enhances the brightness of the freshly squeezed lemon juice. There are a lot of lemons, so we use a potato masher; its large surface area makes quick work of the process. Following Ulmer's wisdom, we add a little honey for a light floral flavor. And we include two variations, mint and ginger, which are also in Ulmer's rotation. When purchasing lemons, choose large ones that give to gentle pressure; hard lemons have thicker skin and yield less juice. Lemons are commonly waxed to prevent moisture loss, increase shelf life, and protect from bruising during shipping. Scrub them with a vegetable brush under running water to remove wax, or buy organic lemons. Don't worry about the seeds in the extracted juice; the entire juice mixture is strained at the end of the recipe.

¾ cup sugar

13 lemons (2 sliced thin, seeds and ends discarded, 11 juiced to yield 2 cups)

56 ounces cold water

½ cup honey

Using potato masher, mash sugar and half of lemon slices in large bowl until sugar is completely wet, about 1 minute. Add water and lemon juice and whisk until sugar is completely dissolved, about 1 minute. Strain mixture through fine-mesh strainer set over serving pitcher, pressing on solids to extract as much juice as possible; discard solids. Stir in honey and remaining lemon slices and refrigerate until chilled, at least 1 hour or up to 3 days. Stir to recombine before serving over ice.

Ginger Lemonade

Mash ½ cup peeled, thinly sliced ginger with sugar and half of lemon slices.

Mint Lemonade

Mash 1 cup fresh mint leaves with sugar and half of lemon slices. Add ½ cup fresh mint leaves to strained lemonade.

Sweet Iced Tea

Serves 4 to 6 ~ Total Time: 10 minutes, plus 1¾ hours steeping and chilling

Sweet tea was called the "house wine of the South" by Truvy (played by Dolly Parton) in the movie *Steel Magnolias*, and indeed this drink has a special place on Southern tables. In her 2008 James Beard Award–winning cookbook, *Screen Doors and Sweet Tea: Recipes and Tales from a Southern Cook*, chef and writer Martha Hall Foose tells us her tea was voted best in the region in *Delta Magazine* in 2004 when she opened Mockingbird Bakery in Greenwood, Mississippi. Foose is a born storyteller as much as a chef, and her cookbooks weave together recipes and rich, whimsical, funny stories about Delta life. In addition to authoring cookbooks, she's flexed her talents in roles from cookbook editor for Pillsbury to food stylist for the movie *The Help*. In 2023, Foose opened Loblolly Bakery in Hattiesburg, Mississippi. To honor Foose, we offer a sip of sweet tea that follows a method similar to her celebrated one. Steeping the tea in room-temperature rather than hot water allows the tea to develop strong flavor without any bitter undertones. Rather than stir in sugar, which can give the tea a gritty quality, we call for a simple syrup that makes it sweet—and smooth. Start with 2 tablespoons of simple syrup and add more to taste. This recipe can easily be doubled. If you have any extra tea, look up Foose's recipe for sweet tea pie. She developed it right after she graduated high school as an entry for a state fair pie baking competition.

6 black tea bags

32 ounces water, room temperature

2–6 tablespoons Simple Syrup (page 489)

1 lemon, sliced thin

1 Tie strings of tea bags together (for easy removal) and place in large bowl along with water; let steep for 45 minutes.

2 Discard tea bags and pour tea into serving pitcher. Add simple syrup and stir to combine. Refrigerate until chilled, at least 1 hour or up to 1 week. Stir in lemon slices and serve over ice.

Martha Hall Foose, James Beard Award–winning cookbook author, writer, and chef.

Chris Granger

Vietnamese Coffee

Serves 1 ~ Total Time: 15 minutes

Vietnamese coffee, renowned both in Vietnam and within Vietnamese communities around the world, has captivated coffee enthusiasts worldwide for its strong yet sweet flavor. This beverage combines darkly roasted robusta coffee beans or an equally intensely flavored bean like Cafe Du Monde (see "Cà Phê or (Ro)Bust(a)!") with sweetened condensed milk. We recommend brewing Vietnamese robusta coffee for this recipe; however, other varieties of robusta or arabica coffee can be used. To substitute Cafe Du Monde coffee, reduce coffee to ¾ ounce. Vietnamese coffee is traditionally brewed using a phin filter, which is composed of four parts—a filter body, a perforated press disk, a perforated plate, and a lid. (We do not use the lid for this recipe.) This recipe was developed using a 10- to 12-ounce phin filter. If unavailable, a small coffee filter–lined fine-mesh strainer set over a liquid measuring cup can be substituted. Serve over ice, if desired.

1   ounce medium-grind dark roast robusta coffee

1   cup boiling water, divided

2   tablespoons sweetened condensed milk, plus extra for sweetening

Add coffee to body of phin filter and arrange perforated press disk on top. Place filter body on perforated plate and set on top of serving cup. Pour ¼ cup boiling water over coffee and let sit for 30 seconds to bloom. Pour remaining ¾ cup boiling water over coffee and let sit until all liquid has passed through filter, about 6 minutes. Remove phin filter and stir 2 tablespoons condensed milk into coffee. Adjust sweetness of coffee with extra condensed milk to taste. Serve.

CÀ PHÊ OR (RO)BUST(A)!

The dandelion-yellow cans of Café Du Monde just appeared at our local Việt supermarket one day. There was abundance, and as immigrants, we were not used to excess, or ever having enough. The deep earthiness of the chicory blend reminded the growing Vietnamese community in Texas of the cà phê they once had back home. Café Du Monde replaced the General Foods International Coffees—small tins of instant coffee with exciting names like Suisse Mocha, French Vanilla Café, and my personal favorite, Café Vienna—our family made do with. (For refugees, canned items that lasted beyond their best-by date and tasted as good as the day they were packed, a decade later, were precious.)

The first Café Du Monde stand opened in 1862 in New Orleans. Five years earlier, across the world, the French introduced the *Coffea arabica* plant to the Vietnamese in 1857. The first cà phê plantation in Vietnam flowered decades later in 1888. Today, Vietnam is the second largest producer of coffee in the world, but most Vietnamese coffee crops are no longer arabica. They are *Coffea canephora*—robusta.

For those of us who grew up without access to beans from our ancestral land, Vietnamese coffee usually meant a can of sweetened condensed milk and a can of Café Du Monde. It was the ritual and process, more than the ingredients themselves. Food assimilation was both necessary for our survival and a way to remember home.

Café Du Monde is Vietnamese American, but not exclusively. In the same way, Filet-O-Fish from McDonald's, hush puppies from Long John Silver's, thighs and wings from Popeyes, and "fine dining" at La Madeleine are a part of the Vietnamese Texan culinary canon, but not exclusively. Countless immigrant foodways intersect. In order to survive, we make do.

by Doris Hồ-Kane

Texan owner and pastry chef of Bạn Bè Vietnamese American bakery in Brooklyn, New York

A POWERFUL INFUSION

I grew up in Houston and celebrated Juneteenth annually. In my community it was a festive, boisterous day of music and prayer, all fueled by a huge spread of delicious, inviting treats. From sweets to meats, the tables were covered with limitless red foods and drinks. Why was all the celebratory food and drink red? To answer that, we need context.

In 2021, June 19 became a federal holiday called Juneteenth National Independence Day, making it the first new holiday since the Reverend Dr. Martin Luther King Jr.'s birthday became one in 1983. But Juneteenth isn't new; emancipation has been celebrated in one form or another (at first mostly in Texas and Louisiana) since the enslaved were freed. The day has been known by names such as Black Freedom Day, Jubilee Day, Manumission Day, and the 19th of June.

"For a long time, Juneteenth wasn't the only emancipation celebration," says Adrian Miller, author of the James Beard Award–winning book Soul Food. "African Americans across the country marked various milestones in the struggle for freedom on different dates, although that patchwork of community traditions faded over time.

Wherever and whenever these celebrations took place, it didn't matter what drink the hosts served—a carbonated beverage, lemonade, Kool-Aid, or punch—it just had to be red."

Red drink is rooted in West Africa. West Africans have long used their native plant hibiscus, also known as roselle, to make a popular hospitality drink called bissap. Water is infused with hibiscus flowers (usually dried). Sweeteners (such as cane syrup), as well as fragrant, bright-tasting citrus, ginger, and other spices, are added to balance the bitterness. Enslaved West Africans brought memories of the drink to the Americas during the slave trade.

"Hibiscus was easily transplanted in the Caribbean because of the similarity in climate," Miller says. "In Jamaica, the plants bloom around Christmas, and sorrel, a local and beloved riff on bissap, was created. Without regular access to hibiscus, the captives who arrived in temperate climates in North America relied upon fruit and dyes to create the desired color. The generic term 'red drink' was born. The extended family of crimson-colored beverages are a nod to bissap, even if they don't have the same ingredients."

So now, as a professional bartender, I know that our Juneteenth drinks are red because of cultural memory. But as a kid, the preparation felt like the lead-up to Christmas. What could be better than a day with my friends, family, neighbors, and church community, eating and drinking treats? Watermelon, barbecue, soda, cakes, balloons—it was even better than Christmas! The special Juneteenth red drink for us kids was ice-cold Big Red soda. Bottles of the crimson beverage rested in ice chests, while hibiscus iced tea (that was sometimes spiked with alcohol) was served out of large punch bowls or gallon jugs for the adults.

by Tiffanie Barriere

award-winning mixologist and beverage historian known as The Drinking Coach

Hibiscus Iced Tea

Serves 4 to 6 ~ Total Time: 45 minutes, plus 1 hour chilling

Avoid letting the tea boil, as that can make it too bitter. Strain out the solids, let the tea cool, and add cane syrup for sweetness (start with the smaller amount and add more to taste if you like a slightly sweeter tea). Use whole dried hibiscus flowers, not ones that have been cut and sifted. If you can find only ones that have been cut and sifted, use the weight listed (1½ ounces), not the volume. This recipe can easily be doubled.

48	ounces water	1	(½-inch) piece ginger, peeled and sliced thin
1½	ounces whole dried hibiscus flowers (about 1½ cups)	1	cinnamon stick
6	(3-inch) strips orange zest plus 2 tablespoons juice	1	star anise pod
6	(2-inch) strips lemon zest plus 2 tablespoons juice	1	whole clove
		2–4	tablespoons cane syrup

1 Bring water, hibiscus flowers, orange zest and juice, lemon zest and juice, ginger, cinnamon stick, star anise, and clove to simmer in large saucepan over medium heat. Reduce heat to low and steep until mixture is fragrant and flavors meld, about 20 minutes.

2 Strain mixture through fine-mesh strainer into large bowl or container. Refrigerate until chilled, at least 1 hour or up to 10 days.

3 Transfer strained tea to serving pitcher and stir in cane syrup. Serve in ice-filled glasses.

Hibiscus Tea Cocktail

Makes 1 cocktail ~ Total Time: 5 minutes

We developed this recipe using dark rum, but you can use golden or light rum, bourbon, gin, tequila, or vodka.

6	ounces Hibiscus Iced Tea	Mint sprig
1½	ounces dark rum	Lemon slice

Fill collins glass with ice. Add tea and rum. Stir to combine. Garnish with mint sprig and lemon. Serve.

PETAL POWER

We prefer to make this tea with whole dried hibiscus flowers (which are technically the calyxes) because the strained tea is cleaner than when made with cut and sifted flowers. Here's what the whole dried flowers look like.

NAMES FOR HIBISCUS TEA

This beautiful beverage is known by different names in different parts of the world; in the United States, Celestial Seasonings makes a popular hibiscus tea called Red Zinger. Here are some of the drink's many names.

Agua de Jamaica
(Latin America, notably Mexico)

Bissap
(West Africa, notably Senegal)

Sobolo
(Ghana)

Sorrel
(the Caribbean, notably Jamaica)

Zobo
(Nigeria)

Cherry Bounce

Serves 12 to 14 (Makes about 4 cups) ~ Total Time: 10 minutes, plus 1 month steeping

"Where cherry bounce flows, mischief frequently follows." With this sentence, Kat Kinsman captures the cherry bounce effect in her article "Blame It on the Cherry Bounce" for *Food & Wine*. With its high alcohol content, the drink straddles the line between infused liqueur and cocktail. It's sweet and fruity yet strong and can be sipped as is or combined with other ingredients for a cocktail. Making it involves combining cherries, sugar, and booze and then letting time do the work.

Martha Washington was known to make large batches of cherry bounce as a way to preserve seasonal cherries while making a flavorful sipper. George Washington wrote in his notes that he packed a canteen of Martha's cherry bounce (alongside canteens of port and Madeira) for a trip west across

the Allegheny Mountains in 1784. Some recipes for cherry bounce call for whiskey. *Joy of Cooking* has a version calling for just "alcohol." But Washington was one of many to opt for brandy. She also added spices to hers, which gives it a nice warming quality and makes it a good fit for the holidays (if yours lasts that long past cherry season).

A quality brandy makes a difference here. We suggest seeking out one that is moderately aged, such as VSOP. We prefer the flavor and convenience of frozen sour cherries in this recipe. Feel free to use an equal weight of stemmed and pitted fresh sour cherries, if they are in season. If necessary, an equal amount of frozen mixed sweet and sour cherries can be substituted. Save the empty brandy bottle; you can use it to store the cherry bounce once it is ready.

1   (750-ml) bottle brandy
1¼   cups sugar
1   pound frozen sour cherries
2   whole allspice berries (optional)
1   whole clove (optional)

1   Whisk brandy and sugar in large bowl or container until sugar has nearly dissolved. Stir in cherries, then stir in allspice and clove, if using. Cover and store in cool, dark place for 1 month, stirring mixture weekly.

2   Set fine-mesh strainer in 8-cup liquid measuring cup or large bowl. Strain brandy mixture through strainer; discard spices and reserve cherries for another use. Transfer cherry bounce to jar and seal. (Cherry bounce can be stored in cool, dark place for up to 2 years; stir before enjoying.)

Brandied Cocktail Cherries

These cherries are an excellent garnish for your whiskey- or brandy-based cocktails or served with your favorite chocolate or ice cream desserts.

Transfer drained cherries from Cherry Bounce to 2-cup jar and cover with 1 recipe Simple Syrup (page 489); you may not need all of syrup. (Cocktail cherries can be refrigerated for up to 2 months.)

THE TRUE WASHINGTON CHERRY STORY

George Washington may not have actually chopped down that cherry tree, but Martha Washington was really known for her cherry bounce recipe. Martha recorded the recipe printed below in her journals. Please note: There aren't typos in this transcription; the spelling was accurate for the time.

"Extract the juice of 20 pounds well ripend morrella cherrys. Add to this 10 quarts of old french brandy and sweeten it with white sugar to your taste—To 5 Gallons of this mixture add one ounce of spice such as cinnamon, cloves and Nutmegs of each an Equal quantity slightly bruisd and a pint and half of cherry kirnels that have been gently broken in a mortar—After the liquor has fermented let it stand close-stoped for a month or six weeks then bottle it remembering to put a lump of Loaf Sugar into each bottle."

Portrait of Martha Washington.

Library of Congress

ALL ABOUT COCKTAILS

Spirit-swirled cocktails relate fascinating stories of the South—some stories that food doesn't reach. They honor the role of women in providing during Prohibition. They reveal inequality (women behind the stove were historically accepted, behind the bar they were not). They celebrate creativity. You don't need a full bar to retell those stories through recipes. Learn what you'll need to make cocktails at home and some helpful techniques.

Equipment

You'll use the following items for the cocktail recipes in this book, but you'll also find them infinitely useful for other cocktails you may make at home.

Shakers

You need only one kind of shaker. The choice is yours. We prefer the accuracy of the Boston shaker and use it to develop our recipes.

Boston Shaker

The choice of bartenders everywhere (and us), this consists of a bottom stainless-steel cup and a top cup. We like top cups that are made of tempered (safety) glass. The glass allows you to see your ingredients as you add them, which helps prevent error.

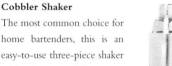

Cobbler Shaker

The most common choice for home bartenders, this is an easy-to-use three-piece shaker with a bottom mixing cup, a built-in strainer on top, and a cap to seal it. Metal and plastic components will be less likely than glass to break.

Mixing Glass

A straight-sided glass with a pouring spout is our choice for stirring cocktails over ice. Since glass is a better insulator than metal, a mixing glass made of its namesake material will chill your cocktail more thoroughly.

Bar Spoon

A long twizzle-handled stainless-steel bar spoon is essential to achieve maximum chilling with minimal dilution when stirring drinks with ice.

Strainers

The julep is one of the most iconic Southern cocktails. We have two recipes in this chapter, so we think the julep strainer is a worthwhile addition to your home bar in addition to the Hawthorne strainer (if you own a Boston shaker) and conical strainer to fit over a glass for a second strain.

Julep Strainer

This strainer predates the Hawthorne strainer and was developed for mint julep imbibers to hold over their cups to keep from getting a face full of crushed ice and mint. It fits well into a mixing glass, so we use it for stirred cocktails.

Hawthorne Strainer

This strainer is made of a flat circular piece of metal with holes, bordered by a flexible spring. It fits neatly into a Boston shaker to catch ice and other solids. Look for one with a tight spring, which will catch smaller pieces of ice and solids and will make for a better-strained cocktail.

Conical Strainer

We double-strain cocktails into the glass using a fine-mesh conical strainer. This provides further insurance against solid ingredients ending up in your glass and also prevents errant ice shards from diluting your cocktail.

Ice Cube Trays

We recommend 1-inch silicone or rubber ice cube trays to make ice for shaking cocktails and 2-inch trays to make ice for serving.

Muddler

A muddler is purpose-built for smashing fruit and herbs in a shaker. We prefer an unvarnished wood muddler at least 9½ inches long with a 1½-inch flat head and a comfortable, indented grip.

Jigger

A graduated jigger with ounce and tablespoon markings that you can read from above is best for measuring spirits.

Channel Knife

Use the channel knife part of a zester to make thin citrus twists, which impart a delicate citrus aroma to cocktails.

Mastering Muddled Cocktails

Originally known as toddy sticks, muddlers are one of the oldest purpose-built cocktail tools, dating back more than 200 years. They were originally used to crush chunks of sugar into water for toddies and other early cocktails such as juleps. Their purpose has evolved over the years, but the basic design of today's muddlers hasn't changed much—although you will now find them made from stainless steel or plastic as well as from wood.

Muddling quickly infuses fresh flavor elements from solid ingredients directly into a cocktail: Think of the cooling sensation of crushed mint or the fragrant intensity of citrus peel. This simple technique creates exciting opportunities for flavor pairings because of the range of ingredients that you can muddle. Fresh herbs, spices, fruits, and even vegetables are all fair game.

Muddling technique is not complicated. About 30 seconds is sufficient time to crush raw ingredients, releasing their juices or expressing their aromatic oils. (Longer muddling times can occasionally lead to "swampy" flavors, especially if muddling fresh herbs.) So whether it's a Mint Julep (page 486), our New-Fashioned (page 488), or a muddled creation of your own, break out your muddler and let the creative juices flow.

How to Muddle Fresh Herbs

1   Add herb leaves and simple syrup, if using, to base of cocktail shaker or mixing glass.

2   Hold cocktail shaker or glass with 1 hand. Gripping muddler with other hand, press firmly into herbs, rotating handle slightly as you progress, until herbs are broken down and fragrant, about 30 seconds.

How to Muddle Fresh Fruits

1   Cut fruit into small pieces, then add to base of cocktail shaker or mixing glass.

2   Hold cocktail shaker or glass with 1 hand. Gripping muddler with other hand, press firmly into fruit, rotating handle slightly as you progress, until fruit is broken down and all juice has been expressed, about 30 seconds.

Using a Boston Shaker

A cobbler shaker is very straightforward to use, which is part of the appeal at home. The Boston shaker, our preference, requires a little explanation. Here's how to properly shake things up.

1   Assemble ingredients in mixing glass, then fill with ice. Invert mixing glass and its contents into shaker tin and angle glass so that 1 side is flush with tin. Firmly tap base of glass with heel of hand to form tight seal.

2   Hold base of shaker tin firmly with 1 hand and base of mixing glass firmly with other hand. Using vigorous back-and-forth motion (ice should hit both ends of shaker), shake cocktail as specified in recipe.

3   To break seal, position shaker on counter with mixing glass on top and angled toward you. Grip side of shaker tin with 1 hand and, using heel of other hand, firmly tap rim of tin on opposite side. (You may have to do this more than once.) Remove mixing glass.

4   Fit Hawthorne strainer onto shaker tin and decant cocktail into chilled serving glass, using conical strainer if directed.

Mint Julep

Makes 1 cocktail ~ Total Time: 10 minutes

Alba Huerta was so inspired by the julep she named her Houston, Texas, bar after the cocktail. We learned in her book by the same name, *Julep: Southern Cocktails Refashioned,* that while the julep is famously known as a bourbon cocktail, the first recorded Southern julep was actually a mix of mint, sugar, cognac, peach brandy, and lots of ice. This was an exclusive drink at the time: Cognac and peach brandy were pricey. Ice was a luxury since it was expensive to procure and hard to store, especially outside of port cities (this was before ice cube trays, when ice was cut from lakes and shipped).

The aspirational qualities of the julep gave way to those signature frosted sterling silver cups and, Huerta speculates, the drink's popularity. Bourbon was more affordable and readily available throughout the South, so much so it was often used as trading currency. Following the lead of the wealthy, others mixed bourbon with their sugar, mint, and ice for juleps. And that's what you'll see most commonly today. Huerta's fascination with the cocktail inspired the seven julep cocktails in her book.

Here we offer two of our own versions: a classic julep and a rye-basil one. We muddle the herb leaves with simple syrup to release the aromatic oils, and stir in the liquor and ice before straining the cocktail into a serving vessel and topping it with a mound of crushed ice and a sprig of fresh herbs. Huerta says, "It's important that the drink be delicious from first sip to last. The trick is to make sure that the alcohol content [the strength of the drink] is sufficient to stand up to that dilution over time [from melting ice] but not so strong that it knocks the drinker over the head and makes it unwise to consider having a second." She opts for a bourbon that is mid-80s to 90-proof.

⅓ cup fresh mint leaves, plus mint sprig for garnishing

½ ounce Simple Syrup (page 489)

2 ounces bourbon

1 Add mint leaves and simple syrup to mixing glass and muddle until fragrant, about 30 seconds. Add bourbon, then fill glass three-quarters full with ice. Stir until mixture is just combined, about 15 seconds.

2 Double-strain cocktail into chilled old-fashioned glass or julep cup half-filled with crushed ice. Top with additional crushed ice to form mound above rim of glass. Garnish with mint sprig and serve.

Rye-Basil Julep

Substitute basil for mint and rye whiskey for bourbon. Garnish with basil sprig.

ALL HAIL THE QUEEN

Maggie Bailey distilled her first batch of moonshine at age 17 in Harlan County, Kentucky, to support her family in the early years of Prohibition (the ban on manufacture, sale, and transport of alcohol in the early half of the twentieth century). Making and selling moonshine became her life's work, as did supporting her community.

Bailey was arrested a total of 38 times for her endeavors but convicted and sentenced to jail just once. Otis Doan, Bailey's friend and lawyer, explained in an interview with NPR that this was in part because even members of the local judiciary were fans of Bailey. "People in the community just loved Maggie. Maggie was the type of person that bought food for families if they were having hard times. She helped send people to school, to college in her community." In a county that struggled with poverty for decades, Bailey lived modestly

Maggie Bailey, Queen of the Mountain Bootleggers.

Helen Halcomb

herself but bought coal to give out to neighbors to heat their homes.

Bailey stayed in business until she was 95, earning herself the nickname Queen of the Mountain Bootleggers. Even when Prohibition ended, Harlan County remained a dry county, meaning alcohol sales were illegal. So Bailey, often dressed in a print dress topped with an apron, continued to sell her moonshine and other alcohol out of her house. Doan says that she knew everyone and would ask customers about how their parents were doing: "She reminded you of your grandmother" (albeit one who was a self-taught expert in the Fourth Amendment's protection against unreasonable search and seizure). Bailey never drank herself, and when sad things were happening in the world she was known to say, "I'm glad I'm just a good old-fashioned bootlegger." She died in 2005 at the age of 101.

by Morgan Bolling

Old-Fashioned

Makes 1 cocktail   ~   Total Time: 10 minutes

In the 1960s and 1970s (and even today, to some extent) bourbon was largely (and woefully) considered an old man's drink. Joy Perrine, the self-dubbed Bad Girl of Bourbon, has challenged that. Perrine started bartending in her early 20s in Saint Croix, where she made mostly rum cocktails. Both of her parents were rumrunners (see page 495) during Prohibition, so rum ran through her veins. She eventually left the island in 1978 to move to Kentucky, a state that just six years earlier had removed its ban on female bartenders.

Perrine quickly fell in love with bourbon. In an interview with Liquor.com, she says, "I knew there were similarities between rum and bourbon, because the rum industry buys the used bourbon barrels [to age the rum] since the bourbon industry can only use the barrels one time. So I just started playing with bourbon the way I had with rum."

Perrine started adding homemade syrups and infusions to bourbon, a maneuver that was frowned upon by the mostly male bartending community. She encountered their contempt in an interview she did with *Esquire* early on in her Kentucky bartending days. "They [*Esquire*] said, 'You're ruining the product. You should only drink this product neat, blah, blah, blah.' I told them, 'Hey, there are some people who just don't like the taste of whiskey straight. So if I make a cocktail and convert them to being a bourbon drinker, then who cares?'"

Clientele (of all genders) fell in love with Perrine's bourbon cocktails. On the rare occasion someone didn't like one of her drinks, she flashed a black widow spider tattooed across her hand, which sent the message: "No one fucks with me." Perrine went on to write *The Kentucky Bourbon Cocktail Book* and *More Kentucky Bourbon Cocktails* (both co-authored with Susan Reigler). She was also the first female bartender inducted into the Kentucky Bourbon Hall of Fame in 2016. Here we have two drinks dedicated to Perrine: a traditional old-fashioned, and one inspired by her New-Fashioned in *The Kentucky Bourbon Cocktail Book*.

Many recipes call for muddling sugar cubes and fruit in the bottom of a rocks glass, but sugar cube size varies, so using simple syrup instead ensures consistency of flavor. The citrus bitters add a subtle citrus element and complexity when combined with the woodsy notes of old-fashioned aromatic bitters. If you wish, you can use only old-fashioned aromatic bitters in this cocktail, a total of ¼ teaspoon.

2   ounces bourbon
1   teaspoon Simple Syrup (recipe follows)
⅛   teaspoon old-fashioned aromatic bitters
⅛   teaspoon citrus bitters
     Orange twist
     Cocktail cherry

Add bourbon, simple syrup, old-fashioned aromatic bitters, and citrus bitters to mixing glass, then fill three-quarters full with ice. Stir until mixture is just combined and chilled, about 15 seconds. Strain cocktail into chilled old-fashioned glass half-filled with ice or containing 1 large ice cube. Garnish with orange twist and cocktail cherry and serve.

New-Fashioned

Makes 1 cocktail   ~   Total Time: 15 minutes

You may use fresh or cocktail cherries here.

¼   lemon, cut into 4 pieces, plus lemon slice
     for garnishing
2   sweet cherries, pitted
2   ounces bourbon
1   ounce limoncello
⅛   teaspoon old-fashioned aromatic bitters
⅛   teaspoon citrus bitters
1   ounce sparkling wine, chilled

Add lemon pieces and cherries to base of cocktail shaker and muddle until broken down and all juice has been expressed, about 30 seconds. Add bourbon, limoncello, old-fashioned aromatic bitters, and citrus bitters, then fill shaker with ice. Shake mixture until just combined and chilled, about 5 seconds. Strain contents of shaker into collins glass. Add sparkling wine and, using bar spoon, gently lift bourbon mixture from bottom of glass to top to combine. Top with additional ice and garnish with lemon slice. Serve.

MAKING A CITRUS TWIST

Simple Syrup

Makes about 8 ounces
Total Time: 15 minutes

¾ cup sugar
5 ounces warm tap water

Whisk sugar and warm water in bowl until sugar has dissolved. Let cool completely, about 10 minutes, before transferring to airtight container. (Syrup can be refrigerated for up to 1 month; shake well before using.)

A citrus twist is an elegant garnish.

1   Use channel knife to remove 3- to 4-inch strand, working around circumference of citrus in spiral pattern to ensure continuous piece. (If you don't have a channel knife, remove 3- to 4-inch strip zest with vegetable peeler, then slice zest lengthwise into slender strips.)

2   To garnish with citrus twist, curl strand tightly to establish uniform twist, then place in cocktail or on edge of glass.

Planter's Punch

Serves 8 ~ Total Time: 10 minutes, plus 2 hours chilling

It can be hard to nail down a definitive origin story for planter's punch. Some legends say the Planters Hotel in Charleston, South Carolina, a 19-century retreat for wealthy rice planters, served the first citrus-rum libation. Other stories claim the sweet tropical drink was first served by a Caribbean planter's wife to cool her enslaved laborers. Today, most cocktail historians agree planter's punch was probably invented in Jamaica, an island nation that was once a member of the British West Indies, by mixing dark rum, citrus and/or pineapple juice, and a splash of grenadine.

In 1973, British food writer Elisabeth Lambert Ortiz published *The Complete Book of Caribbean Cooking*, a book that reviewers described as a classic, one that shined a light on the diversity of the region's fare—from its distinctive ingredients, cooking methods, and utensils to its various global influences. The book includes four versions of planter's punch: two Jamaican options featuring dark rum and lime juice, or a combination of lime and orange juices; a Puerto Rican–style drink that calls for both light and dark rums; and one that represents all islands with light rum, lime juice, and orange juice.

Planter's punch evolved to be a deeply loved cocktail sipped on in warm locations throughout the South. It's been on the International Bartenders Association's Official Cocktail List (the 50 most-requested cocktails from the IBA) since the list was created in 1951. And planter's punch is indeed delicious. For our version, we took inspiration from the recipe published by *Cook's Country* editor in chief Toni Tipton-Martin in her 2023 recipe book *Juke Joints, Jazz Clubs, and Juice*. The recipe captures the essence of all three of Ortiz's drinks as well as a formula Tipton-Martin found in a 1990 Jamaican cookbook by Helen Willinsky. We use a mix of aged rum (like Myers's) and white rums. The combination strikes a good balance of caramel flavor and booziness. Pineapple, orange, and lime juices give this tropical punch balanced fruitiness. Rather than use grenadine, we opt for bitters combined with homemade simple syrup for controlled sweetness.

12 ounces pineapple juice	**1** Combine all ingredients in serving pitcher or large container. Cover and refrigerate until well chilled, at least 2 hours or up to 3 days.
8 ounces aged rum	
8 ounces white rum	
8 ounces orange juice (2 oranges), plus orange slices for garnishing	
4 ounces lime juice (4 limes)	**2** Stir punch to recombine. Serve in chilled old-fashioned glasses half-filled with ice, garnishing individual portions with orange slice.
2 ounces Simple Syrup (page 489)	
1 teaspoon old-fashioned aromatic bitters	

RAISING A GLASS TO PUNCH

Punch may conjure images of an overly sweet large-batch drink. In the article "The Great Punch Comeback" for *Our State* magazine, Kathleen Purvis refers to that type of punch as "'church punch'—fruity and frothy, with an iceberg of sherbet floating in it." Similarly, Sara Camp Milam (see page 474) calls these grand bowls of nonalcoholic beverages "Church Lady Punch" in *The Southern Foodways Alliance Guide to Cocktails*—"festive without being scandalous."

But the history of punch in the United States is soaked with alcohol. Punch became popular in the American colonies, where rum was a ubiquitous spirit. Caribbean rum was made as an indirect by-product of sugar production. This rum was different from the rum we know today. Milam writes, "That early rum was famously foul; watering it down and adding citrus, sugar, and spices helped to numb the burn." In the later 1700s, punch was the drink of choice for militias since it could be made in large batches and with different alcohol contents. It remained the convivial tavern choice until drinking and gathering habits changed in the 1800s.

But while punch fell out of vogue in the rest of the United States, it remained popular in the South. Milam explains how punch transitioned from "communal to clubby," becoming a part of debutante balls and New Orleans carnival krewes (a type of social club).

Prohibition changed the nature—and formula—of punch once again, leading to sweeter versions that masked the taste of low-quality alcohol. And it highlighted gender divides in punch habits and the growing popularity of the boozeless versions. "In 18th-century England, and in Colonial America," Milam says, "the drinkers gathered around the punch bowl would have been overwhelmingly male. By the mid-20th century, punch—especially the non-alcoholic kind—was a ladies' drink. Whereas rum punch was served in taverns, nonalcoholic punch was, and is, a drink for luncheons, showers, church socials, and funerals." These sweet, nonalcoholic punches that "fueled female spaces" often relied on Jell-O or a fruit juice concentrate, and they were a staple in community church cookbooks.

Although the idea of punch has come to evoke thoughts of a ladies' luncheon rather than a night at a sophisticated bar, spirit-spiked punches are having a revival with modern mixologists. At a place as high-end as the Ritz-Carlton in Charlotte, North Carolina, guests can imbibe a daily punch at the hotel's bar, the Punch Room.

by Morgan Bolling

Plum Shrub Syrup

Makes about 2 cups ~ Total Time: 15 minutes, plus 24 hours macerating

At its most basic, a shrub is a sweet-tart combination of fruit juice, sugar, and vinegar. Predating the invention of refrigeration, shrubs were popular in the South as a way to extend the life of freshly picked fruit. Today, shrubs are purely about enjoyment rather than necessity. In fact, they've seen a resurgence in popularity in recent years, thanks in part to the bartending trend of returning to classic methods and to health communities touting the benefits of certain vinegars. You can find shrubs in both cocktails and nonalcoholic drinks.

Making fruit shrub syrup at home is really simple and is all about the fruit: Macerate it, strain the juice (save the solids to top desserts!), and then stir in the vinegar to give it tangy complexity. Bursting with sweet, tart, fresh fruit flavor, this shrub syrup is phenomenal stirred into seltzer (we like to use a ratio of 1 part shrub to 3 parts seltzer) for a shrub soda or used as a fruity base for cocktails such as a refined Plum Reviver. The shrub syrup is best made with fresh, juicy, well-ripened plums of any variety. You can substitute white wine vinegar or cider vinegar for the red wine vinegar.

2¼	pounds plums, pitted and chopped coarse
1½	cups sugar
3	tablespoons red wine vinegar

1 Combine plums and sugar in large bowl; stir and mash gently with rubber spatula or wooden spoon until plums are well coated with sugar. Cover and refrigerate for 24 hours, stirring every 6 to 8 hours to dissolve sugar.

2 Transfer plum mixture to fine-mesh strainer set over 8-cup measuring cup or large bowl, scraping any remaining fruit-and-sugar mixture from bowl with rubber spatula. Stir and press gently on solids to extract as much syrup as possible, taking care not to press fruit pulp through strainer; reserve fruit solids for another use. Stir in vinegar. (Shrub syrup can be refrigerated for up to 1 month; shake before using.)

Peach Shrub Syrup
Substitute equal weight of peaches for plums.

WOMEN IN DISTILLING

Traveling around the Southern states to research my book *Distilling the South: A Guide to Southern Craft Liquors and the People Who Make Them*, I racked up visits to more than 50 distilleries. Most were run by men, but I did meet a few expert women: Kristi Croxton, co-owner of James River Distillery in Richmond, Virginia; Becky Harris, the head distiller at Catoctin Creek in Purcelleville, Virginia; Melissa Katrincic, maker of Conniption Gin at Durham Distillery in North Carolina; and Troy Ball at Troy & Sons in Asheville, North Carolina. But still, just a few.

The distilling industry loves to crow about the increase in women in distilling. In 2022, according to Distillingwomen.com, 160 U.S. distilleries were led by women; that is only 8 percent of the 2,063 active distilleries. That's a disappointing number when you consider that American distilling started out as women's work. In colonial America, particularly in the agricultural South, making what people grew into what people drank happened in kitchens. And kitchen work was women's work, often enslaved women's work.

European settlers came from a place where drinking water was dangerous, and fresh water in the colonies wasn't much better. Journals and diaries about visiting the South in the 18th century often recounted the local habit of drinking spirits from breakfast until long after dinner.

Mary Randolph, cousin to Thomas Jefferson and the author of *The Virginia House-Wife*, written in 1824, included a section on "Cordials," from ginger wine to ginger beer. First Lady Martha Washington's *Booke of Cookery* included concoctions like metheglin, a version of mead made with molasses instead of honey.

Those early farm fermentations weren't particularly stable, so by the 18th century, stills were becoming important—and expensive—kitchen equipment. Making apples and peaches into brandy made something stronger that would keep much longer.

Since then, the craft distilling world has become more diverse. Fawn Weaver, the CEO of Uncle Nearest in Tennessee, and her master distiller, Victoria Eady Butler, have won accolades for their whiskeys and bourbons that honor Nathan "Nearest" Green, who was hired by a young Jack Daniel after the Civil War to be his distiller. Green wasn't given credit in the story of the Jack Daniel Distillery until Weaver and Butler, a descendant of Green's, started their distillery in 2017. Today, it's one of the fastest-growing brands in the country. And in Charleston, South Carolina, Ann Marshall and Scott Blackwell, founders of High Wire Distilling Co., create spirits from heritage grains as part of their mission to "enhance flavor, celebrate farmers, preserve rural lands, and make drinking an agricultural act."

You can take women out of the kitchen, but you can't take us out of your whiskey.

by Kathleen Purvis

food journalist and author of Distilling the South: A Guide to Southern Craft Liquors and the People Who Make Them

Plum Reviver

Makes 1 cocktail ~ Total Time: 10 minutes

Figuratively meaning to wake the dead, the corpse reviver no. 2 belongs to a family of pre-Prohibition cocktails that were thought to be hangover cures. Typically it's made with equal parts gin and Lillet Blanc, orange liqueur, fresh lemon juice, and a touch of absinthe. For a fruitier take, we use our Plum Shrub Syrup in place of the orange liqueur and lemon juice. The traditional Lillet Blanc elevates the fruity, tangy notes of the shrub syrup, while the herbal botanicals of London dry gin round out the libation. An absinthe-rinsed glass leaves just a hint of anise on the palate for a pleasantly distinct finish. You can substitute Herbsaint or another dry, anise-forward liqueur, such as Ricard or dry anisette, for the absinthe.

¼	ounce absinthe
1½	ounces Plum Shrub Syrup
1	ounce London dry gin
1	ounce Lillet Blanc
	Plum wedge

1 Pour absinthe into chilled cocktail glass, then tilt and rotate glass to coat with absinthe; pour off excess liquid and set glass aside.

2 Add shrub syrup, gin, and Lillet Blanc to cocktail shaker, then fill shaker with ice. Shake mixture until fully combined and well chilled, about 15 seconds. Strain cocktail into chilled cocktail glass. Garnish with plum wedge and serve.

Rum Runner

Makes 1 cocktail ~ Total Time: 10 minutes

In honor of the female rumrunners (see "The Ladies of Rum Row"), we created our own version of this boozy cocktail made with rum (we like aged), fruit juices, and fruit liqueurs. Be sure to use fresh lime juice and fresh orange juice here for the lightest taste and balanced flavor. This cocktail traditionally relies on blackberry liqueur and we love it here, but it can be hard to find at liquor stores. If you prefer, you can substitute black raspberry liqueur or Chambord, but the drink will be a little sweeter with a less vibrant hue.

2	ounces aged rum
1½	ounces lime juice (2 limes)
1	ounce orange juice, plus orange slice for garnishing
1	ounce pineapple juice, plus pineapple slice for garnishing
1	ounce banana liqueur
½	ounce blackberry liqueur or black raspberry liqueur
⅓	ounce grenadine
	Cocktail cherry
	Blackberries

Add rum, lime juice, orange juice, pineapple juice, banana liqueur, blackberry liqueur, and grenadine to cocktail shaker, then fill with ice. Shake mixture until just combined and chilled, about 5 seconds. Strain cocktail into chilled hurricane glass or old-fashioned glass half-filled with crushed ice. Top with additional ice and garnish with orange slice, pineapple slice, cocktail cherry, and blackberries. Serve.

THE LADIES OF RUM ROW

Cocktail culture in Florida is a visible gesture toward colonial and diasporic histories of the Caribbean region. Often built on rum and flavored with tropical fruit and bright citrus, these popular mixed drinks form a cultural bridge across the Florida Straits to places like Cuba, cradle of the modern mojito; Puerto Rico, where the piña colada reigns as the national drink; and Saint Thomas in the U.S. Virgin Islands, home to an early version of the bushwacker (see page 496), a sweet spin on the white Russian.

According to local folklore, the rum runner was first served at a bar in the Florida Keys that needed to clear shelf space for a new liquor order. Made of both light and dark rums, pineapple and orange juices, banana and blackberry liqueurs, and grenadine, the potent punch was given a name that alludes to the history of liquor smuggling that brought rum from Caribbean sugar plantations to South Florida speakeasies during Prohibition.

Despite the historically male-dominated nature of the liquor industry, many women were able to carve out entrepreneurial space for themselves smuggling contraband spirits, including everything from Caribbean rum and Canadian whiskey to French champagne and English gin, into and around the United States during the 1920s. Gertrude "Cleo" Lythgoe, also known as the Queen of Rum Row or the Bahama Queen, was the first woman to hold a liquor license before setting up a highly profitable wholesale liquor business in Nassau. Gloria de Casares, married to a wealthy Argentinian merchant, founded the Gloria Steamship Company. When one of her ships was apprehended in London, it was found to be carrying 10,000 cases of whiskey.

Gertrude "Cleo" Lythgoe, the Queen of Rum Row, sipping on rum, of course.

Vintage_Space / Alamy Stock Photo

And then there was Spanish Marie, who was estimated at one point to be worth $1 million. Born to a Mexican mother and Swedish father, Marie Waite took over a successful rum-running enterprise from her husband, Charlie Waite ("king of the rumrunners"), after he was killed in a skirmish with the Coast Guard. She commanded a flotilla of speedboats that at one point numbered as many as 15, communicating with them through secret codes in Spanish that she transmitted over radios she had installed on the vessels as they traveled between Havana and Key West. Her reign, while prosperous, was not long. She was arrested in Coconut Grove, near Miami, in 1928, and again in Pensacola in 1931, and again in 1938 for driving under the influence. Today, a Key West distillery makes a rum in her honor, and a brewery is named for her in Miami.

by Carlynn Crosby

writer, scholar of historic foodways in Florida, and editor at the University Press of Florida

Bushwacker

Makes 4 cocktails   ~   Total Time: 10 minutes

This milkshake-like cocktail, originally made with dark crème de cacao, rum, chocolate ice cream, and coconut milk, was invented in 1975 by Angie Conigliaro, a bartender from Saint Thomas in the U.S. Virgin Islands. But the bushwacker gained popularity as the signature drink of Pensacola, Florida, thanks to Linda Taylor Murphy. After visiting Saint Thomas, Linda brought the cocktail to her Pensacola bar, the Sandshaker Lounge. She gave it her own twist (less chocolaty), and in only five years' time, the bar was selling so many, they had to switch from individually making them in a blender to using a frozen drink machine to keep up with demand.

For our version we use a can of coconut milk to let the coconut flavor shine through, and we achieve the chocolate flavor with finely chopped bittersweet bar chocolate. In lieu of the traditional drizzle of chocolate syrup, we save some of the chopped chocolate to sprinkle on top of the finished whipped cream–topped drink. Do not substitute light coconut milk here.

1	(14-ounce) can coconut milk
6	ounces aged rum
4	ounces coffee liqueur
4	ounces crème de cacao
½	cup bittersweet chocolate, finely chopped, plus extra for garnishing
20	ounces (5 cups) ice cubes
	Whipped cream
	Toasted coconut
	Cocktail cherries

Add coconut milk, rum, coffee liqueur, crème de cacao, chocolate, and ice to blender (in that order) and process until smooth, about 45 seconds, scraping down sides of blender jar as needed. Pour into chilled hurricane or old-fashioned glasses. Garnish with whipped cream, toasted coconut, extra chocolate, and/or cherries. Serve.

MILK PUNCH TWO WAYS

Two very different cocktails share the name "milk punch." The version that is more commonly associated with the South is creamy and rich. Often called brandy milk punch or bourbon milk punch, it's made with milk, nutmeg, brandy, bourbon, and/or rum—it's almost like an eggless eggnog. While it's served throughout the South, it's especially popular in New Orleans. It's often a day drink, equally as fitting on a holiday morning, at a birthday lunch, or at a tailgate.

Then there is clarified milk punch (also sometimes called English milk punch after its place of origin). It's clear as water but, seemingly magically, silky-textured, with mellow, harmonious flavors. This is achieved through a process that takes some time: Citrus juice or another acidic ingredient is combined with rum, brandy, dark beer such as porter or stout, and sugar. Milk is added; the milk curdles in the presence of the acidic ingredients, and the punch is strained to remove the curds. The process clarifies the drink, brings all the flavor elements into balance, and preserves the drink from spoilage. While this version originated in England, bartenders all over the South (as well as other regions of the United States) embrace it and play with this concept.

Alex Anderson, who has shaken drinks in her hometown of Atlanta, as well as in Miami and New Orleans, is one such bartender who makes clarified milk punch with a unique twist. Her Nordic Honey Punch, a seasonal drink she serves at Cure, a bar she tends in New Orleans, has Scandinavian flavors: She heats vermouth, Gran Classico, honey, and milk in a saucepan. She then stirs in lemon juice, followed by aquavit, and strains the drink before serving it over ice with dill—a unique spin on a Southern favorite.

We've provided recipes for both versions of milk punch. The drinks give you a taste of the old and new South, respectively.

by Morgan Bolling

Southern Milk Punch

Makes 1 cocktail
Total Time: 5 minutes

Using light cream in this creamy brandy cocktail gives the drink a full body without masking the flavor of the booze. It's perfect for any occasion, night or day. If you can't find light cream, you can substitute 1 ounce milk and 1 ounce heavy cream. A quality brandy makes a difference here. We suggest seeking out one that is moderately aged, such as VSOP. This recipe can be doubled.

2   ounces light cream
1¼   ounces brandy
½   ounce Simple Syrup (page 489)
½   teaspoon vanilla extract
   Ground nutmeg

1   Add light cream, brandy, simple syrup, and vanilla to cocktail shaker and vigorously shake until mixture is foamy, 30 to 45 seconds.

2   Fill shaker with ice, then shake mixture until fully combined and well chilled, about 10 seconds. Strain cocktail into chilled old-fashioned glass. Sprinkle with nutmeg and serve.

Clarified Milk Punch

Makes 12 cocktails
Total Time: 10 minutes, plus 7 hours draining and chilling

Our recipe for clarified milk punch models the classic English version. The draining process in step 2 takes about 4 hours to complete but is necessary in order to get the clearest punch possible. For an accurate measurement of boiling water, bring a full kettle of water to a boil and then measure out the desired amount.

15   (3-inch) strips lemon zest plus 6 ounces juice (4 lemons)
8   ounces Lemon Syrup (recipe follows)
22   ounces aged rum
16   ounces boiling water
10   ounces brandy
6   ounces porter or stout beer
16   ounces whole milk

1   Add lemon zest and lemon syrup to large bowl and muddle until fragrant, about 30 seconds. Stir in rum, boiling water, brandy, beer, and lemon juice, then gently stir in milk until curds form. Cover and refrigerate until flavors meld, at least 2 hours or up to 24 hours.

2   Line fine-mesh strainer with double layer of coffee filters and set over serving pitcher or large container. Working in batches, gently pour rum-milk mixture into prepared strainer and let drain completely, about 4 hours; discard solids. Cover punch and refrigerate until well chilled, about 1 hour. Serve in chilled cocktail or cordial glasses. (Milk punch may be refrigerated for up to 1 month.)

Lemon Syrup

Makes 8 ounces ~ Total Time: 10 minutes, plus 30 minutes cooling

¾   cup sugar
5   ounces water
2   teaspoons grated lemon zest

Heat sugar, water, and lemon zest in small saucepan over medium heat, whisking often, until sugar has dissolved, about 5 minutes; do not boil. Let cool completely, about 30 minutes. Strain syrup through fine-mesh strainer into airtight container; discard solids. (Syrup can be refrigerated for up to 1 month; shake well before using.)

Ponche Navideño

Serves 12 ~ Total Time: 1½ hours

Mexican ponche navideño (which means "Christmas punch") is a winter drink infused with fruit and warm spices. The Spaniards brought ponche to their colonies, including Mexico, centuries ago.

While recipes vary from person to person, the preparation typically involves simmering such ingredients as sweet and sour tejocotes (a fruit that resembles crab apples), tamarind pods, piloncillo (raw cane sugar), guava, and cinnamon sticks in water until the spices release their flavors and the fruits become tender. Often, spirits like rum, brandy, or tequila is added to the brew or held to the side until the kids are served.

As with many delicious Mexican foods and drinks, ponche is popular across the border in Texas and in other places with large Latin American populations. Until 2015, however, tejocotes were banned from being imported to the United States. In a 2013 article for SFGate, Maria Gaura writes, "Despite being a must-have holiday ingredient for millions of American households, these knobby little delicacies have a tenuous legal status in the United States. Tejocotes have long been banned from import, and the trees are rare on this side of the border. So forbidden fruits flood into the country during the holiday season, making them one of the most-smuggled items on the U.S.–Mexican border."

Happily, tejocotes now appear in the United States, especially in the fall and winter in many Latin markets; "limited legal imports" are allowed by the USDA. It is common for their skin to be covered in black dots or patches, and this should not be considered a sign of deterioration. If you can't find or order them, Mexican chef Pati Jinich offers crab apples as a substitute in her recipe, and that works here as well. This recipe calls for piloncillo, also known as panela or panocha. Other varieties of granulated cane sugar can be substituted. The delicate flavor of Ceylon cinnamon is preferred here; if substituting cassia cinnamon, reduce the amount to two 3-inch sticks. While Mexican Cream guava is traditionally added to ponche, other varieties can be used.

Q&A: PATI JINICH ON MEXICO AS THE DEEP SOUTH OF THE SOUTH

Pati Jinich is a TV personality, cookbook author, and educator. Her TV show *Pati's Mexican Table* has won James Beard Awards and has been nominated for multiple Emmys. In 2021, she launched a docuseries, *La Frontera with Pati Jinich*, in which she shares the experiences of the people and their food culture along the United States–Mexican border. We sat down with Jinich to learn how she bridges the border.

Can you tell us some of your story and how you decided to create *Pati's Mexican Table*?
I'm from Mexico City, born and raised; all my family is there. I'm a former political analyst focused on the history of Mexico and its evolution. I ended up moving to the United States and wanted to continue that academic path focusing on where Mexicanness, Mexican people, and Mexican food are going north and south of the border, and building bridges between Mexicans in Mexico and the United States.

And as I shifted focus to food I mostly wanted to have a Mexican talk about Mexican food in the United States. I hadn't seen that before. I felt like America's palate was hungry and open by the time I switched careers.

And even though we have this long border between us, I feel like there are a lot of misconceptions between Mexicans and Americans. I wanted to show how we can enrich the lives of Americans or anyone in the world. And we have so much to give and share. There's a lot of power in meals and sitting together, in that you can share who you are with food in front of you. I started *Pati's Mexican Table*. The mission hasn't changed: I want people to share their stories and their food without interpreting and without interventions.

I understand it wasn't totally easy. In an interview with Les Dames you said that creating this show was an act of defiance. Can you talk more about that?
Yeah, it definitely wasn't easy. My accent was a huge problem, people told me it was too strong and viewers wouldn't understand me. It was excruciatingly difficult to get the

12	cups water
½	ounce whole dried hibiscus flowers (about ½ cup)
2	(6-inch) stalks sugarcane
12	ounces tejocotes, ends trimmed
8	ounces piloncillo
2	(6-inch) tamarind pods, shelled and deveined
1	cup prunes
2	(4-inch) Ceylon cinnamon sticks
1	pound guava, cut into ½-inch-thick wedges
1	large Gala or Fuji apple, peeled, cored, and cut into ¾-inch pieces
12	ounces blanco tequila, white rum, or vodka

1 Bring water to boil in Dutch oven over high heat. Reduce heat to low, add hibiscus, and let steep for 10 minutes. Using slotted spoon, discard hibiscus.

2 Using sharp knife, remove outer peel from sugarcane stalks. Halve each stalk lengthwise, then cut each half lengthwise into 3 strips. Add sugarcane, tejocotes, piloncillo, tamarind, prunes, and cinnamon to pot and bring to boil. Reduce heat to medium-low, cover, and simmer, stirring occasionally, until flavors meld and piloncillo has fully dissolved, about 20 minutes.

3 Stir in guava and apple and simmer, covered, until softened, about 10 minutes. Off heat, stir in tequila. (Ponche can be refrigerated for up to 3 days; bring to brief simmer before serving.) Serve in warmed mugs, garnishing individual portions with tejocotes, sugarcane, guava, and apple.

funding. People gave all these labels and judgments—they didn't want Mexican food. People said it was too ethnic or niche. But I just pushed through.

Can you offer advice for anyone who is starting out who wants to work in a creative field?
Once you decide to go in and do something, or start something new, don't beat yourself up every few months. Wait 10 years, then look back and judge. I was ready to throw in the towel the first year, and the second, and again the fourth. My first cookbook I pitched to 39 publishers before one said yes. And the show—I have no idea, but it was a lot of networks. And social media doesn't help.

It seems like everyone is already so accomplished. People aren't sharing their struggles.

When you're in a creative field like this, often you're an entrepreneur—it's a lot of entrepreneurial work to create a show and a book. My husband has always told me I have the toughest, most horrible boss, which is me. I don't cut myself slack. I feel like in the past couple years I've learned to cut myself slack. Chill a little and be kind to yourself.

And can you talk about what it means to be Southern? I know you've lived in the United States for 25 years; do you identify as "Southern"?
I do identify as Southern because Mexico is

the deep South. Mexico is the South of the South. I'm very happy you guys included me [in this book]. And Mexican food hasn't *made* its way to the South; it has *been* an intrinsic part of the South. A lot of the South was Mexico before it was "Southern."

I feel most at home in the U.S.–Mexico borderlands. I think that's the place where I can be unapologetically multidimensional: Mexican, and American, and an immigrant, and the granddaughter of refugees from Poland and Austria. In the borderland you get that space that defines so much of food and cooking—you get a little bit of everything. I think everyone is a mosaic of sorts.

SOUTHERN WOMEN IN THE BREWHOUSE

In Southerners' glasses, throughout history, there has been sweet tea, lemonade, Coca-Cola, and whiskey distilled from Kentucky corn or Maryland rye. Brandies, wines, cordials, and shrubs were flavored with the fruits, herbs, and flowers that perfumed Southern orchards and gardens.

Also in Southerners' glasses: beer. And where there was beer, there were the women who brewed it. Brewing beer in the South has always been an unlikely craft, for reasons environmental, political, economic, and cultural alike. Still, Southern women of every era have brewed. They have done so with ingenuity, skill, and even bravery.

In the early years of American history, the South's warm climate made it easier to distill spirits than brew beer, especially before the popularization of mechanical refrigeration in the late 19th century. Compared to the Northeast and upper Midwest, the 19th-century South counted fewer large cities, fewer European immigrants, less developed transportation networks, and lesser access to certain raw ingredients—especially barley, the traditional grain for brewing beer. Together, these factors meant less brewing expertise and a more challenging journey for ingredients to get to brewers and beer to get to consumers.

Nevertheless, women in the early South brewed beer as a regular kitchen chore, akin to baking bread. All members of a household, even children, drank low-alcohol "small" beer. Many of the South's first brewers were enslaved women. Their enslavement, coupled with the mundane nature of their work, meant that these brewers and the beers they created were unlikely to be recorded as the stuff of history. Creative researchers can uncover parts of their stories, though.

In early 1800s North Carolina, for example, a young woman named Patsy Young escaped from her enslaver—twice, at least—and supported herself and her young daughter, Eliza, by brewing beer and baking cakes. The path taken by Young as a fugitive and her skill as a brewer surface in unexpected sources, such as the "runaway ads" that sought her recapture, census returns, local newspaper reporting, and agricultural histories of the region. Similarly, one of the first American cookbooks, *The Virginia House-Wife*, included recipes for ginger, spruce, and molasses beers, which used brown sugar and molasses in place of malted barley. Young and other women brewers of their time brewed small batches of English- and Dutch-style ales, whose flavors, as well as the tepid temperatures at which they were served, would be unfamiliar to many contemporary beer lovers.

Once the country industrialized in the late 1800s and early 1900s, brewing moved out of the home and into large breweries, transitioning from a domestic task to a professional industry made up almost entirely of men (many of them were immigrants who had brought lager-brewing expertise from Europe). At the same time, early temperance movements turned several Southern states dry several years before the arrival of national Prohibition in 1920. Even after Prohibition's repeal in 1933, many Southern locales took restrictive stances on alcohol production and sales. Mississippi and Alabama did not legalize homebrewing until 2013, becoming the last American states to do so.

But by the early 21st century, women—together with Americans of color—formed a small but mighty minority of brewers and brewery owners in the South, as across the nation. In 2013, Kristie Nystedt opened Raleigh Brewing Company in Raleigh, North Carolina, as well as stores selling commercial brewing and home-brewing equipment. Leah Wong Ashburn became the CEO of Highland Brewing Company in Asheville, North Carolina, in 2015. When Highland Brewing opened in 1994 (founded by Ashburn's father, Oscar Wong), it initiated a boom in small craft breweries in the region. These include Cherokee-owned 7 Clans Brewing, headed by Morgan Owle-Crisp. In 2022, 7 Clans released We're Still Here, a harvest saison brewed with locally grown honeynut squash, stone-ground cornmeal, and organic sassafras. Computer scientist Briana Brake is the founder and brewmaster of Spaceway Brewing Co., North Carolina's first Black woman–owned brewery; she gives Afrofuturism-inspired names and can label designs to the cardamom stout, double IPA, and cream ale she brews. Whereas Brake imagines the future, Eamoni Collier looks to ancient history—specifically, Egyptian women brewers—when she brews a blonde ale with chamomile and honey and a pale ale with rose hip and rose petals at Urban Garden Brewing in Washington, D.C.

Today, a flourishing women's beer culture in the South is powered by homebrew clubs and supply shops; organizations such as the Pink Boots Society, which awards educational scholarships to women brewers; local and state governments that encourage small entrepreneurs; and passionate consumers. These networks empower Southern women to brew on. They will continue to quench the region's thirst, as they have for generations, and fill Southern glasses with new flavors, styles, and inspirations.

by Theresa McCulla, PhD

curator and historian of American history and identity through food and drink, and author of Insatiable City: Food and Race in New Orleans

Briana Brake, founder of Spaceway Brewing Co. (left); Morgan Owle-Crisp, head of 7 Clans Brewing (top right); and Eamoni Collier, founder of Urban Garden Brewing (bottom right).

Lissa Gotwals (left), Jeremy Wilson Photography (top right), and Priscilla Lima Ledesma (bottom right)

SAINT JULIE

Butter, cayenne, a li'l bit of attitude: Those are the three core ingredients to Julie Mabry's legendary crawfish boil that packs just as much punch as the woman behind this Sunday tradition at her cherished Houston-based lesbian bar, Pearl Bar.

I met Julie in 2020 while filming The Lesbian Bar Project, a documentary endeavor I co-created that aims to bring greater awareness to lesbian queer bars around the world. These were the early days of the COVID-19 pandemic, when everything felt on the brink of collapse, a feeling even more acute within the hospitality industry.

Julie overcame addiction, loss, and economic disadvantages to open and maintain Pearl. She combatted an environment in which people vehemently disagreed about COVID-era rules and protocols and she was forced to take on numerous hands-on roles to keep her business alive. Julie is sober and in her darkest hour, for the first time in 9 years, she contemplated drinking again during the catastrophic Texas energy grid failure back in February of 2021, which left her business without power for several days. Instead, though, she put all her mental energy into what she does best: show up for her community and her bar.

Pearl's patrons and staff have affectionately dubbed her Saint Julie because of the lengths she'll go to protect those she loves. Every Sunday, when crawfish are in season, all walks of life travel to Pearl to enjoy Julie's crawfish boil. Julie isn't afraid to get her hands dirty. She and a small team prepare the crawfish themselves; if anyone knows the Texas summer, that's no easy feat. And in the winter, even through the bitter cold, Julie holds her weekly steak nights. It's just Julie behind the grill, making sure all her patrons get their steak just as they like it (she'll tell you steak should be rare and bloody, but she doesn't discriminate).

Pearl Bar isn't just a place to get a good crawfish boil, steak, or drink. It's a home away from home, a place where people can just relax, be or find themselves, and live out loud without any judgment. Julie is the center of this magic. She is a fearless leader and a relentless fighter.

by Erica Rose

award-winning director with a focus on bold and unapologetic queer and female-driven stories

Michelada

Makes 4 cocktails ~ Total Time: 10 minutes

Sometimes known as a beer bloody Mary, Michelada is one of several well-known cocktails made with beer. This Mexican beer cocktail made its way to the United States via Texas. While the michelada is purported to be a hangover cure, it can be enjoyed by anyone who likes a cocktail with a kick. Use a well-chilled Mexican lager. Our favorite is Tecate, but Corona Extra or Modelo will also work. We recommend Cholula or Tapatío hot sauces for their flavor and thicker consistencies. If using a thinner, vinegary hot sauce such as Tabasco, which is spicier, start with half the amount called for and adjust to your taste after mixing. Do not use bottled lime juice here.

2¼	teaspoons kosher salt, divided	8	teaspoons hot sauce, plus extra for serving
¼	teaspoon chili powder	2	tablespoons Worcestershire sauce
8	ounces lime juice (8 limes), plus lime wedges for serving	4	(12-ounce) Mexican beers, chilled

1   Combine 2 teaspoons salt and chili powder on small plate and spread into even layer. Rub rims of 4 pint glasses with 1 lime wedge to moisten, then dip rims into salt mixture to coat. Set glasses aside.

2   Combine lime juice, hot sauce, Worcestershire, and remaining ¼ teaspoon salt in 2-cup liquid measuring cup, stirring to dissolve salt. Fill prepared glasses with ice and divide lime juice mixture evenly among glasses. Fill glasses with beer. Serve with lime wedges, extra hot sauce, and remaining beer, topping off glasses as needed.

Shandy

Makes 1 cocktail
Total Time: 5 minutes

This crisp beer cocktail is the perfect cooler on the hottest of Southern summer days. You can make one, just for you, with the most ease. We love to use our homemade Lemonade (page 476) here, but store-bought also works. Use a lager such as Budweiser or Pabst Blue Ribbon. For a refreshing drink, make sure that both ingredients are cold before combining them.

8   ounces cold lemonade
8   ounces cold beer

Add lemonade to chilled pint glass. Top with beer. Serve.

HOLIDAY MUST-DRINKS

A creamy, rich, booze-spiked drink is a staple for many around the holidays. And in Miami, you can find a handful of these drinks from different diasporas within a few-block radius. Recipes vary from home to home, but here's a breakdown of some of the standards.

Coquito: Coquito (meaning "little coconut" in Spanish) is a celebrated holiday drink among Puerto Rican families. Dominicans and Cubans in Miami also make their own versions of this creamy coconut drink. "Christmas isn't Christmas in Miami until your fridge has at least two bottles of coquito chilling," Amy Reyes, editor of Miami.com, says. It can have eggs but more often doesn't; coconut milk and/or cream provide its creamy but not superthick texture, one Reyes described as similar to Baileys Irish Cream.

Eggnog: While it's not certain where in the world eggnog originated, it came to the United States with English settlers. This drink is a mix of sugar, milk or cream, and eggs. It's often finished with some nutmeg and spirits such as bourbon, brandy, or rum.

Kremas (sometimes called Cremasse or Cremas): Similar to coquito but more heavily flavored, this drink is served in Miami's Little Haiti neighborhood for all sorts of celebrations. While its ingredients can vary within the island of Haiti, in the United States it's most common to find thick versions that are flavored with coconut. Nadege Fleurimond, chef and author of *Haiti Uncovered: A Regional Adventure into the Art of Haitian Cuisine*, says it's typically made with clairin, a clear liquor that is made from sugarcane. That's hard to find in the United States, so the spirit of choice is Rhum Barbancourt. Flavorings include warm spices, vanilla, and lime.

Ponche Crema: As of 2021, Miami-Dade and Broward Counties had the largest population of Venezuelan immigrants in a metropolitan area in the United States, so it's no surprise you'll find Venezuelan ponche crema in many homes and restaurants throughout the area. Ponche crema is made with eggs, milk (whole, sweetened condensed, and/or evaporated), and rum. Sometimes boxed flan mixes are incorporated to enhance the eggy richness. Citrus zest, vanilla, and/or spices may be added to the mix.

Crema de Vie: The *Miami Herald* reported in 2017 that Miami-Dade County was home to nearly 700,000 Cuban-born residents, higher than any other county in the United States. So Cuban crema de vie (meaning "cream of life") is a drink that brings a lot of joy to life in this area. This drink is made with egg yolks, milk (whole, sweetened condensed, and/or evaporated), sugar, and vanilla. Sometimes spices are added. It's typically consumed after dinner during the holiday season.

Eggnog

Serves 6 to 8 ~ Total Time: 25 minutes, plus 1 hour chilling

This version of eggnog is creamy (but not too heavy), just a touch sweet, and fortified with a definite note of spirit. Cooking the eggnog results in a velvety texture and avoids the safety concerns of serving uncooked eggs. Using some heavy cream in addition to the milk and whipping half of the cream before adding it to the eggnog makes for a richer sip. We opt for dark rum here, but you can substitute brandy or bourbon, if desired.

12	ounces heavy cream, divided
6	large egg yolks
6	tablespoons sugar
24	ounces whole milk
¼	teaspoon table salt
4	ounces dark rum
¼	teaspoon ground nutmeg, plus extra for serving

Nonalcoholic Eggnog

Substitute root beer for dark rum.

1 Whisk 6 ounces cream, egg yolks, and sugar in medium bowl until thoroughly combined and pale yellow, about 30 seconds; set aside. Bring milk and salt to simmer in medium saucepan over medium-high heat, stirring occasionally.

2 When milk mixture comes to simmer, remove from heat and, whisking constantly, slowly pour into yolk mixture to temper. Return milk-yolk mixture to saucepan. Place over medium-low heat and cook, whisking constantly, until mixture reaches 160 degrees, 1 to 2 minutes.

3 Immediately pour eggnog into clean bowl. Stir in rum and nutmeg. Fill slightly larger bowl with ice and set eggnog bowl in ice bowl. Refrigerate until eggnog registers 40 degrees, 1 to 2 hours, stirring occasionally.

4 Just before serving, using stand mixer fitted with whisk attachment, whip remaining 6 ounces cream on medium-low speed until foamy, about 1 minute. Increase speed to high and whip until soft peaks form, 1 to 3 minutes. Whisk whipped cream into chilled eggnog. Serve, garnished with extra nutmeg. (Eggnog can be covered and refrigerated for up to 24 hours.)

Coquito

Serves 8 to 10 ~ Total Time: 10 minutes, plus 1 hour chilling

Like many holiday sippers, there are nuances to each family's coquito recipe that make it their own. This version is served over ice—but some folks prefer drinking it chilled, without ice. With both a can of coconut milk and a can of cream of coconut, it has plenty of creamy coconut richness. Vanilla, cinnamon, and nutmeg provide warm spiciness. Blending the drink right before serving time ensures that everything is fully combined; plus it gives the cocktail a delightful bit of frothiness. Different families suggest using different kinds of rum. Whichever you decide, we suggest looking for a Puerto Rican brand such as Don Q or Palo Viejo.

1	(15-ounce) can cream of coconut
1	(14-ounce) can coconut milk
1	(12-ounce) can evaporated milk
10	ounces light rum
1	teaspoon vanilla extract
½	teaspoon ground cinnamon
¼	teaspoon ground nutmeg, plus extra for serving

1 Whisk all ingredients in large pitcher until combined. Refrigerate for at least 1 hour or up to 3 days.

2 Just before serving, working in 2 or 3 batches, transfer mixture to blender and process until slightly frothy, about 1 minute per batch. Serve over ice, garnished with extra nutmeg.

Recipe sharing is a powerful historical tradition simultaneously linking generations of Southern women to both the past and the present. Tucked loosely into cookbooks, swiftly copied into handwritten correspondence, or clipped from newspapers, recipes and shared cooking knowledge served as a kind of cultural capital with which women could cultivate new friendships, foster allies, and even make an enemy or two. As society evolved and technology sped up, our relationships to food and cooking reconfigured, and the way we share recipes changed, too. The delicious dishes remained, but the cultural legacy of those recipes was often limited to the footnotes or disappeared altogether. Today, many of us source our recipes from websites, blogs, and other digital publications that understandably prioritize the food, but downplay the full story of how a recipe came to be. The opportunity for cultural connection still exists in these virtual spaces, if only we take the time to cultivate it.

As you learned from reading and using this cookbook, women's history has been told through a purposefully narrow lens, especially when it came to our contributions to the world of food and cooking. For generations, women were relegated to the kitchen and food-related labor, but in our gendered assignment found opportunities for agency and creativity. As it turns out, feeding people is an important responsibility. While women had been documenting their recipes and cooking knowledge in cookbooks both personal and published for centuries, the late 1800s saw a radical shift as women turned that expertise into a scientific profession. Nineteenth-century domestic scientists aimed to validate and uplift their fellow women's work in the home and a few decades later, as the consumer market set its sights on women's purchasing power, home economists hoped to further the work of their foremothers.

These powerful moments of progress, however, were consistently dismissed as good for the advancement of women's domestic labor, but not important to the broader advancement of the food industry or the general consuming public. Since the dawn of quantifying recipes, while women were marginalized by their male peers, white and upperclass women turned around and did the same to their even more underrepresented sisters. The legacy of this process exists to some degree in all of our kitchens today; it is now our duty and our honor to give credit where it is due and celebrate the fruits (at times, quite literally) of the labor of the women who came before us.

Inspired by the foundational history of this work, but aware of the need to reach beyond the exclusive confines of the historical archives, the contributors whose bios follow extracted the scholarship of Southern women's food history and served it up to you, the people. Historically labeled as "sentimental writing" and maligned as unimportant texts within the scope of rigorous academic work, we considered Southern women's narratives and personal correspondence on food and cooking equally as important as their recipes, and in the process, reclaimed culinary knowledge that has lasting power. We are grateful to the diverse team of women and women-identifying folks on the following pages who collaboratively provide a broader notion of what it means to be a Southern woman in the world of food.

And much like the flexible boundaries of the South, our contributors give context to recipes that exist as both a set of prescribed ingredients as well as a shared idea, open to a bit of interpretation. Some recipes have been passed down through the generations, changing with each new hand; others were standardized years ago and exist, to this day, unquestioned even when they don't turn out so well. Then there are recipes that are simply new-to-us, but come from cultures who have been cooking from them for centuries and were only recently brought to this part of the South. These "new" recipes combine with our older ones to create something entirely different, but still decidedly Southern—American.

Through this book, we expanded the notion of the Southern table to include new recipes, as well as those that have been lost, forgotten, or even stolen. Each recipe, each story, each participant represents an interpretation of what it means when Southern women cook.

by KC Hysmith

CONTRIBUTOR BIOGRAPHIES

REEM ASSIL is an award-winning chef, speaker, and community-builder working at the intersection of food and social justice. With more than 20 years of nonprofit and food industry experience, Assil builds her vision for a more socially and economically just world. She owns the bakery and restaurant Reem's California and is the author of the cookbook *Arabiyya: Recipes from the Life of an Arab in Diaspora.*

LINDSAY AUTRY is a multi-disciplinary culinary and media professional with experience in culinary instruction, testing and developing recipes, live-event hosting, culinary production, and food writing. She is the owner of Meet Me in Your Kitchen, through which she offers cooking and baking classes both virtually and in person.

TIFFANIE BARRIERE is an award-winning mixologist, beverage historian, educator, and influencer in the cocktail industry. She is passionate about sharing African American culture and its influences on the American cocktail space. She currently lives in Atlanta, Georgia, and is recognized on all social platforms as The Drinking Coach.

VICTORIA BOULOUBASIS is an award-winning freelance journalist, food writer, and filmmaker from North Carolina. Her work aims to dispel myths about the Global South—its people and places—against the backdrop of complex social, political, and personal histories. She often tells stories at the intersection of food, labor, and immigration.

ADDIE BROYLES is a freelance writer, editor, and consultant. She is a veteran of the newspaper industry, including a 13-year stint as a food columnist for the *Austin American-Statesman.* She currently writes the *Invisible Thread,* a weekly newsletter about the things that connect us that we cannot see. A native of the Missouri Ozarks, she now lives in Austin, Texas.

KATIE BUTTON is an award-winning chef and the co-founder of Cúrate in Asheville, North Carolina—a collection of restaurants, online marketplace, wine club, and culinary journeys designed to connect people with the Spanish experience and lifestyle. She has also written a cookbook: *Cúrate: Authentic Spanish Food from an American Kitchen.*

ANNE BYRN is an award-winning food writer and best-selling cookbook author. She trained in French cuisine in Paris, and worked as the food editor of the *Atlanta Journal-Constitution* for 15 years. She has written many cookbooks, including *The Cake Mix Doctor* series and, most recently, *Baking in the American South: 200 Recipes and Their Untold Stories.*

SHERI CASTLE is the host of *The Key Ingredient*, an Emmy-winning cooking show from PBS. She is also an award-winning food writer, cookbook author, recipe developer, and cooking teacher. She was named one of 20 Living Legends of Southern Food by the Southern Foodways Alliance. She is known for her rich storytelling and culinary expertise.

SHAUN CHAVIS is a food and health journalist based in Atlanta, Georgia. She's worked or written for Serious Eats, Time Inc. Books, *Real Simple*, *Health*, Sharecare, How Stuff Works, Allrecipes, SouthernLiving.com, and CookingLight.com. Shaun has a MLA in Gastronomy and a Certificate in the Culinary Arts from Boston University

ASHLEY CHRISTENSEN is a James Beard Award–winning chef and restaurateur in Raleigh, North Carolina. She is involved in a number of nonprofits and organizations, including the Frankie Lemmon Foundation, the Southern Smoke Foundation, and the Southern Foodways Alliance. She wrote *Poole's: Recipes and Stories from a Modern Diner* and *It's Always Freezer Season: How to Freeze Like a Chef with 100 Make-Ahead Recipes.*

LINDA CIVITELLO, PHD, is a food historian and author of the award-winning books *Cuisine and Culture: a History of Food and People* and *Baking Powder Wars: the Cutthroat Food Fight That Revolutionized Cooking*. She has taught food history at universities and culinary schools, appeared on TV and radio to share her expertise, cooked professionally, and also worked in the film industry. She is currently writing her next book, *Food and Film from Prohibition to James Bond*.

SARAH COLE is the owner and head chef of Abadir's, an Egyptian eatery and grocery shop in Greensboro, Alabama. She is also a small-plot farmer, writer, good-food-for-all advocate, and community organizer.

CARLYNN CROSBY is a Florida-bred writer, editor, and scholar primarily focused on historic foodways in Florida. She is pursuing a PhD at the University of Florida examining the relationship between citrus farming and creative experimentation for Florida writers such as Harriet Beecher Stowe, Marjorie Kinnan Rawlings, and Laura (Riding) Jackson.

KELLEY FANTO DEETZ, PHD, is a public historian dedicated to researching the history of enslaved Africans and African Americans, elevating their stories, and amplifying the need for acknowledgment and reconciliation. She is the author of the critically acclaimed *Bound to the Fire: How Virginia's Enslaved Cooks Helped Invent American Cuisine*. Deetz is the Vice President of Collections and Public Engagement at Stratford Hall and a Visiting Scholar in the Department of African American Studies at the University of California, Berkeley.

VON DIAZ is an Emmy Award–winning documentarian and food historian. She is the author of *Islas: A Celebration of Tropical Cooking* and *Coconuts and Collards: Recipes and Stories from Puerto Rico to the Deep South*. Her work has been featured in the *New York Times*, the *Washington Post*, *Bon Appétit*, and *Food & Wine*. She has also taught food studies and oral history at Duke University and the University of North Carolina at Chapel Hill, and works as an editor and producer at StoryCorps.

NADIA DOMEQ is a freelance recipe developer based in Miami, Florida. She is a graduate of Boston University's culinary arts program and enjoys cooking food from her native country, Colombia.

ALI DOMRONGCHAI is a Florida-born, North Carolina–raised food writer who grew up around her family's Thai restaurant, which ignited her initial curiosity about how food connects people. Her work can be found in *Food & Wine*, *Travel + Leisure*, Allrecipes, EatingWell, and more.

LISA DONOVAN is a *New York Times* columnist, James Beard Award–winning writer, and chef. Her recipes and writing have appeared in the *Washington Post*, Eater, *Saveur*, and *Food & Wine*. Her memoir, *Our Lady of Perpetual Hunger*, earned her a Les Dames d'Escoffier International M.F.K. Fisher Prize.

BELINDA ELLIS is a food editor, baker, and author of *Biscuits: A Savor the South Cookbook*. She was previously the test kitchen manager for White Lily Flour, and is now a training specialist for Blackberry Farm, a luxury country resort in Walland, Tennessee.

ASHLEY ENGLISH is a teacher and writer who lives in Candler, North Carolina. She is the author of 11 books, including *Canning and Preserving: All You Need to Know to Make Jams, Jellies, Pickles, Chutneys and More*; *A Year of Pies: A Seasonal Tour of Home Baked Pies*; and *The Essential Book of Homesteading: The Ultimate Guide to Sustainable Living*.

SKYE ESTROFF is known as "Atlanta's Food Expert" on TV, radio, and podcasting. She hosted and executive produced the *Foodie Road Trip* TV show and hosts the weekly *Skye's the Limit* podcast. She has a degree in Dietetics from the University of Georgia and is a regular food judge of culinary competitions and a contributor to local, regional, and national media.

AMY C. EVANS is an award-winning artist, writer, and documentarian based in Houston, Texas. She conducted the fieldwork for *The Mississippi Delta Hot Tamale Trail* documentary project during her tenure as lead oral historian for the Southern Foodways Alliance. Her stories and paintings appear in *A Good Meal Is Hard to Find: Storied Recipes from the Deep South*, which she co-wrote with Mississippi-based chef and cookbook author Martha Hall Foose.

LISA FAIN is the seventh-generation Texan behind the regional food blog *Homesick Texan*. A James Beard Award–winning writer, she has authored three cookbooks, including *The Homesick Texan Cookbook*.

MARCIE COHEN FERRIS, PHD, is a scholar and writer who has studied, documented, and taught about Southern foodways, material culture, and the Southern Jewish experience. She has written and edited several books, including *Edible North Carolina: A Journey Across a State of Flavor*. She is a professor emeritus in American Studies at the University of North Carolina at Chapel Hill, an editor for *Southern Cultures*, and Senior Leadership Advisor for UNC's Center for the Study of the American South.

DIANE FLYNT writes about fruit, farming, and the South and is an orchardist in the Virginia Blue Ridge Mountains. She founded Foggy Ridge Cider, the South's first cidery, in the late 1990s and produced celebrated cider until 2018. She is the author of *Wild, Tamed, Lost, Revived: The Surprising Story of Apples in the South*.

DEBRA FREEMAN is an award-winning writer and podcaster with a focus on Black foodways throughout America, but particularly in Virginia and the greater South. She is host and creator of *Setting the Table*, which was named podcast of the year by the IACP in 2023. She is the food editor for *Style Weekly* in Richmond, Virginia, and the executive producer and host of the forthcoming documentary *Finding Edna Lewis*.

AMETHYST GANAWAY is an award-winning chef, food writer, recipe developer, and content creator. Her area of expertise is the culture and foodways of the South, African Americans, and the African diaspora.

HOLLY GLEASON is a Nashville-based writer, academic, and artist development consultant who has extensively covered and collaborated with women in country music. She conceived and edited the essay collection *Woman Walk the Line: How the Women in Country Music Changed Our Lives* and, with Miranda Lambert, co-authored the *New York Times* best-selling cookbook *Y'all Eat Yet?: Welcome to the Pretty B★tchin' Kitchen*.

MERCEDES GOLIP is a chef and experienced consultant and creative producer in the marketing world. She is also a casual food stylist, recipe tester and developer for media outlets and blogs. She is the creator of My Venezuelan Kitchen, a project for hosting Venezuelan-inspired pop-up dinners and teaching cooking classes.

CYNTHIA GRAUBART is a James Beard Award–winning cookbook author, cooking teacher, and culinary television producer. She produced the groundbreaking series *Nathalie Dupree's New Southern Cooking*. She is a member of Les Dames d'Escoffier International and is currently working on a history of community cookbooks in Georgia.

ROBIN LEE GRIFFITH has lived and traveled the world cooking and learning about the local culinary diasporas. She manages a 145-acre working farm in eastern North Carolina and is a co-owner of Mermosa Wines out of Oregon. She served as president of the Charleston, South Carolina, chapter of the Les Dames d'Escoffier International and is working on three cookbook projects and a television show.

MELISSA GUERRA is a food historian, authority on the foodways of the Americas, and eighth-generation Texan living on a working cattle ranch. She authored *The Texas Provincial Kitchen* and *Dishes from the Wild Horse Desert: Norteño Cooking of South Texas*. She is a member of Les Dames d'Escoffier International, a founding board member of Foodways Texas, and a member of the executive committee of the Culinary Institute of America's Latin Cuisines Advisory Council.

SANDRA A. GUTIERREZ is an award-winning journalist, author, food historian, and professional cooking instructor. She is a celebrated expert on Latin American foodways and United States Southern Regional cuisine. She has written five cookbooks, including *Beans and Field Peas: A Savor the South Cookbook* and *Latinísimo: Home Recipes from the Twenty-One Countries of Latin America*.

DORIS HỒ-KANE is the Texas-born-and-raised owner and baker behind Bạn Bè, a Vietnamese American bakery in Brooklyn, New York. She is also the proud daughter of Vietnamese refugees, a historian, an archivist, and the founder of 17.21 Women, an archive of East and Southeast Asian trailblazers whose legacies have been obscured by traditional history-telling. She is currently working on a book based on her research.

VIVIAN HOWARD is an award-winning cookbook author, TV personality, chef, and restaurateur from Deep Run, North Carolina. Her cookbook *Deep Run Roots: Stories and Recipes from My Corner of the South* was a *New York Times* best seller. She created and stars in the public television shows *Somewhere South* and *A Chef's Life*, for which she has won Peabody, Emmy, and James Beard awards.

KYLE TIBBS JONES co-founded *The Bitter Southerner*, which is on a mission to make the South, and the world, a better place. The James Beard Award–winning media brand tells stories through a Southern lens via its print magazine, books, podcasts, and commerce. Jones hosts the podcast BATCH and is the author of *Your Heart Is Your Home*, *The Bitter Southerner*'s first children's book. Originally from the small northern Georgia town of Dalton, Jones now lives in Athens, Georgia.

REBECCA LANG is a food writer, cooking instructor, television personality, and ninth-generation Southerner. She has written eight cookbooks, including *The Southern Vegetable Book: A Root-to-Stalk Guide to the South's Favorite Produce* and *Y'all Come Over: Charming Your Guests with New Recipes, Heirloom Treasures, and True Southern Hospitality*.

COURTNEY LEWIS, PHD, is an associate professor at Duke University, the inaugural director of Duke's new Native American Studies Initiative, and an enrolled citizen of the Cherokee Nation. Her research explores the themes of American Indian sovereignty, economic justice, Indigenous food and plant entrepreneurship, and more. She is the author of *Sovereign Entrepreneurs: Cherokee Small-Business Owners and the Making of Economic Sovereignty*.

VALLERY LOMAS is the winner of *The Great American Baking Show* and the first Black winner of the *Great British Bake Off* franchise. She is a frequent columnist and contributor to the *New York Times* and the author of the cookbook *Life Is What You Bake It*. She writes the "Baking a Case" column for the *Wall Street Journal* and frequently appears on the History Channel. Her hometown is Baton Rouge, Louisiana.

RONNI LUNDY is a James Beard Award–winning author and a food and culture writer with 40 years of experience writing about southern Appalachia. She worked as a journalist at the *Louisville Times* before writing her first cookbook, *Shuck Beans, Stack Cakes, and Honest Fried Chicken*. Her most recent cookbook is *Victuals: An Appalachian Journey, with Recipes*. She is a founding member of the Southern Foodways Alliance.

KEIA MASTRIANNI is a writer and the baker behind Milk Glass Pie, a cottage bakery located on the farm she runs with her husband in western North Carolina. It has been featured in *Southern Living*, the *Local Palate*, and *Garden & Gun* and on the PBS show, *The Key Ingredient*. She is the former editor of *Crop Stories*, an independent zine focused on the agricultural South, and is also the co-author of *Bruce Moffett Cooks: A New England Chef in a New South Kitchen*.

THERESA MCCULLA, PHD, is a curator, public historian, and James Beard Award–winning writer. Her work investigates how Americans have used material and visual culture to understand race, ethnicity, and gender, especially in the realm of food and drink. Her new book is *Insatiable City: Food and Race in New Orleans*.

NANCIE MCDERMOTT is a food writer and cooking teacher based in Chapel Hill, North Carolina. She has authored 14 cookbooks, including *Southern Soups and Stews: More than 75 Recipes from Burgoo and Gumbo to Etoufée and Fricassee*. Her *Southern Living* cover story on Thanksgiving pies was nominated for a James Beard Award.

SARA CAMP MILAM is the Southern Foodways Alliance's managing editor. She has cowritten or collaborated on three cookbooks, including the James Beard Award–winning cookbook *I Am From Here: Stories and Recipes from a Southern Chef* with Vishwesh Bhatt and *The Southern Foodways Alliance Guide to Cocktails* with Jerry Slater.

NIKKI MILLER-KA is a food and travel writer, award-winning culinary expert, and content creator based in North Carolina. Her work has appeared in *Food & Wine*, *Southern Living*, HuffPost UK, Eater, *Forbes*, and more. She's worked in every part of the food industry from pantry cook to catering manager, pastry chef, recipe developer, private chef, and restaurant reviewer for the *Greensboro News & Record*.

SHANE MITCHELL is a journalist and author. She has five James Beard Awards. Her next book is *The Crop Cycle: A History with Southern Roots*.

ERIN BYERS MURRAY is the editor-in-chief at *The Local Palate* magazine, which celebrates the food culture of the South, and the author of *Grits: A Cultural and Culinary Journey Through the South*. She is the recipient of the Les Dames d'Escoffier International M.F.K. Fisher Award for excellence in culinary writing and the New England Society Book Award. Her writing has been featured in *Food & Wine*, the *Boston Globe*, HuffPost, *Wine & Spirits*, and three editions of the *Best Food Writing* series.

DAWN ORSAK is a fourth-generation Texas Czech. She has been a special events coordinator for the Texas State Historical Association, an executive director of the Texas Hill Country Wine and Food Festival, and in 2019 she was inducted into Les Dames d'Escoffier International. She is the author of the forthcoming cookbook *Kolach Culture: Cooking in Texas Czech Kitchens*.

MM PACK has been a private chef and food writer-historian since 1998. She grew up on the Texas Gulf Coast and is a graduate of Rice University, the University of Texas School of Information Science, and the California Culinary Academy. She's an advisory board member of Foodways Texas and a media awards judge for the James Beard Foundation. She writes articles and does presentations about foods that have shaped Texas and its history.

SUSAN PUCKETT is a James Beard Award–nominated food journalist and editor who has authored or collaborated on more than a dozen books. A native of Jackson, Mississippi, Susan was the food editor for the *Atlanta Journal-Constitution* for nearly 19 years and today, as a freelance writer, contributes to its food section as well as to other media outlets. Her book *Eat Drink Delta: A Hungry Traveler's Journey Through the Soul of the South* is considered a classic.

KATHLEEN PURVIS is a former *Charlotte Observer* food editor with more than 25 years of experience writing about food, cooking, and Southern food culture. She has written three books, including *Distilling the South*, with liquor trails covering 11 southeastern states. Her work has been included in the anthologies *Best Food Writing* and *Cornbread Nation*.

HANNA RASKIN is a food critic, journalist, and the founder of the *Food Section*, an award-winning newsletter covering food and drink across the American South. She previously served as food editor of the *Post and Courier* in Charleston, South Carolina, where her work earned the James Beard Foundation's inaugural Local Impact Journalism prize. She is a founding member of Foodways Texas, and is active in the Southern Foodways Alliance.

JENN RICE is an acclaimed culinary art and travel journalist telling inventive stories within the food and beverage industry. She is a freelance writer for top national media outlets and has bylines in *Food & Wine*, *Vogue*, Eater, Tasting Table, *GQ*, and more. She is known for spotlighting her home state of North Carolina whenever possible.

ERICA ROSE is an award-winning writer and director with a focus on bold, unapologetic queer and female-driven stories. Her docuseries *The Lesbian Bar Project* won Emmy and GLAAD awards and screened at the Sundance Film Festival. It has received over 1 billion impressions.

KIM SEVERSON is a Pulitzer Prize–winning journalist, speaker, recipient of four James Beard Awards, and the author of four books, including *Spoon Fed: How Eight Cooks Saved My Life.* A national food correspondent for the *New York Times*, she lives in Atlanta, Georgia.

REBECCA SHARPLESS, PHD, is a professor of history at Texas Christian University. She is the author of *Grain and Fire: A History of Baking in the American South* and *Cooking in Other Women's Kitchens: Domestic Workers in the South, 1865–1960*. She is past president of the Southern Association for Women Historians and a board member of Foodways Texas.

JULIA SKINNER, PHD, is the author of the award-winning *Our Fermented Lives: A History of How Fermented Foods Have Shaped Cultures and Communities* as well *The Fermentation Oracle: Readings and Recipes to Take You on a Magical Culinary Journey*. She is the owner of Root—a fermentation and food history company in Atlanta, Georgia—a writing coach, a fermentation educator, and a food historian. She is currently writing *The Essential Food Preserving Handbook*.

TAMBRA RAYE STEVENSON is a celebrated scholar, nutrition advocate, and founder of WANDA and NativSol Kitchen, focusing on uplifting the voices of women and the foodways of Africa and the diaspora. She is a member of Les Dames d'Escoffier and serves as a judge for the James Beard Foundation Awards. Her work has been featured in academic journals, TED, the *Washington Post*, *Forbes*, and EatingWell.

KAYLA STEWART is a James Beard Award–winning food and travel journalist and cookbook author. She contributes to publications such as the *New York Times*, *Food & Wine*, and *Travel + Leisure*. With Emily Meggett, she is the co-author of the James Beard Award–nominated, *New York Times* best-selling cookbook *Gullah Geechee Home Cooking: Recipes from the Matriarch of Edisto Island*.

KENDALL VANDERSLICE is a baker, writer, and speaker who has made a career out of exploring the intersection of food, faith, and culture. In 2018, she was named a James Beard Foundation national scholar for her work on food and religion. She is the author of *By Bread Alone: A Baker's Reflections on Hunger, Longing, and the Goodness of God* and *Bake and Pray: Liturgies and Recipes for Baking Bread as a Spiritual Practice*.

ANDREA WEIGL is a former newspaper journalist and documentary film producer, and a current food writer and publicist in Raleigh, North Carolina. She worked as a producer on the PBS TV shows *A Chef's Life* and *Somewhere South* starring North Carolina chef Vivian Howard. She is the author of *Pickles and Preserves: A Savor the South Cookbook*.

JAN WHITAKER is a writer and consumer historian with a focus on department stores and restaurants. She is author of the book *Tea at the Blue Lantern Inn: A Social History of the Tea Room Craze in America*. She is the creator and author of the blog *Restaurant-ing Through History*, which is about the history of American restaurants.

CRYSTAL WILKINSON was Poet Laureate of Kentucky, and she currently teaches writing at the University of Kentucky, where she is a Bush-Holbrook Endowed Professor. A recent fellowship recipient of the Academy of American Poets, she is the award-winning author of *Praisesong for the Kitchen Ghosts: Stories and Recipes from Five Generations of Black Country Cooks*, a culinary memoir, and *Perfect Black*, a collection of poems. Her short stories, poems, and essays have appeared in numerous prestigious journals and anthologies.

LIZ WILLIAMS is a food historian, podcaster, and the founder of the Southern Food and Beverage Museum and the National Food and Beverage Foundation. She hosts *Tip of the Tongue*, a podcast on the individuals and issues at the intersection of food, drink, and culture. She has written several books about New Orleans's culinary history, including *Lift Your Spirits: A Celebratory History of Cocktail Culture in New Orleans* and *Nana's Creole Italian Table: Recipes and Stories from Sicilian New Orleans*.

PSYCHE A. WILLIAMS-FORSON, PHD, is an author, speaker, and scholar of African American foodways, life, and culture. Her books include *Building Houses out of Chicken Legs: Black Women, Food, and Power* and the James Beard Award–winning *Eating While Black: Food Shaming and Race in America*. She also serves on the board of the Southern Food and Beverage Museum and is a founding member of the Southern Foodways Alliance.

VIRGINIA WILLIS is a chef and James Beard Award–winning cookbook author, TV and video personality, content creator, motivational speaker, and social media influencer. Her cookbooks include *Secrets of the Southern Table: A Food Lover's Tour of the Global South* and *Bon Appetit, Y'all: Recipes and Stories from Three Generations of Southern Cooking*. She is also the founder of Good and Good for You, a lifestyle brand featuring healthy recipes, best-life living tips, self-care techniques, and ideas and inspiration.

BRONWEN WYATT is a writer and pastry chef with nearly two decades of experience in restaurants across the United States, including in New Orleans, Louisiana; Baltimore, Maryland; San Francisco, California; and Portland, Maine. In 2020, she established Bayou Saint Cake, a boutique cake studio specializing in imaginative layer cakes featuring seasonal Southern produce. Wyatt lives in a century-old shotgun house in New Orleans.

ASHLEY ROSE YOUNG, PHD, is the historian for the Smithsonian Food History Project, where her research explores the intersection of race, ethnicity, and gender in American food culture. She is the host of the Smithsonian's live cooking demonstration series, Cooking Up History, where she has cooked alongside many of the dynamic women who are keepers of Southern culinary traditions. She is co-authoring a book on Lena Richard, the first Black woman to host her own cooking show on TV.

RAFIA ZAFAR, PHD, is professor emerita of English, African and African American Studies, and American Culture Studies at Washington University in Saint Louis, Missouri. She holds a PhD in the History of American Civilization from Harvard University. Her book *Recipes for Respect: African American Meals and Meaning* is filled with intriguing stories about Black food history. She began her career in foodways in college and was one of the first employees of Giorgia DeLuca, founder of the renowned food emporium Dean & DeLuca in New York City.

SELECTED BIBLIOGRAPHY

The editors drew from the following books and citations. It is a selected list referenced in building the content; you will find many more books and articles specifically mentioned among the pages of this cookbook. The ones listed here and elsewhere are encouraged for further reading.

Bryan, Lettice. *The Kentucky Housewife.* Stereotyped by Shepard & Stearns, 1841.

Child, Lydia Maria. *The Frugal Housewife.* Marsh & Capen, and Carter & Hendee, 1829.

Cooley, Angela Jill. *To Live and Dine in Dixie: The Evolution of Urban Food Culture in the Jim Crow South.* University of Georgia Press, 2015.

Edge, John T. *The Potlikker Papers: A Food History of the Modern South.* Penguin Press, Reprint edition 2017.

Egerton, John. *Southern Food: At Home, on the Road, in History.* University Of North Carolina Press, Reprint edition 1993.

Engelhardt, Elizabeth S.D. *A Mess of Greens.* University of Georgia Press, 2011.

Ferris, Marcie Cohen. *The Edible South: The Power of Food and the Making of an American Region.* The University of North Carolina Press, 2014.

Ferris, Marcie Cohen and KC Hysmith. *Edible North Carolina: A Journey Across a State of Flavor.* The University of North Carolina Press, 2022.

Fisher, Abby and Karen Hess. *What Mrs. Fisher Knows about Old Southern Cooking: Soups, Pickles, Preserves, Etc.: In Facsimile with Historical Notes.* Applewood Books, Reprint edition 1995.

Fox, Minnie C. *The Blue Grass Cook Book (Classic Reprint).* Forgotten Books, 2017.

Franklin, Sara B. *Edna Lewis: At the Table with an American Original.* University of North Carolina Press, 2018.

Harris, Jessica B. *High on the Hog: A Culinary Journey from Africa to America.* Bloomsbury USA, 2012.

Harris, Jessica B. and Tara Donne. *Rum Drinks: 50 Caribbean Cocktails, from Cuba Libre to Rum Daisy.* Chronicle Books, 2010.

Heckert, Amanda and Garden and Gun. *Southern Women: More than 100 Stories of Innovators, Artists, and Icons.* Harper Wave, 2019.

Hess, Karen, *The Carolina Rice Kitchen, second edition: The African Connection.* University of South Carolina Press, 2022.

Junior League of Charleston. *Charleston Receipts.* Favorite Recipes Press, Reprint edition 2021.

Lewis, Edna. *The Taste of Country Cooking: The 30th Anniversary Edition of a Great Southern Classic.* Knopf, 2006.

Lewis, Edna, and Scott Peacock. *The Gift of Southern Cooking: Recipes and Revelations from Two Great American Cooks.* Knopf, 2003.

Meacham, Sarah H. *Every Home a Distillery: Alcohol, Gender, and Technology in the Colonial Chesapeake.* Johns Hopkins University Press, Reprint edition 2009.

Milam, Sara Camp, Jerry Slater, and Southern Foodways Alliance. *The Southern Foodways Alliance Guide to Cocktails.* University of Georgia Press, 2017.

Miller, Adrian. *Black Smoke: African Americans and the United States of Barbecue.* The University of North Carolina Press, 2021.

Miller, Adrian. *The President's Kitchen Cabinet: The Story of the African Americans Who Have Fed Our First Families, from the Washingtons to the Obamas.* University of North Carolina Press, 2017.

Miller, Adrian. *Soul Food: The Surprising Story of an American Cuisine.* University of North Carolina Press, 2013.

O'Connell, Libby H. *The American Plate: A Culinary History in 100 Bites.* Sourcebooks, 2014.

O'Meara, Mallory. *Girly Drinks: A World History of Women and Alcohol.* Hanover Square Press, 2021.

O'Neill, Molly. *American Food Writing: An Anthology with Classic Recipes.* Library of America, 2007.

Randolph, Mary. *The Virginia Housewife Or, Methodical Cook: A Facsimile of an Authentic Early American Cookbook,* Dover Publications, Reprint edition 1993.

Roahen, Sara, et al. *Southern Foodways Alliance Community Cookbook.* University of Georgia Press, 2010.

Russell, Malinda. *A Domestic Cook Book: Containing a Careful Selection of Useful Receipts for the Kitchen.* Self-published, 1866.

Rutledge, Sarah. *The Carolina Housewife.* W.R. Babcock, 1847.

Shapiro, Laura. *Perfection Salad: Women and Cooking at the Turn of the Century.* University of California Press, 2008.

Sharpless, Rebecca. *Grain and Fire: A History of Baking in the American South.* University of North Carolina Press, 2022.

Simmons, Amelia. *American Cookery.* Andrews McMeel Publishing, Reissue edition 2012.

The Second Savor the South Cookbooks, 10 Volume Omnibus E-Book. The University of North Carolina Press, 2017.

The Third Savor the South Cookbooks, 5 Volume Omnibus E-Book. The University of North Carolina Press, 2021.

Tipton-Martin, Toni. *The Jemima Code: Two Centuries of African American Cookbooks.* University of Texas Press, 2015.

Tipton-Martin, Toni. *Jubilee: Recipes from Two Centuries of African American Cooking.* Clarkson Potter, 2019.

Twitty, Michael W. *The Cooking Gene: A Journey Through African American Culinary History in the Old South.* HarperCollins, 2018.

Nutritional Information for Our Recipes

To calculate the nutritional values of our recipes per serving, we used The Food Processor SQL by ESHA research. When using this program, we entered all the ingredients, using weights wherever possible. We also used our preferred brands in these analyses. Any ingredient listed as "optional" was excluded from the analyses. If there is a range in the serving size, we used the highest number of servings to calculate nutritional values. We did not include additional salt or pepper for food that's seasoned to taste.

	Cal	Total Fat (g)	Sat Fat (g)	Chol (mg)	Sodium (mg)	Carbs (g)	Fiber (g)	Total Sugars (g)	Protein (g)
No. 1 The Bread Basket									
Hoecakes	203	7	3	9	203	30	1	3	4
Quick Cornbread	240	9	5	55	240	34	0	12	4
Cornbread Mix	880	1	0	0	1310	200	2	66	26
Sweet Potato Cornbread	246	10	6	83	281	34	3	6	5
Ginger Honey Butter	20	2	1	5	25	1	0	1	0
Fresh Corn Muffins	332	12	6	59	289	52	2	19	6
Cardamom Brown Sugar Butter	80	8	5	20	29	3	0	3	0
Corn Spoonbread	260	15	8	125	470	26	2	8	10
Pan de Campo	440	10	6	65	230	81	0	54	6
Drop Biscuits	160	8	5	20	290	19	1	1	3
Baking Powder Biscuits	230	12	5	10	400	26	1	1	4
Pat-in-the-Pan Buttermilk Biscuits	340	16	10	43	291	42	1	3	6
Angel Biscuits	230	12	5	10	450	26	1	1	3
North Carolina Cheese Biscuits	554	22	12	60	626	70	2	6	19
Sawmill Gravy	360	25	8	95	630	10	6	6	21
Chocolate Gravy	160	10	6	25	90	18	2	14	2
White Sandwich Bread	234	4	2	10	208	41	1	6	7
Easy Crescent Rolls	211	9	5	52	144	28	1	5	5
Pan de Jamón	280	6	3	60	710	41	1	11	14
Dollywood Cinnamon Bread	330	15	19	40	370	44	1	21	3
Alabama Orange Rolls	489	21	13	78	321	68	2	27	7
Conchas	480	23	10	65	440	56	2	13	9
Beignets	754	76	5	16	80	17	1	3	3
No. 2 Soul-Satisfying Breakfasts									
Buttermilk Pancakes	325	12	6	86	392	45	1	9	10
Pain Perdu with Chantilly Crème	540	33	18	160	450	54	2	24	9
Quick Yeasted Waffles	408	20	11	110	381	47	2	10	10
Buttery Blueberry Maple Syrup	158	4	2	10	103	32	1	28	0
Fried Boneless Chicken Thighs	550	24	4.5	120	1850	50	1	1	35
Spicy Lime Honey	60	0	0	0	280	17	6	16	0
Light Rolls	280	10	4.5	15	320	39	1	3	6
Country Ham with Red-Eye Gravy	290	16	6	85	3070	4	0	3	32
Black Pepper Candied Bacon	231	11	4	56	299	14	0	13	18
Homemade Breakfast Sausage	344	28	9	82	285	3	1	2	19
Texas Breakfast Tacos	555	32	10	391	726	42	3	3	22
Salsa Roja	17	0	0	0	190	4	1	2	1
Homemade Taco-Size Flour Tortillas	137	6	1	0	99	18	1	0	2

	Cal	Total Fat (g)	Sat Fat (g)	Chol (mg)	Sodium (mg)	Carbs (g)	Fiber (g)	Total Sugars (g)	Protein (g)
No. 2 Soul-Satisfying Breakfasts, continued									
Eggs Hussarde	910	66	36	695	2100	35	1	5	41
Migas	375	24	6	381	489	21	3	3	18
Hash Browns	294	14	2	0	402	40	5	2	5
Kolaches	293	14	8	62	218	35	1	9	6
Klobásníky	274	16	6	49	386	24	1	3	8
No. 3 Eat with Your Hands									
Southern Cheese Straws	52	4	2	10	35	4	0	0	2
Appetizer Biscuits	80	3.5	2	10	120	10	0	1	2
Beer Cheese	190	15	10	50	390	3	0	1	11
Roast Country Ham	680	28	9	235	9010	8	0	7	93
Pimento Cheese	290	26	12	55	400	2	0	0	12
Hot Cheddar Crab Dip	215	15	8	78	439	7	1	3	15
Chile con Queso	210	16	8	40	350	6	0	5	10
Vidalia Onion Dip	282	27	8	38	321	4	0	2	7
Fire Crackers	320	23	3	0	520	24	0	0	2
Savory Benne Wafers	40	2.5	1	5	110	2	0	0	1
Basic Deviled Eggs	60	5	1	95	79	0	0	0	3
Hard-Cooked Eggs	72	5	2	186	71	0	0	0	6
Truffled Egg Salad	240	22	4.5	255	540	1	0	0	8
Boiled Peanuts	321	28	4	0	1232	9	5	3	15
Candied Pecans	180	16	1.5	0	120	9	2	6	2
Pickled Shrimp	383	28	4	183	1050	10	1	8	23
Shrimp Rémoulade	429	31	5	289	642	4	1	1	35
West Virginia Pepperoni Rolls	513	26	10	65	853	49	2	3	18
Natchitoches Meat Pies	370	23	5	55	650	28	0	1	12
No. 4 From the Garden									
Buttermilk Coleslaw	80	4.5	1	5	380	8	3	5	2
Red Slaw	100	2	0	0	317	20	3	16	1
Pickled Cucumber and Onion Salad	36	0	0	0	245	8	1	6	1
Tomato Salad with Onion	120	10	1.5	0	400	8	2	5	2
Watermelon Salad	191	12	4	17	609	18	2	12	4
Peach and Burrata Salad	240	15	6	35	540	22	1	21	10
Killed Salad	228	16	6	29	408	12	1	11	7
Grilled Ramps	45	3.5	0.5	0	5	3	1	1	1
Squash Casserole	349	27	8	0	35	18	2	6	10
Creamed Corn	167	6	3	11	495	29	3	10	5
Esquites	170	11	4	20	450	15	2	3	5
Grit Cakes with Beans and Summer Squash	430	12	2	0	1190	67	1	7	14
Stewed Collards	146	9	3	13	185	11	8	1	8
Green Beans with Ham and Potatoes	223	10	3	46	831	17	4	4	19
Tamatar and Bhindi Dal Tadka	350	9	3	5	1380	51	27	3	18
Tomato Pie	430	33	0.5	70	490	26	3	5	10
Cowboy Caviar	130	6	0.5	0	540	15	3	3	6
Three-Bean Salad	140	7	1	0	380	17	5	6	5
Southern-Style Baby Lima Beans	280	11	4.5	15	1110	31	7	1	15
Sweet Potato Casserole	400	12	8	34	401	70	7	27	5

	Cal	Total Fat (g)	Sat Fat (g)	Chol (mg)	Sodium (mg)	Carbs (g)	Fiber (g)	Total Sugars (g)	Protein (g)
No. 5 Rice or Grits									
Boudin Balls	130	4.5	1	70	430	12	0	1	10
Rémoulade	90	10	1.5	5	160	1	0	0	0
Everyday White Rice	234	0	0	0	199	52	0	0	4
Chicken Bog	524	25	7	111	800	46	1	3	26
Hoppin' John	639	40	11	70	1380	46	2	3	23
Shrimp Middlins	360	15	4.5	85	980	39	3	2	11
Cajun Rice Dressing	413	22	10	137	755	34	3	3	19
Red Beans and Rice	490	12	3	20	1140	74	7	3	21
Habichuelas Guisadas con Calabaza	344	10	2	16	999	48	11	6	20
Sofrito	5	0	0	0	0	1	0	0	0
Sazón	20	0	0	0	1750	3	1	0	1
Arroz con Tocino	436	22	8	22	702	52	0	0	6
Chicken and Shrimp Jambalaya	470	11	3	170	930	58	1	5	35
Gullah Lowcountry Red Rice	440	23	8	35	1300	46	2	4	11
Calas	290	9	1	70	320	46	0	11	7
Extra-Cheesy Grits	400	23	13	64	606	27	1	5	20
Shrimp and Grits	627	33	17	288	1565	47	3	8	35
Fried Whole Branzino with Grits	1630	132	47	264	1356	63	4	4	50
No. 6 In the Stew Pot									
Brunswick Stew	464	19	5	169	1322	35	4	11	40
South Carolina Barbecue Hash	363	20	7	165	754	12	2	7	32
Kentucky Burgoo	960	47	15	295	1690	51	5	8	78
Chicken Broth	200	18	5	50	340	0	0	0	9
Smoky Chicken, Sausage, and Shrimp Gumbo	880	56	13	180	1450	31	4	7	66
Lowcountry Shrimp and Okra Stew	308	17	5	124	1271	13	4	3	27
Chili con Carne	580	26	11	220	1360	19	6	3	70
Carne Guisada	708	29	9	92	1076	75	7	7	39
Eastern North Carolina Fish Stew	330	15	5	257	1062	15	2	4	34
Viet-Cajun Shrimp Boil	850	43	22	585	3330	44	5	10	71
Stuffed Turkey Wings	793	49	10	192	1621	24	3	6	61
Beef Yakamein	624	25	8	185	1477	55	3	7	45
Chicken and Pastry	578	32	10	165	684	37	1	5	34
Smothered Chicken	370	6	1.5	160	1280	21	2	3	53
Delta Hot Tamales	470	29	11	55	1200	39	5	1	15
No. 7 Fried and True									
One-Batch Fried Chicken	750	20	4	165	1940	74	2	3	62
Lard-Fried Chicken	820	46	16	195	1740	33	0	0	61
North Carolina Dipped Fried Chicken	820	37	3.5	180	4380	62	1	12	54
Nashville Hot Fried Chicken	840	54	12	200	1260	30	0	1	53
Chicken-Fried Chicken	780	28	9	155	2120	79	1	7	48
Crab Croquettes	732	59	11	133	583	36	2	5	15
Crispy Fried Shrimp	295	17	3	70	407	30	1	6	6
Fried Catfish	755	51	5	76	725	47	2	5	27
Comeback Sauce	191	20	3	8	307	4	0	2	0
Puffy Tacos	300	15	3	30	540	31	3	1	12
Gobi Manchurian	400	22	3	0	2100	46	3	6	6
Fried Okra	480	39	3	35	630	30	3	2	5
Churros with Mexican Chocolate Sauce	1101	107	11	32	113	36	2	21	4
Fried Peach Pies	350	16	6	25	410	47	1	20	5

	Cal	Total Fat (g)	Sat Fat (g)	Chol (mg)	Sodium (mg)	Carbs (g)	Fiber (g)	Total Sugars (g)	Protein (g)
No. 8 Sandwich Icons									
Cuban Sandwiches	1190	64	26	185	3340	90	1	3	57
Cuban Roast Pork with Mojo	360	19	4.5	100	2490	15	1	11	31
Cuban Bread	520	13	5	10	880	84	1	0	13
Shrimp Po' Boys	890	51	9	260	1120	64	4	7	29
Lemongrass Chicken Bahn Mi	830	49	8	200	1730	50	2	16	46
Bahn Mi Pickles	25	0	0	460	4	0	1	4	0
Tomato Sandwiches	471	35	5	11	499	32	4	6	7
Homemade Garlic Mayo	140	15	1.5	10	85	0	0	0	0
Ultimate BLT Sandwiches	914	74	19	88	1286	36	6	9	26
Surry Ground Steak Sandwiches	440	27	8	60	950	31	1	7	18
Bacon, Lettuce, and Fried Green Tomato Sandwiches	1357	97	12	223	1144	92	5	10	29
Fried Onion Burgers	452	26	11	84	549	28	2	5	26
Muffulettas	660	37	10	70	2110	57	0	7	25
Pickle-Brined Fried Chicken Sandwiches	700	40	5	90	1200	57	1	4	25
Chicken Salad with Fresh Herbs	382	26	4	120	438	1	0	0	34
Ham and Swiss Football Sandwiches	470	28	14	80	760	30	0	4	23
No. 9 Skillet Suppers & Casserole Comfort									
Blackened Salmon	525	38	13	140	506	2	1	0	41
Cast Iron Baked Chicken	794	47	18	270	824	3	1	0	64
Tamale Pie	623	34	11	104	866	52	9	5	29
Keftedes	864	65	17	255	849	3	1	0	64
M'sakhan	500	21	3.5	110	860	37	4	7	40
Roasted Pork Shoulder with Peach Sauce	260	7	2.5	70	1600	19	1	18	22
Shrimp Curry	240	10	5	235	1710	10	1	5	26
Cider-Brined Pork Chops with Apples and Onions	360	12	2.5	95	370	29	4	19	33
Bourbon Chicken	504	18	3	213	1975	33	0	27	47
Pad Thai	480	24	2.5	145	770	47	1	11	20
Pan-Seared Maryland-Style Crab Cakes	440	31	6	175	1252	17	1	8	23
Cheese Enchiladas	555	36	15	70	591	36	5	3	24
Macarona Béchamel	480	22	5	100	930	45	4	8	26
Savory Noodle Kugel	269	9	2	150	274	36	2	3	11
Southern Chicken Spaghetti	570	24	14	115	1510	51	3	7	36
King Ranch Casserole	583	35	19	155	948	30	5	5	38
Cornbread Dressing	376	16	8	132	650	41	2	9	16
No. 10 Outdoor Cooking (& Eating)									
Grilled Steak Fajitas	821	48	10	98	1413	59	4	8	40
Smoked Chicken Wings	552	37	13	272	603	13	1	10	40
Texas Barbecued Brisket	900	60	23	285	420	0	0	0	83
Texas Smoked Beef Ribs	670	25	10	321	1193	2	1	0	110
North Carolina Barbecued Pork	389	26	9	128	637	1	0	0	36
Memphis Wet Ribs	340	23	8	80	1240	17	1	14	16
Alabama Smoked Chicken	940	73	18	270	1010	2	0	1	65
Easy All-Purpose Barbecue Sauce	122	4	0	0	564	23	1	19	1
South Carolina Mustard Sauce	40	0	0	0	220	10	0	9	0
Eastern North Carolina–Style Barbecue Sauce	64	0	0	0	1199	13	0	12	0
Lexington-Style Barbecue Sauce	76	0	0	0	441	16	1	11	1
Alabama White Barbecue Sauce	190	20	3	10	380	2	0	1	0

	Cal	Total Fat (g)	Sat Fat (g)	Chol (mg)	Sodium (mg)	Carbs (g)	Fiber (g)	Total Sugars (g)	Protein (g)
No. 10 Outdoor Cooking (& Eating), continued									
Pimento Mac and Cheese	613	40	24	118	554	43	2	7	20
Green Spaghetti	480	19	10	60	1090	62	3	6	15
Strawberry Pretzel Salad	480	25	15	70	390	62	3	44	4
Backyard Barbecued Beans	350	17	5	35	1000	36	2	16	13
Smashed Potato Salad	304	20	3	65	470	28	4	4	5
No. 11 Flavor, Preserved									
Pepper Vinegar	5	0	0	0	130	1	0	0	0
Easy Homemade Hot Sauce	25	2	0	0	105	3	0	2	0
Quick Tomato Salsa	20	0	0	0	330	5	0	2	1
Quick Tomatillo Salsa	40	2.5	0	0	90	5	1	3	1
Ají Picante	35	2	0	0	101	3	1	2	1
Refrigerator Pickled Okra	22	0	0	0	143	4	1	2	1
Candied Jalapeños	54	0	0	0	87	14	0	13	0
Quick Pickled Jalapeños	5	0	0	0	50	1	0	1	0
Quick Pickled Watermelon Rind	20	0	0	0	35	5	0	5	0
Quick Bread and Butter Pickles	10	0	0	0	105	2	0	2	0
Dill Pickle Chips	10	0	0	0	115	2	0	1	0
Chow-Chow	25	0	0	0	340	5	1	5	0
Apple Butter	50	0	0	0	20	10	0	9	0
Preserved Peaches in Syrup	260	0	0	0	0	66	2	64	1
Grapefruit–Arbol Chile Marmalade	45	0	0	0	0	12	0	12	0
Red Pepper Jelly	45	0	0	0	10	11	0	11	0
Homemade Peanut Butter	210	18	3	0	150	8	3	2	9
Scuppernong Jelly	35	0	0	0	0	8	0	8	0
Dandelion Jelly	25	0	0	0	5	6	0	6	0
No. 12 Everyday Treats									
Peach Cobbler	330	9	5	25	330	58	2	38	5
Simple Blueberry Cobbler	312	13	8	39	260	44	1	30	6
Peach Dumplings	322	12	8	32	343	50	2	25	4
Apple Pandowdy	420	23	15	90	310	51	4	32	3
Strawberry Sonker	427	17	10	43	609	68	4	42	4
Strawberry Cornmeal Shortcakes	479	29	18	105	437	50	2	21	7
Chocolate Éclair Cake	494	28	16	66	346	58	2	40	6
New Orleans Bourbon Bread Pudding	686	38	23	248	406	67	2	40	11
Bourbon Sauce	93	7	5	22	20	3	0	3	1
Huguenot Torte	550	21	2.5	125	390	86	2	74	8
Rich Vanilla Ice Cream	344	23	14	200	118	30	0	30	5
Bourbon Balls	48	3	0	0	3	3	1	3	0
Sea Foam Candy	136	7	1	0	19	19	1	18	1
Pralines	133	13	4	15	69	5	1	4	2
Peanut Brittle	200	9	2.5	10	190	29	1	27	3
Chocolate-Marshmallow Sandwich Cookies	490	24	15	30	310	69	4	32	6
Stuffed Red Velvet Cookies	248	25	13	86	150	6	1	4	2
Moravian Cookies	34	1	1	3	20	5	0	2	0
Cowboy Cookies	181	14	6	35	82	15	1	14	1
Oat Guava Cookies	240	9	6	35	95	36	1	22	3
Gingerbread Snack Cake	311	9	1	37	226	54	1	36	4
Pound Cake	439	26	15	154	230	48	0	31	5

	Cal	Total Fat (g)	Sat Fat (g)	Chol (mg)	Sodium (mg)	Carbs (g)	Fiber (g)	Total Sugars (g)	Protein (g)
No. 13 Celebration Sweets									
Bourbon Butterscotch Pudding	440	32	19	175	260	36	0	32	4
Bananas Foster	460	18	11	60	210	64	2	52	3
Chocolate Soufflés	309	19	11	157	102	31	2	28	7
Caramel Cake	908	49	29	217	528	112	1	80	9
Smith Island Cake	655	37	20	116	317	81	2	60	6
Apple Stack Cake	700	16	10	70	570	129	0	69	10
Blackberry Jam Cake	750	34	21	160	450	103	0	72	6
Lady Baltimore Cake	640	26	9	35	380	93	2	71	7
Chocolate-Lemon Doberge Cake	950	57	29	205	310	97	0	85	7
Coconut Layer Cake	782	53	36	127	361	73	1	55	6
Hummingbird Cake	972	58	21	124	538	109	3	79	9
Porter Plum Pudding Layer Cake	610	31	13	90	410	76	1	61	6
Texas Chocolate Sheet Cake	389	22	8	38	87	49	2	37	3
King Cake	439	15	5	59	195	69	2	33	8
Double-Crust Pie Dough	370	23	15	65	370	34	0	2	5
Single-Crust Pie Dough	180	11	7	30	150	17	0	1	2
Aunt Jule's Pie	266	18	12	62	108	25	2	21	3
Fresh Peach Pie	152	1	0	0	51	36	3	31	2
Thoroughbred Pie	574	38	14	77	286	54	3	34	6
Bourbon Whipped Cream	56	5	3	17	4	1	0	1	0
Brûléed Buttermilk Pie	390	19	11	205	450	46	0	29	8
Lemon Chess Pie	454	22	11	147	237	61	1	44	5
French Silk Chocolate Pie	456	32	18	107	126	42	2	28	4
Key Lime Pie	621	26	14	155	530	88	2	55	11
Banana Pudding Pie	537	25	13	166	349	71	1	54	8
No. 14 Southern Sippers									
Lemonade	130	0	0	0	10	35	0	31	0
Sweet Iced Tea	20	0	0	0	5	5	0	4	0
Vietnamese Coffee	120	3.5	2	15	55	21	0	21	3
Hibiscus Iced Tea	54	0	0	0	19	14	1	10	0
Cherry Bounce	200	0	0	0	0	21	1	21	0
Mint Julep	170	0	0	0	0	11	1	9	0
Old-Fashioned	150	0	0	0	0	4	0	4	0
New-Fashioned	220	0	0	0	0	13	0	12	0
Simple Syrup	35	0	0	0	0	9	0	9	0
Planter's Punch	190	0	0	0	0	15	0	12	0
Plum Shrub Syrup	164	0	0	0	1	42	1	40	1
Plum Reviver	150	0	0	0	0	14	0	13	0
Rum Runner	280	0	0	0	1	38	0	25	0
Bushwacker	600	30	24	0	20	41	1	22	3
Southern Milk Punch	300	18	11	85	20	13	0	13	1
Clarified Milk Punch	260	1.5	0.5	5	20	18	1	15	1
Lemon Syrup	70	0	0	0	0	19	0	19	0
Ponche Navideño	240	0	0	0	0	16	4	35	2
Michelada	170	0	0	0	979	19	0	2	2
Shandy	190	0	0	0	15	35	0	30	1
Eggnog	318	22	13	197	131	16	0	15	6
Coquito	342	18	16	10	57	27	0	25	4

Conversions and Equivalents

Some say cooking is a science and an art. We would say that geography has a hand in it too. Flours and sugars manufactured in the United Kingdom and elsewhere will feel and taste different from those manufactured in the United States. So we cannot promise that the loaf of bread you bake in Canada or England will taste the same as a loaf baked in the States, but we can offer guidelines for converting weights and measures. We also recommend that you rely on your instincts when making our recipes. Refer to the visual cues provided.

The recipes in this book were developed using standard U.S. measures following U.S. government guidelines. The charts below offer equivalents for U.S. and metric measures. All conversions are approximate and have been rounded up or down to the nearest whole number.

Example:
1 teaspoon   =   4.9292 milliliters, rounded up to 5 milliliters
1 ounce   =   28.3495 grams, rounded down to 28 grams

CONVERTING FAHRENHEIT TO CELSIUS

We include temperatures in some of the recipes in this book, and we recommend an instant-read thermometer for the job. To convert Fahrenheit degrees to Celsius, use this simple formula:

Subtract 32 degrees from the Fahrenheit reading, then divide the result by 1.8 to find the Celsius reading. For example, to convert 160°F to Celsius:

$160°F - 32 = 128°$

$128° \div 1.8 = 71.11°C$ rounded down to 71°C

VOLUME CONVERSIONS

U.S.	Metric
1 teaspoon	5 milliliters
2 teaspoons	10 milliliters
1 tablespoon	15 milliliters
2 tablespoons	30 milliliters
¼ cup	59 milliliters
⅓ cup	79 milliliters
½ cup	118 milliliters
¾ cup	177 milliliters
1 cup	237 milliliters
1¼ cups	296 milliliters
1½ cups	355 milliliters
2 cups	473 milliliters
2½ cups	591 milliliters
3 cups	710 milliliters
4 cups (1 quart)	1 liter
4 quarts (1 gallon)	4 liters

WEIGHT CONVERSIONS

Ounces	Grams
½	14
¾	21
1	28
1½	43
2	57
2½	71
3	85
3½	99
4	113
4½	128
5	142
6	170
7	198
8	227
9	255
10	283
12	340
16 (1 pound)	454

Index

Note: Page references in *italics* indicate photographs.